PARADOXES OF GENDER

Judith Lorber

PARADOXES OF GENDER

YALE UNIVERSITY PRESS
New Haven and London

Published with assistance from the foundation established in memory of Philip Hamilton McMillan of the Class of 1894, Yale College.

Designed by Jill Breitbarth and
set in Perpetua and Copperplate Gothic types by
The Composing Room of Michigan, Inc.
Printed in the United States of America by Vail-Ballou Press,
Binghamton, New York.

Library of Congress Cataloging-in-Publication Data

Lorber, Judith.
    Paradoxes of gender / Judith Lorber.
        p.   cm.
    Includes bibliographical references and index.
    ISBN 0-300-05807-1 (cloth)
          0-300-06497-7 (pbk.)
    1. Sex role.   2. Gender identity.   3. Social institutions.
    4. Feminist theory.   I. Title.
    HQ1075.L667   1994
    305.3—dc20   93-23459
                                             CIP

A catalogue record for this book is available from the
British Library.

The paper in this book meets the guidelines for
permanence and durability of the Committee on Production
Guidelines for Book Longevity of the Council on Library
Resources.

10   9   8   7   6   5   4   3

For Jesse, Julian, and Gabrielle,

and again, for Matt

Unless the past and future were made part of the present by
memory and intention, there was, in human terms,
no road, nowhere to go.

—Ursula Le Guin, *The Dispossessed*

CONTENTS

Part III. The Politics of Gender

PREFACE

This book has been two years in the writing and twenty years in the thinking. I taught my first sex roles course in 1972; it was a new course, called Male and Female in American Society. A few years later, I got the name changed to Sociology of Gender. A few years after that, I taught my first women's studies course. (Actually, I taught a precursor of all these courses in 1970—a two-credit, large-enrollment course called, of all things, Courtship and Marriage!) These titles in many ways chart the development of the field, which was paralleled by my own intellectual development in thinking about the relationships between women and men, relationships we took for granted in the days of "courtship and marriage."

Sociologists for Women in Society (sws) started twenty years ago, too. In addition to countless absorbing conversations about gender with women whose thinking was also evolving, sws gave me the opportunity of being the founding editor of *Gender & Society* from 1986 through 1990. In this position, I had the privilege of helping to develop feminist social science theory and research. As editor I was able to hone my own ideas about gender, particularly its social construction.

The language of this book reflects the style I developed as editor of *Gender & Society*. I made a distinction between gender as a social phenomenon and the social phenomenon of biological sex. Gender, sexuality, and sex are distinct concepts in this book. "Women" and "men" are not equated with "females" and "males" and are not assumed to be heterosexual. Where "sex" is used, it connotes a biological or physiological category that is also socially constructed. I distinguish sex from sexuality, because sexual orientation, identification, and

ix

sexual practices are similarly socially constructed and have their own genealogy and politics.

In an effort to bring more precision to the designation of racial ethnic groups, particularly in a country as heterogeneous as the United States, I have tried to indicate the groups' social relationship to each other as "dominant group and subordinated group," rather than "majority" and "minority," which are clearly misnomers.

For authors who use their birth name and their married name, both last names are used in the text. In the citations in parentheses only the final name is given, and the references are alphabetized by the first letter of the final name, following English-language practice. The exceptions are women who follow Hispanic usage, where both names are integral as final names. In Oriental names, I have used the first name as the family name, the second name as the given name.

The bibliography, long as it is, is by no means exhaustive. For the most part, the citations represent the works that were most interesting to me and most important to scholars in the area, as indicated by frequency of citation. However, a glance at the references in publications in any of the specialized areas will demonstrate that their depth and breadth far exceed my limited listing. I concentrated on publications since 1980, but many of the ideas, theories, and premises of feminist scholarship were first presented in the early 1970s in books and papers that have become classics. Although many of the early journal articles have by now been reprinted, some in many anthologies, I have tried to cite the earliest appearance in order to give the reader an idea of how feminist thinking has developed.

The last chapter of the book is a greatly revised version of "Dismantling Noah's Ark," originally published in *Sex Roles* 14 (1986): 567–80.

For helping me organize and refine the concepts presented in this book, I am indebted to my students at the CUNY Graduate School, who commented on early drafts of chapters of the book, and the members of the gender seminar at Bar Ilan University, who commented on later drafts. Patricia Yancey Martin, Barbara Katz Rothman, and Dafna Izraeli, who read the entire manuscript, have my heartfelt thanks. I am also grateful to Susan Farrell for being a sounding board for my ideas during the years she was managing editor of *Gender & Society* and for supplying me with many pertinent articles during the time I was writing this book.

My thanks also to Susan Zimmerman, who gave me the citations on Renaissance cross-dressing and the theater and *The Roaring Girl,* Daphne

Achilles, who lent me her copy of *The Exultation of Inanna,* and David Abrams and Diane Kelly for a wonderful firsthand experience of prehistoric cave art in France with Past Times Tours.

My editor, Gladys Topkis, recognized the worth of my ideas about gender from a very sketchy proposal and gave me the impetus to launch this project. Elliot Weininger, Susan Farrell, and Sharon Sherman did the indispensable runs back and forth from the various CUNY libraries. Helga Feder and the CUNY Graduate School Mina Reese Library staff have my gratitude for filling with dispatch my endless requests for interlibrary loan books. During 1992–93, when I was finishing the book, I had the benefit of a sabbatical fellowship in Israel that was funded by the United States–Israel Educational Foundation (Fulbright Award).

Most of all, I am indebted to all those feminists who have done the research and developed the theories of gender I used. My book is a synthesis of their gigantic and heroic endeavors. If I have taken feminist ideas a little farther by showing the underlying structure and processes of what I call the social institution of gender, it will pay off some of my great debt to the feminist scholarship of the past twenty years.

INTRODUCTION

When a new field of study emerges, it is usually based theoretically and in research practice on premises and problems current at the time. But as research brings in data that do not fit into accepted theory, the field begins to go through what Thomas Kuhn (1970) calls a scientific revolution. Eventually, if the field is to progress, it needs a new *paradigm:* new theories and new research questions.

In this book, I offer a new paradigm of gender—*gender as a social institution.* Its focus is the analysis of gender as a social structure that has its origins in the development of human culture, not in biology or procreation. Like any social institution, gender exhibits both universal features and chronological and cross-cultural variations that affect individual lives and social interaction in major ways. As is true of other institutions, gender's history can be traced, its structure examined, and its changing effects researched.

My concept of gender differs from previous conceptualizations in that I do not locate it in the individual or in interpersonal relations, although the construction and maintenance of gender are manifest in personal identities and in social interaction. Rather, I see gender as an institution that establishes patterns of expectations for individuals, orders the social processes of everyday life, is built into the major social organizations of society, such as the economy, ideology, the family, and politics, and is also an entity in and of itself.

When studies of gender started, the field was called "sex roles." The perspective of sex roles is psychological and focused on individual attitudes and attributes. Sex-role theorists argue that what children learn from their families, teachers, picture books, and school books produces masculine and feminine attitudes, motivations, and personalities that will fit children into their adult roles. Although change can take place later in life, many sex-role characteristics, such as women's parenting abilities, seem to be fixed for life. Since the liberal feminists who were promulgating the new field of sex roles believed in progress and change, the field had a built-in contradiction—where was change to take place? Reeducation and resocialization of adults? Or new, nonsexist patterns of socialization of children, which would require waiting a generation for change to take place? If parents and teachers enacted traditional sex roles, who was to institute the new, nonsexist patterns for the new generation? And what would be the content of future, androgynous roles? The concept of roles as the connection between individuals and society is useful for exploring how the consensus and contradictions of social structure play out in interpersonal relations (Komarovsky 1992), but the roles women and men play don't explain gender as a social institution any more than the jobs people have explain the economy as a social institution.

Radical feminists like Catharine MacKinnon (1982) threw down a powerful challenge to liberal feminists, arguing that sex and gender are a worldwide system of domination of women by men through control of women's sexuality and procreative capacity. In the radical feminist view, the sex-gender system of women's oppression is deliberate, not accidental, and pervades other social institutions—the family especially, and also the mass media and religion, which produce the justification for women's subordination. Radical feminists are particularly critical of such modern social-control agencies as law and the criminal-justice system because they allow men to rape, batter, prostitute, and sexually harass women with few legal restrictions.

Marxist feminists like Heidi Hartmann (1976) and Michèle Barrett ([1980] 1988) also locate women's oppression in the structure of society. In contrast to the radical feminists' focus on sexuality, Marxist feminists focus on the gendered division of labor. They argue for the equal importance of gender and class oppression and analyze the ways in which two parallel institutions— the economy (capitalism) and the family (patriarchy)—structure women's lives. Marxist feminists argue that work in the marketplace and work in the home are inextricably intertwined structures and that both exploit women. Recent theories claim that patriarchy, the ideological dominance of women by men, is located both in the family and in the workplace (Walby 1986, 1990).

Psychoanalytic feminists, such as Nancy Chodorow (1978), Luce Irigaray ([1974] 1985), Juliet Mitchell (1975), and Gayle Rubin (1975), building on the ideas of Freud, Lacan, and Lévi-Strauss, have argued that gender is an idea of difference that emerges from family relationships, particularly mothering.

In the feminist psychoanalytic perspective, gender is embedded in the unconscious and is manifest in sexuality, fantasies, language, and the incest taboo. The focus is on sexuality as a powerful cultural and ideological force that oppresses women because it is inscribed in bodies and also in the unconscious.

For radical, Marxist, and psychoanalytic feminists, *patriarchy* is a central concept, but each perspective conceptualizes it somewhat differently. For radical feminists, patriarchy is *the* central concept—the structure and process of men's misogynist domination of women through violent control of their sexuality and childbearing. For Marxist feminists, women's patriarchal domination by their husbands in the home goes hand in hand with their exploitation as workers in the capitalistic marketplace (Hartmann 1981b; Young et al. 1981). For psychoanalytic feminists, patriarchy is the symbolic rule of the father through gendered sexuality and the unconscious.

"Patriarchy" has been used so commonly by feminists of every perspective to stand for "what oppresses women" that it sometimes seems to be the theoretical equivalent of phlogiston—what causes fire to burn—before the discovery of oxygen. More than all men's individual actions, patriarchy is simultaneously the process, structure, and ideology of women's subordination. While different aspects of women's subordination are teased out and dissected, the connections among the parts are left to "patriarchy." More recently, some Marxist feminists have been developing a theory of women's subordination that connects psychological development, sexual dominance, production, procreation, child care, and ideology (Hartsock 1983; Walby 1990). They want to look at patriarchy in all aspects of society at once to see how each form of men's exploitation of women supports and reinforces the others.[1]

I have chosen not to use the term "patriarchy" as an explanatory concept because of its overuse and slippery conceptualization, but I have quoted many passages that do discuss patriarchy as "what men do that subordinates or exploits women." My focus is *gender* because this term badly needs precise definition and clearer conceptualization or it will go the way of patriarchy. Although I see patriarchy, or men's subordination and exploitation of women, as the salient feature of gender as a social institution in many societies, including late twentieth-century postindustrial countries, gender is not synonymous with patriarchy or men's domination of women. *Gender* is a more general term encompassing all social relations that separate people into differentiated gendered statuses. I argue that inequality of the statuses of women and men was a historical development and that, as feminist research from a racial ethnic perspective has shown, there are cross-cutting racial and class statuses within each gender status that belie the universal pattern of men's domination and women's subordination implied by the concept of patriarchy.

Feminists writing from a racial ethnic perspective, such as bell hooks (1984) and Patricia Hill Collins (1989), have argued that it is incorrect to build research and feminist theory on a binary opposition of women and men when race and social class produce many categories of women and men that form hierarchical stratification systems in many societies. In that stratification system, race, class, and gender intersect to produce domination by upper-class white men *and* women and subordination of lower-class women *and* men of color.[2]

Such theorists in men's studies as R. W. Connell (1987), using a concept of hegemonic masculinity—economically successful, racially superior, and visibly heterosexual—have similarly developed the idea of a multiplicity of masculinities. In particular, they have shown how the practices of power are layered and interwoven in a society and have argued that gender dominance and its ideological justification include men's subordination and denigration of other men as well as men's exploitation of women (Carrigan, Connell, and Lee 1987).[3]

Cultural feminists—Judith Butler (1990), Donna Haraway (1989, 1991), Jane Flax (1990), and Marjorie Garber (1992), for example—also challenge the concept of gender categories as dual and oppositional. Their theories are rooted in the French feminist critique of psychoanalytic concepts of gendered sexuality and language.[4] But where the French feminists' political stance has been to valorize women's sexuality and its evocation in literature, cultural feminists claim that sexuality and gender are shifting, fluid categories. By teasing out the intertwined strands of the socially constructed body, self, desire, and symbolic representation, cultural feminists critique a feminist politics based solely on women as a subordinated status, presenting instead a more subversive view that undermines the solidity of a social order built on concepts of two sexes and two genders.[5]

The concept of gender as constructed was explored by American feminists in the 1970s, particularly Suzanne Kessler and Wendy McKenna ([1978] 1985). Building on Harold Garfinkel's (1967, 116–85) ethnomethodological analysis of how "Agnes," a transsexual, constructed a conventional womanhood, Kessler and McKenna argued that gender *and* sex are socially constructed. Their important point, that there is neither an essential sex dichotomy nor an essential gender dichotomy, was absorbed into liberal feminism. But liberal feminism emphasized only the social construction of femininity and masculinity and their translation into family and work roles. Cynthia Fuchs Epstein's *Deceptive Distinctions* (1988) is an extensive critique of the scientific premises of gender dichotomies, but it does not probe deeply enough into the way the dichotomies of sex, sexuality, and gender are built into the organization and politics of all social institutions, the interactions of everyday life, and the consciousness of self we call identity. The work on psychoanalysis and politics that the French feminists were doing in the 1970s was not translated into English until the 1980s. It is only now, in the 1990s, that a full-fledged analysis of gender as wholly constructed, symbolically loaded, and ideologically enforced is taking place in American feminism.

In this book, I have used theoretical ideas of all of these strands of feminism and drawn on research on the social aspects of gender from anthropology, history, sociology, social psychology, sociolinguistics, men's studies, and culture studies. I have tried to fit these pieces together into a coherent picture of gender as a process of social construction, a system of social stratification, and an institution that structures every aspect of our lives because of its embeddedness in the family, the workplace, and the state, as well as in sexuality, language, and culture. The intent of this book, however, is not to valorize that institutionalization but to call its naturalness and inevitability into question. My politics is that of feminist deconstructionism, and my aim in this book is to challenge the validity, permanence, and necessity of gender. For that reason, I have not used the feminist "we," but refer to women in the third person. I agree with Judith Butler that an inclusive, monolithic concept of "woman" denies the multiplicity, complexity, and historical and geographical location of genders (1990, 142).

Paradoxes of Gender

This book is called *Paradoxes of Gender* because, when examined closely, much of what we take for granted about gender and its causes and effects either does not hold up or can be explained differently. For example, despite the evidence that women and men are more similar than different, the institution of gender continues to create and maintain socially significant differences between women and men (Hess 1990). What seems to be relevant—gender differences—is a means, not an end. The point of these differences is to justify the exploitation of an identifiable group—women. If one set of differences is successfully challenged, another set will take its place (Reskin 1988). As Joan Wallach Scott says, "Gender is a constitutive element of social relationships based on perceived differences between the sexes, and gender is a primary way of signifying relationships of power" (1988a, 42).

A second major paradox is the origin of gender and, especially, gender inequality. Because gender is ubiquitous in human society, the belief has been that it must be genetic or physiological and that gender inequality is ultimately based on procreative differences. But a close examination of females' and males' relationship to procreation reveals that it is females who are at an advantage, not males:

> Women's ability to bear babies in contrast to men's inability to do so, is a potential source of power unmatched in modern times by any physical advantages men have. . . . Usually, in civilized societies, varying degrees of compensations have been created for the deprived. . . . In the case of fertility, however, instead of repairing the disabled—that is, men—they have received compensation in the form of social customs that give them power over the able—that is, over women's bodies— and fertility. (Tangri 1976, 896)

This paradox is resolved if gender is conceptualized as a social institution often rooted in conflict over scarce resources and in social relationships of power. Gender inequality structures the unequal conditions of procreation, not the other way around (Rich 1977). Where women and men are different but not unequal, women's birth-giving is not a source of subordination. Indeed, for much of human history, people worshiped goddesses of fertility; statues of these goddesses can be found in every archaeological museum.

Gender is a human invention, like language, kinship, religion, and technology; like them, gender organizes human social life in culturally patterned ways. Gender organizes social relations in everyday life as well as in the major social structures, such as social class and the hierarchies of bureaucratic organizations (Acker 1988, 1990). The gendered microstructure and the gendered macrostructure reproduce and reinforce each other. The social reproduction of gender in individuals reproduces the gendered societal structure; as individuals act out gender norms and expectations in face-to-face interaction, they are constructing gendered systems of dominance and power.[6] Gender has changed in the past and will change in the future, but without deliberate restructuring it will not necessarily change in the direction of greater equality between women and men.

Order of the Book

The usual order of most books (and courses) on gender is to start with individuals and show how they are gendered through socialization and through selective learning of gender norms and roles. These learned patterns are projected into adult men's and women's behavior in families and in the labor force. Adults' behavior is said to create men's and women's unequal social and political status in any society. The order of such explanations implies that individual actions construct social institutions and therefore that changes in individual behavior can topple social institutions.

It is true that without individual actions (voluntary or coerced) there would be no social institutions, since the social structures we call "gender," "government," "family," "economy," and so on must be enacted every day in order to continue and in that enactment are strengthened or weakened, sustained or resisted (D. E. Smith 1987a). Nonetheless, social institutions, except in periods of revolutionary or anarchic upheaval, exist *prior* to any individual's birth, education, and social patterning. The patterned and intertwined structures of work, family, culture, education, religion, and law are gendered, and they deeply and continuously shape the lives of individuals, starting at birth (or even before, when the sex of the fetus is known). Through gendered personalities and identities, these patterns are internalized and willingly reenacted.

The familiar data about women and men in the economy, education, the media, law, medicine, and politics are the concrete manifestations of an underlying structure—the social institution of gender. The concept of gender as an institution explains work patterns (why do occupational gender segregation and stratification persist?), family patterns (why is housework mostly women's responsibility?), norms of sexuality (why is there violence against women?), the micropolitics of authority (why are there so few women leaders?), and symbolic cultural representations (why are they seen through men's eyes?).

The book expands on and documents these ideas. Although many paradoxes of gender are discussed throughout the book, each chapter takes up a particular paradox of gender:

Why does gender simultaneously construct difference and sameness?

Why are the phenomena of bodily experiences gendered?

Why, given the variety of sexual behaviors and relationships, do we speak of only two opposite sexes?

Why don't transvestites, transsexuals, hermaphrodites, and the institutionalized third genders in some societies affect the conceptualization of two genders and two sexes?

Why are most of our cultural images of women the way men see them, not the way women see themselves?

Why was inequality of women and men the consequence of humans' invention of gender when originally the gendered division of labor was a means of cooperatively expanding the food supply and ensuring the survival of children?

Why are all women expected to have children and care for them in modern society? How does this responsibility coopt women into a system of inequality?

Why is domestic work the wife's responsibility in modern societies even when she earns more than half the family income?

Why does gendered segregation of jobs and lower compensation of work done by women persist throughout industrialized economies despite the enormous variety of types of work and work skills?

Why, when women can be found in substantial numbers in many occupations and professions, are there so few women in positions of authority in modern industrialized societies?

Why do societies established for equality (including, in some revolutionary cases, gender equality) still exhibit substantial and systematic gender inequality?

Why, since gender is socially constructed, is it so difficult to eradicate or even minimize?

Although each chapter explores one topic, the overall frame of gender as a social institution means that the discussion of gender structures and practices in one chapter resonates with themes in other chapters. The three parts are intertwined as well: gendered practices produce the social institution of gender, which in turn constrains social practices; structure and practices simultaneously sustain and are legitimized by the micropolitics of everyday life and the macropolitics of state power.

Where Are We Going?

The enormous weight of history and current institutionalized practices makes it seem as if there is no way out—no way to make significant and lasting changes in the social institution of gender. Yet changes are made every day (another paradox of gender). There is constant tension between individual and group resistance and social control, between the exceptions and the rules. Indeed, the rules of existing institutions are constantly being revised and repaired (Hilbert 1987). Human beings are both orderly and rebellious; they like knowing what to expect from others, even if they protest and challenge.

Feminists have resisted and rebelled as scholars, researchers, and activists (Chafetz and Dworkin 1986; Rowbotham 1989). The "known world" looks very different through women's eyes. As activists, feminists have promulgated reforms of existing institutional laws, rules, and norms. As researchers, feminists have made evident the built-in oppression of women in patterns of behavior that are taken for granted, particularly concerning sexuality and violence. As theorists, feminists have turned inside out the categories of production and social reproduction by demonstrating that housework and child care are unpaid *work* for the family and for society, and that paid work is so deeply gendered that there seem to be built-in sexual taboos about how women can earn money. Lesbian feminists and gay men particularly, through their open rebellions, have changed ideas of normalcy and deviance in sexual mores, living arrangements, and parenting.

But I do not think it is inevitable that gender categories will gradually blur under the weight of evidence of the similarities of women and men, or that by gradual erosion, gender will stop being the major determinant of how the work of modern society is allocated and the rewards distributed. Pendulum swings are common and social exigencies often excuse greater oppression of one group by another. It can certainly happen to women and men.[7]

In the United States during World War II, women were recruited for work in defense plants, steel mills, and other heavy industry. Day-care centers were set up in many workplaces because of the desperate need for workers. But despite women's evident ability to handle heavy physical labor and their desire to keep working and earning high wages, gender segregation of jobs persisted, and women were fired when the war ended (Milkman 1987). The day-care centers were abandoned, and the 1950s were conservative, family-oriented, and gender-segregated.[8] In Islamic countries that have become more fundamentalist, women have put on the veil over their blue jeans; more problematic, they have been stripped of all their civil rights (Kandiyoti 1991; Moghadam 1989). With the crumbling of communism and the turn to capitalist economies in Eastern Europe, women workers expect to be fired first, and liberal abortion laws are under challenge from resurgent Catholic hierarchies.[9]

Change can go the other way, too. The Persian Gulf War of 1990–91 sent 35,000 U.S. servicewomen to the frontlines, including mothers of small children, some of whom volunteered.[10] They were 6 percent of the total force of 541,425, and 10 percent of those who were killed.[11] Although the disruption of family life may lead to promulgation of protective rules once again, U.S. servicewomen attained widespread public recognition of their role. ("Our men and women in the Armed Services" was the slogan of the day.) Indeed, a few months after the end of the war, the U.S. House of Representatives voted to allow women to be combat pilots (*New York Times* 1991d).[12]

The paradox of women fighting and dying to protect and liberate countries that don't allow their women to vote, drive cars, or appear in public unveiled seems to have raised the consciousness of women in both cultures.[13] American servicewomen had to wear long sleeves off their bases, be accompanied into town by a man and have him pay, and use the back doors of gymnasiums and other facilities. Under orders from generals and politicians, they conformed, but grudgingly; they would have liked servicemen to give up their prerogatives in sympathy.[14] At the same time, forty-seven Saudi women were empowered enough to stage a drive-in, which resulted in eight hours of questioning by the police, harassment by the religious authorities, and loss of jobs, but also acts of support from kinsmen (*Ms. Magazine* 1991).

Because consciousness of oppression does not always lead to a push for action (Davis and Robinson 1991) and rebels are frequently publicly punished, individuals are more likely to conform than to rebel. Not surprisingly, those advantaged by the social institution of gender want to maintain the status quo, but the not-so-privileged also have an investment in a going social order that gives them some bargaining power.[15] Rebellion is hard on individual lives—it can eat up a person's livelihood, emotions, and freedom. Unless rebellion is a major group effort, supported by a substantial number of women and men, it is not likely to make a dent in an existing major institution like gender.

Real change would mean a conscious reordering of the organizing principles of social life (women take care of children, men go to work) with awareness of hidden assumptions (children have different attachments to mothers than to fathers) and latent effects (men need to suppress the feminine in themselves and can't allow women to have any authority over them). Change is unlikely to be deep-seated unless the pervasiveness of the social institution of gender and its social construction are made explicit.[16] The prime paradox of gender is that in order to dismantle the institution you must first make it very visible, which is the purpose of this book.

Part I

PRODUCING GENDER

[Gethenians] do not see each other as men or women. This is almost impossible for our imagination to accept. What is the first question we ask about a newborn baby?

—*Ursula Le Guin (1969, 94)*

"NIGHT TO HIS DAY": THE SOCIAL CONSTRUCTION OF GENDER

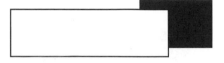

Talking about gender for most people is the equivalent of fish talking about water. Gender is so much the routine ground of everyday activities that questioning its taken-for-granted assumptions and presuppositions is like thinking about whether the sun will come up.[1] Gender is so pervasive that in our society we assume it is bred into our genes. Most people find it hard to believe that gender is constantly created and re-created out of human interaction, out of social life, and is the texture and order of that social life. Yet gender, like culture, is a human production that depends on everyone constantly "doing gender" (West and Zimmerman 1987).

And everyone "does gender" without thinking about it. Today, on the subway, I saw a well-dressed man with a year-old child in a stroller. Yesterday, on a bus, I saw a man with a tiny baby in a carrier on his chest. Seeing men taking care of small children in public is increasingly common—at least in New York City. But both men were quite obviously stared at—and smiled at, approvingly. Everyone was doing gender—the men who were changing the role of fathers and the other passengers, who were applauding them silently. But there was more gendering going on that probably fewer people noticed. The baby was wearing a white crocheted cap and white clothes. You couldn't tell if it was a boy or a girl. The child in the stroller was wearing a dark blue T-shirt and dark print pants. As they started to leave the train, the father put a Yankee baseball cap on the child's head. Ah, a boy, I thought. Then I noticed the gleam of tiny earrings in the child's ears, and as they got off, I saw the little flowered sneakers and lace-trimmed socks. Not a boy after all. Gender done.

Gender is such a familiar part of daily life that it usually takes a deliberate disruption of our expectations of how women and men are supposed to act to pay attention to how it is produced. Gender signs and signals are so ubiquitous that we usually fail to note them—unless they are missing or ambiguous. Then we are uncomfortable until we have successfully placed the other person in a gender status; otherwise, we feel socially dislocated. In our society, in addition to man and woman, the status can be *transvestite* (a person who dresses in opposite-gender clothes) and *transsexual* (a person who has had sex-change surgery). Transvestites and transsexuals carefully construct their gender status by dressing, speaking, walking, gesturing in the ways prescribed for women or men—whichever they want to be taken for—and so does any "normal" person.

For the individual, gender construction starts with assignment to a sex category on the basis of what the genitalia look like at birth.[2] Then babies are dressed or adorned in a way that displays the category because parents don't want to be constantly asked whether their baby is a girl or a boy. A sex category becomes a gender status through naming, dress, and the use of other gender markers. Once a child's gender is evident, others treat those in one gender differently from those in the other, and the children respond to the different treatment by feeling different and behaving differently. As soon as they can talk, they start to refer to themselves as members of their gender. Sex doesn't come into play again until puberty, but by that time, sexual feelings and desires and practices have been shaped by gendered norms and expectations. Adolescent boys and girls approach and avoid each other in an elaborately scripted and gendered mating dance. Parenting is gendered, with different expectations for mothers and for fathers, and people of different genders work at different kinds of jobs. The work adults do as mothers and fathers and as low-level workers and high-level bosses, shapes women's and men's life experiences, and these experiences produce different feelings, consciousness, relationships, skills—ways of being that we call feminine or masculine.[3] All of these processes constitute the social construction of gender.

Gendered roles change—today fathers are taking care of little children, girls and boys are wearing unisex clothing and getting the same education, women and men are working at the same jobs. Although many traditional social groups are quite strict about maintaining gender differences, in other social groups they seem to be blurring. Then why the one-year-old's earrings? Why is it still so important to mark a child as a girl or a boy, to make sure she is not taken for a boy or he for a girl? What would happen if they were? They would, quite literally, have changed places in their social world.

To explain why gendering is done from birth, constantly and by everyone,

we have to look not only at the way individuals experience gender but at
gender as a social institution. As a social institution, gender is one of the major
ways that human beings organize their lives. Human society depends on a
predictable division of labor, a designated allocation of scarce goods, assigned
responsibility for children and others who cannot care for themselves, common values and their systematic transmission to new members, legitimate
leadership, music, art, stories, games, and other symbolic productions. One
way of choosing people for the different tasks of society is on the basis of their
talents, motivations, and competence—their demonstrated achievements.
The other way is on the basis of gender, race, ethnicity—ascribed membership
in a category of people. Although societies vary in the extent to which they use
one or the other of these ways of allocating people to work and to carry out
other responsibilities, every society uses gender and age grades. Every society
classifies people as "girl and boy children," "girls and boys ready to be married," and "fully adult women and men," constructs similarities among them
and differences between them, and assigns them to different roles and responsibilities. Personality characteristics, feelings, motivations, and ambitions flow
from these different life experiences so that the members of these different
groups become different kinds of people. The process of gendering and its
outcome are legitimated by religion, law, science, and the society's entire set
of values.

In order to understand gender as a social institution, it is important to
distinguish human action from animal behavior. Animals feed themselves and
their young until their young can feed themselves. Humans have to produce
not only food but shelter and clothing. They also, if the group is going to
continue as a social group, have to teach the children how their particular
group does these tasks. In the process, humans reproduce gender, family,
kinship, and a division of labor—social institutions that do not exist among
animals. Primate social groups have been referred to as families, and their
mating patterns as monogamy, adultery, and harems. Primate behavior has
been used to prove the universality of sex differences—as built into our
evolutionary inheritance (Haraway 1978a). But animals' sex differences are
not at all the same as humans' gender differences; animals' bonding is not
kinship; animals' mating is not ordered by marriage; and animals' dominance
hierarchies are not the equivalent of human stratification systems. Animals
group on sex and age, relational categories that are physiologically, not socially,
different. Humans create gender and age-group categories that are socially,
and not necessarily physiologically, different.[4]

For animals, physiological maturity means being able to impregnate or conceive; its markers are coming into heat (estrus) and sexual attraction. For humans, puberty means being available for marriage; it is marked by rites that demonstrate this marital eligibility. Although the onset of physiological puberty is signaled by secondary sex characteristics (menstruation, breast development, sperm ejaculation, pubic and underarm hair), the onset of social adulthood is ritualized by the coming-out party or desert walkabout or bar mitzvah or graduation from college or first successful hunt or dreaming or inheritance of property. Humans have rituals that mark the passage from childhood into puberty and puberty into full adult status, as well as for marriage, childbirth, and death; animals do not (van Gennep 1960). To the extent that infants and the dead are differentiated by whether they are male or female, there are different birth rituals for girls and boys, and different funeral rituals for men and women (Biersack 1984, 132–33). Rituals of puberty, marriage, and becoming a parent are gendered, creating a "woman," a "man," a "bride," a "groom," a "mother," a "father." Animals have no equivalents for these statuses.

Among animals, siblings mate and so do parents and children; humans have incest taboos and rules that encourage or forbid mating between members of different kin groups (Lévi-Strauss 1956, [1949] 1969). Any animal of the same species may feed another's young (or may not, depending on the species). Humans designate responsibility for particular children by kinship; humans frequently limit responsibility for children to the members of their kinship group or make them into members of their kinship group with adoption rituals.

Animals have dominance hierarchies based on size or on successful threat gestures and signals. These hierarchies are usually sexed, and in some species, moving to the top of the hierarchy physically changes the sex (Austad 1986). Humans have stratification patterns based on control of surplus food, ownership of property, legitimate demands on others' work and sexual services, enforced determinations of who marries whom, and approved use of violence. If a woman replaces a man at the top of a stratification hierarchy, her social status may be that of a man, but her sex does not change.

Mating, feeding, and nurturant behavior in animals is determined by instinct and imitative learning and ordered by physiological sex and age (Lancaster 1974). In humans, these behaviors are taught and symbolically reinforced and ordered by socially constructed gender and age grades. Social gender and age statuses sometimes ignore or override physiological sex and age completely. Male and female animals (unless they physiologically change) are not interchangeable; infant animals cannot take the place of adult animals.

Human females can become husbands and fathers, and human males can become wives and mothers, without sex-change surgery (Blackwood 1984). Human infants can reign as kings or queens.

Western society's values legitimate gendering by claiming that it all comes from physiology—female and male procreative differences. But gender and sex are not equivalent, and gender as a social construction does not flow automatically from genitalia and reproductive organs, the main physiological differences of females and males. In the construction of ascribed social statuses, physiological differences such as sex, stage of development, color of skin, and size are crude markers. They are not the source of the social statuses of gender, age grade, and race. Social statuses are carefully constructed through prescribed processes of teaching, learning, emulation, and enforcement. Whatever genes, hormones, and biological evolution contribute to human social institutions is materially as well as qualitatively transformed by social practices. Every social institution has a material base, but culture and social practices transform that base into something with qualitatively different patterns and constraints. The economy is much more than producing food and goods and distributing them to eaters and users; family and kinship are not the equivalent of having sex and procreating; morals and religions cannot be equated with the fears and ecstasies of the brain; language goes far beyond the sounds produced by tongue and larynx. No one eats "money" or "credit"; the concepts of "god" and "angels" are the subjects of theological disquisitions; not only words but objects, such as their flag, "speak" to the citizens of a country.

Similarly, gender cannot be equated with biological and physiological differences between human females and males. The building blocks of gender are *socially constructed statuses*. Western societies have only two genders, "man" and "woman." Some societies have three genders—men, women, and *berdaches* or *hijras* or *xaniths*. Berdaches, hijras, and xaniths are biological males who behave, dress, work, and are treated in most respects as social women; they are therefore not men, nor are they female women; they are, in our language, "male women."[5] There are African and American Indian societies that have a gender status called *manly hearted women*—biological females who work, marry, and parent as men; their social status is "female men" (Amadiume 1987; Blackwood 1984). They do not have to behave or dress as men to have the social responsibilities and prerogatives of husbands and fathers; what makes them men is enough wealth to buy a wife.

Modern Western societies' *transsexuals* and *transvestites* are the nearest equivalent of these crossover genders, but they are not institutionalized as third genders (Bolin 1987). Transsexuals are biological males and females who

have sex-change operations to alter their genitalia. They do so in order to bring
their physical anatomy in congruence with the way they want to live and with
their own sense of gender identity. They do not become a third gender; they
change genders. Transvestites are males who live as women and females who
live as men but do not intend to have sex-change surgery. Their dress, appearance, and mannerisms fall within the range of what is expected from members
of the opposite gender, so that they "pass." They also change genders, sometimes temporarily, some for most of their lives. Transvestite women have
fought in wars as men soldiers as recently as the nineteenth century; some
married women, and others went back to being women and married men once
the war was over.[6] Some were discovered when their wounds were treated;
others not until they died. In order to work as a jazz musician, a man's
occupation, Billy Tipton, a woman, lived most of her life as a man. She died
recently at seventy-four, leaving a wife and three adopted sons for whom she
was husband and father, and musicians with whom she had played and traveled,
for whom she was "one of the boys" (*New York Times* 1989).[7] There have been
many other such occurrences of women passing as men to do more prestigious
or lucrative men's work (Matthaei 1982, 192–93).[8]

Genders, therefore, are not attached to a biological substratum. Gender
boundaries are breachable, and individual and socially organized shifts from
one gender to another call attention to "cultural, social, or aesthetic disso-
nances" (Garber 1992, 16). These odd or deviant or third genders show us
what we ordinarily take for granted—that people have to learn to be women
and men. Men who cross-dress for performances or for pleasure often learn
from women's magazines how to "do femininity" convincingly (Garber 1992,
41–51). Because transvestism is direct evidence of how gender is constructed,
Marjorie Garber claims it has "extraordinary power . . . to disrupt, expose,
and challenge, putting in question the very notion of the 'original' and of stable
identity" (1992, 16).

Gender Bending

It is difficult to see how gender is constructed because we take it for granted
that it's all biology, or hormones, or human nature. The differences between
women and men seem to be self-evident, and we think they would occur no
matter what society did. But in actuality, human females and males are physiologically more similar in appearance than are the two sexes of many species of
animals and are more alike than different in traits and behavior (C. F. Epstein
1988). Without the deliberate use of gendered clothing, hairstyles, jewelry,

and cosmetics, women and men would look far more alike.[9] Even societies that do not cover women's breasts have gender-identifying clothing, scarification, jewelry, and hairstyles.

The ease with which many transvestite women pass as men and transvestite men as women is corroborated by the common gender misidentification in Westernized societies of people in jeans, T-shirts, and sneakers. Men with long hair may be addressed as "miss," and women with short hair are often taken for men unless they offset the potential ambiguity with deliberate gender markers (Devor 1987, 1989). Jan Morris, in *Conundrum,* an autobiographical account of events just before and just after a sex-change operation, described how easy it was to shift back and forth from being a man to being a woman when testing how it would feel to change gender status. During this time, Morris still had a penis and wore more or less unisex clothing; the context alone made the man and the woman:

> Sometimes the arena of my ambivalence was uncomfortably small. At the Travellers' Club, for example, I was obviously known as a man of sorts—women were only allowed on the premises at all during a few hours of the day, and even then were hidden away as far as possible in lesser rooms or alcoves. But I had another club, only a few hundred yards away, where I was known only as a woman, and often I went directly from one to the other, imperceptibly changing roles on the way—"Cheerio, sir," the porter would say at one club, and "Hello, madam," the porter would greet me at the other. (1975, 132)

Gender shifts are actually a common phenomenon in public roles as well. Queen Elizabeth II of England bore children, but when she went to Saudi Arabia on a state visit, she was considered an honorary man so that she could confer and dine with the men who were heads of a state that forbids unrelated men and women to have face-to-unveiled-face contact. In contemporary Egypt, lower-class women who run restaurants or shops dress in men's clothing and engage in unfeminine aggressive behavior, and middle-class educated women of professional or managerial status can take positions of authority (Rugh 1986, 131). In these situations, there is an important status change: These women are treated by the others in the situation as if they are men. From their own point of view, they are still women. From the social perspective, however, they are men.[10]

In many cultures, gender bending is prevalent in theater or dance—the Japanese kabuki are men actors who play both women and men; in Shakespeare's theater company, there were no actresses—Juliet and Lady Macbeth

were played by boys. Shakespeare's comedies are full of witty comments on
gender shifts. Women characters frequently masquerade as young men, and
other women characters fall in love with them; the boys playing these masquerading women, meanwhile, are acting out pining for the love of men
characters.[11] In *As You Like It,* when Rosalind justifies her protective cross-
dressing, Shakespeare also comments on manliness:

> Were it not better,
> Because that I am more than common tall,
> That I did suit me all points like a man:
> A gallant curtle-axe upon my thigh,
> A boar-spear in my hand, and in my heart
> Lie there what hidden women's fear there will,
> We'll have a swashing and martial outside,
> As many other mannish cowards have
> That do outface it with their semblances.   (I, i, 115–22)

Shakespeare's audience could appreciate the double subtext: Rosalind, a
woman character, was a boy dressed in girl's clothing who then dressed as a
boy; like bravery, masculinity and femininity can be put on and taken off with
changes of costume and role (Howard 1988, 435).[12]

   M Butterfly is a modern play of gender ambiguities, which David Hwang
(1989) based on a real person. Shi Peipu, a male Chinese opera singer who sang
women's roles, was a spy as a man and the lover as a woman of a Frenchman,
Gallimard, a diplomat (Bernstein 1986). The relationship lasted twenty years,
and Shi Peipu even pretended to be the mother of a child by Gallimard. "She"
also pretended to be too shy to undress completely. As "Butterfly," Shi Peipu
portrayed a fantasy Oriental woman who made the lover a "real man" (Kondo
1990b). In Gallimard's words, the fantasy was "of slender women in chong
sams and kimonos who die for the love of unworthy foreign devils. Who are
born and raised to be perfect women. Who take whatever punishment we give
them, and bounce back, strengthened by love, unconditionally" (D. H. Hwang
1989, 91). When the fantasy woman betrayed him by turning out to be the
more powerful "real man," Gallimard assumed the role of Butterfly and,
dressed in a geisha's robes, killed himself: "because 'man' and 'woman' are op-
positionally defined terms, reversals . . . are possible" (Kondo 1990b, 18).[13]

   But despite the ease with which gender boundaries can be traversed in
work, in social relationships, and in cultural productions, gender statuses
remain. Transvestites and transsexuals do not challenge the social construction
of gender. Their goal is to be feminine women and masculine men (Kando

1973). Those who do not want to change their anatomy but do want to change their gender behavior fare less well in establishing their social identity. The women Holly Devor called "gender blenders" wore their hair short, dressed in unisex pants, shirts, and comfortable shoes, and did not wear jewelry or makeup. They described their everyday dress as women's clothing: One said, "I wore jeans all the time, but I didn't wear men's clothes" (Devor 1989, 100). Their gender identity was women, but because they refused to "do femininity," they were constantly taken for men (1987, 1989, 107–42). Devor said of them: "The most common area of complaint was with public washrooms. They repeatedly spoke of the humiliation of being challenged or ejected from women's washrooms. Similarly, they found public change rooms to be dangerous territory and the buying of undergarments to be a difficult feat to accomplish" (1987, 29). In an ultimate ironic twist, some of these women said "they would feel like transvestites if they were to wear dresses, and two women said that they had been called transvestites when they had done so" (1987, 31). They resolved the ambiguity of their gender status by identifying as women in private and passing as men in public to avoid harassment on the street, to get men's jobs, and, if they were lesbians, to make it easier to display affection publicly with their lovers (Devor 1989, 107–42). Sometimes they even used men's bathrooms. When they had gender-neutral names, like Leslie, they could avoid the bureaucratic hassles that arose when they had to present their passports or other proof of identity, but because most had names associated with women, their appearance and their cards of identity were not conventionally congruent, and their gender status was in constant jeopardy.[14] When they could, they found it easier to pass as men than to try to change the stereotyped notions of what women should look like.

Paradoxically, then, bending gender rules and passing between genders does not erode but rather preserves gender boundaries. In societies with only two genders, the gender dichotomy is not disturbed by transvestites, because others feel that a transvestite is only transitorily ambiguous—is "really a man or woman underneath." After sex-change surgery, transsexuals end up in a conventional gender status—a "man" or a "woman" with the appropriate genitals (Eichler 1989). When women dress as men for business reasons, they are indicating that in that situation, they want to be treated the way men are treated; when they dress as women, they want to be treated as women:

By their male dress, female entrepreneurs signal their desire to suspend the expectations of accepted feminine conduct without losing respect and reputation. By wearing what is "unattractive" they signify that they are not intending to display their physical charms while engaging in public activity. Their loud, aggressive banter contrasts with the modest demeanor that attracts men. . . . Overt signalling of a suspension of the rules preserves normal conduct from eroding expectations. (Rugh 1986, 131)

For Individuals, Gender Means Sameness

Although the possible combinations of genitalia, body shapes, clothing, mannerisms, sexuality, and roles could produce infinite varieties in human beings, the social institution of gender depends on the production and maintenance of a limited number of gender statuses and of making the members of these statuses similar to each other. Individuals are born sexed but not gendered, and they have to be taught to be masculine or feminine.[15] As Simone de Beauvoir said: "One is not born, but rather becomes, a woman . . . ; it is civilization as a whole that produces this creature . . . which is described as feminine." (1952, 267).

Children learn to walk, talk, and gesture the way their social group says girls and boys should. Ray Birdwhistell, in his analysis of body motion as human communication, calls these learned gender displays *tertiary* sex characteristics and argues that they are needed to distinguish genders because humans are a weakly dimorphic species—their only sex markers are genitalia (1970, 39–46). Clothing, paradoxically, often hides the sex but displays the gender.

In early childhood, humans develop gendered personality structures and sexual orientations through their interactions with parents of the same and opposite gender. As adolescents, they conduct their sexual behavior according to gendered scripts. Schools, parents, peers, and the mass media guide young people into gendered work and family roles. As adults, they take on a gendered social status in their society's stratification system. Gender is thus both ascribed and achieved (West and Zimmerman 1987).

The achievement of gender was most dramatically revealed in a case of an accidental transsexual—a baby boy whose penis was destroyed in the course of a botched circumcision when he was seven months old (Money and Ehrhardt 1972, 118–23). The child's sex category was changed to "female," and a vagina was surgically constructed when the child was seventeen months old. The parents were advised that they could successfully raise the child, one of identical twins, as a girl. Physicians assured them that the child was too young to have formed a gender identity. Children's sense of which gender they belong to usually develops around the age of three, at the time that they start to group objects and recognize that the people around them also fit into categories—big, little; pink skinned, brown-skinned; boys, girls. Three has also been the age when children's appearance is ritually gendered, usually by cutting a boy's hair or dressing him in distinctively masculine clothing. In Victorian times, English boys wore dresses up to the age of three, when they were put into short pants (Garber 1992, 1–2).

The parents of the accidental transsexual bent over backward to feminize the child—and succeeded. Frilly dresses, hair ribbons, and jewelry created a pride in looks, neatness, and "daintiness." More significant, the child's dominance was also feminized:

> The girl had many tomboyish traits, such as abundant physical energy, a high level of activity, stubbornness, and being often the dominant one in a girls' group. Her mother tried to modify her tomboyishness: ". . . I teach her to be more polite and quiet. I always wanted those virtues. I never did manage, but I'm going to try to manage them to—my daughter—to be more quiet and ladylike." From the beginning the girl had been the dominant twin. By the age of three, her dominance over her brother was, as her mother described it, that of a mother hen. The boy in turn took up for his sister, if anyone threatened her. (Money and Ehrhardt 1972, 122)

This child was not a tomboy because of male genes or hormones; according to her mother, she herself had also been a tomboy. What the mother had learned poorly while growing up as a "natural" female she insisted that her physically reconstructed son-daughter learn well. For both mother and child, the social construction of gender overrode any possibly inborn traits.

People go along with the imposition of gender norms because the weight of morality as well as immediate social pressure enforces them. Consider how many instructions for properly gendered behavior are packed into this mother's admonition to her daughter: "This is how to hem a dress when you see the hem coming down and so to prevent yourself from looking like the slut I know you are so bent on becoming" (Kincaid 1978).

Gender norms are inscribed in the way people move, gesture, and even eat. In one African society, men were supposed to eat with their "whole mouth, wholeheartedly, and not, like women, just with the lips, that is halfheartedly, with reservation and restraint" (Bourdieu [1980] 1990, 70). Men and women in this society learned to walk in ways that proclaimed their different positions in the society:

> The manly man . . . stands up straight into the face of the person he
> approaches, or wishes to welcome. Ever on the alert, because ever
> threatened, he misses nothing of what happens around him. . . . Con-
> versely, a well brought-up woman . . . is expected to walk with a
> slight stoop, avoiding every misplaced movement of her body, her head
> or her arms, looking down, keeping her eyes on the spot where she will
> next put her foot, especially if she happens to have to walk past the
> men's assembly. (70)

Many cultures go beyond clothing, gestures, and demeanor in gendering
children. They inscribe gender directly into bodies. In traditional Chinese
society, mothers bound their daughters' feet into three-inch stumps to enhance their sexual attractiveness. Jewish fathers circumcise their infant sons to
show their covenant with God. Women in African societies remove the clitoris
of prepubescent girls, scrape their labia, and make the lips grow together to
preserve their chastity and ensure their marriageability. In Western societies,
women augment their breast size with silicone and reconstruct their faces with
cosmetic surgery to conform to cultural ideals of feminine beauty. Hanna
Papanek (1990) notes that these practices reinforce the sense of superiority or
inferiority in the adults who carry them out as well as in the children on whom
they are done: The genitals of Jewish fathers and sons are physical and psychological evidence of their common dominant religious and familial status; the
genitals of African mothers and daughters are physical and psychological
evidence of their joint subordination.[16]

Sandra Bem (1981, 1983) argues that because gender is a powerful
"schema" that orders the cognitive world, one must wage a constant, active
battle for a child not to fall into typical gendered attitudes and behavior. In
1972, *Ms. Magazine* published Lois Gould's fantasy of how to raise a child free
of gender-typing. The experiment calls for hiding the child's anatomy from all
eyes except the parents' and treating the child as neither a girl nor a boy. The
child, called X, gets to do all the things boys *and* girls do. The experiment is so
successful that all the children in X's class at school want to look and behave
like X. At the end of the story, the creators of the experiment are asked what
will happen when X grows up. The scientists' answer is that by then it will be
quite clear what X is, implying that its hormones will kick in and it will be
revealed as a female or male. That ambiguous, and somewhat contradictory,
ending lets Gould off the hook; neither she nor we have any idea what someone
brought up totally androgynously would be like sexually or socially as an adult.
The hormonal input will not create gender or sexuality but will only establish

secondary sex characteristics; breasts, beards, and menstruation alone do not produce social manhood or womanhood. Indeed, it is at puberty, when sex characteristics become evident, that most societies put pubescent children through their most important rites of passage, the rituals that officially mark them as fully gendered—that is, ready to marry and become adults.

Most parents create a gendered world for their newborn by naming, birth announcements, and dress. Children's relationships with same-gendered and different-gendered caretakers structure their self-identifications and person-alities. Through cognitive development, children extract and apply to their own actions the appropriate behavior for those who belong in their own gender, as well as race, religion, ethnic group, and social class, rejecting what is not appropriate. If their social categories are highly valued, they value themselves highly; if their social categories are low status, they lose self-esteem (Chodorow 1974). Many feminist parents who want to raise andro-gynous children soon lose their children to the pull of gendered norms (T. Gordon 1990, 87–90). My son attended a carefully nonsexist elementary school, which didn't even have girls' and boys' bathrooms. When he was seven or eight years old, I attended a class play about "squares" and "circles" and their need for each other and noticed that all the girl squares and circles wore makeup, but none of the boy squares and circles did. I asked the teacher about it after the play, and she said, "Bobby said he was not going to wear makeup, and he is a powerful child, so none of the boys would either." In a long discussion about conformity, my son confronted me with the question of who the conformists were, the boys who followed their leader or the girls who listened to the woman teacher. In actuality, they both were, because they both followed same gender leaders and acted in gender-appropriate ways. (Actors may wear makeup, but real boys don't.)

For human beings there is no essential femaleness or maleness, femininity or masculinity, womanhood or manhood, but once gender is ascribed, the social order constructs and holds individuals to strongly gendered norms and expectations. Individuals may vary on many of the components of gender and may shift genders temporarily or permanently, but they must fit into the limited number of gender statuses their society recognizes. In the process, they re-create their society's version of women and men: "If we do gender appropriately, we simultaneously sustain, reproduce, and render legitimate the institutional arrangements. . . . If we fail to do gender appropriately, we as individuals—not the institutional arrangements—may be called to account (for our character, motives, and predispositions)" (West and Zimmerman 1987, 146).

The gendered practices of everyday life reproduce a society's view of how women and men should act (Bourdieu [1980] 1990). Gendered social arrangements are justified by religion and cultural productions and backed by law, but the most powerful means of sustaining the moral hegemony of the dominant gender ideology is that the process is made invisible; any possible alternatives are virtually unthinkable (Foucault 1972; Gramsci 1971).[17]

For Society, Gender Means Difference

The pervasiveness of gender as a way of structuring social life demands that gender statuses be clearly differentiated. Varied talents, sexual preferences, identities, personalities, interests, and ways of interacting fragment the individual's bodily and social experiences. Nonetheless, these are organized in Western cultures into two and only two socially and legally recognized gender statuses, "man" and "woman."[18] In the social construction of gender, it does not matter what men and women actually do; it does not even matter if they do exactly the same thing. The social institution of gender insists only that what they do is *perceived* as different.

If men and women are doing the same tasks, they are usually spatially segregated to maintain gender separation, and often the tasks are given different job titles as well, such as executive secretary and administrative assistant (Reskin 1988). If the differences between women and men begin to blur, society's "sameness taboo" goes into action (G. Rubin 1975, 178). At a rock and roll dance at West Point in 1976, the year women were admitted to the prestigious military academy for the first time, the school's administrators "were reportedly perturbed by the sight of mirror-image couples dancing in short hair and dress gray trousers," and a rule was established that women cadets could dance at these events only if they wore skirts (Barkalow and Raab 1990, 53).[19] Women recruits in the U.S. Marine Corps are required to wear makeup—at a minimum, lipstick and eye shadow—and they have to take classes in makeup, hair care, poise, and etiquette. This feminization is part of a deliberate policy of making them clearly distinguishable from men Marines. Christine Williams quotes a twenty-five-year-old woman drill instructor as saying: "A lot of the recruits who come here don't wear makeup; they're tomboyish or athletic. A lot of them have the preconceived idea that going into the military means they can still be a tomboy. They don't realize that you are a *Woman* Marine" (1989, 76–77).[20]

If gender differences were genetic, physiological, or hormonal, gender bending and gender ambiguity would occur only in hermaphrodites, who are born with chromosomes and genitalia that are not clearly female or male. Since gender differences are socially constructed, all men and all women can enact the behavior of the other, because they know the other's social script: "'Man' and 'woman' are at once empty and overflowing categories. Empty because they have no ultimate, transcendental meaning. Overflowing because even when they appear to be fixed, they still contain within them alternative, denied, or suppressed definitions." (J. W. Scott 1988a, 49). Nonetheless, though individuals may be able to shift gender statuses, the gender boundaries have to hold, or the whole gendered social order will come crashing down.

Paradoxically, it is the social importance of gender statuses and their external markers—clothing, mannerisms, and spatial segregation—that makes gender bending or gender crossing possible—or even necessary. The social viability of differentiated gender statuses produces the need or desire to shift statuses. Without gender differentiation, transvestism and transsexuality would be meaningless. You couldn't dress in the opposite gender's clothing if all clothing were unisex. There would be no need to reconstruct genitalia to match identity if interests and life-styles were not gendered. There would be no need for women to pass as men to do certain kinds of work if jobs were not typed as "women's work" and "men's work." Women would not have to dress as men in public life in order to give orders or aggressively bargain with customers.

Gender boundaries are preserved when transsexuals create congruous autobiographies of always having felt like what they are now. The transvestite's story also "recuperates social and sexual norms" (Garber 1992, 69). In the transvestite's normalized narrative, he or she "is 'compelled' by social and economic forces to disguise himself or herself in order to get a job, escape repression, or gain artistic or political 'freedom'" (Garber 1992, 70). The "true identity," when revealed, causes amazement over how easily and successfully the person passed as a member of the opposite gender, not a suspicion that gender itself is something of a put-on.

Gender Ranking

Most societies rank genders according to prestige and power and construct them to be unequal, so that moving from one to another also means moving up or down the social scale. Among some North American Indian cultures, the hierarchy was male men, male women, female men, female women. Women produced significant durable goods (basketry, textiles, pottery, decorated leather goods), which could be traded. Women also controlled what they produced and any profit or wealth they earned. Since women's occupational realm could lead to prosperity and prestige, it was fair game for young men— but only if they became women in gender status. Similarly, women in other societies who amassed a great deal of wealth were allowed to become men— "manly hearts." According to Harriet Whitehead (1981):

> Both reactions reveal an unwillingness or inability to distinguish the sources of prestige—wealth, skill, personal efficacy (among other things)—from masculinity. Rather there is the innuendo that if a person performing female tasks can attain excellence, prosperity, or social power, it must be because that person is, at some level, a man. . . . A woman who could succeed at doing the things men did was honored as a man would be. . . . What seems to have been more disturbing to the culture—which means, for all intents and purposes, to the men—was the possibility that women, within their own depart- ment, might be onto a good thing. It was into this unsettling breach that the berdache institution was hurled. In their social aspect, women were complimented by the berdache's imitation. In their anatomic aspect, they were subtly insulted by his vaunted superiority. (108)

In American society, men-to-women transsexuals tend to earn less after surgery if they change occupations; women-to-men transsexuals tend to in- crease their income (Bolin 1988, 153–60; Brody 1979). Men who go into women's fields, like nursing, have less prestige than women who go into men's fields, like physics. Janice Raymond, a radical feminist, feels that transsexual men-to-women have advantages over female women because they were not socialized to be subordinate or oppressed throughout life. She says:

> We know that we are women who are born with female chromosomes and anatomy, and that whether or not we were socialized to be so- called normal women, patriarchy has treated and will treat us like women. Transsexuals have not had this same history. No man can have the history of being born and located in this culture as a woman. He can have the history of *wishing* to be a woman and of *acting* like a woman, but this gender experience is that of a transsexual, not of a woman. Surgery may confer the artifacts of outward and inward female organs but it cannot confer the history of being born a woman in this society. (1979, 114)

Because women who become men rise in the world and men who become women fall, Elaine Showalter (1987) was very critical of the movie *Tootsie,* in which Dustin Hoffman plays an actor who passes as a woman in order to be able to get work. "Dorothy" becomes a feminist "woman of the year" for standing up for women's rights not to be demeaned or sexually harassed. Showalter feels that the message of the movie is double-edged: "Dorothy's 'feminist' speeches . . . are less a response to the oppression of women than an instinctive situational male reaction to being treated like a woman. The implication is that women must be taught by men how to win their rights. . . . It says that feminist ideas are much less threatening when they come from a man" (123). Like Raymond, Showalter feels that being or having been a man gives a transsexual man-to-woman or a man cross-dressed as a woman a social advantage over those whose gender status was always "woman."[21] The implication here is that there is an experiential superiority that doesn't disappear with the gender shift.

For one transsexual man-to-woman, however, the experience of living as a woman changed his/her whole personality. As James, Morris had been a soldier, foreign correspondent, and mountain climber; as Jan, Morris is a successful travel writer. But socially, James was far superior to Jan, and so Jan developed the "learned helplessness" that is supposed to characterize women in Western society:

> We are told that the social gap between the sexes is narrowing, but I can only report that having, in the second half of the twentieth century, experienced life in both roles, there seems to me no aspect of existence, no moment of the day, no contact, no arrangement, no response, which is not different for men and for women. The very tone of voice in which I was now addressed, the very posture of the person next in the queue, the very feel in the air when I entered a room or sat at a restaurant table, constantly emphasized my change of status.
>
> And if other's responses shifted, so did my own. The more I was treated as woman, the more woman I became. I adapted willy-nilly. If I was assumed to be incompetent at reversing cars, or opening bottles, oddly incompetent I found myself becoming. If a case was thought too heavy for me, inexplicably I found it so myself. . . . Women treated me with a frankness which, while it was one of the happiest discoveries of my metamorphosis, did imply membership of a camp, a faction, or at least a school of thought; so I found myself gravitating always towards the female, whether in sharing a railway compartment or supporting a political cause. Men treated me more and more as junior, . . . and so, addressed every day of my life as an inferior, involuntarily, month by

month I accepted the condition. I discovered that even now men prefer
women to be less informed, less able, less talkative, and certainly less
self-centered than they are themselves; so I generally obliged them.
(1975, 165–66)[22]

Components of Gender

By now, it should be clear that gender is not a unitary essence but has many
components as a social institution and as an individual status.[23]

As a social institution, gender is composed of:

Gender statuses, the socially recognized genders in a society and the norms
and expectations for their enactment behaviorally, gesturally, linguistically, emotionally, and physically. How gender statuses are evaluated depends on historical development in any particular society.

Gendered division of labor, the assignment of productive and domestic work
to members of different gender statuses. The work assigned to those
of different gender statuses strengthens the society's evaluation of
those statuses—the higher the status, the more prestigious and valued the work and the greater its rewards.

Gendered kinship, the family rights and responsibilities for each gender
status. Kinship statuses reflect and reinforce the prestige and power
differences of the different genders.

Gendered sexual scripts, the normative patterns of sexual desire and sexual
behavior, as prescribed for the different gender statuses. Members of
the dominant gender have more sexual prerogatives; members of a
subordinate gender may be sexually exploited.

Gendered personalities, the combinations of traits patterned by gender
norms of how members of different gender statuses are supposed to
feel and behave. Social expectations of others in face-to-face interaction constantly bolster these norms.

Gendered social control, the formal and informal approval and reward of
conforming behavior and the stigmatization, social isolation, punishment, and medical treatment of nonconforming behavior.

Gender ideology, the justification of gender statuses, particularly, their
differential evaluation. The dominant ideology tends to suppress criticism by making these evaluations seem natural.

Gender imagery, the cultural representations of gender and embodiment of
gender in symbolic language and artistic productions that reproduce

and legitimate gender statuses. Culture is one of the main supports of the dominant gender ideology.

For an individual, gender is composed of:

Sex category to which the infant is assigned at birth based on appearance of genitalia. With prenatal testing and sex-typing, categorization is prenatal. Sex category may be changed later through surgery or reinspection of ambiguous genitalia.

Gender identity, the individual's sense of gendered self as a worker and family member.

Gendered marital and procreative status, fulfillment or nonfulfillment of allowed or disallowed mating, impregnation, childbearing, kinship roles.

Gendered sexual orientation, socially and individually patterned sexual desires, feelings, practices, and identification.

Gendered personality, internalized patterns of socially normative emotions as organized by family structure and parenting.

Gendered processes, the social practices of learning, being taught, picking up cues, enacting behavior already learned to be gender-appropriate (or inappropriate, if rebelling, testing), developing a gender identity, "doing gender" as a member of a gender status in relationships with gendered others, acting deferent or dominant.

Gender beliefs, incorporation of or resistance to gender ideology.

Gender display, presentation of self as a certain kind of gendered person through dress, cosmetics, adornments, and permanent and reversible body markers.

For an individual, all the social components are supposed to be consistent and congruent with perceived physiology. The actual combination of genes and genitalia, prenatal, adolescent, and adult hormonal input, and procreative capacity may or may not be congruous with each other and with sex-category assignment, gender identity, gendered sexual orientation and procreative status, gender display, personality, and work and family roles. At any one time, an individual's identity is a combination of the major ascribed statuses of gender, race, ethnicity, religion, and social class, and the individual's achieved statuses, such as education level, occupation or profession, marital status, parenthood, prestige, authority, and wealth. The ascribed statuses substantially limit or create opportunities for individual achievements and also diminish or enhance the luster of those achievements.

Gender as Process, Stratification, and Structure

As a social institution, gender is a process of creating distinguishable social statuses for the assignment of rights and responsibilities. As part of a stratification system that ranks these statuses unequally, gender is a major building block in the social structures built on these unequal statuses.

As a *process,* gender creates the social differences that define "woman" and "man." In social interaction throughout their lives, individuals learn what is expected, see what is expected, act and react in expected ways, and thus simultaneously construct and maintain the gender order: "The very injunction to be a given gender takes place through discursive routes: to be a good mother, to be a heterosexually desirable object, to be a fit worker, in sum, to signify a multiplicity of guarantees in response to a variety of different demands all at once" (J. Butler 1990, 145). Members of a social group neither make up gender as they go along nor exactly replicate in rote fashion what was done before. In almost every encounter, human beings produce gender, behaving in the ways they learned were appropriate for their gender status, or resisting or rebelling against these norms. Resistance and rebellion have altered gender norms, but so far they have rarely eroded the statuses.

Gendered patterns of interaction acquire additional layers of gendered sexuality, parenting, and work behaviors in childhood, adolescence, and adulthood. Gendered norms and expectations are enforced through informal sanctions of gender-inappropriate behavior by peers and by formal punishment or threat of punishment by those in authority should behavior deviate too far from socially imposed standards for women and men.

Everyday gendered interactions build gender into the family, the work process, and other organizations and institutions, which in turn reinforce gender expectations for individuals.[24] Because gender is a process, there is room not only for modification and variation by individuals and small groups but also for institutionalized change (J. W. Scott 1988a, 7).

As part of a *stratification* system, gender ranks men above women of the same race and class. Women and men could be different but equal. In practice, the process of creating difference depends to a great extent on differential evaluation. As Nancy Jay (1981) says: "That which is defined, separated out, isolated from all else is A and pure. Not-A is necessarily impure, a random catchall, to which nothing is external except A and the principle of order that separates it from Not-A" (45). From the individual's point of view, whichever gender is A, the other is Not-A; gender boundaries tell the individual who is like him or her, and all the rest are unlike. From society's point of view, however, one gender is usually the touchstone, the normal, the dominant, and the other is different, deviant, and subordinate. In Western society, "man" is A, "wo-man" is Not-A. (Consider what a society would be like where woman was A and man Not-A.)

The further dichotomization by race and class constructs the gradations of a heterogeneous society's stratification scheme. Thus, in the United States, white is A, African American is Not-A; middle class is A, working class is Not-A, and "African-American women occupy a position whereby the inferior half of a series of these dichotomies converge" (P. H. Collins 1990, 70). The dominant categories are the hegemonic ideals, taken so for granted as the way things should be that white is not ordinarily thought of as a race, middle class as a class, or men as a gender. The characteristics of these categories define the Other as that which lacks the valuable qualities the dominants exhibit.

In a gender-stratified society, what men do is usually valued more highly than what women do because men do it, even when their activities are very similar or the same. In different regions of southern India, for example, harvesting rice is men's work, shared work, or women's work: "Wherever a task is done by women it is considered easy, and where it is done by [men] it is considered difficult" (Mencher 1988, 104). A gathering and hunting society's survival usually depends on the nuts, grubs, and small animals brought in by the women's foraging trips, but when the men's hunt is successful, it is the occasion for a celebration. Conversely, because they are the superior group, white men do not have to do the "dirty work," such as housework; the most inferior group does it, usually poor women of color (Palmer 1989).

Freudian psychoanalytic theory claims that boys must reject their mothers and deny the feminine in themselves in order to become men: "For boys the major goal is the achievement of personal masculine identification with their father and sense of secure masculine self, achieved through superego formation and disparagement of women" (Chodorow 1978, 165). Masculinity may be the outcome of boys' intrapsychic struggles to separate their identity from that of their mothers, but the proofs of masculinity are culturally shaped and usually ritualistic and symbolic (Gilmore 1990).

The Marxist feminist explanation for gender inequality is that by demeaning women's abilities and keeping them from learning valuable technological skills, bosses preserve them as a cheap and exploitable reserve army of labor. Unionized men who could be easily replaced by women collude in this process because it allows them to monopolize the better paid, more interesting, and more autonomous jobs: "Two factors emerge as helping men maintain their separation from women and their control of technological occupations. One is the active gendering of jobs and people. The second is the continual creation of sub-divisions in the work processes, and levels in work hierarchies, into which men can move in order to keep their distance from women" (Cockburn 1985, 13).

Societies vary in the extent of the inequality in social status of their women and men members, but where there is inequality, the status "woman" (and its attendant behavior and role allocations) is usually held in lesser esteem than the status "man." Since gender is also intertwined with a society's other con-structed statuses of differential evaluation—race, religion, occupation, class, country of origin, and so on—men and women members of the favored groups command more power, more prestige, and more property than the members of the disfavored groups. Within many social groups, however, men are advantaged over women. The more economic resources, such as education and job opportunities, are available to a group, the more they tend to be. monopolized by men. In poorer groups that have few resources (such as working-class African Americans in the United States), women and men are more nearly equal, and the women may even outstrip the men in education and occupational status (Almquist 1987).

As a *structure,* gender divides work in the home and in economic produc-tion, legitimates those in authority, and organizes sexuality and emotional life (Connell 1987, 91–142). As primary parents, women significantly influence children's psychological development and emotional attachments, in the pro-cess reproducing gender. Emergent sexuality is shaped by heterosexual, homo-sexual, bisexual, and sadomasochistic patterns that are gendered—different for girls and boys, and for women and men—so that sexual statuses reflect gender statuses.

When gender is a major component of structured inequality, the devalued genders have less power, prestige, and economic rewards than the valued genders. In countries that discourage gender discrimination, many major roles are still gendered; women still do most of the domestic labor and child rearing, even while doing full-time paid work; women and men are segregated on the job and each does work considered "appropriate"; women's work is usually paid less than men's work. Men dominate the positions of authority and leadership in government, the military, and the law; cultural productions, religions, and sports reflect men's interests.

In societies that create the greatest gender difference, such as Saudi Arabia, women are kept out of sight behind walls or veils, have no civil rights, and often create a cultural and emotional world of their own (Bernard 1981).

But even in societies with less rigid gender boundaries, women and men spend much of their time with people of their own gender because of the way work and family are organized. This spatial separation of women and men reinforces gendered differentness, identity, and ways of thinking and behaving (Coser 1986).

Gender inequality—the devaluation of "women" and the social domination of "men"—has social functions and a social history. It is not the result of sex, procreation, physiology, anatomy, hormones, or genetic predispositions. It is produced and maintained by identifiable social processes and built into the general social structure and individual identities deliberately and purposefully. The social order as we know it in Western societies is organized around racial ethnic, class, and gender inequality. I contend, therefore, that the continuing purpose of gender as a modern social institution is to construct women as a group to be the subordinates of men as a group. The life of everyone placed in the status "woman" is "night to his day—that has forever been the fantasy. Black to his white. Shut out of his system's space, she is the repressed that ensures the system's functioning" (Cixous and Clément [1975] 1986, 67).

The Paradox of Human Nature

To say that sex, sexuality, and gender are all socially constructed is not to minimize their social power. These categorical imperatives govern our lives in the most profound and pervasive ways, through the social experiences and social practices of what Dorothy Smith calls the "everyday / everynight world" (1990, 31–57). The paradox of human nature is that it is *always* a manifestation of cultural meanings, social relationships, and power politics; "not biology, but culture, becomes destiny" (J. Butler 1990, 8). Gendered people emerge not from physiology or sexual orientation but from the exigencies of the social order, mostly, from the need for a reliable division of the work of food production and the social (not physical) reproduction of new members. The moral imperatives of religion and cultural representations guard the boundary lines among genders and ensure that what is demanded, what is permitted, and what is tabooed for the people in each gender is well known and followed by most (C. Davies 1982). Political power, control of scarce resources, and, if necessary, violence uphold the gendered social order in the face of resistance and rebellion. Most people, however, voluntarily go along with their society's prescriptions for those of their gender status, because the norms and expectations get built into their sense of worth and identity as a certain kind of human being, and because they believe their society's way is the natural way. These beliefs emerge from the imagery that pervades the way we think, the way we see and hear and speak, the way we fantasy, and the way we feel.

There is no core or bedrock human nature below these endlessly looping processes of the social production of sex and gender, self and other, identity and psyche, each of which is a "complex cultural construction" (J. Butler 1990, 36). *For humans, the social is the natural*. Therefore, "in its feminist senses, gender cannot mean simply the cultural appropriation of biological sexual difference. Sexual difference is itself a fundamental—and scientifically contested—construction. Both 'sex' and 'gender' are woven of multiple, asymmetrical strands of difference, charged with multifaceted dramatic narratives of domination and struggle" (Haraway 1990, 140).

What would happen . . . if suddenly, magically, men could menstruate and women could not? . . . The answer is clear—menstruation
would become an enviable, boast-worthy, masculine event.

— Gloria Steinem (1978a, 110)

Believing Is Seeing: Biology as Ideology

Freud claimed that anatomy is destiny, but Aristotle believed that destiny was determined by one's place in the social order, not only as a man or a woman but as a free man or a slave. Until the eighteenth century, Western philosophers and scientists believed that there was one sex and that women's internal genitals were the inverse of men's external genitalia (Dean-Jones 1991; Laqueur 1990a). And so, what they saw was that the womb and vagina were the penis and scrotum turned inside out: "The more Renaissance anatomists dissected, looked into, and visually represented the female body, the more powerfully and convincingly they saw it to be a version of the male's" (Laqueur 1990a, 70).[1]

Current Western thinking sees women and men as so different physically as to sometimes seem two species. The bodies, which have been mapped inside and out for hundreds of years, have not changed. What has changed are the justifications for gender inequality. When the social position of all human beings was believed to be set by natural law or was considered God-given, women and men of different classes had their assigned places. When scientists began to question the divine basis of social order and replaced faith with empirical knowledge, they now saw that women were very different from men in that they had wombs and menstruated. Such anatomical differences had to destine them for an entirely different social life than men.

In actuality, the basic bodily material *is* the same for females and males; except for procreative hormones and organs, female and male human beings have similar bodies (Naftolin and Butz 1981). Furthermore, as has been known since the middle of the nineteenth century, male and female genitalia develop from the same fetal tissue, and so because of various genetic defects, infants can be born with ambiguous genitalia (Money and Ehrhardt 1972; Fausto-Sterling 1993).[2] When they are, sex assignment can be quite arbitrary. Suzanne Kessler (1990) interviewed six medical specialists in pediatric intersexuality and found that whether the infant with XY chromosomes and anomalous genitalia was categorized as a boy or a girl depended on the size of the penis. If the penis was very small, the child was categorized as a girl, and sex-change surgery was used to make an artificial vagina: "The equation of gender with genitals could only have emerged in an age when medical science can create credible-appearing and functioning genitals, and an emphasis on the good phallus above all else could only have emerged in a culture that has rigid aesthetic and performance criteria for what constitutes maleness. . . . There is a striking lack of attention to the size and shape requirements of the female genitals, other than that the vagina be able to receive a penis" (20).[3] In medieval Islamic law, whether the child urinated as a female or male was the determining criterion, but it also involved judgment by the inspecting person (Sanders 1991, 77–78).[4] In the late nineteenth century, the presence or absence of ovaries was the determining criterion of gender assignment for hermaphrodites, since a woman who could not procreate was not a complete woman (20).

Yet, in Western societies, we see two discrete sexes and two distinguishable genders because our society is built on two classes of people, women and men. Practically every form you fill out asks whether you are male or female, even though your physiology and biology may be irrelevant to what the form is used for. And everyone, including transvestites, transsexuals, and hermaphrodites, dutifully ticks off one box.[5] That is because everyone is gendered. Every child is categorized as a "girl" or a "boy," every adult as a "woman" or a "man." Once the gender category is given, the attributes of the person are also gendered: Whatever a woman is has to be "female"; whatever a man is has to be "male." Analyzing the social processes that construct the categories we call "female and male," "women and men," "homosexual and heterosexual" uncovers the ideology and power differentials congealed in these categories. Bodies differ in many ways physiologically, but they are completely transformed by social practices to fit into the salient categories of a society, the most pervasive of which are "female" and "male" and "women" and "men." In the social construction of two sexes and two genders today, one is constructed to be superior, the other to be inferior.

Neither sex nor gender is a self-evident category. Combinations of incongruous genes, genitalia, and hormonal input are ignored in sex categorization, just as combinations of incongruous identity, sexuality, appearance, and behavior are ignored in the social construction of gender statuses. Menstruation, lactation, and gestation do not demarcate women from men. Only some women are pregnant and then only some of the time; some women do not have a uterus or ovaries. Some women have stopped menstruating temporarily, others have reached menopause, and some have had hysterectomies. Some women breast-feed some of the time, but some men lactate (Jaggar 1983, 165n). Menstruation, lactation, and gestation are individual experiences of womanhood (Levesque-Lopman 1988) but not determinants of the social categories "female" or "woman." Similarly, "men are not always sperm-producers, and in fact, not all sperm producers are men. A male-to-female transsexual, prior to surgery, can be socially a woman, though still potentially (or actually) capable of spermatogenesis" (Kessler and McKenna [1978] 1985, 2).

The reliance on only two sex and gender categories in the biological and social sciences is therefore epistemologically spurious. Most research designs do not investigate whether physical skills or abilities are really more or less common in women and men (C. F. Epstein 1988). They start out with two social categories ("women," "men"), assume they are biologically different ("female," "male"), look for similarities among them and differences between them, and attribute what they have found for the social categories to sex differences (Gelman, Collman, and Maccoby 1986). These designs rarely question the categorization of their subjects into two and only two groups, even though they often find more significant within-group differences than between-group differences (Hyde 1990). They also assume that if any differences occur early in childhood, they must be due to genetics, not social learning, even though there is ample evidence that once gender is assigned, boy and girl children are handled and reacted to quite differently.

Take the phenomenon of boys' boisterousness or girls' physical awkwardness in Western societies. When little boys run around noisily, we say, "Boys will be boys," meaning that physical assertiveness has to be in the Y chromosome because it is manifest so early and so commonly in boys. But are boys universally, the world over, in every social group, a vociferous, active presence? Or just where they are encouraged to use their bodies freely, to cover space, take risks, and play outdoors at all kinds of games and sports? Conversely, what do we mean when we say, "She throws like a girl"? We usually mean that she throws like a female child, a carrier of XX chromosomes. After all, she's only four or five, so how could she have learned to be so awkward? In fact, she throws like a person who has already been taught to restrict her movements, to protect her body, to use it femininely:

> Not only is there a typical style of throwing like a girl, but there is a more or less typical style of running like a girl, climbing like a girl, swinging like a girl, hitting like a girl. They have in common first that the whole body is not put into fluid and directed motion, but rather . . . the motion is concentrated in one body part; and . . . tends not to reach, extend, lean, stretch, and follow through in the direction of her intention. (Young 1990, 146)[6]

The girl who experiences her body in such a limited way at an early age is a product of her culture and time. Girls and boys who are given tennis rackets at the age of three and encouraged to become champions use their bodies similarly. After puberty, boys will have more shoulder and arm strength and concentrated bursts of energy; girls will have more stamina, flexibility, and lower-body strength. Training, the sport, and physical exercise enhance, compensate, or override these different physical capabilities, as well as individual differences in musculature and athletic ability.

Sociobiologists have argued that inexorable workings of the genes create markedly different male and female behavior (E. O. Wilson 1975, 1978). Sociobiological and biosocial research designs and interpretations of data have been extensively criticized as inadequate proof that biological sex alone produces gendered behavior.[7] Put briefly, "any evaluation of the heritability of sex differences in behavior is hampered by . . . [an] interaction problem: males and females immediately enter different environments by virtue of their anatomical sex alone" (McClintock 1979, 705). The evidence of interaction between hormonal output and social situations suggests that the situation seems to influence hormone levels as much as hormone levels influence behavior.[8] Physical bodies are always social bodies: "The body, without ceasing to be the body, is taken in hand and transformed in social practice" (Connell 1987, 83).

Gendering begins prenatally when amniocentesis reveals the sex of the child; it gets a gendered name. If it is the "wrong sex," an unwanted sex, it may be aborted. Once the sex category is assigned, the pressures toward sex and gender congruity are so strong that sex-change operations are used to create anatomy congruent with "inappropriate" gender identity and gender behavior. As Margit Eichler says: "The rationale for sex reassignment surgery seems to be based on a circular logic which goes like this. Sex determines character.

This is natural. Therefore, cases in which biological sex does not result in the expected sex identities are unnatural. Consequently, we need to change the biological sex (i.e., nature) in order to uphold the principle that biological sex determines one's character" (1989, 289).

What Sports Illustrate

Sports illustrate the ways bodies are gendered by social practices and how the female body is socially constructed to be inferior. To begin with, competitors are rigidly divided into women and men. When gender assignment is contested, chromosomes are now used to determine in which category the athlete is to compete. However, an anomaly common enough to be found in several women at every major international sports competition is the existence of XY chromosomes that have not produced male anatomy or physiology because of a genetic defect. Because these women are women in every way significant for sports competition, the prestigious International Amateur Athletic Federation has urged that sex be determined by simple genital inspection (Kolata 1992a). Transsexuals would pass this test, but it took a lawsuit for Renée Richards, a man-to-woman transsexual, to be able to play tournament tennis as a woman. She finally did so, despite male sex chromosomes (Richards 1983). Oddly, neither basis for gender categorization—chromosomes or genitalia—has anything to do with sports prowess (Birrell and Cole 1990).

In the Olympics, in cases of chromosomal ambiguity, a woman must undergo "a battery of gynecological and physical exams to see if she is 'female enough' to compete. Men are not tested" (Carlson 1991, 26). The purpose is not to categorize women and men accurately but to make sure men don't enter women's competitions, where, it is felt, they will have the advantage of size and strength. This practice sounds fair only because it is assumed that all men are similar in size and strength and different from all women. Yet in Olympics boxing and wrestling matches, men are matched within weight classes. Some women might similarly successfully compete with men in many sports. Women did not run in marathons until about twenty years ago. In twenty years of marathon competition, women have reduced their finish times by more than an hour and a half; they are expected to run as fast as men in that race by 1998 and might catch up with men's running times in races of other lengths within the next fifty years because they are increasing their fastest speeds more rapidly than men are (Fausto-Sterling 1985, 213–18).[9]

Once women and men are separately categorized, assumptions about their physiology and athletic capabilities influence rules of competition; subsequent sports performances than validate how women and men are treated in sports competitions. Gymnastic equipment is geared to slim, wiry, prepubescent girls and not to mature women; conversely, men's gymnastic equipment is tailored for muscular, mature men, not slim, wiry, prepubescent boys. Boys could compete with girls but are not allowed to do so; women gymnasts are left out entirely (*New York Times* 1989b). Girl gymnasts are just that—little girls who will be disqualified as soon as they grow up (Vecsey 1990). Men gymnasts have men's status. In women's basketball, the size of the ball and rules for handling the ball change the style of play to "a slower, less intense, and less exciting modification of the 'regular' or men's game" (Watson 1987, 441). There is no opportunity for women to play by men's rules in public competition. In the 1992 Winter Olympics, men figure skaters were required to complete three triple jumps in their compulsory program; women figure skaters were forbidden to do more than *one*. These rules penalized artistic men skaters and athletic women skaters (Janofsky 1992). For the most part, Western sports are built on physically trained men's bodies: "Speed, size, and strength seem to be the essence of sports. Women *are* naturally inferior at 'sports' so conceived. But if women had been the historically dominant sex, our concept of sport would no doubt have evolved differently. Competitions emphasizing flexibility, balance, strength, timing, and small size might dominate Sunday afternoon television and offer salaries in six figures" (English 1982, 266).

Organized sports are big business and thus who has access and at what level is a distributive or an equity issue. The overall status of women and men athletes is an economic, political, and ideological issue that has less to do with individual physiological capabilities than with their cultural and social meaning and who defines and profits from them.[10] Some twenty years after the passage of Title IX of the U.S. Civil Rights Act, which forbade gender inequality in any school receiving federal funds, the *goal* for participating in collegiate sports in the next five years and for scholarships and funding is 60 percent men, 40 percent women (Moran 1992).

How access to and distribution of rewards (prestigious and financial) are justified is an ideological, even moral, issue (Birrell 1988, 473–76; Hargreaves 1982). One way is that men athletes are glorified and women athletes ignored in the mass media. Michael Messner and his colleagues found that in 1989 in the United States, men's sports got 92 percent of the television coverage and women's sports 5 percent, with the remaining 3 percent mixed or gender-neutral (Messner, Duncan, and Jensen 1993). In 1990, in four of the top-selling newspapers in the United States, stories of men's sports outnumbered those on women's sports 23 to 1. Messner and his colleagues also found an implicit hierarchy in naming, with women athletes most likely to be called by their first names, followed by Black men athletes; only white men athletes were routinely referred to by their last names. Similarly, women's collegiate sports teams are named or marked in ways that symbolically feminize and trivialize them—the men's team is called Tigers; the women's, Kittens (Eitzen and Baca Zinn 1989).[11]

Assumptions about bodies and their capacities are crafted in ways that make unequal access and distribution of rewards acceptable (Hudson 1978; Messner 1988). Media images of modern men athletes glorify their strength and power, even their violence (Hargreaves 1986). Media images of modern women athletes tend to focus on feminine beauty and grace (so they are not really athletes) or on their thin, small, wiry androgynous bodies (so they are not really women). In coverage of women's Olympic sports,

> loving and detailed attention is paid to pixie-like gymnasts; special and extended coverage is given to graceful and dazzling figure skaters; the camera painstakingly records the fluid movements of swimmers and divers. And then, in a blinding flash of fragmented images, viewers see a few minutes of volleyball, basketball, speed skating, track and field, and alpine skiing, as television gives its nod to the mere existence of these events. (Boutilier and SanGiovanni 1983, 190).[12]

Extraordinary feats by women athletes who were presented as mature adults might force sports organizers and audiences to rethink their stereotypes of women's capabilities, as elves, mermaids, and ice queens do not. Sports, therefore, construct men's bodies to be powerful; women's bodies to be sexual: "The meanings in the bodily sense of masculinity concern, above all else, the superiority of men to women, and the exaltation of hegemonic masculinity over other groups of men which is essential for the domination of women" (Connell 1987, 85).

Competitive sports have become, for boys and men as players and as spectators, a way of constructing a masculine identity, a legitimated outlet for violence and aggression, and an avenue for upward mobility.[13] For men in Western societies, physical competence is an important marker of masculinity.[14] As Erving Goffman (1963a) says: "There is only one complete unblushing male in America: a young, married, white, urban, northern, heterosexual Protestant father of college education, fully employed, of good complexion, weight, and height, and recent record in sports" (128).

Given the association of sports with masculinity in the United States, women athletes have to manage a contradictory status. One study of women college basketball players (Watson 1987) found that though they "did athlete" on the court—"pushing, shoving, fouling, hard running, fast breaks, defense, obscenities and sweat" (441), they "did woman" off the court, using the locker room as their staging area: "While it typically took fifteen minutes to prepare for the game, it took approximately fifteen minutes after the game to shower and remove the sweat of an athlete, *and* it took another thirty minutes to dress, apply make-up and style hair. It did not seem to matter whether the players were going out into public or getting on a van for a long ride home. Average dressing time and rituals did not change" (443).

Another way women manage these status dilemmas is by redefining the activity or its result as feminine or womanly (Mangan and Park 1987). Thus, women bodybuilders claim that "flex appeal is sex appeal" (Duff and Hong 1984, 378). Ironically, this gloss of sexuality on women's bodybuilding almost cost a woman army officer her command when photographs of her in her "bikini posing suit" were printed in an army newspaper (Barkalow and Raab 1990, 203–09).

Such a redefinition of women's physicality affirms the ideological subtext of sports that physical strength is men's prerogative and justifies men's physical and sexual domination of women.[15] When women demonstrate physical strength, they are labeled unfeminine: "It's threatening to one's takeability, one's rapeability, one's femininity, to be strong and physically self-possessed. To be able to resist rape, not to communicate rapeability with one's body, to hold one's body for uses and meanings other than that can transform what *being a woman means*" (MacKinnon 1987, 122). Resistance to that transformation, ironically, was evident in the policies of American women physical education professionals throughout most of twentieth century. They minimized exertion, maximized a feminine appearance and manner, and left organized sports competition to men (Birrell 1988, 461–62, Mangan and Park 1987).

Women Get Sicker, But Men Die Quicker

Not only for athletes but for everyone, social practices transform the body and invest it with cultural and symbolic meaning.[16] In the nineteenth century, the physical strength and stamina of African-American slave women were exploited and those of the European-American mistresses of plantations in the pre–Civil War South ignored. Slave women worked side by side with slave men in the fields, plowing and harvesting; slave women and their mistresses did arduous manual domestic labor.[17] The image of woman as fragile and incompetent, physically and mentally, was not shaken by the very evident capabilities of women (Jordanova 1989). As Sojourner Truth told the Women's Rights Convention in Akron, Ohio, in 1852, "Look at me! Look at my arm! . . . I have plowed, and planted, and gathered into barns, and no man could head me—and ain't I a woman?" (quoted in hooks 1981, 160). Her famous statement pointedly illustrates how all women were diminished by nineteenth-century concepts of womanhood—physically capable working-class women and women slaves were considered inferior as women; physically fragile upper- and middle-class women, full-fledged women, were an economically dependent class.[18]

Today, in countries with Westernized medical systems, gender, combined with race and social class, strongly affects health and longevity not through physiological factors but through different work and family responsibilities, risk-taking, health and illness behavior, and marital and economic status.[19] Women tend to have more illnesses and to see physicians more often because of the stresses of routinized jobs, child care, care of elderly parents, and the "double day" of work and housework. Men are more prone to chronic and life-threatening diseases, such as heart attacks, but tend to be healthier mentally and physically if they are married than married women are. In the United States, unequal access to prenatal care is an important factor in the high rate of low-birthweight babies among African-American women, and a host of lifetime traumas are implicated in the high rates of early death among African-American men.[20]

Until quite recently, insurance companies paid out retirement insurance at higher rates to men than to women, arguing that women lived longer than men (Harrison, Chin, and Ficarrotto 1992). They did not make racial or ethnic distinctions, even though European Americans outlive people of color in the United States by about ten years. European-American women's life expectancy is greater than that of African-American men by about fifteen years; the racial gap for each gender is about eight years. Thus, middle-class European-American women have the longest potential life span in the United States, but they are also most likely to need professional nursing care in old age because they outlive their husbands (Ory and Warner 1990). African-American men, conversely, are more likely to suffer trauma or die young from homicide, suicide, or accidents (Gibbs 1988a, 1988b).

In the research on gender differences in rates of illness and death, as in other areas where biology and social circumstances are intertwined, it is extremely difficult to separate out the effects of biological sex. According to Lois Verbrugge, who has worked on the problem for many years, "the vulnerabilities and the resistances that males and females typically receive at conception, or how aging processes and social exposures alter the size and character, are not known. The single greatest need in population studies of sex differences in health and mortality is operational measures of that biological substrate" (1989a, 296). The real problem is that a purely biological substrate cannot be isolated because human physiology is socially constructed and gendered.

"If Men Could Menstruate"

Despite the strong evidence of women's overall physical hardiness, *all* women in the United States are considered unfit for certain kinds of work and physical activity because of their procreative physiology. Medically, premenstruation, menstruation, pregnancy, childbirth, and menopause are alleged to disable women either physically or psychologically.[21] Contraceptive use may result in side effects, and abortions in moral stigma, making women who have taken responsibility for their physical condition "double deviants"—they have a physical problem, and they are blamed for it (Lorber 1967). Similarly, women who choose not to have children are criticized for not being complete women, and those who are involuntarily infertile because of their own or their husband's procreative problems are also stigmatized for their childlessness.[22]

What supposedly makes women "real" women—their biology— simultaneously makes them second-class citizens. Only women's procreative potential is used to determine where they can and cannot work, although studies have shown that toxic chemicals and other occupational hazards are equally likely to affect sperm production.[23] Thus, women's procreative physiology ideologically justifies their marginal status as workers. Hidden in this discussion is women's knowledge of the procreative risks of their work, and even the possibility of their use of it to limit their childbearing. English women potters who used lead in their work in the early twentieth century when abortion was illegal seem to have turned its hazardous effects to their own ends: "A local doctor found in one sample of 77 women pottery workers, who used lead, eight had experienced 21 still-births; 35 admitted to having a total of 90 miscarriages. In spite of the risks women potters employed lead to bring on abortions. It was apparently a local truism that to marry a girl lead worker would ensure a marriage where family size could be easily limited" (Grieco and Whipp 1986, 135–36). In a definitive decision, the U.S. Supreme Court declared in 1991 that employers could not use protection of the fetus as a rationale for barring fertile women from hazardous jobs (Greenhouse 1991).

Employers now can leave the decision up to workers themselves (including men at risk of sperm deformity), reduce all workers' exposure to occupational hazards, or equip them with protective devices (Kilborn 1991).

Another example of discrimination against women on the basis of their physiology is the use of menstruation to call into question women's intellectual and physical capabilities. Since it is women, a subordinate group, who menstruate, menstruation has been used as a pervasive justification for their subordination (Delaney, Lupton, and Toth 1977). Notions of pollution were replaced in nineteenth-century Europe and America by scientific studies of the detrimental effects of higher education on women's ability to menstruate (Bullough and Voght 1973; Vertinsky 1990, 39–68).[24] In the late 1970s, as women increasingly entered athletic competitions, similar scientific studies showed that women who exercised intensely would cease menstruating because they would not have enough body fat to sustain ovulation (Brozan 1978). But when one set of researchers did a year-long study that compared sixty-six women—twenty-one who were training for a marathon, twenty-two who ran more than an hour a week, and twenty-three who did less than an hour of aerobic exercise a week—they discovered that only 20 percent of the women in *any* of these groups had "normal" menstrual cycles every month (Prior et al. 1990). The dangers of intensive training for women's fertility were exaggerated as women began to compete in arenas formerly closed to them.

Premenstrual tension is another purportedly biological phenomenon that undermines women's social status (Rittenhouse 1991). It was described and attributed to hormonal causes sixty years ago; since then, most research has followed the biomedical model—defining it as *a* syndrome, with *a* cause, *a* pathology located in the *individual*. Critics have noted that there is confusion about what it is, when it occurs, whether it is a single syndrome, and what its effects are.[25] The notorious connection between premenstrual tension and crimes, suicides, and other destructive actions may be due to emotional stress that causes both changes in the menstrual cycle and pathological behavior; women taking important examinations are as likely to be premenstrual or menstruating as women committing crimes are (Parlee 1982a).

Some women experience premenstrual bodily changes, others emotional ups-and-downs, and still others a combination of both, in mild, moderate, and severe forms: "The emotional states most commonly reported in studies of PMS are tension, anxiety, depression, irritability, and hostility. Somatic complaints include abdominal bloating, swelling, breast tenderness, headache, and backache. Behavioral changes frequently reported are an avoidance of social contact, a change in work habits, increased tendency to pick fights (especially with a spouse / partner or children), and crying spells" (Abplanalp 1983, 109). Many women have mild symptoms (just as many women have mild menstrual discomfort); the incidence of severe syndromes (or debilitating menstrual periods) is much less common.

Many women and men experience mood swings by the day of the week; for women, these may modify or intensify menstrual-cycle mood swings (Hoffmann 1982; Rossi and Rossi 1977). Mary Brown Parlee (1982b) found that individual women were less likely to attribute psychological mood swings to menstrual cycles than to other causes, such as reactions to difficulties at work or at home; when the data were grouped, however, the influence of menstrual cycles was magnified because the other patterns were idiosyncratic. Daily self-reports gave "a picture of what might be called 'premenstrual elation syndrome' that is the opposite of the negative one embodied in the stereotype of premenstrual tension" (Parlee 1982b, 130). Retrospective reports from these same women described their feelings in stereotypical terms.

One woman physician sardonically commented that perhaps the effects of what is defined as premenstrual syndrome—anger and irritability—stand out because this behavior is in contrast to three weeks of pleasant sociability (Guinan 1988). Emily Martin (1987) suggests that from a feminist perspective, premenstrual tension can be positive—not only a release of ordinarily suppressed anger at the everyday put-downs women are subject to, but a different kind of consciousness, concentration, and creativity: "Does the loss of ability to concentrate mean a greater ability to free-associate? Loss of muscle control, a gain in ability to relax? Decreased efficiency, increased attention to a smaller number of tasks?" (128).

Menopause, too, has been defined as a disease, and social factors are discounted.[26] Western culture imposes a negative connotation of distance, a sense that body and mind are separate, on women's experience of menstruation, menopause, pregnancy, and childbirth.[27] Western women are given no chance to contemplate their bodies as located in time and place and as *theirs,* the way men in our culture experience erections and orgasms as extensions of themselves. Unlike Western societies, where bodily and social statuses are frequently disjointed (Rossi 1980), Native American and other cultures link women's and men's age cycles to the community. For women, menstrual and birthing rituals become integrative and celebratory rites of passage (Buckley and Gottlieb 1988; Powers 1980). Peruvian women gain full adulthood around the time of menopause, reaping social and financial benefits and freedom from daily chores and from large extended families (E. A. Barnett 1988).[28]

What women may ignore as a routine, tolerable occurrence becomes a syndrome, a pathology, an "illness," when it is so labeled by the medical profession (Dodd 1989; Fisher 1986). Although there certainly are women who could benefit from medical amelioration of disabling premenstrual, menstrual, and menopausal conditions, they are not necessarily the majority (Yankauskas 1990). Nonetheless, all women are said to suffer from (and make others suffer in turn) the "horrors" of "that time of the month" or "that time of life." In our society, these syndromes denigrate women as a group and justify their less-than-fully-human social status.[29] Since adult women will be experiencing one or another of these physiological conditions throughout their lifetime, to the extent that women are defined by their biology, they are all "sick" most of the time.

Dirty Little Secrets

In large ways and small, sex differences are invoked to justify what are gendered differences in social status (C. F. Epstein 1988). Men's supposed greater strength rationalizes the gendered division of work even when it is machinery that does the actual physical labor: "Two qualities are combined in men's work . . .: physical competence and technical competence. The men bind these two together and appropriate both qualities for masculinity. Each affords a little power. Not much, just a modicum of power that is enough to enable men to lever more pay, less supervision and more freedom out of management" (Cockburn 1985, 100). This "greater strength" is also socially constructed, and it builds into gender stratification at work and in society in general:

> Small biological differences are turned into bigger physical differences which themselves are turned into gambits of social, political and ideological power play. Females are born a little smaller than males. This difference is exaggerated by upbringing, so that women grow into adults who are less physically strong and competent than they could be. They are then excluded from a range of manual occupations and, by extension, from the control of technology. The effect spills over into everyday life: ultimately women have become dependent on men to change the wheel of a car, reglaze a broken window or replace a smashed roof slate. Worse, women are physically harassed and violated by men: women are first rendered relatively weak; the weakness is transformed to vulnerability; and vulnerability opens the way to intimidation and exploitation. It is difficult to exaggerate the scale and longevity of the oppression that has resulted. (Cockburn 1983, 204)

Meta-analysis of studies of gender differences in spatial and mathematical ability found that men have a large advantage in the ability to mentally rotate an image, a moderate advantage in visual perception of horizontality and verticality and in mathematical performance, and a small advantage in the ability to pick a figure out of a field (Hyde 1990). It could be argued that these advantages explain why, within the short time that computers have become ubiquitous in offices, schools, and homes, work on them and with them has become gendered: Men create, program, and market computers, make war and produce science and art with them; women microwire them in computer factories and enter data in computerized offices; boys play games, socialize, and commit crimes with computers; girls are rarely found in computer clubs, camps, and classrooms.[30]

But women were hired as computer programmers in the 1940s because "the work seemed to resemble simple clerical tasks. In fact, however, programming demanded complex skills in abstract logic, mathematics, electrical circuitry, and machinery, all of which . . . women used to perform in their work. Once programming was recognized as 'intellectually demanding,' it became attractive to men" (Donato 1990, 170). Grace M. Hopper, a woman mathematician and pioneer in data processing, was famous for her work on programming language (Perry and Greber 1990, 86). By the 1960s, programming was split into more and less skilled specialties, and women's entry into the computer field in the 1970s and 1980s was confined to the lower-paid specialties. At each stage, employers invoked women's and men's purportedly natural capabilities for the jobs they were being hired to do (Donato 1990).

It is the taken-for-grantedness of such everyday gendered behavior that supports the belief that the widespread differences in what women and men do must come from biology. To take one ordinarily unremarked scenario: In modern societies, if a man and a woman who are a couple are in a car together, he is much more likely to take the wheel, even if she is the more competent driver. Molly Haskell (1989) calls this phenomenon "the dirty little secret of marriage: the husband-lousy-driver syndrome" (26). Men drive cars whether or not they are good drivers because men and machines are a "natural" combination (Scharff 1991).[31] Yet because some young men drive recklessly as proof of their masculinity, auto insurance is particularly expensive for men under the age of twenty-five in much of the United States. The connection between ability to drive and social power is explicit in Saudi Arabia, which forbids women from driving cars at all (LeMoyne 1990b).

In the early days of the automobile, feminists coopted the symbolism of mobility as emancipation: "Donning goggles and dusters, wielding tire irons

and tool kits, taking the wheel, they announced their intention to move
beyond the bounds of women's place" (Scharff 1991, 68). Driving enabled
them to campaign for women's suffrage in parts of the United States not served
by public transportation, and they effectively used motorcades and speaking
from cars as campaign tactics (67–88). Sandra Gilbert also notes that during
World War I, women's ability to drive was physically, mentally, and even
sensually liberating:

> For nurses and ambulance drivers, women doctors and women mes-
> sengers, the phenomenon of modern battle was very different from
> that experienced by entrenched combatants. Finally given a chance to
> take the wheel, these post-Victorian girls raced motorcars along for-
> eign roads like adventurers exploring new lands, while their brothers
> dug deeper into the mud of France. . . . Retrieving the wounded and
> the dead from deadly positions, these once-decorous daughters had at
> last been allowed to prove their valor, and they swooped over the
> wastelands of the war with the energetic love of Wagnerian Valkyries,
> their mobility alone transporting countless immobilized heroes to safe
> havens. (1983, 438–39)

Social Bodies and the Bathroom Problem

People have different genitalia, different secondary sex characteristics, different contributions to procreation, different orgasmic experiences, different
patterns of illness and aging. But we all experience our bodies differently, and
these experiences change as we grow, age, sicken, and die. The bodies of
pregnant and nonpregnant women, short and tall people, those with intact and
functioning limbs and those whose bodies are physically challenged are all
different. But the salient social categories group these attributes in ways that
ride roughshod over individual experiences.[32]

Gender categories are split by other social constructions of physiological
attributes. African-American men share a privileged gender status with
European-American men with regard to the women of their racial category,
but African-American men and women are both discriminated against because
of the color of their skin (hooks 1984). A tall woman and a short man, in a
society that favors tall men and short women, have similar social
experiences—they both are somewhat stigmatized in dating and marriage
(Goffman 1963a). A physically challenged man and woman are both rendered
socially sexless in the United States (Zola 1982a). The man, however, may be

admired for asserting strong willpower in overcoming dependency, even while relying on a supportive woman; the woman may remain a social dependent but, ironically, not have anyone to care for her (Fine and Asch 1985).

Physical differences between male and female bodies certainly exist—a roomful of naked people would tell us at least that—but these differences are socially meaningless until social practices transform them into social facts. The social transformation of female and male physiology into a condition of in-equality is well illustrated by the bathroom problem. Most buildings that have gender-segregated bathrooms have an equal number for women and for men. When there are crowds, there are always long lines in front of women's bathrooms but rarely in front of men's bathrooms. Modern women's clothing and their need to sit or squat when urinating lengthen the time they take in the bathroom (underpants, girdles, pantyhose, and pants have to be taken down to allow women to use the toilet); men's bathrooms often have urinals as well as stalls. Little boys are more likely to go to the bathroom with a woman than little girls are with a man. Women who are pregnant have to urinate often; men do not get pregnant, but prostate problems may send them to the bathroom as often as pregnant women. Menstruating women take longer in a bathroom; men do not menstruate, and neither do postmenopausal women, but the need to urinate frequently increases with age, especially in women. Older people take longer to urinate, and there are likely to be more elderly women than elderly men, since women live longer than men.

The cultural, physiological, and demographic combinations of clothing, frequency, menstruation, age, and child care add up to generally greater bathroom use by women than men. Thus, although an equal number of bathrooms *seems* fair, true equity would mean providing more women's bath-rooms or allowing women to use men's bathrooms for a certain amount of time (Molotch 1988).[33] Yet the gender boundaries supposedly dictated by biological differences between females and males create symbolic social spaces we rarely breach, even when they present identity problems:

> As public accommodations more and more often serve a multilingual clientele, the words "men" and "women" or "ladies" and "gentlemen" have been replaced by signs showing a figure dressed in [men's] clothes—trousers—and a figure dressed in [women's] clothes—a skirt or dress. Yet no one (except perhaps transvestites and transsex-uals) interprets these signs literally or mimetically. A woman in pants would not ordinarily go through the door marked with a figure in pants, nor would a priest in a soutane or a Hare Krishna advocate in robes head

for the door with the skirt. . . . Cross-dressers who want to pass prefer to read the stick figures literally: those in pants, in there; those in skirts, in here. (Garber 1992, 13–14)

My friends and I have "liberated" many men's rooms, but one woman was arrested (though fortunately acquitted) for having done so (*New York Times* 1990).

The bathroom problem is the outcome of the way gendered bodies are differentially evaluated in Western cultures: Men's social bodies are the measure of what is "human." West Point's curriculum is devised to produce military leaders, and physical competence is used as a significant measure of leadership ability (Yoder 1989). When women were accepted as cadets, it became clear that the tests of physical competence, such as the ability to scale an eight-foot wall rapidly, had been constructed for male physiques—pulling oneself up and over, using upper-body strength. Rather than devise tests of physical competence for women, West Point provided boosters that mostly women used, but that lost them test points (in the case of the wall, a platform). Finally, the women themselves figured out how to use their bodies successfully. Janice Yoder (1989) describes this situation: "I was observing this obstacle one day, when a woman approached the wall in the old prescribed way, got her fingertips grip, and did an unusual thing: she walked her dangling legs up the wall until she was in a position where both her hands and feet were atop the wall. She then simply pulled up her sagging bottom and went over. She solved the problem by capitalizing on one of women's physical assets: lower-body strength" (530). Thus, if West Point is going to measure leadership capability by physical strength, women's pelvises will do just as well as men's shoulders.

Gray's *Anatomy,* in use for a hundred years, well into the twentieth century, presented the human body as male. The female body was shown only where it differed from the male (Laqueur 1990a, 166–67).[34] Denise Riley says that if we envisage women's bodies, men's bodies, and human bodies "as a triangle of identifications, then it is rarely an equilateral triangle in which both sexes are pitched at matching distances from the apex of the human" (1988, 197). Catherine MacKinnon also contends that in Western society, universal "humanness" is male because

virtually every quality that distinguishes men from women is already affirmatively compensated in this society. Men's physiology defines most sports, their needs define auto and health insurance coverage, their socially defined biographies define workplace expectations and successful career patterns, their perspectives and concerns define quality in scholarship, their experiences and obsessions define merit, their objectification of life defines art, their military service defines citizenship, their presence defines family, their inability to get along with each other—their wars and relationships—define history, their image defines god, and their genitals define sex. For each of their differences from women, what amounts to an affirmative action plan is in effect, otherwise known as the structure and values of American society. (1987, 36)

They have sex fingers to fingers. They have sex belly to belly. They have sex genital tubercle to genital tubercle. . . . There are no sexes to belong to, so sex between creatures is free to be between genuine individuals—not representatives of a category. They have sex. They do not have a sex. Imagine life like that.

—*John Stoltenberg (1990, 27)*

How Many Opposites? Gendered Sexuality

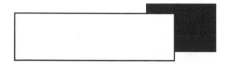

In the 1950s, Alfred Kinsey used a seven-point scale to place people on a heterosexual-homosexual continuum of sexuality, from all male-female sexual acts to all male-male or all female-female. What was revolutionary at the time were Kinsey's statistics showing that a significant proportion of Americans fell into the middle ranges of the scale: They had engaged in both heterosexual and homosexual sex. The problem with the scale was its uni-dimensionality and counting of discrete acts, which could not assess their historical, social, cultural, or personal meanings (McWhirter, Sanders, and Reinisch 1990). The Romans, for instance, would have used an entirely different scale to place people, one based not on sexual practices per se but on the power they represented: "Penetration and power were associated with the prerogatives of the ruling male elite; surrendering to penetration was a symbolic abrogation of power and authority—but in a way that posed a polarity of domination-subjection rather than of homosexual-heterosexual. It was generally acceptable for a member of a less powerful group to submit to penetration by a member of a more powerful one" (Boswell 1990a, 17).

Kinsey's open approach to sexual behavior is still quite unusual. Sexological researchers and sex therapists, using a biological model, view sexuality as a "universal force or drive residing inside the body in some observable and perhaps measurable quantity" that can be repressed, twisted, or expressed in healthy or unhealthy ways (Irvine 1990, 185). "Healthy" or "normal" is defined as physiological sexual relations between human females and human males.

In psychoanalytic theories, sexualities are fantasy-laden erotic and emotional attachments established early through family life and parenting, latent in childhood, powerful in puberty, and relatively constant into old age. The psychological components of sexuality are fantasy, desire, and passion, not a universal drive or sexual acts (Stein 1989). A heterosexual identity as a woman or a man whose sexual desires are oriented toward members of the opposite gender is believed to be the result of the successful outcome of the Oedipus complex.[1] The psychoanalytic view of transsexuality and homosexuality claims that gender identity and sexual orientation are formed early, and thus if gender identity is not congruent with genitalia or sexual orientation is not heterosexual, it is not a matter of choice. Although some psychoanalysts have considered homosexuality and transsexuality pathological conditions that are treatable, many homosexuals and transsexuals feel that their gender identity and sexuality are fixed for life.[2]

The social-construction perspective focuses on the cultural and historical context in which sexuality is learned and enacted, or "scripted." Social constructionists argue that cultures and societies organize sexual practices into approved, permitted, and tabooed patterns that are internalized by individuals and that the meanings of sexual behavior vary greatly over time and place. In this view, ideas about sexuality have a history, structure, and politics that affect any individual's developing sexual desires and behavior. In the social-constructionist view, which reflects the overall perspective of this book, sexualities are multiple, not unitary, and not physiologically or psychologically fixed for life; all are socially shaped. Approved practices are actively encouraged; permitted practices are tolerated; and tabooed patterns are stigmatized and often punished. Heterosexuality is as much a product of learning, social pressures, and cultural values as homosexuality. All sexual desires, practices, and identities not only are gendered but reflect a culture's views of nature, the purpose of life and procreation, good and evil, pleasure and pain; the discourses about them are permeated with power.[3]

The milieu and the politics of identity shape the meaning of sexual experiences. Under colonialism and slavery, Black women and men were forced into sexual identities that were the opposites of white sexual identities (P. H. Collins 1990, 68–70). Black women were raped and impregnated by white masters and then accused of sexual licentiousness (Omolade 1983; Simson 1983). Black women's and white women's legal standing as accusers of Black men and white men in rape cases reflected these sexual identities. As Kimberlé Crenshaw says:

> Rape statutes generally do not reflect *male* control over *female* sexuality, but *white* male regulation of *white* female sexuality. . . . When Black

women were raped by white males, they were being raped not as
women generally, but as Black women specifically. Their femaleness
made them sexually vulnerable to racist domination, while their Black-
ness effectively denied them any protection. This white male power
was reinforced by a judicial system in which the successful conviction of
a white man for raping a Black woman was virtually unthinkable.
(1991, 68–69)[4]

Black men were psychologically emasculated and socially desexualized so that
they could be trusted as field workers and house servants. In Africa, Black men
were preferred by white women as servants ("house boys") and child-carers
("nurse boys") because white employers considered Black women both sexually threatening and domestically untrainable (K. T. Hansen 1990).[5] The
supposed reaction—exaggerated masculinity in Black men and assertive femininity in Black women—have become twentieth-century mythologies.[6]

What Counts as "Sex"?

Supposedly normal sexual practice is genital and orgasmic, no matter who the
partners are, although men as well as women enjoy many forms of sexual
arousal and satisfaction that are not genitally specific.[7] Nonetheless, what
counts as "sex" in Western culture is genital contact. In Blumstein and
Schwartz's (1983) study of American couples, 67 percent of the homosexual
men said they had had sex three or more times a week in the first two years of
their relationship, similar to heterosexual cohabitors (61 percent) but more
than married heterosexuals (45 percent) and much more than lesbians living
together (33 percent).[8] One reason for lesbians' seemingly low sexual frequency could be that in this study "having sex" was defined too narrowly.
Interviews with lesbians revealed that cuddling, touching, and hugging
were considered sexual activities, not just "foreplay" (197). Furthermore,
among lesbians, "having sex" is much more prolonged than among heterosexual couples, and so it is rather difficult to count "how many times" (Frye
1990).

How are "times" counted by heterosexual couples, anyway? "By orgasms?
By *whose* orgasms?" Marilyn Frye asks (1990, 308). In the current script for
heterosexual sex, the term *foreplay* refers to the "preliminaries preceding the
main event." From a heterosexual woman's perspective, it can *be* the main
event: "Women like foreplay before, during, and after" (Laws and Schwartz
1977, 56).[9] For many woman, sexuality is diffuse and emotionally laden:

"Feminine sexuality, unlike the mediation of the visible which sustains phallic desire, is of the register of touching, nearness, presence, immediacy, contact" (Gallop 1982, 30). Mariana Valverde says that because lesbian relationships reflect mother-daughter love, they are more emotionally encompassing and more powerfully erotic than heterosexual relationships are for women: "Because of this 'emotionalism' that women are conditioned to have, and the inevitable associations of the lover's body with the nurturing, all-powerful body of the mother, love between women can create some of the strongest bonds in human experience" (1985, 90–91). But some heterosexual and lesbian women also enjoy sadomasochistic sex.[10] For some men, heterosexual as well as homosexual, objectified sexuality is not "good sex" (Stoltenberg 1990, 101–14).

Physiologically, a woman's orgasms are the same whether she masturbates, uses a vibrator, is masturbated, performs cunnilingus with a woman or a man or has it done to her, is penetrated by a penis, is caressed all over her body, or plays out a fantasy. She may be less likely to be orgasmic through penile penetration than through other sexual practices. A man's orgasms are physically the same no matter what arouses him to the point of ejaculation. But for both, the sensuality and emotional quality vary sexual experiences. Irving Kenneth Zola, whose legs are wasted from polio, described making love with a severely paralyzed woman: "And so the hours passed, ears, mouths, eyes, tongues inside one another. And every once in a while she would quiver in a way which seemed orgasmic. As I thrust my tongue as deep as I could in her ear, her head would begin to shake, her neck would stretch out and then her whole upper body would release with a sigh." (1982b, 216). Such lovemaking is not a substitute for the "real thing"; it *is* the real thing.

Gendered Sexual Statuses

Sexuality is physically sexed because female and male anatomies and orgasmic experiences differ.[11] It is gendered because sexual scripts differ for women and for men whether they are heterosexual, homosexual, bisexual, transsexual, or transvestite (Gagnon and Simon 1973; Laws and Schwartz 1977). Linking the experience of physical sex and gendered social prescriptions for sexual feelings, fantasies, and actions are individual bodies, desires, and patterns of sexual behavior, which coalesce into gendered sexual identities. These identities, however various and individualized, are categorized and socially patterned into gendered sexual statuses. There are certainly more than two gendered sexual statuses: "If one uses the criteria of linguistic markers alone, it suggests that people in most English-speaking countries . . . recognize four genders: women, lesbian (or gay female), man and gay male" (Jacobs and Roberts 1989, 439). But there are not the variety there could be.[12]

In Western societies we could say that, on the basis of *genitalia,* there are *five sexes:* unambiguously male, unambiguously female, hermaphrodite, transsexual female-to-male, and transsexual male-to-female; on the basis of *object choice,* there are *three sexual orientations:* heterosexual, homosexual, and bisexual (all with transvestic, sadomasochistic, and fetishistic variations); on the basis of *appearance,* there are *five gender displays:* feminine, masculine, ambiguous, cross-dressed as a man, and cross-dressed as a woman (or perhaps only three); on the basis of *emotional bonds,* there are *six types of relationships:* intimate friendship, nonerotic love (between parents and children, siblings and other kin, and long-time friends), eroticized love, passion, lust, and sexual violence; on the basis of *relevant group affiliation,* there are *ten self-identifications:* straight woman, straight man, lesbian woman, gay man, bisexual woman, bisexual man, transvestite woman, transvestite man, transsexual woman, transsexual man (perhaps fourteen, if transvestites and transsexuals additionally identify as lesbian or gay).[13] Sexual practices are even more varied (Freud called human beings "polymorphously perverse"). One can have sexual relations with men, women, both, one at a time or in groups, with oneself, or with no one (celibacy); one can erotically cross-dress or have sexual relations with cross-dressers; one can have sadomasochistic sex; one can have sex with animals, use fetish objects, pornography, sexual devices; and so on and on.[14] But on the basis of current social recognition in Western cultures, there are only four gendered sexual statuses: heterosexual woman, heterosexual man, lesbian, gay man.[15]

These gendered sexual statuses encompass a variety of feelings and experiences. Complementary differences and mirrorlike sameness create the possibilities for different kinds of relationships. Heterosexual lovers are not only different physically; because they are different genders, they may not share leisure-time interests and may spend less time together than homosexual lovers, who have same-gendered social lives and so "can combine this need for friendship and their need for romantic love in one person" (Blumstein and Schwartz 1983, 183). Any two gay men or two lesbians, however, can be as different from each other as any two heterosexuals, and so can their relationships (Valverde 1985, 58; Weston 1991, 137–64).

Because Western culture constructs sexuality as well as gender dichotomously, many people whose sexual experiences are bisexual are forced to choose between a heterosexual and homosexual identity as their "real" identity

(Rust 1992, 1993; Valverde 1985, 109–20). In contemporary American society, boys identify themselves or are identified as homosexuals earlier and on the basis of fewer same-gender sexual experiences than girls because one of the main components of hegemonic masculinity is constant sexual interest in women. Femininity, in contrast, is not contradicted by a romantic attraction to other girls or women. Yet for both genders, self-identified heterosexuals can be sexually attracted to those of their own gender, and many have had homosexual relationships. Similarly, self-identified homosexuals have heterosexual relationships, including marriage. Were bisexuality a legitimate sexual category, the boundaries between heterosexuality and homosexuality would blur not only for them but for their sexual partners: "Unless bisexuals confine their romantic involvements to other bisexuals, they probably engage in the most intimate of social relationships with both homosexuals and heterosexuals, again blurring the social and political boundaries between these two types of people" (Rust 1992, 383n).[16]

Gender Identities and Sexual Identities

A sexual identity or orientation involves desired and actual sexual attraction and fantasies, not just behavior. It also includes emotional preferences, social preferences, self-identification, and a heterosexual or homosexual life-style (Klein, Sepekoff, and Wolf 1985). All sexual identities and orientations—heterosexual, homosexual, bisexual, transsexual, transvestite—are responses not just to psychic constructs but also to social and cultural strictures and pressures from family and friends. Paula Rust's research on bisexual and lesbian sexual identity found that 90 percent of the 323 self-identified lesbians who answered her questionnaire had had heterosexual experiences, 43 percent after coming out as lesbians (1992, 1993). They discounted these experiences, however; what counted for them were their current relationships. The 42 women who identified themselves as bisexual, in contrast, put more emphasis on their sexual attraction to both women and men.

Although same-gender sex has occurred throughout history all over the world, homosexual identities have not, and when they do occur they have different content, connotations, and functions in different societies (Blackwood 1985; McIntosh 1968). John D'Emilio argues that in Western societies "capitalism has created conditions that allow some men and women to organize a personal life around their erotic/emotional attraction to their own sex" because it provides the opportunity for young people to get jobs and live away from their families (1983a, 104). They did not identify themselves as a separate group, however, until the end of the nineteenth century, when prominent sexologists, such as Krafft-Ebing, typologized and categorized them according to supposedly uniform characteristics.

Krafft-Ebing's work popularized the terms *heterosexual* and *homosexual* and contrasted them as "different-sex/same-sex eroticisms—two symmetrical, polarized erotic desires, mental states, and persons" (Katz 1990, 16). However, physical anatomy, sexual desire and practices, social roles, and public identities do not necessarily coalesce into uniform and constant combinations, but often cross-cut and shift with time. The majority of the homosexual men in the United States studied by a number of researchers did not cross-dress or pretend to be girls as children, did not want to be girls, did not play with dolls, had boys as friends, and were not called "sissies" (Troiden 1988, 119). Lesbians were more likely to have engaged in cross-gendered activities when they were young, and there was a tradition of "butch" or masculinized role play in working-class lesbian communities in the 1940s and 1950s.[17] Now that previously masculine activities, such as playing baseball, have become acceptable for young girls, as has unisex clothing, the scope of cross-gendered marks of differentness predicting a nonconventional adulthood for women has considerably diminished.

The question of how similar lesbians are to heterosexual women depends on what lesbians and heterosexual women one is talking about. Nineteenth-century women were supposed to be passionless but arousable by love of a man; therefore, two women together could not possibly be sexual. The emotionally passionate relationships of long-term women friends who displaced their husbands from the marriage bed so they could sleep together during long visits were considered perfectly normal (Smith-Rosenberg 1975). In the 1920s, the flapper was sexually assertive but still subordinate to men (Trimberger 1983). The independent, sexually aggressive lesbian of the time, like Stephen Gordon in Radclyffe Hall's *The Well of Loneliness,* was a social man (Newton 1984). In the 1950s "the butch was expected to be both the doer and the giver; the fem's passion was the butch's fulfillment" (Kennedy and Davis 1989, 244). Lesbians playing the "fem" role were extremely feminine in their dress, demeanor, and expressions of sexuality. There were also butch-fem role exchangers ("roll overs" or "kikis") who played both parts. Up to the 1960s, many women professionals and activists, most of whom did not identify as lesbians, were nonetheless able to break the mold of conventional women's roles because of their deeply emotional, supportive friendships with other women, which may or may not have been sexual (Cook 1977, 1979, 1992, 7–20). In sexual practices and other behavior, as well as in dress and use of cosmetics, lesbians are now so varied that Faderman calls them a "tower of Babel community" (1991, 271–302).

Gay men have varied from super-macho to campily feminine, but many are as conventionally masculine in their dress and demeanor as most heterosexual men.[18] Much of the research and discussion of homosexuality in men in the twentieth century has revolved around "how do you know one?" Until quite recently, the goal was to identify the marks of incipient or actual homosexual proclivities so that this orientation could be treated or the sexual deviant isolated. Homosexual practices were likely to be punished by expulsion from school, a prison term, or dishonorable discharge from the military if the boys or men were discovered in a sexual act. Since both heterosexual and homosexual men have either remained bachelors or dated, married, and fathered children biologically or socially, and since many married men have heterosexual and homosexual sex outside of marriage with prostitutes, in one-night stands, or in long-term love affairs, one wonders why homosexual sex among men has been so condemned during the twentieth century in Western cultures.

The answer would seem to lie in the contradiction between men's overt and covert relationships with each other (Herek 1986). Frye says that men's heroes and love objects are other men whether they are heterosexual or homosexual: "The people whom they admire, respect, adore, revere, honor, whom they imitate, idolize, and form profound attachments to, whom they are willing to teach and from whom they are willing to learn, and whose respect, admiration, recognition, honor, reverence and love they desire . . . those are overwhelmingly, other men" (1983, 135). Men's work lives, because of the gendered division of labor they have fought so bitterly to preserve, are gender-segregated, as is much of men's leisure time and networking. Men have justified the privileges of these gender-segregated social worlds by their masculinity, which they have demonstrated by their sexual desire for women, economic support of wives and children, and, as soldiers, policemen, and firefighters, physically protecting them. When men's domination is challenged, as it was by women's claim for the vote around the turn of the century, one type of response is masculinizing homosocial activity, like the Boy Scouts, a defense against the feminization of public life (Kimmel 1987a).

Women's challenges to conventional gender roles and gendered behavior continued during the twentieth century. With other social changes in technology, employment, and opportunities for upward mobility, conventional bases of masculinity eroded (Ehrenreich 1983). Men therefore more and more sharply defined their differentness from women, and, in the process, defined homosexuals as "not-men" because they, like women, were sexually penetrated by men. But men who engaged in sexual activity with other men were discovered everywhere—in every profession and occupation, in the sports arenas and the exclusive clubs, in the military, the police, the fire departments—not just in the arts and in feminine fields like clothing design. Hence, the preoccupation with identification and extirpation of homosexuals. Otherwise, how would men know whom they could trust, confide in, and rely on without danger of being seduced? Since the invitation to homosexual sex itself was stigmatizing, the only protection for masculine men was to make sure their homosocial worlds were free of the contamination of homosexual men.

Lesbianism during this period was much less visible as a social problem, but was publicly condemned whenever women as a group broke out of their conventional gender roles. The medicalization of the female "invert" occurred at the turn of the century, when the suffragist movement was flourishing in the United States and England. Lesbianism surfaced again as a social problem after World War I; its visibility in the form of the "mannish woman" was part of the reaction to the increased sexual and social freedom for heterosexual women (Trimberger 1983; Smith-Rosenberg 1985, 245–96). Lesbians were treated less harshly in the U.S. military during World War II, when women's new roles were thought to be only for the duration of the war, than they were after the war, when the resurgence of traditional expectations made any woman in the work force a deviant.[19] Since the social-change movements of the 1960s, people identifying as homosexuals have formed a powerful social movement of their own and have gained some legitimation (D'Emilio 1983b).[20]

In sum, homosexual identities reflect social mores about sexual deviance and conformity as well as overall gender norms for heterosexual women and men. As a result of this interplay of gender and sexuality, lesbians first identified with homosexual men in their resistance to sexual discrimination, but after experiencing the same gender discrimination as women in the civil rights and draft-resistance movements, they turned to the feminist movement, where, unhappily, they experienced hostility to their sexuality from heterosexual women. Subsequently, some lesbian feminists have created an oppositional, woman-identified, separatist movement that identifies heterosexuality as the main source of the oppression of women.[21]

Sexual Conformity and Deviance

In the social construction of sexuality, much of the moral strictures involve the politics of permissibility. Certain practices are actively encouraged and others punitively forbidden. In between are shifting levels of tolerance, with the tabooed sexual practices done clandestinely or, in periods of change, openly and defiantly. These gray-area behaviors may move to the permitted-but-not-encouraged level, but they can just as easily be harshly and legally condemned (G. Rubin 1984). In Europe in the Middle Ages and Reniassance, for example, adults openly fondled children's genitals (Ariès 1962, 100–27). Today, such behavior is considered criminal or sick in many Western communities. For a society, and especially for pubescent girls and boys, sexual politics establish the boundaries between conformity and deviance and warn of the dire consequences of whatever practices are considered immoral or unsafe. In our time, unwanted pregnancies, infertility, venereal diseases, and AIDS have been considered punishments for nonconforming sexuality.[22] At the opposite end of the sexuality spectrum, voluntary celibacy or lifelong chastity has, in some religions, been a mark of holiness. In Roman Catholicism, only celibate men can be priests, which has kept control of church doctrine and property in the hands of a small select group (Ranke-Heinemann 1990).

The social construction of sexuality is tied into the social construction of gender by marking off categories of who it is proper to mate and have children with. Societies encourage some sexual practices as demonstrating proper manliness or womanliness—marks of marriageability. Thus, in Papua New Guinea, homosexual fellatio makes men of adolescent boys (Herdt 1981). Among the ancient Romans, fellatio was condemned as highly immoral, although Roman husbands were expected to have anal sex with their young slave boys. In contrast, among the Romans, "relationships that were illicit, immoral, and above all, loathsome . . . were passivity in free men, excessive compliance in women, cunnilingus, finally lesbianism, especially in the active partner" (Veyne 1985, 33).

For more than two thousand years, in a broad belt across the middle of Africa, clitoridectomies and infibulation (scarring of the labia to create adhesions that keep most of the vaginal opening closed until marriage) have been used to ensure women's virginity until marriage and to inhibit wives' appetites for sex after marriage.[23] Ironically, these mutilating practices do neither, but result in the infliction of pain as part of normal sexuality. One of the Sudanese men Hanny Lightfoot-Klein interviewed said that his wife's evident suffering was preferable to no reaction at all (1989, 8). Wives' immobility during intercourse is a mark of a good woman—that is, one who is not sexually arousable. But a common signal of desire and receptivity among wives in this area is their perfuming their skin with sandalwood smoke, a pungent odor that can be smelled from a distance: "The meaning of the ceremony is tacitly agreed upon, and no verbalization or other act of agreement is needed. The woman can now behave in a way that totally negates her intent. She can now act out the role of the ravaged, while he acts out the role of the ravager, or she can be dutifully acquiescent to her husband's sexual demands while seeming to have no interest or pleasure whatsoever herself" (Lightfoot-Klein 1989, 88). In Lightfoot-Klein's interviews with women throughout the Sudan who had clitoridectomies and infibulation, 90 percent described experiencing full orgasms during intercourse once the period of excruciatingly painful opening through penile penetration was over (80–102).[24] However, Asma El Dareer's survey of 2,375 women, almost all of whom had had full infibulation, found that only 25 percent experienced sexual pleasure all or some of the time (1982, 48).

Circumcision of boys is much more common and occurs in societies throughout the world. Where it is associated with sexuality, it is for women's and men's pleasure. Another practice, subincision, where the penis is cut through and flattened and urination is subsequently done squatting, seems to occur in imitation of kangaroos, who can copulate for up to two hours (Gregersen 1983, 100–10).

The pressure of patrilineal inheritance has produced equally complex paradoxes in the social construction of women's and men's sexuality in Western cultures. During the Renaissance, women's as well as men's orgasms were thought necessary for conception; men who wanted heirs wanted women who were easily aroused but not until they were married (Laqueur 1990a, 99–103). Upper-class boys and girls were kept physically separate or carefully chaperoned when they were together because it was assumed that otherwise, like Romeo and Juliet, they would immediately fall in love and have sexual intercourse, ruining their parents' marital arrangements for them (Goode 1959). Young men were encouraged to use slaves, servants, and prostitutes for casual sexual intercourse. Homosexual behavior among young men was not a major problem as long as they eventually married; girls' and married women's passions for their female friends were considered normal (McIntosh 1968; Smith-Rosenberg 1975).

Since men of property had to produce male heirs, they had to be potent enough to impregnate their wives, but once married, their energies were supposed to go to amassing wealth or status for their families. Married wealthy or aristocratic women who had had children were, until the nineteenth century, socially and sexually available for flirtations, seductions, and love affairs with marriageable young men waiting to inherit enough property to support a wife. Anna Clark (1987) describes eighteenth-century sexual norms as clearly class-based:

> While languishing young wives read bourgeois novels which warned
> them to protect their chastity as their most precious jewel, great ladies
> of the court openly engaged in illicit affairs and illegitimate ménages,
> relying on their wealth to protect them from scandal. . . . [Working-
> class women] flirted, fought, and drank in the streets, ran stalls in
> fishmarkets, and carried vegetables to Covent Garden Market; they
> sold themselves in alleys or high class brothels, or lived with men with
> or without the bourgeois bonds of legal marriage. . . . Their . . .
> sexuality was celebrated in ballads but denigrated by the upper classes;
> their safety was protected by their own bravery but endangered by the
> violence they faced every day. (21)[25]

From the sixteenth to the eighteenth century in Europe, the belief that
women's orgasms were necessary to procreation assured wives' rights to
sexual pleasure; more accurate knowledge of procreation eroded those rights
in the nineteenth century (McLaren 1984, 28–29).[26] Orgasm was now considered irrelevant to maternity, and passionlessness was a good woman's moral
shield (Cott 1978). Married or not, she was expected to monitor herself and
any men in her presence. Should a woman be raped, infertile, pregnant by the
wrong man or at the wrong time, too lustful for her husband, or too emotionally involved in a love affair, her status as a good woman was ruined. In
communities where a family's honor depended on the virginity of its unmarried women and the chastity of its wives, death rather than dishonor was the
preferred fate (K. Z. Young 1989). The famous fictional adulterers, Anna
Karenina and Emma Bovary, however, did not commit suicide because their
husbands found out about their love affairs. They became too passionate about
their lovers and consequently voracious, jealous, and ultimately miserable.
They committed suicide because they were too emotional. They might just as
easily have killed their lovers or the women to whom their lovers were turning
their attentions. All of these "crimes of passion" disrupted the bourgeois
family, which was governed by norms of strictly controlled sexuality and
passion (Shapiro 1991).[27] Some women were marked as "whores" by their
social class, race, or poverty (Davis 1983, 3–29). They were stereotyped as
"more sexual" than the daughters of good families. Well-born young virgins,
however, were kept chaste and marriageable by locking them up, chaperoning
them, and, in the Victorian era, curing them of a propensity to masturbate by
subjecting them to clitoridectomies.

In the eighteenth and nineteenth centuries in Europe and the United
States, formerly private and unremarked sexual behaviors, such as homosexual

practices, children's masturbation, and women's selling or bartering sex for gifts, money, or favors, was brought into public discourse and became subject to control and regulation by medicine and law, which had supplanted religion as the prime agencies of social control (Foucault 1978; Weeks 1985, 1989). Prostitution (known as "vice") became a career and was viewed as evidence of a debased moral identity. Working-class women who had been able to augment their poor salaries or survive in hard times by selling sex were publicly stigmatized by vice campaigns.[28] Condemned as sources of disease and moral pollution, they were subjected to medical examinations and treatment under contagious disease acts or sent to prison as lawbreakers. Their customers, of course, were rarely included in these clean-up campaigns, although the ostensible intent was to protect wives and unborn children from the scourge of syphilis. It was as difficult for middle-class feminists as for men reformers to see the working-class woman who sold sex as someone making a rational decision: "Middle class reformers could not grasp the motivations, moral codes, and survival strategies of poor women—that prostitution could appear as a viable alternative to low wages and lack of employment options. . . . Consequently, they advocated protection rather than punishment, which translated into policies that imposed strong controls over young women's lives, work, leisure, and relationships" (Hobson 1987, 5). The result, as with so much other sexual behavior, was to transform formerly private acts into a public problem and stigmatize the women involved.

Today, prostitution is likely to be part of other illegal activity, especially selling drugs, but even where it is not, it is usually an illegal way of making money (Miller 1986). Margo St. James, organizer of COYOTE (Call Off Your Old Tired Ethics), campaigned to treat prostitution as freely chosen work (Jenness 1990). Kathleen Barry (1979), however, considers prostitution a form of sexual slavery because men control the trade. Christine Overall, attempting to reconcile the two positions, comes to the conclusion that it "makes sense to defend prostitutes' entitlement to do their work but not to defend prostitution itself as a practice under patriarchy" (1992, 723). In a society in which women have fewer resources than men, and poor women, especially those from disadvantaged racial groups, have few economic choices and a degraded status, prostitution is intrinsically exploitive.

Homosexual practices, prohibited in the Judeo-Christian Bible, have been variously ignored, condemned as sinful, punished as a crime, and treated as a mental illness. In England and the United States, all nonprocreative sex was called "sodomy" until the late nineteenth century (Weeks 1989, 106–07). The codification of homosexuality as a stigmatized identity was a product of the medicalization of sexuality and the same Victorian campaigns for the social purity of the family that brought prostitution under legal control. Paradoxically, regulation of sexual behavior led to public discussion that "provided the space for new sexual localizations: for indeed sharper sexual identities" (Weeks 1989, 107). The more self-awareness and self-labeling, the more other homosexuals were sought out, creating communities, subcultures, and the possibilities of resistance and rebellion against the legal and medical control that created the homosexual underground in the first place (Plummer 1981a, 29).

In current Western sexual discourse, sexual pleasure is a right for women and men, but what is considered normal sex is still narrowly defined as heterosexual, genital, orgasmic, and ideally, emotionally expressive (L. B. Rubin 1990). Although experimental sexual behavior and impermanent relationships are permissible for both women and men, both are supposed to strive for a long-term relationship founded on mutual affection, companionship, and sexual fidelity. Family laws and policies apply only to long-term heterosexual cohabitators in marriagelike relationships (Parker 1990, 126–57). Gay and lesbian communities have claimed legitimacy for homosexual couples by arguing that their relationships are based on the same kind of romantic love. Heterosexual marriages and heterosexual and homosexual relationships incorporate a great variety of sexual practices, including love affairs, transvestism, bisexuality, sadomasochism, and even celibacy, but the ideal type of relationship has been conventionalized as a sexually monogamous, emotionally satisfying bond between two loving companions. The ideology of long-term love and friendship has been heightened by the AIDS epidemic.[29]

Heterosexual Asymmetry

In Western society, as in other societies, sexual norms differ for women and for men. When an ethnically diverse sample of 272 New York City college women and men and 170 pedestrians in Manhattan and Albany were asked to select the ten things they would wish for the most from a list of forty-eight, the wish that generated the largest and most consistent gender difference was "To have sex with anyone I choose." It was chosen by 28 percent of the men but only 6 percent of the women (Ehrlichman and Eichenstein 1992). The gender differences were consistent across age ranges and religiousness. In a second study of only college students, the question was reworded, "To make love with whomever I wish," and 96 students, who ranged in age from seventeen to twenty-five, were asked to rate this and the other wishes on a four-point scale. Of the women, 4.3 percent said they would want this wish very much and 46 percent rejected it; of the men, 25 percent rated it highly and 24.8 percent rejected it. Responses to the wish "To have a completely satisfying sexual relationship with one and only one person my whole life" were: highest rating, 53.4 percent of the women and 33.4 percent of the men; lowest rating, 14.2 percent of the women and 13.9 percent of the men.

The narratives on their sex lives written by 237 white, middle-class, mostly heterosexual college students in the 1980s showed that women as well as men felt that they had a right to experiment sexually, that men as well as women were romantic, and that everyone believed that sex with affection was the best kind (Moffatt 1989, 181–270). There were few women or men who wanted "casual sex without guilt *and* the deeper pleasures of romance; the meaning of sex with commitment *and* the thrill of the quick sexual encounter" (221). To be sexually eclectic, a man had to be able to respect his sex partner whether their relationship was casual or long term. Similarly, "to be an authentic sexual liberal, a woman, correspondingly, had to stop believing that if she fooled around she was a slut. Also, like a male romantic, she had to modify the neotraditional woman's stance so that she herself could enjoy casual sex without commitment" (223).

These studies showed both gender differences and significant overlap in current attitudes toward sexual behavior, but in the context of heterosexual relationships, women and men seem to be at cross-purposes. Perhaps the greatest paradox of modern gendered sexuality in Western cultures is that boys and girls grow up and form emotional bonds in homosocial worlds, but they are expected, once they reach puberty, to fall in love and sexually desire a member of the opposite gender while not giving up their same-gender friendships (A. Rich 1980; Sherrod 1987). For heterosexual men, norms of masculinity forbid both open displays of affection for other men and rejection of their friendship for that of women (Herek 1986). Women who become heterosexual relegate their emotional bonds with other women to "backup," while they pursue their dream of trying to find one man to invest in emotionally for a long-term relationship.[30]

A corollary paradox is that femininity is framed by a relationship with one man that is romantic first and sexual later, but masculinity is framed by sexual conquests of many women and only secondarily by an emotional attachment to one. To be considered feminine, a woman has to pry a man loose from his friends and cleave him to her; sex is her lure. To prove he is masculine, a man has to show his friends he is a sexual conqueror; an emotional attachment to one woman can feel like a trap (Ehrenreich 1983). In their peer groups, the closeness of men's bonding is masked by sex talk, especially boasting of sexual conquests: "Men need to shoot the breeze, talk shit, chase women and run the jungle together" (Simmons 1992, 401).[31] The heterosexual boy's goal is conquest: "To the young man, the woman becomes, in the most profound sense, a sexual object. Her body and mind are the object of sexual games, to be won for his personal aggrandizement. Status goes to the winner, and sex is prized not as testament of love but as testimony to control of another human being" (Anderson 1990, 114).

The contradictions of men's continuing attachment to their friends and sexual objectification of women, and women's needing their friends for emotional solace while they pursue unrewarding romances have been depicted in the songs, folklore, and fortune-telling rituals in the Russian working class before the Communist Revolution, in the bawdy songs and stories of today's working-class Mexican men, in the street lore of late-twentieth-century African Americans, in the sexual fantasies of white middle-class college students of the 1980s, and in the sexualization of adolescent girls in Germany in the 1970s.[32]

Through peer-group socialization, heavily reinforced by mass-media and other cultural depictions, boys learn *their* version of sexuality and seduction, and girls learn *their* version of romantic love: "The girls have a dream, the boys a desire" (Anderson 1990, 113): "This dream involves having a boyfriend, a fiancé, a husband, and the fairy-tale prospect of living happily ever after with one's children in a nice house in a good neighborhood—essentially the dream of the middle-class American life-style, complete with nuclear family" (115). Both white and Black middle-class women who have the opportunity for careers are encouraged by their peer culture to put their professional plans on hold and pursue romance while they are in college (Holland and Eisenhart 1990; Komarovsky 1985). For many working-class and poor girls, the gap between their romantic fantasies and the gritty reality of their lives is enormous; for young women of color it can be a chasm.[33]

Women who succeed in their romantic pursuits very often find that the emotional return on their time and effort is disappointing, because heterosexual men have learned in the course of growing up to be emotionally independent of their mothers, and by extension, of all women (Chodorow 1976). Implicit in the cliché that women want to talk love and men want to make love is the dilemma of modern heterosexual relationships: "She keeps asking for something she can understand and is comfortable with—a demonstration of his feelings in non-sexual ways. He keeps giving her the one thing he can understand and is comfortable with—his feelings wrapped up in a blanket of sex" (L. B. Rubin 1976, 147).[34] Given these asymmetrical patterns, it is hardly surprising that modern heterosexual relationships are fraught with emotional and sexual tensions. The strongest relationships, heterosexual, homosexual, or lesbian, tend to be those between two people who are not only lovers but friends.

Battered Love

Sexual relationships that go awry may end in physical violence. The incidence of lovers' and husbands' brutally beating and raping their partner is horrifyingly high.[35] The average yearly number of recorded acts of violence against women in the United States from 1979 to 1987 was 56,900 by husbands, 216,100 by divorced or separated husbands, and 198,800 by boyfriends (Harlow 1991, 1). Paradoxically, abusive relationships often seem very romantic at the beginning, because the men are especially attentive: "They showed constant concerns with the woman's whereabouts and activities, a desire to be with them all the time, intense expressions of affection, and wanted an early commitment to a long-term relationship. . . . Over time, though, such behavior is increasingly seen by the woman as intrusive, possessive, and controlling" (Frieze and Browne 1989, 186). By the time of the first episode of violence, the man has split the woman from her friends and family, leaving her isolated and dependent on him emotionally and often economically. Even if she gets a job and finds another place to live, she may feel she has no one else to rely on. The emotional bonds forged at the beginning of the relationship, before the abuse started, remain powerful on both sides.[36]

Men whose masculinity is tied to norms of dominance but who do not have the economic status to back up a dominant stance are likely to be abusive to the women they love, either psychologically or physically, and often both (L. E. Walker 1984; Yllö 1984). James Ptacek's interviews with eighteen men in a counseling program for husbands who battered found that they felt they had a right to beat their wives: "There is a pattern of finding fault with the woman for not being good at cooking, for not being sexually responsive, for not being deferential enough, . . . for not knowing when she is 'supposed' to be silent, and for not being faithful. In short, for not being a 'good wife'" (Ptacek 1988, 147). Women who stay in such relationships are likely to have been well socialized into the emotionally supportive feminine role but to be socially or economically superior to the men who batter them. Beth Richie (1992) found that the twenty-six African-American battered women she interviewed had had girlhoods of relative privilege and thought they could be ideal wives and mothers. These gender patterns set the stage for battering, and other factors trigger the behavior.

Men's use of violence to control women is deliberate and carefully orchestrated to instill fear, self-blame, and submission (Adams 1988). Threats and beatings alternate with contrition and concessions. Many women who stay in such a relationship respond with a defensive pattern of "learned helplessness" (L. E. Walker 1984). Both patterns may be the outcome of abuse witnessed and experienced in their childhood families.[37]

The question always arises of why a woman who is repeatedly savagely beaten and raped to the point of suffering not just bruises and black eyes but broken bones and traumatic wounds stays with her abuser. Julie Blackman's interviews with 172 battered women found that they did not have a sense of injustice over what was happening to them because they could not see any alternatives outside of the situation (1989, 67–82). Even women who had acted on alternatives, such as calling the police or going to shelters for battered women, did not feel that they had severed the relationship (153–66). The African-American battered women Richie interviewed felt they could not admit to their families that they had failed to live up to their early promise as "good girls." They also felt they could not go to the police because their batterers had embroiled them in illegal activities (1992).

The women who feel they cannot leave are in a situation similar to that of hostages. They feel their survival depends on becoming special to the person who threatens their life but from whom they cannot escape (Graham, Rawlings and Rimini 1988). A woman in a battering relationship feels she must distinguish herself from "all women," against whom her batterer expresses seemingly uncontrollable rage. So she placates him and tries to appeal to his warmer, friendlier, kinder side, suppressing her terror and rage. If she does escape, she is likely to experience a psychological aftermath of fear that he will retaliate for any subsequent punishment or negative actions against him. Such fears are not unwarranted, since ex-husbands and former boyfriends are three times more likely to assault women than husbands and current lovers (Harlow 1991, 2).

When a battered woman kills her abuser, she does so not out of reciprocal violence but out of a feeling that the man's rage has escalated and now threatens her life or that of her children.[38] Cynthia Gillespie says that in the most common scenario, the woman who kills her abuser says that he threatened to beat or kill her and lunged at or attacked her. She used a kitchen knife or his gun to defend herself and killed him accidentally. She then called the police or ambulance and was found "sitting on the floor cradling her husband's head in her lap begging him not to die. This story was played out, with minor variations, so many times that I sometimes had the feeling that I was reading the same case over and over again" (1989, ix). Less commonly, a battered woman kills the man who has been abusing her when he is asleep or passed out drunk, but for the same reasons. She thinks she will not survive otherwise. In court, despite the marks of self-defense and a long history of horrible beatings, if the woman has no eyewitness doubt is often cast on her credibility and truthfulness and the seriousness of the danger she was in.[39]

R. Emerson and Russell Dobash have argued that learned helplessness, dependence, and isolation define wifehood itself and that the pattern of increasing possessiveness and sexual jealousy is normal behavior for a husband (1979, 77–93). Wife beating was once approved in most communities and is still condoned today where there is an ideology of men's authority over their wives. Marital rape has only recently been accorded recognition as a genuine sexual assault.[40] The lackadaisical response of doctors, nurses, and the police to battering reflects these mores.[41] But when there is no communal approval or the violence is so extreme no one would condone it, a man who uses it to control has to separate the woman from her friends and family. Most women in long-term heterosexual relationships have same-gender friends to turn to for solace, advice, and support; without them, a battered woman is truly a prisoner of romantic love (McConnell 1992; Richie 1992).

Forbidden Love

The incest taboo is thought to be universal, yet the definition of incest depends on how kin are defined, not on the closeness of the biological relationship. In some societies, a woman is not allowed to marry her father's brother's son because he belongs to the same kin group she does, but she is supposed to marry her father's sister's son because he is a member of a different kin group. Both are similarly close cousins.[42] If the universality of the incest taboo is confined to the nuclear family—fathers and daughters, mothers and sons, and brothers and sisters—then the frequency of sexual relationships between fathers and daughters and even fathers and sons is a phenomenon that needs explaining.[43]

One explanation claims that young girls can be sexually seductive. Although children as well as young adolescents have sexual desires, "it is the adult, not the child, who determines the sexual nature of the encounter, and who bears the responsibility for it" (Herman 1981, 42). A second explanation blames the mother, who is said to be deficient in her maternal duties, first, by not satisfying her husband's or partner's sexual needs and, second, by not protecting her daughter from him. In a more common situation, the mother is physically or emotionally ill and may be hospitalized or otherwise absent for long periods. A daughter then takes over her domestic duties, including nurturing other children and becoming the father's emotional outlet: "For the daughter, the duty to fulfill her father's sexual demands may evolve almost as an extension of her role as 'little mother' in the family" (Herman 1981, 45). That explanation of the circumstances that lead to father-daughter incest, however, rests on the assumption that the father and children cannot share the household chores, that other child-care arrangements cannot be made, and that "fathers are entitled to female services within their families, no matter what the circumstances" (Herman 1981, 49).[44]

Judith Herman's interviews with forty white women in Massachusetts who had had sexual relationships with their biological, step-, or adoptive fathers when they were prepubescent (the average age was nine) found that the dynamics of father-daughter incest came out of a complex triangle made up of a powerful father, a powerless mother, and a privileged but exploited child. The mothers were mostly full-time homemakers who had numerous pregnancies or were alcoholic, depressed, or psychotic. Some were also battered by their husbands. The daughters rejected their mothers as weak or incompetent. They described their fathers as hard workers and good providers, gifted, likable, intelligent, but "perfect patriarchs" whose authority was never questioned. The daughters received special favors, gifts, and privileges from their fathers, and they spent a lot of time together, without the other children.[45] As a result, "some remembered that, as children, they had frankly adored their fathers" (Herman 1981, 82). A sexual relationship initiated within that family structure seemed almost inevitable:

> These daughters, in short, were alienated from their mothers, whom they saw as weak, helpless, and unable to nurture or protect them. They were elevated by their fathers to a special position in the family, in which many of the mothers' duties and privileges were assigned to them. They felt obligated to fulfill this role in order to keep their families together. Moreover, their special relationship with their fathers was often perceived as their only source of affection. Under these circumstances, when their fathers chose to demand sexual service, the daughters felt they had absolutely no option but to comply. (83)

But even where mothers and daughters were estranged, if the mother retained power in the family, she was able to prevent a seductive father from acting on his desires: "The most effective barrier to overt incest thus appeared to be not the father's impulse control, but the degree of social control exerted by the mother" (124). Father-daughter incest, then, like wife battering, is an extreme end of men's domination over women in the family: "It is like seeing normal patterns . . . reflected in a distorting mirror" (L. Gordon 1989, 205).

Masculinity and Rape

In modern societies where violence is endemic, men engage in and are victims of violence more often than women, but women feel much more vulnerable because they are subject to a continuum of sexual assault that includes obscene phone calls, flashing, verbal harassment on the street and at work, and physical attacks not only from strangers but also from co-workers, bosses, dates, boyfriends, kinfolk, and husbands.[46] Sex crimes against women—rapes and Jack-the-Ripper murders—are almost mythic metaphors for men's dominance and women's submission: "This fixed iconography—'the nude spread-eagled body of a woman'—recurs in many cases of sex crime and, like overt mutilation, serves to communicate female defeat, degradation, and destruction" (Caputi 1987, 8).

Serial murders and mass murders of women are open war.[47] Rape, however, is so common that it takes a particularly brutal gang rape to make headlines. During the week in which a white investment banker jogging in Central Park in New York City was gang-raped and beaten into unconsciousness in a highly publicized attack (April 16–22, 1989), twenty-eight girls and women, aged eight to fifty-one, mostly Black or Hispanic, were also raped—in the street, waiting for a train, visiting a friend (Terry 1989). In the United States, the FBI estimates, there is one rape every six minutes. These statistics do not include forced sex by dates, boyfriends, and husbands, which is often not considered "real rape" legally and is rarely reported to the police (Estrich 1987).[48] Yet the U.S. National Crime Survey data for 1979–87, which is based on field surveys, not police reports, reveal that in 52 percent of the completed rapes of women and girls twelve years of age and over, the offender was an intimate of the victim and, in an additional 38 percent, was known to the victim (Harlow 1991, 7). According to these data, strangers complete less than half their rape attempts.[49]

What is considered "real rape" is therefore much less common than what is only beginning to be recognized as "date rape."[50] A better way of defining rape, which could be applied to any sexual activity involving any number of people of any age or sex, is to think of a continuum of consent: Points along the continuum would include mutually expressed desire; seduction or invitation and clearly expressed agreement; psychological coercion and reluctant agreement; and physical coercion eliciting either active resistance or a passive giving-in. The defining points then become the issue. The minimum criterion for a definition of rape would be physical coercion, even if the reaction was not active resistance. Physical coercion should include deliberate inducement to heavy drinking or drug use. In a definition of rape, I would also include psychological coercion, imposed by threats of a job loss, or a bad evaluation or grade, or loss of love, or some other punitive action, and also promises of a job, a raise, a promotion, a good evaluation or grade, or some other advantage. For a child or mentally handicapped person who could not understand what they were agreeing to, seduction or invitation would also have to be defined as rape, although not for competent, aware adults. What is clearly not rape is mutually expressed desire for certain sexual practices. If the line is drawn at certain activities and that line is violated, it is rape.

Theories regarding rape-proneness of a community have included economic inequality in industrialized countries and the level of other kinds of violence in nonindustrial countries (Sanday 1981b; Schwendinger and Schwendinger 1983). One study found that the incidence of rape in states in the United States varied by level of social disorganization, sex-magazine circulation, and gender inequality (Baron and Straus 1987).[51] Another study compared fifteen college-student date-rapists, most of whom were white, with a matched control group of nonrapists and found that the most significant difference was that the rapists described their fathers, mostly all successful professionals, as physically and emotionally distant (Lisak 1991). The control group of men were closer to their fathers emotionally, yet both groups said they wanted to be like their fathers, suggesting that the rapists had learned to make themselves emotionally numb.

The radical feminist perspective on rape is that in practice and as a threat to all women, it is a form of social control by dominant men (Brownmiller 1975; MacKinnon 1982). From the subordinated men's point of view, rape of "their" women is a way of humiliating them as well. Women's exoneration of "our" men as not capable of such brutality is, in this view, a false loyalty (Hoerning 1988). Peggy Reeves Sanday, however, found that rape as punishment was a cultural phenomenon only in rape-prone societies, which were also characterized by the use of rape as a ceremonial act of manhood. Her cross-cultural analysis of ninety-five nonindustrial societies found that in 18 percent there was a high incidence of rape and concomitant cultural approval, and in 47 percent rape was rare or absent and culturally condemned (1981b, Table 2, 9). In the rape-free societies, women were respected for their procreative and productive roles, power was balanced between women and men, interpersonal violence was minimized, and the natural environment was revered. In contrast, in rape-prone societies, men were dominant and regarded women as property, hostility was fostered between women and men, and sexual assault was part of the generalized use of violence in social conflict.

Even in a rape-prone society, all men do not rape. To find out under what circumstances men in the United States commit rape, Diana Scully and Joseph Marolla interviewed 114 convicted rapists and compared them to 75 other felons in the same prisons (Scully 1990). The rapists they interviewed were poorly educated and had held low-status jobs; many were serving sentences for more than one crime, including 11 percent who had been convicted of murder. The majority were under thirty-five years old; 54 percent were Black and 66 percent of their victims were white; 46 percent were white, and two of their victims were Black.[52] More than half had not lived with their biological parents when growing up, and about half had grown up in violent families; one-third had been beaten as children; and less than 10 percent had experienced child-hood sexual abuse. Their adolescent and adult sex lives had been active and unremarkable. As adults, 59 percent were religiously affiliated, and 46 percent were either married or cohabiting at the time of the rape. The felons who were committed for crimes other than rape had similar social backgrounds, so there was nothing in upbringing or social characteristics that distinguished the rapists.

The subjects fell into three types: forty-seven admitted to raping the victims and corroborated what was in their records, but they underplayed the level of violence they had used; thirty-three admitted sexual contact with their victims but denied that it was rape; thirty-four denied having any sexual contact with the victims at all. The eighty men who admitted to the sexual contact for which they were serving time tended to be hostile toward women and held rigid beliefs that women should be sexually faithful and men should be tough, fearless, and athletic; they should conquer women sexually and defy authority. They also tended to believe that women's own behavior causes men to rape, that women could avoid rape if they tried, that women secretly want to be raped and enjoy it, and that women use the charge of rape vindictively against innocent men. These beliefs were also held by the other felons, but the rapists adhered to them more strongly.

Three-quarters had been drinking at the time of the rape. The men who admitted to sexual violence attributed their actions to alcohol; those who denied they had raped blamed what happened on their *victims'* drunkenness. Of those who admitted to the rape, 80 percent described a stressful precipitating event, mostly involving being let down by their wives or girlfriends, but only 25 percent of the deniers talked of being upset prior to the rape. Those who admitted raping felt the act had been aberrant and were now remorseful, but they said they had gotten satisfaction at the time out of degrading and humiliating their victim. Scully calls rape a low-risk, high-reward crime, deliberately undertaken for a variety of reasons: to get revenge against the women in their lives, to gain sexual access to an unwilling or unavailable woman, to have impersonal sex, to feel powerful, or to enjoy a "bonus" while committing another crime. These men's victims were not individuals but members of a category, women, a means to an end: "Admitters and deniers were similar in one very important respect. The majority did not experience guilt or shame during or immediately following their rapes, nor did they report feeling empathy for their victims at that time. Instead of the emotions that may have constrained their sexually violent behavior, these men indicated they felt nothing or they felt satisfied" (135).

The social context of gang rapes shows that these rapes are also rooted in gender norms of masculinity and a sexual double standard that blames the woman for complicity.[53] But in addition, gang rapes or date rapes that turn into gang rapes are part of men's bonding rituals in Western cultures.

In a cultural analysis of gang rapes in the United States, Reeves Sanday (1990) found a common pattern: "A vulnerable young woman, one who is seeking acceptance or who is high on drugs or alcohol, is taken to a room. She may or may not agree to have sex with one man. She then passes out, or is too weak or scared to protest, and a train of men have sex with her" (1). This pattern appears to be widespread not only among fraternities but in many other exclusively male contexts at colleges and universities in the United States, such as organized sports. Similar behavior occurs outside universities where men band together in clubs, work groups, athletic teams, military units, and business conventions—in all the settings associated with the term 'stag party.' " (4).[54]

Reeves Sanday argues that this behavior is a manifestation of both homosociality and homophobia: "In group sex, homoerotic desire is simultaneously indulged, degraded, and extruded from the group. The fact that the woman involved is often unconscious highlights her status as a surrogate victim in a drama where the main agents are males interacting with one another" (12–13). The sexual show of masculinity is for each other, to show they are "real men." Men close ranks around one another when accused of gang rapes, and their families and communities also support their behavior by decrying the promiscuity or irresponsibility of the victim and the unfairness of the legal system (Chancer 1987; Martin and Hummer 1989). Gender norms are upheld: Good girls don't get raped; good boys could not possibly be real rapists.

Sexuality and Social Constraints

Gendered sexual statuses are such powerful political, legal, and ideological constraints on individuals' sexuality and emotional relationships that alternative statuses are almost unthinkable. The men-to-women transsexuals whom Anne Bolin interviewed described the transitional phase of gradually looking and acting more and more like a woman while still living as a man as a gender limbo (1988, 89–105).[55] Sexual practices, fantasies, and identities for everyone are profoundly shaped by cultural representations of femininity and masculinity and reinforced by legal and medical means. Every culture has hegemonic or morally dominant forms of sexuality that are considered right and proper for children, for young and adolescent boys and girls, and for adult men and women. At the same time, other patterns may be prominent enough to be more or less acceptable alternatives to the dominant pattern. All these patterns evolve unevenly and usually carry over elements of past patterns. Therefore, they often exhibit contradictions, fault lines, and contested terrains (Foucault 1978).

Sexuality could certainly be organized less restrictively in Western societies. It is doubtful, though, that any and all sexual practices would be treated neutrally or not become marked by economic and power interests. Even if some future utopia were not gendered, sexuality is likely to be organized with norms of appropriateness, if not with moral strictures, in the service of community interests. Democratic states may restrict the undue burdens they place on what citizens do with their bodies, but in the end, bodies belong as much to the community as they do the individual: "Human sexuality is—and always has been, since our species began—the creation of people themselves, in social groups" (Caulfield 1985, 360). Whoever has power in the community will be influential in determining what sexualities will have moral hegemony.

> This thing here, you call this a person? There is no such thing
> as a person who is half male half female.
>
> —*Meira Weiss (forthcoming)*

MEN AS WOMEN AND WOMEN AS MEN: DISRUPTING GENDER

The French writer Colette felt that she was a "mental her-maphrodite" but had "a sturdy and perfectly female body" (Lydon 1991, 28). When she offered to travel with a noted womanizer, he said that he traveled only with women: "Thus when Damien declares that he travels only with women, implying that a woman is what Colette is *not,* the only linguistically possible conclusion is that she must be a man. But she and we know this not to be the case, despite her willingness to admit to a certain 'virility.' What then, can Colette legitimately call herself?" (29).[1] Cool and rational androgynous women are social men, one step removed from the "mannish lesbian" (Newton 1984). Men who use a highly emotionally charged vocabulary may be judged romantic geniuses, but their masculinity may be somewhat suspect, as was Byron's (Battersby 1989).

The history of a nineteenth-century French hermaphrodite illustrates the impossibility of living socially as both a woman and a man even if it is physi-ologically possible (J. Butler 1990, 93–106). Herculine Barbin, who was raised in convents as a girl, after puberty, fell in love with a young woman and had sexual relations with her. At the age of twenty-two, Herculine (usually called Alexina) confessed the homosexuality to a bishop, and after examination by two doctors, was legally recategorized as a man and given a man's name. But Herculine's genitals, as described in two doctors' reports, were ambiguous: a one-and-a-half-inch-long penis, partly descended testicles, and a urethral opening (Foucault 1980, 125–28). One doctor reasoned as follows:

> Is Alexina a woman? She has a vulva, labia majora, and a feminine urethra, independent of a sort of imperforate penis, which might be a

monstrously developed clitoris. She has a vagina. . . . These are completely feminine attributes. Yet, but Alexina has never menstruated;
the whole outer part of her body is that of a man, and my explorations
do not enable me to find a womb. Her tastes, her inclinations, draw her
toward women. At night she has voluptuous sensations that are followed by a discharge of sperm; her linen is stained and starched with it.
Finally, to sum up the matter, ovoid bodies and spermatic cords are
found by touch in a divided scrotum. These are the real proofs of
sex. . . . Alexina is a man, hermaphroditic, no doubt, but with an
obvious predominance of masculine sexual characteristics. (127–28)

But Barbin, now called Abel, did not feel he was fully a man socially because he
did not think any woman would marry him, and at the age of thirty, he ended a
"double and bizarre existence" as a suicide. The doctor who performed the
autopsy felt that the external genitalia could just as well have been classified as
female, and that, with a penis-clitoris capable of erection and a vagina, Barbin
was physiologically capable of bisexuality (128–44). But there was no social
status of man-woman.

What would have become of Herculine Barbin one hundred years later?
Surgery to remove the testicles, enlarge the vagina, and make the penis
smaller? Then hormones to produce breasts and reduce body hair? Or closure
of the vaginal opening, release of the testes, cosmetic surgery to enlarge the
penis? Having been brought up as a girl, but loving a woman, would Barbin
have identified as a "man," a "lesbian," or a "bisexual?" Would the woman who
loved him as a woman accept him as a husband? Without surgery or gender
reassignment, would Herculine and Sara have been accepted as a lesbian couple
today? Without surgery, but with gender reassignment, would Abel and Sara
have been accepted as a heterosexual couple? Would Barbin have used a
gender-neutral name, dressed in a gender-neutral way? What sex would be on
her or his official documents? What kind of work would he or she have done?[2]

One possibility was documented in 1937. A hermaphrodite named Emma
who had a penislike clitoris as well as a vagina was raised as a girl. Emma had
sexual relationships with a number of girls (heterosexual sex) and married a
man with whom she also had heterosexual sex, but continued to have women
lovers (Fausto-Sterling 1993). She refused to have vaginal closure and live as a
man because it would have meant a divorce and having to go to work. Emma
was quite content to be a physiological bisexual, possibly because her gender
identity was clearly that of a woman.

Anne Fausto-Sterling says that "no classification scheme could more than
suggest the variety of sexual anatomy encountered in clinical practice" (1993).

In 1992, a thirty-year-old Ethiopian Israeli whose social identity was a man was discovered at his army physical to have a very small penis and a very small vagina. Exploratory surgery revealed vestigial ovaries and vestigial testicles, a uterus, and fallopian tubes. He was XY, but when he was classified a male at birth it was on the basis of how the external genitalia looked, and the penis took precedence. Because he had been brought up as a man and wanted to have this identity supported physiologically, his penis was enlarged and reconstructed, and the vagina was closed and made into a scrotum. Testosterone was administered to increase his sexual desire for women.[3]

"Penis and Eggs"

When physiological anomalies occur today in places with sophisticated medical technology, the diagnosis, sex assignment, and surgical reconstruction of the genitalia are done as quickly as possible in order to minimize the intense uncertainty that a genderless child produces in our society (Kessler 1990). Other cultures, however, are more accepting of sex and gender ambiguity.

In the Dominican Republic, there has been a genetic phenomenon in which children who looked female at birth and were brought up as girls produced male hormones at puberty and virilized. Their genitalia masculinized, their voices deepened, and they developed a male physical appearance (Imperato-McGinley et al. 1974, 1979). They are called *guevedoces* (penis at twelve) or *machihembra* (male-female) or *guevotes* (penis and eggs). According to one set of reports, sixteen of nineteen who were raised as girls gradually changed to men's social roles, working outside the home, marrying, and becoming heads of households (Imperato-McGinley et al. 1979). One, now elderly, who immigrated to the United States, felt like a man, but under family pressure, lived as a woman. One, still in the Dominican Republic, had married as a woman at sixteen, had been deserted after a year, continued to live as a woman, and wanted surgery to be a "normal" woman. Not all those who lived as men had fully functioning genitalia, and all were sterile.

The physicians who studied thirty-three of these male pseudohermaphrodites (biologically male with ambiguous-appearing genitalia at birth) claim that the nineteen who decided without medical intervention that they would adopt men's identities and social roles despite having been raised as girls "appear to challenge both the theory of the immutability of gender identity after three or four years of age and the sex of rearing as the major factor in determining male-gender identity" (Imperato-McGinley et al. 1979, 1236). Their report stresses the effects of the hormonal input and secondary male sex characteristics at puberty, despite the mixture of reactions and gradualness of the gender changeover.

Another physician (Baker 1980) questions whether the pseudohermaphrodites were reared unambiguously as girls, given their somewhat abnormal genitalia at birth, and an anthropologist (Herdt 1990) claims that culturally, the community recognized a third sex category, since they had names for it. Although the medical researchers described the parents' reactions during the course of the virilization as "amazement, confusion, and finally, acceptance rather than hostility" (Imperato-McGinley et al. 1979, 1235–36), the researchers' interviews with the pseudohermaphrodites revealed that as children, they had always suffered embarrassment because of their genitalia and had worried about future harassment whether they chose to live as women or as men. That is, they were never unambiguously girls socially, and their appearance and sterility undercut their claims to be men. Nonetheless, most chose to live as men. Virilization was not total, but it provided the opportunity for the choice of the more attractive social role.[4] According to the medical researchers, "In a domestic setting, the women take care of the household activities, while the affected subjects work as farmers, miners or woodsmen, as do the normal males in the town. They enjoy their role as head of the household" (Imperato-McGinley et al. 1979, 1234).

In Papua New Guinea, where the same recessive genetic condition and marriage to close relatives produce similar male pseudohermaphrodites, the culture does have an intergender category (*kwolu-aatmwol*). Many of these children were identified by experienced midwives at birth and were reared anticipatorily as boys (Herdt 1990; Herdt and Davidson 1988). Although the kwolu-aatmwols went through boys' rituals as they grew up, their adult status as men was incomplete ritually, and therefore socially, because they were sterile and also because they were embarrassed by the small size of their penises. They rarely allowed themselves to be fellated by adolescent boys, a mark of honor for adult men, although some, as teenagers, in an effort to become more masculine, frequently fellated older men. In their behavior and attitudes, they were masculine. Their identity as adult men was stigmatized, however, because they did *not* participate in what Western societies consider homosexual (and stigmatized) sex practices but in that culture made them fully men (Herdt 1981).

The pseudohermaphrodites who were reared as girls, either because they were not identified or their genital anomalies were hidden, did not switch to living as men when they virilized. Rather, they tried very hard to live as women, but were rejected by the men they married. Only at that point did they switch to men's dress, but they were even more ostracized socially, since they did not undergo any men's rituals. According to Gilbert Herdt and Julian Davidson: "Once exposed, they had 'no place to hide,' and no public in which to continue to pose as 'female.' It was only this that precipitated gender role change. Yet this is not change to the male role, because the natives know the subjects are not male; rather they changed from sex-assigned female to turnim-men, male-identified *kwolu-aatmwol*" (1988, 53). Thus, neither childhood socialization nor pubescent virilization nor individual preference was definitive in the adult gender placement of these male pseudohermaphrodites. Their assigned status was problematic men; away from their home villages, they could pass as more or less normal men. One was married, but to a prostitute; he had been "ostentatiously masculine" as an adolescent, was a good provider, and was known as "a fearless womanizer" (Herdt and Davidson 1988).

Switching Genders

Transsexuals have normal genitalia, but identify with the members of the opposite gender. Since there is no mixed or intermediate gender for people with male genitalia who want to live as women or people with female genitalia who want to live as men, transsexuals end up surgically altering their genitalia to fit their gender identity. They also undergo hormone treatment to alter their body shape and hair distribution and to develop secondary sex characteristics, such as breasts or beards. Transsexuals do not change their sex completely (Stoller 1985, 163). Their chromosomes remain the same, and no man-to-woman transsexual has a uterus implant, nor do women-to-men transsexuals produce sperm. They change *gender;* thus, the accurate terms are *man-to-woman* and *woman-to-man,* not *male-to-female* and *female-to-male.*

Discussing only men-to-women transsexuals, Richard Docter sees the process as one in which more and more frequent cross-dressing reinforces the desire to completely switch genders:

> The cross-gender identity seems to grow stronger with practice and with social reinforcements of the pseudowoman. In unusual cases, the end result is a kind of revolution within the self system. The balance of power shifts in favor of the cross-gender identity with consequent disorganization and conflict within the self system. One result can be a quest to resolve the tension through sexual reassignment procedures or hormonal feminization. (1988, 3)

Transsexuals, however, have also indicated a sense from an early age of being in the wrong body (Morris 1975). Sexologists and psychiatrists have debated whether this anomalous gender identity is the result of biology, parenting, or retrospective reconstruction.[5]

The social task for transsexuals is to construct a gender identity without an appropriately gendered biography.[6] To create a feminized self, men-to-women transsexuals use the male transvestite's "strategies and rituals" of passing as a woman—clothing, makeup, hair styling, manicures, gestures, ways of walking, voice pitch, and "the more subtle gestures such as the difference in ways men and women smoke cigarettes" and the vocabulary women use (Bolin 1988, 131–41). Creating a new gender identity means creating a paper trail of bank, educational, and job history records; drivers' licenses, passports, and credit cards all have to be changed once the new name becomes legal (145–46). Significant others have to be persuaded to act their parts, too. Discussing men-to-women transsexuals, Anne Bolin notes:

> The family is the source of transsexuals' birth and nurturance as males and symbolically can be a source of their birth and nurturance as females. Thus, when their families accept them as females, refer to them by their female names, and use feminine gender references, it is a profound event in the transsexuals' lives, one in which their gender identity as females is given a retroactive credence. . . . The family is a significant battleground on which a symbolic identity war is waged. . . . Because an individual can only be a son or daughter [in Western societies], conferral of daughterhood by a mother is a statement of the death of a son. (1988, 94)

The final rite of passage is not only passing as a visibly and legally identifiable gendered person with a bona fide kinship status but passing as a *sexual* person. For Bolin's men-to-women transsexuals, "the most desirable condition for the first passing adventure is at night with a 'genetic girlfriend' in a heterosexual bar" (140).

Some transsexuals become gay or lesbian. In Anne Bolin's study population of seventeen men-to-women transsexuals, only one was exclusively heterosexual in orientation (1988, Fig. 1, 62). Nine were bisexual, and six were exclusively lesbian, including two transsexuals who held a wedding ceremony in a gay church.[7] Justifying the identification as lesbian by a preoperative man-to-woman transsexual who had extensive hormone therapy and had developed female secondary sexual characteristics, Deborah Heller Feinbloom and her co-authors argue that someone "living full-time in a female role must be called

a woman, albeit a woman with male genitalia (and without female genitalia),"
although potential lovers might not agree (1976, 69).[8] If genitalia, sexuality,
and gender identity are seen as a package, then it is paradoxical for someone to
change their anatomy in order to make love with someone they could easily
have had a sexual relationship with "normally." But gender identity (being a
member of the group, women or men) and gender status (living the life of a
woman or a man) are quite distinct from sexual desire for a woman or man. It
is Western culture's preoccupation with genitalia as the markers of both
sexuality and gender and the concept of these social statuses as fixed for life
that produces the problem and the surgical solution for those who cannot
tolerate the personal ambiguities Western cultures deny.[9]

Gender Masquerades

Transvestites change genders by cross-dressing, masquerading as a person of a
different gender for erotic, pragmatic, or rebellious reasons. Since they can
put on and take off gender by changing clothes, they disrupt the conventional
conflation of sex, sexuality, and gender in Western cultures much more than
transsexuals do.

François Timoléon de Choisy was a seventeenth-century courtier, histo-
rian, ambassador, and priest who was "indefatigably heterosexual" but a constant cross-dresser. The Abbé de Choisy married women twice, once as a
woman, once as a man, and both spouses had children by him. He survived the
turmoil of gender ambiguity by going to live in another community or country
when the censure got too vociferous (Garber 1992, 255–59). The Chevalier
(sometimes Chevalière) d'Eon de Beaumont, a famous cross-dresser who lived
in the eighteenth century, seems to have been celibate. Because d'Eon did not
have any sexual relationships, English and French bookmakers took serious
bets on whether d'Eon was a man or a woman. Physically, he was a male,
according to his birth and death certificates, and he lived forty-nine years as a
man (259–66). He also lived thirty-four years as a woman, many of them with
a woman companion who "was astounded to learn that she was a man" (265).
Garber asks: "Does the fact that he was born a male infant and died with the
male organs perfectly formed' mean that he was, in the years between, a man?
A 'very man'?" (255). A man in what sense—physical, sexual, or gendered?

Some men who pass as women and women who pass as men by cross-
dressing say they do so because they want privileges or opportunities the other
gender has, but they may also be fighting to alter their society's expectations
for their own gender. One of her biographers says of George Sand:

While still a child she lost her father, tried to fill his place with a mother whom she adored, and, consequently, developed a masculine attitude strengthened by the boyish upbringing which she received at the hands of a somewhat eccentric tutor who encouraged her to wear a man's clothes. . . . For the rest of her life she strove, unconsciously, to recreate the free paradise of her childhood, with the result that she could never submit to a master. . . . Impatient of all masculine authority, she fought a battle for the emancipation of women, and sought to win for them the right to dispose freely of their bodies and their hearts. (Maurois 1955, 13)[10]

Natalie Davis calls these defiers of the social order disorderly women. Their outrage and ridicule produce a double message; they ask for a restoration of the social order purified of excesses of gender disadvantage, and their own gender inversion also suggests possibilities for change (1975, 124–51).[11]

During the English Renaissance, open cross-dressing on the street and in the theater defied accepted gender categories.[12] In early modern England, the state enforced class and gender boundaries through sumptuary laws that dictated who could wear certain colors, fabrics, and furs. Cross-dressing and wearing clothes "above one's station" (servants and masters trading places, also a theatrical convention) thus were important symbolic subverters of social hierarchies at a time of changing modes of production and a rising middle class (Howard 1988). Since seventeenth-century cross-dressing up-ended concepts of appropriate sexuality, the fashion was accused of feminizing men and masculinizing women: "When women took men's clothes, they symbolically left their subordinate positions. They became masterless women, and this threatened overthrow of hierarchy was discursively read as the eruption of uncontrolled sexuality" (Howard 1988, 424).

The way the gender order was critiqued and then restored can be seen in a famous Renaissance play about a cross-dressing character called the "roaring girl." The Roaring Girl, by Thomas Middleton and Thomas Dekker, written in 1608–11, was based on a real-life woman, Mary Frith, who dressed in men's clothes and was "notorious as a bully, whore, bawd, pickpurse, fortune-teller, receiver [of stolen goods], and forger" (Bullen 1935, 4). She also smoked and drank like a man and was in prison for a time. She lived to the age of seventy-four. In Middleton and Dekker's play, this roaring girl, called Moll Cutpurse, becomes a model of morality. She remains chaste and thus free of men sexually and economically, unlike most poor women, as she herself points out:

> Distressed needlewomen and trade-fallen wives,
> Fish that must need bite or themselves be bitten,
> Such hungry things as these may soon be took
> With a worm fastened on a golden hook.   (III, i, 96–97)

Her cross-dressing allows her to observe and question the ways of thieves and pickpockets not to learn to be a criminal but to protect herself. She can also protect any man who marries her:

> You may pass where you list, through crowd most thick,
> And come off bravely with your purse unpick'd.
> You do not know the benefits I bring with me;
> No cheat dares work upon you with thumb or knife,
> While you've a roaring girl to your son's wife.   (V, ii, 159–63)

But she feels she is too independent to be a traditional wife:

> I have no humour to marry; I love to lie a' both sides a' the bed myself:
> and again, a' th' other side, a wife, you know, ought to be obedient, but
> I fear me I am too headstrong to obey; therefore I'll ne'er go about it.
> (II, ii, 37–41)

Her other reason for not marrying is that men cheat, lie, and treat women badly. Should they change, "next day following I'll be married," to which another character in the play responds: "This sounds like doomsday" (V, ii, 226–27), not likely to happen soon.

Despite her gloomy views on men and marriage, Moll helps a young couple marry by pretending to be wooed by the man. His father, who has withheld his consent for his son's original choice, is so outraged that his son is thinking of marrying Moll Cutpurse that he willingly consents to the son's marriage to the woman he has loved all along. Thus, rather poignantly, Moll's independence and street smarts are invidious traits when compared to those of a "good woman." Her cross-dressing is not a defiance of the gender order; rather it places her outside it:

> 'tis woman more than man,
> Man more than woman; and, which to none can hap
> The sun gives her two shadows to one shape;
> Nay, more, let this strange thing walk, stand, or sit,
> No blazing star draws more eyes after it.   (I, i, 251–55)

Moll Cutpurse's social isolation means that the gender order does not have to change to incorporate her independence as a woman: "a politics of despair . . . affirms a seemingly inevitable exclusion of marginal genders from the territory of the natural and the real" (J. Butler 1990, 146).

Affirming Gender

In most societies with only two gender statuses—"women" and "men"—those who live in the status not meant for them usually do *not* challenge the social institution of gender. In many ways, they reinforce it. Joan of Arc, says Marina Warner (1982) in discussing her transvestism, "needed a framework of virtue, and so she borrowed the apparel of men, who held a monopoly on virtue, on reason and courage, while eschewing the weakness of women, who were allotted to the negative pole, where virtue meant meekness and humility, and nature meant carnality" (147). A masculine woman may be an abomination to tradition, but from a feminist point of view, she is not a successful rebel, for she reinforces dominant men's standards of the good: "The male trappings were used as armor—defensive and aggressive. It . . . attacked men by aping their appearance in order to usurp their functions. On the personal level, it defied men and declared them useless; on the social level, it affirmed male supremacy, by needing to borrow the appurtenances to assert personal needs and desires . . .; men remain the touchstone and equality a process of imitation" (Warner 1982, 155).[13]

Joan of Arc said she donned armor not to pass as a man but to be beyond sexuality, beyond gender. She called herself *pucelle,* a maid, but socially, she was neither woman nor man. She was an "ideal androgyne"; "She could thereby transcend her sex; she could set herself apart and usurp the privileges of the male and his claims to superiority. At the same time, by never pretending to be other than a woman and a maid, she was usurping a man's function but shaking off the trammels of his sex altogether to occupy a different, third order, neither male nor female, but unearthly, like the angels" (Warner 1982, 145–46). When Joan was on trial, she was denuded of her knightly armor and accused of female carnality, and then she was burned at the stake—as a woman and a witch. Twenty-five years later, at her rehabilitation trial, and in 1920, when she was declared a saint, she was presented as a sexless virgin, amenorrheic and possibly anorectic.

As a heroine today, Joan of Arc is more likely to be a symbolic Amazon, a woman warrior, than an ideal androgyne, sexless and saintly. The ambiguity of her gender representation was corroborated by one of the first women to enter West Point to be trained with men as an army officer. On her first day in the dining hall, Carol Barkalow "was startled to find among the depictions of history's greatest warriors the muralist's interpretation of Joan of Arc. There she stood in silver armor, alongside Richard the Lion Hearted and William the Conqueror, sword uplifted in one hand, helmet clasped in the other, red hair falling to her shoulders, with six knights kneeling in homage at her feet" (1990, 27). As Barkalow found later, the warrior maid had set little precedent for the acceptance of women as military leaders. The mixed-gender message of the portrait was prescient, for the main problem at a coed military academy seemed to be one of categorization. Women army officers were suspect as women when they looked and acted too much like men, but they were a puzzlement as soldiers when they looked and acted like women.

Other Genders

There are non-Western societies that have third and fourth genders that link genitalia, sexual orientation, and gender status in ways different from Western cultures. These statuses demonstrate how physical sex, sexuality, and gender interweave, but are separate elements conferring different levels of prestige and stigma.

The Native American berdache is an institutionalized cross-gendered role that legitimates males doing women's work. The berdache can also be a sacred role, and if a boy's dreaming indicates a pull toward the berdache status, parents would not think of dissenting. Although it would seem logical that societies that put a high emphasis on aggressive masculinity, like the Plains Indians, would offer the berdache status as a legitimate way out for boys reluctant to engage in violent play and warfare, berdaches do not occur in all warlike tribes and do occur in some that are not warlike (W. L. Williams 1986, 47–49).[14]

Berdaches educate children, sing and dance at tribal events, carry provisions for war parties, and have special ritual functions (H. Whitehead 1981, 89; W. L. Williams 1986, 54–61). Among the Navahos, berdaches not only do women's craft work but also farm and raise sheep, which are ordinarily men's work: "Beyond this, because they are believed to be lucky in amassing wealth they usually act as the head of their family and have control of the disposal of all the family's property" (W. L. Williams 1986, 61).

Berdaches are legitimately homosexual:

Homosexual behavior may occur between non-berdache males, but the cultures emphasize the berdache as the usual person a man would go to for male sex. With the role thus institutionalized, the berdache serves the sexual needs of many men without competing against the institution of heterosexual marriage. Men are not required to make a choice between being heterosexual or being homosexual, since they can accommodate both desires. Nevertheless, for that minority of men who do wish to make such a choice, a number of cultures allow them the option of becoming the husband to a berdache. (108–09)

Since homosexual sex does not make a man into a berdache, Walter Williams makes a distinction between homosexuality, as sex between two men, and *heterogender* sex, between a man and a berdache: "The berdache and his male partner do not occupy the same recognized gender status" (96). Two berdaches do not have sexual relations with each other, nor do they marry. In some cultures, the berdache's husband loses no prestige; in others, he does, coming in for kidding for having an unusual sexual relationship, like a young man married to an older woman (113). Sometimes the husband is kidded because the berdache is a particularly good provider. The berdache's husband is not labeled a homosexual, and if a divorce occurs, he can easily make a heterosexual marriage.

The berdache is not the equivalent of the Western male homosexual (Callender and Kochems 1985). The berdache's social status is defined by work and dress and sometimes a sacred calling; the social status of modern Western homosexual men is defined by sexual orientation and preference for men as sexual partners (H. Whitehead 1981, 97–98). The berdache's gender status is not that of a man but that of a woman, so their homosexual relationships, like those of heterosexuals, are heterogendered; homosexual couples in Western society are homogendered.

The Plains Indians had a tradition of *warrior women,* but a cross-gender status for younger women was not institutionalized in most Native American tribes (Blackwood 1984, 37). Harriet Whitehead argues that because men were considered superior in these cultures, it was harder for women to breach the gender boundaries upward than it was for men to breach them downward (1981, 86). Walter Williams speculates that every woman was needed to have children (1986, 244). The tribes that did allow women to cross gender boundaries restricted the privilege to women who claimed they never menstruated (H. Whitehead 1981, 92). Young women could become men in societies that were egalitarian and tolerant of cross-gendered work activities (Blackwood 1984). Among the Mohave, a girl's refusal to learn women's tasks could lead to her being taught the same skills boys learned and to ritual renaming, nose piercing, and hair styling as a man. At that point, her status as a man allowed her to marry a woman and to do men's work of hunting, trapping, growing crops, and fighting. She was also expected to perform a man's ritual obligations. Because divorce was frequent and children went with the mother, cross-gendered females could rear children. Adoptions were also common. Sexually, cross-gendered females were homosexual, but, like berdaches, their marriages were always heterogendered—they did not marry or have sexual relationships with each other.[15] Among less egalitarian Native American societies, a legitimate cross-gender status, *manly hearted woman,* was available for postmenopausal women who acquired wealth (H. Whitehead 1981, 90–93). In some African cultures today, a wealthy woman can marry a woman and adopt her children as a father (Amadiume 1987).

Lesbians in Western societies differ from cross-gendered females in Native American and African societies in that they do not form heterogendered couples. Both women in a lesbian couple continue to be identified socially as women; neither becomes a "husband." If they have children, neither becomes a "father"; both are mothers to the children (Weston 1991).

Hijras, a group in northern India, consider themselves intersexed males who have become women; many, but not all, undergo ritualistic castration (Nanda 1990). They serve both a legitimate cultural function as ritual performers and an illegitimate sexual function as homosexual prostitutes. Sometimes they are considered women, sometimes men, but they are deviant in either status not because of their sexuality but because they don't have children. Hijras are required to dress as women, but they do not imitate or try to pass as ordinary women; rather, they are as deviant as women as they are as men:

> Their female dress and mannerisms are exaggerated to the point of caricature, expressing sexual overtones that would be considered inappropriate for ordinary women in their roles as daughters, wives, and mothers. Hijra performances are burlesques of female behavior. Much of the comedy of their behavior derives from the incongruities between their behavior and that of traditional women. They use coarse and abusive speech and gestures in opposition to the Hindu ideal of demure and restrained femininity. Further, it is not at all uncommon to see hijras in female clothing sporting several days growth of beard, or exposing hairy, muscular arms. The ultimate sanction of hijras to an abusive or unresponsive public is to lift their skirts and expose the mutilated genitals. The implicit threat of this shameless, and thoroughly unfeminine, behavior is enough to make most people give them a few cents so they will go away. (Nanda 1986, 38)

Hijras live separately in their own communal households, relating to each other as fictive mothers, daughters, sisters, grandmothers, and aunts. Occupationally, they sing and dance at weddings and births, run bathhouses, work as cooks and servants, and engage in prostitution with men; or they are set up in households by men in long-term sexual relationships. The hijras Serena Nanda interviewed came from lower-class, middle-caste families in small cities and said they had wanted to dress and act as women from early childhood. They left home because of parental disapproval and to protect their siblings' chance for marriage (65).

Hijras worship Bahuchara Mata, a mother-goddess. Shiva is also sometimes worshiped by hijras as a deity who is half-man, half-woman. In the great Indian legend, the *Mahabharata,* one of the heroes, Arjuna, lives for a year in exile as a woman, doing menial work and teaching singing and dancing. Those who were not men and not women were blessed by Ram in the Hindu epic, *Ramayana.* In addition to these Hindu religious connections, Islam is also involved in hijra culture. The founders of the original seven hijra communal "houses," or subgroups, were said to be Muslim, and in keeping with this tradition, modern houses also have Muslim gurus. This religious legitimation and their performance of cultural rituals integrate hijras into Indian society, as does the Indian tradition of creative asceticism. Young, sexually active hijras, however, are seen by the elders as compromising the ascetic sources of their legitimacy.

Hijras seem to resemble transvestite performers (female impersonators or "drag queens") in modern Western society. But transvestite performers do not have roots in Western religious tradition, nor are they castrated. Castrated hijras do not have the same social status as men-to-women transsexuals in Western societies, since transsexuals act as normal women, and hijras do not. In some respects, hijras resemble the castrati of European operatic tradition.

In the seventeenth century, because the Roman Catholic church forbade women to sing in public, women's parts were sung by castrati, boys whose testicles were removed in adolescence so their voices would remain soprano. Throughout the eighteenth century, castrati and women singers both appeared on the operatic stage, often in competition, although the castrati had the advantages of far superior training, respectability, church support, and fame. There was constant gender reversal in casting and plot. Women contraltos sang men's roles in men's clothes (now called "trouser roles"); soprano castrati sang the "leading ladies" in women's costumes (*en travesti*); and both masqueraded in plots of mistaken or hidden identity in the clothes of the role's opposite but their actual gender.

Casanova, in his memoirs, tells of being sexually attracted to a supposed castrato, Bellino, in the early 1740s. This attraction totally confounded his notorious ability to "smell" a woman in his presence, so he was much relived, when he seduced Bellino (in anticipation of homosexual sex), to find out that Bellino was a woman soprano posing as a eunuch in order to sing in Rome. Of course, she sang women's roles. She had heterosexual sex with Casanova, although this womanizer was just as ready to make love with a man (Ellison 1992).[16]

A third type of institutionalized intermediate gender role are the xaniths of Oman, a strictly gender-segregated Islamic society in which women's sexual purity is guarded by their wearing long, black robes and black face masks when in public and not mingling with men other than close relatives at home (Wikan 1982, 168–86). Xaniths are male homosexual prostitutes who dress in men's clothes but in pastel colors rather than white, wear their hair in neither a masculine nor a feminine style, and have feminine mannerisms. They sing and eat with the women at weddings and mingle freely with women, but they maintain men's legal status. (Women are lifelong minors; they must have a male guardian.) They are not considered full-fledged women because they are prostitutes, and women, in Oman ideology, may engage in sexual acts only with their husbands. The xaniths' social role is to serve as sexual outlets for unmarried or separated men, and thus they protect the sexual purity of women. The men who have sexual relations with them are not considered homosexual, because supposedly they always take the active role.

Xaniths live alone and take care of their own households, doing both men's work—the marketing—and women's work—food preparation. Being a xanith seems to be a family tradition in that several brothers will become xaniths. They move in and out of the gender status fairly easily, reverting to manhood when they marry and successfully deflower their bride. To be considered a man, a groom must show bloody evidence of defloration or accuse his bride of not having been a virgin. A xanith, therefore, who shows he has successfully deflowered a virgin bride becomes a man. Just as a female in Oman culture is not a woman until she has intercourse, a male is not a man until he successfully consummates his marriage. A woman, though, can never revert to the virgin state of girlhood, but a man can revert to xanithhood by singing with the women at the next wedding.

In the sense that passive homosexual sex rather than heterogendered behavior is the defining criterion of status, the xanith is close to the feminized homosexual prostitute in Western culture, but not, according to Unni Wikan, to homosexual men in other Middle Eastern cultures:

Homosexual practice is a common and recognized phenomenon in many Middle Eastern cultures, often in the form of an institutionalized practice whereby older men seek sexual satisfaction with younger boys. But this homosexual relationship generally has two qualities that make it fundamentally different from that practiced in Oman. First, it is part of a deep friendship or love relationship between two men, which has qualities, it is often claimed, of being purer and more beautiful than love between man and woman. . . . Second, both parties play both the active and the passive sexual role—either simultaneously or through time. (1982, 177)

One or the Other, Never Both

Opportunities for multiple genders vary over time and place. Michel Foucault, in the introduction to Barbin's memoirs, says of the concept "one true sex":

Biological theories of sexuality, juridical conceptions of the individual, forms of administrative control in modern nations, led little by little to rejecting the idea of a mixture of the two sexes in a single body, and consequently to limiting the free choice of indeterminate individuals. Henceforth, everybody was to have one and only one sex. Everybody was to have his or her primary, profound, determined and determining sexual identity; as for the elements of the other sex that might appear, they could only be accidental, superficial, or even quite simply illusory. (1980, viii)

Yet, in Western societies, despite our firm belief that each person has one sex, one sexuality, and one gender, congruent with each other and fixed for life, and that these categories are one of only two sexes, two sexualities, and two genders, hermaphrodites, pseudohermaphrodites, transsexuals, transvestites, and bisexuals exhibit a dizzying fluidity of bodies, desires, and social statuses. According to Annie Woodhouse, "punters" are men "who don't want to go to bed with a man, but don't want to go bed with a real woman either." So they go to bed with men dressed as women (1989, 31). The ambiguous appearance of the women Holly Devor (1989) interviewed was typed as "mannish," and so they had difficulty being considered "opposite" enough for heterosexual relationships. As lesbians, not only was their appearance acceptable, but they could, and did, sexually excite other women when passing as men, as did Deborah Sampson, the woman who fought in the American Revolution in a man's uniform, and Nadezhda Durova, the Russian "cavalry maiden" in the

Napoleonic Wars (Durova 1989; Freeman and Bond 1992). Marjorie Garber writes of Yvonne Cook, a man who dresses as a woman, considers herself a lesbian, and has a woman lover who dresses as a man (1992, 4).

All these components can shift back and forth over days, weeks, months, and years. With unisex clothing, gender can change in minutes, depending on the context and the response of others to gender cues. Bisexuals have long-term serial relationships with women and men but may define themselves as either heterosexual or homosexual. Transvestites consciously play with sexual and gender categories. Gay men, lesbians, and bisexuals cross Western culture's sexual boundaries but do not always challenge gender norms. Transsexuals, in their quest for "normality," often reaffirm them. Through their "subversive bodily acts," all demonstrate the social constructedness of sex, sexuality, and gender (J. Butler 1990, 79–141). But they have not disrupted the deep genderedness of the modern Western world. And to maintain genderedness, to uphold gender boundaries, the "impulses toward, or fear of, turning into someone of the opposite sex" that many ordinary, normal people feel have to be suppressed (Stoller 1985, 152).

The norms, expectations, and evaluation of women and men may be converging, but we have no social place for a person who is neither woman nor man. A man who passes as a woman or a woman as a man still violates strong social boundaries, and when transsexuals change gender, they still cross a great divide. In this sense, Western culture resembles the intensely gendered world of Islam, where all the rules of marriage, kinship, inheritance, purity, modesty, ritual, and even burial are challenged by people of ambiguous sex (Sanders 1991). Rather than allowing the resultant social ambiguity to continue, medieval Islamic jurists developed a set of rules for gendering hermaphrodites: "A person with ambiguous genitalia or with no apparent sex might have been a biological reality, but it had no gender and, therefore, no point of entry into the social world: it was unsocialized" (Sanders 1991, 88). As in modern Western society, a person who was neither woman nor man had no social place and could have no social relationships without disturbing the social order: "What was at stake for medieval Muslims in gendering one ungendered body was, by implication, gendering the most important body: the social body" (89). The social body in modern Western society, both for the individual and the group, is, above all, gendered.

Suppose Godot's a woman, what then?
—*Mary O'Brien (1989, 83)*

WAITING FOR THE GODDESS: CULTURAL IMAGES OF GENDER

In *Sexual Politics,* Kate Millett, one of the first of the current feminist critics of modern culture, commented sardonically on Freud's theory of the origins of civilization:

> One of Freud's happiest thoughts along this line is an entertaining specimen of his logical processes, and a particularly quaint instance of his unflagging enthusiasm for glorifying the inestimable male organ. Speculating on how man discovered fire, Freud concludes that it was the result of "instinctual renunciation" of the impulse to extinguish the fire by urinating on it. It must be perfectly clear to all that the female could not discover fire because she could not renounce the impulse to urinate on it, lacking as she does the only adequate organ of long-distance urination. Here one had an extreme and pristine case of how, anatomically, woman is disqualified from contributing to the advancement of knowledge. (1970, 201)

In her book, Millett shows how men's phallus-worship and fear of castration are played out in the sexual and symbolic imagery in the novels of D. H. Lawrence, Henry Miller, and Norman Mailer, and the plays of Jean Genet— "sexual politics at the fundamental level of copulation" (6). In *Intercourse* (1987), Andrea Dworkin argues that men's fear of becoming women turns sexual intercourse into rape in the works of Leo Tolstoy, Gustave Flaubert, Kobo Abe, Tennessee Williams, James Baldwin, and Isaac Bashevis Singer. According to Millett and Dworkin, these writers depict men's need to objectify and sexually dominate women in order to allay their fears of castration and homosexuality.

Like other radical feminists, they claim that the symbolic sexual plunder of women in high culture and the mass media is often no different from the explicit sexual violence in hard-core pornography.[1] Both demean and exploit women. Catharine MacKinnon says: "In pornography the violence *is* the sex. The inequality is the sex. Pornography does not work sexually without hierarchy. If there is no inequality, no violation, no dominance, no force, there is no sexual arousal" (1987, 160).[2]

Pornography portrays women as sexual objects of men's lust and at the same time as sexually demanding and virtually insatiable; it portrays men as objectified by their enlarged penises, always sexually arousable and performance-perfect. The sex act is genitally specific and ends in explosive orgasms for the man and the woman—the "money shot" (Brod 1990; L. Williams, 1989). In her discussion of the pornographic portrayal of orgasm, Linda Williams notes that it is male-focused not only for ideological reasons; there is also the problem of the representation of female orgasm: "The irony . . . is that, while it is possible, in a certain limited and reductive way, to 'represent' the physical pleasure of the male by showing erection and ejaculation, this maximum visibility proves elusive in the parallel confession of female sexual pleasure. Anatomically, female orgasm takes place . . . in an 'invisible place' that cannot be easily seen" (1989, 49).

Women depict sexual desire in visual pornography without necessarily being aroused; in enacting sexual desire, men *have* to be aroused: "The male actor cannot merely depict arousal, because the audience looks for his erection as the sign of arousal. The only men who could depict arousal without enacting it are those who could sustain an erection in the absence of arousal" (Soble 1986, 129). Men's evident sexual prowess in visual pornography glorifies them as superstuds, but sex for a price is by definition prostitution when women do it, so acting in pornographic films or live sex acts or posing for pornographic photography debases them (Soble 1986, 129–30).[3] As audience, men spectators can identify with the studs and feel powerful; women feel cheap, embarrassed, or disgusted.[4]

In pornography and in popular culture, penises are usually visualized as "hard, tough, weapon-like," making their owners potent, powerful, and authoritative (Dyer 1985, 31). The fragility of male genitals is rarely symbolized:

> Male genitals are fragile, squashy, delicate things: even when erect, the penis is spongy, seldom straight, and rounded at the tip, while the testicles are imperfect spheres, always vulnerable, never still. There

are very exceptional cases where something of the exquisiteness and softness of the male genitals is symbolized. . . . Far more commonly the soft, vulnerable charm of male genitals is evoked as hard, tough, and dangerous. It is not flowers that most commonly symbolize male genitals but swords, knives, fists, guns. (Dyer 1985, 30)

Nonpornographic cinema uses "a range of fetish substitutes for the visible truth of women's sexual difference" (49), but most of the sexual imagery in Western culture does not depict women's sexuality as experienced by women. Sandra Gilbert and Susan Gubar (1988) argue that men publishers and critics are uncomfortable with women writers' images of women and sexuality. Some of these sexual metaphors appear in women novelists' and poets' descriptions of animals, birds, insects, flowers, jewels, water, and landscapes: "the Black Valley, the Divide, the Red Deeps," and "the little hard nut, the living stone, something precious in miniature to be fondled with the hand or cast away in wrath" (Moers 1977, 370, 387, 369–401). Such imagery is rarely used when men write about women. Rather, women's sensuality is more likely to be expressed as maternity, as in medieval art: "Is it possible that man and woman no longer even caress each other except indirectly through the mediation between them represented by the child? Preferably male. Man, identified with his son, rediscovers the pleasure of maternal coddling: woman retouches herself in fondling that part of her body: her baby-penis clitoris" (Irigaray 1981b, 102). This metaphor of maternal sexuality resonates with Freudian oedipal and phallic imagery.

Even when an author evokes women's sensuality with sensitivity and nuance, as James Joyce does in Molly Bloom's extended soliloquy in *Ulysses*, she is defined by her sexuality, not her womanhood: "and I thought well as well him as another and then I asked him with my eyes to ask again yes and then he asked me would I yes to say yes my mountain flower and first I put my arms around him yes and drew him down to me so he could feel my breasts all perfume yes and his heart was going like mad and yes I said yes I will Yes" ([1922] 1986, 643–44). Molly Bloom has the last word, but does she? The S in her last "yes" leads back to the beginning of *Ulysses*, to "Stately, plump Buck Mulligan . . . bearing a bowl of lather on which a mirror and a razor lay crossed. . . . He held the bowl aloft and intoned:—*Introibo ad altare Dei*" (3). Throughout the book, Leonard Bloom, not Molly, wanders through Dublin and through time and Western culture; Molly stays in bed.[5] Molly Bloom's perfumed breasts may break the spell of Buck Mulligan's mock prayer, but in Western culture, women's sensuality, sexuality, and procreative powers are controlled for men and by men, who are thus free to (re)create themselves in their fathers' image.

The Male Gaze

A culture's symbolic system communicates obvious and subliminal meanings. Ordinary language reflects gender hierarchies in conscious and deliberate devaluation (as in referring to adult women as "girls") and in careless language that renders women invisible (referring to men and women peers as "the guys").[6] In a "wickedary," a feminist dictionary, Mary Daly and Jane Caputi (1987) reclaim common words for women—hag and crone, spinster, glamour and charm, Amazon. They give the original meaning of these pejoratives—old women, one who spins, magic spells, woman warrior.

Symbolic language, however, does not just name in ways that praise and denigrate; symbolic language reflects and creates the culture's "unconscious." Freudian psychoanalytic theory sees Western culture as embedded in the Oedipus complex, in which the young boy represses his emotional attachment to his mother and identifies with his more powerful father because he is afraid that otherwise, like her, he will lose his penis. Patriarchal culture in this analysis is the sublimation of men's suppressed infantile desire for the mother and fear of the loss of the phallus, the symbol of masculine difference. Since women don't have a phallus to lose, they don't participate in the creation of the culture. Their wish for a phallus and repressed sexual desire for their fathers is transformed into wanting to give birth to a son; men's repressed sexual desires and fear of the father's castration are transformed into cultural creations. For Jacques Lacan, the influential French writer on psychoanalysis, sexuality, and gender, women know that their relationship to culture is negative "because at the very moment of the acquisition of language, she learns that she lacks the phallus, the symbol that sets language going through a recognition of difference; her relation to language is a negative one, a lack" (E. A. Kaplan 1983, 310).[7]

Semiotic analysis of the subtext of cultural productions has deconstructed art, films, fiction, and the mass media to show how they legitimate men's cultural domination, in particular, the creation of women as the objects of their sexual fantasies—"the male gaze."[8] In film criticism, for instance: "Dominant (Hollywood) cinema is seen as constructed according to the unconscious of patriarchy, which means that film narratives are constituted through a phallocentric language and discourse that parallels the language of the uncon-scious. Women in film, thus, do not function as signifiers for a signified (a real woman), . . . but signifier and signified have been elided into a sign that represents something in the male unconscious" (E. A. Kaplan 1983, 310). What women represent is the sexual desire and emotionality that men must repress in order to become like their fathers—men who are controlled and controlling.

Women as performers cannot escape men's voyeuristic gaze: Men film-makers look at them, men actors look at them, and men spectators look at them. Thus, no matter what role women play, they are sexualized because men look at them as desired or despised objects, and "men do not simply look; their gaze carries with it the power of action and of possession that is lacking in the female gaze" (E. A. Kaplan 1983, 311). Women stars are turned into fetishes and women characters into discreet objects of desire (Mulvey 1989, 14–16). Symbolically, then, *all* the pretty women are prostitutes.

Many nineteenth-century paintings by men were of prostitutes, and in their paintings of artists' models, ballerinas, and bartenders, Linda Nochlin points out, the women selling services are also selling themselves sexually (1988, 34n, 37–56). As Luce Irigaray says: "For woman is traditionally use-value for man, exchange-value among men. Merchandise, then" (1981c, 105). Commenting on the prima donnas of Western opera and concert halls, Elizabeth Wood says: "They have been consistently described in erotic images of thinly disguised exotic libertinism. The contrast between the ways in which women competing with men for professional power have been trivialized, and ways in which female 'stars' have been glamorized, exemplifies the 'madonna-whore' dichotomy in men's perception of women. For success, women must frequently serve the linked economic and erotic aspects of dominant culture" (1980, 295).

Teresa de Lauretis notes that while cinematic actresses complicitly portray the images of men's desire and thus attract men as spectators, heterosexual women spectators collude in these sexual and economic enterprises not only by watching but by incorporating the images men present to them as part of their own gendered sexual identities: "This manner of identification would uphold both positionalities of desire, both active and passive aims: desire for the other, and desire to be desired by the other. This, I think, is in fact the operation by which narrative and cinema solicit the spectators' consent and seduce women into femininity: by a double identification, a surplus of pleasure produced by the spectators themselves for cinema and for society's profit" (1984, 143).[9]

The 1980s saw the spectacular stardom of Madonna, who travestied the madonna-whore dichotomy with her name, her tarty clothes, and her hit record, *Like a Virgin* (McClary 1991, 148–66). She deliberately perverted conventional sexual norms with "counternarratives of female heterosexual desire" and converted feminine clothing, such as sexy bustiers, into symbols of power (McClary 1991, 165; Pareles 1990). Madonna has created an aggressively feminized erotic vocabulary and made a lot of money flouting the conventions of the dominant culture, selling herself sexually while symbolically critiquing conventionally gendered sexuality. Madonna's exaggeration and parody of femininity makes its artifice explicit; in contrast, many earlier culture heroines, like Marilyn Monroe, who also seemed to be "female female impersonators," did not distance themselves from their highly feminized public personae (L. J. Kaplan 1991, 261).[10] Madonna's look in music performances, actually modeled on Monroe's, says, "This is how women have been made by men." By signaling that she is making her image *herself,* Madonna recuperates her sexuality. She does what Julia Kristeva says young women must now do—show that sexuality is, above all, symbolic: "The sharpest and most subtle point of feminist subversion brought about by the new generation will henceforth be situated on the terrain of the inseparable conjunction of the sexual and the symbolic" (1981, 21).

Suffering's Melody

Women in Western cultural productions have represented not only men's sexual desires but also the extravagant emotions the hero cannot express without losing his manliness.[11] Once Western culture equated masculinity with rationality, to "lament" was to be feminine (Clément [1979] 1988, 118; McClary 1991, 50). In cultural productions, women have lamented the loss of their children, their husbands, and their homelands, but since the nineteenth century, women's laments are mostly about lost love. Romantic heroines in opera are "sexually frenzied madwomen" who die in the last act. But there is subtle subtext here. By their symbolic sacrifice, these heroines uphold men's rational social order. As Catharine Clément, in *Opéra, or The Undoing of Women,* says: "Beyond the romantic ideology, lines are being woven, tying up the characters and leading them to death for transgression—for transgressions of familial rules, political rules, the things at stake in sexual and authoritarian power. That is what it is all about" ([1979] 1988, 10).

Susan McClary (1991) locates the beginning of the operatic identification of women, sexuality, emotion, and rebellion in the seventeenth century, when

the shift in gender representation was bound up with the more general crisis in all forms of authority—political, economic, religious, and philosophical. . . . Significantly, composers and librettists grant the right to launch attacks on traditional authority not only to women characters, but also to servants, who complain constantly about class oppression. Although such grievances are blunted somewhat by being put into the mouths of women and grotesque comic characters, these moments of resistance may reveal—and yet conceal—more general dissatisfaction with powerful social institutions: critiques are safer, after all, when displaced onto marginalized Others. (51)

But order is restored, both politically and operatically, and at the end of the opera heroines are "trotted out to sing hymns of faith to male authority" (51).

By the nineteenth century, the voice of rebellion was heard again, and once again, it was the voice of the feminine Other. Carmen, seducer, sensualist, and free spirit, is "somewhat whore, somewhat Jewess, somewhat Arab, entirely illegal, always on the margins of life" (Clément [1979] 1988, 49). Her otherness, McClary (1991) says, is clearly represented in the music: "Her principal musical motif . . . is made up of the illicit augmented-second interval that had long been the musical sign for the Jew, the Arab, the all-purpose racial Other; this is the motif that finally is forcibly expunged by the final triad of the opera" (64).

Carmen, McClary points out, is a man's fantasy of liberatory sexuality, both dangerous and attractive, indeed, attractive because it is dangerously subversive and uncontrollable (56–67): "Infuriatingly, the male-constructed Carmen refuses to be contained in accordance with José's fantasies; she says 'no' to his 'lyric urgency,' talks back, makes sexual demands, takes other lovers" (59). Because the nineteenth-century opera audience was, ultimately, properly bourgeois, their alter ego, the rebellious Don José (or Pinkerton or Alfredo) had to be punished, and for that Carmen (or Butterfly or Violetta) had to be sacrificed: "Someone (a colonial, nonwhite, non-Christian, lower-class female character) actually has to die as a result of José's mind/body crisis" (66). Thus, while the operatic hero finally suffers emotionally and is a better man for it, it is the operatic heroine who dies: "Carmen, in the moment of her death, represents the one and only freedom to choose, decision, provocation. She is the image, foreseen and doomed, of a women who refuses masculine yokes and who must pay for it with her life" (Clément [1979] 1988, 48). The music becomes more and more dissonant, but both socially and tonally, order is restored: "Carmen and Lulu are killed like vampires with stakes through the heart. . . . The monstrosity of Salome's sexual and chromatic transgressions is such that extreme violence seems justified—even demanded—for the sake of social and tonal order" (McClary 1991, 100).

Thus is perpetrated an opera-loving feminist's dilemma: How can one enjoy the spectacle of women being sacrificed to expunge the emotional and sexual excesses that threaten a properly gendered social order where men are rational (not "crazy in love") and women are submissive (not sexually free and rebellious)? As Clément says, "Reading the texts, more than in listening at the mercy of an adored voice, I found to my fear and horror, words that killed, words that told every time of women's undoing. . . . How beautiful is suffering's melody" ([1979] 1988, 22).[12]

Today, homosexual men, many with AIDS, are creating music that expresses love, grief, anger, and ironically, the madness or dementia that the H.I.V. virus often causes (Crutchfield 1992). One of the songs in *The AIDS Quilt Songbook 1992,* Chris DeBlasio's "Walt Whitman in 1989," with text by Perry Brass, is based on Whitman's account of the deaths of Civil War soldiers he nursed, thus linking AIDS deaths to a universal masculine theme, death in war.[13] Culturally, though, these productions, too, may ultimately be seen as bracketing degenerate and pathological emotions and thus purifying the social order rather than expressing everyone's helpless rage over early painful death.[14]

Off with Her Head

Alice Jardine says that "legitimacy is part of that judicial domain which, historically, has determined the right to govern, the succession of kings, the link between father and son, the necessary paternal fiction, the ability to decide who is the father—in patriarchal culture" (1985, 24). "Gynesis"—putting "the feminine, woman, and her obligatory . . . historical connections" into modern culture—is profoundly disrupting (25). Before a new symbolic or social order can be constructed, there can be a feeling of chaos, of unreality, of losing one's mind. This chaos is projected onto woman even if it is men who are rebelling. Men artists have represented social upheaval as ferocious, mad, witch women; women artists have simply depicted women revolutionaries (Gullickson 1991; Nochlin 1988, 22–29).

When they are not dismissed or ignored, women rebels and revolutionaries pay a very high price for their questioning of the "revealed truths." Charlotte Perkins Gilman created an extended metaphor of the psychological and cultural imprisonment of a rebellious woman in *The Yellow Wallpaper:*

> On a pattern like this, by daylight, there is a lack of sequence, a defiance
> of law, that is a constant irritant to a normal mind. . . . the pattern is

torturing. You think you have mastered it, but just as you get well underway in following, it turns a back-somersault and there you are. It slaps you in the face, knocks you down, and tramples upon you. It is like a bad dream. . . . At night in any kind of light, in twilight, candle light, lamplight, and worst of all by moonlight, it becomes bars! The outside pattern I mean, and the woman behind it as plain as can be. ([1892] 1973, 25–26)

By the time the woman tears off the paper, she has lost her mind and creeps about like an animal.

Kristeva retells a Chinese story of how decapitation of their women commanders brought a Chinese general's 180 wives in line: "It's a question of submitting feminine disorder, its laughter, its inability to take drumbeats seriously, to the threat of decapitation. If man operates under the threat of castration, if masculinity is culturally ordered by the castration complex, it might be said that the backlash, the return, on women of this castration anxiety is its displacement as decapitation, execution, of woman, as loss of her head" (1981, 43). "Head" here is both women's thought, which is muffled in the language, metaphors, and symbols of Western phallocratic culture, and women's sexuality, located in the clitoris, which is bypassed in intercourse with men, and in some cultures, literally cut off in prescribed clitoridectomy. As Jane Marcus (1987) suggests: "The brutal cutting out of woman's tongue in the Procne and Philomel myth represents more than the rapist's desire to silence his victim. For the tongue is not only a verbal instrument, it is a sexual instrument, an organ of pleasure as well as an organ of speech. It challenges phallic supremacy at both levels. Woman's tongue is a threat to the Phallus as law, and to the phallus as penis" (143).

Medusa's Laugh

Rather than reassuring men of their masculinity by submitting to their symbolic sexual domination, Hélène Cixous, in "The Laugh of the Medusa," says women must use their heads and their mouths for themselves: "Woman must write herself: must write about women and bring women to writing, from which they have been driven away as violently as from their bodies—for the same reasons, by the same law, with the same fatal goal" (1976, 875).

As an assertion of woman's power, display and portrayal of the vagina (comparable to the mouth of the Medusa) has been used in women's rituals in Africa and Greece and by contemporary American women artists, such as Judy

Chicago in *The Dinner Party* (Ardener 1987).[15] In 1973, Maryse Holder described women artists' recent work that presented women's bodies as playfully and powerfully erotic: "The frecuncy, the fecuntitty, of cuntassy. The most striking and uniform aspect of the two shows I saw at the Erotic Art Gallery was the metaphoric treatment of women's anatomy. Cunts appeared as fruit, primarily, or leaves, park swings, elements of landscape" (1988, 2).

Appropriated as an icon of strength, the Medusa's laughing mouth (women's sexuality) is liberating for women: "You have only to look at the Medusa straight on to see her. And she is not deadly. She is beautiful and she is laughing" (Cixous 1976, 885). The look of the Medusa (the phallic or castrating woman) turns men to stone. Women's direct gaze at men strips them of their mystery. Add iconoclastic laughter, and phallocentrism has had it. As Mary Daly says: "There is nothing like the sound of women really laughing. The roaring laughter of women is like the roaring of the eternal sea. . . . One can hear pain and perhaps cynicism in the laughter of Hags. . . . But this laughter is the one true hope, for as long as it is audible there is evidence that someone is seeing through the Dirty Joke" (1978, 17).

Women's laughter and parodies of heterosexuality must be carefully contained if men are to continue to dominate. In Iran, for instance, sexually explicit dance dramas (*baziha*) are performed by women for women at festivities, such as weddings, circumcisions, and after the birth of a child (Safa-Isfahani 1980). Women play the men's roles—lovers, husbands, menservants—and the central women's roles: nubile daughters, pregnant women of ambiguous marital status, and embattled wives. There are also standard older women's roles—mother, mother-in-law, older friend, and midwife. The expression of sexuality can go as far as a striptease, but it is not an erotic display for other women. The reason for the stripping is that the woman is pretending to be bitten by ants: "Thus, the symbolic tearing off of veils might . . . be viewed as an affirmation and celebration of the female body, or even a comic unmasking of the mystification of the female body by men and man-centered culture. Not only is woman's body exposed, but it is brought down-to-earth by evoking the physical sensation of crawling ants" (42).

The texts of the baziha depict Iranian women as active, erotic, resistant, and independent: "the baziha represent women as relatively autonomous subjects rather than objects, . . . whose axis of desire, value, thought, and action lies within themselves rather than the male world outside" (51). But they can only act these roles ritualistically, on special occasions, and as a game: "Like plays or rituals, the baziha create a 'distance' and an effect of 'estrangement' from daily life as it is ordinarily lived, perceived, and defined. From this distance and perhaps because of it, the baziha redefine or create another order of reality, a relatively self-contained 'play world' which in various degrees can disguise, accentuate, or transform the norms and concepts dominating ordinary life" (52). The point of the games is that women's laughter and sexuality do not spill out into the ordinary, male-dominated world of Iranian women; unlike the "laugh of the Medusa," Iranian women's laughter is not liberating.

The Lesbian Metaphor

For some feminists, the only way women can create themselves culturally is to separate from men; for them, the lesbian is a metaphor for an independent, woman-identified woman: "I prefer to reserve the term *Lesbian* to describe women who are women-identified, having rejected false loyalties to men on all levels" (Daly 1978, 26n).[16] The lesbian metaphor transforms love between women into an identity, a community, and a culture. The subtext of women's love and friendship with other women runs through many cultural productions by women, but in most cultural productions by men, women seem to live in a social vacuum when they are not with men (Abel 1981). The lesbian metaphor highlights this subtext and its corollary that sexual love between women is one end-point of a continuum that starts with mother-daughter love. Thus, lesbian imagery is not a mirror opposite of the representation of men's sexuality and relationships, but a new language, a new voice:

> Once a Lesbian identifies herself as a *lesbian,* she brings all of her earlier experiences with and feelings for other women into focus. . . . Crossing into this territory, she begins to remember experiences she had "forgotten," recalling women and her feelings for them that she had analyzed or named differently; she examines memories of her past from a new perspective. Events and experiences that once "made no sense" to her are now full of meanings she had ignored, denied or discarded. Reconceiving herself as a Lesbian, she doesn't change or revise women, events, and experiences in her past; she reinterprets them, understands them anew from her Lesbian Perspective in the present. (Penelope 1990, 93)

Culturally, the lesbian is "that core of self-knowledge, power, and creativity that is potentially in all women" (Farwell 1988, 111) but that is evoked and sustained by women-identified communities.[17] The lesbian metaphor encompasses women's sexuality, women "writing the body," mother-daughter love, and the cultural community of women, not just sexual love between women. It celebrates the bonds of love that classical psychoanalysis deplores: "The paradigmatic relationship of this community is the mother-daughter relationship, the return of the woman to her original love" (Farwell 1988, 113), the love she is supposed to renounce in order to become a wife and mother:

> You look at yourself in the mirror [*la glace,* frozen]. And already you see your own mother there. And soon your daughter, a mother. Between the two, what are you? And what space is yours alone? In what frame must you contain yourself? And how to let your face show through, beyond all the masks?
>
> It's evening. As you're alone, as you've no more image to maintain or impose, you strip off your disguises. You take off your face of a mother's daughter, of a daughter's mother. You lose your mirror [frozen] reflection. You thaw. You melt. You flow out of yourself. (Irigaray 1981a, 63)

Irigaray's mirror imagery is a takeoff on Freud's observation that when a baby recognizes his (*sic*) reflection in the mirror, he knows he is not his mother and thus establishes an individual identity (ego).[18] Irigaray depicts both the beauty and the dangers of women's reidentification with women. On the one hand, there is unity ("one does not stir without the other"—a metaphor for lesbian sexuality and community),. but there is also the problem of lack of individuality, of submergence in the loved one.

In Lacanian psychoanalytic theory, women lack a sense of individuality or *différence* because they don't have the symbolic phallus that separates boys from their mothers and is the source of men's engagement with patriarchal culture. Countering this theory in "Ce sexe qui n'en est pas un" ("This sex which is not one"), Irigaray says that a women does not need a phallus for sexuality or creativity; all she needs is herself because as a woman, she is "two": "A woman 'touches herself' constantly without anyone being able to forbid her to do so, for her sex is composed of two lips which embrace continually. Thus, within herself she is already two—but not divisible into ones—who stimulate each other" (1981b, 100). Culturally, a woman can speak for herself and for other women with her own two lips; she doesn't need men or men's language: "We don't need to be produced by them, named by them, made sacred or profane by them" (Irigaray 1980, 74). Women have their own source of power—to Audre Lorde, the power of the erotic: "When I speak of the erotic, then, I speak of it as an assertion of the lifeforce of women; of that creative energy empowered, the knowledge and use of which we are now reclaiming in

our language, our history, our dancing, our loving, our work, our lives"
(1984, 55).

Not Lavender, But Purple

Other feminists have argued that women's culture does not have to reject men
and men's culture to celebrate women. For African-American feminists, like
Alice Walker, what is needed is a vision of strong, proud women who can be
heterosexual, homosexual, bisexual. Walker has called this perspective "womanist":

> Usually referring to outrageous, audacious, courageous or *wilful* behav-
> ior. Wanting to know more and in greater depth than is considered
> "good" for one. . . . A woman who loves other women, sexually
> and / or nonsexually. Appreciates and prefers women's culture,
> women's emotional flexibility (values tears as natural counterbalance
> of laughter), and women's strength. Sometimes loves individual men,
> sexually and / or nonsexually. Committed to survival and wholeness of
> entire people, male *and* female. Not a separatist, except periodically,
> for health. Traditionally universalist. . . . Traditionally capable. . . .
> Loves music. Loves dance. Loves the moon. *Loves* the Spirit. Loves love
> and food and roundness. Loves struggle. *Loves* the Folk. Loves herself.
> *Regardless*. . . . Womanist is to feminist as purple is to lavender. (1983,
> xi–xii)

Womanists find their symbolic language in what women produce in everyday life: not paintings, but quilts; not symphonies, but folk songs; not ballet,
but wedding dances. Food, the dishes to eat it from, the embroidered table-
cloth, are quintessential elements of women's culture; all this imagery is in
Judy Chicago's *The Dinner Party*. Elsa Barkley Brown shows how African-
American women's history and culture are reflected in the quilts they made:
Their patterns form a "polyrhythmic, 'nonsymmetrical,' nonlinear structure
in which individual and community are not competing entities" (1989, 926).
Patricia Hill Collins notes that African-American modes of discourse tend to
use "call-and-response" dialogues, and their cultural productions and knowledge claims rest also on an "ethic of caring—the value placed on individual
expressiveness, the appropriateness of emotions, and the capacity for empathy" (1989, 67). African-American women writers and blues singers, she
argues, have redefined themselves as forceful people drawing strength and self-
respect from one another (1990, 91–113).

Sometimes womanist cultural vocabularies are universal, understood by women everywhere, and sometimes they are specific to women's different racial and ethnic groups. The question is whether they are specific to the *women* of the group, or whether the emphasis is on ethnic consciousness that is shared with the men of the group. Trinh Minh-ha claims the choice cannot be made between ethnicity and womanhood: "You never have / are one without the other" (Trinh 1989, 104). Gayatri Chakravorty Spivak says that the concept of the *subaltern* (the insurgent subordinate) is gendered; thus, consciousness of subordination and the forms of struggle have to be different for women and men (1988, 215–21). The man who is Other needs to find the voice suppressed by the dominant men; the woman who is Other needs to find the voice suppressed by both dominant *and* subordinate men.

African and African-American women have a gender-specific aesthetic. Women's art in sub-Saharan Africa uses female imagery and media to create life-history rituals for women and to validate women's identity and lineages (Aronson 1991). In both Africa and America, women's music accompanies rituals of birth, puberty, marriage, and death and also everyday activities like preparing food (T. V. Jackson 1981). Some Indian women writers have been able to find imagery of strong women in their culture's mythology. The epic Indian moral myth *Mahabharata* has many important, active heroines, such as Draupadi, whom the god Krishna keeps clothed when she resists being shamefully undressed and whose menstrual blood is a badge of honor. Draupadi is married to five brothers: "Within a patriarchal and patronymic context, she is exceptional, indeed 'singular' in the sense of odd, unpaired, uncoupled. Her husbands, since they are husbands rather than lovers, are *legitimately* pluralized. No acknowledgement of paternity can secure the Name of the Father for the child of such a mother" (Spivak 1988, 183). Draupadi becomes a modern heroine of Indian resistance in a story by Mahasweta Devi.[19] Maxine Hong Kingston found the strength to be a woman writer in a ghostly Chinese predecessor:

> After I grew up, I heard the chant of Fa Mu Lan, the girl who took her father's place in battle. Instantly I remembered that as a child I had followed my mother about the house, the two of us singing about how Fa Mu Lan fought gloriously and returned alive from war to settle in the village. I had forgotten this chant that was once mine, given me by my mother, who may not have known its power to remind. She said I would grow up a wife and a slave, but she taught me the song of the war-

rior woman, Fa Mu Lan. I would have to grow up a warrior woman.
(1976, 24)

"Money Creates Taste"

When women produce culture, they have the chance to portray women
differently than men artists do (Grigsby 1990). An eighteenth-century illustra-
tion shows a Japanese woman artist, Mu-Me, painting a woman and a finished
painting of another woman (Fister 1988, 47). In this triple image, all the
women—the painter and her two paintings—are fully visible. The painter,
surrounded by her brushes and paint, is shown in the act of making art.
Professional women artists flourished in Japan in the late seventeenth and
eighteenth centuries in the hedonistic urban cultures of Edo, Kyoto, and
Osaka, the *ukiyo,* or "floating worlds." Much of their work has since disappeared (Fister 1988, 47–54).

Sofonisba Anguissola, one of the professional women artists who emerged
in the sixteenth-century Italian Renaissance, was known for her self-portraits.
When a woman paints a self-portrait it can be a valorization of herself as an
artist; it can also mean that the work is being done clandestinely, for she is her
own model. Anguissola's self-portraits had other ambiguous implications.
According to Ann Sutherland Harris and Linda Nochlin (1976, 26–32), Anguissola was a rarity at the time, and as "the object of much curiosity and
admiration" (27), she became a cult figure, with her self-portraits much in
demand. Although she was handsomely rewarded financially and her example
encouraged other women artists, "her curiosity value as a new phenomenon, a
female painter," classed her "with dwarfs, fools, and other court amusements,"
and her assessment by the influential critic Vasari was "polite but limited" (31).

About eight years later, in 1630, Artemisia Gentileschi made *Self-portrait
as the Allegory of Painting.* Her face intense and focused, framed by strong arms
holding brush and palette, "the artist emerges forcefully as the living embodiment of the allegory. Painter, model and concept are one and the same"
(Garrard 1989, 354). This self-portrait is a confident, unambiguous display of
her artistry by a painter who had been working professionally since girlhood.
During her lifetime, Gentileschi had an international career in which she
imbued familiar artistic prototypes, such as Judith cutting off the head of
Holofernes, with a mixture of masculine and feminine elements, transforming
them into heroes with cross-gendered traits (Garrard 1989, 7–8). Toward the

end of her life, however, she painted more voluptuous heroines, such as Bathsheba, perhaps to sell better (136–37).

The ideological power of gendered assumptions and the "all-pervasive certainty about gender difference itself" (Nochlin 1988, 2) are not automatically challenged by the presence of women artists, writers, or composers: "Symbolic power is invisible and can be exercised only with the complicity of those who fail to recognize either that they submit to it or that they exercise it. Women artists are often no more immune to the blandishments of ideological discourses than their male contemporaries, nor should dominant males be envisioned as conspiratorially or even consciously forcing their notions upon women" (Nochlin 1988, 2–3). Women tend to use the conventional cultural symbols because men are the cultural arbitrators. Men may not be conscious conspirators, but they dominate training, criticism, and markets in the production of culture and have often deliberately kept women out of all these areas. In order to gain visibility, artists, composers, and playwrights need people to sponsor them—show their paintings, play their music, produce their plays. Since white men control artistic resources in Western societies, women have a hard time gaining access to museum and gallery display, orchestral or operatic performance of their works, and production of their plays. For women of color, it can be doubly difficult (Burman 1988). Although the audiences for novelists and poets are private, they do need to be published, and men writers have frequently been favored over women writers by men publishers (Tuchman 1989).[20]

The spiraling power of reputation in the aesthetic and commercial evaluation of artists is a well-known phenomenon.[21] Fame accrues to a few visible, highly sought-after artists.[22] Most art hanging in museums, according to John Berger (1977), was produced for a market; only some have the quality of "greatness." To be recognized as "great," an artist needs to be trained in a tradition and then take it further or break with it. The artist's vision has to be recognized as original and worthy by critics who publicize the breakthrough, by a public that consumes and buys the new art, and by other artists who take up the artist's fresh view. All these reputation makers are likely to be men who tend to value what men, not women, produce. Many women artists who have become famous, like Georgia O'Keeffe, had men sponsors.[23]

One particularly telling fact about women artists in Western culture is that until the late nineteenth century, they were completely excluded from drawing and painting classes that had nude models, the capstone of training for professional artists well into the twentieth century (Sheehy 1987). Furthermore, Nochlin says, "It was argued by defenders of traditional painting in the nineteenth century that there could be no great painting *with* clothed figures, since costume inevitably destroyed both the temporal universality and the classic idealization required by great art" (1988, 159). Thus, her answer to the perennial question of why there have been no great women artists in Western art is that it was "*institutionally* made impossible for women to achieve artistic excellence, or success, on the same footing as men, *no matter what* the potency of their so-called talent, or genius" (1988, 176).

Once the production of culture became a profession in Western societies, entry demanded professional training, and a career demanded public exhibition. Women artists and musicians especially, but also writers, needed a window of opportunity to have access to professional training, tools of their craft, patronage, and a network of supportive colleagues (Tuchman 1975). Gaye Tuchman (1989) notes that nineteenth-century women novelists were successful because they had an audience of literate middle-class women readers who had the time to read and the money to buy books. When the genre of the novel became established and writing them brought some prestige, women novelists were edged out by men, in a kind of cultural gentrification (208).

For many women creators of culture whose biographies are known, birth into a family of artists or musicians, or the help of a father or mother was almost indispensable. Elizabeth Wood says of women musicians:

> There is overwhelming evidence that the significant parent for most women musicians is their mother, in contrast to the significance of paternal support cited by women artists. Female systems of kin, friendship, and mentorship are crucial not merely for emotional interaction but for formal skill sharing and career shaping. Maternal support systems have exerted a powerful influence on the cultural process, ranging from "low-level" domestic personal interactions and identifications, through which musical talent is discovered early and first contacts are made with instruments, concerts, and teachers, to more organized alliances which establish opposition to "higher-level" cultural authorities. Courageous older, established women mentors, role models, musical mothers, effective and generous "patrons," have forced access for women to musical education, maturation, and career options. (1980, 293–94)

In a lovely extended metaphor, "Virginia Woolf and Her Violin: Mothering, Madness, and Music," Marcus (1987, 96–114) shows that when Woolf had mothering mentors, she produced her wonderful literary music, and when she did not, discordant voices in her head took over. She and Ethel Smyth, a composer, had help from many women: "Women had recognized genius in both Woolf and Smyth, and they had given them the teaching, discipline, and love which they needed to survive" (113).

For many women musicians, the outlets for their productions were what Wood calls "closed systems"—women's music clubs, all-women orchestras, and private teaching. This constriction, she says, characterizes most Western women musicians, "regardless of racial, regional, and socioeconomic background" (294).[24] Although Ellen Taaffe Zwilich and Shulamit Ran have won Pulitzer Prizes, they and earlier women composers, such as Amy Beach, Fanny Mendelssohn Hensel, and Clara Schumann, are rarely played in concerts or broadcasts.[25]

A New Vocabulary from the Old?

If women's cultural productions are to constitute a new voice, they not only need to be heard, read, and seen by everyone, but they must also use a distinctive symbolic vocabulary that can speak to men as well as well women. Twentieth-century modernity gave women cultural producers the opportunity to forge a new symbolic vocabulary of gender, but for the most part, women were not cultural revolutionaries.[26] Cubist and abstract painters, stream-of-consciousness novelists, atonal composers, and modern-dance choreographers created new visual, verbal, and musical vocabularies, which have achieved such widespread critical and public recognition that they are now synonymous with Western culture. Modernity could also have provided the language for deconstructing gender categories: "The modernist poem, with its abrupt shifts, ellipses, breaks and apparent lack of logical construction is a kind of writing in which the rhythms of the body and the unconscious have managed to break through the strict rational defenses of conventional social meaning" (Moi 1985, 11).

Yet, though there have been many wonderful women producers of twentieth-century modern culture, and "mind, body, sexuality, family, reality, culture, religion, and history were all reconstrued" (B. K. Scott 1990, 16), except for some modern-dance choreography produced by men as well as by women, the categories "woman" and "man" were not created anew and the predominance of men in cultural productions was rarely even questioned.[27] Some women and men have deliberately blurred gender boundaries, creating heroes who are sometimes men, sometimes women, like Virginia Woolf's Orlando, but these transmuted characters inhabit and ultimately re-create a gendered world (Garber 1992). Feminist science-fiction writers have created nongendered worlds as critiques of the conventional social structure of gender.[28] But for the most part, accepted gender categories are the context for cultural productions by women as well as by men.

Where could a new feminist symbolic vocabulary come from that would not only evoke women's experiences but also resonate with deep-rooted cultural traditions? Although myths in Western culture have often repressed women's experiences or subverted them to men's uses, there is much subterranean symbolism that could be the core of a new cultural vocabulary.[29] The first recorded poet so far discovered was a woman, a Sumerian princess and priestess named Enheduanna (Hallo and Van Dijk 1968). She was the daughter of Sargon, who founded the Mesopotamian Empire about four thousand years ago. One of the revered goddesses of this culture was the powerful Inanna-Ishtar, to whom Enheduanna wrote a hymn of praise:

> In the guise of a charging storm you charge.
> With a roaring storm you roar.
> With Thunder you continually thunder.
> With all the evil winds you snort.
> Your feet are filled with restlessness.
> To . . . the harp of sighs you give vent to a dirge.   (19, ll. 28–33)

Like the Medusa, Inanna's "glance is terrible . . . flashing" (31, ll. 128–31).

There is conjecture that the original Old Testament was written by a woman, "J," a royal member of King Solomon's court (H. Bloom 1990). Her point of view is ironic and celebrates women as much as men: In the story of Moses, "what could be more charming, more beautifully self-aware, than a fable of deliverance in which the Egyptian princess is wholly benign, knows Hebrew, and rejects the male violence of her father? And what could be more cunning than J's use of the sister of Moses, who is sent to observe and is thus available to offer the princess the most proper of Hebrew wet nurses, the baby's own mother?" (243). In Jewish tradition, midrashim are retellings and reinterpretations of biblical texts. Judith Plaskow says that feminists have written midrashim on Lilith (Adam's first wife), Miriam (Moses' sister), and Sarah (Abraham's wife) that describe the Garden of Eden, the Exodus, and the sacrifice of Isaac from a woman's point of view (1990, 53–56).

Origin myths are another source of woman-empowering symbols. According to Peggy Reeves Sanday, origin myths are "a projection of a people's perception of the phenomenon of human birth and of their experience with their environment" (1981a, 56). The gender of the creator reflects what the people think is the source of universal power: "Female creators originate from within something—such as earth or water—and create from their bodies. Male, animal, and supreme being creators originate from without—such as the sky or another land—and produce people magically. Couple creators, on the other hand, originate from within and without but they tend to produce by natural reproductive processes" (57). Origin myths reflect food production— hunting is linked to external origins, and plant gathering to internal origins (67). Origin symbolism is also related to child-rearing practices—fathers are more intimate with their children in societies with female creators than in societies with male creators (Sanday 1981a, 60–64). In the latter societies, men are disassociated from women as well as from their children, and "suspicion, competition, sexual antagonism, and rigid sexual segregation characterize many of these societies" (63). These origin myths are kept even after the production of food shifts, but if a group migrated or was conquered, they may have ambiguous origin myths or more than one.

In the Judeo-Christian Book of Genesis, for instance, there are two versions of the creation of humans, and several tellings of each. In one version, as William Phipps (1989) notes, the creator is a possibly androgynous deity: "Elohim pronounces, 'Let us make humanity in our image, after our likeness.' The text then states, 'Elohim created humanity male and female in the divine image'" (3). In the second version, first Adam is made from the earth and then Eve from his rib, as a "suitable partner" (32). Thus, in the first origin myth, male and female are equal reflections of the creator; in the second, even though woman is made from man, the two are socially equal (12). In the later tellings, the creator becomes male, and it is a puzzle as to how his image can be female as well; man's partner becomes "an help meet for him," not quite an equal. In J's version, "six times the space [is given] to woman's creation as to man's; it is the difference between making a mud pie and building a much more elaborate and fairer structure" (Bloom 1990, 180). Reeves Sanday argues that when the early Jews escaped from Egypt and went into Canaan, they first adopted the feminized and sexualized Canaanite religion, but then, in an effort to maintain their own identity and to stop intermarriage with Canaanite women (Abraham insisted that his only son, Isaac, marry a woman from his homeland, not from Canaan), they rejected that religion and purified their own (1981a, 215–31). This ambiguity and tension, according to Reeves Sanday, is reflected in the two Judeo-Christian stories of creation.[30]

For early human beings, the symbol of the origin of life may have been a fertile woman. Widely dispersed throughout Europe and Siberia in prehistoric sites 15,000 to 25,000 years old are little statuettes and amulets of women, obviously pregnant or emphasizing breasts or buttocks. Some are just a simple

Y-shape or a round object with a vulval slit.[31] Other objects found at these sites have markings said to be a lunar count, days from first crescent to full moon to first crescent again, and some of the female figurines are similarly marked (Marshack 1972, 288–330). Some objects have engravings showing seasonal plants and pregnant animals. There are also engraved symbolic phalluses, but female imagery seems to predominate. Alexander Marshack, who argues in *The Roots of Civilization* (1972) that the essence of human symbolic cognition is "thinking in time," asks:

> Which *aspect* of the female process or myth is being depicted, symbol-ized, or given story? Is it the menstrual, the pubertal, the copulative, the pregnant, or the milk giving? . . . Is it the general image of the mother "goddess," the ancestress of the tribe? Or is it the female aspect which is related to birth and rebirth in all life and nature and, therefore, to a "female property"? Is it related to biological or seasonal cycles? Is the image related to the lunar cycle via the story of birth, death, and rebirth and by comparisons between the lunar and the menstrual cycles? (283)

Two anthropological studies of menstruation suggest that such symbolic link-ages of women and time persist in some cultures (Knight 1988; Lamp 1988).[32]

Linking origin imagery and women's experiences to symbolic time as expressed in musical language, Janika Vandervelde has written a series of compositions called *Genesis* (McClary 1991, 112–31). In contrast to "the standard narrative of tonal striving, climax, and closure" of Western music (114), *Genesis II* begins with "a musical image of childbirth: the pulsation of a fetal heartbeat, the intensifying strains of labor, and the sudden emergence into a fresh and calm new world" (116). The new world, however, has not left men's time behind:

> The fresh new world that comes into being as a result of this prologue contains two kinds of music, each organizing time in a different way. On the one hand, we are presented with a minimalistic "clockwork" pattern in the piano: a pattern that repeats cyclically but which, be-cause it is internally marked by asymmetries of rhythm and pitch, is endlessly fascinating, almost like the facets of a crystal that seem to change with each turn. . . . It creates a sense of existence *in* time that is stable, ordered, yet "timeless." (McClary 1991, 117–18)

Cyclical time seems to be women's time, represented here in musical lan-guage.

> And on the other hand, we have the string parts . . . [that] present us
> with the goal-oriented gestures of self-expression and striving
> that . . . are explicitly *not* content with living in the present moment
> but that seek to expand horizons and to defy social convention, gestures
> that trade the very hope of future stability for a never-ending chase
> after the elusive chimeras of progress, change, and finally the transcen-
> dence and obliteration of time. (116–19)

Linear time that eventually obliterates cyclical time seems to be men's time,
again represented in musical language. Vandervelde uses standard musical
notation in ways that represent two contrasting images of time, cyclical and
linear. They seem to be symbolically gendered, but they could just as well
represent two different ways of being in the world, both equally valued.

Women Are Always There; You Just Have to Look

In an essay on Martin Heidegger's *Being and Time* and Samuel Beckett's *Waiting
for Godot,* Mary O'Brien notes that there are no women in them (1989, 83–
102). Heidegger's transcendental Being and everyday being are both men.
Because men do not give birth, O'Brien argues, they do not have the intimate
connection to past and future that women have. They can only passively wait.
Heidegger never notices the absence of women in his philosophy; Beckett's
play, however, suggests that sometimes those who wait for Godot know that
"bereft of the integrative power of women in the reproductive process, men
stand alone, alienated from the natural world and from species continuity"
(94). In *Waiting for Godot:*

> Brooding over all is a presence without definition, a possibility, a threat
> and a promise which Beckett names: Godot. The tragi-comedy is a
> remarkable evocation of is-ness without clutter, complete in the essen-
> tials of human life except for one. There are no women. Womanhood,
> however, is there in the same way as Godot is there. . . . Further,
> there are children, a boy or perhaps two boys, who "come from" Godot
> as messengers of the fact that although Godot is rendered as invisible,
> Godot *must exist,* just as this Dasein in all his tortuous aspects, his
> divisions, must have been, as these boys also were, born of woman. But
> if Godot is a woman, then all the interrogation in the world will not
> reveal a fecundity which is absolutely negated. There is no dialectic of
> birth and death, of subject and species, no tension of natural and
> historical time, no being and no Being. (87–88)[33]

There once were goddesses of life and death, symbols of birth and fertility, displaying ample breasts and pregnant bellies, showing stretch marks, holding a child. Their names were Asherah, Astarte, Inanna, Ishtar, Hathor, Isis, Aphrodite, Demeter, Venus, Freya, Al-Lat, Al-Uzza, Al-Manat. When patriarchal monotheism destroyed these images of women as idols, the symbol of fertility became the many-seeded pomegranate ubiquitous in Judaic decorative art, the daughters of Allah, and the Christian Madonna.[34] Woman, the symbolic life-giver, has not really disappeared.

What is the world like with women in it? Women's visions are different from men's, not because women and men are biologically different, but because in a culture dominated by men, the questions women ask and the answers that they come up with can be subversive. Just producing culture in their own right is a form of rebellion. I would like to see men, too, produce culture that undermines phallocentrism, but for the time being, it may be sufficient for women cultural producers to turn the world upside down:

> Spinners Spinning Widdershins—turning about face—feel / find an Other Sense of Time. We begin by asking clock-whys and then move on to counter these clock-whys with Counterclock Whys—Questions that whirl the Questioners beyond the boundaries of Boredom, into the flow of Tidal Time / Elemental Time. This is Wild Time, beyond the clocking / clacking of clonedom. It is the Time of Wicked Inspiration / Genius, which cannot be grasped by the tidily man-dated world. (Daly and Caputi 1987, 279)

Part II

GENDER IN PRACTICE

What is produced by cooperative human labor is not just food, shelter, tools, and artifacts, but also the symbolic conceptions that reproduce the social organization essential for future production.

—*Minna Davis Caulfield (1985, 352)*

OUT OF EDEN:
THE SOCIAL EVOLUTION OF GENDER

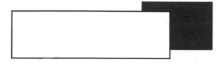

Rayna Rapp, a feminist anthropologist, devised a song for her baby daughter, Mireille Rapp-Hooper, that takes her through monkeydom, primate ancestry, upright locomotion, stereoscopic vision, and opposable thumb past the extinct branches of early humans to Homo sapiens. It ends with:

> This is the story
> My darling Mira
> That science tells us of our worth
> Welcome to culture
> My dearest daughter
> It's the greatest show on earth.[1]

If gender is not a by-product of mammalian sexual reproduction, its genesis must be sought in human culture and social patterns. We must go back to a time before calendar time, to prehistoric time, to find the social origins of gender. Because we have only hints of how prehistoric humans lived, the behavior of the great apes, our evolutionary cousins, is frequently invoked to explain gender differences in humans (Haraway 1989). There is, however, a qualitative divide between animal behavior and human behavior, and that divide is culture. Humans are certainly animals (omnivorous viviparous mammals—we eat everything, bear live young, and breast-feed them), and animals have social organization, such as pair bonding and territorial bands. But humans' physical, sexual, and social relationships reflect a consciousness of their personal and group identification, their moral values, and their sense of time. For humans, behavioral patterns are almost completely the result of

123

learning and are imbued with moral and symbolic meaning. Humans think about the past and the future, not just the present, and their actions reflect this expanded sense of time. Human culture should not be opposed to animal nature; for humans, *culture is natural;* it is what distinguishes Homo sapiens from higher primates.

The important behavioral patterns of nonhuman primates are mother-child bonding and matrifocal genealogies that are the center of the group, with dominance hierarchies among males forming cross-cutting ties. Sexual mating patterns vary by social grouping and environment, and a variety of adults of either sex watch and protect the young, but do not share food with them once they can feed themselves.[2] The important human behavioral patterns are the social construction of gender and age statuses, a gendered division of productive labor and child care, institutionalized sharing of food with kin, and rules for distribution of surplus food and inheritance of permanent property. These patterns, which determine power and privilege, are human inventions and are produced through social interaction.

Primates, Hominids, and Humans

Primate behavior, as a story about human origins, has variously emphasized universal male domination and universal female cooperativeness (Haraway 1978b, 1989). But what can the evolution of humans from primates tell us about *gender*—the categorization of people into social statuses and the patterns of their relationships and interactions?

Hominids diverged from primates several million years ago. Like higher primates, hominids lived in social groups of varying ages and both sexes and used tools (Lancaster 1974), but for hominids, tool use and food gathering for later consumption and sharing were important transitional behaviors. More food could be gathered if hands were free, so bipedalism and eye-hand coordination became important evolutionary changes (Tanner 1981, 133–262; Zihlman 1978). Children and sick or elderly adults would survive if food was shared, so "share and share alike" became important for group survival (Leibowitz 1986).

Mothers, offspring, and female siblings were probably the central core of the social group, with adult males in a marginal status:

Mothers, as the socializers, were the carriers of group tradition; the social and technical inventions of females were passed on to their offspring during the socialization process and eventually became part of the behavioral repertoire of the transitional population as a whole. The mother-offspring relationship is of fundamental importance to the transmission of technical innovations and environmental information necessary to the establishment of gathering as a basic form of ecological adaptation. (Tanner 1981, 149)

Unlike higher primates, human females do not have estrus, a seasonal period of sexual responsiveness during which impregnation can occur. Since hominid females were always potentially interested in sex, hominid males were likely to have been encouraged to share in feeding infants as a way of gaining access to their mothers (Tanner 1981, 163–67; Zihlman 1981): "Females probably had sex more frequently with those males who were around more often, playing with offspring, helping in protection, occasionally sharing meat and foraged plants, and who were generally friendly" (Tanner 1981, 164).

Archeological evidence shows that hominids were more efficient and skillful tool makers and users than primates, and thus were able to expand the amount and variety of food they could obtain. Gathering extra food and sharing hunted animals were early forms of production, but they were un-differentiated by sex and involved the children (Leibowitz 1986, 48–51). In order to gather food and also carry infants and toddlers, it is likely that female hominids created a carrying bag out of an animal skin—the sling (Tanner 1981, 195).[3] According to Adrienne Zihlman (1981), gathering and hunting were not opposed ways of acquiring food. Many similarities between them suggest that hunting arose out of gathering technology and therefore that females and males could have done both: "One might . . . make a case for hunting as a specialized form of gathering—'gathering' small reptiles, conies, rodents, and so on, and building on this to go after small and young herbivores, and on to larger herbivores" (109).

The major adaptive patterns that differentiate humans from primates and hominids are walking upright and using hands for more tasks, a longer period of infant development and dependence, the loss of estrus, more continuous involvement of adult males in food gathering and sharing, the use of fire, and symbolic interaction. Animal communication is gestural and emotionally expressive. Human language uses symbols—names for things real and imagined that have meaning within the context of the situation or the group's social organization. Symbolic language permits humans to "think in time," to incorporate the past and future into present action. The use of fire by Homo erectus about 500,000 years ago not only led to the ability to change the material environment but also produced a concept of change over time:

> Fire is "alive." It must be tended; it needs a home and a place out of the great winds, the heavy rains, the deep snows; it must be constantly fed; it sleeps in embers and can die, yet it can also be blown back to life by the breath; it can burn a hand; it sputters angrily and brightly with animal fat; it dies entirely in water; it whispers, hisses, or crackles, and therefore has a variable "voice"; it uses itself up, transforming a large weight of wood to gray ash, while climbing by smoke and savor to the sky, at last disappearing in the wind; one can carry its spirit or "life" on a burning branch or ember to make a second fire. (Marshack 1972, 113)

These human capabilities—potentially continuous sexual responsiveness, the use of fire, the invention of tools to make food acquisition more efficient, value-laden social relationships, and a sense of time—are the bases for the transformation of physiological sex and age differences into gender statuses, kinship, and, eventually, gender inequality.

Gender as a Functional Invention

Every society, in order to survive, has to feed the adults and the children, to mind the children until they are old enough to take care of themselves, and to teach them the ways of the society. These are the constants. The variable is how food is obtained and processed—the technology. The cultural solutions to putting the technology together with the survival necessities are gender, kinship, and the division of labor.

Humans of the Paleolithic period were primarily foragers. The main sources of food were wild vegetables, nuts, fruits, and grass-eating animals. Animals were not tracked; they were scavenged from predators' leavings or from dead or dying animals. A larger supply of meat, bones, and furs was obtained in drive hunts, where a band of men, women, and older children forced animals over cliffs or into swamps or pits. The foraging band was nomadic, at least seasonally, because a large territory had to be covered in order to obtain enough to eat. Caves or temporary shelters of branches, reeds, and skins were "home." There was no permanent property; an individual's accumulation of possessions had to be movable. The main tools were the digging stick, the flint knife, and the carrying sling. The need to carry infants on long gathering treks and to breast-feed them until they had enough teeth to chew up wild vegetables meant that births were probably spaced several years apart.

The foraging band was communal and sociable, with little age or sex division in activity. Were there gender differences at all, and were women and men evaluated differently? Eleanor Leacock argues on the basis of eth-nographic data about recent foraging groups that in early human societies, individual abilities, not gender statuses, were salient: "Individual autonomy was a necessity, and autonomy as a valued principle persists to a striking degree among the descendants of hunter-gatherers. It was linked with a way of life that called for great individual initiative and decisiveness along with the ability to be extremely sensitive to the feelings of lodge-mates" (1981, 139). Margaret Power describes the "extraordinarily egalitarian" social organization of for-agers, both human and primate, as a mutual dependence system of smaller and larger groups, with individual autonomy, charismatic leadership, and fluid membership (1991, 9). Within the local group, there are two subgroups—the more mobile childless, active adults and near-adults of both sexes, and the more sedentary child rearers, dependent young, and the elderly of both sexes. Shifting band membership scatters parents, children, and siblings among several bands, which bond into larger groupings who meet periodically.

With more elaborate tools and sophisticated use of fire came the ability to harden spear points, straighten spear shafts, and bend wood into bows. These new weapons changed hunting practices (Leibowitz 1986, 64). Larger animals could now be tracked and killed a few at a time by smaller groups. Hunting by tracking would be difficult for those minding children and for females in advanced pregnancy or nursing, but it could be done by adolescents of either sex and the other adult females, as well as by adult males (Estioko-Griffin and Griffin 1981). The new form of projectile hunting demanded new skills, however. These included spear throwing, archery, and following a track; skinning, butchering, and cooking; "processing skins and hides; converting them into clothing and carrying devices, and making hunting equipment and the tools to process foods and hides. Setting up and maintaining the shelters *cum* workshops where all of these activities take place were even more de-manding" (Leibowitz 1986, 65).

One of the consequences of this greater technological complexity was that it took longer for children to become productive members of the group. Since increased food production meant that fertility increased and more children lived, the tasks were divided, for pragmatic reasons, between child-minders and non-child-minders.[4] Child-minders gathered and processed food and hides and made the necessary tools for these tasks, and non-child-minders tracked animals and made spears, spear-throwers, and bows and arrows. Women who were pregnant or nursing and other less mobile members of the tribe minded the children while they foraged for edible plants, trapped small animals, cooked, tanned, and turned hides into clothing and shelter. As Jane Beckman Lancaster (1974) says, "Clearly, with the long years that it takes for the human child to develop and learn adult roles and skills, there was no other way once gathering and hunting had developed as a major adaptive stance for the division to have evolved except between males and females. There is no need to posit special 'killer' or 'maternal' instincts in males and females to explain the assignment of these roles" (79).

In subsistence societies, where every able-bodied adult contributes labor, work in food production has to be compatible with the work of caring for infants and small children; if it isn't, either few children will survive or the adults will have too little to eat. Judith K. Brown argues that it is not pregnancy and childbirth that determines the gendered division of work, but the first few years of care of a child. The general principle is that "if the economic role of women is to be maximized, their responsibilities in child care must be reduced or the economic activity must be such that it can be carried out concurrently with child care" (1970, 1075). The exigencies of child-minding—small children demand a constantly attentive eye and have needs that must be met more or less on demand, such as frequent feeding and sleeping—dictate the type of work that child-minders can successfully carry out:

> Subsistence activities . . . compatible with simultaneous child watching . . . do not require rapt concentration and are relatively dull and repetitive; they are easily interruptible and easily resumed once interrupted; they do not place the child in potential danger; and they do not require the participant to range very far from home. . . . Activities . . . incompatible with simultaneous child watching . . . require rapt concentration, cannot be interrupted and resumed, are potentially dangerous, and require that the participant range far from home. (J. K. Brown 1970, 1075–76)

According to Janet Siskind, the gendered division of ways of getting food in gathering and hunting societies makes it possible "for men to undertake wide-ranging tasks of uncertain productive results secure in the knowledge that they can count on appropriating the certain production of women's labor. That is, one can only afford the luxury of spending a day chasing a kangaroo, which may or may not end up as dinner, if it is possible to count on a meal, at least, of roots" (1978, 865). The repetitiousness and routine in work compatible with child-minding also makes it reliable: "If women are given the major responsibility for nurturing infants and small children, then not only must these tasks be compatible with productive work . . . but women must produce a dependable source of food to keep small children satisfied" (879n).

The tasks do not divide so clearly between hunting and gathering. A study of child care among the Aka Pygmies, who use nets to capture animals and hunt in family groups, found that mothers transported the infant to the hunting site and assisted with the family net, putting the infant down to do so:

> Occasionally, it was difficult to tell if the parent was more interested in the protection of the infant or capturing game. Several instances were recorded where the mother holding the infant placed the infant alone on the ground, and ran to capture the animal. The infant was left alone about 10 m. from the parent, often crying, until the parent killed the animal. . . . Instead of bringing the infant close to the net where the capture took place and where it would be possible to see the infant, the mothers said they preferred to be unencumbered so they could run faster to make sure the game did not get away. (Hewlett 1987, 303–04)

The more deliberate hunting practices needed trained skills, however, and the increased food supply meant a rise in the number of children born who lived and had to be cared for. A gendered division of labor in which child-minders gathered and non-child-minders hunted was an efficient way to produce food *and* children. That the division reflected two physiological sexes did not mean that the cause was sex differences in personality or that procreation automatically produced nurturance capabilities in women. The gendered division of labor grew out of the exigencies of expanded food production and child-minding; it was a cultural solution to a technological problem that resulted in changed social organization. The expanded social groups needed practical arrangements that organized the living and working spaces and the patterns of interaction within them (Hillier and Hanson 1984; Mellars 1985). Over time, through repetition, these arrangements became routinized, then expected, and then required (Bourdieu [1980] 1990). Legitimation through rituals turned many of these practices into powerful norms and mores. Who did what was no longer a matter of convenience or consensus. Instead of individual choice based on personal talents and proclivities, or practical solutions to problems as they occurred, a group of people was assigned the same kind of work to do. In order to have stability in the allocation of tasks, social groups now divided their members into recognized categories—"women," "men," "girls," "boys."

When many people are socially located in similar positions, they acquire a status, a symbolically evaluated place in the social order. The emergence of statuses encourages rites of passage that mark changes in status, and status markers, such as headgear, clothing, tools, weapons, and decorated objects that allow everyone to know who has what status. Among the Paleolithic peoples of the European continent, visual records, such as art hidden deep in caves, may have been used to record and to recall these social arrangements and statuses in a way that enhanced their sacredness, but everyday activities and objects, such as pots, through their use by one group of workers, also became status identifiers. [5]

Since productive tasks in the expanded gathering and hunting groups needed practiced skills, assignment to each set of workers had to take place well before the tasks had to be done. Once food production and other activities were divided between the socially constructed categories of women and men, children had to be divided into their gender categories as soon as they could feed and dress themselves and walk longer distances, and had enough manual dexterity to start to learn their appropriate tasks. They then spent their time with the adult members of their assigned category, who taught them their share of the productive work.

At the same time, girls and boys learned the symbolic behavior appropriate to their future adult gender status. Where there is significant separation of women and men, much of this symbolic behavior relates the person to the members of the other status and is age-graded. That is, girls and boys had to be taught not only how to work as women and men but how to behave toward girls and boys their own age and toward women and men their parents' and grandparents' age. They also learned how women and men were supposed to act toward each other, as well as how everyone actually did act toward each other. In the process, the children identified with the members of their gender category, and because they were rewarded for it, they came to want to act in the prescribed ways. In this way, gender statuses were reproduced in daily activity.

Why Kinship?

The division of food production and other survival tasks between women and men meant that they had to exchange the fruits of their labor in order for all their skills to be available to one another. Children could no longer be cared for by any adult; they had to be the responsibility of particular men and women. The same would be true of old people. Although prehistoric societies cannot be assumed to be the same as contemporary nonindustrial societies, which have evolved as long as Western civilizations have, recurrent broad patterns evident in recent societies have been used to interpret the archaeological evidence of how prehistoric people may have lived (Ehrenberg 1989, 14–20).

One of the main ways nonindustrial societies organize and order food production and distribution and raise future members of the group is through kinship. Kinship also legitimates sexual relationships, allocates responsibilities for children among adults, and creates alliances outside the immediate family and the clan. Kinship is not an emanation of sociability and affection emerging out of long-term living together (the basis of primate bonding) but a complex social network that organizes the production and distribution of food, shelter, and gifts, and the social reproduction of new members of the group.[6]

Although we mostly think of kinship as public recognition of sexual relationships (marriage), and the assignment of specific children to individual men and women who have the obligation for their care, feeding, and teaching (filiation), kinship can occur between adults and children who do not have a blood relationship (adoption), and between adults of the same sex who may or may not have a sexual relationship, but who are heterogendered: Men married to berdaches are married to social women; women married to manly hearted women are married to social men.

Because the division of labor is gendered, and kinship organizes the claims of those doing women's and men's work on one another's production, kinship is necessarily gendered. The people occupying the gendered kinship statuses do not have to be biologically congruent or even heterosexual, and the recipro-cal exchange can take place between brothers and sisters. As Sylvia Junko Yanagisako and Jane Fishburne Collier point out: "There is a wide range of activities in which people participate besides heterosexual intercourse and parturition that contribute to the birth of viable babies and to their devel-opment into adults. These activities, in turn, involve and are organized by a number of relationships other than those of parenthood and marriage" (1987, 31).

Gendering extends to children because men and women separately train them in order to reproduce themselves socially. This training is an investment in the children's future labor, a "lien over time, the claim of both men and women over the future production of children" (Siskind 1978, 873). Unless they are strictly segregated, however, girls and boys can learn each other's work. If they persist in doing the work of the other gender, and the work is strictly divided between women and men with little overlap, they will be ostracized unless their society permits gender shifts, as happens when boys become berdaches; they will be women and do women's work when they grow up.

In some societies, sisters and brothers are the exchangers in the gendered division of labor and have reciprocal rights and responsibilities for the sister's children. Although they could physically produce children together, incest taboos against permanent sexual relationships between brothers and sisters, fathers and daughters, and mothers and sons ensure that children will marry out of the immediate kinship group (Gailey 1987, 47). The advantage of marrying out is that it expands the network of kin—of those responsible for each other (Lévi-Strauss 1956, [1949] 1969).

Where there is a food surplus or other valued goods, the kinship rules decide who controls and distributes it to whom. The type of technology determines whether child-minding is compatible with the main food production and therefore whether child-minders can be significant food producers, but the kinship rules set out obligations and privileges for women and men, and so are the more significant determinants of whether women and men have equal opportunities to gain power and prestige in a society.[7]

Were Men or Women Valued More?

Foraging groups are egalitarian—each individual's skills are respected; food is shared and consumed quickly; leaders are those who persuade a few others to go along with what he or she suggests (Power 1991, 37–49). The fluidity of group membership defuses hostility and violence, so that foraging groups anthropologists have studied tend to be described as kind, generous, affectionate, hospitable, and cooperative, as well as egalitarian (18–21). Such social flexibility was a successful pattern of survival among what are called "immediate-return" groups.

Ideally, gatherers and hunters should have been equally valued, since both brought in food, but men may have needed an incentive to bring the meat they hunted back to those in the home camp. As Peggy Reeves Sanday says:

> Since women are the potential bearers of new additions to the population, it would scarcely be expedient to place them at the front line at the hunt and in warfare. In addition, there are such questions as: What

would there be for men to do if women hunted, warred, or ruled? How would men acquire the "reason for being" that comes to women automatically? . . . Because men must sometimes gamble with their lives, power and prestige are the incentive that motivates them to hunt and defend territory and are the reward for being very nearly expendable in terms of the group's ultimate survival. (1981a, 115)[8]

An equally plausible argument can be made for women being valued more than men, and there is some evidence that Paleolithic cultures venerated women, especially fertile women. Salvatore Cucchiari (1981) imagines a possible pre-gender human society and a "gender revolution." He argues that "bisexual hordes" had fluid work allocation (gathering, intergroup trading, child-tending, camp maintenance), with perhaps a core group doing each task. Child-tending was shared among adults, and even breast-feeding was shared among nursing mothers. Pre-gender sexuality played down anatomical differences and ignored the connection between sex and pregnancy. Sexual relations did not create bonds or group membership or identity: "intense and unrestricted sexual expression within the horde is compatible with social relations. . . . Sexuality is peripheral to group organization and self-identity and therefore poses no threat to interpersonal relations" (46).

Cucchiari argues that eventually there was an ideological gender revolution: "The model of pre-kinship society . . . contains a dynamic or dialectic between unitarian ideology, with its insistence on sharing one's life experiences, and the biological asymmetry or exclusivity of proto-women's ability to have and suckle children. Once this exclusivity becomes a firm part of consciousness, the crisis in pre-kin society becomes acute and must be resolved" (50). As a result of these new ideas, women became sacred, the breasts and vagina became the symbol of childbearing and of the status "woman," and this new status was linked to an established category, "child-nurser." According to Cucchiari, this difference between those-who-nurse and those-who-do-not-nurse created an almost sacred division between woman and not-woman. For the first time, the facts of anatomical femaleness and maleness and the facts of procreation, he argues, took on symbolic meaning and became part of human culture as gender (50–52). He cites Paleolithic cave art that dates from 35,000 to 10,000 years ago and the little statues of women that have been found in widely dispersed archaeological sites throughout Europe as the symbolic representation of new and sacred gender statuses. The "Venus" figurines or "mother goddesses" have very large breasts, large buttocks, and thick thighs, usually considered symbols of female fertility. According to Elisabeth Badinter, they could also have represented woman's procreative power, the counterpart of the physical and metaphysical power of the hunter (1989, 26).

Researchers of Paleolithic art have argued that the central animals in cave art, the bison and the horse, are gendered, too, but they have attributed symbolic femaleness and maleness to the animals found in painted caves in opposite ways (Laming 1959; Leroi-Gourhan 1968, 1981).[9] Whether Paleolithic symbols are gendered at all is questionable (Ucko and Rosenfeld 1967; Marshack 1972). A number of sexless figures have been found, and they outnumber the female figurines in western Europe (Hadingham 1979, 223–25). One researcher argues that the bison and the horse, often painted alternately red and black, depict linked clans, families, or other kinship groups (Laming-Empéraire 1971, cited in Hadingham 1979, 203), which may have been more important socially than the gender statuses within them because they ordered many groups living in the same territory and established relationships over time. What Paleolithic people were painting and worshiping may have been neither women nor men, but representations of their kinship links through time and space.

Although women may not have been worshiped as sacred, they most likely had a high status in the Paleolithic period that continued into the Neolithic era, when plants and animals were domesticated, since they were both food producers and child producers:

> Peoples who carried their crops with them as they emigrated or who remained in an area where their ancestresses first experimented with plant domestication probably maintained the web of meanings that mediate female social and ritual authority. To break the equation of maternity with fertility of the soil would, in the minds of such peoples, threaten the wellspring of plant and human life. Maternity and fertility of the soil are equated because as women bring forth new life from their bodies, plants burst forth from the earth. The earth spirit is female. (Sanday 1981a, 120)

In any society, if the productive work the women do in conjunction with child-minding is the main way the group is fed and women also control the distribution of any surplus they produce, they have power and prestige. If the subsistence work of a group is not compatible with child-minding, women's power and prestige are usually low—men will provide most of the food and distribute the surplus. Because women must feed the children, what they produce may have to be consumed immediately, so there may be no surplus or

whose wife refuses to garden, gather, or cook, however, could well go hungry" (Coontz and Henderson 1986, 132).

A man needs a permanent relationship with a woman to have both a reliable provider of daily subsistence and maintenance and a claim to children. Within the social group, "marriage enables a man to become an effective social actor. He can play the role of host and invite others to share the hearth, food, and, in some cases, sexual services provided by his wife. As a man with recognized interests to protect, he can speak up and expect to be heard in public gatherings. And, as an individual whose basic needs are provided, he can devote his time to building the exchange networks that enhance social influence and prestige" (Collier and Rosaldo 1981, 284). A man needs alliances with his wife's kinsmen in order to ensure that they will persuade or allow her to marry him, will not take her back if she wants to leave him, and will support the legitimacy of his claims to her services and children if she takes a lover. That is, it is precisely because men need women more than women need men that men have to form alliances with other men to get and keep wives.

In order to understand why men exchange women and why marriages create gender inequality, Fishburne Collier says that "we must . . . add another character to Lévi-Strauss's triad consisting of a woman, her brother, and her husband: her lover" (1988, 228). Women's relationships with their lovers and their brothers are egalitarian; women's relationships with their husbands are not:

> With brothers, women engage in voluntary exchanges of goods and services, but do not have sex relations. With lovers, women engage in direct and voluntary exchanges of goods, services, and sex. And with husbands, women have sexual relations, but engage in exchanges of goods and services that are forced. . . . Husbands cannot engage in direct and voluntary exchanges with wives because a husband must distribute his products according to prior obligations. (228)

A husband's obligations are to the men who helped him get his wife and will help him keep her. He needs their help because, given wives' exploitation, marriages are inherently unstable (229).[14] By allying with other men to back their claims on a woman's labor and sexuality and on her children, men transform private quarrels between women and men into public conflicts. "In classless societies, quarrels over women between men, or between husbands and women's kin, are endemic," as are demands for compensation between women's and men's kin groups (226).

Fishburne Collier argues that wives leave husbands for lovers in order to have more egalitarian relationships and that brothers-in-law band together to bring them back or to get compensation for the husband, but Karen Sacks (1979) claims that even in patrilineal societies women have rights in their own lineages as sisters and in their husbands' lineages as mothers: "Sisters have a claim on a brother's products or labor. Perhaps more importantly, they also have a claim on the labor of the junior members of their own lineage. Often this is phrased as a return for their having provided their brother with the wherewithal to marry and have children. Thus brothers' claims to their own children's labor are shared with the claims of their sisters and the children's mother" (120).[15]

Structurally, in classless societies where kin groups are the units of production, women who go to live with their husbands' families are workers in one place but still claimants to their own families' production. Similarly, in matrilocal societies, men who go to live with their wives' families work for them but reap the benefits of the work of their sisters' husbands. Thus, in Sacks's view, even though women are exchanged in marriage for brideservice or bridewealth, and their work as wives benefits their husbands, they still, as sisters, maintain an egalitarian reciprocity with some men—their brothers (1979, 119–23). A study that tested Sacks's relationship among kinship, production, and women's status found that the crucial variable was control of property, which enhanced women's kin-group leadership and domestic authority (Hendrix and Hossain 1988, 448).

In sum, gender relationships in classless societies are both conflictual and cooperative, with potentially disruptive alliances of men against women and women against men, but there are also coalitions of women and men, such as brothers and sisters or mothers and sons, that create the reciprocal relationships that keep the society together.

Were Women Inventors of Their Own Subordination?

At what point did gender inequality emerge? Can buried bones tell us whether Paleolithic women and men were differently evaluated? First, the sex of skeletons and parts of skeletons have to be accurately determined. Once distinguished, they can tell archaeologists age at death, illnesses, likely cause of death, nutritional status, what kinds of foods were eaten, and what kinds of repetitive physical movements the individual carried out.[16] Evidence of differences in the value of women and men can be gleaned from nutritional status, infant mortality rates, and proportion of men to women at grave sites.

The kinds and quality of grave goods are additional evidence of status, but subject, as Margaret Ehrenberg points out, to common misinterpretation. The sex of the skeleton is often used to establish the interpretation of what carved spear throwers or other valuable goods mean: When these implements are buried with men, they are considered evidence of hunting and high rank; if they are buried with women, they are considered evidence of the rank of the women's mate or father (1989, 29–31). Ehrenberg suggests combining the evidence of age and burial goods: Valuable goods buried with those who died young are likely to have been inherited; when buried with women or men who died at older ages, they are likely to be evidence of the person's own activities and social ranking.

Given that interpretation, women and men in the Upper Paleolithic period were equal, since in the graves discovered, they were equally likely to have been buried with valued artifacts. In the earlier Middle Paleolithic, only the graves of men have stone or bone implements, and in the later Mesolithic period, men were more likely than women to have received special treatment in their burials (Ehrenberg 1989, 61–62). The substantially egalitarian status of women and men during most of the Paleolithic period reflected their equal contribution to subsistence; any surplus from hunting, which would have increased men's prestige, was quickly consumed, and there was a fluid kinship system. (See table 6.1).

In the next major stage of human evolution, around twelve thousand to ten thousand years ago, the domestication of plants and animals (the "Neolithic revolution"), women's status was high. According to one theory, already settled communities around the Mediterranean experienced food shortages when the climate got drier, and the plant gatherers began to set aside some grain seeds for planting instead of eating them all (McCorriston and Hole 1991). Since gathering was women's work, plant domestication was also probably women's invention.[17] Settling down in one place and growing food meant that women could be pregnant more often; the population explosion required that more land be cultivated and more animals be domesticated, so gradually, for more and more groups of people, gathering and hunting became outmoded as the primary form of food production.

Another important invention, pottery (molded and fired clay) was also probably an outcome of women's work in gathering and cooking plant foods and processing hunted animals. With sedentary life, women's earliest inventions, the digging stick and the sling that carried infants and the food that was gathered, were replaced by the hoe and pottery. If grains, vegetables, fruits, and nuts were planted in one place, producing a more reliable supply than if they were foraged over a large territory, there would be a surplus that needed

Table 6.1.   Technology and the Status of Women

| | Type of Technology | | | |
	Gathering-Hunting	Horticultural	Agricultural, Herding	19th-Century Industrial
Compatible with child-minding	Gathering	Yes	No	No
Control of surplus	Men (products of hunt)	Women (products of garden-ing)	Men who own land or herds	Men who own means of production
Residence rule	Fluid	Matrilocal	Patrilocal	Neolocal
Inheritance	No permanent property	Matrilineal or patrilineal	Patrilineal	Patrilineal
Control over procrea-tion	Children spaced by nursing and mother's fertility	Women, but high birth-rate and high infant mortality	Men, to have sons by legal wife	Men who own property
Women's status	Men and women relatively equal	High	Low	Low

storing in large pottery jars. Both the hoe and pottery, which may very well have been women's inventions, were significant technological advances that gradually transformed other aspects of social life.

The increase in the food supply and sedentary communities meant that more children could be born and fed: They did not have to be carried on gathering treks and could be fed cereals at an early age (Ehrenberg 1989, 88–89). Women's work therefore increased; there was more food to be grown and processed, and more children to mind. If the men of the community still hunted once the land was cleared, the gendered division of labor would have deepened. A second consequence was stratification:

> Another consequence of the ability to keep material possessions and to store food was that for the first time some people could accumulate

more than others. If someone needed a tool or an emergency supply of food that someone else had in surplus, it could be borrowed or accepted as a gift, and the borrower would become indebted to the lender or giver. So wealth, debt and obligation, and hence social stratification based on differential ownership, could have begun to develop for the first time in the Neolithic period. (Ehrenberg 1989, 88)

Archaeological evidence of living arrangements and burial practices and ethnographic inference suggest that Neolithic communities, such as Çatal Hüyük, were matrilineal and matrilocal, and that women had considerable authority because they controlled the distribution of food.[18] Houses were large, accommodating a mother, her daughters, their husbands, and their children. Women, as the planters and reapers, had claims to the surplus. Husbands, as incoming members of the family, could be expelled if their behavior was undesirable. They could return to their mothers' hearth; it would be difficult for them to gather a warring band, since their brothers and other kinsmen would be scattered in many women's households.

Neolithic female figurines have been found in many sites in southeastern Europe and southwestern Asia, as well as in the Aegean Sea islands. Although their significance for documenting the status of women has been debated, Marija Gimbutas (1989) argues that the imagery and symbolism of the art of this period represent an iconography of the Goddess as life-giver, renewer of the eternal earth, regenerator of the dead, unfolder of endless energy.[19] Such imagery would reflect women's status during the Neolithic period, which was high because of their great contribution to subsistence, their share in the distribution of the surplus, and the matrifocal kinship system.

Around five thousand years after the discovery of agriculture and pottery, a major shift in human technology in the settled areas took place, and with it, crucial changes in the gendered division of labor and women's status.[20] With settlement and food growing, the population of settled communities expanded and moved into less fertile territory. So that seeds could be planted more deeply, the iron plow was invented. Animals such as cattle and sheep, instead of being hunted for meat, were herded, domesticated, used for milk, wool, and pulling plows, and slaughtered for food and ritual sacrifice.

The division of labor shifted. Men turned from hunting to herding and from clearing land to farming it with plows. Like hunting, this work was not compatible with child-minding. Women concentrated on food processing, which now included making cheese and yogurt out of raw milk, important forms of food. Their horticultural skills went into gardening, and they also took care of fowl and eggs. All the tasks of carding wool and flax, spinning it into thread, and weaving it into cloth became women's and children's work.

Control over property shifted from women to men and became more unequal. Large-scale herding and more intensive farming increased the value of domestic animals and land. There were also implements and cloth to be traded. Warfare, raiding, and alliances by marriage among geographically dispersed groups were the social result. Men consolidated their landholdings and herds of sheep and cattle; those who owned hired those who did not own; slaves were captured in warfare and became workers and servants. Children were valued as workers and as bonds in the alliances. Women's value as food producers and distributors of surplus declined; they were now more valued as child producers.

Some men's ownership of large tracts of land and herds made them dominant in their communities. These men stayed put; when they married, their wives moved to their villages far from their own kin. Sons inherited their fathers' land and herds and were taught their skills. Daughters did not inherit but were given a share in the property as dowry; they learned their mothers' skills in weaving, food processing, gardening—and birthing and caring for children. These skills were transportable; women went as productive partners to their husbands' homes, but without a claim to their husbands' property, they were junior partners. Their social status depended on the size of their dowry, which in turn depended on the status of their birth families. Those men and women who did not own land and herds, did not inherit it, or did not marry those who owned it worked for the owners as peasants and servants. Their children grew up as peasants and servants.

The greater importance of patrilineal descent meant that the daughters and wives of landowners had to be sexually controlled (Lerner 1986). Virginity at marriage and severe punishment for adulterous women were the means of ensuring paternity of the children born within marriage. Rape was a violation of another man's property and a way of punishing wayward women. The children of a marriage belonged to the father. The laws were those of the property-owning fathers. One god (a father-lord-king) replaced goddesses of fertility: "When Adam is transferred to the Garden of Eden, he is called to a state of service to God. He is forbidden to partake of the goddess symbol—the tree of knowledge of good and evil. The act of eating in this passage has been frequently equated with sexuality. In fact, ritual sex was common in sacred Canaanite shrines marked by the tree symbol of the goddess" (Sanday 1981a, 223).

Agricultural societies in the fertile crescent around the Mediterranean Sea about five thousand years ago developed the most extreme form of gender inequality. Women's status was low because of their reduced contribution to production, men's ownership of property and control over the distribution of the surplus, and the kinship system, which served men's interests. Many parts of the world, such as Africa and Melanesia, retained horticulture, matrilineality, and a high status for women, but in Western civilization and its culture and social patterns, property-owning men came to have much more power and prestige than the women of their class well into the modern era.[21] These agrarian feudal societies were the true patriarchies: The landowning fathers ruled, and sons inherited everything. As for women, the end of the story of the Garden of Eden in the King James version of the Bible sums up their fate: "Thy desire shall be to thy husband, and he shall rule over thee."

Don't pity the infants who died here on the Alto do Cruzeiro.
Don't waste your tears on them. Pity us instead. Weep for
their mothers who are condemned to live.

—*Nancy Scheper-Hughes (1992, 425)*

ROCKING THE CRADLE:
GENDERED PARENTING

In late 1992, a unique four-inch clay figurine, three thousand years old, was found in the Negev Desert in Israel (Ronnen 1992). It depicts the inside and outside of a woman's body. The arms form an oval, womblike frame around twin embryos clutching at her breasts, and the hands open the vulva in preparation for childbirth. The hair frames an expressive face. On each thigh is an ibex standing by a tree, the symbol of life, growth, and fertility in many ancient Middle East cultures. The figurine may be a representation of a Canaanite goddess named Asherah, wife of El, head of a pantheon, and mother of seventy divine sons. She is also called Qudshu, goddess of fertility.[1] One of the many little figures of voluptuous or pregnant women made by European pre-Christian and Middle Eastern peoples, the Canaanite figurine transforms the procreative female body into a cultural representation of the concept of fertility. The repeated ovals, the inside-outside perspective, and the use of symbols make it into a work of art similar to the statues and paintings of Mary and the infant Jesus of Christian cultures. The figurines glorify women's fecundity; the madonnas create an image of holy motherhood.

Berthe Morisot's 1879 painting *Wet Nurse and Julie,* an impressionist depiction of a woman nursing an infant, is not an updated madonna and child, but an implicit dual work scene—the nursing woman is feeding Morisot's child for wages, while Morisot is making a painting of them for exhibition and sale. According to Linda Nochlin,

> this painting embodies one of the most unusual circumstances in the history of art—perhaps a unique one: a woman painting another woman nursing her baby. Or, to put it another way, introducing what is

144

not seen but what is known into what is visible, two working women confront each other here, across the body of "their" child and the boundaries of class, both with claims to motherhood and mothering, both, one assumes engaged in pleasurable activity which, at the same time, may be considered production in the literal sense of the word. What may be considered a mere use value if the painting was produced by a mere amateur, the milk produced for the nourishment of one's own child, is now to be understood as an exchange value. In both cases—the milk, the painting—a product is being produced or created for a market, for profit. (1988, 38–39)

The little prehistoric figurines of hip-heavy, large-breasted women and the goddesses of fertility, Raphael's madonnas and the worship of the Virgin Mary, and Morisot's depiction of shared maternity by working women all socially constructed motherhood and encouraged emulation by the women of the time.

As a working mother, Morisot was not unusual in hiring a wet nurse; wet-nursing was a booming business in preindustrial France (Otis 1986; Sussman 1982). From the seventeenth to the nineteenth centuries, Parisian women were expected to send their children to the country to be wet-nursed for the first two or three years, even though the babies risked neglect, illness, and even death. Most of the women who used rural wet nurses were independent artisans and shopkeepers who could not afford to stop work to nurse and care for their infants and small children, but even if they could, "wet-nursing was so normal a part of the life cycle that it required an independent mind, a strong will, and even courage on the part of a mother to keep her newborn baby and nurse it herself" (Sussman 1982, 67).

In eighteenth-century France, indifference to the fate of their children was not emotional self-protection against sorrow over their probable early death but, according to Elisabeth Badinter, a choice to pursue their own interests: "It was not so much because children died like flies that mothers showed so little interest in them, but rather because the mothers showed so little interest that the children died in such great numbers" (1981, 60). It was not until the end of the eighteenth century that well-to-do women in France were urged by philosophers and economists to feed and care for their children themselves (Badinter 1981, 117–201). The child had become more valuable as a future worker and citizen. In order to ensure the survival of more children, parenthood was redefined to enhance the importance of mothers. These new views gave wives more authority within their families but diminished women's opportunities to make a mark in the larger society: "The inquiring, ambitious, bold woman of an earlier period was transformed into a modest and reasonable creature, whose ambitions no longer reached out beyond the family" (Badinter 1981, 146). It took many years before the concept of mother love as natural, spontaneous, and central to womanhood became generally accepted by French women. After it was, women who did not want children, did not nurse their children, were not personally attentive to all their children's needs, and did not sacrifice their own desires to that of their children were condemned as unnatural and abnormal: "Between the saint and the slut there was an unbridgeable chasm" (Badinter 1981, 238).[2]

Mary O'Brien (1981), a former midwife, has argued that the separation of men from the immediate experience of reproduction is alienating in a profound existential sense. She claims that once women start to menstruate, they have a conscious link to potential procreation and through procreation, to the history of the human race. Men's procreative consciousness, in contrast, is that of alienation, of losing control of his seed: "Paternity is in fact an abstract idea" (p. 29).[3] The image of the good mother, in contrast, is that of someone intimately bound to her children in physical and emotional symbiosis, loving but asexual, self-sacrificing, putting the children's welfare before her own or anyone else's.

Although it may make good evolutionary sense for a mother to bond to her helpless newborn, whether she actually will may depend on the social worth of both the mother and the child. For very poor women, the emotional bonding that has come to be taken for granted as part of mothering in the modern Western world may be an unaffordable luxury; their children may not even be named until it is clear they will live beyond the first year (Scheper-Hughes 1992).[4] African-American women who mothered white children as paid domestics often had to leave their own children to fend for themselves so they could make the money to feed, clothe, and educate them (Dill 1980). In order to earn a living, some poor women have placed older children in orphanages or with foster parents or have boarded out their infants (Bellingham 1986; Broder 1988). The wisdom of Solomon, that the "real mother" is the one who would give up her son rather than see him killed ignores real mothers who *have* killed their children rather than see them grow up as slaves or suffer slow death through starvation (Ashe 1991; Morrison 1987). Good, loving mothers also send their beloved sons to war.

Who Shall Live, and Who Shall Die?

Depending on the circumstances of their birth and their parents' resources, some children are not cared for at all. In New York City today, newborns, some alive, some dead, are discarded in trash cans and garbage bags, down chutes and into dumpsters, usually anonymously. But one baby, found in a yellow plastic bag, was dressed in new clothes—a T-shirt, a diaper, and flowered pajamas—and wrapped in a white blanket with ribbon around it and a note attached, which read, "Please take care of my girl. She was born April 26, 1991 at 12:42 pm. Her name is April Olivia. I love her very much. Thank you. She died at 10:30 am on April 29, 1991. Sorry."[5] This mother was clearly attached to her child and probably had been during the months of pregnancy, but when a fetus might have to be aborted or a child killed or abandoned, it is not thought of as human.[6]

In nineteenth-century rural Bavaria, women servants worked to the minute of birth, left the child where it was born, and went back to work, denying that they were ever pregnant. Many of these abandoned infants were born in privies and "experienced and described as feces or frequently as clotted blood, as something unclean and sick which is rejected. . . . The unborn child produced no picture, no projection, no fantasy about its existence after its birth or its presence in the life of its mother or in the future of a family. It remained in an ambiguous indeterminateness, a marginal state" (Schulte 1984, 89). In the poorest quarters of twentieth-century Brazil, "the sickly, wasted, or congenitally deformed infant challenges the tentative and fragile symbolic boundaries between human and nonhuman, natural and supernatural, normal and abominable" (Scheper-Hughes 1992, 375). Meira Weiss's firsthand observations of two hundred Israeli families with severely disabled children revealed that they were often treated as "monsters"—physically abused, emotionally neglected, and isolated in dark, bare, tiny bedrooms or corridors (1994).

The lines between stillbirths, accidental deaths, neglect, and infanticide are not clear. Whether infanticide is considered deliberate or accidental has often depended on how the birthing woman is morally judged (Hoffer and Hull 1981). In eighteenth-century England, if the defendant could show preparation for the child, the claim of stillbirth was believed, and the defendant was acquitted of murder. It was called the "benefit-of-linen" defense (Hoffer and Hull 1981, 68–69). Another successful defense was "want-of-help"—the defendants argued that they tried to obtain help, but their cries were not heard, a door was locked, they became ill, or they fell on the way to getting help. Here the crime was reduced to negligence. Failure to tie off the umbilical cord or to prevent injury to the child in an unassisted birth was presumed to show not "murderous intent but a lack of skill or self-possession" (69). Women also successfully pleaded ignorance of being in labor; as in Bavaria, many infants "fell" into privies (70–71).

Under conditions of high infant mortality, the deaths of unwanted children seem to be barely noticed, and local practices may exacerbate the risks of infant mortality. In the nineteenth century, in one French town, almost half of the babies sent from Paris to wet nurses died in the first nine days of life (Fuchs 1984, 201 and Table 6.5, 203). Given the conditions of meager, dirty, insect-infested housing, poor food, and germ-laden water, it's a wonder any child survived. Laundry was done twice a year, and adults didn't wash themselves either. Most children died of diarrhea, dehydration, and gastroenteritis, the classic child-killers of poverty. The wet nurse's child was little better off than the foundling who was boarded out, and the foundling may have had more clothes, since they were supplied by the state (Fuchs 1984, 192–234).

High infant mortality is still prevalent where there is a scarcity of food, and water is contaminated by feces, urine, and waste. In late-twentieth-century Brazil, for example, the deaths of children are routine. Publicly, "child death has yet to seize the imagination of political leaders, administrative and civil servants, physicians, and priests or religious officials as an urgent and pressing social problem about which 'something must be done.' Rather, there is a failure to see or recognize as problematic what is considered the norm (as well as normal, expectable) for poor and marginal families" (Scheper-Hughes 1992, 272). England did not make registration of births compulsory until 1907. Starting in 1834, deaths and their actual causes (not "old age" or "wasting") had to be recorded, but authorities did not record the infant mortality rate until 1875. Malnutrition and diarrhea, the main killers of young children, were not considered diseases until the twentieth century. Diarrhea was "trivial," and infant "wasting" was not attributed to hunger. Marasmus, kwashiorkor, and other diseases of malnutrition are the causes of death of adults as well as children in famines, but are common killers of children in every neglected, poverty-stricken area in the world (Scheper-Hughes 1992, 274).

In the Alto do Cruzeiro, an extremely poor section of Brazil, mothers "are forced to participate in the community's 'space of death' by making innumer-able, little 'selections' that have life-and-death consequences. Mothers must decide on the quality and strength of the powdered milk and *mingua* [gruel] given to young and older, stronger and weaker children; on the claims to the small amount of carefully filtered and boiled water that is kept in a special clay pot; who shall receive emergency medical care; and who will get a new pair of sandals" (Scheper-Hughes 1992, 407). Bottle-feeding is lethal since it is the product of powdered milk and unboiled water, unsterilized bottles and nipples, and no refrigeration. Yet powdered milk or Nestlés are fathers' gifts to their children—the more milk brought, the more a mark of father's love.

The more a child is valued, the more the mother's milk is devalued as not sufficiently nourishing (316–26).

The women of the Alto do Cruzeiro know their children die because they are hungry, the water they drink is "filthy with germs," they have no shoes or clothing, and their medical care is worthless. Mothers must leave their babies alone so they can work for pay. They know that above all, their children need more food to survive. And yet they will claim that their children do not die of hunger, even though they are described as wasted, withered, shriveled up, shrunk "to nothing." Why this denial? "The alternative—the recognition that one's own child is slowly starving to death—is too painful given the role that mothers sometimes play in reducing food and liquid." This slow infanticide is a strategy used to feed the children most likely to live, rather than those born "wanting to die" (1992, 315–16):

> What mothers expectantly looked for in their newborn infants were qualities that showed a readiness for the uphill struggle that was life . . . . Active, quick, responsive, and playful infants were much preferred to quiet, docile, inactive infants, infants described as "dull," "listless," and "spiritless." . . . A particularly lethal form of negative feedback sometimes resulted when Alto mothers gradually withdrew from listless infants whose "passivity" was the result of hunger itself. (316)

Scarce resources, including mother love, must be reserved for those who have the best chance of surviving.

Worthless and Priceless Children

In the survival stakes, social worth is crucial. Parents do not necessarily value all their children equally, and the social value of children has fluctuated widely.[7] The policies of states toward unwanted children depend on who will have the financial responsibility for them; the policies of religious bodies tend to emphasize the morals of the mothers. The children themselves are frequently not a major concern.

In early modern Europe, when few families could feed more than three children, 10 to 40 percent of the children registered as born were abandoned, even in times of prosperity (Boswell 1988, 15–16). From ancient Rome to medieval Europe, parents of illegitimate children or of too many to feed or too many of one gender often left them where they could be found by someone who wanted children (Boswell 1988). Sometimes the fates were kind to them:

Their foster parents loved them and treated them well, or their biological parents had a change of heart or fortune and recovered them. Many, however, were turned into slaves, child prostitutes (including boys), crippled beggars, or eunuchs by those who took them in (111–32). In early medieval Europe, many "surplus" children were donated as permanent gifts to monasteries and convents (Boswell 1988, 228–55). The practice was called "oblation" or "offering" and occurred over a thousand years. Whether or not they wanted to be nuns or priests, these children had to stay; the oblate who left was excommunicated.

By the late Middle Ages, the establishment of foundling hospitals provided a place to dispose of unwanted children. "A major benefit of the foundling-home system was that the problem of unwanted children was removed from the streets and the view of ordinary citizens. The children disappeared behind institutional walls, where specialists were paid to deal with them, so that parents, relatives, neighbors and society could forget" (Boswell 1988, 423). The death rate from communicable diseases in these institutions could be as high as 90 percent (421–27). This unintended consequence of what was in theory an improvement over abandoning children in the streets or selling them in the marketplace may very well have been its latent function—passive, hidden infanticide.

In twelfth-century France, abandoned newborns were deposited in a *tour,* which was a revolving cradle located in an opening in the tower of a hospice or a shelter for the sick. Foundlings were cared for by wet nurses or foster parents until they were three or four and then returned to the hospice until they were seven, when they were apprenticed. The church encouraged the anonymous use of the tour as an alternative to abortion and infanticide. But the state wanted to know the name and status of the mother in order to force her or the father to take responsibility for the child (Fuchs 1984).[8] Although fathers could legally recognize their illegitimate children, almost none did, and the Napoleonic Code, designed to protect the bourgeois husband and father, expressly forbid *recherche de la paternité*—seeking out and legally petitioning the father for financial support. In 1912 the right to petition a *single* man for payment for his child's food was granted (Fuchs 1992, 37, 69). There was very little adoption in France because the only reason for it was to provide an heir. Nieces and nephews were felt to be more appropriate heirs, since "the children of unwed mothers were . . . seen as potentially immoral, criminal, deviant, or subnormally intelligent. They were the pariahs of society" (Fuchs 1984, 30).

The practice of abandonment in a tour, wet nursing, return to the church-run refuge, and apprenticeship continued in France from the twelfth to the sixteenth centuries. Then the monarchy began to administer the hospitals, and some separate refuges were set up for orphaned (not abandoned and presumed illegitimate) infants and children. With this distinction, the children were morally judged by their parentage: *pauvre orphelins* were the result of misfortune, but *enfants trouvés* represented vice, depravity, and crime. In contrast, by the seventeenth century, children of upper- and middle-class families were thought of as innocent and pure (Ariès 1962, 15–133).

During the French Revolution, the state assumed responsibility for orphans and abandoned children, and all were called *enfants de la patrie* (Fuchs 1984, 18). The policy of anonymous abandonment and state responsibility was codified at the beginning of the nineteenth century; the number of tours was increased, and all hospitals were required to have them. The result was controversy over whether ease and anonymity of abandonment encouraged immoral behavior or prevented abortion and infanticide. The opponents of the tours won out; most were shut by the late 1850s, and the one in Paris by 1862 (Fuchs 1984, 19–45).

A similar practice of abandoning children to institutions when they could not be cared for by a widowed or deserted mother occurred in the United States in the nineteenth century, when "child savers" set up orphanages and foster parentage for poor children, such as the Children's Aid Society (Bellingham 1986, S41–51). The parents' strategy was thus to get them food, clothing, shelter, and some education or training. These children knew who their mother was and where to find her. From the parents' point of view, this solution to family poverty was temporary and not intended to permanently sever family ties despite the legal turnover of custody to social welfare agencies. The state, however, wanted to remove the children from parents they considered immoral and depraved, because they defined neglect as cruelty to children (L. Gordon 1989, 27–58).

Before the nineteenth century, except for the firstborn son, children were not valued by aristocratic or bourgeois French families, and so turning an infant over to a wet nurse, without supervision or visits, might have been a more or less purposeful strategy of limiting the number of children in a family (Badinter 1981, 49).[9] In contrast, in the United States in the twentieth century, only 1.5 percent of the recorded births are available for adoption, and more than 2 million couples want to adopt. As a result, childless couples are willing to pay tens of thousands of dollars for adoption, a surrogate mother, or high-technology infertility treatment. These costs are not the market value of a child; most capitalist countries have laws against selling babies. The payment is for the services of doctors, lawyers, adoption agencies, or surrogate mothers. The child is today of such high value that its worth is intrinsic and emotional, virtually sacred (Zelizer 1985, 22–55).[10] Yet some may be discarded as worthless. From 1980 to 1986, in Israel, a country in which women are encouraged to have at least three children and that pays ample child allowances, 68.4 percent of 250 infants born with very visible deformities in three hospitals were abandoned by their parents in the hospital (Weiss 1994). In the Middle Ages, such children were given permanently to the church "with the most pious of vows" (Boswell 1988, 298).

Sons and daughters often do not have equal worth. The sex ratio (proportion of boys to girls or women to men) is revelatory of a society's evaluation of girl and boy children. The selective infanticide that is usually the result of poor economic resources often kills girls, not boys (Johansson 1984). Analyzing the sex ratios in the ninth-century tax census called the "polyptych of Saint Germain-des-Prés," which listed the people living on lands belonging to a monastery over a generation, Emily Coleman (1976) found that the sex ratio ranged from 110.3 to 252.9 men for each 100 women, and among children, from 115.7 to 156.2 boys to each 100 girls. The smaller the farm and the larger the family on it, the more imbalanced the sex ratio in favor of men and boys. At that time, women who did not marry were entitled to support, and though women contributed to the farm economy, the farm could only support a limited number. The society was patrilocal, so if there were many women kin already living on the farm, the men could not bring wives in; "the number of baby girls that could be encouraged, or allowed, to survive was closely related also to the number of wives and adult spinsters that already took their sustenance from it" (61). Where infanticide of female infants was not deliberate, the value of boys as future workers in agricultural communities meant that they were likely to be fed better and get more attention when ill, resulting in a gender-skewed mortality rate (Hammel, Johansson, and Ginsberg 1983).[11]

The social worth of sons in Far Eastern countries is still far greater than the social worth of daughters, so limits on family size has had tragic consequences for women and girls. Africa, Europe, and North America have a sex ratio of 105 boys to 100 girls, considered balanced because more boys than girls are born to compensate for the higher natural death rate of male children. In China, India, Bangladesh, and West Asia, the sex ratio is 94 girls to 100 boys, and in Pakistan it is 90 girls to 100 boys. Given the number of men, there should have been about 30 million more women in India today and 38 million more women in China (Sen 1990). Although the manifest intent of female infanticide and abortions of female fetuses is to prevent the birth of unwanted daughters, the latent effect could be to lower the overall birthrate to well below the replacement level unless wives are imported.[12]

What of the women who are forced to abort a female fetus or kill a newborn daughter? Barbara Katz Rothman, in her study of the emotional effects of amniocentesis, found that of twenty-six women who learned they were carrying daughters, twenty-four were very pleased; the other two women already had three daughters (1986, 148–51). The twenty-four women expecting sons were not as happy about the prospect as our culture would predict—eight were pleased, ten were disappointed, and six were ambivalent. Only two out of the twelve who were expecting their first child were pleased that it was male; five were neutral, and five were disappointed whether it was to be a firstborn son or another son in an all-boy family or a mixed-gender family. Katz Rothman argues that women may prefer daughters because "the fetus who is male is *other,* an intruder in the female body. The more patriarchal, the more traditional the woman, the more that is true" (151).[13]

Think then of the tragedy of having to abort a daughter because you must have a son *and to know that it will be the only child you will have,* as in China. Yet not to do so is to incur family wrath and perhaps divorce or death.

Bargaining over Begetting

Norms, mores, religious rules, economic conditions, and family patterns all regulate fertility directly through contraception and abortion before birth and infanticide and abandonment postnatally, as well as indirectly through the age at which women and men may marry, the imposition of sexual abstinence for various reasons during marriage, and customs regarding remarriage after the death of a spouse or divorce.[14] Physiological fertility control comes with prolonged nursing and also nutritional health of women of childbearing age, but both are influenced by social norms about how long children should be breast-fed, the food supply, its distribution, and who gets first chance to eat.

When a country wants to encourage births, social policies encourage every woman to have children and take care of them. The poor and pregnant women who were immoral "fallen women" in France from 1830 to 1870 became the future mothers of needed workers and soldiers from 1870 to 1914 (Fuchs 1992, 56–76). A change in attitudes toward out-of-wedlock births occurred around the same time in England, Germany, the United States, and Russia because a long depression and a drop in the birthrate produced fears of depopulation. The beginning of the French welfare state shifted policies from punishing women who had "too many children" to helping them to have healthy children. At the end of the nineteenth century, a French subcommission on infant mortality recommended, for all mothers, married or single,

> reduced work during the last stages of pregnancy, prenatal medical care and rest, four-week paid maternity leaves, mutual maternity insurance programs, more convalescent homes for postpartum mothers, an increase in free maternity hospitals, and sufficient financial support so that women, regardless of marital status, could nurse their infants. The subcommission also recommended well-baby clinics, free sterilized milk to mothers who could not nurse, infant care centers, and a wide variety of maternal and family aid. The subcommission sought to protect a woman through her pregnancy and the first few years of her child's life, but one thing it did not protect: her right to choose whether or not she wanted to be pregnant. They agreed to outlaw the sale of contraceptives or any information pertaining to contraception and abortion. (Fuchs 1992, 60)

Conversely, as prosperity rises, more food is produced, maternal health improves, and the neonatal mortality rate drops. In order to prevent a population explosion, states intervene to decrease births, encouraging married couples to have fewer, healthier, better-educated children. The decline in the number of children born to working-class married couples in England and Wales in 1900–39 resulted from changing employment patterns and information about birth control provided by health agencies and clinics (Gittens 1982). Throughout the twentieth century, the same decline in fertility rates to replacement level (a bit above two children per couple) or below occurred in all Western countries, whether they were capitalist or communist and whether the labor force participation of women was high or low. For instance, Cuba, in 1979–80, had a 1.6 total fertility rate with 28.1 percent of the women of childbearing age employed outside the home, while Czechoslovakia, where 72.4 percent of the women in that age group were in the labor force, had a fertility rate of 2.1. The United States' fertility rate in 1980 was 1.9 with about a 60 percent labor force participation for women (Anker 1985).[15]

Capitalist economic development results in decreased fertility because the potential for wage earning reduces control by the men heads of families over the labor of their children (Folbre 1983). Although unmarried daughters and sons may be obligated to turn over part of their wages to their father, they are less likely to support their parents in their old age once they form their own households, unless they materially raise their economic status through education. Investing in the education of a few children, rather than having many children who will work for the extended family, does not, however, reduce the cost of those children to the mother. Her work now includes helping to pay for the children's education and the commodities of a higher-status household. In addition, she is expected to take responsibility for the children's emotional and intellectual development. Thus, in terms of the mother's investment, the cost of a few, carefully brought up children seems to be as high as the cost of many children who assist her and earn money for her (Mueller 1982).

Because the woman's status in her family may depend on motherhood, infertility is more detrimental socially for women than for men. Even in modern Western societies, they have more at stake but less bargaining power in the decisions over what to do about not being able to conceive.[16] Whether the woman or the man is infertile, the woman is the one who usually seeks help. If she is determined to try to have a biological child with her partner, she has to assure his willingness to undergo whatever procedures physicians deem appropriate to their medical situation. She will also need his sympathy and emotional support throughout the days, months, and often years of repeated attempts to get pregnant (Lorber and Greenfeld 1990). An infertile man might want to forget about having children entirely, or he might find the examinations, tests, and semen production challenging to his identity as a man. Given his stress over his infertility, he might be unwilling or unable to provide much emotional support (Lorber and Bandlamudi 1993)

The newest procreative technology, in vitro fertilization (IVF), or out-of-the-body conception, has been used in both female and male infertility. This method involves giving a woman hormones to make her produce more than one ovum a month, removing the ova, fertilizing them with sperm in a petri dish, and incubating the gametes for a day or two until the resultant cell division produces an embryo that can be implanted in the woman's womb (Fredericks, Paulson, and DeCherney 1987). In male infertility, IVF provides a technological means for a man who has low sperm count, poor sperm motility, or badly shaped sperm to impregnate and for his fertile partner to have *his* child. In theory, extracorporeal fertilization should work better than using collected sperm for insemination because a very small amount of good sperm is needed to fertilize an egg in a petri dish. But the current procedures for injecting the sperm into the nucleus of the ovum often produce defective embryos, and very few of these couples end up with a baby (Oehninger, Stecker, and Acosta 1992; Tournaye et al. 1992).

Unfortunately, all the procedures, which involve not only the administering of hormones and surgery but many blood tests and sonograms, have to be undergone by the woman, who may be able to conceive with a much simpler procedure, donor insemination. If motherhood and not pregnancy is her goal, she may prefer to adopt. But if she refuses to undergo fertility treatments, her partner's opportunity to have a biological child in this relationship is lost. He has everything to gain and less to undergo. This imbalance in the demands of treatment sets up the dynamics of gender bargaining in male infertility (Lorber 1987b, 1989b; Lorber and Bandlamudi 1993).

When her male partner is infertile, a woman's ability to conceive does not necessarily enhance her bargaining power in the relationship. Like the wife who earns more than her husband, she usually needs to do an extraordinary amount of emotional labor to repair the damage to his sense of masculinity (Hochschild 1989a, 82–86, 220–28). She takes on the burden of *his* infertility, considering herself infertile as well, since she is unable to have a child with him (Greil, Leitko, and Porter 1988). By doing most of the emotional work and by defining his infertility as "our infertility," the woman maintains the covertness of the imbalanced power relations (Komter 1989). She cannot demand and may not even expect gratitude for this emotional labor, for, as Arlie Hochschild notes: "For a gift to be a gift, it must feel like one. For it to feel like a gift, it must seem something extra—something beyond what we expect normally" (1989b, 95).

Willingness to undergo repeated trials of IVF, even if they are unsuccessful, seems to be a rational decision for women.[17] Going through IVF proves to themselves, their mates, and family members that they have done everything they could to have a biological child together (Lorber and Greenfeld 1990). These latent gains are what make IVF so popular throughout the world, despite its low success rate of about 15–25 percent in female infertility and zero to 10 percent in male infertility. The discourse of infertility and the new procreative technologies frames personal narratives in terms of social loss, biological pressures, and technological hope (S. Franklin 1990). Hence, doing IVF is often an obligatory rite of passage not only to try to have a child but also to try "to reach a secondary objective as a necessary substitute, that is, protection against social stigmatization and a means to obtain social recognition as an involuntary childless woman" (I. Koch 1990, 240–41). For many women, it is a no-choice "choice."[18]

Who Owns the Child?

The biological parents may not be legally responsible for a child; social fathers and mothers are. Social fathers and mothers may not be the caretakers;

frequently nurses, nannies, and governesses are. In matrilineal societies, the Western father's role is split between the biological father and the mother's brother—the maternal uncle is the social father, legally responsible for his sister's children. In the African-American community, women kin and neighbors mother each other's children, and Latinas act as co-madres (Collins 1990, 118–37).

Not only parenting but fertilization and pregnancy and birth can be split up among several women and men. In one case, a woman donated an ovum that was fertilized in vitro by her brother-in-law's sperm and gestated by his wife, the donor's sister; the gestator and sperm donor were legally named the social parents, and the ovum producer was called "aunt" (Leeton et al. 1986). In another case, one sister donated the ovum, the sperm was donated by a friend, and another sister gestated the fetus; the social parents were the egg donor and her husband; this time, the gestator was called "aunt" (Leeton et al. 1988). In the third case, a woman gave birth to triplets conceived with her daughter's ova and her son-in-law's sperm; these genetic parents were also the social parents, and the gestator was called "grandmother" (Michelow et al. 1988).[19]

Despite all these variations, a "family" in modern Western culture continues to be defined as two parents with one or more children, a social designation that overrides the genetic or physiological connection between the adults and children involved. These social designations determine who is legally responsible for the child's welfare and upbringing and also who has rights to the child. Legitimizing claims to children are the function of reproductive rituals in kin-based societies and custody contests in societies with legal systems. Children are valuable assets in kin-based societies; where clansmen form strong groups, pregnant and birthing women are kept under surveillance or confined to prevent abortions, infanticide, and exchange of infants (Paige and Paige 1981, 167–208). Where men's groups are not strong, a man who wants to make sure his claim to a child will be recognized often engages in couvade—observing food taboos, restriction of work or warfare, and sometimes seclusion during his wife's delivery and immediately after.[20] In modern Western societies, the husband's presence in the delivery room, immediate bonding with the newborn, and staying home from work for a week or two after the birth may be a modern version of couvade, a form of laying claim to a child.

The father in modern Western families still has more rights than responsibilities with regard to children, and the mother has more responsibilities than rights. The husband's wishes often prevail in when and how many children a couple have, even though it is the wife who will bear and care for them (Lorber

1987b). The presumption since the 1920s, however, has been that after divorce, children of "tender years" belong with their mothers, a drastic shift from the nineteenth century, when legally children belonged to their fathers (Derdeyn 1976). Although the tender-years doctrine leaves the children with the mother, it can force her into celibacy and continued economic dependency on her former husband; if she cohabits or leaves the children in someone else's care to take paid employment, she risks being labeled an unfit mother, and the father may sue for custody. More gender-neutral legal approaches consider the best interests of the child or recommend joint custody.[21] However, Geoffrey Greif's survey of 1,136 divorced men who had custody of their children found that there was still a presumption in favor of the mother; only 221 had won a court case. In most of the other cases, the mother relinquished custody or older children chose to live with the father (1985, 36–46). A new approach is to award custody to the parent who is the primary caretaker or to whom the child has a primary attachment, without regard to gender. Thus, demonstration of intimate involvement with a child from birth is no doubt helpful in sustaining men's custody claims in modern society, especially since an "unfit" primary caretaker can be denied custody.[22]

By the late nineteenth century in the United States, the value of children for middle- and upper-class families had become "priceless" (Zelizer 1985). Having only intrinsic value, children were not supposed to be used to benefit their parents; rather, parents were supposed to nurture a child's individuality. From this point of view, making children contribute to the family economy, restricting girls' activities to preserve their virginity, and beating a child for not obeying became instances of child abuse.[23] The worst abuse, however, for which agencies for the prevention of cruelty to children were formed, was neglect, and mothers were held to blame since they were responsible for their children's physical and emotional welfare (L. Gordon 1989). Under conditions of late-nineteenth-century urban immigrant life in the United States and during the 1930s Great Depression, parents were hard-pressed to feed and clothe their children adequately unless mothers as well as fathers earned money. But a mother's absence from the home was defined as abusive neglect, although without her earnings, especially if she was the head of the household, the children would not have adequate food, clothing, or shelter, conditions also defined as abusive neglect. In either case, poverty-stricken mothers, especially if they had no man in the home, "could not conform to norms of domesticity, since they by necessity worked outside the home, or tried to; or their domesticity was suspect because they were paupers, dependent on charity or the state. Failing domesticity, they by definition failed at proper femininity and mothering" (L. Gordon 1989, 84). The outcome was that their children were often made wards of the state and put into charity institutions.

Child Care as Work

If the fragmentation of procreation is a relatively recent phenomenon, the maintenance and socializing of children has long been shared among caretakers and teachers. The work components of early child care are feeding, bathing, dressing, and toilet training; older children must be provided with meals, clothing, and a place to live. The work of socialization entails educating children and sometimes training them to take over their parents' social position. Like other forms of work, these jobs are assigned to people of different statuses and are differentially rewarded: "Historically, amid shifting household and social structures, the tasks of caring for newborn babies have been accomplished through various combinations of parents, family and kin, friends and neighbors, domestic servants, extramural sitters, wet nurses, professionals, industries such as diaper service and home-milk delivery, bureaucratic social agencies, and the product market" (Sussman 1982, 1–2). The economy and ideology of a culture determine the value of children of different social backgrounds and hence the value of the work involved in socially reproducing them.

Child care also produces an emotional relationship between the caretakers and the children, and the work involved is qualitatively different from other forms of work: "One does not (cannot) produce another human being in anything like the way one produces an object such as a chair. Much more is involved, activity that cannot easily be dichotomized into play or work. Helping another to develop, the gradual relinquishing of control, the experiencing of the human limits of one's actions—all these are important features of women's activity as mothers" (Hartsock 1983, 236).[24] This emotional labor may not be highly valued. The culture determines whether the emotional bonding of caring is considered an integral part of good child development or is seen as an incidental by-product that may or may not be useful to the way child care is managed (Eyer 1992; Riley 1983).

Not all full-time mothering is emotionally intense, nor is all intensive mothering done by women. Barbara Risman (1987), in her study of fifty-five men who became single fathers because of their wives' death, desertion, or relinquishment of custody, found that their relationships with their children were as intimate as those of single mothers and mothers in traditional marriages. Although intensive mothering involves attachment and eventual detachment, women who cared for their own and other mothers' children in their own homes had to juggle these emotions simultaneously. Margaret Nelson (1990) found that these care providers, who had stayed home to be with their own children, paid less attention to them than they wanted, and they also had to be careful not to get too emotionally attached to the children they were caring for on a monetary basis.[25]

Why Women Mother

If mother love is not the same the world over and throughout time, why do women do most of the primary child care? Alice Rossi argues that women and not men are genetically programmed to invest time and energy in child care (1977, 1984). In her original argument about the biosocial origins of women's parenting, Rossi linked the hormonal input during pregnancy and lactation to the development of mother-child bonding and child-care skills.[26] In a later paper, Rossi placed more emphasis on male and female styles of parenting, which she claimed are "rooted in basic sexual dimorphism" that gives women greater sensitivity and consequent fine-tuned acuity to infants' cues for attention. It is not giving birth, she felt, that makes women instinctively better parents than men but their overall physiological makeup. Men, however, could receive compensatory training that would make them better parents than they would be naturally. But even if men and women do share parenting equally, Rossi argues, it will not erase the biosocial differences: "Men bring their maleness to parenting, as women bring their femaleness" (Rossi, 1984, 10). When men parent *alone* as single parents, however, they exhibit a range of involvement and competence, even with young children (Greif 1985, 73–86).[27] It therefore could be argued that what seems like a natural aptitude for parenting in women is the result of their doing it so much more frequently and consistently than men.

Nancy Chodorow, in *The Reproduction of Mothering* (1978), relied on psychoanalytic object relations theory to explain why women want to mother and why most are good mothers. Chodorow argues that since women are the primary parents, the emotional bond between them and their daughters is not severed in the same way that the emotional bond between sons and their mothers is in the resolution of the Oedipus complex. Girls do not develop such strong ego boundaries, and therefore, when they grow up, they find it easier to bond with *their* children, thus reproducing the same mother-child bond they had early in life. Boys, on the other hand, develop strong ego boundaries in the process of distancing themselves from their mothers in order to solidify their masculine identity. Getting involved in intensive child care can elicit disturbing emotions in men. Lynne Segal notes that some men have expressed a psychological fear of fatherhood: "The intense emotions aroused in men watching childbirth and handling infants take them back to the emotionality, generalized sensuality and tenderness of childhood so utterly tabooed in most areas of adult masculinity. Fatherhood can thus threaten men's whole perceptions of themselves as adults, arousing jealousy and anxieties of inadequacy, leaving them feeling tired, confused, vulnerable, insecure and rejected" (1990, 42).[28]

Women also feel incompetent and emotionally vulnerable as new mothers (Oakley 1980), but they want to take care of a child because their relationships with the significant men in their lives are not too satisfying. According to Chodorow, women cannot get the emotional bonding they want from men, but they can from their children:

> As a result of being parented by a woman, both sexes are looking for a return to this emotional and physical union. A man achieves this directly through the heterosexual bond which replicates for him emotionally the early mother-infant exclusivity which he seeks to recreate. He is supported in this endeavor by women, who, through their own development, have remained open to relational needs, have retained an ongoing inner affective life, and have learned to deny the limitations of masculine lovers for both psychological and practical reasons. (Chodorow 1976, 464)

Women's more permeable ego boundaries make them more open to their children's needs, and they are therefore the better parent. The psychological patterns Chodorow describes reproduce the gendered division of child care in families with heterosexual parents, but lesbians who have deep and intense relationships with women also want children, as do homosexual men.[29] Furthermore, the involvement of fathers in parenting varies enormously in societies throughout the world.

What Do Fathers Do?

For Western culture, consider the typical scenario for fathers' initial involvement with their newborns once hospital births became common in the 1920s.[30] The wife, upon realizing she had missed a period, would see her doctor alone. She would announce the impending event to her husband and then consult her mother and other women about prenatal care and layettes. During the birth, she would be in the care of the medical staff, who delivered her child, using anesthetics, episiotomies, and often forceps. The husband would be pacing the floor of the waiting room. When the doctor announced the birth and the sex of the child, the father rushed back to work or to his friends or a bar, passing out cigars. He would take a day off from work to bring his wife and baby home, and all the rest, except perhaps for some middle-of-the-night bottles, would be up to her.

In the typical scenario today for many young couples, both husband and wife hover over a home pregnancy test and then go off together to tour the birthing center or obstetrics floor of a hospital. They practice breathing together in prenatal classes and view the fetus on a sonogram (learning the sex). He is present at the birth, usually as coach, and she is a conscious and full participant in pushing out the baby even though she has a fetal monitor strapped around her abdomen. The father holds the newborn, sometimes before the mother, and takes time off from work for a week or two to help care for and bond with the infant. He tries to be present for breast-feeding and frequently takes the baby walking in a sling or pram.

In both scenarios, what is expected and routinized constructs the birth and parenting experience for both the woman and the man; these norms also define womanhood and manhood. Sonia Jackson notes: "The presence of the father at birth is now so clearly expected in Britain that it is probably as hard for a man to stay out of the delivery room as it was for him to get in only a decade ago" (1987, 37).[31]

Men's involvement in pregnancy and birth in Western societies, however, has not resulted in equal responsibility for child care. The mother still does most of the work not because she is more nurturing or competent but because the culture ideologically and practically structures women's and men's parenting behavior and the time spent in paid work (Shelton 1992). Commenting on modern fathers, Lynne Segal says that all the research shows "a change in men's *attitudes* towards childcare, a change in their *experiences* of fatherhood, and . . . a change in psychological perspectives on the importance of the father's role. What proves harder to find is convincing evidence that there has been a change in the amount of practical work men actually do as fathers" (1990, 33).

Michael Lamb (1987), in assessing the amount of child care performed by fathers throughout the world, notes that there are three levels of a caretaker's involvement with children: *accessibility*—or being on call near the child but not directly engaged in care; *direct interaction or one-on-one care*—holding, feeding, bathing, dressing, playing with, helping with homework, reading to the child, and so on; and *responsibility*—continually thinking about the child's

emotional, social, and physical development and welfare, and making arrangements for babysitting, sick care, doctor visits, school visits, and playtime.
Responsibility is the work that in postindustrial Western society most typifies
what mothers do as opposed to what fathers do: "It is hard to quantify the time
involved, particularly because the anxiety, worry, and contingency-planning
that comprise parental responsibility often occur when the parent is ostensibly
doing something else" (Lamb 1987, 8).

Lamb found that in two-parent families in the United States in which
mothers did not work outside the home, fathers spent about 20 to 25 percent
of the time that mothers spent in direct interaction with children, and about a
third of the time in being accessible. They assumed no responsibility for
children's care or rearing. In two-parent families where both mothers and
fathers were employed thirty or more hours a week, fathers interacted with
children 33 percent of the time that mothers did and were accessible 65
percent of the time that mothers were, but they assumed no more responsibility for children's welfare than when mothers were full-time homemakers.
In fact, the higher proportional level of their day-to-day child care was due to
employed mothers' spending less time with the children; it did not reflect
more actual time spent with children by the father.[32] The overall pattern for all
regions, ethnic groups, and religions in the United States was that fathers spent
more time with sons than with daughters and were more likely to play with
them than do things for them.

Cross-nationally, in Western societies, fathers' involvement in child care
ranges from almost none to some. The description of fathers' and mothers'
interaction with newborn infants in a traditional Italian village sounds like a
sitcom of the bumbling, all-thumbs father and competent wife surrounded and
backed up by women relatives (New and Benigni 1987). Whatever fathers did,
even when it was done well, was ignored, ridiculed, or done over. The women
were full-time homemakers, and mothering was their highly praised role.

In countries where fathers give a hand, such as Ireland, England, Australia,
Israel, and the United States, all change diapers, put the baby to bed, and
comfort the baby during the night.[33] A study of forty-eight Irish infants and
their families found that when their babies were one month old, 15 percent of
the fathers regularly got the baby up in the morning, and 26 percent did so at
one year; 46 percent put a new baby to bed, and 21 percent, the one-year-old;
3 percent dressed the baby in the morning, but none did so for the older child;
48 percent changed the newborn's diapers, and 35 percent, the one-year-
old's; 4 percent took the new baby for a walk, and 15 percent, the older child
(Nugent 1987, 182–83). More than half fed and sang to their new babies, a

third soothed them at night, and almost all talked to, played with, and picked them up when they were crying during the day. This behavior stayed about the same through the infants' first year.

What could encourage fathers to be more involved in child care? First, just doing it produces skills, ease, and confidence, so it's been suggested that mothers have to be willing to give up some of their power and authority in this area.[34] Work organizations could make it possible for fathers to spend more time with their children. In Sweden, however, where parental leave is offered to fathers as well as mothers, most men do not alternate taking extended time off with the mothers of their children. Swedish fathers or mothers can take parental leave for the first year of their child's life, with nine months almost fully compensated. Parents get child sick leave at 90 percent compensation, and either can reduce his or her working time up to two hours a day, with a reduction in pay, until the child is eight years old. In addition, fathers of newborns may stay home for ten days at 90 percent pay.[35] In 1986, about 85 percent of men took advantage of the ten "daddy days," but only 27 percent took paid leave from their jobs to care for the new baby on a long-term basis (Haas 1991; Moen 1989, 26). In the Nordic countries, men who share the extended parental leave tend to be one of three types—husband of high-earning women with intensive commitment to their work; young fathers not yet in the labor force, such as students (but their wives have to be working for the family to get the paid leave time); or older fathers whose position in the labor market is very secure (Kaul 1991).

Flexible schedules might be a more acceptable way to structure fathering than extended time away from a job. But in Sweden, in 1977, married men with children worked the longest average day. One-third of the men with children under seven worked over ten hours a day, whether their wife was employed full or part time (C. P. Hwang 1987, 171).[36] The men with the most negative attitudes toward sharing parental leave were self-employed or worked mostly with men; the more positively oriented worked mostly with women. In general, employers were not enthusiastic about men taking parental leave, although most of the men who did so did not experience negative reactions on their return, and many of their bosses and coworkers were openly positive about it.

Although more recent data indicate a bit more involvement of Swedish men in child care (Sandqvist 1992), what Carl Philip Hwang concludes has not changed: "In reality, many Swedish fathers do not want to stay home" (1987, 130). The reason may be that they do not get much payoff from it, socially or psychologically. Hwang studied seventeen men who took parental leave of about three months when their first child was around five months old. He found no difference in their relationship with their children when he compared them with fathers who did not stay home at all. The children preferred their mothers whether or not they had stayed home and whether or not the fathers had stayed home. But, it should be noted, the mothers had taken care of the children from birth and had stayed home longer than the fathers had. However, he also found no difference in the mothers' relationship with the children when he compared those who did and did not stay home after the birth. In all cases, the mothers "were consistently more affectionate. . . . They talked to them, smiled, and laughed more often; they performed more activities to care for the child; and they held the child more than the fathers did" (131). Good effects of fathers' greater involvement with children are more likely to come from the double attention a child gets, from mothers being able to pursue a career or other interests, and from the mutually supportive family context that emerges.

A similar range of paternal involvement occurs in nonindustrialized societies, but fathers' help is more direct. A study of child care among the Aka Pygmies used variations in holding infants and small children as "a direct form of paternal investment, an observable and, consequently, a measurable behavior essential to the survival of the Aka infant" (Hewlett 1987, 295). The Aka Pygmies live in camps of about twenty-five to thirty-five people, related patrilineally or by marriage. They spend 56 percent of the time net-hunting moderate-sized animals, 27 percent gathering vegetable food, and 17 percent in village work for another tribe. Most of the camp members, men and women, young and old, participate in net hunts. The study group comprised fifteen families with infants between one and eighteen months old. Eight of the children were girls, and seven were boys. In 264 hours of observation, fathers held infants 8.7 percent of the time. In the base camp, where infants one to four months old were held all the time, the mother held them 51 percent of the time, the father 22 percent of the time, and others 27 percent of the time. On net hunts, mothers held children of all ages almost 90 percent of the time they were held, and that was almost all the time. Fathers held infants 6.5 percent and older children 2.4 percent of the time. Fathers held infants on the way home, since the mothers carried the meat. This reciprocity is only one of the husband-wife exchanges in this culture, and Barry Hewlett argues that the greater the number of such exchanges, the greater the likelihood that fathers will do child care (1992).

In the camps, the fathers held the children, usually carrying on a conversation with other adult men, while the mothers were busy collecting firewood or preparing a meal. Neither mothers nor fathers voluntarily picked up an infant; they were handed the child, or the child initiated the attention. Mothers picked up infants to care for them; fathers because the infant gestured or called to be picked up. *Others* picked up children because they felt like it. Yet fathers almost as well as mothers knew "the early signs of infant hunger, fatigue, and illness—as well as the limits in their ability to soothe the infant" (320). "Fathers also: offered their nipple to the infant when the infant tried to nurse, often cleaned dirt from the infant's nose, chest, and hair as they held the infant; picked lice from their hair; cleaned mucus from their nose; and cleaned them after they urinated or defecated (often on the father)" (326).

How much a father held an infant depended on whether the child was under a year old, was the firstborn, and whether the father lived with the mother and child, all of which tended to be correlated with his being a younger man. Another important factor was status. Fathers who invested highly in their children tended to have no brothers, few other relatives, late and monogamous marriages, wives from distant clans who had no kin in the group, small hunting nets, few hunting companions, and low status. High-status fathers invested more time in status maintenance—visiting other camps and talking with other men—than in child care. For fathers with fewer social resources, children were more valuable.

Shared Parenting

When a couple truly shares parenting, the result is that the child has two primary caretakers (Ehrensaft 1987). Although some parents end up sharing parenting because each holds a full-time job, for parents who share by choice, it is a deliberate effort to give the child a more gender-neutral upbringing not by having each parent do exactly the same thing but by dividing chores and the time spent with the child equitably.[37] Thus, where the mother breast-feeds, the father changes the diapers and walks the floor with a baby who doesn't want to go back to sleep right away.

The middle-class urban and academic couples whom Diane Ehrensaft (1987) studied found it easy to divide the *work,* but the mothers tended to take on more of the psychological and emotional management, particularly the "worrying," partly because they were brought up to be emotion managers. Women feel on call for their children all the time; men do not. Men can more easily distance themselves from their children, letting them cry, not paying attention to their every move, and not thinking about them at work. On the other hand, another father, writing of his own experiences, felt that he was the worrier, not his wife:

> I am far guiltier of the stereotypical vices of motherhood—the neuro-
> tic worry about Hannah's physical and mental well being, unfounded

premonitions of danger, excessive emotional demands, and general nudginess—than is Gail. In short, my experiences—ignoring for the moment a vast ethnographic and somewhat smaller historical litera-ture—make me suspect the naturalness of "mother" or "father" in any culturally meaningful sense. (Laqueur 1990b, 209)

The women Ehrensaft interviewed felt that the boundaries between them-selves and their child were fluid, and they had to struggle to maintain their own autonomy. The men she interviewed said they had literally fallen in love with their children and wanted to be with them because they were so fascinating and lovable. The intensity of the men's feelings for their children reversed the conventional parental triangle; instead of the fathers being jealous of the time the mothers spent with the children, wives felt left out of the father-child "couple" (1990, 150–58). Ehrensaft argues that, socially, women *are* mothers; men *do* fathering (1987, 93–117). One outcome of women's identification of themselves as mothers was their concern for how their children were dressed. A father would dress his child in whatever was at hand; the mother carefully put together appropriate attractive outfits because the way the child looked in school and at parties and family gatherings reflected upon her, not him (59–65).

Scott Coltrane's study of twenty dual-earner couples who shared the care of older children found that the fathers felt they were being socialized as adults to become nurturing parents (1989). They felt they were learning to "con-struct and sustain images of themselves as competent fathers" (483). But they had started out with the expectation they could be nurturant, and "the success-ful practice of sharing child care facilitated the development of beliefs that men could nurture like women" (485). In contrast, Barbara Risman interviewed men who became single parents out of necessity because their wives had died or left them with the children (1987). These single fathers became "mothers" whose relationships with their children were intimate and nurturing. Men who parent in this manner are considered unusual in modern societies, as are women who invest more time and energy in their careers than in their children. But the men who "mother" get praised for doing something excep-tional; the women who "father" are criticized for denying their "essential nature" as women.

A Labor of Love

The current construction of motherhood in Western cultures claims that women naturally feel unconditional love for their children and want to nurture them, especially when they are babies. But the phenomenon we call mothering is a learned experience, and the doing of it by anyone develops skills, competence, and emotional relationships. As Barbara Katz Rothman says:

> Mothering, like everything else in life, is best learned by doing. I think that the mothering women have done has taught many of us skills of listening to what is said and to what is not said. I think in mothering we hone our empathic abilities, learn to understand the vulnerability in others without profiting from it. I think that the experience of mothering teaches people how to be more emotionally and intellectually nurturant, how to take care of each other. It is not the only way we learn that lesson, but it is hard to mother and not learn it. (1989, 226)

Women who have prime responsibility for child care, even though they may work full time outside the home, must live part of their lives in a world of reciprocity and cooperation, personal responsibility and sharing, physical contact and affection—a gemeinschaft world.[38] Talcott Parsons's (1951, 45–67) analysis of role patterns in modern societies reflects the shift from gemeinschaft—close-knit, face-to-face, personalized social relationships—to gesellschaft—fragmented, scattered, impersonal social interaction. The patterned characteristics of what he called gemeinschaft or socioemotional roles are ascribed statuses, particularistic standards of competence, diffuse functions, affective relationships, and collectivity orientation. The patterned characteristics of what he called gesellschaft or instrumental roles are achieved statuses, universalistic standards of competence, task-specific functions, affectively neutral relationships, and an individualistic orientation. Instrumental roles allow individuals to garner the rewards of well-defined work measured by recognized standards. In modern society, instrumental roles are the way to succeed in the workplace or political life. Socioemotional roles are not chosen; the work they entail is never-ending; rewards depend on personalized standards; and others come first. They typify family work: "How much house cleaning discharges the moral duty of marriage?" (Acker 1988, 488).

But married women's main responsibility in modern society is not just to keep the house clean; it is to create psychological well-being for family members on a daily basis, a sense of kinship among extended family members during holidays and on ritual occasions, and sociability when friends are invited into the home (di Leonardo 1987). This combination of material and socioemotional labor differentiates women's and men's consciousness. Nancy Hartsock (1983, 231–51) contrasts men's intermittent and often abstract connection to the material reality of everyday life with women's deeper unity of body and mind, emotion and thought:

Masculinity must be attained by means of opposition to the concrete world of daily life, by escaping from contact with the female world of the household into the masculine world of politics or public life. . . . Women's construction of self in relation to others leads in an opposite direction—toward . . . valuation of the concrete, everyday life; a sense of a variety of connectednesses and continuities both with other persons and with the natural world. (1983, 241, 242).[39]

Women's sense of caring and responsibility for others is therefore the *result*, not the cause, of gendered parenting (Rothman, 1989, 226–27). Through their practiced skill at picking up the cues of the needs of others, women are psychologically coopted into wanting to be good mothers, and both the competence and the feelings become a significant part of being a "good woman." This pattern depends on her having adequate material resources for the care of her children and the time to give to psychological nurturance. When men spend time taking care of children, they, too, become nurturant, but they usually do not take complete responsibility for parenting unless they are single fathers, and it does not define them as men.

As family members, heterosexual men in postindustrial Western societies may be as emotionally invested in their mothers as in their wives, fathers, siblings, or friends, but given the norms of masculinity, they are supposed to declare their independence (Rossi and Rossi 1990, 13–14). Some heterosexual men are emotional wanderers, leaving a bit of themselves in many women's households—their mothers', their sisters', their wives', their lovers' (Stack 1975). Other men, especially in countries with a high divorce rate, may resemble rogue elephants, roaming alone, looking for mates with whom to have children. By having biological children in short- or long-term relationships or becoming social fathers to the children of the women they love, heterosexual men hope to obtain heirs, old-age care, and a modicum of immortality. More immediately and directly, they also receive nurturance that helps them thrive physically and emotionally. In modern industrial societies, women's nurturing increases men's life span, improves their mental health, and contributes substantially to their physical health (Gove 1982). Women give their attention and concern to men as well as to children, who cannot thrive without it. But since most men have not learned how to nurture others, women also have to nurture the elderly, the sick, and anyone else in their social milieu who needs tender, loving care (Rossi and Rossi 1990, 495–96).

In sum, the ideology of the good mother has significant latent functions for *men*. Full-time or part-time motherhood for women implies some economic dependence on a man, whose manhood is linked to being economically successful enough to support a wife and children. Gendered parenting thus justifies women's inferior position in the paid labor market. In return for the economic support he provides, a man gets progeny carrying his name, to whom his class values have been transmitted (Kohn 1963; Kohn and Slomczynski 1990, 171–201). The social order that elevates men over women is legitimated by women's devotion to child care, since it takes them out of the running for top-level jobs and political positions and defuses their consciousness of oppression.

Women's decisions to either undergo IVF or not to have children, to have only one because the state limits fertility or ten because their religion prohibits contraception, to care for them personally or have others care for them, to watch them starve or abandon them, to abort children they are not ready for or give them up for adoption, to have amniocentesis and either bear a child with a genetic defect or abort it—these are all no-choice choices, given away by the words "my only choice" or "I had no other choice" (Rothman 1986, 177–216). That's not choice; rather, it is facing an inevitable loss one way or the other and taking moral responsibility for which loss it will be: an aborted fetus or a severely retarded child, feeding one healthy child and starving the sickly one or letting both waste away, aborting a female fetus or losing a husband and home, not having a child and getting an education or having a baby and going on welfare. These choices, for which social groups hold individual women responsible, are not true choices because of lack of services for the disabled, lack of food for the poor, lack of help for single parents, and the overall devaluation of women.

Virginia Held notes that birth and death are natural events transformed into human events because they are imbued with choice, awareness, and imaginative representation:

> Questions of what to give birth for, like questions of what to die for, or questions of what to live for, can be asked even when women have no more control over childbirth than the possibility of refusing to give birth through extreme risk to themselves. . . . Men (and women) can die out of loyalty, out of duty, out of commitment, and they can die for a better future. Women can give birth, or refuse to give birth, from all these motives and others. . . . That women can give birth for reasons should make it clear how very *unlike* a natural, biological event a human birth is. (1989, 366)

But in the social construction of birthing and parenting, women do not have full control over their choices. In societies where men are dominant, they have veto power over women's procreation choices (K. O. Mason 1985; Polatnick 1983). The powerless over and over again feel they have no choices; they will suffer no matter what they choose.[40] Theirs are "Sophie's choices": To save one child from the gas chamber, Sophie, in William Styron's novel, condemns the other to death. She snatches what she can from a social order in which she has very little power to act. Through mothering, modern women support men's dominance. Their willingness to do so for the sake of their sense of self as a woman and the love they have for their children and the men in their lives does not belie the covert coercion to put men's and children's interests before their own.

Domestic labor is not essentially "feminine work"; a woman doesn't fulfill herself more or get less exhausted than a man from washing and cleaning. These are social services inasmuch as they serve the reproduction of labor power.

—*Mariarosa Dalla Costa (1973, 31–32)*

DAILY BREAD:
GENDER AND DOMESTIC LABOR

In this generation of young adults in Western cultures, in households of all men or all women, domestic work is usually rotated or divided fairly equitably. Male homosexual couples tend to take into consideration the time spent in paid work to decide how much housework each does, and lesbians try to divide housework scrupulously equally (Blumstein and Schwartz 1983, 144–54). Heterosexual women and men parcel out domestic tasks to each roommate when they are living in single-gender households. But when they move in with an opposite-gender partner, they often fall into conventional patterns of task allocation that have little to do with how much paid work each does—she cooks, cleans, and shops; he looks after the car and changes the light bulbs. Even married men who like to dress in women's clothes rarely do housework when they are being women (Woodhouse 1989, 94).

The gendered structure of work in modern societies is familiar and seemingly ubiquitous—men do paid work and women do housework. So are the assumed reasons—women bear children and take care of them, so they logically should take care of men's physical and emotional needs as well. Men, because they don't bear children, are responsible for working at a job or running a business to provide the financial support for their wife and children. This neat complementarity assumes a heterosexual, nuclear family household and high enough wages or profits on the part of the male earner to support the whole family. This "ideal family" is achieved by very few people (Baca Zinn 1990).

Family structures and household composition are diverse, and women as well as men (and many children, too) do both paid work and unpaid domestic work.[1] Furthermore, all kinds of activities can be done for family members out of love, kindness, or a sense of duty, or as a regular paid job or a sideline, just as volunteers often do work for which others get paid (Daniels 1987). Domestic work—the labor of physically maintaining a household and those who live in it—has been done without pay by slaves, by loving and not-so-loving kin, and by members of communes, and with pay by servants and professionals (Oakley 1976; Rollins 1985, 21–59). All these domestic workers, paid and unpaid, have been men as well as women. In short, paid and unpaid work is not divided so neatly between the home and workplace, nor is paid and unpaid work so clearly gendered. Yet, within these blurred boundaries, there are gendered patterns—among them, that women tend to do more unpaid domestic work than men do. This pattern is not the result of sex differences in procreation. Women do most of the unpaid work whether or not they have children, and child care is only one part of women's work for their families.

What must be explained is why unpaid domestic work in particular has become a primary responsibility of almost all women in modern societies. Domestic work did not always have the characteristics or the low status it has today. In nonindustrialized societies, household production is necessary for the survival of the family, and both women and men are expected to grow and process food, make tools and implements, weave cloth, make clothes—in short, produce what the members of the household consume. In industrialized societies, keeping a household going, though necessary, has lost its salience; many of the goods and services provided by housewives can be purchased. In fact, the more prosperous the household, the more domestic labor is done by paid workers, not unpaid household members. This principle, that those who have the resources buy their way out of unpaid domestic work, explains why it is women, not men, who do most of the domestic work in modern families— they have fewer economic resources. And the low social value placed on domestic work explains why, when domestic laborers are hired, they tend to be members of the most disadvantaged social groups. But even when women have the resources to buy household help, they tend to retain responsibility for the work, as an indication of their love and concern for their family's welfare.

Domestic Work and Its Value

Domestic work has two major aspects, subsistence production and social reproduction. *Subsistence production* is the provision of food, clothing, and shelter for use by family members or those living in the same household (who may or may not be related by birth, marriage, or adoption). Domestic production, when it is done by household members to produce things they eat, wear, and use in daily living, is usually not compensated with wages or a salary. It is *use-value work*. The same work—cooking, cleaning, doing laundry, and other household maintenance tasks—can also be done for wages. The monetary value of such labor depends on the job market and the structure of the work (part time versus full time, live-in versus day work, professionally trained versus trained on the job).

In modern societies, the wife, the family member most likely to do use-value domestic work for no pay, resembles the highest paid servant—full time, live-in, and skilled—but the housewife-mother does much more than the paid servant.[2] In addition to transforming wages into food, clothing, and shelter and minding the children, her domestic duties include nurturing and teaching the children, giving them and the adults in the household emotional support, and having sexual relations with her husband. Her domestic work frequently also includes caring for sick and elderly family members, maintaining kinship and friendship ties and obligations, entertaining family members and other guests, and, in prosperous families, enhancing the status of her family through conspicuous consumption and service in philanthropic, cultural, and political organizations. The mother often links the family to bureaucratic institutions, such as schools and child welfare agencies.[3]

This expansion of domestic work beyond housework and child care turns it into *social reproduction* or "renewing life as a form of work, a kind of production, as fundamental to the perpetuation of society as the production of things" (Laslett and Brenner 1989, 383). Social reproduction includes

> the activities and attitudes, behaviors, and emotions, responsibilities and relationships directly involved in the maintenance of life on a daily basis, and intergenerationally. Among other things, social reproduction includes how food, clothing, and shelter are made available for immediate consumption, the ways in which the care and socialization of children are provided, the care of the infirm and elderly, and the social organization of sexuality. Social reproduction can thus be seen to include various kinds of work—mental, manual, and emotional—aimed at providing the historically and socially, as well as biologically, defined care necessary to maintain existing life and to reproduce the next generation. (382–83)

Social reproduction is maintaining family members not just physically and emotionally but also socially. Part of social reproduction is preserving and passing on the family's cultural capital to children—style of life, religious and ethnic rituals, and social position (Bourdieu and Passeron [1970] 1977).

Social reproduction and production of goods and services, either unpaid as use-value or paid at market value, are the main divisions of work. Both women and men do production work for pay as well as unpaid social reproduction and use-value work for their family. Men do social reproduction by training sons to do men's work and by engaging in status-producing activities for their families, and many do use-value domestic work, such as repairs, gardening, and even housework. Paid production work and unpaid domestic work jointly support each other, and each has undergone major historical transformations.[4] These transformations have affected how paid and unpaid work is divided between women and men—especially who does domestic work.

Who Doesn't Do Domestic Labor

The present gendered division of labor, where women do paid work but are primarily responsible for housework and child care, is considered a normal and natural outcome of women's procreative capabilities or feminine skills and personality. In actuality, it is the result of historical developments and transformations in technology, the gendered division of different kinds of labor, and the production and control of wealth (Huber 1990). Despite a rhetoric that glorifies women's role in the home and the family, the allocation of most unpaid domestic work and nurturance to women has significant economic and social benefits for men and is exploitive of women's time and energy (Delphy and Leonard 1992). The arrangement may seem natural, but it is the result of the systematic deprivation of married women's rights to control their own property, profits, and wages.

In kinship-based societies, where the family is a work unit and the household is the workplace, those who control any surplus can get others to do all or most of their share of the work (H. L. Moore 1989, 54–62). Those women in the most disadvantaged bargaining position—junior wives and the wives of men with few resources—are therefore likely to do most of the unremunerated production of food, clothing, and shelter. Women in some kin-based societies, however, have considerable bargaining power (Kandiyoti 1988). Where women and men have separate sources of income, as in East and West Africa, husbands and wives are equal bargainers over who should do unremunerated family work, and "conflicts often emerge between spouses as they try to balance the demands of family labor against the time and resources necessary for their individual projects and enterprises" (H. L. Moore 1989, 56).[5]

Before the industrialization of Europe and the United States, and in most developing countries today, producing food, clothing, and shelter was and is use-value work done by and for household members. Any work done for trading or for selling in the marketplace was also done by household members. In farming families, everyone had to contribute to the production of food, clothing, and shelter, including mothers of young children, but since the work was done in the household, it was compatible with child care (Tilly and Scott 1978). Although different tasks were allocated to women and to men, when a lot of work had to get done in a short time or women or men had extra time, they worked together, in both agricultural production and household chores (K. V. Hansen 1989). On large plantations, enslaved women did domestic work for the master's family and for their own, and they also did strenuous work in the fields alongside enslaved men.[6] In towns and cities, artisans who produced goods for sale and shopkeepers, inn keepers, and other providers of services for payment were both women and men, and the workplace was the family's residence.[7] Domestic work and child care were done by women and men servants or older children as well as by the adult women of the household.

With increasing industrialization, more and more goods and services were produced for profit in work that capitalists gradually moved out of the home and into factories and offices. The workers were, in sequence, daughters of farm families, women and children or whole families, and then men and women hired as individuals (Kessler-Harris 1982; Kasson 1976). Initially, production of goods for family use, such as cloth, continued to take place in the home and the surplus was sold or bartered. In the eighteenth century, home industries expanded, with middlemen supplying raw materials and machinery that could be used in the home by adult women and men, helped by children. Since these workers lived in barely furnished cottages, domestic work was minimal (B. Hill 1989, 103–24).

When land began to be used for cash crops, men were the main agricultural workers. Wives did kitchen gardening, kept fowl, and did all the cooking for the farm workers. Daughters went to work in factories or in other people's houses. Families who lost their farms went to work in factories as a family and lived in rented furnished rooms. Once capitalist production was widespread, women and men became rivals for the better-paid jobs. After a long series of conflicts over who would get these jobs, the men prevailed, and women's main responsibility became unpaid domestic work, although many single and married women, including mothers, continued to do paid work as well.

The rise of the bourgeoisie and the ascendance of capitalism in Europe from the seventeenth century on shifted the source of wealth from land to accruing capital. Since wealth increasingly depended on business enterprises, men, to be successful, had to devote more of their time to making money (Davidoff and Hall 1987). Wives and daughters worked in the family businesses; in the most prosperous families, they devoted their time to status-enhancing activities for the family. Men and women servants did the domestic work for bourgeois households, including taking physical care of the children.

In Europe and the United States, until the late nineteenth century, married women's rights to own and control property were severely circumscribed (Holcombe 1983). As Jan Pahl has noted: "The husband who stood in church and promised 'with all my worldly goods I thee endow' was in truth taking possession of his wife's goods and all her future earnings because until the late nineteenth century marriage marked the point at which a woman's property passed into the hands of her husband" (1989, 11). Without control of her own money, a middle-class wife did what her husband wanted, whether it was running his household, helping out in his business, dressing beautifully to show off his wealth, or turning over the profits from her business. What she was not likely to do was domestic labor. That was servant's work.

Working-class husbands controlled not property but the better jobs and their wives' wages. Once food was no longer raised on family farms, several (if not all) family members had to work for wages and pool their income in order to live. At the beginning of the era of industrialization, men workers had the advantage of organizational skills and political power, which allowed them eventually to monopolize the better-paid jobs (Hartmann 1976, 147–69). With greater control of economic resources, they could command the labor of other members of the family.

In England, under the putting-out system, home industries provided work for women and men in the home, where men were legally in control as heads of households; when the work was moved under one roof in factories so workers could be supervised, men sent their wives and children to work and were legally entitled to claim their wages; finally, men were recruited for the factories, where, as supervisors of women's and children's work, they were paid higher wages (Hartmann 1976, 152; Marglin 1978). Since everyone did productive work, domestic work was shared, if it was done at all. Working-class homes were small and meagerly furnished. Domestic work, which included hauling water and fuel from central sources to the home, was women's and children's responsibility, although men also pitched in (B. Hill 1989, 103–24).[8]

By the time married women had gained control of their own earnings at the end of the nineteenth century, the working-class man was agitating for the *family wage,* pay that would be high enough to support a wife and children, so that the wife could become a full-time homemaker.[9] The concept of the family wage "meant that a just wage for men was necessarily higher than a just wage for women. The wage gap, in other words, was essential to implementing the ideal of a family wage" (Acker 1988, 481).[10] The concept of a family wage reduced working-class women's status as wage workers and as family members. Without an income, or with a lesser income that belonged to the family, and with no recognition of the worth of her unpaid domestic labor, the wife did not exchange domestic services for her husband's economic support as an equal: "The husband's pay legally belongs to him and appears to be produced only by him, even though the wife's domestic labor has contributed to his ability to work and in some cases to the work itself" (Acker 1988, 487).

As long as the husband is the primary wage earner, the wife has no control over his job decisions, but her responsibility for maintaining the home allows him veto power over where, when, and how much she works outside the home. The result has been the perpetuation of women's lesser earning power and larger responsibility for domestic work:

> Low wages keep women dependent on men because they encourage women to marry. Married women must perform domestic chores for their husbands. Men benefit, then, from both higher wages and the domestic division of labor. This domestic division of labor, in turn, acts to weaken women's position in the labor market. Thus, the hierarchical domestic division of labor is perpetuated by the labor market, and vice versa. This process is the present outcome of two interlocking systems, capitalism and patriarchy. . . . The resulting mutual accommodation between patriarchy and capitalism has created a vicious circle for women. (Hartmann 1976, 139)

This interdependency is lost, however, if the husband cannot earn enough to support a family. Even a part-time job improves the bargaining power of the working-class wife whose husband is unemployed for long periods, since her earnings often keep the family out of welfare (Wheelock 1990, 148).

It was not until well into the twentieth century that the middle-class housewife did her own housework, took care of her own children, and was also responsible for maintaining family status and kinship connections. The pattern of women's economic dependence on the earnings of one man and a rigid division of paid work and family work did not occur in working-class households or in African-American middle-class households in the United States (Baca Zinn 1990). In those households, women continued to contribute to family income through paid work before and after they had children, and they also maintained the household and took care of the social and emotional needs of its members. The working-class and African-American pattern is the prevailing pattern for women in industrialized countries today. They are compelled to contribute substantially to family income in order to buy the consumer goods the modern household relies on, while at the same time continuing their domestic work (J. Smith 1987).

The chief difference between working-class and middle-class families today is that middle-class women may have enough surplus income to purchase domestic services provided by women who are recent immigrants or members of disadvantaged racial ethnic groups.[11] Upper-class women and men with control of enormous financial resources can devote much of their time to enhancing their prestige and power. Upper-class men's status-enhancing activities tend to increase their wealth and allow them to wield political power, but upper-class women tend to produce status for their husbands, their families, and their communities, not for themselves (Daniels 1988; Ostrander 1984). Their homes are maintained by cadres of servants, and their children are cared for by nannies.

The Angel in the House

The shift from household-based production mostly for family use to profit-making production under the control of capitalists and physically separated from the household privatized and demeaned domestic labor. The Industrial Revolution gradually separated the factory, shop, and office from the household and turned family farms into agribusinesses. Products that had been made at home or grown on the family farm were commodified and had to be bought for home use, but workers' wages were kept low to increase profits (D. E. Smith 1987b). Workers therefore could not buy all of their food, clothing, and shelter ready-made; they had to turn their wages or salaries into food and clothing through additional work—cooking and sewing—and they had to maintain their clothing and household goods through washing, ironing, and cleaning (Boydston 1986). Although necessary and certainly work by any standards, housework by the end of the nineteenth century had been made invisible by not being counted as work in census or economic data in Europe, the United States, and Australia (Folbre 1991). Children could no longer be watched while production was going on. They could, however, be cared for by the person who cooked, cleaned, and did the laundry, who was likely to be a working-class wife and mother. Since housework was not considered real work, child care and the emotional sustenance of all the family were publicly perceived as married women's main work.

The ideology that exalted women's domestic role in creating the home as a refuge from the ruthless public world of commerce reached its heyday in the nineteenth century, undermining feminists' demands for women's rights to control their own property and wages, sign contracts, and keep the profits from their business enterprises.[12] The glorification of the economically dependent wife applied only to middle- and upper-class women whose husbands could fully support their families: "For a middle-class woman of the early nineteenth century, gentility was coming to be defined by a special form of femininity which ran directly counter to acting as a visibly independent economic agent. Despite the fact that women could [now] hold property, their marital status always pre-empted their economic personality" (Davidoff and Hall 1987, 315). These "pure women residing in pristine homes" (Palmer 1989, 137) depended on the dirty work of poor women to do the actual domestic labor: "These oppositional ideas of womanhood—as angelic or slatternly, frail or strong, virginal or sexual, served or serving—have been connected with images of home and the organization of housework since the mid-nineteenth century. . . . At the simplest, ladies were *clean* and servants were *dirty*" (Palmer 1989, 16, 146). The servants who did the work were not expected to have families of their own; if they had children, they boarded them out (Broder 1988).

Psychological and moral family work, however, was the middle- and upper-class wife's responsibility (Zaretsky 1986). The ideology of familism made the nuclear family household the preferred living arrangement and was "the nexus for the various themes—romantic love; feminine nurturance, maternalism, self-sacrifice; masculine protection and financial support—that characterize our conception of gender and sexuality" (Barrett [1980] 1988, 205). This ideology trickled down to working-class wives, many of whom still had to do paid work as well as the physical work of maintaining their households (Cancian and Gordon 1988).

The Class Structure of Domestic Work

Since the nineteenth century, in the traditional middle-class household, the husband's status depended on his ability to provide the economic wherewithal to support his family and also to allow his wife to manage the household and consume conspicuously. Although the running of the home was the middle-class wife's responsibility, his social status depended on her *not* doing the dirty work and on his being able to hire another woman to do it for her.[13] She was then free to fulfill her more genteel responsibilities of acting as hostess, providing companionship, consuming tastefully, performing charity work, and supervising the moral and psychological welfare of her children. In this way, the middle-class husband emulated the upper-class husband. A working-class husband making a good income might also boast that his wife didn't have to "work." But he meant paid work, since his wife usually did all her own housework and child care. By providing all the income for the family so his wife didn't have to get a job or do work for money in her home, the working-class husband was able to emulate the middle-class husband.

By the twentieth century, household appliances, ready-made food and clothing, and self-service shopping supplemented or replaced servants for middle-class housewives in the United States and Europe, increasing, not reducing, their hands-on, use-value work, but giving the illusion of greater autonomy and control.[14] Domestic work may have been "rationalized," but it was neither communalized nor turned into a well-paid job, as feminists recommended (Hayden 1981). Rather, the new appliances increased the individual homemaker's output enough that, even without servants, work in the home could be combined with paid work outside the home "so as to maintain an appropriate level of comfort and decency, if rather inappropriate levels of exhaustion" (R. S. Cowan 1987, 174).

When middle- and upper-class full-time housewives hired other women to do their more tedious and onerous chores and to mind the children, these women came from working-class, immigrant, and other disadvantaged groups (Palmer 1989; Rollins 1985). Restricted in their job opportunities, they worked for other people's families to help their own families survive.[15] Karen Sacks has pointed out that "for white middle-class women, domestic labor may be subordinating to them as women, but if they hire others to do it (mostly Black, Latina, or Asian women), domestic labor becomes (low) paid work—thus gender subordination becomes gender, class, and race subordination" (1989, 539). Paradoxically, women who do domestic work for pay get little social status from it, but they often take pride and gain prestige from the unpaid domestic work they do for their own families:

> A clean house, good meals, and well-mannered responsible children were major sources of pride and status in the black community. . . .
> The elevated social status denied black domestic workers and laun-

dresses by the larger society and even some members of the black community could be found by them in their families and neighborhoods. Not only was women's unpaid labor in their own homes a great source of self-worth and pride; it also provided them with a sense of autonomy and control absent for them in the labor market environment. (Harley 1990, 348–49)[16]

Professional teachers, nurses, psychologists, pediatricians, and social workers have turned many aspects of social reproduction into paid work. These occupations became middle-class women's professions in the twentieth century (Ehrenreich and English 1978). Supplementing the paid work of these women professionals, women family members of all classes are expected to oversee their children's education and represent the family at the school, coordinate and complement the home nursing care of sick and elderly kin, and provide emotional sustenance as well as nutritional sustenance at family meals.[17] Upper-class women construct class and community through philanthropic activities; middle-class women maintain long-distance kin ties; and lower-class women share goods, services, and child care among real and fictive kin as a survival strategy.[18] Thus, through their paid and unpaid work of social reproduction, especially with regard to children's education and upbringing, women sustain and perpetuate the values of the social class structure. These values preserve the hegemony of dominant men by encouraging upper-class women to maintain their family's status as property-owners, middle-class women to foster the upward mobility of their husbands and sons as professionals and managers, and working-class women to affirm the worth of steady paid work (Kohn 1963; Kohn and Slomczynski 1990).

In short, wives and mothers in modern societies have become unpaid "servants to capital," whose work is "central to the distribution of goods in retailing and to the performance of services" (Glazer 1984, 81).[19] Because women's main work is considered social reproduction for their own families, they are paid less as workers. They are also called into the labor force or sent back home according to whether the capitalist economy needs cheap labor; thus they constitute a reserve army of labor that unplanned economies depend on.[20]

Paradoxically, despite all their unwaged work, women are excellent paid workers. One study (Bielby and Bielby 1988) of 1,469 workers found that 65 to 70 percent of the women with family responsibilities worked harder than men:

> Compared with men with similar household responsibilities, market human capital, earnings, promotion opportunities, and job respon-

sibilities, women allocated substantially more effort to work activities. . . . To the extent that women *do* allocate effort away from the
workplace in order to meet family demands, those trade-offs bring
their work effort back to the level of the typical male with no such
family responsibilities. For women to work as hard as men, if not
harder, despite their greater household responsibilities, they must be
able to draw on a reserve of energy that is either not available to the
typical male or, more realistically, that men choose not to draw upon.
(1055–56)

Women in twentieth-century capitalist economies are thus exploited
many times over. Their unwaged domestic work supplements their husband's
low wages; their shopping, tutoring, and home nursing fill the gaps left by
overworked and underpaid retail clerks, teachers, and nurses (most of whom
are women); they work hard and conscientiously at their paid jobs despite
extensive family responsibilities; and the money they earn buys the appliances
and other household goods that keep the capitalist economy going and that
make it possible for them to do domestic work. In all these ways, the domestic
and paid work of women allows men to make jobs and careers their main
commitment and capitalists to accumulate more profits.[21] As a result, men, as
workers, managers, and business owners, command the greater economic
resources, and thus they are able to claim women's unpaid domestic labor.

Whose Welfare Comes First?

Although "a living wage, quality child care, and good work are necessary for
everyone, but especially for women who choose not to share child care with a
man" (Brenner 1987, 455), the thrust of most twentieth-century capitalist
countries' social and legal policies makes it extremely difficult for women
not to depend on a man economically and therefore not to be responsible for
the home and children. Women marry and accept the responsibility for domestic work not because they are naturally nurturant (or domesticated) but
because they are dependent on a man's earnings to keep them out of poverty or
in the middle class, and they are dependent because they are systematically
excluded from better-paid jobs (Walby 1986, 248). Fear of losing the paternalistic protection of a married woman's entitlement to economic support
(and lacking access to decently paid work) led Irish women to defeat the
legalization of divorce as late as 1986 (L. Stone 1990, 420). This solution was
drastic but not necessarily misguided considering that no-fault divorce in the
United States has, according to Lenore Weitzman, "worsened women's condi-

tion, improved men's condition, and widened the income gap between the sexes" (1985, 378).[22]

Dependence on a husband's wages means that widows with children need enough insurance and state-provided benefits to produce the equivalent of a family wage. Other women also need some form of economic support: the older widow who does not work outside the home and has no pension of her own, the divorced mother whose support payments do not replace the family wage since the ex-husband is often supporting another family or reneges on payment agreements, the married mother whose husband is disabled, ill, or unemployed, and the unwed mother trying to maintain a household for her children. All these women fall through the cracks of the traditional family that in theory is supported by a man.

Governments in the United States, Canada, and Europe historically reacted to these women's and children's economic needs by promulgating a series of charity and welfare policies: providing orphanages for the children of widows and deserted wives so they themselves could earn a living, providing a modest pension on a short-term basis to tide over widows with children at home until they could get married again, or placing the whole family of a man who could not work in a poorhouse. Elderly widows had to move in with grown children or other relatives. Divorced and unwed mothers were not considered deserving of help and were left to fend for themselves.[23]

By the end of the nineteenth century and throughout the twentieth, the rise of the welfare state shifted the dependence of women from one man to one man plus the state (W. Brown 1992, Hernes 1984). The new welfare policies first entitled to some form of economic support those men who had had full-time jobs but could no longer work because of illness, disability, a failing job market, or old age; then the widows and children of these men were given a share of their entitlements. Between 1880 and 1920, European states began to give *all* mothers maternity and child health care, food supplements, and cash allowances for their children in order to encourage a rise in the birthrate. It wasn't until the 1950s that unwed and divorced mothers were extended state support in the United States.[24] By this time, most European countries, Canada, and Israel had instituted paid maternity and child-care leave and subsidized child care to enable mothers, married or not, to work outside the home.[25]

The entitlements that working-class men achieved in the twentieth century through unions—a living wage, reasonable hours of work, paid vacations and sick leave, pensions, unemployment benefits, disability coverage, health insurance, and compensation for job-related injuries—are available only to those who work full time in the core economy (B. J. Nelson 1990). Few of those benefits are available to women or men working part time, to piece-workers at home or in sweat shops, and to paid domestic workers. None is available to those who do unpaid work in the home full time. Legally, married women are entitled to "necessities"—food, clothing, and shelter at a level of maintenance (not luxury)—and the housewife herself contributes to that maintenance (Dahl 1984; Weitzman 1974).

In many countries, safety-net policies reflect what Mimi Abramovitz calls the "family ethic." They are based on a model of the middle-class family with a husband employed in an industrial or managerial job and a homemaking wife and mother (1988, 241–66). For example, in the United States, the 1935 Social Security Act originally paid pensions only to retired workers, most of whom were white men. It excluded domestic workers and farmers, the jobs of most African-Americans at that time, as well as many of the occupations urban white women were working in, such as teaching, hospital nursing, and government jobs. Amendments in 1939 expanded benefits to include the wives and widows of covered retirees; their children became eligible for survivors' benefits until they reached the age of eighteen. Divorced women had to rely on their own benefits until 1965, when those who had been married for twenty years or more and had not remarried were granted a portion of their ex-husband's benefits. In 1977, the period of marriage was reduced to ten years, and divorced men became eligible for part of their ex-wife's benefits as well.

In the United States, Social Security policies were so clearly gender-biased that until 1950, the surviving children of a deceased woman who had paid into the system during her lifetime received no benefits if their father was living in the home and had a job. Until the mid-1970s, a widower could receive survivor's benefits only if he could show he had been economically dependent on his wife in the year before her death. Until a 1975 Supreme Court ruling in favor of a young widower who wanted to stay home and care for his young child, an able-bodied widower could not raise his children on the benefits from his late wife's earnings.

Aid to Dependent Children, a carryover of the early twentieth-century mothers' pensions, became part of the 1935 U.S. Social Security Act. It was at that time a separate, temporary allotment meant to help indigent widows keep their children out of orphanages. Aid to Dependent Children became Aid to Families with Dependent Children (AFDC, colloquially known as "welfare") in 1962. It is now a means-tested public assistance program for indigent unwed, separated, and divorced mothers—that is, women "without a man"—as well as for those who live with a man who is disabled or unemployed (Abramovitz

1988, 313–42). The women who are the most penalized by U.S. government policies are those full-time mothers who receive AFDC. Because many have never had the financial cushion of a man's economic support or, given poor opportunities for decently paid jobs in their communities, have never worked outside the home full time, they are totally dependent on the state. The state does not apply the same standards to the "welfare mother" as it does to middle-class mothers; rather, it discourages them from staying home and, especially, from having more children.

The Family Support Act of 1988, intended to reform the U.S. welfare system, mandated child-support payments from noncustodial fathers and job training for mothers whose children were over the age of three when their fathers could not contribute child support. The jobs these poorly educated members of racially disadvantaged communities living in urban ghettos are likely to get are low-paid manufacturing or menial service work in the peripheral economy.[26] These reforms as well as the administration of AFDC consistently wink at the reality of life on welfare; the meager benefits are usually supplemented by illegal or off-the-books work and by pooled income and other help from family and friends who don't live in the household (Edin and Jencks 1992).

The white middle-class traditional family model of a father, mother, and children living in one self-supported household still pervades family policies in the United States.[27] All other kinds of families are measured against this model, and household patterns that deviate from it are treated as pathological. The kinds of family arrangements that are "problems" in the United States are common in Sweden. One-fifth of all Swedish families are headed by one parent; one-fifth of the couples who live together are unmarried; and almost half the births are out-of-wedlock (Gelb 1989, 142; Glendon 1989, 273–77). In the past, Sweden's maternal and child benefits made no distinction among types of families, were not means-tested, and paid women who were in the job market as well as those who were not, but cutbacks may seriously affect women's lives.[28]

Diana Pearce (1990) says that social welfare programs in the United States not only do not address the needs of poor women but exacerbate what she has called the "feminization of poverty."[29] Women make up the majority of single parents after separation and divorce; social welfare programs do not provide them with child care so they can earn a living for themselves and their children. Even middle-class men renege on child-support payments. Money the state collects from fathers repays AFDC; it doesn't go to the mothers. Finally, both middle-class and working-class women are disadvantaged in the job market by low pay and lack of benefits such as health insurance for themselves and their children, affordable child care, and paid leave to care for a sick child. A sensible welfare program would supplement income from paid jobs at a more generous level and also provide medical care and day care, enabling women heads of households to rise out of poverty through a combination of government assistance and their own efforts. Instead, the programs are insidiously designed to keep working-class women poor as welfare recipients, poor as wage-earning heads of households, and, unless they marry a man who has a good job and no other dependents, poor as wives. Whatever their marital status, their level of income makes an extensive amount of domestic labor necessary for survival.[30]

Junior-Partner Wives

When married women do paid work, their second job is still housework and child care. Governments that want to encourage women to perform these dual roles not only need to give them the benefits men receive as paid workers but also need to assure their health and well-being as mothers. The benefits these governments extend to women are access to abortion and contraception, prenatal and maternal health care, paid leave before and after the birth of a child, and paid leave to care for a newly adopted or sick child or an elderly parent. Many of these governments also provide cash allowances for children's expenses and subsidized child care, and they encourage employers to offer working mothers flexible schedules or reduced hours of work.[31] Like welfare, these benefits are given in the interests of the family, not gender equality. The trade-off is that women can expect to be paid less than men and therefore have to depend on an additional salary for a middle-class life-style. Sweden, for example, has had the most generous social policies with regard to benefits to women who work outside the home, but compared to Britain and the United States, it also has had the highest level of gender segregation in the workplace and the highest percentage of women part-time workers.[32]

The United States in 1993 was one of the few modern industrialized countries that had no guaranteed medical insurance for children, no children's allowances, no national paid parental leave, and no subsidized child care. Yet it has had less workplace gender segregation and fewer women working part time than Sweden. By giving working women child-leave benefits and taxing every worker individually, Sweden's state social policies have encouraged women's dual roles. The United States, in contrast, has treated women full-time workers as if they were men, but its lack of mandated paid maternity and child-care leave benefits and tax policies that penalize the second earner has discouraged their continuing to work outside the home once they have children. In 1986, in Sweden, 85.6 percent of women with children under seven were in the paid labor force, compared to 55 percent in the United States (Lewis and Åström 1992, 70–71).

The American government's policies have reflected continued ideological ambivalence over whether mothers should be full-time employees. Women are not denied the right to work full time, and if they do so, they get all the benefits men do, but their pregnancies have been treated like illnesses, abortions have not always been covered by health insurance, and there has been only unpaid leave for births cr child care. Large corporations, which have an economic investment in their highly trained women workers, are likely to provide paid maternity leave and sick-child leave. Child-care services have been a patchwork of providers, usually expensive and often unreliable. Government policies in the United States have encouraged the pattern of women dropping out of the paid work force while their children are young and returning later to full-time but low-paid jobs, stagnant careers, or totally new careers. Sweden's gender-segregated and part-time labor market for women and the United States' encouragement of interrupted careers have both fostered a junior-partner status in two-earner families for married working women with children.[33] Married women's secondary-earner status has then justified their greater burden of domestic labor.

What Women's Money Can't Buy

In all Western countries, married women with full-time jobs do more housework than their husbands even if they work throughout their lives and are high earners. If lack of control over property, junior-partner status, or blocked access to high-paying jobs has been the source of wives' economic powerlessness and consequent obligation to take on the responsibility of family work, how can we explain the persistence of this pattern when wives and husbands are equal earners and even when the wife earns more than her husband? The answer lies in men's greater marital bargaining power, which allows them to avoid doing unpleasant domestic chores, and in the conflation of family work with "womanliness."[34]

By the mid-twentieth century, even economically advantaged middle-class wives in the United States began to supplement the family income with paid work. There were more jobs available for women of color and women immigrants, and so there were fewer servants. Middle-class wives now did their own housework, using sophisticated household appliances—automatic

other words, men do the "nicer" parts of housework, and women are left with the "nasty" parts (M. T. Coleman 1991).

A woman may be better off buying housekeeping services than trying to share housework with the man she lives with, but if most of her discretionary income is allocated to this expenditure and his is not, she has not in any way challenged conventional gender roles (Blumberg and Coleman 1989). Similarly, if the man's income goes for rent and groceries, he can maintain the symbolic role of main provider, even if the family could not maintain its standard of living without the woman's income (Hood 1983, 124–27).[40] Judith Stacey notes that "many people of both genders recoil from the prospect of a fully democratic family regime" because of the psychological and social costs (1991, 258): "A normless gender order, one in which parenting arrangements, sexuality, and the distribution of work, responsibility, and resources all are negotiable and constantly renegotiable, can . . . invite considerable conflict and insecurity" (258–59).[41]

For many heterosexual couples, the gendered division of household labor is not even questioned. In her study of 335 American husband-wife-children families, Sarah Fenstermaker Berk found that despite a stubbornly lopsided division of domestic work in terms of time and task allocation, even in dual-earner households, 94 percent of the husbands considered the situation fair, and 70 percent of wives also felt the amount of domestic work they did should stay the same. She concludes that rational considerations of "who has more time, whose time is worth more, who has more skill, or who has more power" are far less important than normative gendered expectations (1985, 195–96). The wife who keeps her household running and her husband and children nutritionally and emotionally well-fed no matter what else she does is validated *as a woman*; the husband who is a good economic provider but who never does any housework or child care is still validated *as a man*. The work of the modern nuclear family household is "the production of goods and services and what we might call the production of gender. Simultaneously, household members 'do' gender, as they 'do' housework and child care, and . . . the division of household labor provides for the joint production of labor and gender: it is the mechanism by which both the material and the symbolic products of the household are realized" (Berk 1985, 201).

First a kinship and work unit, later an upper- and middle-class status producer and a means for lower-class survival and social mobility, the family, in the modern postindustrial world has become, in Fenstermaker Berk's words, a "gender factory." Women's domestic work is what makes them women, but since the chores are "dirty work," it denigrates them (Palmer 1989, 137–51).

The caring work, the "work of service and sociability" that makes a family a psychological unit, is not considered work at all; rather, it is "an expression of inherent femininity" (DeVault 1991, 9). For these reasons, men usually regard domestic work as either beneath them or unmanly (Mainardi 1970). Men's definition of the situation prevails even when they don't have the economic upper hand, because the gendered norms discount women's paid work as secondary and inflate men's income as the primary support of the household.

Truly egalitarian role sharing means that when a woman and man live together, they both must feel responsible for providing the household's necessities, and both must share what are usually considered women's and men's domestic chores (Haas 1980). For such an outcome, the worth of the woman's job or career has to be acknowledged by both, and the couple must conscientiously and consciously work on the relationship to allow each to maintain a high level of career involvement (Hertz 1986). A study that compared sixty married couples among whom the wives outearned the husbands by a third with sixty couples in the reverse economic situation found that the husband's better earning power *raised* the value of his career over that of the wife's in the eyes of both. The wife's greater earning power gave her career merely an *equal* value. All the careers had comparable prestige value occupationally (Steil and Weltman 1991).

In families with residues of traditional ideology about women's and men's roles, a wife who earns more than her husband may paradoxically be at a psychological disadvantage. The marriage's "economy of gratitude" may make her feel that she owes it to her husband not to ask him to do domestic work since her greater success has already lowered his status in the eyes of their families and friends, if not in their own.[42] Hochschild (1989a) interviewed over a period of years fifty working-class, middle-class, and professional white, African-American, Chicano, and Asian-American men whose wives also worked outside the home. Eighty percent of these men did not share housework or child care at all (173). The few who did earned more or about the same as their wives. None of the men who earned less than their wives did so:

> How much responsibility these men assumed at home was thus related
> to the deeper issue of male power. Men who earn much more than their
> wives already have a power over their wives in that they control a scarce
> and important resource. The more severely a man's identity is finan-
> cially threatened—by the wife's higher salary, for example—the less
> he can afford to threaten it further by doing "women's work" at home.
> (221)

One survey of about 700 white and African-American men in the United States found that men who held nontraditional attitudes toward gender roles were likely to do more household labor (Huber and Spitze 1983, 75–91). The greatest equality comes from psychological role reversal. Among thirty-one married couples who shared economic and family work equally, for 87 percent of the wives, commitment to having a job was very important, whereas over three-quarters of the husbands claimed that career advancement was not of major importance to them (Haas 1982, 752–53).

Just as women have to redefine what a job or career means to them in order to share the provider role equally, men have to redefine the meaning of domestic work to share equally in household maintenance and child care. A study of fifty-six American-born white middle-class men who did a substantial amount of housework because they had the time and inclination showed they did not feel "unmanned" (Beer 1983). More important, housework has to be seen as something beneficial, not demeaning, if those with material or psychological resources are to decide not to buy out of it. William Beer, the author of this study, redefined housework for himself in very masculine terms:

> A day of cooking, cleaning, child care and household management is not unlike climbing a mountain. Some of it is sweaty, gruelling work, but the pleasures, such as sunlight through the mist on Mount Washington, or seeing a toddler learn a new game, are constant enough to make it worth it. . . . Housework may not be Everest, but it is an adventure that awaits any man who wants to forge ahead and meet the challenges of unexplored territory. (1983, xxi)

Women's class situations are characterized by . . . sex segregation,
low wages, intermittent employment, and subordination to men in
the workplace and often at home. Men's class situations are
characterized by . . . sex segregation, higher wages, lifelong
employment, and either dominance over women or little contact
with them in the workplace and dominance in the home.

—*Joan Acker (1989a, 18–19)*

SEPARATE AND NOT EQUAL:
THE GENDERED DIVISION OF PAID WORK

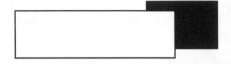

If the gendered domestic division of labor seems currently imper-
vious to change, even more paradoxical is the extent of gender segregation in
paid work in modern industrialized economies. Anyone who takes even a
cursory look around any place of work in industrialized countries can see that
workers doing the same or similar jobs tend to be of the same gender and racial
ethnic group. In a workplace in New York City—for instance, a handbag
factory—a walk through the various departments might reveal that the
owners and managers are white men; their secretaries and bookkeepers are
white and Asian women; the order takers and data processors are African-
American women; the factory hands are Hispanic men cutting pieces and
Hispanic women sewing them together; African-American men are packing
and loading the finished product; and non-English-speaking Eastern European
women are cleaning up after everyone. The workplace as a whole seems
integrated by race, ethnic group, and gender, but the individual jobs are
markedly segregated according to social characteristics.

Although modern industrialized workplaces have different segregation
patterns, one type of sorting is endemic: *Almost every workplace in modern
industrial societies is either gender-segregated or all one gender.* One group of
researchers studying the organization of work in over four hundred firms in
California from 1959 to 1979 found that "men and women shared job assignments in organizations so rarely that we could usually be certain that an
apparent exception reflected coding or key-punch error. . . . We were
amazed at the pervasiveness of women's concentration in organizational
ghettos" (Baron and Bielby 1985, 235). The organizations ranged in size,
extent of bureaucracy, and mixture of occupations, yet in virtually all of them,

women worked with women and men worked with men (Bielby and Baron 1984, 1986); 59 percent were *totally* segregated by gender (Baron and Bielby 1985).

There are women and men workers in most occupations, but the extent of clustering is such that 60 to 70 percent of men (or women) workers in the United States would have to change occupations to desegregate them, a situation that has persisted throughout the twentieth century. During the 1970s, a decade in which women were thought to have made inroads into many occupations previously dominated by men in the United States, only 33 of 537 occupations saw an increase of women workers of at least 9 percent, or twice the percentage increase of women into the paid labor force during that decade (Reskin and Roos 1990, 16–21). In the 1980s, in 22 of these occupations, women's representation increased twice as rapidly as their increase in the labor force as a whole, which was only 2.4 percent. Although most of the new women workers went into occupations where most of the employees were women, those who went into occupations where the workers were predominantly men soon found that their coworkers were becoming predominantly women. For example, women were 33.4 percent of the personnel, training, and labor relations specialists in 1970, 47 percent in 1980, and 58.9 percent in 1988. They were 33.9 percent of the computer operators in 1970, 59.1 percent in 1980, and 66 percent in 1988. Insurance adjusters, examiners, and investigators went from 29.6 percent women to 60.2 percent to 72.2 percent during that period (Reskin and Roos 1990, table 1.6). These occupations had *resegregated*. Thus, the gender composition of blue-collar, white-collar, and professional occupations sometimes reverses, but gender segregation persists (E. Gross 1968; J. A. Jacobs 1989a).

Both women and men workers can be found in occupations where most of the workers are of the opposite gender, but when they change occupations, the trend is toward gender homogeneity.[1] There is occupational change in the opposite direction, too, with women and men going into nontraditional occupations, but the overall outcome of these "revolving doors" is social pressure for continued occupational gender segregation (J. A. Jacobs 1989b).[2] When women and men work in nontraditional occupations, gender typing is often maintained symbolically, as when policewomen view their work as social work and men nurses emphasize the technical and physical strength aspects of what they do (S. E. Martin 1980, 194–99; C. L. Williams 1989, 90).

Specific *jobs* are even more gender-segregated. An analysis of 645 occupational categories in 290 work organizations in California found that over three-fourths of the women (or men) would have to be reclassified to degender the occupational categories, and that 96 percent of the 10,525 different job titles were gender-segregated (Bielby and Baron 1986). Only 8 percent of the 50,838 workers shared job titles with a member of the opposite gender: "Our findings indicate that small differences in job requirements get amplified into large differences in gender composition. . . . With few exceptions, a job was either inappropriate for women or appropriate only for women, regardless of the amount of overlap in the attributes of prospective male and female employees" (Bielby and Baron 1985, 782).[3]

During World War II, which created a national labor power emergency in the United States, there was an influx of millions of women workers into industrial jobs, but the work continued to be gender-typed, and Black women were hired last (Milkman 1987, 49–83). Rosie riveted, former housewives cooked steel, and farmers' wives and daughters ran tractors and threshing machines, but the structure of occupational gender segregation remained intact. Heavy-industry jobs were mechanized and deskilled because women were believed to have dexterity and patience but no strength. Other jobs were feminized by being compared to sewing, filing nails, and cutting out patterns so that they would be appropriate for "housewives." In Detroit's auto industry, more than half the women workers were crowded into five of seventy-two job categories, where only 11 percent of the men worked. In electrical appliance plants converted to military production, almost half the women worked in *one* job category. The gender typing was arbitrary: in one plant, the best welders were women; in another no women welded. However the work was divided between women and men, management insisted that it was "natural." In the military, women were similarly recruited only for the duration of the war, and jobs formerly typed as men's work were retyped as women's work: "Ironically, women's war work—as mediated by official policy and propaganda—actually promoted feminine stereotypes" (C. L. Williams 1989, 28).

The continued reluctance of employers to hire women for men's jobs has led some women who want the better-paid or more adventurous men's jobs to masquerade as men (Matthaei 1982, 192–93; Wheelwright 1989). Other women who could pass for men but want to maintain their status as women have applied for jobs with gender-blind résumés. They work through the probation period passing as men, and then, when they reveal that they are women, threaten a lawsuit if they are fired (Devor 1989, 135–36).

How Segregation Supports Stratification

Occupational gender segregation does not result in separate but equal jobs. Rather, women's work tends to be lower in pay, prestige, and even fringe benefits, such as health insurance (Perman and Stevens 1989). Both occupations and jobs within occupations (as well as professions and specialities within professions) can be ranked on a number of material and subjective factors. In surveys, the gender of the particular worker does not affect the public's prestige ratings of occupations in the United States (Bose and Rossi 1983). But workers themselves rate jobs where most of the workers are women as inferior to jobs where most of the workers are men. The criteria are number and flexibility of hours, earnings, educational requirements, on-the-job training, having a union contract, extent of supervision and place in the hierarchy, repetitiveness, risk of job loss, and being a government employee (Jencks, Perman, and Rainwater 1988). Workers rate women's jobs as better in vacation days and not getting dirty at work, even though, ironically, it is *men* who are more averse to a job's dirtiness! Most full-time jobs of mothers are incompatible with parenting demands; flexibility of schedules and control and timing of work-related tasks are the prerogatives of men managers, not their secretaries (Glass and Camarigg 1992). If wages were used to compensate for unattractive nonmonetary job characteristics, women's jobs would have to pay four times as much as men's jobs for workers to rate them equally.

Race, ethnicity, and national origin are also built into the organization of work.[4] These social characteristics, along with gender, are used by employers to create segregated labor markets. In the primary sector, the best jobs are shaped on an ideal, dominant man's career—long-term continuous work in the same organization, with steady pay raises and a pension at retirement (Acker 1990). Men's gender status is an advantage to them as workers; because they are expected to earn more money when they marry and when they have children, employers tend to view them as better workers than women. Women workers are felt to be entitled only to supplementary wages, whether they are married or single, because they are considered not legitimate workers but primarily wives and mothers.

The structured patterns of opportunities and access far override most individual employers' tastes or individual workers' motivations, ambitions, personal desires, and material needs. By the 1970s in the United States, adolescent girls were considerably less likely than in previous years to plan on entering an occupation where most of the workers were women, especially if they lived in a woman-headed household (Berryman and Waite 1987, 130).[5] But they continued to value working with people, helping others, using their abilities, and being creative; boys wanted jobs with status, high earnings, freedom from supervision, and leadership potential (Marini and Brinton 1987). Those who obtained higher education tended to choose gender-appropriate majors, but with considerable shifting back and forth (J. A. Jacobs 1989b). The jobs women are likely to end up in are more gender-typed and less fulfilling than their occupational aspirations, but ambitious and hardworking men can often reach their early goals.

Women of all educational levels and men disadvantaged because of race, immigrant status, lack of education, or outmoded job skills are profitable workers because they tend to be low-paid; they also get promoted less frequently and therefore receive fewer raises. They can be paid little because the pool of such workers is larger than that of privileged men workers. The size and social characteristics of the pool of low-waged workers are affected by state policies encouraging or discouraging the employment of women, the influx of immigrants, and the flight of capital from one area of a country to another or offshore.[6]

Occupational gender segregation and stratification reflect two parallel and related processes—*segmentation and ghettoization* (Baron and Bielby 1980). Segmented occupations are horizontally or vertically divided into sectors with different educational or credential requirements for hiring, different promotion ladders, different work assignments, and different pay scales (R. Edwards 1979, 163–99). Typically, these segments are gendered and frequently also exhibit racial ethnic clustering. Occupations in which almost all the workers are one gender, however, can also be segmented. For instance, doctors and nurses are gender-segregated segments in medical organizations. Physicians are segmented between those in primary care and hospital-based specialists, who have more prestige and power and higher incomes. Women physicians are often found in primary care (Lorber 1987a, 1991). Nursing is also segmented into registered nurses, licensed practical nurses, nurses' aides, and home health workers (Glazer 1991). Nurses are virtually all women, but the segments are racially differentiated, with the majority of registered nurses in the United States white and Asian American and most of the lower-paid health workers African American and Hispanic (Glenn 1992, 24–31). Men who go into nursing tend to specialize in the more lucrative areas and become administrators (C. L. Williams 1992).

Segmentation is legitimized by bureaucratic rules or legal requirements for qualifying credentials, but ghettoization separates the lower-paid "women's" jobs from the better-paid "men's" jobs within an occupation through informal gender typing. What is dubbed "women's work" or "men's work" has a sense of normality and naturalness, an almost moral quality, even though the justification for such typification is usually an after-the-fact rationalization. Thus, after men left residential for commercial real estate sales jobs in the United States in the 1970s because of a recession, women were hired to sell homes; employers then argued that women were naturals for the job, since they ran homes and knew the neighborhood schools and playgrounds (Thomas and Reskin 1990). The assumption is that the skills, competence, strength, and other qualities needed to do a job are tied up with masculinity and femininity, but gendered identities as workers are constructed in the gendered organization of the workplace and reinforced in training and organizational social occasions.[7] Within gender-typed occupations, jobs or specialties may be gender-typed in the opposite direction. For example, the majority of physicians are men in the United States and women in the Soviet Union, but the same specialities are seen as appropriate for one gender—pediatrics for women and neurosurgery for men (Lorber 1984, 16–30). In both countries, neurosurgery pays better and has more prestige than pediatrics.

Both structural segmentation and normative gender typing that puts some jobs into a low-wage ghetto have the same results. They limit the extent of competition for the better positions, make it easier for privileged workers to justify their advantageous salary scales, and create a group of workers whose lack of credentials or requisite skills legitimate their lower pay (Acker 1989a; Glazer 1991). Credentials and skills, however, as well as experience, are manipulated or circumvented to favor workers with certain social characteristics, as when men with less lower-rank experience in women's jobs are hired as supervisors (C. L. Williams 1992). In addition, femaleness and maleness are stereotypically linked to certain capabilities, such as finger dexterity and physical strength; gender then becomes the discriminant criterion for hiring and not what potential employees can actually do with their hands, backs, and heads (Bielby and Baron, 1986, 790–91).

Promotion ladders are also gender-segregated. Women and men who are not of the dominant racial ethnic group tend not to rise to the top in their work organization, unless practically all the workers are women or men of the same racial ethnic group. White men tend to dominate positions of authority whether or not they are numerically predominant. Even in occupations where the majority of the workers are women, positions of authority tend to be held by men —elementary school teachers are predominantly women in the United States, but principals and superintendents are predominantly men. That is, token men in a woman's occupation tend to be promoted faster than the women workers; the workplace has to be virtually all women for women to be promoted to supervisory positions (Baron and Bielby 1985, 224; C. L. Williams 1992). If bosses of dominant-group men were women or members of subordinate groups, the gendered and racial assumptions of current organizational hierarchies would be challenged (Acker 1989a, 207–23; 1990).

In a country with a racially homogeneous population like China, gender discrimination is especially evident. Membership in the Communist party, a reward for ideological loyalty and work achievements, is a resource for upward mobility into decision-making positions. A study of status attainment among 469 men and 402 women in China found that 21 percent of the men but only 11 percent of the women were party members, and so women were less likely to move into the better sectors of the economy (Lin and Bian 1991). Well-educated men who moved to less advantageous sectors, presumably to manage or administer collectives, retained their earnings and job prestige; well-educated women in similar situations lost their advantages.

These pervasive patterns of occupational segregation and stratification are the result of deliberate actions and also inaction on the part of governments, owners and managers, and organized groups of workers, and change has to come from the same sources.[8] A study of the rate of gender integration from 1979 to 1985 in ninety civil service agencies in California found that it depended on "new approaches to recruitment, selection, and promotion; career development; and job analysis and classification" (Baron, Mittman, and Newman 1991, 1364). Since gender segregation occurs in occupations and professions, job titles, and specific work sites, integration has to involve more than simply increasing the numbers of women (Yoder 1991; Zimmer 1988). True occupational gender equality would mean that women and men of all races would have the same opportunities to obtain professional credentials and occupational training, and would be distributed in the same proportions as they are in the paid work force across workplaces, job titles, occupations, and hierarchical positions. Instead, in most industrialized countries, women are overrepresented in clerical and service jobs, low-prestige professional and technical work, and sales.[9] In developing countries, and in areas of industrialized countries with large numbers of immigrants, women tend to be concentrated in labor-intensive factory work, agriculture, and the informal (off-the-books) economy (Nuss 1989, 42–43).

The gendered division of paid labor dovetails with the gendered division of domestic labor. Low pay and uninteresting jobs encourage single women to marry and married women to devote energy and attention to child rearing and domestic work. Better job opportunities for men encourage them to devote their energy and attention to paid work. Employers (mostly men) benefit from women's cheap labor and men's need to earn more to support a family; men who live with women benefit from women's unpaid labor at home.

From Farm to Factory

Clear-cut gender segregation in production work in Europe and the United States evolved as industries gradually moved from the home to the factory. When the work unit on farms and in towns was the household, women were primarily responsible for cooking and child care, but they also did or super-vised much agricultural work and home industry, such as cheese making and spinning. The overlap of tasks and the frequent need for all hands to pitch in to reap a harvest or get other work finished meant that women and men worked side by side. When women sold their services outside the home, many per-formed the equivalent of housekeeping work for pay, but they were engaged in a great variety of other occupations as well (Schultz and Lantz 1988). Accord-ing to Gerda Lerner, in preindustrial United States,

> the entire colonial production of cloth and clothing and in part that of shoes was in the hands of women. . . . They were butchers, sil-versmiths, gunsmiths, upholsterers. They ran mills, plantations, tan yards, shipyards, and every kind of shop, tavern, and boarding house. They were gate keepers, jail keepers, sextons, journalists, printers, "doctoresses," apothecaries, midwives, nurses, and teachers. Women acquired their skills the same way as did the men, through apprentice-ship training, frequently within their own families. (1979, 183)[10]

In the putting-out system used in the early days of the Industrial Revolu-tion, machine-based commodity production also took place in the home; the whole family did piecework under the authority of the man who was head of the household. He dealt with the capitalist, assigned tasks, and distributed wages. In England and the United States in the early nineteenth century, the first factory workers were white unmarried daughters and younger sons, the less valuable farm workers (Lamphere 1987; Sacks 1989, 521–42). In New England, Francis Cabot Lowell devised a way to attract young white farm girls to work in the textile mills without compromising their marriageability. He boarded them to keep strict watch on their morals and their punctuality and paid them enough to save for a trousseau, pay off a mortgage, or send a brother to college.[11] Increasing competition, however, resulted in overproduction, cuts in wages, and speedups in the pace of work. Not all Lowell women workers could go back home, and those who could lost their independence if they went home without savings. Some protested individually, and the gender-segregated and communal living and working arrangements were also conducive to organized strikes (Dublin 1977; Vogel 1977). These strikes were not successful, however; the gender ideology that women were primarily wives and mothers was used to justify their low pay. The conscious use of family ties by both management and labor has alternately hindered and fostered industrialized women workers' collective action.[12]

An arrangement similar to Lowell's was used in the silk mills in England at the beginning of the nineteenth century and in industrializing Japan at the end of that century (Lown 1990; Tsurumi 1990). Fifteen- to seventeen-year-old girls were indentured in silk and cotton mills, their meager wages going to their families or to the poorhouses from which they came.

Recruiting poor young women as cheap labor for factories is still a common phenomenon in industrialization. Today, Asian and Latin and Central American young women from farming families are sent to work in factories, where they live highly controlled lives, sleeping in dormitories and eating meager meals, just as the nineteenth-century factory girls did: "Women, typically aged sixteen to twenty-four, constitute 80 to 90 percent of the export-processing labor in Mexico, Southeast Asia, and other export platform nations. . . . Within a single generation, the process has created a female proletariat in export zones throughout the world" (Tiano 1990, 196). Seung-Kyung Kim's (1990) firsthand research on women workers in the Korean economic "miracle" showed that the young women worked in electronics factories to pay for their family's upward mobility. They lived in crowded rooms and ate sparingly in order to save their salaries to pay for the college tuition of brothers and to bring money to their own marriages. But they couldn't save enough to become truly upwardly mobile. Since their blue-collar worker husbands did not make enough to support a family, they ended up as married women with children, working again but in less attractive jobs. As married women, they were barred from the electronics industry, where employers wanted a rapid turnover so wages could be kept low.

In the *maquiladoras,* the Mexican border industries, where 85 to 90 percent of the workers are women, there is a similar division between the electronics industries, which offer somewhat better working conditions and higher pay but hire only young single women, and the smaller, less modern apparel factories, which employ older women supporting children and pay less (Fernández-Kelly 1984). In Puerto Rico's "Operation Bootstrap," women were recruited into manufacturing industries that in 1980 paid the lowest weekly salaries—apparel ($54.12), textiles ($55.85), and leather products ($57.28). In the two better-paid areas where women workers predominated— electrical ($76.49) and professional and scientific instruments ($73.99)— their salaries were not as high as those where men workers predominated— machinery ($80.70), metal ($80.44), and chemicals ($102.44) (Ríos 1990).

Neither nineteenth- nor twentieth-century industrialization benefited African-American and Hispanic women in the Western Hemisphere; as slaves, they did both field work and domestic work, and as free labor, they tended to work as domestic servants, laundresses, seamstresses, and neighborhood entrepreneurs rather than in factories.[13] In the global economy today, Third World women workers are likely to be more exploited than men workers, whether they migrate to a city, work in a factory and send money back to their farm-based families, or stay in a rural area doing triple duty growing food, keeping house, and earning money any way they can to supplement what their migrating husbands send them.[14] In developing countries and in poor families in industrialized countries, women's paid work particularly benefits children, since women are more likely than men to buy food, clothing, and other family necessities with extra income.[15] In Ghana, a " 'strong' woman is a wife mother who can provide independently of her husband and / or household head during the hungry season. In households where women have other income sources throughout the year from brewing and speculating in grain, this ideology leads to *their income* being used to provide staple food during the hungry season" (Whitehead 1981, 101).

Men Workers versus Women Workers

In the search for cheap labor and greater control over the work process, capitalists moved production out of the home, paid each waged worker individually, and pitted women against men in the competition for increasingly necessary waged jobs (S. O. Rose 1987). The labor conflicts of the nineteenth and twentieth centuries were not just between waged workers and capitalists for higher pay, shorter hours, and better working conditions but also between women and men waged workers—women to maintain a place in the industrialized labor market that would give them economic independence; men to monopolize the better-paid jobs so they could support an economically dependent wife who would devote time to domestic labor and child care.

In the early period of industrialization, the interests of capitalists and working-class men coincided; later, they clashed. Sylvia Walby (1986) suggests that employers preferred women factory workers during early industrialization because they were cheaper and more docile, and male heads of households were happy to have the extra income.[16] When factories replaced farms, men also became factory workers: "As factory employment expanded, it became the source of a greater proportion of all paid work and this changing pattern threatened men's interests. This employment threatened to become a source of power for women from which men could be relatively excluded. . . . If women were to earn their way and work long hours away from home, and men did not, then men would find their control over women significantly reduced" (Walby 1986, 110).

At first, men were recruited to the factory as supervisors of women and children (Marglin 1978, n84), but later generations competed with women for the best-paid work. In an effort to preserve their pay differentials, the men's unions designated some machines as "women's machines" and others as "men's machines." Job segregation and stratification, buttressed by women's status as wives and mothers and men's as heads of households, also legitimated men's higher pay rates: "The individualized wage and gender ideology together changed women and men from coparticipants in domestic industry to competitors in the factory. Job segregation by gender among machine operatives was a solution both to economic competition and to the threat of a reordering of the gender hierarchy" (S. O. Rose 1987, 165). When they could not sustain these arbitrary designations, men workers agitated for supervisory positions and training in machine repair (Bradley 1986).

Another solution to the competition for jobs between women and men workers was protective labor legislation. These laws limited where and for how many hours women could work in a factory on the grounds that family life suffered from women's poor health or lack of time for domestic labor (Kessler-Harris 1982, 180–214). In actuality, families suffered as much from men's as women's occupational health hazards and low pay, and working-class urban living quarters were small and meagerly furnished. Women who worked in the informal economy supplied cheap prepared food and laundry services and boarded babies (Broder 1988; Walby 1986, 115).

The women workers themselves were not happy about protective legislation that limited their earning power, pointing out that not all women were married. What was to become of their livelihood if women were forbidden to work in certain industries and their hours of work were restricted? An 1849 survey found that 70 percent of the men operatives were in favor of the ten-hour day, but only 55 percent of the women were, though the women were the supposed beneficiaries (Walby 1986, 119–22). Morality was invoked to support legislation that forbade women from working at night. Freer sexuality is symbolic of the independence of women who can earn their own living.[17] But single women did not work at night because it cut into their social life. The abolition of night work meant less flexible allocation of time for domestic duties, and so it was opposed by married women (Kessler-Harris 1982, 190–95).[18]

This concern that working-class women's economic independence would make them unfit or unwilling wives and mothers was, in the nineteenth century, an issue for middle-class as well as working-class men that somewhat overrode capitalists' interests in higher profits (Lown 1990, 172–201; Walby 1986, 116–17). However, the ultimate effect of the protective labor legislation passed in the United States in the late nineteenth and early twentieth centuries was to increase the numbers of married working-class women in manufacturing but to decrease their earnings. More crucial, it solidified the gender segregation of jobs and excluded women from some of the better-paying industries and from better-paid shifts. The protection from overwork was in name only, as employers often moved maintenance duties to the women workers' own time or speeded up the work process. The paradoxical effect on men workers was that it increased competition because women were paid less, and so they eventually supported the principle of equal pay for the same work.

Today, the argument that women should not be permitted to do hazardous work when pregnant (or potentially pregnant) or work long hours when they have small children similarly ignores the dangers of the workplace for men's physiological ability to become fathers and the restriction on the time they have available to spend with their children.[19] Protective legislation reinforces women workers' status in the labor market as primarily wives and mothers who need the state's protection and a husband's income. It discourages men as well as women workers from collectively bargaining for what they *both* need to make it possible for them to earn a living and take care of their families—safe working conditions, high wages, and manageable hours.

Gender and Technology

The presence of machines does not distinguish men's and women's work. In fact, more women than men work with machines, even in offices (Form and McMillen 1983). Women operatives assemble machinery and electronic components in factories, and white-collar women run office machines; men operatives run large, impressive cranes and forklifts, and white-collar men design and service machines (Cockburn 1983, 1985). Women workers' ability to use all types of machinery during wartime, when there are few men workers, illustrates that it is not capability but monopolization of valued skills that segregates workers by gender and justifies paying women less:

> Technological skills are a source of power and where men were in possession of all other vehicles of power, from state organization to marriage, it would have been surprising to find women in possession of mechanical powers. The "mighty five" devices—level, wedge, screw, wheel, and inclined plane—that made it possible to move mountains and build pyramids were the technical armory of men. . . .
>
> The technological skills, defined as male property, were therefore both a cause and an effect of male supremacy. (Cockburn 1985, 21, 24)

Although women operatives were the showpiece of the Lowell textile mills in the early days of the Industrial Revolution in America, in many of the later factories men operated the machines, and lower-paid women "gave raw materials a preliminary screening and sorting, put finishing touches on the final product, scanned finished goods for flaws, sorted and graded them, washed them, folded them, labeled them, or packed them for shipping" (McGaw 1982, 808).

Men do not always monopolize machinery without a battle. The Linotype, patented in 1885, cast type for newspapers on a machine whose keyboard resembled a typewriter's, but was different. Employers wanted to hire women as Linotype operators but were opposed by the men in the International Typographical Union (Baron 1987). The union men argued that the work was masculine because the molten metal used gave off heat and gases and the work was exhausting: "Men printers were forced to emphasize the physical attributes necessary for the job because keyboard work—where the definition of the work as intellectual resided—was increasingly associated with natural female attributes" (Baron 1987, 71). In the process, men workers went along with employers' emphasis on increased output through "masculine" endurance and speed. Thus, though employers might have preferred lower-paid women workers, whom they felt were also neater and harder working than men, they could not compete with the demand for women clerical workers. Men continued to dominate printing and to consider the work masculine; in actuality, the work process was speeded up and productivity increased, compensating employers for men's comparatively higher wages.

When computer typesetting replaced the Linotype in the 1970s, the keyboard was deliberately designed like the typewriter keyboard in order to allow employers to switch from unionized blue-collar men workers to nonunionized white-collar women workers, and not always without a strike (Roos

1990). The occupation feminized, going from 17 percent women in 1970 to 56 percent by 1980 and to 74 percent by 1988, because to the men workers, the work was now typing, and typing was for women (Cockburn 1983; Roos 1990). If they did retrain, the men "complained that everything about their work reminded them of 'women's work': the keyboard layout, the plastic machine, the operator's posture, and the association of typing with women. They described the conditions as not masculine enough and less virile than the hot-metal composing room" (Roos 1990, 285). It was not technology per se that first masculinized then feminized printing, but the monopolization and gender typification of the earlier technology by unionized men craft workers, who could then command high pay, and fifty years later, their being pushed out or leaving when nonunion lower-paid women workers were brought in by employers.

In contrast, the typewriter seems to have been aimed at women clerical workers right from the beginning (M. W. Davies 1982; Srole 1987). In the nineteenth century, women worked in family businesses as clerks and copyists, and also did copying at home for low pay: "Copyists were temporary workers, comparable to modern Kelly Girls, who were paid by the piece to do tasks involving writing. The work consisted of simple duties such as making copies of correspondence, addressing receipts, or making entries in ledgers. The skills required were negligible, since transcription requires few skills other than literacy and penmanship" (Cohn 1985, 67). The typewriter increased clerks' and copyists' output and pay but not enough to make the work attractive to men, who valued clerking only when it was a stepping-stone into management.

Office work did not become women's work because it was deskilled; it wasn't particularly skilled to begin with (Glenn and Feldberg 1977). "Scientific management" may have actually upgraded clerical work by rationalizing it and encouraging the use of machines, such as Addressographs, postage meters, adding machines, staplers, and, of course, the typewriter, and by making it full-time work (Cohn 1985, 81–89; M. W. Davies 1982, 97–128). By the early twentieth century, the typical clerical worker was no longer an ambitious, literate young man but an upwardly mobile working-class woman with a high school education or a downwardly mobile daughter of a middle-class father whose business had failed (M. W. Davies 1982, 51–78).

Although the private secretary was a step up from clerical work, the job description was that of a virtual "office wife." For the office pool typist, the work was the white-collar equivalent of factory work.[20] The computer and word processor have replaced the typewriter, but the pay is still low, especially for women of color, and the use of advanced technology by women churning out data entries has not increased their autonomy, prestige, or chance for promotion.[21] Indeed, computer data processing seems to have brought women clerical workers full circle, back to part-time, temporary, or home-based piecework (Crompton and Jones 1984, 42–77).

Where men once monopolized the heavy machinery of the nineteenth-century Industrial Revolution, today they monopolize the technological, computerized knowledge that gives them an advantage in getting jobs with more autonomy and higher pay in many kinds of work and work organizations, including those organized communally.[22] One study of the distribution of workers in computer-related occupations found that 60 percent of white men were computer scientists or programmers, as were 42 percent of men of other racial ethnic groups, and three-quarters of the white women and women of color were computer operators or data entry keyers (Glenn and Tolbert 1987). The mean earnings in these jobs in 1983 were $28,383 for the scientists, $21,946 for the programmers, $14,245 for the operators, and $11,700 for data processors.

How to Make a Woman's Job

The continued division of workers into gender- and race-segregated jobs and work sites and its spread to office work derive from the conflict between employers' needs for cheap labor in order to maintain high profits and from men workers' resistance to women and to men of different racial ethnic groups as colleagues (Walby 1986). Since employers hire women in order to reduce their wage bill, women must work for less in order to work for pay at all. The question is not why an occupation or workplace has mostly women workers (all should by economic reasoning) but why most of the workers in some occupations are men, or why, within the same occupation, some firms use exclusively women and some exclusively men (Cohn 1985, 17–23).

Denise Bielby and William Bielby suggest that "an astute employer would do better by statistically discriminating against men" (1988, 1056) because women are conscientious hard workers. But men workers, particularly if they are entrenched and organized, can keep women workers out by denying them technological training and access to apprentice programs and professional schools and by refusing them membership in unions or professional organizations.[23] Employers have to hire men if the men have monopolized the skills needed to use certain machinery or the requisite educational credentials or if women are legally forbidden to work at night or to hold hazardous jobs. Employers who are buffered from having to minimize labor costs because their firms do not have to show a profit can afford to hire white men, or they may turn to disadvantaged or immigrant men who will work for as low wages as white women (Cohn 1985, 18). In the long run, state-supported exclusionary strategies are likely to be politically unpopular since the result is higher labor costs (Walby 1990, 53–55). Much more common is the division of the work force into a large lesser-paid group (women and disadvantaged men), whose work is divided into small, repetitive components, and a smaller better-paid group (usually dominant men), who supervise and administer or who monitor expensive machinery.

Women are cheap labor not because they are willing to work for low pay but because women's work is structured to justify minimal salaries. Most women's jobs are broken into small units with flat learning curves (after a brief training period, few advantages accrue to experience) and short promotion ladders. These women are rarely promoted, and they are discouraged from staying on so long that they have to be given pay raises and time toward a pension. But even the routinization and blocked mobility do not deter women from staying on a job that pays a decent salary. As a result, administrators have to find other ways to encourage turnover.

In Britain in the late nineteenth century, employers used marriage bars to preserve a cheap labor pool of women clerks. They were hired only if they were single and had to quit when they married. Such synthetic, or deliberately produced, turnover was not chosen by the women; it was imposed on them, for raises were tied to years of service. Young girls out of school were hired at sixteen; the expectation was that they would quit in five years and be replaced with another young woman at an entry-level salary. The marriage bar was imposed about eight years after the feminization of the clerical labor force in the British post office, when it was evident that left to their own devices, married women would keep their jobs. Later, "dowries," or substantial cash bonuses, were offered after six years of service to women who were getting married, with the understanding, of course, that they would quit. But most worked for four to seven years beyond the minimum before they married, so they had the additional money they saved *and* the cash bonuses. Women held onto their jobs on an average of thirteen years (Cohn 1985, 91–115). As Samuel Cohn says, "when offered better-than-average employment, women were willing to defy both organizational incentives and social convention in order to keep it" (1985, 108).

Other inducements have also been used to create turnover and maintain low wage scales for women. When hospitals expanded at the beginning of the twentieth century in the United States, administrators solved the problem of finding cheap labor by opening nursing schools and attracting poor young women with the promise of food, board, and training. The women were exploited for three years and then turned out as independent workers who competed for private patients with the nursing students sent into homes by hospitals; they were not upgraded into permanent staff (Ashley 1976).

Today, women's professions—nursing, social work, librarianship, elementary school teaching—are structured so that women can leave for several years to take care of their babies and return to work when the children start school. The compressed workday or shifts are supposed to coincide with children's school hours, and work can frequently be found close to home. Thus, these occupations have characteristics of women's work, including the low pay that presumably is a trade-off for compatibility with caring for children (Etzioni 1969; Grimm and Stern 1974).

Teaching, which today seems tailored to women's lives as wives and mothers, was compatible with *men's work* in nineteenth-century rural America: "When teaching was a relatively casual occupation that could be engaged in for fairly short periods of time, it was attractive to men in a variety of circumstances. A farmer could easily combine teaching in the winter with caring for his farm during the rest of the year. A potential minister, politician, shopkeeper, or lawyer could teach for a short period of time to gain visibility within the community" (Strober 1984, 152). When schools grew in size and were age-graded, with a curriculum devised for each grade, formal credentials were required and the teaching term was lengthened. But instead of raising wages to the level where a middle-class man could support a family, school boards kept them low, and "an ideological crusade was waged in favor of women's entry into teaching" (Strober 1984, 153). Teaching was turned into the ideal profession for single, educated, middle-class women, who were supposedly patient and nurturant, who could live on low pay, and who could learn skills for future motherhood. In the United States, women teachers were fired when they married up until World War II (Goldin 1990, 162) and were put on leave when pregnant until the 1960s. Today, for women, teaching has the structural characteristics of women's work—low wages, little autonomy, and high turnover; for men who predominate as principals and superintendents, it has the structural characteristics of men's work—stability, chances for promotion, and high wages (Spencer 1988).

Office Temps and Homeworkers

Whether women participate in the labor force depends on economic necessity, job opportunities, family responsibilities, and subjective commitment to working outside the home.[24] Kathleen Gerson (1985) found in her interviews with seventy-two college-educated white women that some who had planned careers ended up staying home with their children because they lived in a community where they could not get jobs or had no access to child care; others who had planned to be full-time mothers ended up as full-time career women because they did not marry or did not have children, or they married and had children but then divorced and had to support themselves and their children. If the workplace is pleasant, the pay good, and the health benefits generous, young pregnant women tend to continue working after giving birth (Glass 1988). If they have another baby and have good child-care arrangements, they are even more likely to return to their jobs.

Married working-class women throughout the world have no choice about taking on paid work to provide their families with necessities their husbands cannot or will not supply, and they often work at several jobs, some off the books and some in illegal work.[25] When women cannot work outside the home because of family responsibilities (not only children but an elderly parent or a sick husband may need to be cared for) or because their husbands oppose it, they often do home-based work, not intermittently, but steadily over a period of years.[26]

Middle-class people tend to think of a paid job as a nine-to-five permanent position in a store, office, or factory. But many jobs are not full time, and many are done in workers' residences. Some are not even officially counted as "work" (Bose 1987). A large proportion of part-time and home-based workers are women with families, who need these jobs as a way of juggling two kinds of domestic responsibilities—unpaid household maintenance and paid work that buys food and clothing and pays the rent (Benería and Roldán 1987). Women's jobs are frequently structured as part-time or home-based waged work so that workers can be paid less and cannot demand fringe benefits, such as medical insurance and paid vacations (Allen and Wolkowitz 1987; Beechey and Perkins 1987). Veronica Beechey and Tessa Perkins's analysis of the growth of the women's part-time labor market in England in the 1970s and 1980s showed that when flexibility in hiring practices was necessary because of hourly, daily, or seasonal peaks, employers used built-in overtime or double shifts in men's jobs and organized women's jobs around part-time temporary (in England, "casual") work schedules. Beechey and Perkins argue: "There is nothing *inher-ent* in the nature of particular jobs which makes them full-time or part-time. They have been constructed as such, and such constructions are closely related to gender" (1987, 145–46). They are race-based as well; as the work becomes less prestigious, more immigrant women and women of disadvantaged racial ethnic groups are hired.

Many women's occupations have been degraded. The job of saleswoman was once a full-time retail clerk in a posh urban department store (Benson 1986). It has deteriorated to part-time work in suburban malls and taking telephone orders for catalog sales. Most women clerical workers once had permanent, full-time jobs. Today, they are likely to be part-time or temporary or home-based data processors. Factory owners have relocated in developing countries in their search for the cheapest labor. In this century, women apparel workers went from sewing at home or in sweatshops to well-paid union jobs back to sweatshops and sewing at home. Every time a job is degraded, the work process is increasingly broken down into smaller and more repetitive components and the wages earned go down.[27] The employer cuts out more and more capital investment and overhead, lowers the wage bill, eliminates fringe benefits, and hires only the workers needed for the particular job or season (Beechey and Perkins 1987, 142–44; Safa 1981).

When employers convert jobs into part-time work, their rationale is that they want to attract women with small children, but their real reason is that they want to have a flexible supply of workers and to save money on training, health and disability insurance, vacation days, sick pay, and pensions (Beechey 1987, 149–67; Beechey and Perkins 1987). Home-based waged work is similarly sold as compatible with child care and housekeeping, but it is structured by contractors to be "low-paid, irregular and unskilled" (Allen and Wolkowitz 1987, 62). Most paid work done in the home by women workers is not free-lance self-employment but piecework in an "invisible assembly line" system of production analogous to the putting-out system of cottage industries prevalent at the start of the Industrial Revolution (Marglin 1978; Mies 1982, 53–71). The paradox is that these new cottage industries are found in the most highly industrialized countries, such as Britain or the United States, where "women working at home produce everything from clothes, shoes and quilts to windscreen wipers and industrial transmission belts. They process insurance claims, peel vegetables, and do company accounts. In India and Bangladesh homeworkers assemble electrical components, roll cigarettes, and make cane furniture and many other goods" (Allen and Wolkowitz 1987, 1). Dorinne Kondo worked part time in a small factory in modern Tokyo. In the same block where the factory was located, she found home-based workers stamping metal parts and plastic accessories, making shoes, folding boxes, sewing uniforms, weaving mats, carving umbrella handles, lacquering trays, ironing shirts, and even sharpening pencils (1990a, 4–6).

Kathleen Christensen (1988) interviewed one hundred home-based women workers in the United States who were independent contractors, worked in family businesses, or did piecework. She found that for married women with children, the disadvantages outweighed the purported advantages of autonomy, flexible schedules, and parenting full time. Their work was not taken seriously; their time was encroached on; they had no opportunity to learn new skills, be promoted, or find out what was going on in their work organization; they could easily be let go or given less work, and if they were self-employed, a recession could make serious inroads into their businesses.

Part-time and home-based waged work are not, for most women, ways to reduce their double day but ways "to fit paid work into the laborious, caring unpaid work of looking after their households" (Allen and Wolkowitz 1987, 86). Because men are relatively free of responsibilities for care of children, the elderly, and the sick, and for cooking, cleaning, and laundry, they are available for the better-paid, steadier, full-time jobs with fringe benefits. Part-time and home-based women workers may end up doing the equivalent of full-time work, but without good pay, a chance for promotion, and paid sick leave or vacations. That they have traded off fringe benefits and decent wages for flexibility in scheduling their work and family responsibilities is a myth (Allen and Wolkowitz 1987, 109–34, 166). The suppliers of work control when and how much they work, and their presence at home increases the domestic calls on their time: "The real situation is that homeworking permits the worker to go on working until she drops. It allows her to extend the working day into . . . evening and night work, and the working week into a full seven days" (125).

Job Queues and Labor Queues

The exigencies of capital accumulation segregate and stratify women and men of different racial ethnic groups into subdivisions of workers that range from valuable and relatively well-paid professionals, managers, sellers, and technicians in the core economy to first-line job holders—full-time clerks, assemblers, and supervisors—to second-line seasonal and part-time white-collar and blue-collar workers, down to "externals," subcontracted workers in sweatshops and home-based work (Beechey and Perkins 1987, 142–44). Men of the dominant racial ethnic group monopolize the better positions; all women and men of subordinate racial ethnic groups compete for the lower-ranked jobs not as individuals but as members of segregated labor markets— groups of workers defined more by their social characteristics than their capabilities.

Despite twenty years of legislation mandating nondiscrimination in the United States, the better a job is ranked by workers, the more likely it still is to be held by a well-educated white man of high-status background and extensive work experience (Jencks, Perman, and Rainwater 1988).[28] As the members of subordinate racial ethnic groups garner more social resources, they move into the better sectors of the economic system, but the women do not benefit as much as the men from the group's upward mobility. The men, as putative heads of households, monopolize the better opportunities for education, jobs, and starting businesses (Almquist 1987). Women of different racial ethnic groups, however, compete with each other, and as with men, being white is often an advantage (Glenn and Tolbert 1987; Glazer 1993). In teaching, for example, 82.5 percent of Black women teachers were employed in the public sector in fifteen large U.S. cities in 1983, compared to 66.7 percent of white women teachers (E. Higginbotham 1987, table 4.3).

The processes that sort women and men of different racial ethnic groups into segregated unequal jobs are a matching of ranked workers and jobs, or what Barbara Reskin and Patricia Roos (1990) conceptualize as *queues* of workers and jobs. Workers are ranked by employers from their first picks to their last. Jobs are ranked by workers similarly. Lower-ranked workers get the chance to move into better jobs than they have held in the past when these jobs are abandoned by favored workers, or there are too few of these workers to go around, such as in wartime. The process works the other way, too; when there are too few of the best jobs for the preferred workers, as in a recession, only the best qualified or experienced will get them; those with fewer credentials and less seniority move down the queue, bumping out lesser-ranked workers. When workers are moving up, the best qualified usually get the better jobs. But if gender segregation is so rigid that men will not apply or be hired for "women's work," when manufacturing jobs decline or are taken elsewhere, women in service, sales, and clerical work may continue to work as men's unemployment rates soar.[29]

Workers rank jobs, Reskin and Roos argue, on the basis of payoff for education and experience in fringe benefits, prestige, autonomy, security, and chances of promotion. For some workers, having any job may be an improvement over economic dependency (Segura 1989). Employers' preferences for workers, however, are not so uniform. Some will rank gender and race above qualifications; others will choose the most highly qualified of the preferred race and gender and then go down the line, looking for the most qualified each time. Another variable employers factor in is the going pay scale for the workers they want; they may have to settle for less preferred workers to see more of a profit or sacrifice some profits to avoid protests from highly paid entrenched workers.

Although worker demographics, industry growth, and employer preferences produce change in occupational gender composition, Reskin and Roos argue that the main factor that redistributes workers of different races and genders is change in the structure of the work process and in the quality of particular *jobs* within occupations, which can be manipulated by employers. That is, jobs can be automated and deskilled or made part time or home-based to justify reducing labor costs, with a few better-paid workers retained in supervisory positions.

Examining shifts in the gender makeup of the U.S. work force in the 1970s, Reskin and Roos focused on changes in occupational characteristics— such as working conditions, skills needed, unionization, education level, extent of unemployment, part time versus full time, and earnings—in jobs where the increase in women's representation was at least twice as great as the increase in women workers between 1970 and 1980, when women's proportion of the U.S. labor force increased from 38 percent to 42.6 percent. To discover what caused the disproportionate influx of women workers into occupations such as personnel manager, computer operator, insurance agent, and real estate salesperson, and the outcome of that "feminization," their research team visited workplaces, interviewed practitioners, gatekeepers, and experts, and consulted industry and academic reports, government, union, trade, and professional publications, census data, and court records. They found that jobs became available to women because they lost their attractiveness for white men. They were deskilled, earnings declined, there was less autonomy, and working conditions deteriorated. In some cases, employers helped the process along by finding better jobs in the organization for men incumbents or by making a position a part-time job. Government pressure on employers to hire more women was effective only in very visible jobs, such as broadcasting. Some employers invoked gender stereotypes to claim, after the fact, that the job was particularly appropriate for women workers.

Why did women want these downgraded jobs? Simple—they were better than the women's jobs they had before. Ironically, however, as more women took the downgraded jobs vacated by men, the more the job, work site, or occupation resegregated—became predominantly women's work. The most common outcome in the 1970s was not a complete turnover, but ghettoization; for the same occupation, men and women did different jobs at different work sites or in different kinds of organizations. The women's jobs moved down the queue, and the women who were hired later did not move up at all: "Though women did make progress in desegregating traditionally male occupations, by the time women gained access to them, the occupations had lost much of their attraction to men and were becoming less advantageous for women as well. Women's success in these occupations was in large measure hollow" (Reskin and Roos 1990, 87). As Michael J. Carter and Susan Boslego Carter titled their summing up of women's putative progress in the professions, "Women Get a Ticket to Ride after the Gravy Train Has Left the Station" (1981).

During shifts of labor queues up and down the job ladder, the potential for conflict between women and men and members of dominant and subordinated racial ethnic groups is high. Dominant men want to perpetuate the work conditions that justify their high pay; employers who want to reduce their labor costs degrade the work process so they can hire cheaper labor, and then these new workers are accused of depressing the job's qualifications and skills. Gender segregation of jobs is historically the way employers have kept their men workers satisfied, while expanding the number of cheaper women workers (Walby 1986, 154). Such job divisions undercut unions that want to organize women and demand the same pay for them as similarly situated men workers. In a growing or stable job market, dominant men have much less resistance to incoming new types of workers, since they do not see them as competition (Swerdlow 1989). In those cases, the job may come closer to being integrated on gender and race.

In general, though, when the gravy train stays in the station, white men continue to be the predominant workers in the better paid, most prestigious jobs with good working conditions, as Natalie Sokoloff found in her analysis of gender and race shifts in professions in the United States between 1960 and 1980 (1988). Black men, severely underrepresented in the most prestigious professions over these two decades, nevertheless almost doubled their representation, as did white women, while Black women increased their representation fivefold. But though white men were no longer a majority of all professionals by 1980, they were still 86.1 percent of the *prestigious* professionals, such as lawyer, doctor, or scientist.

Reaching Out for Diversity: Affirmative Action

Affirmative action was a policy developed in the United States after the passage of the Civil Rights Act of 1964, which forbade discrimination in education, training, hiring, promotion, and salaries on the basis of race and gender. It was soon found that with no plan of action, educational and business organizations continued to recruit, train, and hire men for "men's" jobs and women for "women's" jobs, whites for "white" jobs, and members of other racial ethnic groups for "minority" jobs (Hillsman and Levenson 1975; Levinson 1975). The recruiters argued that they could not find more than a few "tokens."

Affirmative action guidelines instructed organizations that the proportion of students, apprentices, new workers, and workers at every level should reflect the proportion of people of every race and gender in the general population, provided they had suitable qualifications. The next policy step was to ensure a qualified supply of white women and women and men of disadvantaged racial and ethnic groups. If the affirmative action goal was more Black women managers, then business schools had to recruit more Black women students. Recruiters for business schools under affirmative action pressure went to Black colleges and recruited, and then recruiters for firms under affirmative action pressure went to the business schools to recruit for entry-level jobs. As they all found more than a few qualified "tokens," a number of gender and racial barriers were broken.

Women and disadvantaged men are more likely to want to desegregate white men's jobs than vice versa, although out-of-work men have taken "women's" jobs, such as telephone operator. When AT&T desegregated after a successful affirmative action suit, 16,300 men became telephone operators, but they were predominantly temporary workers; the better-paid craft jobs for which women now had to be hired were automated (Hacker 1979). Without constant monitoring, affirmative action guidelines were simply ignored, and employers continued to recruit on the basis of gender stereotypes about women's and men's jobs and family commitments (Collinson, Knights, and Collinson 1990).

On the positive side, organizations have successfully changed specific career ladders by creating "bridge" jobs that allow already-hired clerical employees to obtain on-the-job administrative or technical experience in order to qualify for managerial positions. Because interested groups of workers must monitor these and other affirmative action processes, particularly in politically and economically powerful corporations, having a large percentage of women workers is helpful, as is having women in executive positions (Yoder, Crumpton, and Zipp 1989). When funding comes from the state, it can sometimes be withheld for noncompliance with affirmative action directives. But a generation of affirmative action has barely disturbed deeply entrenched patterns of occupational segregation and stratification by gender and race in the United States.

The Wage Gap

Equal pay for equal work is a generally accepted principle that not only guarantees that women doing men's work receive a man's salary but also ensures that an employer cannot undercut men's wages by hiring women at a cheaper rate (Kessler-Harris 1990, 81–112). The shifting boundaries of occupational gender segregation maintain the principle and undermine it at the same time. Women and men do not do "equal" work—they do different work, or the same work in different industries, or the same work in a different part of a work organization under a different job title (Goldin 1990, 58–82; Strang and Baron 1990). As William Bielby and James Baron say: "men's jobs are rewarded according to their standing within the hierarchy of men's work, and women's jobs are rewarded according to their standing within the hierarchy of women's work. The legitimacy of this system is easy to sustain in a segregated workplace" (1987, 226).

The result is the familiar gendered wage gap. In the United States, the ratio of white women's to white men's wages for full-time, year-round work rose from .46 to .56 from 1890 to 1930, but from 1950 to 1980 hovered around .60 and rose to about .65 by 1989 (Blum 1991, 29; Goldin 1990, 59). The ratio is somewhat better when Black and Hispanic women and men workers are compared, but only because men of color earn less than white men. Most of the early increase in white women's wages was due to their greater work experience and education, but most of the later increase was due to the decline in white men's earnings. The dollar value of "human capital" factors, such as education and experience, is consistently less for all women and for men of subordinate racial ethnic groups than for dominant-group men workers, and this unexplained difference is attributed to the "wage discrimination" that occurs in industrialized countries.[30]

Wage discrimination occurs in two major ways: Wage scales of jobs, occupations, sectors, and segments where dominant-group men are in the majority are consistently higher, and in *any* job, women and subordinate-group men tend to be paid less as workers. Gender differentials are more prevalent than racial gaps. Men who do "women's work" earn less than men who work in occupations where most of the workers are men, but they tend to earn more than the women in these occupations because they are promoted faster. Women who do "men's work" earn more than women who do "women's work" because the occupation or profession as a whole is likely to be better paid; however, since women in "men's work" are not likely to be promoted as fast or as high as their men colleagues, if at all, they rarely outearn men.

In addition to the wage gap produced by the proportion of women to men workers and by the gendered inequalities in advancement, occupations that encompass authority or supervision pay more than similar jobs that do not need managerial skills, and jobs that require workers to deal with clients in an interpersonal or nurturant way pay less than similar non-people-oriented jobs (England 1992). Since authority is more likely to characterize higher-level jobs, where men predominate, and nurturance the lower-level jobs where the majority of the workers are women, all the types of wage discrimination coincide.

Pay Equity or Comparable Worth

One way of achieving pay equity in the face of persistent gender segregation is to compare the actual work content of women's and men's jobs and to pay the same salaries for those that are equally complex or skilled or have similar responsibilities. The strategy of comparable worth is to break a job down into components that add up to points. Such components can be education or training needed to get the job, skills needed to do the job, the extent of responsibility for others' work and for finances, dangerousness, dirtiness, and so on. Evaluation schemes usually assign "worth points" for knowledge and skills, mental demands, accountability, and working conditions.[31]

Comparable worth or pay equity lawsuits claim that women and men workers in jobs with the same number of points should be paid the same in order to redress gendered wage discrimination. For example, in Minnesota, the highest grade of clerk-typists, all women, earned $1,274 a month, while senior highway maintenance workers, almost all men, earned $1,521 a month. In the pay equity evaluation, the clerk-typist job was given 169 points; the highway maintenance job 154 points (Evans and Nelson 1989, table 1.1, 9). In San Jose, California, before the implementation of a pay equity plan, a nurse earned $9,120 a year less than a fire truck mechanic; a legal secretary made $7,288 a year less than an equipment mechanic; the mayor's secretary made 47 percent less than a senior air conditioning mechanic (Blum 1991, 82–83).

The choice of components and how they are weighted in the evaluation scheme tend to favor certain kinds of jobs and workers.[32] Dangerous or dirty working conditions tend to be rewarded with extra points, but boredom from routinized and heavily supervised work is not usually considered an adverse working condition. As a result, assembly line and data processing workers get fewer points than construction workers (Amott and Matthaei 1988). Management knowledge and skills always get a large number of points, but the invisible work done for managers by administrative support workers, such as editing, maintaining office machinery, keeping the boss's calendar, tactfully screening phone calls and visitors, and attending to myriad details, does not (Amott and Matthaei 1988; Mine 1988). All of these job evaluation assumptions disfavor women, who tend to work in routinized, heavily supervised, white-collar jobs and whose skills are often considered natural attributes. Nursing, for example, has been considered women's "natural talent," and so, even though nurses are indispensable in the modern hospital and in short supply, their wages are not high, compared to doctors' salaries (Corley and Mauksch 1988; Reverby 1987).

In Oregon, there was a battle between the consultants hired to set up the evaluation system and the feminist members of the state's Task Force on Compensation and Pay Equity over how many levels of human relations skills should be recognized (Acker 1989a, 61–103). Were "ordinary courtesy" and the ability to communicate factual information basic skills and therefore not worth too many points? What level of human relations skill did a clerical worker who worked for several bosses have? As much as a highway mainte-nance worker in a work team? The top-level ratings tended to favor upper-level management; tautologically, what managers did were high-level skills deserving of many points, which translated into high pay; "skill is often an ideological category imposed on certain types of work by virtue of the sex and power of the workers who perform it" (Phillips and Taylor 1980, 79). What lower-level workers did concerning interpersonal relationships was consid-ered "basic." In California, knowing what job characteristics would be assigned points, women workers helped to educate each other to describe their jobs in terms that would pay off, not in terms likely to be discounted. For example, librarians did not describe their job as checking out books but as managing the annual book-buying budget and maintaining a million-dollar book collection (Blum 1991, 75–77).

In the United States, Black women are clustered in lower-level clerical jobs and in the public sector, the areas where comparable worth has been most frequently applied. Their salaries in the jobs where they are overrepresented are compensated at a lower rate than jobs held by mostly white women, and their families are heavily dependent on their income. Comparable worth might benefit Black women workers even more than white women workers, espe-cially where the underlying goal is a form of poverty relief.[33]

Radical Remedies, Radical Effects

Despite its purported radical implications, the comparable worth strategy does not restructure the economy, eliminate workplace hierarchies, flatten out major wage differentials, or remove other forms of gender inequities. It has, however, made women aware of who their allies and enemies are at different

hierarchical levels and taught them how to organize, how to shape the evaluation of their jobs, and how to insist on pay levels commensurate with *their*
evaluation of their worth. [34]

The race, gender, and class inequities revealed by comparable worth job
evaluations belie the ideology that worth in the labor market is based on effort,
productivity, or contribution to profit (Baron and Newman 1990). By defining
what women do in their typical jobs (nursing, teaching, social work, office
managers, child-care workers) as skilled, and paying commensurately, comparable worth could raise the value of those underpaid qualities of "nurturance,
community, and relational abilities" (Kessler-Harris 1990, 125). Since much of
women's work would then pay as well as lower-level men's work, there would
be little reason for men to shun such jobs as nurse or clerk, or to keep women
out of such jobs as train engineer or electrician.

It is unlikely, however, that occupational gender segregation and stratification would be eliminated. Comparable worth will not address hiring discrimination based on the gender or race of the worker or inequities in discretionary
raises and promotion; these are affirmative action issues. And even the objec-
tives that comparable worth is designed to address—unbiased assessment of
job demands and commensurate financial compensation—are rarely accomplished without serious compromise. Organizational politics and the power of
some groups of workers determine who benefits from comparable worth.
One extensive study in Washington State found that the determination of
comparative wage levels was "shot through with subjectivity, arbitrariness, and
interest-group politics, virtually from beginning to end" (Bridges and Nelson
1989, 654). In Oregon, the preservation of organizational hierarchy and class
boundaries took precedence over recognition of the management skills involved in women's support jobs, such as office supervisor and secretary. If
women's management abilities were considered job-related skills and not
natural feminine talents, the large gap between what those jobs pay and what
men managers are paid would have been seriously challenged (Acker 1989a,
208–17).

Thus, though pay equity might even out women's and men's wages at
lower levels, it preserves the gap between these levels and upper-level management dominated by white men: "the idea that some jobs are worth more
than others is reinforced under comparable worth" (Evans and Nelson 1989,
13). In addition to salary levels, jobs are ranked on prestige, autonomy,
authority, location, and working conditions. Pay equity does not do away with
large stratification differences or with the restrictive effects of professional
training and other forms of gatekeeping. In addition, as long as employers

control the work process, they can fragment jobs into part-time and sub-contracted work, shift offices and plants to locations where labor is cheaper, automate jobs, and retain only a few high-priced workers (Malveaux 1987). Since workers of different genders, races, and ethnic groups are distributed very unevenly across the resultant hierarchies, these class-producing processes reproduce the major gendered and racial ethnic inequities as well (Acker 1989a, 210). In this sense, comparable worth is hardly radical:

> A radical strategy would argue for raising the pay of the lowest-paid workers, most of whom are women and minorities, on the grounds that everyone who contributes his or her labor deserves a comfortable and secure existence. This strategy would not only protest the under-valuation of women's work but also argue that existing salary differen-tials among jobs, especially between management and nonmanagement jobs, are unnecessarily large. And it would argue that if we are looking at the work people do, then we should ask whether that work is productive, safe, and interesting, and whether it allows people to use their talents and skills and to develop new ones. (Brenner 1987, 461)

Giving all workers the opportunity to do intrinsically and materially rewarding work would radically alter gender, class, and race stratification in paid work. It would also radically alter domestic work by giving women the same economic resources as men and equalizing their bargaining power, and it would eliminate much of the pool of domestic service workers. Either all the members of a household would have to do housework, or, more likely, more and more household services would be commodified. If domestic services were not gender- and race-stratified, we might see married white men rou-tinely cooking, cleaning, doing laundry, and scrubbing toilet bowls for pay— or for love.

Part III

THE POLITICS OF GENDER

> You're proposing your interpretation of the universe, and for
> that you need to have the recognition of your colleagues. You must
> assert that this is a good idea, the right interpretation, and that *you*
> thought of it, because all three of those things have to be accepted
> by your colleagues. It doesn't do your career any good to have the
> theory accepted, without anyone giving you the credit.
>
> —*Harriet Zuckerman, Jonathan R. Cole, and John T. Bruer (1991, 103)*

GUARDING THE GATES:
THE MICROPOLITICS OF GENDER

Twenty-five years ago, Muriel F. Siebert bought a seat on the New York Stock Exchange, the first woman to be permitted to do so. In 1992, receiving an award for her accomplishments, she said bluntly that despite the numbers of women coming into high finance, the professions, and government, the arenas of power are still overwhelmingly dominated by men (Henriques 1992). The numbers bear her out.

In 1980 in the United States, only two women were chief executive officers of the largest corporations, the Fortune 500. They were Katherine Graham, chief executive of the Washington Post Company, and Marion O. Sandler, co–chief executive of Golden West Financial Corporation, in Oakland, California. In 1985, there were three: Graham, Sandler, and Elisabeth Claiborne of the Liz Claiborne clothing company. In 1990, there were also three: Graham, Sandler, and Linda Wachner of the Warnaco Group, Inc., New York. In 1992, Charlotte Beers became chief executive of Ogilvie & Mather Worldwide, the fifth largest international advertising agency, with billings of $5.4 billion, making her the world's highest ranking woman executive in that field (Elliott 1992). Linda Wachner (earning $3.1 million in 1991) was the first woman in *Fortune*'s "roster of exorbitantly paid executives" (Strom 1992). Thus, in the past decade, in the United States, where women composed between 42.4 and 45.4 percent of the work force, and numbered between 42.1 and 53.5 million, a total of five women were heads of the largest corporations (Marsh 1991).[1] When *Fortune* culled the lists of the highest paid officers and directors of 799 U.S. industrial and service companies, out of 4,012 it found 19 women, or less than one-half of 1 percent (Fierman 1990).

The belief that upward mobility and leadership positions would automatically follow if women increased their numbers in the workplace greatly underestimated the social processes that get some people onto the fast track and systematically derail others. These processes are used by those at the top to ensure that those coming up will be as similar as possible to themselves so that their values and ideas about how things should be done will be perpetuated. The markers of homogeneity are gender, race, religion, ethnicity, education, and social background. The few heterogeneous "tokens" who make it past the gatekeepers first must prove their similarity to the elite in outlook and behavior. The numbers at the bottom in any field have little relation to the numbers at the top, where power politics is played and social policies are shaped.

The gender segregation so evident in the modern work world is exacerbated at the top echelons of business, the professions, and politics by gendered concepts of authority and leadership potential. Women are seen as legitimate leaders only in areas considered of direct concern to women, usually health, education, and welfare. Women's accomplishments in men's fields tend to be invisible or denigrated by the men in the field, and so women rarely achieve the stature to be considered leaders in science or space, for example.[2] The U.S. National Aeronautics and Space Administration put twenty-five women pilots through rigorous physical and psychological testing from 1959 to 1961. Thirteen demonstrated "exceptional suitability" for space flight, but neither they nor seventeen women with advanced science degrees were chosen to be astronauts or space scientists, even though the Russians had sent Valentina Tereshkova into space in 1963 (McCullough 1973). As Gloria Steinem said, recalling these invisible women almost twenty years later, women's demonstrating they have the "right stuff" turns into the "wrong stuff" without the approval of the men in charge (1992).

When a leader is chosen among colleagues, women are often overlooked by the men of the group, and there are usually too few women to support one another. Even where women are the majority of workers, men tend to be favored for positions of authority because women and men will accept men leaders as representing their general interests but will see women as representing only women's interests (Izraeli 1984). As a result, men in occupations where most of the workers are women, such as nursing and social work, tend to be overrepresented in high-level administrative positions, and women in occupations where most of the workers are men rarely reach the top ranks (C. L. Williams 1989, 95–98; Zunz 1991).

When men choose a woman for a position of power and prestige, she is often considered "on probation." For example, an Israeli woman physician who was made head of a prestigious department of obstetrics and gynecology where she was the only woman told me that a year later, the men colleagues who had chosen her told her that they were now enormously relieved. She had not made any serious mistakes, so their decision to choose her as head of the department was validated. She was furious that they had felt she had to prove herself; she had been their colleague and friend for seventeen years, and they surely should have known her worth and her leadership capabilities. At that point, she said, she realized that her men colleagues had never really considered her "one of them."[3]

The Glass Ceiling

The pervasive phenomenon of women going just so far and no further in their occupations and professions has come to be known as the *glass ceiling*. This concept assumes that women have the motivation, ambition, and capacity for positions of power and prestige, but invisible barriers keep them from reaching the top. They can see their goal, but they bump their heads on a ceiling that is both hidden and impenetrable. The U.S. Department of Labor defines the glass ceiling as "those artificial barriers based on attitudinal or organizational bias that prevent qualified individuals from advancing upward in their organization into management level positions" (L. Martin 1991, 1).

A recent study of the pipelines to power in large-scale corporations conducted by the U.S. Department of Labor found that the glass ceiling was lower than previously thought—in middle management. Members of disadvantaged groups were even less likely than white women to be promoted to top positions, and the upper rungs were "nearly impenetrable" for women of color (L. Martin 1991). A random sample of ninety-four reviews of personnel in corporate headquarters found that of 147,179 employees, 37.2 percent were women and 15.5 percent were minorities. Of these employees, 31,184 were in all levels of management, from clerical supervisor to chief executive officer; 16.9 percent were women and 6 percent were minorities. Of 4,491 managers at the level of assistant vice president and higher, 6.6 percent were women and 2.6 percent were minorities. Thus, in this survey, the higher the corporate position, the smaller the proportion of women; if the numbers of women in the top ranks had been proportional with the number of women in the lower ranks, over a third of the vice presidents, presidents, and executive officers would have been women. There was no separate breakdown of these figures for women of color, but another report cited by the Labor Department indicated that they make up 3.3 percent of the women corporate officers, who make up only 1 to 2 percent of all corporate officers.

Karen Fulbright's (1987) interviews with twenty-five African-American women managers found fifteen who had reached the level of vice president, department head, or division director in oil, automobile manufacturing, tele-communications, and banking, or had moved rapidly up the hierarchy. The factors in their upward mobility were long tenure, a rapidly growing company, or a Black-owned or operated company. The others had experienced blocked mobility, despite positioning themselves on career tracks that were known to be the routes to the top.

Similar attrition in the numbers of women at the top has been found in public-sector jobs in the United States. As of 1990, 43.5 percent of the employees in lower-level jobs were women, but they were only 31.3 percent of the department heads, division chiefs, deputies, and examiners in state and local government agencies (*New York Times* 1992a). African-American women were 9.8 percent of the workers at lower levels, 5.1 percent at the top levels.

The ways that most people move up in their careers are through *networking* (finding out about job opportunities through word-of-mouth and being recom-mended by someone already there), *mentoring* (being coached through the informal norms of the workplace), and *sponsorship* (being helped to advance by a senior colleague). In civil service bureaucracies, where promotion depends on passing a test or getting an additional credential, those who receive encour-agement and advice from senior members of the organization tend to take the qualifying tests or obtain the requisite training (Poll 1978). In the sciences, research productivity depends to a significant degree on where you work, whom you work with, and what resources are available to you.[4] All these processes of advancement depend on the support of colleagues and superiors, which means that in a workplace where men outnumber women and whites outnumber any other racial ethnic group, white women and women and men of disadvantaged racial ethnic groups have to be helped by white men if they are to be helped at all.

An in-depth study of nine Fortune 500 companies with a broad range of products and services located in different parts of the country found that despite differences in organizational structure, corporate culture, and person-nel policies, the same practices results in a glass ceiling for women, especially women of color (L. Martin 1991, 4–5). These practices were recruitment policies for upper-management levels that depended on word-of-mouth net-working and employee referrals. When "head hunters" were used, they were not instructed to look for women and men of social groups underrepresented at managerial levels. The few white women and women and men of color who were already hired were not given the opportunity to build up their credentials or enhance their careers by assignment to corporate committees, task forces, and special projects. These are traditional avenues of advancement, since they bring junior members into contact with senior members of the organization and give them visibility and the chance to show what they can do. There was no monitoring of evaluation or compensation systems that determine salaries, bonuses, incentives, or perks to make sure that white women and women and men of color were getting their fair share. In general, "monitoring for equal access and opportunity, especially as managers move up the corporate ladder to senior management levels where important decisions are made, was almost never considered a corporate responsibility or part of the planning for develop-mental programs and policies" (L. Martin 1991, 4). In short, none of the white men in senior management saw it as their responsibility to sponsor white women or women and men of color to be their replacements when they retired.

Men in traditional women's occupations report the opposite phenome-non. Their minority status turns out to be a career advantage. Christine Williams's study of seventy-six men and twenty-three women in nursing, teaching, librarianship, and social work in the United States, whom she inter-viewed from 1985 to 1991, found that the men were tracked into the more prestigious, better-paying specialties within the occupation, and urged by their mentors, mostly other men, to move into positions of authority. Most of these men were white, so they were the most advantaged workers.[5] For them not to move up to supervisory and administrative positions was considered inap-propriate. As a result, they were on a "glass escalator," Williams says: "Often, despite their intentions, they face invisible pressures to move up in their professions. As if on a moving escalator, they must work to stay in place" (1992, 256). But they sometimes faced a glass ceiling at higher levels. The affirmative action policies of many institutions make the women deans and heads of departments in the women's areas too visible for them to be replaced by men (257).

Although these processes may seem benign, the imbalance of lower-level workers with disadvantaged social characteristics compared to upper-level workers with advantaged social characteristics implies a deliberate, though unstated, policy of hostility and resistance that deepens with each additional mark of disadvantage. Kimberlé Crenshaw presents a graphic analysis of who can make it through the glass ceiling:

Imagine a basement which contains all people who are disadvantaged on the basis of race, sex, class, sexual preference, age and / or physical ability. These people are stacked—feet standing on shoulders—with those on the bottom being disadvantaged by the full array of factors, up to the very top, where the heads of all those disadvantaged by a single factor brush up against the ceiling. . . . A hatch is developed through which those placed immediately below can crawl. Yet this hatch is generally available only to those who—due to the singularity of their burden and their otherwise privileged position relative to those below—are in the position to crawl through. Those who are multiply-burdened are generally left below. (1991, 65)

Bands of Brothers

Parallel to the formal organization of a large, modern workplace, which is structured as a task-related, bureaucratic hierarchy, is the informal organization, which is based on trust, loyalty, and reciprocal favors (Lorber [1979] 1989a). Because the unspoken rules are often as significant to the way business is conducted as the written rules, colleagues want to work with people who know what goes without saying: "In order that men [sic] may communicate freely and confidentially, they must be able to take a good deal of each other's sentiments for granted. They must feel easy about their silences as well as about their utterances. These factors conspire to make colleagues, with a large body of unspoken understandings, uncomfortable in the presence of what they consider odd kinds of fellows" (Hughes 1971, 146).

Personal discretion and reliability are particularly necessary for those in positions of authority because of the uncertainties they face (Kanter 1977a, 47–68). According to Dianne Feinstein, former mayor of San Francisco who was elected to the U.S. Senate in 1992, women have to bend over backward to prove not only their competence but their trustworthiness:

Women have to prove themselves effective and credible time and time again. Experience has taught me that the keys to a woman's effectiveness in public office are to be "trustable": to give directions clearly and to follow up, to verify every statement for accuracy, to guard her integrity carefully, and to observe the public's trust one hundred percent. Most important, she must be a team player and build relationships with her colleagues that are based on integrity and respect. (Cantor and Bernway 1992, xv)

Almost twenty years ago, Margaret Hennig and Anne Jardim predicted that conscientious and hard-working women would find it difficult to get out of middle management because their performance was geared to formal training and bureaucratic responsibilities. They felt that if women knew that senior management relies on informal networking, gathering extensive sources of knowledge from areas other than one's own, planning, policy-making, and delegating responsibility to reliable subordinates, they would be able to move up corporate career ladders (1976, 55–68).[6] Career mobility, however, does not depend only on competent performance and other efforts by the ambitious individual. To move up, a young person's worth has to be recognized and encouraged by those in the upper echelons. Promising young men of the right social characteristics are groomed for senior management by "godfathers" or "rabbis"—sponsors who take them under their wing and see to it that they learn the informal organizational rules for getting ahead. Promising young women are left to fend for themselves (Lorber 1981).

Brotherly trust among men who are business associates goes back to the nineteenth century. Before the creation of the impersonal corporation, each partner in an enterprise was personally responsible for raising capital and making a profit. Credit depended on personal trustworthiness; bankruptcy was a personal tragedy (Davidoff and Hall 1987, 198–228; Silver 1990). In these transactions, the active players were all men. Women were passive partners; their money was used by kinsmen and men friends who acted as trustees. In order to cement the brotherly bonds among men who were in business together, women were encouraged to marry cousins or their brothers' partners; two sisters often married two brothers, or a brother and sister married a sister and brother: "Free choice marriage controlled in this way provided a form of security in binding together members of the middle class in local, regional and national networks, a guarantee of congenial views as well as trustworthiness in economic and financial affairs" (Davidoff and Hall 1987, 221).[7]

In twentieth-century businesses, professions, and politics, trust and loyalty are built not through kin ties (which is considered nepotism) but through *homosociality*—the bonding of men of the same race, religion, and social-class background (Lipman-Blumen 1976). These men have the economic, political, professional, and social resources to do each other favors. Women with the same social characteristics may be included in men's circles when they have equivalent wealth, power, and social position (C. F. Epstein 1981, 265–302; Lorber 1984, 57–63). Most men and women, however, relate to each other socially only in familial or sexual roles (G. Moore 1990).

Homosociality starts early. In childhood play, boys separate themselves from girls and become contemptuous of girls' activities in their efforts to keep themselves apart.[8] This segregation, attributed to boys' needs to establish their masculinity, makes friendship between girls and boys difficult because it is discouraged by same-gender peers. Gender grouping is not perfect in mixed-gender schools but is broached by social class and racial ethnic cross-currents and sometimes by the organizing activities of teachers (Thorne 1990).[9] In adulthood, whenever men and women come together as equals, in coed schools and workplaces that are not gender-segregated, cross-gender friendships are undermined by intimations of sexual attraction (O'Meara 1989). One study of white middle-class young adults found that the women preferred same-gender friendships more than the men did because the men were more interested in them sexually than as companions (S. M. Rose 1985). The men invested more time and attention in their friendships with men than they did in their friendships with women, while the women gave as much emotional support to their men friends as they did to their women friends. Letty Cottin Pogrebin (1987, 311–40) feels that the main reason that women and men are rarely intimate friends is that they are rarely true equals.

Many working women are expected as part of their job to smile, be cordial, sympathetic, agreeable, and a bit sexy.[10] Men workers are supposed to display masculine emotions—coolness under fire, rationality, and objectivity, which are part of the performance of power (Sattel 1976). The qualities men want in women in the workplace as well as in the home—sympathy, looking out for the other person, understanding the nuances and cues of behavior, caretaking, flattering them sexually—keep women out of the top ranks of business, government, and the professions. Such qualities are gender-marked as "womanly"; they are also subordinating (Ridgeway and Johnson 1990).

Much of men's workplace small talk is about sports or sex. Replaying the weekend's games gives men the chance to compete and win vicariously (Kemper 1990, 167–206). Sexist jokes establish the boundaries of exclusion, and if the men are of the same race or religion, so do racist and anti-Semitic or anti-Catholic jokes. Sexist joking also keeps men from revealing their emotional bonds with each other and deflects their anger from their bosses onto women.[11] Women who can talk and joke like men may be allowed entry into the men's brotherhood, as honorary men, but then they cannot protest against sexism and sexual harassment, even if they themselves are the victims.[12]

Although men or women may be "odd fellows" in their workplace or job, the pressures of being a woman in a man's job and a man in a woman's job are quite different. Men nurses can talk cars and sports with men physicians. In doing so, they affiliate with a higher status group, affirm their masculinity, and gain a benefit from these informal contacts in more favorable evaluations of their work. Men physicians' status is too high to be compromised by chatting with men nurses (or flirting with women nurses). Men who are openly homosexual, however, may face discrimination from men supervisors (C. L. Williams 1992, 259). Women physicians socialize with women medical students, interns, and residents, but not with women nurses.[13] Women physicians' status is more tenuous, and they end up in a bind. They need to get along with the women nurses so that their work proceeds efficiently, yet they lose status if they bond with a lower-status group as women. Women physicians need to build colleague relationships with the men physicians who are their peers, but these men may not treat them as equals. They also need to seek sponsors among senior men who can help them advance their careers, but these men may not want them as protégées.

Because men know the power of homosocial bonding, they are discomfited when women do the same thing and often accuse such women of lesbianism, particularly because women's attentions are turned to each other and not to them. As Carol Barkalow said of the military:

> They often appear to possess an irrational fear of women's groups, believing that, in their midst, men will be plotted against, or perhaps worst of all, rendered somehow unnecessary. If women soldiers do try to develop a professional support network among themselves, they are faced with the dilemma that something as simple as two women officers having lunch together more than once might spark rumors of lesbianism—a potentially lethal charge, since even rumored homosexuality can damage an officer's career. (1990, 167–68)[14]

Women officers who want to bond without innuendoes of homosexuality often turn to sports, which is as legitimate a place to build trust and loyalty among women as it is among men.[15]

For the most part, as colleagues, friends, and wives, women are relegated to acting as audience or sex objects for men. According to Kathryn Ann Farr (1988), who studied a group of upper-class white men whose bonding preserved their race and class as well as their gender privileges, wives and girlfriends were needed to serve as foils for the men's exclusive sociability. The women listened as the men talked about their exploits. When the men went off on an escapade, their women warned them against getting into too much trouble, prepared food for them, and stayed behind. The men defined the boundaries of their homosocial world by excluding women, just as they maintained its racial and class exclusivity by keeping out the "wrong" kind of men. The irony is that they built their superior status in a direct and immediate way by denying their own wives and girlfriends the privileges of their race and class. In this way, the domination of men over women in their own social group is sustained, and the women collude in the process:

> These men do not view themselves as sexist, and they do not appear to be viewed by the women *with whom they interact* as sexist. In their choice of wives and girlfriends, the majority of these men seem to value independent and intelligent women. Yet their socialization into a male-dominated environment and a culture in which male sociability is highly valued causes them to think and act in ways that conflict with their intellectual assessments of the worth of and the value of social relationships with women. (Farr 1988, 269)[16]

By excluding women who share their social characteristics from their social space, these men never have to treat women as equals or as serious competitors for positions of power.[17]

The "Mommy Track"

If they could not exclude women completely or relegate them to subordinate positions, men have reduced competition and encouraged turnover by refusing to hire married women or mothers and by encouraging women employees who get married or have children to quit. Marriage bars were used against women schoolteachers, stewardesses, and other occupations in the United States well into the twentieth century and are still used today in other countries (Brinton 1989; Goldin 1990, 160–84). When the marriage bar fell out of use in the United States in the late 1950s, partly because there was a dearth of young single women workers, it was replaced by what Claudia Goldin calls "the pregnancy bar" (1990, 176). The ideology that children need full-time mothering produced turnover not at marriage but at first pregnancy.

Discriminating against women workers and job applicants who are married, pregnant, or mothers is now illegal in the United States; informally, however, these practices have been replaced by a tacit or openly acknowledged "mommy track." Ostensibly intended to make it easier for married women with children to continue managerial and professional jobs, the "mommy track" offers flexible working hours and generous maternity leave to women but not men in dual-career marriages to ameliorate the pressures of family and work (Rodgers and Rodgers 1989). But women are penalized for taking advantage of these policies, because once they do, their commitment to achieving top-level positions is called into question (Kingson 1988). The secondary result and, I would argue, latent function of these "mommy tracks" is to derail women who were on fast tracks to the top. As Alice Kessler-Harris says: "To induce women to take jobs while simultaneously restraining their ambition to rise in them required a series of socially accepted constraints on work roles. Unspoken social prescription—a tacit understanding about the primacy of home roles—remained the most forceful influence. This is most apparent in professional jobs where the potential for ambition was greatest" (1982, 231).

Until quite recently in many Westernized countries, the more prestigious professions, such as medicine, law, and the sciences, and the upper-level managerial sector of business were thoroughly dominated by men.[18] Men were easily able to keep women out because they were gatekeepers in several ways: They determined admissions to professional and managerial training schools; they controlled recruitment to and from such schools; and they determined promotion policies. With the advent of affirmative action in the United States, many women have become doctors, lawyers, scientists, and administrators, and they have become formidable competition for men. The "mommy track" keeps women professionals and managers in lower-paid, lower-prestige ranks. This exclusion from top-level positions is considered legitimate because they are mothers. The assumption is that women could not possibly handle the responsibility of leadership and the responsibility for their children's welfare at the same time, but they are never given the chance to try (Covin and Brush 1991). It is also taken for granted that mothers, never fathers, will supervise their children's day-to-day care.[19] "Mommy tracks" thus reinforce and legitimate the structural glass ceiling, the processes of exclusion, and the justifying stereotypes.

Paradoxically, "mommy tracks" are not the way most married women professionals and executives with children organize their careers. Such women order their lives so they can be productive.[20] Jonathan Cole and Harriet Zuckerman's interviews with seventy-three women and forty-seven men scientists, eminent and rank and file, who received their doctorates between 1920 and 1979 found little difference in the rates and patterns of publication of the men and women, the married and single women, and the childless women and those with children (1991). A woman with an endowed chair in a major department of behavioral science was married four times, divorced three times, and had four children by three different husbands, but the largest dip in her publication rate came in a year when there were no changes in her personal life (167). The rate of publication for all these scientists depended on stage of career, extent of collaboration, and the completion of projects. The women they interviewed were successful scientists as well as wives and mothers not because of a "mommy track" but because they carefully timed both marriage and childbearing, had child care and household help, and cut out leisure-time activities that had no professional payoff.[21]

When women put their families before their careers, they are often responding to a generalized cultural mandate that is mediated through direct pressures from their husbands at home and other women's husbands in the workplace (Cockburn 1991). These men, according to Mirra Komarovsky, have inconsistent ideas about their women peers:

> Some of the revealed inconsistencies are: . . . the right of an able woman to a career of her choice; the admiration for women who measure up in terms of the dominant values of our society; the lure but also the threat that such women present; the low status attached to housewifery but the conviction that there is no substitute for the mother's care of young children; the deeply internalized norm of male occupational superiority pitted against the principle of equal opportunity irrespective of sex. (1976, 37)

These inconsistencies are resolved by rewarding men's efforts to move up in their careers but not rewarding women's efforts, and both rewarding and punishing women for taking care of their families—rewarding them as women and punishing them as professionals, managers, and politicians. Should any woman not make the appropriate "choice" to put her family before her career, both she and her husband often face subtle and not-so-subtle harassment from their men colleagues. African-American women and men may have more egalitarian norms and expectations about women's ambitions, but these women face discrimination from white men on two counts and may be competing with African-American men for the same few "minority" positions (Fulbright 1987). Women may feel it is their choice to stay home with their small children and to limit their career commitments, but their choices are constrained by real and direct social pressures (Gerson 1985; Komarovsky 1985, 225–68).

The Salieri Phenomenon and the Matthew Effect

What happens when women can't be excluded from the workplace and don't choose to put family before career, but instead become men's competitors?

The unspoken practices of the informal organization of work make women particularly vulnerable to the covert undercutting I have called the *Salieri phenomenon,* after the highly placed composer who allegedly sabotaged Mozart's career (Lorber 1984, 8–10). In Peter Shaffer's play *Amadeus,* Salieri never openly criticizes Mozart to the emperor who employs both of them; he simply fails to recommend him enthusiastically. Salieri also suggests that Mozart be paid much less than the musician he is replacing. Mozart later thanks Salieri for his help in getting a position; he blames the emperor for the low salary (P. Shaffer 1980, 71–72). Salieri's damning with faint praise is one way women are undermined by their men colleagues and bosses, often without being aware of it.

Nijole Benokraitis and Joe Feagin (1986) describe other ways men subtly undercut women: *condescending chivalry,* where a boss protects a woman employee from what could be useful criticism; *supportive discouragement,* where a woman is not encouraged to compete for a challenging position because she might not make it; *friendly harassment,* such as being joshed in public when visibly pregnant or dressed for a social occasion; *subjective objectification,* or being grouped with "all women"; *radiant devaluation,* when a woman is given extravagant praise for doing what is considered routine when men do it–the "dancing dog" effect; *liberated sexism,* such as inviting a woman for an after-work drink but not letting her pay for a round; *benevolent exploitation,* where a woman is given all the detail work so she can learn the job, but a man takes credit for the final product; *considerate domination,* such as deciding what responsibilities a married woman can and cannot handle, instead of letting her determine how she wants to organize her time; and *collegial exclusion,* thoughtlessly scheduling networking meetings for times women are likely to have family responsibilities. These practices undermine a woman's reputation for competence in the eyes of others and her abilities in her own eyes, making it less likely that she will be visible to gatekeepers or considered a legitimate competitor for a position of power.

Once out of the fast track for advancement, it is very difficult to accrue the necessary resources to perform valued professional activities. Those who have access to personnel, work space, and money have the opportunity to do the kind of work that increases their reputation, brings the approval of superiors, and garners additional rewards and promotions. The circular proliferation of prestige, resources, and power is the *Matthew effect.* As attributed to Christ in the Gospel according to Matthew, those who have faith become more and more favored and those who do not sink lower and lower: "For whosoever hath, to him shall be given, and he shall have more abundance: but whosoever hath not, from him shall be taken away even that he hath." (Bible, King James version, 25:29).

The Matthew effect in science was first described by Robert Merton (1968) and Harriet Zuckerman (1977) to explain the "halo" that winning the Nobel Prize confers. The process of accumulating advantages in science, however, starts with the scientist's working at a prestigious university or laboratory that encourages the kind of research and productivity that wins Nobel Prizes.[22] Women scientists are disadvantaged by positions that give them fewer resources and less encouragement to do high-quality work and by a lesser payoff for their achievements in recognition, rewards, and additional resources. Citations of published papers by others in a field are a form of visibility that adds to the researcher's or scholar's reputation (Astin 1991). According to Marianne Ferber (1986, 1988), women tend to cite other women more than men cite women, and the fewer women in a field, the greater the citations gap. As a result of the accumulation of disadvantages, women often have stop-and-go careers that may start out well, but then founder (Lorber and Ecker 1983).[23]

Two brilliant twentieth-century women scientists who were loners had totally different fates that had little to do with the value of their scientific work. One of them, Rosalind Franklin, was a well-born Jewish woman scientist who launched a productive career in England in the 1950s. Her crucial contribution to the discovery of the double-helix structure of DNA was minimally acknowledged in the initial announcement by James Watson and Francis Crick in 1953.[24] She herself was denigrated by Watson in his widely read book, *The Double Helix* (1968). His description of her and her work is a classic example of the Salieri phenomenon: "Rosy . . . spoke to an audience of about fifteen in a quick, nervous style. . . . There was not a trace of warmth or frivolity in her words. And yet I could not regard her as totally uninteresting. Momentarily I wondered how she would look if she took off her glasses and did something novel with her hair. Then, however, my main concern was her description of the crystalline X-ray diffraction pattern" (68–69).[25] What Franklin was describing was nothing less than a clear X-ray picture of the DNA molecule that actually showed its helical structure! Watson paid little attention to what she had reported for over a year. Working alone, Franklin tried to envisage the three-dimensional structure her photographs of DNA suggested; she alternately played with and rejected a helical model. Watson subsequently was shown her best picture without her knowledge by the man who ran the laboratory she worked in, Maurice Wilkins; to Watson, "the pattern shouted helix" (Judson 1979, 135).

Wilkins could have been the collaborator Franklin needed to help her make an inductive leap, but according to Franklin's biographer, they "hated one another at sight. . . . Only too evidently the antipathy was instant and mutual" (Sayre 1975, 95). Horace Freeland Judson calls the conflict between Wilkins and Franklin "one of the great personal quarrels in the history of science" (1979, 101), noting but underplaying the gendered overtones. Wilkins insisted he hired Franklin to do the X-ray diffractions on DNA; Franklin's friends insisted that she thought she had been given control of the project and "was profoundly angered" by being treated as an assistant rather than a colleague by Wilkins (148).[26] At thirty-one, she was eight years older than Watson and a little younger but "much further along professionally than Crick" (148). Yet Wilkins, Watson, and Crick regularly corresponded, conversed, and ate together (159); Franklin's only associate was a graduate student, and as a woman, "she was denied the fellowship of the luncheon club organized by the senior common room" at King's College, London, where her laboratory was located (148).

Franklin died of cancer in 1958, at the age of thirty-seven; Watson, Crick, and Wilkins were awarded the Nobel Prize in physiology or medicine in 1962. Only in a contrite epilogue to his book, published in 1968, did Watson pay tribute to Franklin:

> The X-ray work she did at King's is increasingly regarded as superb. . . . We both came to appreciate greatly her personal honesty and generosity, realizing years too late the struggles that the intelligent woman faces to be accepted by a scientific world which often regards women as mere diversions from serious thinking. Rosalind's exemplary courage and integrity were apparent to all when, knowing she was mortally ill, she did not complain but continued working on a high level until a few weeks before her death. (225–26)[27]

Another woman scientist, also a loner but luckier because she lived to see her work rewarded with science's highest honor, was Barbara McClintock. She published a landmark paper in 1931 that established the chromosomal basis of genetics and, in 1945, was elected president of the Genetics Society. In the 1950s, the field became dominated by the Watson-Crick model of genetics, in which DNA produces RNA, and RNA produces protein. The research that McClintock published in that decade, which showed that the process was not so straightforward and that genes could "jump," or transpose, was ignored: "In spite of the fact that she had long since established her reputation as an impeccable investigator, few listened, and fewer understood. She was described as 'obscure,' even 'mad'" (Keller 1983, 10).

In 1960, McClintock described the parallels between her own work and that of other scientists, but these scientists did not reciprocate and cite her work. Except for two other women scientists, she was ignored at Cold Spring Harbor Laboratory where she had worked since 1941 (Watson became director in 1968), but she had nowhere else to go. McClintock lived long enough to see "startling new developments in biology that echo many of the findings she described as long as thirty years ago" (Keller 1983, x), and she was awarded the Nobel Prize in medicine in 1983, when she was eighty-one years old. She died on September 2, 1992, at the age of ninety, her work "widely celebrated as prescient" (Kolata 1992b).

The Salieri phenomenon and the Matthew effect are two sides of the same coin. Those who benefit from the Matthew effect receive acknowledgments from their colleagues for good work, which builds their reputation and brings them financial and professional rewards. The work of those subjected to the Salieri phenomenon is not recognized; they do not get credit for good performance, and their careers are stymied. But reputations must be constantly maintained; even those who have built up social credit can lose it, and reversals of fortune are not uncommon. Because women do not have a protective "status shield," they are easy targets for jealous, threatened, or hostile Salieris. Certainly, not all women are future Mozarts, but even those who are may never be heard.[28]

Inner Circles, Friendly Colleagues, and Tokens

The discriminatory aspects of the sorting and tracking that occur in every occupation and profession with long career ladders are obscured because colleagues who are not considered for the top jobs are not fired. They simply fail to make it into the inner circle. Colleagues are organized, informally, into three concentric circles—*inner circles, friendly colleagues*, and *isolated loners*.[29] Power is concentrated and policy is made in inner circles, which are usually homogeneous on gender, race, religion, ethnicity, social class, and education or training. Friendly colleagues usually have some, but not all, of the social characteristics members of the inner circle have. Although they are not totally excluded from the informal colleague network, they are rarely groomed to be part of the inner circle. Women with excellent credentials and work performance in occupations and professions dominated by men tend to end up friendly colleagues if they are of the same race and social class as the men of the inner circle and do similar kinds of work; otherwise, they become loners. Women professionals have formed their own separate colleague groups or professional networks, but many ambitious women do not want to be professionally segregated. They often try to fit in with the men or work on their own and hope that their worth will eventually be recognized by the gatekeepers of their profession or occupation.

Although inner circles tend to be homogeneous on gender, religion, race, ethnicity, education, and class background, a few people with different social characteristics may be accepted if they have a respected sponsor and demonstrate that in all other ways, they are just like the others. They are the true "tokens" (J. L. Laws 1975). They are actively discouraged from bringing more of their kind into the inner circle or from competing for the very top positions in the organization. Tokens usually are eager to fit in and not embarrass their sponsor, so they do not challenge these restrictions or the views, values, or work practices of the inner circle. Indeed, they may outdo the others in upholding the prevailing perspectives and exclusionary practices. That is why token women tend to be "one of the boys."

In order to get support from senior men, a senior woman may end up in the paradoxical position of making a stand for women by proving she is just like a man. A woman physician I interviewed was passed over by one set of gatekeepers in favor of her younger brother for the top position in a hospital department. She went over their heads to more powerful men, who vouched for her "manliness." She said:

> I do give a hoot about titles and I'm enough of a feminist not to let them promote my brother over me. I have put in many years more of service, and I'm a far better dermatologist than my brother. They tried to do this to me because I'm a woman. Those, excuse the French, assholes, said to me, "Do you mind us promoting your brother over you? He needs the honor." And I said, "For the sake of the women who follow after me, I mind." . . . And they said, "Well, if you come to our meetings, we can't tell dirty jokes, and we can't take off our shoes." I said, "Bull to that one. I know just as many dirty jokes as you do, and I always take off my shoes." All the board of trustees laughed like hell when they heard about it. They all said, "For God's sake, promote her." Most of them were patients of mine anyway. It's a stupid thing to say to a woman doctor. I don't care for me, but I want to make sure that the

next generation gets a fair shake and doesn't get it in the eye. (Lorber
1984, 61–62)

Unfortunately, token junior women cannot afford to be so outspoken.

In 1977, Rosabeth Moss Kanter predicted that as the number of work-
group peers with different characteristics significantly increased, they would
lose their token status and characteristics and be better integrated into the
group.[30] They would be able to express individual differences and sponsor
others with similar social characteristics for leadership positions. When they
became almost half of the group, they could become a recognized subgroup,
with alternative views and work practices and their own inner circles. Subsequent research on what came to be called the "Kanter hypothesis" showed that
as the numbers of women approach 15 percent, paradoxically, they are *more*
not less isolated, as she had predicted. They are cut off from organizational
information flows, are not able to acquire the loyal subordinates that leaders
depend on, and are not central in the organizational structure (Olson and
Miller 1983; South et al. 1982a, 1982b). Because they lack the protection of a
sponsor that tokens have, they may be subject to open and covert harassment.
When the occupation is symbolically masculine, such as police work or the
military, additional numbers of women rarely break down the interactional
barriers, and they continue to be loners.[31] Being few in number, therefore,
may result in a more favorable position than a more balanced gender mix, since
an increase may be seen as a threat to those in the majority (Toren and Kraus
1987; Wharton and Baron 1987).

Why are men professionals and managers reluctant to allow substantial
numbers of women into elite inner circles or to support the ambitions of more
than a select safe few for leadership positions? Competition is one reason. Yet
other men are competitors, too. Catholic and Jewish men physicians, once also
subject to discriminatory quotas in American medical schools, are more
successfully integrated than women into the prestigious ranks of the medical
profession. It could be that men feel their profession will "tip" and become
feminized if too many women are in high-paid, high-prestige, and high-power
positions (Lorber 1991). Just as one group seems to fear the neighborhood will
go downhill when too many of a devalued group move in, men professionals
may be afraid that if too many women become leaders, their profession will
become women's work, and the men in it will lose prestige, income, and their
control over resources (Blum and Smith 1988; Reskin 1988).

People from subordinate social groups do not become half of the work
group unless the occupation, profession, or job specialty loses its prestige and
power (Carter and Carter 1981). The leaders, however, tend to stay on and

continue to choose successors to the top positions who are like themselves, not like the new people who outnumber them. The men in colleague groups of mostly women and the whites in groups of mostly people of color (at least in the United States) tend to remain the supervisors and administrators. As administrators, dominant white men need to keep productivity high and costs low. If the members of formerly excluded groups can be relegated to the necessary lower-paid and less prestigious jobs (such as primary care in medicine), administrators can keep costs down and use the increasing numbers of white women and women and men of color who are highly trained professionals and managers without disturbing the status quo.[32]

Gender and Authority

Are men so much more acceptable in positions of authority because women "do power" differently? There tend to be two models of women's leadership styles: women are exactly like men, and women are different, but equally competent (Adler and Izraeli 1988a).[33] How women or men act does not give the whole picture; women's and men's leadership styles are socially constructed in interaction and heavily influenced by the situational context and how others perceive them. If women in positions of authority tend to be more accessible, to grant more autonomy, but also to be more demanding of subordinates to perform well, the reason may be that they are in weaker positions in the organization and have fewer resources.[34] They need subordinates' help but may be unable to reward them with raises or other perks. As a result, they ask more of subordinates but are also more likely to give concessions to those who are loyal to them, which may be perceived as contradictory behavior.

Authority in a woman is granted in a woman-dominated situation, such as nursing, but questioned where authority is defined as a masculine trait, such as in police work or the military.[35] In 1986, 10.4 percent of all uniformed U.S. Army personnel were women, but they have been underrepresented in the higher ranks. In 1988, there were nine women who were one-star generals in the U.S. military, 1.2 percent of the total, and none of higher rank. Women constituted 2 percent of the colonels, 3.5 percent of the lieutenant colonels, and 7.1 percent of other officer ranks (Barkalow and Raab 1990, 280–81). In 1991, a woman, Midshipman Juliane Gallina, was chosen the U.S. Naval Academy's brigade commander, student leader of 4,300 midshipmen. Ironically, her appointment came six months after a survey found that a "considerable segment" of students, faculty, and staff believed women had no place in the Naval Academy (New York Times 1991b).

A woman leader is expected to be empathic, considerate of other's feelings, and attuned to the personal (Lorber 1985). If she is not, she is likely to be called "abrasive." As the editor of the prestigious *Harvard Business Review,* Rosabeth Moss Kanter has been publicly faulted for her confrontational management style by her associates, even though her predecessor, a man, had similar problems in his first year (A. L. Cowan 1991). Her high status as a Harvard Business School professor, corporate consultant, and author of internationally known books on management did not protect her from open criticism by her colleagues.

On the other hand, a more conciliatory style may be criticized by men and women colleagues as insufficiently authoritative. Despite the increase in women managers in the past twenty years, men and women at all career stages, including undergraduate and graduate business students, stereotype the good manager as "masculine" (Powell 1988, 145–50). Nonetheless, there are situations where a nonconfrontational approach is highly appropriate. In medicine and police work, quintessential masculine professions in American society, being able to listen and take the role of the other person may be more productive than a distancing, authoritative stance in eliciting information or deflecting conflict (S. E. Martin 1980; West 1984, 51–70). Conciliation and using the other person's views can be threatening to men in police work who have learned to rely on physical force and to men doctors for whom medical expertise is the ultimate authority.

If the goal for women in men-dominated situations is to be treated as if they were men, they are in a double bind, and so are the men (Chase 1988). If the women act like men, they challenge men's "natural" right to positions of power. If the women act like women, they don't belong in a situation where they have to take charge (that is, act like a man). As Susan Ehrlich Martin says of policewomen on patrol: "The more a female partner acts like a police officer, the less she behaves like a woman. On the other hand, the more she behaves like a woman, the less protection she provides, the less adequate she is as a partner—although such behavior preserves the man's sense of masculinity. The way out of the bind is simple: keep women out of patrol work" (1980, 93–94).[36]

Producing "Face"

All these processes of legitimation and validation that build the reputations of stature and ability needed by a competitor for a position of power and prestige take place in face-to-face interaction.[37] In everyday encounters, people present themselves the way they would like to be responded to—as powerful leaders, cooperative colleagues, deferential underlings, more or less intimate friends, possible sexual partners. The ways people dress, gesture, talk, act, and even show emotion produce social identities, consciously or unconsciously crafted for different arenas and a variety of occasions.[38] Ritual behavior, such as bows and handshakes, and the rules of protocol—who goes through a door first, who sits where, who calls whom by their first name—reproduce status hierarchy or create status equality. Ordinary conversations become covert battlegrounds: Who talks more, who interrupts, whose interests are discussed, who gets sustained attention or short shrift, all indicate who has the social upper hand.[39] Whom one walks with or stands with—or puts space between—demonstrates affiliation, hostility, or respect, as does eye contact, touching, and other forms of "body politics."[40] These "face" productions are such delicate balances of power and deference that they can easily be disrupted by rudeness or embarrassment (Goffman 1967, 97–112; Scheff 1988). Secret stigmas, such as deviant behavior in the past or present, or even by members of one's family or by intimate friends, can contaminate a seemingly upright identity if revealed (Goffman 1963a). In face-to-face interaction, accidental attributes, such as beauty or height, may add to social status, and obvious physical deformities often detract from it.[41]

These presentations of self take place in social contexts, and the responses of others validate, neutralize, deny, or subvert them. Status signals, whether they are verbal or nonverbal, practical or symbolic, can be understood only in the social context and only by people who have learned their meaning (Hodge and Kress 1988). You need to know the symbolic language of everyday social interaction to be able to tell who is the boss and who is the employee, who are friends and who are enemies. Signals can be manipulated to shore up or subvert the status quo, or they can be used deliberately in open resistance or rebellion.

These status productions are part of "doing gender" (or of doing race, ethnicity, religion, or social class). In doing gender, as West and Zimmerman point out, "men are also doing dominance and women are doing deference" (1987, 146). That is, in face-to-face interaction, what is being produced, reinforced, or resisted is the society's whole system of social stratification. This system endows women and men, people of different racial ethnic groups and religions, and those with greater or lesser economic resources with different social worth. Everyday interaction reenacts these power and prestige differences because people with different status characteristics are seen as legitimately superior or inferior by the others in the situation. When people are evaluated highly, the others take what they have to say seriously, follow their suggestions, and defer to their judgment. Those who have low status in the eyes of the others are not listened to, their advice is ignored, and their bids for leadership are simply not acknowledged. Status superiors are granted the benefit of the doubt if they make a mistake; status inferiors have to prove their competence over and over again.

The pattern of structured power and prestige in face-to-face interaction replicates the ranking of social characteristics in the larger society because people are seen not as individuals but as representatives of their race, religion, gender, education, occupation, and so on. If everyone in a group has the same social characteristics, then natural leaders and followers emerge; in a group of friends, there is usually one person who is the ringleader. But when the social characteristics of people in a group differ, the social characteristics have more salience than personal characteristics—the woman who leads other women follows when men are present. The solo man does not dominate in a group of women, but he is listened to more than the solo woman is in a group of men (Johnson and Schulman 1989). The size of the group, its status mix, endurance, and purpose determine its structure of power and prestige, but the patterns are constant: Status superiors lead because others feel they have the right to lead; they don't have superior status because they lead. Most of the time, the building up and tearing down of "face" goes unnoticed, but conflicts and confrontations reveal that the vital subtext is the social production of prestige and power (Morrill 1991).

Producing Power

The week I started to write this chapter was the week of the U.S. Senate Judiciary Committee hearings on Professor Anita Hill's allegations of sexual harassment by Judge Clarence Thomas, nominee to the Supreme Court. These encounters dramatized status production and destruction, and the interplay of race, class, and gender with evaluations of performance and social worth. They laid bare the social processes of upward mobility, and how these differ for women and men of the same race. "The scalding contest was not only about race and sex, and women and men. It was about power, and who knows how to use it more effectively" (Dowd 1991c).[42]

Both Clarence Thomas and Anita Hill are African Americans who were born into poverty and segregation, and both received their law degrees from Yale University, one of the most prestigious law schools in the United States, during a time of nationally approved and implemented affirmative action. They met when they worked together in the administration of President

Ronald Reagan. Judge Thomas, then thirty-three years old, was at the Department of Education and then head of the Equal Employment Opportunities Commission (EEOC), the body set up to implement the civil rights laws against discrimination. Professor Hill, then twenty-five years old, worked for Judge Thomas in both organizations for several years.

Professor Hill contended that on and off during this time, at both workplaces, she had been subject to Judge Thomas's repeated requests for dates, as well as descriptions of the sexual acts in pornographic movies he had seen, the size of the breasts and penises of the actors in those movies, the size of his own penis, and his own sexual prowess. She had told few people of the incidents—two women friends, a man she was dating who lived in another city, and the dean at a school considering her for an appointment six or seven years later. They testified before the Judiciary Committee that she had been very upset and uncomfortable talking about it, although she had offered none of the graphic details that she was asked to make public at the reconvened hearings.

Judge Thomas denied the allegations categorically and made his own charges that he was the victim of a particularly ugly brand of racism, the stereotyping of African-American men as nothing more than sexual animals. He called it a "high-tech lynching," but it was Anita Hill who was verbally lynched by the senators who supported Judge Thomas. The judge's supporters on the Judiciary Committee accused Professor Hill of being a vindictive scorned woman, the tool of anti-Thomas political interests, a fantasizer, and a schizophrenic. The members of the Judiciary Committee who were against confirming Judge Thomas were circumspect when they questioned him, and rambling and disjointed with his witnesses. They did not ask him anything about what was rumored to be his well-known interest in pornography. They called no experts to testify on sexual harassment, its effects, or common responses, but listened respectfully to the rambling, self-serving account of a man who had met Anita Hill at a large party.

Professor Hill's accusation of sexual harassment by Judge Thomas was called into question because she had followed him from the Department of Education to the EEOC and had kept in touch with him professionally after she left the EEOC for a teaching position, once asking him for a needed reference, once to come to her campus as a speaker, and at other times requesting help for others or materials for seminars and grants. She had telephoned him about ten to fifteen times in the decade after she left Washington, D.C. When he came to speak at the school where she had her first teaching job, she participated in the social events around his visit and drove him to the airport. A witness to their interaction said it was very friendly and relaxed.

Judge Thomas's supporters on the Judiciary Committee said over and over that they could not understand why Anita Hill had followed him from one organization to another after he had harassed her. She said that for several months before he took the new position, he had not engaged in lewd talk or pressured her for dates, as he had started seeing someone seriously. After they both moved to EEOC, she said he harassed her again. His relationship had not worked out, and he was also going through a divorce. Pro-Thomas members of the committee also said they could not understand why she had maintained a cordial professional relationship with him in the ensuing years. One of Professor Hill's witnesses tried to explain why by talking about her own experience, which included "touching," and said that as a Black woman you learn to "grit your teeth and bear it" so that you can get to a position where you do not need the support of your harasser any longer.

Professor Hill said she had followed Thomas to EEOC because she was afraid she could not otherwise find employment commensurate with her credentials and abilities. She had been a corporate lawyer and did not want to return to that sector of law. Although this motivation for continuing a relationship with someone she said had subjected her to disgusting talk was challenged by witnesses for Judge Thomas, the evidence of her career path bears out her restricted opportunities. At the time of the alleged incidents, Professor Hill was an African-American woman professional in her twenties, a graduate of a highly prestigious law school, just beginning her career. The position she went to after she left EEOC was with Oral Roberts University, a small low-status school (now defunct).[43] Judge Thomas was an African-American man in his thirties, appointed by the president to direct a large federal agency. He was being groomed for further appointments in Republican circles and was described by one witness as "a rising star." Professor Hill's continued reliance on Judge Thomas for reference letters, speaking engagements, positions for others, and materials on civil rights enhanced her career and standing at her workplace and in the profession. Despite a high level of professional activities, such as research and attendance at conventions of the American Bar Association, she could not afford to alienate an important professional contact.

The women who testified for Judge Thomas lauded him for his respect for women and the help he gave them; except for one, none was a professional. They called Anita Hill "stridently aggressive," "arrogant," "opinionated," "hard," "tough," "ambitious," and "aloof." They suggested that her motivation was that she resented not being his main assistant at EEOC, as she had been at the Department of Education, or that she "had a crush on him" and was scorned.

As a professional woman, Professor Hill realized too late that Clarence Thomas was more interested in her sexually than professionally and was not going to be helpful in advancing her career at EEOC. She said that he had said when she left EEOC that if she ever talked about what he had done, it would ruin *his* career. She did not talk about it publicly, and in turn, he filled any request from her. She had nothing to gain by going public when she finally did so, and she said she would not have done so had she not been approached by staff of the Judiciary Committee, who had been told of rumors that Judge Thomas had been involved in sexual harassment at EEOC.

The Judiciary Committee was made up of fourteen upper-middle-class white men. The Senate, which had to vote to confirm the nomination, consisted of ninety-eight men, almost all white, and two white women. More of the senators (including the Republican woman) and, according to polls, more of the American people, believed him than her (Kolbert 1991b). After a weekend of testimony by Professor Hill and Judge Thomas and witnesses for and against her and for him, and a day of debate in the full Senate, on October 16, 1991, he was confirmed, 52–48, to a lifetime term on the Supreme Court. Professor Hill went back to her teaching job, with applause from her colleagues and students and later awards from professional women's groups.[44]

Sexual Harassment as Discrimination

Barbara Gutek (1985) found that 67.2 percent of 393 men would be flattered if asked to have sex by a woman coworker, but 62.8 percent of 814 women would be insulted by a sexual invitation from a male colleague (table 1, p. 96). Demands for sexual relations by superiors as the cost of keeping a job or advancing in it is quid pro quo, a long-standing ugly phenomenon of work life for heterosexual and lesbian women of all classes and races, and also for many women college and graduate students.[45] Most people understand the unfairness when someone who needs a job or a grade is subject to unwanted sexual advances, verbal or physical. But sexual talk, gestures, and other behavior inappropriate to a work environment or to a professional or student-teacher relationship also constitute discrimination against the targets. This concept of sexual harassment as discrimination, first advanced by Catharine MacKinnon (1979), was promulgated in EEOC guidelines in 1980 but was not upheld in the courts in this or other countries until the late 1980s (Lewin 1991a; Weisman 1989).

The concept of harassment as discrimination emerged in the United States when white women and women and men of color were hired in workplaces and accepted in training institutions from which they had been excluded. Women in blue-collar jobs tend to come up against sexual harassment and other forms of interpersonal resistance when they successfully break into white men's work worlds, especially when they are women of color and have low-status jobs (Gruber and Bjorn 1982). The intent of such harassment is to make work life so unpleasant that the woman will quit. Women who enter formerly all-men managerial or professional schools or workplaces are likely to be subject to sexual innuendoes or remarks about their physical appearance, which are aimed at undercutting their poise and work performance. The aim is to induce them to shrink from visibility and assertiveness, the hallmarks of the person who becomes a leader in a field.

Only recently, and only in a very few instances, have formal complaints or grievances been filed and lawsuits instituted over persistent episodes of sexual harassment of women or of homosexual men. The reason for not making the incidents public is that the accuser is often not supported by colleagues or bosses, and in many cases, the harasser is the boss (Schneider 1991). When the incidents, such as embarrassing sexual remarks or jokes at meetings, are between peers, they are frequently condoned or at least not halted or criticized by those present. Neither senior men nor women are likely to put a stop to such incidents while they are happening or to chastise the harasser and offer support to the person harassed in private afterward. These "microinequities" are not considered serious enough for a lawsuit, but "in the daily lives of working women, it is precisely these small, taken-for-granted comments, jokes, and physical acts, each individually unlikely to force a woman to initiate administrative action, that may accumulate in the long-term feeling and experience of harassment" (Schneider 1985, 104).[46]

Recently, feminists have begun to speak of a continuum that runs from *gender harassment,* which is inappropriately calling attention to women's or men's bodies, sexuality, and marital status, to *sexual harassment,* which is turning a professional, work or student-teacher relationship into a sexual relationship *that is not wanted by one of the people involved and that is coercive because the initiator has some power over the other person.*[47] The defining criterion for gender harassment is that the person's gender or sexual persuasion is used to comment on the individual's capabilities or career commitment. The defining criterion for sexual harassment is that the behavior is *inappropriate* for the situation; what should be a gender-neutral situation is turned into an *unwanted* sexual situation, and the initiator or instigator has *power,* which makes it difficult for those subject to the harassment to protest, leave, complain to others, or take action without jeopardy to their own status. The immediate reaction to gender and sexual harassment is likely to be discomfort, anger, feelings of powerlessness, inability to work, or feeling demeaned. These feelings may be suppressed if the person feels he or she has no choice but to continue in the situation or relationship.

Even senior women have faced such continued harassment. Several months before Anita Hill's allegations, a woman neurosurgeon, Dr. Frances K. Conley, a fifty-year-old full professor at Stanford Medical School and head of the Faculty Senate, resigned after sixteen years on the faculty.[48] She said she had been subject to continuous verbal sabotage of her professional status, such as comments on her breasts at meetings and being called "honey" in front of patients. Dr. Conley was the only woman faculty member in neurosurgery and one of two full professors in the department. The other, the acting head of neurosurgery, was going to be made chair of the department. He was the man she said was constantly insulting to her and to other women. Her women colleagues and the women medical students reported the long-standing practice of men physicians' use of pictures of naked women in lectures. If women complained or argued, they were labeled "premenstrual." Women medical students have always been subject to sexist practices, but women now constitute almost 40 percent of the classes in the United States. Rather than abating, gender and sexual harassment as a means of curbing the ambitions of women has persisted as the number of women in medicine has increased.[49]

"Speak-out" sessions reveal many incidents of gender and sexual harassment and how situations are differently perceived by women and by men. Neither type of harassment is likely to diminish using only formal methods of complaint and censure because both are so pervasive at every level in every workplace where women and men work together. The best remedy is clear indication from senior men, in a public setting, that *all* women employees, trainees, and students are to be treated *neutrally*—which does not mean coldly and distantly, but in a cordial, friendly, but not sexual manner. Most people do know the difference; they make such distinctions all the time in relating to their friends' spouses, for instance.

It takes a very well-established woman to stand up for her professional status successfully, and she needs the support of senior men. Dr. Conley finally agreed to return to the Stanford Medical School faculty because the administration appointed a task force on discrimination and also set up committees to review claims of sexual harassment. A follow-up interview showed that her actions paid off. Mary Roth Walsh (1992) reported that Conley has become the Anita Hill of American medicine, giving speeches all over the country and garnering awards from feminist organizations. Dr. Gerald Silverberg, the chair who had harassed Conley and many other women who were prepared to testify against him, resigned, made a formal apology, and was attending gender sensitivity classes and counseling sessions!

Women who live on the economic margins and women at the beginning of their careers cannot be expected to counter the constant sexist commentary that men use to guard the boundaries of what they feel is their turf. Nor can sympathetic men in similar positions. Not much support can be expected from senior men, who often engage in gender and sexual harassment themselves. So it is up to senior women to use whatever power they have for social change. They can no longer remain silent: "Woman must put herself into the text—as into the world and into history—by her own movement" (Cixous 1976, 875).[50]

Oh, liberty, what crimes are committed in thy name.
—*Madame Manon Roland (L. Kelly 1987, 121)*

THE VISIBLE HAND:
GENDER AND THE STATE

During the 1980s, while Margaret Thatcher was prime minister of Great Britain, the lord mayor of London was also a woman. With Elizabeth II as queen, that was a remarkable concentration of women leaders in a modern society, but it didn't make England a matriarchy. Parliament as well as other government institutions were dominated by men, and Thatcher's régime showed that a woman head of state is no guarantee of support for women's rights. Her government reduced child-care provisions, maternity benefits, and work rights for women (Gelb 1989, 59).

Women's civil status has fluctuated in Western societies; it has not improved with the rise of the modern state or the spread of Western ideas of individual liberty. Paradoxically, as states become more democratic, elite women lose power, but middle-class and poor women do not gain. There were periods in ancient Greece and Rome and in medieval Islamic and European societies when elite women had a higher status than upper-class women did in the eighteenth and nineteenth centuries in England, France, and the United States.[1] Women who are part of a landowning aristocracy derive power from their family's status. They often have inheritance rights or act as agents and managers so that the extended family's property can be kept intact. Women lost the right to inherit and control property in ancient Greece and Rome when entrepreneurial nuclear families supplanted landowning extended families as the main production units (Arthur 1977). The European Renaissance, by elevating the individual over the family, similarly reduced the power of aristocratic women members of families that had owned great tracts of land, since they had often substituted for their kinsmen in the feudal period (Coontz and Henderson 1986; J. Kelly 1984).

Women's rights as citizens were circumscribed even in new countries that wanted to attract them. In the early 1700s in colonial America, Pennsylvania offered single women who immigrated to that colony seventy-five acres, and Salem, Massachusetts, offered them "maid lotts" (Abramovitz 1988, 46). This inducement to unmarried white women came with strings attached. The understanding was that the land was a dowry with which to marry; when some women landowners chose not to, the offer was rescinded. Maryland gave women landowners seven years to find a husband or lose their land. When the American colonies overthrew British rule in 1776, they retained the English marriage and inheritance laws that forbade married women from acting as autonomous economic agents (Salmon 1979). Many of the white women who came to the English colonies in America and Australia were vagrants, prostitutes, and convicts who had been banished or poor women who indentured themselves to a prosperous person who paid their transportation. Others were young women who voluntarily or after kidnapping were sold as wives. Black women and men came as both indentured servants and as slaves. Whether they came voluntarily or in chains, they all endured miserable crossings on overloaded ships and then had no civil rights in their new country (Abramovitz 1988, 27–50). The signers of the Declaration of Independence addressed their plea for legitimation to "the opinions of mankind." Their assertion of the self-evident truths that "all men are created equal, that they are endowed by their Creator with certain unalienable Rights, that among them are Life, Liberty and the pursuit of Happiness" was not intended for the ears of any woman or of men who were indentured servants, slaves, or Native Americans.

Revolutions have shifted power among men of different social classes, and some women have gained civil rights previously denied them, but modern revolutions have not given women equal political power with the men of their social class. The bourgeois citizen who usurped political power from the hereditary aristocracy in England was first a property-owning man and then any free man, but never a woman: "After the Glorious Revolution of 1688, English wives would remain for another two hundred years in the paradoxical situation of being the legal chattels of husbands who were constantly boasting that they lived in a society unique in the world for its devotion to the principles of liberty" (L. Stone 1990, 18).

The major modern revolutions in France, Russia, and China transformed men's class relationships, putting formerly subordinate men in control of the state. The women of these newly dominant classes, active participants in the making of these revolutions, ended up politically subordinate to the men. In each case, women's support for the revolution was ensured with promises of change in their civil and marital status. After the revolutions succeeded, loyal women leaders were passed over in favor of men whose political base the revolutionary governments needed in order to consolidate and stabilize their power. Women's interests were often sacrificed in order to ensure the cooperation of formerly oppressed men. Not only was women's continued support for the new régimes taken for granted, but in times of turmoil, women's traditional roles as mothers and subordinate wives were revived by the government in an attempt to restore the social order.

Socialist and communist ideology stresses the economic base of women's oppression and therefore locates the source of their liberation in the transformation from private to state control of the economy and women's full employment in the paid sector.[2] This solution to the problem of gender equality was revealed as an illusion during recurrent economic crises in the Soviet Union and Central European countries. Work remained gender-segregated, and women were generally paid less than men and were less likely to be in positions of authority (Lin and Yanjie 1991; Jancar 1978, 12–37). Waged work under socialism was not seen by women as liberating, since they still had almost full responsibility for unwaged housework and child care, a burden not completely relieved by state-supported paid maternity leave, child allowances, nurseries, and day care:

> The focus on "Militant Sunday, Tired Monday" is not a struggle to socialize housework like the Great Leap Forward efforts to establish public canteens, laundries, and child care centers. Chinese policy planners now favor short-term solutions like improving the toys for grandparent-raised children and encouraging husbands to take a fairer share of privatized housework, shopping, and child care responsibilities. National responsibility for public and socialized facilities that would alleviate the double day of working women is no longer a high priority on the Chinese agenda. (Dalsimer and Nisonoff 1987)

Women revolutionaries and their feminist ideas have been discredited as "sell-outs" along with the rest of the communist rhetoric (Burawoy and Lukács 1992, 83–83). These women had confined their work to "women's issues" in order to maintain whatever power they had in governments that continued to be dominated by men (Browning 1987).

Most recently, women have participated in all the "velvet revolutions" that overturned the Central European Communist governments, but without the prop of state-imposed quotas, the percentage of women in the parliaments of these countries dropped precipitously after the fall of communism: in the former Czechoslovakia, from 29.5 percent in 1989 to 8.7 percent in 1991; in Hungary, from 20.9 to 7 percent; in Romania, from 34.4 to 3.6 percent; in

Bulgaria from 21 to 8.5 percent; and in the former German Democratic Republic from 38 to 20.2 percent (Dölling 1991; Ragab 1992).[3] The push to privatize state socialist economies has resulted in high unemployment for women and reduced child care and maternal leave benefits for those who still have jobs.[4]

The conditions of women's subordination and exploitation changed under both capitalism and state socialism, but the outcomes have been remarkably similar. In all industrialized countries, married women and mothers of small children are in the paid labor force and are also the primary unpaid domestic workers. Their overburdening leads the state to institute ameliorative policies such as paid parental leave. These policies ease women's double burden but reduce their earning power because they, rather than the father, are likely to stay home to care for children. Policies that diminish gender segregation of the job market and mandate equitable pay for women's work would go much further in encouraging men's participation in child care, since the men most likely to share parental leave are those whose wives are high earners (Kaul 1991).

The double burden of work inside the home and in the work force remains a significant barrier to women's political activism. The time needed to serve in organizations, go to meetings, learn political skills, cultivate mentors and sponsors, and do the infighting and campaigning necessary to advance a political career would constitute a *third* job.[5] Ambitious married women with children are therefore rarely able to rise high in government. The men who make state policies promote the gendered division of labor that exploits women as workers and as family members. The advantageous outcome for men's continued political domination suggests a conspiracy against women, but it is through seemingly gender-neutral policies that rarely serve women's interests that the state "plays a part in the oppression of women" (McIntosh 1978, 255).[6]

Gender, Property, and Power

The very visible way that states empower certain groups (or rather, the way certain groups empower themselves through their control of the ruling apparatuses of the state) is the legal code governing ownership and inheritance of property, the chief economic resource. These laws replaced the rules that determined the distribution of what is produced among the members of kin-based societies. In these societies, women usually have rights to their family's production surplus as sisters and to their own as wives (Sacks 1979). Among the Celts and Germanic tribes through the first century of the present era, women could inherit and pass on property from their birth and marital families (V. Muller 1985). In Islamic medieval societies, the daughters, sisters, and wives in elite Mamluk families owned and managed extensive property of their own and managed that of kinsmen (Ahmed 1992, 105–06; Petry 1991). In European societies that did not allow women to own or inherit property directly, if there were no adult sons, daughters or wives managed their fathers' or husbands' property in their absence.[7] The women who ran the great castles and estates (the chatelaines, or keepers of the keys) oversaw both production and domestic work, and propertyless women and men provided the labor (McNamara and Wemple 1974). In medieval Europe, when priests could marry, women's power extended to church affairs: "Wherever we look during this period, we find no really effective barriers to the capacity of women to exercise power. They appear as military leaders, judges, castellans, controllers of property. Though barred from the priesthood, they even exercised vast power over the church as a result of their family positions" (McNamara and Wemple 1974, 113).

Indicative of their social independence throughout the feudal period in Europe was women's freedom to engage in extramarital love relationships, which were condoned as long as they had already produced a male heir (J. Kelly 1984, 27). However, as David Herlihy (1984, 396) points out, "Even limited sexual promiscuity has the result of obscuring lines of descent through males" and strengthening matrilineal ties. When women owned property, they willed it as they wished, often to women kin (Anderson and Zinsser 1988, 1:425). What was important was to keep property—land or a business—in the extended family, the woman's or the man's.

Women in European medieval society retained their family names, and children were frequently identified by the mother's name (the matronymic) not because the father was unknown but because mothers wielded considerable economic power and were well known in their communities (Herlihy 1976). It wasn't until the eleventh and twelfth centuries that elite families grouped along male descent lines, assumed a single family name, and limited daughters' inheritances to a dowry (Herlihy 1984, 397–98). Women took their husbands' names in France from the thirteenth century on, but in England, they did not until the seventeenth century (Anderson and Zinsser 1988, 1:337).

Why Women Did Not Have a Renaissance

Frederick Engels ([1884] 1972) attributed the subordination of women to the institutions of the family, private property, and the state. The rise of the state (which has occurred in many different times in different parts of the world) diminishes the power of extended kin groups and therefore also the power of the men who head those groups. In feudal societies, the men who owned large tracts of land commanded the labor and loyalty of the people living on it, using them to war on each other to gain new territory. Some of the bloodiest battles erupted between brothers over who would inherit the family's property. In the twelfth and thirteenth centuries, the rule of primogeniture, passing all the family property on to the eldest son, was instituted throughout Europe. Younger sons (cadets) were given military commissions, trained for the priest-hood, or, during the colonial era, sent abroad. "The near-sanctity accorded to the rights of property and male primogeniture" disinherited elite women (L. Stone 1990, 350); all they were now entitled to was a dowry. The same strict lines of succession, however, meant that women in the ruling families became the heads of the absolute monarchies of Europe from the fifteenth to the eighteenth centuries when there were no legitimate male heirs (Anderson and Zinsser 1988, 2:44–61).[8]

With the breakup of feudal estates, elite women lost considerable bargain-ing power, since they no longer brought the prestige of a great family to marriage, and they had fewer kinsmen to call on in case of conflicts with their husbands. Although aristocratic women retained some of their prerogatives and status, and widows of capitalist entrepreneurs in the thirteenth to seven-teenth centuries were able to run successful businesses (Anderson and Zinsser 1988, 1:424–30), married women in England and Europe became increas-ingly financially dependent on their husbands. The father in the nuclear family, not the patriarch of the clan, now had domestic power over his wife and chil-dren through control of the family's property (Delaisi de Parseval and Hurstel 1987; L. Stone 1979). This control further restricted women's status:

> As part of this institutionalization of civil power at the expense of aristocratic kin groups, there grew up a new emphasis on the conjugal bond and the civil legitimacy of marriage. Where marriage once united corporate kin groups, it now broke them up, as husband and wife were urged—and often legally obliged—to identify with each other rather than with their kin. . . . The new public, hierarchical nature of au-thority put an end to the informal and delegated powers that aristo-cratic women had exercised by virtue of their family position. (Coontz and Henderson 1986, 150, 151)

Women's activities were confined to their household, and they were con-trolled sexually to ensure that the children born of the marriage had been fathered by their husband.[9] As Joan Kelly pointed out, European women did not benefit from the Renaissance (1984, 19–64): "The startling fact is that women as a group, especially among the classes that dominated Italian urban life, experienced a contraction of social and personal options that men of their classes either did not, as was the case with the bourgeoisie, or did not experience as markedly, as was the case with the nobility" (1984, 20).

Liberty and Equality for Men Only

In prerevolutionary France, widowed noblewomen and groups of religious women had some political rights; in 1789, the Declaration of the Rights of Man did away with the privileges of the aristocracy and clergy and left women with no political rights at all (Linda Kelly 1987, 32–33). "Universal suffrage" was proclaimed when all *men* in France got the vote in 1848, but Frenchwomen did not vote until 1945 (Reynolds 1987a).[10]

In the French Revolution, women played a vital part in political debates and street battles but never broke free of their subordinate status. Rather, they were condemned as carriers of disorder (Gullickson 1991). Bourgeois and market women and enlightened women aristocrats were part of the political ferment, the mass protests, and the storming of barricades.[11] Women were members of "fraternal" political clubs, but the ideological rhetoric of *liberté et egalité* did not extend to *sororité*. Despite the efforts of the Marquis de Condorcet, a liberal aristocrat, and the protest speeches of Etta Palm D'Aelders, a young, Dutch-born, single woman, the new French constitution of 1791 was based on the 1789 Declaration of the Rights of Man and of the Citizen, which explicitly did not include women.

For the French Revolution to have espoused political equality for women, more than a handful of its theorists would have had to take an intellectual leap beyond the Enlightenment view that women's subordination to men and confinement to domestic duties were attributable to nature (Proctor 1990). Those women whose writing, speeches, and actions violated traditional expectations were vilified in the popular press, on the floor of the National Assembly, and in numerous salacious and satirical pamphlets (Proctor 1990, 131–51). After Charlotte Corday's assassination by Jean-Paul Marat, outspoken women were condemned not only as antirevolutionary but as sexually unnatural.

Olympe de Gouges, a poorly educated butcher's daughter, playwright, and pamphleteer, published a separate Declaration of the Rights of Woman and the Female Citizen in 1791, which called for freedom of thought, government employment, property rights, better education, political participation, and reform of the marriage laws. Linda Kelly points out the "sinister resonance" of Article X: "woman has the right to mount the scaffold; she has equally the right to mount the rostrum" (1987, 38). De Gouges, who favored a constitutional monarchy, offered to defend the king at his trial (79–80). She was guillotined as a royalist in 1793.

Working-class Parisian women used street protests to demand cheaper food, and middle-class women formed societies to agitate for civil rights; in 1793, they merged in the Society of Revolutionary Republican Women, "a family of sisters."[12] Its presidents were Claire Lacombe, an actress, and Pauline Léon, a chocolate maker who supported her widowed mother and younger siblings. At first praised by the militant Jacobins for revolutionary zeal, the society and its supporters were later virulently condemned as monstrous women in the political upheavals of 1793 (Proctor 1990, 154–66). The heroine of the militant revolutionaries had been Théroigne de Méricourt; "in her habitual [red] riding habit, pistols and sabre by her side," she was "in the forefront of the mob" that stormed the Tuileries and imprisoned Louis XVI in 1792 (Linda Kelly 1987, 58). But when she called for unity between the moderates and militants a year later, "she was attacked by a band of women . . . who stripped her and flogged her brutally—such public flog- gings, humiliating their (generally female) victims, were a relatively common feature of mob justice" (90). Her fate was confinement to a lunatic asylum, where she died in 1807.

The French revolutionary government gave women, who fought in mili- tias and in the army, some of the civil rights they had demanded, but not the right to vote or to be a member of any governing body. As the revolution became more repressive, women's societies were banned, and women were forbidden to speak at the governing assemblies. Robespierre's Republic of Virtue, which instituted the repressive Reign of Terror in the closing years of the revolution, urged women to support the state by "republican mother- hood." In 1804, the Napoleonic Civil Code restored the authority of husbands and fathers in marriage and divorce and also "deprived women of the right to perform as civil witnesses, to plead in court in their own name, or to own property without the husband's consent" (Landes 1988, 145–46). The only right that women kept was entitlement to an equal share in inheritance, "the one tangible legacy of the Revolution" (Linda Kelly 1987, 157).

"Covered" Women

In eighteenth- and nineteenth-century Europe and the United States, the rise of the entrepreneur transformed land as wealth into fluid capital. In order to be able to buy, sell, mortgage, and rent property to make a profit or raise money for investment in businesses, husbands needed to be free of feudal marriage rules, which set aside as untouchable a certain portion of their property for their widows and heirs. Instead of bringing marriage into contract law and allowing women to set the economic terms of their status as wives, mothers, and widows, married women's rights to control property and make contracts were restricted on the basis of their gender and marital status (Pateman 1988). As *femes covert,* wives' legal existence was covered by their husband. The only wives who were free to make contracts were *femes sole,* whose husbands were away for long periods at war or at sea; like the aristocratic women of the feudal era, they were given the power to run their husbands' businesses in their absence. Except for these wives, who acted as their husbands' agents, the lifelong legal status of women became that of children; as unmarried women they were ruled by their fathers or brothers, as married women, by their husbands, and as widows, by their sons.

In English common law, before the eighteenth century, a widow was entitled to one-third of her husband's estate upon his death. Changes in the law and legal decisions allowed husbands to replace this dower right to land with a more flexible (but usually less valuable) guaranteed income as a widow (jointure), keeping the property itself out of her control. During the marriage, a wife was usually given a variable amount of "pin money" and household funds, which she was more or less free to use as she wished, except that if she used this money as capital, the proceeds or the original funds themselves could revert to her husband (Staves 1990, 131–61). Furthermore, these entitlements could be abrogated if the wife was caught in sexual misconduct, euphemistically called "criminal conversation."

Compared to European women in the Middle Ages, bourgeois women were freer to choose whom they married, and they had more influence over how their children were raised, but they lost everything if they were caught in adultery. A married woman who was not rich enough to get a full divorce (which, until 1857 in England, literally took an act of Parliament) or had no family who could arrange a financial settlement was powerless before the late nineteenth century:

A separated wife faced exceptionally severe penalties. Unless she was protected by a private deed of separation, she was in practice virtually an outlaw. All the income from her estate was retained by her husband, as well as all future legacies which might come to her. All her personal property, including her future earnings from a trade and her business stock and tools, were liable to seizure by her husband at any moment.

She was unable to enter into a legal contract, to use credit to borrow money, or to buy or sell property. All her savings belonged to her husband. And finally, all her children were controlled entirely by their father, who was free to dispose of them as he wished, and to deprive their mother of any opportunity ever to speak to them again. These were the conditions which tended to make marital breakdown at the insistence of the wife a rarity. (L. Stone 1990, 4–5)[13]

Yet women married. As spinsters their opportunities for work were few and low paid, so they were as economically dependent on their fathers or brothers as wives were on husbands (B. Hill 1989, 221–39; Shanley 1989, 9–10). The unmarried daughters of fathers who went bankrupt became governesses or overworked "poor relations" in the households of prosperous kin who would take them in; their only other recourse to maintaining the same style of living was to become a rich man's mistress (L. Stone 1979, 329).

Depriving women of the right to control property meant that wives could be used to procreate heirs and to socially reproduce what the bourgeois men had created through their "own efforts" without the husbands giving up any economic power. Women's legal subordination in modern capitalist societies was therefore deliberate but was glossed over with an ideology of fragile womanhood in need of men's protection:

New forms of capital required novel methods of restraining women. It was never the laws of property alone which prevented the myriad middle-class women who owned capital from using it actively. Rather, it was the ways in which the laws of inheritance and the forms of economic organization (the trust, the partnership, the family enterprise) intersected with definitions of femininity. The active generation of lasting wealth was virtually impossible for women. (Davidoff and Hall 1987, 451)

In the nineteenth century, this intricate combination of law, kinship, and gender made bourgeois men into successful entrepreneurs and bourgeois women into lifelong economic dependents whose contributions to capital accumulation were invisible (Davidoff and Hall 1987, 198–315). The sons' inheritances were theirs to invest; their obligations, as they became heads of families, were to support their wives, unmarried sisters, widowed mothers, and other needy women relatives. Their formal and informal education and adult associations with other men taught them how to invest and manage money. Daughters' inheritances were given in trust, to be used for support if they were widowed with young children, and then to be passed on to their sons. Managed by men trustees, women's property was an important source of capital for family and community enterprises, but the women themselves neither saw the profits nor reaped social power from investment decisions. Women's obligations as dependents was to provide personal services to fathers, husbands, and brothers, to marry men their kinsmen could do business with, and to have their children (Davidoff and Hall 1987, 281; P. D. Hall 1978). Their contribution to family businesses as manufacturers, inventors, account keepers, clerks, secretaries, and publicists was part of their services as dependents, so it was unremunerated and unremarked.

Free at Last?

By the end of the nineteenth century in England, thanks to the efforts of feminists, the Married Women's Property Acts of 1870, 1874, and most of all, 1882 gave all married women some economic rights. Only a generation earlier, separated and deserted wives' property and earnings were protected from being seized by penurious returning husbands (Shanley 1989, 35–39). Similar laws were passed in the United States and other European countries.[14] But the Married Women's Property Acts of the nineteenth century benefited only women with their own property or income. The laws that gave married women the right to separate ownership of property denied them the right to a claim on their husbands' property or earnings in a divorce or separation because spouses' property was no longer commingled (Smart 1984, 46–49).

Twentieth century reforms in divorce laws that give married women a claim on all marital property and their husbands' future earnings have partly undone the nineteenth-century reforms. In some countries, the concept of *deferred community* allows each spouse to control his or her own property and earnings during the marriage, retaining the spousal independence of the old marriage reforms, but if there is a divorce, the property is shared equally to ensure the economically disadvantaged spouse a continued means of support (Glendon 1989, 118). Even though the new community property laws shield the full-time homemaker and part-time earner from destitution in case of divorce, they are not entirely beneficial, because in order to split communally owned real estate, one party has to buy out the other or the family residence has to be sold. A common compromise is to defer the property split, letting the spouse with custody use the family residence until the children are grown (Smart 1984, 118).

Women who control their own property or income can support themselves and their children and pass their property on to their children, regardless of who the father is. Such rights belonged to a small group of free women of color in parts of the South in the United States before the Civil War (Schweninger 1990). Although white wives were "covered" by their husbands legally, white men gave their freed Black mistresses and daughters a start in establishing their own businesses and buying property, including slaves. Since free Black women could not legally marry white men and could lose their property rights by marrying one of the few freed Black men or their freedom by marrying slaves, they had to be economically independent to survive:

> For some, the long road from slavery to freedom had consumed their most productive years; for others, it took a substantial effort to extricate their children or family members from bondage. They were forced to deal with oppressive laws, the violent hostility of whites, tenuous and sometimes volatile relationships with black men, and the difficulties of maintaining "normal" family relations in the midst of slave society. Yet they struggled to overcome these difficulties through hard work and the acquisition of property. (Schweninger 1990, 26)[15]

After the Civil War, these women were in the paradoxical position of having to choose between autonomous control of their property and marrying a newly freed slave who, like a white husband, would control his wife's assets. They gave up their economic independence and "overwhelmingly chose to live in stable families with their husbands and children" (Schweninger 1990, 30)[16]

Postsuffrage Politics

In the United States and England, generations of organized feminists mobilized, agitated, and went to jail for suffrage, and then women were rewarded with the right to vote for their efforts in World War I (Chafetz and Dworkin 1986; Kraditor [1965] 1981). Women have had the right to vote in most democracies for less than a hundred years, and nowhere constitute half of any national government. In addition to Margaret Thatcher, as of October 1993, thirteen women have been elected or appointed prime ministers or presidents: Kim Campbell of Canada, Tansu Ciller of Turkey, Edith Cresson of France, Gro Harlem Brundtland of Norway, Vigdis Finnbogadottir of Iceland, Mary Robinson of Ireland, Golda Meir of Israel, Violeta Barrios de Chamorro of Nicaragua, Khaleda Zia of Bangladesh, Benazir Bhutto of Pakistan, Indira Gandhi of India, Corazon Aquino of the Philippines, and Hanna Suchocka of Poland.[17] The governing bodies of these countries, however, have been mostly men, and few of these leaders have had a feminist agenda.[18] They have tended to be party leaders or widows or daughters of male rulers. Even with increasing economic independence and political clout, women are more likely to organize effectively around local community issues than around national political questions.[19] Since the decisions of national and international capitalists, who are almost all men, affect local business owners, who are also predominantly men, women's effectiveness even in local community politics is "discounted" by men's economic power (Blumberg 1984).

The working-class men in the nineteenth- and twentieth-century union movements in Europe and the United States often turned against women workers as competitors in their fight for higher wages and better working conditions.[20] The outcome was paternalistic state policies in the form of protective labor legislation that forbade employers from making women work overtime, on night shifts, or in hazardous areas. The obverse side of these policies was to cut women off from the source of higher wages. In the twentieth century, men industrial workers in Western democracies fought for and obtained government-guaranteed protections from labor-market vicissitudes, such as unemployment insurance, minimum wages and maximum hours, sick leave and health insurance, and retirement pensions. The additional benefits that working women need, such as low-cost prenatal and maternal health care, paid parental leave, affordable child care, and medical insurance for children and those who are not full-time paid workers, are less likely to be universal entitlements or guaranteed fringe benefits in capitalist countries. They are usually made available when the economy needs women workers.

Free elections have not produced many women politicians representing women's interests. In order to be elected, women have to be loyal to their parties and their general political base. They are not likely to rally behind a feminist agenda or form a women's party. A few women in leadership positions who have a feminist perspective but do not have a feminist constituency are not likely to alter the status quo very much. They must rely on the goodwill of the men around them to maintain their positions, and these men rarely want to make major changes in the direction of gender equality because it would mean giving up their own privileges. Joyce Gelb's analysis of politics in the United States, Britain, and Sweden has shown that criticisms of men's domination and agitation for change are more likely to come from autonomous feminist political activity outside of the government (1989). But without women in government to supervise and implement new policies in a way that empowers rather than exploits women, these policies are often watered down.

Women are clients and employees of modern states, but they do not control the government policies that affect their lives as paid workers, mothers, and housewives. In that sense, they are still second-class citizens: "The citizen role . . . is a masculine role. It links the state and the public sphere. . . . But it also links these to the official economy and the family. And in every case the links are forged in the medium of masculine gender identity rather than . . . in the medium of a gender-neutral power. Or, if the medium of exchange here is power, then the power in question is masculine power" (N. Fraser 1989, 127).[21]

The Soviet Solution to the Woman Question

At the meeting of the New York branch of the International Workingman's Association in the late 1860s that came to be known as the First International of the Communist Party, the American-born socialists had a large contingent of women, including the militant suffragist Victoria Woodhull. The American section fought to have women's emancipation linked to workers' rights. They were adamantly opposed by the German-born trade unionists, for whom the class struggle was a workers' struggle alone. After an open conflict between the two groups, "Karl Marx himself recommended the expulsion of the American section on the ground that they gave 'precedence to the women's question over the question of labor.'" (Buhle 1983, xiv).[22] For the German immigrant socialists, women's role was "guardian of the proletarian family," not an independent worker and political agent (Buhle 1983, 8).

Marx's own views on "the woman question" were contradictory; he considered women and men workers to be a genderless class, subsuming women's emancipation in the struggle against capitalist exploitation, but he also understood women's subordinate position as workers' wives (Landes 1989). In *Women under Socialism,* originally published in 1879, August Bebel presented women both as workers to be freed from capitalist tyranny along with men and as wives whose subjugation to their husbands would end when private property was abolished.[23] Under socialism, according to Bebel, women as industrial workers and farmers would be as important to the working class as men were, but women as wives and mothers would also regenerate the working-class family that had been ground down under capitalism.

Vladimir Lenin was a proponent of women's rights, adding a clause, "complete equality of rights for men and women," to the draft program of the Communist Party, which was included when the program was adopted in 1903.[24] Without the imprimatur of the men leaders, men within the socialist and communist movements ignored or resisted implementing the views of women theorists and organizers, such as Inessa Armand, Vera Figner, Emma Goldman, Aleksandra Kollontai, Rose Luxemburg, Vera Zasulich, and Clara Zetkin. Both women and men socialists and communists wanted working-class women to commit to their cause and not to the feminist cause, whose emphasis on the right to vote was excoriated as "bourgeois." The men leaders held out the promise of political, economic, and marital rights for working-class women as inducements to work for the overthrow of capitalism, but they frequently reneged on implementation.[25]

Leon Trotsky called the strike of women textile workers in 1917 the first day of the Russian Revolution.[26] Women continued at the forefront, as political organizers and factory and farm workers. They were fighters as well as nurses in the civil war that followed. The first working women's conference was held in Petrograd as soon as the revolutionary government was in power. Spearheaded by Kollontai, the women instituted a sickness insurance fund, lighter work for pregnant women, and sixteen weeks' free pre- and postnatal care at new maternity clinics. In 1918, the Department for the Protection of Motherhood and Infancy was organized, and in 1919, the Working and Peasant Women's Department of the Communist Party (the Zhenotdel). The first head of the Zhenotdel was Armand, who died of cholera in 1920, and the second was Kollontai, who was removed in 1922 after she publicly clashed with Lenin over workers' autonomy. Her successor was Sofia Smidovich, who had little status in the Communist Party, and who shifted the Zhenotdel's goals from abolition of the traditional family and equal representation of women in the government and party to maternity leave, child care, full employment for women, the liberation of Muslim women, and delegate conferences (Clements 1979, 220–21).[27]

Under Russia's tsarist laws, husbands had control of their wives' property and their freedom to travel, custody of the children in divorce, and the right to beat their wives. The new Matrimonial Codes established civil marriage, equality of rights between husband and wife, and easy divorce with community property rules. Women could keep their own names, citizenship, passports, and identity cards. Legal distinctions between legitimate and illegitimate children and formal and informal marriages were abolished. In 1920, abortion was legalized.

In practice, it was as difficult to establish equality between women and men as it was to structure a classless society. In an address to the 1925 Third All-Union Conference on Protection of Mothers and Children, Leon Trotsky contrasted the building of a power station with the "terrifying backwardness" of the little villages surrounding it when he said that "everyday life is fearfully conservative, incomparably more conservative than technology" (1970, 36). The peasant family, still governed by patrilocal and patrilineal kinship rules, was in direct conflict with the individualistic premises of the new Family Code. Parents and husbands, especially in rural areas, beat and even killed daughters and wives who attempted to live by the new emancipated ways.

But the men of the Communist Party played as much a part in impeding the establishment of equality between women and men as the peasantry did. In the 1920s, they set up few communal nurseries and kitchens. Hundreds of thousands of homeless children roamed the country, stealing, begging, and selling sex to survive. Industrial jobs for women were scarce, or only unskilled work was available. Men coworkers were contemptuous of Zhenotdel representatives. Within the Communist Party, the necessary economic conditions for "free love" were debated, but the social and psychological conditions for women's unrepressed sexuality was a taboo subject.[28] Abortion became the chief means of limiting pregnancies. Few of the supposedly liberated men shared cooking, cleaning, or child care, and some revolutionaries who called for women's rights in public forbade their wives to attend the meetings.

These problems were addressed in practical ways by the thousands of women who came to Moscow for the 1927 All-Union Congress of Working and Peasant Women, a time of severe economic conditions (Goldman 1989). The women delegates recognized that better skills, higher salaries, and state-provided child care would give them the economic independence they needed to support themselves and their children. The party's response was to try to restore women's traditional roles by rescinding the troublesome new matrimonial and family laws that had produced the high rates of divorce and illegitimate children. The Zhenotdel was abolished in 1929. Legal marriages and large families were officially encouraged in the 1930s. Homosexuality was made a criminal offense in 1934, and abortions were abolished in 1936 (to be legalized once again in 1955).[29] Individual parents were responsible for their children, but unwed mothers could not petition for child support from the father. Divorces were harder to obtain (a less restrictive policy was reinstated in 1964). Homeless children were adopted by peasant families who needed extra workers.

Once again, for women, the reality of everyday life belied the official policy of motherhood in the service of the Soviet. The forced collectivization of agriculture and rapid industrialization in the 1930s radically transformed women's roles as workers and as family members. Paradoxical as it seems, the attempts to restore the family's traditional functions went along with a vast expansion of educational opportunities for women, the spread of a network of institutions for the education and care of children, and the enactment of protective labor legislation and social programs designed to ensure the compatibility of women's domestic responsibilities with industrial employment. The changes reverberated across the whole range of social institutions including, most importantly, the family itself. (Lapidus 1978, 96)

This social transformation of Soviet work and family life was intensified by the need for women workers in World War II. By the post–World War II period, Soviet women were better-educated, skilled workers, many of whom had grown up with the idea that they could be pilots and engineers. Although many still did heavy, unskilled labor and farm work, the majority of the physicians were women, as were many other professionals.[30] Even rural areas had village nurseries. Because employment was mandatory, most women remained in the paid work force full time for most of their lives, although not as the equals of men workers. The birthrate went down, and the divorce rate went up (Jancar 1978, 38–69).

Women's political participation was concentrated in all-women *zhensovety,* local committees of up to fifty members whose concerns tended to be pragmatic issues of work and child care (Browning 1987). On the national level, a small number of women were appointed deputy heads of legislative bodies or heads of ministries of health, education, or light industry. Only two women were ever members of the ruling Politburo. The representation of women in the Central Committee never rose above 5 percent, and after the first years of the revolution, women had little input into policy decisions.[31] There may have been comparatively more women in the dissident movements in the Soviet Union and Communist Central European countries, but their leaders, over almost twenty years, have also all been men (Browning 1985; Jancar 1978, 88–121).[32]

Communist ideology predicted that labor force participation would free women from economic dependence and therefore raise their status. In actuality, women in the Soviet Union had many of the same disadvantages as working women in other industrialized countries—occupational gender segregation, unequal pay, and limited access to managerial positions. Although Soviet women had paid maternity leave and state-subsidized child care, abortion was the main form of limiting the number of children to one or two in urban areas. The burden of housekeeping, given the shortage of consumer goods and consequent long lines for food and clothing, was considerably greater for Soviet women than women in capitalist countries, and Soviet husbands were less likely to help with housework than husbands in France, England, or the United States.

The "woman question" in the Soviet Union was solved the way it was in most capitalist countries, by reinforcing the gendered division of labor that communist ideology originally questioned (Buckley 1989a). The idea of communal services and shared housework was supplanted by policies of shorter work hours, longer maternity leaves, and part-time work for women. These policies were responses to a falling birthrate and the continued need for women as industrial workers and farmers. They were justified by assumptions of women's natural capacity for nurturance and perpetuated by socialization and education based on an ideology of intrinsic psychological sex differences.[33] This ideology, tailored to changing political needs, legitimated both Soviet women's recruitment to the paid labor force and encouragement to have children and Soviet men's resistance to sharing political power and housework (Buckley 1989b).

Soviet family life was strong, but given the lack of serious state concern for women's double burden, not quite in the way Soviet men leaders intended. After marriage and one birth, many Soviet women divorced and lived with their divorced or widowed mothers, who did most of housework and child care and were in turn looked after by their daughters when they grew old. Writing before the breakup of the Soviet Union, Francine du Plessix Gray described this scene:

> So on that afternoon in Leningrad I looked around at the homey living room in which my hostess and her very independent daughter were graciously pouring tea, its walls hung with travel souvenirs from Poland, Hungary, and India, its mantelpiece and tables filled with photographs of what seemed to be exclusively female ancestors—mothers, grandmothers, great-aunts, with nary a male in sight. Observing this female intimacy, these tokens of indissoluble mother-daughter ties, I thought of those gaily painted *matrioshka* dolls that are a staple of Russian folk art: Breaking apart at the stomach to spill out many identical dolls, parthogenetic females fitting snugly into the next, generation after generation. (1990, 53)

China: Iron Girls Without a Voice

The fate of Soviet women in the last seventy-five years seems like a roller-coaster ride, from the paid labor market to domestic duties and back again, from sexual freedom to the iconography of Russian motherhood to single heads of households.[34] But for Chinese women, this century has been one long contradiction. The fate of Chinese women after the Communist Revolution demonstrates that the patriarchal family can survive women's entry into paid work (Johnson 1983; Stacey 1983). Urban Chinese women tend to work in low-paid jobs and continue to be held responsible for the physical and emotional welfare of their families. Women in rural areas, the largest part of the Chinese population, are still tightly bound to their husband's kin. The allocation of land to every peasant in the 1950s made wives more valued; they were therefore paradoxically *less* free to get a divorce and custody of their children, who also had a share in the land distribution.

At the end of the nineteenth century, China was virtually colonized by Japan, the United States, and Great Britain (Siu 1982). Cash crops of tea and opium replaced farming for food; silk cloth was exported, and the cotton cloth peasants wore was imported. Food prices were high, and sharecropping, loan sharking, and famines added to the peasants' misery. Women's farm work was marginal to the family economy, and their independent source of income, cotton spinning, had dried up. If they weren't killed at birth, young girls were sold as child-wives, concubines, prostitutes, and indentured factory workers whose wages were paid to their families. Poor women were commodities: "Men could, and frequently did, exchange their female kin for money, whether in marriage, adoption, or sale into slavery or prostitution" (Gates 1989, 799).

The daughters of wealthier families, forced into hated arranged marriages, sometimes committed suicide (Witke 1973a).[35] Women who stayed married were virtually buried in the patriarchal, patrilocal, and patrilineal extended families and village clans that structured traditional Chinese society (Johnson 1983, 1–26). As in-marrying strangers, their status was that of a servant to the family, especially if their bride price had been high and they hadn't brought in a compensatory dowry. Poor girls who had been adopted as foster daughters and future daughters-in-law in the "minor marriage" form were even more exploited and oppressed. The will of young girls was sapped by foot-binding and vicious punishments for any disobedience. Their only way out was to live long enough to produce sons and manipulate their filial devotion. When the sons married docile girls whom the mothers helped select, the cycle started again. In this way, "women, through their actions to resist passivity and male control, became participants with vested interests in the system that oppressed them" (Johnson 1983, 21).

The May Fourth Movement, in the early part of the twentieth century, targeted the family as the locus of social and economic transformation and also pushed for women's suffrage. A women's resistance movement flourished from 1902 to 1912 among middle-class students who had been sent to Japan to be educated. Ironically, the women's cause was anti-imperialism, especially against Japan, as well as education and marriage reform. One of their leaders was Qui Jin, who was killed in the 1911 revolution that deposed the Ch'ing dynasty and promised women the vote but failed to give it to them. Women cotton mill workers went on strike in 1919 for better working conditions, especially for child laborers, and for higher wages and job security; other strikes by women textile workers followed. Over a thousand women marched in anti-imperialist demonstrations in 1919, and the Hunan Women's Association got one of its members, Wang Changguo, elected to the Hunan Provincial Assembly. The Guomingdang, which took power in 1912, formed a Woman's Bureau in 1923 and coopted many of the women's associations (Gilmartin 1989; Siu 1982).

When the Chinese Communist Party (CCP) was formed in 1920, it reached out to both well-educated and peasant women with a program of marriage reforms and distribution of land to every adult, including women. The men of the party, such as Chen Duxiu, a leader of the earlier May Fourth Movement, felt that women's emancipation was particularly crucial if China was to become a modern nation. The first woman member of the CCP was Miao Boying. Other prominent women members at the time were Liu Qingyang, Xiang Jingyu, Yang Kaihui, Gao Junman, and Wang Huiwu. The First Party Congress, held in 1921, set up a women's action program, which included establishing a school and publishing a journal (Gilmartin 1989).

The political activism of these and other women was a radical break with the docile self-effacing behavior prescribed by Confucian precepts and reinforced by family pressure. Paradoxically, many women CCP leaders owed their positions to their marriages to powerful men in the party, a phenomenon that can be traced to women's embeddedness in men's kinship networks in the traditional family structure (Johnson 1983, 1–26). According to Christina Gilmartin, Wang Huiwu, the head of the CCP women's action program, never had formal Communist Party membership but was appointed because she was married to Li Da, one of the three members of the Central Bureau of the First Party Congress (1989, 86–91). Li Da was officially head of the Shanghai Common Girls' School, even though Wang Huiwu had planned it, designed the curriculum, selected the teachers, and was in charge of running it: "Such contradictions . . . seemed to go unnoticed by Communist men in Shanghai, who believed themselves to be firm upholders of social emancipation for Chinese women, and thus saw no need to subject their assumptions about women's access to formal positions within the party hierarchy to rigorous scrutiny" (Gilmartin 1989, 88). When Li Da was removed from the Central Committee at the Second Party Congress in 1922, the journal and the school were closed down. Wang Huiwu did not have the support or the financial resources to maintain these centerpieces of the women's action program alone.

The Second Party Congress chose Xiang Jingyu, wife of Cai Hesen, a member of the Central Committee, to officially head the formally constituted Communist Women's Bureau. An experienced revolutionary who had participated in the student movements of 1919, she worked with all the women's groups in the country that were fighting for political, economic, and social rights—suffragists, professional organizations, students and teachers, workers' unions and strikers, and the feminist press. As a good Communist, however, she was critical of the suffragists and most sympathetic to the striking women workers (Leith 1973).[36] In opposition to her husband, she supported a united front with the Guomingdang and was officially head of its Women's Movement Committee as well. When, in 1925, the Guomingdang refused to grant women the vote, Xiang led the women in both parties in national protests that radicalized them and verified her belief in their revolutionary potential. But she lost her position on the CCP Central Executive Committee and was removed from the head of the Women's Bureau when she divorced her husband and broke with her high-ranking lover. She went to the Soviet Union to study in 1926 and did not even have delegate status to the CCP Fifth Party Congress in 1927, which gave women high positions in the party hierarchy in recognition of their role in mobilizing support for the revolution (Gilmartin 1989, 91–97). Despite all the work she had done for the party, "as an unattached female, she lost her access to the world of high politics in the CCP. Xiang's experiences showed that a woman had to be related to an important male figure in the CCP in order to both gain and retain an influential position in the party hierarchy, and that the quality of her performance in the position had little bearing on the matter" (97).

The Guomingdang and the CCP violently broke their alliance in 1927. The Guomingdang gave women the vote and other legal rights in 1928, but like the Soviet Union during a time of upheaval, tried to restore order by returning women to their traditional status in the family. The Guomingdang dismantled its Women's Department, suppressed women's associations, propagandized for traditional women's roles, and allowed the "White Terror" to spread. Women who cut their hair, used cosmetics, danced, wore short sleeves or trousers, and in other ways visibly proclaimed themselves "modern" were severely punished by their families, and in the "White Terror," hundreds were tortured, mutilated, and killed. Among them was Xiang Jingyu, who was executed on May 1, 1928.

The CCP was driven out of the cities by the Guomingdang army under Chiang Kai-shek's leadership, and in 1935, retreated to the northwest provinces in the Long March. There, of necessity, they lived with the poor peasants, recruiting and eventually mobilizing them to the Communist cause.[37] Japan invaded China in 1937, and from 1938 to 1945, the two nations were at war. During this period, until their successful defeat of the Guomingdang in 1948, the Red Army and the CCP under Mao Zedong's leadership forged the political structure and ideology of their future government. Although their base had originally been urban factory workers, women as well as men, they now had to recruit peasant men for the Red Army and for membership in the party. In order to ensure the loyalty of these men, the CCP sacrificed peasant women's interests. The new CCP policies always paid lip service to the need to free women from the feudal family, but the resistance of men and older women meant that marriage and divorce reforms were not implemented until the 1950s and always took a back seat to the distribution of land to poor peasants.

In the 1950s, everyone got a piece of land, including women and children, but women were unable to leave their husbands and take their children with them because they could not get divorces without the permission of the men in the village council. Divorce meant the loss of considerable property for the men in the family and so was resisted to the point of beatings and murders. Politically, marriage laws that gave women greater rights in choice of husband, where to live, and custody of their children meant that poor young peasant men, who had been promised a family life by the Communists before the revolution, might not get their reward. Land without a wife was worthless to a peasant man, and so without admitting to their collusion in the restoration of the patriarchal family, which had been severely disrupted by the poverty in China before the revolution, the Communists nevertheless restored it.[38]

The 1950 Marriage Reform Law finally outlawed arranged and forced marriages, bride prices and dowries, polygamy, and child brides; it permitted divorce, enabled women to gain custody of their children, and allowed widows to remarry. It also set a minimum age for marriage for both partners. It was revolutionary in that it undermined the two-thousand-year-old Chinese family structure that had been the primary economic and property-owning unit and a major means of social control. The effect for many women, however, was not liberation because the land they were given by the government during this period locked them into their husbands' villages.

Trying to get out of distasteful arranged marriages, women initiated 75 percent of the divorce cases, and these were almost half of all civil cases in major Chinese cities following the promulgation of the new marriage law. The grounds the women cited were polygamy, adultery, desertion, forced or child marriage, and physical cruelty. The women seeking divorces were accused of promiscuity by local women's associations and ostracized by their communities. Once a woman left her husband's household, she could not farm her own land alone. But she had no place else to go, since her parents would not take her back, and there were no facilities in the countryside for living alone. Nonetheless, when women couldn't get a divorce, many committed suicide. Conversely, some were murdered by their husbands when they tried to leave. (Not surprisingly, the highest incidence of murder was in the cases charging cruelty.) According to Barbara Wolfe Jancar, "the marriage law revolutionized women's status with one hand and with the other took away the traditional protective infrastructures that had surrounded women in the past, leaving them prey to all the expressions of frustration and resentment the law occasioned" (1978, 132).

Few women emerged as leaders for women's issues after the revolution. According to government policy, women had to be heard in the village councils discussing land reform, since they were equal beneficiaries, but their organizations were subsidiary to the men's decision-making forums. To be legitimate leaders, women had to be both virtuous and militant, a contradiction in terms to the peasants. Those most likely to be militant were the least likely to be virtuous:

> Some had been rented out to landlords and other men to pay off a husband's or a father's debts. Others had lost their husbands and lived unmarried with other men. Some, without family ties, eked out an existence as prostitutes or scavengers, one of the few ways a familyless woman could survive. . . . It was apparently very difficult to find women leaders who met both the class standards and the moral standards set down by male cadres. One strongly suspects that the language was circular—if women were militant (i.e., outspoken, assertive, daring to break away from traditional restrictions which kept them in their place) they were not considered virtuous women by the men any longer. (Johnson 1983, 77)

Even young women who had not been tainted by sexual immorality were vilified: "Iron Girls were unwomanly, unmarriageable, unattractive, in short, 'false boys'" (M. B. Young 1989, 241).

During the disruptive Cultural Revolution of 1966–69, a struggle over values, attitudes, and patterns of behavior, women were "depicted as especially venal, or authoritarian, or brutal" (M. B. Young 1989, 240). When women were able to express their anger, it was boundless: Writers commented on "the quite stunning ferocity of female middle-school students against figures of authority (up to and including beating people to death)" (238).[39] Teenaged Chinese women found the Cultural Revolution liberating because they were sent into the countryside, freed of familial constraints, and made team leaders—"physically sprung loose from a home, school, or work environment" (239). One talked of riding horses very fast at night. They suffered sexual abuse and rape, but they also had an opportunity for sexual experimentation until the Cultural Revolution turned puritanical.

For women as a whole, the Cultural Revolution's emphasis on inculcating a proletarian revolutionary ideology undermined the struggle to relieve the double burden of family and economic responsibilities. The Women's Federation was disbanded as "bourgeois," and women were recruited into local political organizations, adding a third job to their work load. They did not attain significant power because they were supposed to represent peasants' not women's interests, and men, with their kinship ties in the villages, were better representatives (Johnson 1983, 178–93).

The economic policies of the 1970s brought Chinese women solidly into the waged labor market in agriculture, handicrafts, and factory work, but did not free them from sexist work practices (Dalsimer and Nisonoff 1987). Chinese women workers cluster in light industries (textiles, appliances, handicrafts), agriculture, and the service sector. These industries are understaffed, and the pace of work is intense; the heavy industries, where most men work, are overstaffed. The women's jobs also pay less than the men's jobs, and within integrated industries, women are in the lower wage grades. Subsidized services, such as transportation, housing, schools, health care, and child care, are provided through the workplace and are not uniform; women are underrepresented in the industries that provide the better social services. In addition, "model workers" get bonuses and the chance for education or Communist Party membership, and only 25 percent of the model workers are women. Women are underrepresented in upper levels of management and are most likely managers of staff services or "women's work"—well-being and family planning. The restored All-China Women's Federation sees itself as an organization for children as well as women and is charged with creating new crèches, nurseries, and after-school programs.

Like Lenin, Mao subscribed to the Marxist belief that women's productive labor would end their exploitation, but in China as in the Soviet Union (and in capitalist democracies), rural and urban women have ended up as lower-paid workers who rarely rise to positions of authority and who do the additional work of housekeeping and child care (Croll 1981). As in all countries, state demographic policies regulate procreation, but with a population in the billions, China has a far more restrictive one-child policy (Croll, Davin, and Kane 1985). The result is that Chinese girls, because of the continued cultural preference for boys, are now disappearing by the millions—aborted, killed in infancy, given up for adoption, placed in orphanages, or simply not legally registered (Kristof 1991, 1993; WuDunn 1991). When they live, most are dutiful daughters, wives, and daughters-in-law (Davis-Friedmann 1985). Women in China may have unbound feet and unbound minds, but without the power to rear many sons and still not having an equal status with men, their avenues of resistance and independence have been cut off yet again.

Had the revolution's promises to women been carried through, Margery Wolf notes, "women might now be valued members of the workforce, sharing leadership positions in the countryside, earning as much as their brothers, and being as much or more of a blessing to their parents in their old age" (1985, 272). Instead, Chinese women are supposed to be productive "iron girls" but also pretty enough, young enough, chaste enough, and unthreatening enough to get a husband—"marriage remains virtually compulsory" (Honig and Hershatter 1988, 336). Once married, not necessarily to a man of her own choosing, it is the woman's responsibility to maintain a "peaceful, harmonious family." In order to do so,

> women should learn the arts of adornment, but refrain from their undue exercise; women should be filial toward parents and in-laws, but modern, independent, antifeudal; women should certainly follow the dictates of state population policy and are of course the primary child rearer, but they must learn, from professional experts, how to avoid spoiling the single child; women should fully participate in the drive to realize the four modernizations (in agriculture, industry, science and technology, and defense), but they might just want to take three, four, or even ten years maternity leave as well. Romantic love is an acceptable socialist notion, but women are responsible for controlling their own and male sexual behavior and sex itself should be indulged in only after marriage and strictly within its confines. (M. B. Young 1989, 244)

For Women, All Revolutions Have Failed

Women have gone out in the streets and risked their lives alongside men in all social movements. As Michelle Wallace said of the civil rights movement in the United States: "Women are hard workers and they require little compensation.

Women are sometimes willing to die much more quickly than men. Women vote. Women march. Women perform tedious tasks. And women cannot be paid off for the death and the suffering of their children" ([1978] 1990, 81).[40] Yet women themselves have never had a revolution. They are mobilized to add to a revolution's supporters, but once a revolution succeeds, women are exploited as paid and unpaid workers in modernizing governments, or as bulwarks of traditionalism and the family in revolutions of national and religious revival (Moghadam 1993a, 1993b; Molyneux 1985).

In the French Revolution, women began as political activists and ended as glorified mothers, personifications of the regenerated country: "Women had sacrificed for the republic and in return the Jacobins honored the importance of women *within the family* in revolutionary France. Gone were the Amazons, the activists, the petitioners for women's rights, the clubs of revolutionary women" (Graham 1977, 250). Women demonstrated in the streets in favor of twentieth-century Islamic revolutions, but with their ideology of the purity of women, many postrevolutionary Islamic states have revoked women's civil liberties. They are under men's control even more than women were in Western countries before the end of the nineteenth century (Kandiyoti 1991; Moghadam 1989, 1993a, 1993b).[41] In Iran, the fundamentalist state has instituted the following policies:

> (1) the compulsory veil; (2) the segregation of women in public institu-
> tions; (3) lowering the marriage age from eighteen to thirteen; (4) the
> reinstitution of polygamy and temporary marriage; (5) the reinstate-
> ment of divorce and child custody as unilateral rights of men; (6) the
> reintroduction of male guardianship, especially for travel; (7) the re-
> striction of female employment (including the requirement of the male
> guardian's written permission . . .); (8) the illegalization of abortion;
> (9) the closing of day-care centers; (10) . . . a woman's value is
> deemed half as that of a man [for retribution]; women's inheritance is
> also 50%, (11) sexual offenses such as adultery [and repeated homosex-
> uality] are punishable by death. (Moghadam 1989, 46)

Now that the new republics of the former Soviet Union and the state socialist Central European countries are instituting market economies based on private capital, women workers are losing the state supports and child-care services that encouraged their full employment.[42] They have been fired from inefficient industries; in modernized factories, their skills are being replaced by high-tech machinery and robots, or better-trained men workers are hired. If foreign capital investment in sweatshop production creates a demand for low-waged workers, women will be hired again in capacities similar to women in underdeveloped countries (Moghadam 1990b). Some women managers have bought enough shares in privatized enterprises to continue in their positions of authority; the likelihood, though, is that many more men will do so than women, and the women will start smaller, home-based businesses or continue to work in women-dominated sectors of the economy, including agriculture.[43] The lives of women teachers, doctors, nurses, and administrators in those countries may improve, since they may be able to buy food without standing in long lines and may be able to afford household appliances. But increased consumption will probably foster the need for the two-earner household. Women's status will then depend on the extent to which their governments encourage their dual roles as paid workers and mothers or emphasize their familial duties, and that will depend on the rates of unemployment.

Women who help make successful revolutions do not have a significant central role in institutionalizing the revolution because issues continue to be gendered. The state, economy, and defense are men's issues; the home, family, children, and procreation are women's issues, problems to be solved once a revolution is solidified.[44] Women's interests are frequently sacrificed for the support of groups resistant to revolutionary social change. In Latin American countries, such as Nicaragua, the right to abortion was shelved to keep the support of the Roman Catholic church (Molyneux 1985; Wessel 1991). Women are not seen as legitimate shapers of the government, economy, and defense, although their recruitment as workers may be crucial to industrialization and military mobilization. Abortion, child care, and who is responsible for cooking and cleaning are not central revolutionary problems to men, although the strength of the family may be an ideological rallying cry.

Under the guise of a rhetoric of gender equality, the decisions of post-revolutionary governments exploit women as paid workers in the labor force and as unpaid workers in the home. In particular, access to abortion is a litmus test of the status of women. The postcommunism situation in Hungary is typical of how states control women's lives:

> It is rather intriguing that in the middle of a deep economic crisis, political chaos and social insecurity, when the very foundations of society are to be reshaped, abortion has become a primary question in almost all post-socialist countries. There is a clear economic reason for it: the neo-classical type of economic restructuring will create massive unemployment, and it is easier and more comfortable to get rid of the

female workforce. . . . It also has an ideological message: the new conservative, right-of-center government puts the emphasis on the family. . . . And women are expected to be the pillars, the caryatids of a newly painted, but badly designed old building, namely the unequal and oppressive traditional family. (Kiss 1991)

Although religious, cultural, ethnic, and political rhetoric are all invoked to support policies emancipating women or returning them to the service of their families, the underlying goal is not women's interests or gender equality but the state's interests in women as industrial workers, farmers, and breeders. When the rhetoric is unpacked, the gender biases are individualism, independence, and economic self-reliance for men, and economic dependence on a man and service to the family for women (Sapiro 1990). The revolutions of the 1990s, therefore, are likely to be a reprise of the last 350 years— "democratization with a male face" (Moghadam 1990a).

Making a Feminist Revolution

What would it take for feminists to become significant players in a revolution? According to Antonio Gramsci, "A social group can, and indeed must, already exercise 'leadership' before winning governmental power (this indeed is one of the principal conditions for the winning of such power)" (1971, 57). Women would need organizations, programs, and legitimacy as political leaders, and they would have to mobilize other key groups to join *them*. Jack Goldstone, building on Theda Skocpol's (1979) concept of marginal elites, notes that they have the potential to become the key to structural transformation in a revolution:

Marginal elites are groups that have an upper-class education and access to national debates over political and social issues, yet at the same time are also restricted . . . from any prospect of active participation in the highest levels of government and society. Such marginal elites take the lead in articulating and seeking to implement alternative social orders; their presence or absence is thus a critical factor in the spread of "transformative" ideologies. (Goldstone 1991, 42)

With prior national organizations, programs, and leaders, feminists could, during and after a revolution, take the lead in promulgating their viewpoint and forming coalitions with other groups.

But disruptive revolutions are chancy bets; they are more likely to lead to dictatorship and repression than to democracy and freedom (Goldstone 1991, 477–82).[45] Rather than waiting for the next societal breakdown, feminists could start a revolution for themselves by developing the organizations, programs, and leadership for a state that is truly gender-neutral. For women and men to be equal, this vision needs to go far beyond reform of any present gendered social structure. A feminist revolution needs an ideological vision of societal transformation that reflects a critical knowledge of current institutional practices (D. E. Smith 1990). Feminist revolutionaries would have to redefine the terms of political discourse and challenge the premises and taken-for-granted assumptions of everyday life in order to produce ideas for a society that is not built on the exploitation of women in the workplace and in the home. They need to "suspend commitment to the game . . . in order to reduce the world, and the actions performed in it, to absurdity, and to bring up questions about the meaning of the world and existence which people never ask when they are caught up in the game" (Bourdieu [1980] 1990, 66–67).

A feminist theory of the state has barely been imagined;
systematically, it has never been tried.

—*Catharine A. MacKinnon (1989, 249)*

DISMANTLING NOAH'S ARK:
GENDER AND EQUALITY

The defeated Equal Rights Amendment to the United States Constitution read simply, "Equality of rights under the law shall not be denied or abridged by the United States or any state on account of sex." Equal rights for women is a goal that resonates with individualism and freedom of choice. Yet that goal failed because, legally, in order to be treated alike, people have to *be* alike, and the prevailing belief in Western societies is that women and men are intrinsically different. Biological rationales for gender inequality not only are still part of the taken-for-granted assumptions of everyday reality in Western countries; they are built into public policy and law.[1] As a result, the liberal feminist goal of equality for women in Western societies will probably, as Robert Connell sardonically points out, have as little effect in countering men's domination of women as the rallying cries of liberal philosophers that all *men* were equal had in countering rich men's domination of poor men: "Liberal feminism took the doctrine of 'rights' seriously and turned it against the patriarchal model of citizenship. 'Equal rights' is more than a slogan; it is a wholly logical doctrine that is as effective against the 'aristocracy of sex' as the doctrine of the 'rights of man' was against the aristocracy of property" (Connell 1990, 512).

If women and men are alike, unlike treatment is inequality, but if they are not alike, dissimilar treatment is appropriate. As Catharine MacKinnon says:

> Gender is socially constructed *as difference* epistemologically, and sex discrimination law bounds gender equality *by difference* doctrinally. Socially one tells a woman from a man by their difference from each

other, but a woman is discriminated against on the basis of sex only
when she can first be said to be the same as man. A built-in tension
exists between this concept of equality, which presupposes sameness,
and this concept of sex, which presupposes difference. Sex equality
becomes a contradiction in terms, something of an oxymoron. (1990,
215)[2]

Less emphasis on masculinity and femininity in bringing up children,
depiction of diverse behavior by women and men in the mass media, and
encouraging men's access to jobs traditionally filled by women and women's
access to jobs traditionally filled by men are familiar ways feminists have
recommended to avoid creating *unnecessary* differences—that is, differences
that go beyond the biological. The alternative goal—equity—recognizes
differences but tries to compensate for them by giving women benefits or
protections, such as maternity leave or assignment to nonhazardous work. The
goal of equality and of equity are actually the same: "for women to be in some
way the same as men, whether this sameness be interpreted as identical
treatment or as access to the same opportunities" (Jaggar 1990, 250).[3]

Much of the debate over gender equality revolves around procreation and
sexuality (Kay 1985). The subjects of the debate seem to be females and males,
not women and men. Females and males are physiologically different, so if
they are treated differently, it is supposedly not an equal-rights problem. But a
closer look at the way women are treated in Western societies clearly indicates
that although the rationale is biological, the differential treatment is political.
In bureaucratic organizations, the workers and, more crucially, the people in
the top positions, are expected to be *male:*

It is the man's body, its sexuality, minimal responsibility in procreation,
and conventional control of emotions that pervades work and organizational processes. Women's bodies—female sexuality, their ability to
procreate and their pregnancy, breast-feeding, and child care, menstruation, and mythic "emotionality"—are suspect, stigmatized, and
used as grounds for control and exclusion. . . . To function at the top
of male hierarchies requires that women render irrelevant everything
that makes them women. (Acker 1990, 152, 153)

In order for female workers to be treated the same as male workers, their
biological differences are considered disabilities that are not their fault. For
example, in order to give females time off while pregnant and immediately
after childbirth without discriminating against males, pregnancy in the United

States is treated the way a male disability like a prostate infection would be, as an illness. The problem is that *women* are still discriminated against because their time off for pregnancy and childbirth is held against them as workers, whereas men's time off from work because of illness is not. Responsible women workers (especially the career-oriented) are supposed to use efficient contraception to time their pregnancies and childbirths, just as they are supposed to work out efficient child-care arrangements. But their ability to do so is heavily influenced by government policies on access to contraception and abortion, by employers' policies on maternity leave, and by the availability of affordable child care in their community.

Procreative and parenting statuses are rooted in social policies, not biological differences. Another example is fetal protection regulations, which usually concern potentially fertile women and developing fetuses, but not men, even though the same toxic substances affect sperm and can result in fetal malformation. Furthermore, as Elaine Draper points out, "Women have usually not been barred from all jobs that entail toxic risks, but only from the relatively high-paying production jobs traditionally held by men. . . . Significantly, the question of exclusion has not come up in jobs where the industry is heavily dependent on women workers. Those jobs may involve serious health risks, but where women are a majority, no one advocates removing all fertile women" (1993, 94). Women hospital workers are exposed to radiation and powerful anesthetics and assemblers in electronics factories are exposed to potentially harmful solvents, but no one suggests barring them from these jobs.

The status of women and men is as much an issue of power and privilege as is the status of people of different races and social classes. To *not* ask why a social category called "men" has power over a social category called "women" is to accept the assumption that men's domination is natural and to seek for natural causes. In theories of race, it is the very categories themselves that are problematic, that are questions for theoretical analysis: Are they cultural divisions, structural divisions, or deliberate social constructions by the dominant group whose purpose is to justify the continuation of its dominance? Either way, "as myth and as a global sign, . . . it superimposes a 'natural' unity over a plethora of . . . differences" (E. B. Higginbotham 1992, 270).[4] Once pulled apart, the discourse of race reveals the social structural underpinnings that maintain racial inequality.

In *Capital,* Karl Marx provided the theory of class as relations to the means of production—that is, classes are social groupings with a material base, personal consequences, and ideological justification. The two classes (capitalists, or owners of the means of production, and the proletariat, or exploited workers) are inherently unequal not because of some intrinsic characteristics, although that was long the prevailing belief, but because of the different relations of each to the means of production and their conflictual interdependence. For race and class, then, the relational and political aspects of the categories are clear. The dominant groups define themselves and the subordinate groups as they construct and justify the boundaries of exclusion and power.

The concept of gender, however, has been theoretically grounded in sexuality and procreation. This conceptualization undermines the feminist focus on the relational aspects of women's and men's social status and the political aspects of gender inequality. I am arguing that gender inequality is located solely in the structure of gendered social practices and institutions. Procreation and sexuality are constructed as conditions of subordination within the social institution of gender; the social institution of gender is not built on procreation and sexuality. Human sexual reproduction is universal, but gender inequality is not. The gender status of women affects the social construction of sexuality, fertility, pregnancy, childbirth, and parenting, not the other way around. Responsibility for the work in the domestic sphere is an outcome of women's gender status, not its cause.

Feminist Theories of Gender Inequality

Many feminist theories of gender inequality locate women's subordination in their procreative or sexual status as mediated through gendered social practices and institutions. Janet Saltzman Chafetz, for example, argues that "specialization in the productive / public sphere undergirds superior advantage and, conversely, specialization in the reproductive / domestic forms the basis of extensive disadvantage" (1984, 118). Since women bear the main burden of childbirth, child care, and housework, she argues that they are often at a disadvantage and never have an advantage over men. Social variables influence the extent of women's disadvantage, but the constant is that "nowhere are women, considered categorically, systematically more advantaged than men" (117).[5]

For Rae Lesser Blumberg (1984), it is not procreation but women's role as child minders, combined with a lack of control over the surplus they produce, that produces gender inequality. When the technology is such that women's work is fully compatible with child minding *and* the kinship or legal rules allow them to control the surplus they produce, women are men's social equals.

Although Lesser Blumberg's theory allows for gender equality under those circumstances, she assumes, as does Saltzman Chafetz, that if women bear babies, they will automatically become the primary parents. Other child-care arrangements are possible, including care by a designated group of men and women. If women have the main responsibility for child care, it is because of structural arrangements, not because of biology. Furthermore, the very important variable in gender inequality—the kinship or legal rules that determine whether or not women may use the surplus they produce or inherit family property—is certainly an outcome of gender as a social institution, not of sexual reproduction.

According to Judith Buber Agassi (1989), the Israeli kibbutz, as originally structured, provides an illuminating lesson in the construction and maintenance of structured gender inequality. On the Israeli kibbutz, rearing the children was not the biological mothers' sole responsibility but that of the kibbutz as a whole. But though domestic and production work was shared among the members of the kibbutz, women did the communal child rearing, laundry, much of the kitchen work, and some productive work, and men did most of the communal productive work and were in charge of administration of the kibbutz. This gendered division of labor was not necessitated by women's procreating and breast-feeding, since each woman usually had two to four children and nursed them for six months each. Allocating women to lifelong communal domestic work and child care and men to communal production and management was a social decision that resulted in a structure of gender inequality. Women and men could have rotated both types of work.

Women and men kibbutz members were not equal because the work they did was not equally valued:

> No member or resident there exchanges labor power for cash. It follows, then, that women's reproductive work should not be devalued in the kibbutz. But work in the communal service branches, which is performed overwhelmingly by women, has for decades been regarded there as of lesser value, as not "productive," and is of lower prestige than work done primarily by men in agriculture, industry, and administration, which is highly valued. (Agassi 1989, 172)[6]

The preference for producers is explained by Marx's theory of surplus value. In any economic system that produces goods that are not consumed or used by the producers, work that results in a surplus that can be sold produces a valuable profit. Whoever controls this surplus has a vital source of social power in the community.

Another evaluative distinction between women and men that has its roots in social organization, not biology, is the differential treatment of women and men waged workers in modern industrialized societies. Why are women workers routinely paid less than equivalent men workers when they are also producers of surplus value? Marxist feminist theorists, such as Michèle Barrett ([1980] 1988), Heidi Hartmann (1975, 1981a, 1981b), Maria Mies (1986), Natalie Sokoloff (1980), and Sylvia Walby (1990), base their theories of gender inequality on women's dual roles as paid *and* unpaid workers. Women are exploited in both capacities. They are low-waged workers throughout the world, which increases profits, and because they have few economic resources, they must do domestic labor either to warrant a better-paid man's economic support or to stretch their own wages (J. Smith 1984). Each form of exploitation reinforces the other, and both are justified by an ideology of natural sex differences:

> Women are considered not only to have naturally nimble fingers, but also to be naturally more docile and willing to accept tough work discipline, and naturally more suited to tedious, repetitive, monotonous work. Their lower wages are attributed to their secondary status in the labor market which is seen as a natural consequence of their capacity to bear children. . . . Indeed the phenomenon of women leaving employment . . . when they get married or pregnant is known as "natural wastage," and can be highly advantageous to firms which periodically need to vary the size of their labor force so as to adjust to fluctuating demand for their output in the world market. (Elson and Pearson 1981, 149)

If responsibility for child care is construed as part of domestic labor and not as the outcome of physiology, the Marxist feminist theory of gender inequality is fully social structural.

Exploiting Women

As a group, men own most of the private property, monopolize the better jobs, and make the laws. The outcome of this inequality is men's double exploitation of women in the job market and in the home. Even if they have no other privileges, men reap the advantages of women's domestic labor. Procreative differences are not the cause of women's exploitation but its justification. Women are subordinated in all industrial societies not because they are child bearers or child minders but because owners, managers, and governments depend on them as low-paid, accessible, responsible workers. They are the primary child carers not because of their procreative capabilities but because they are economically disadvantaged and have little choice but to do the unwaged work of social reproduction. Each form of exploitation of women's labor reinforces the other. Women's economic value as waged and unwaged workers is the *main* reason for their subordination in modern societies; they are the "last colony" (Mies, Bennholdt-Thomsen, and von Werlhof 1988).[7]

An often-cited United Nations report (1980) claims that women do two-thirds of the world's work, receive 10 percent of the income, and own 1 percent of the property. Underlying that statement is the world economic system that exploits working-class women and, in particular, women of color by paying them barely subsistence-level wages so that they must expand their nonwaged work in order to maintain their families.[8] Working-class women's labor as unpaid housewives and poorly paid domestic servants, child carers, sex workers, subsistence farmers, sellers and traders of petty commodities, and pieceworkers in the home and in sweatshop factories, combined with middle-class women's work as low-paid office workers, service workers, teachers, nurses, librarians, and social workers, adds up to two-thirds of the world's work at one-tenth of the world's income.[9] The exploitation of women as waged and unwaged workers swells the profits of a small number of capitalists, the men who own 99 percent of the world's private property. It also increases the accumulation of surplus in state-owned economies. The ideology of women's intrinsic sex differences and propensity for love and service mystifies what is in reality simple exploitation—exploitation that is compounded for economically disadvantaged women and women of color (Attwood 1990; Sokoloff 1980).

As paid workers, women as a group are cheap expendable labor. They enter the work force as a distinct segment when the work process is deliberately broken down into assembly line components, either in one workplace or spread over several, sometimes in different countries. Most women's work in the global economy is "precarious, sporadic, poorly paid and unprotected" (Bennholdt-Thomsen 1988, 160). As clerks, data processors, and service personnel in large-scale organizations and state agencies, keeping information flowing and clients "cooled out," women are "reliable workers who can be counted upon, even when distant from management, to act on its behalf" (Tancred-Sheriff 1989, 50). Whether they do manual labor or white-collar work, women's replaceability as workers makes them too vulnerable to resist the myriad forms of exploitation they encounter in the paid workplace.

Working-class women are exploited the most in the job market and in the home. They are systematically deprived of well-paying jobs and so provide cheap labor in the world's factories and offices. Because they do not have a secure place in the labor market, they continue to be exploitable as low-paid domestic workers, dependent on better-paid workers to supplement their inadequate income. In their own homes, their unpaid domestic labor swells capital accumulation because the workers in the household do not have to buy the goods and services they provide for free, and so employers can keep wages down. Working-class women need their husbands' economic support, so they continue to shoulder the burden of the double day. If a working-class woman earns as much or more than her husband, she might insist on their sharing domestic work. But if she overcompensates for her higher salary by taking responsibility for all the child care and housework, she might be unable to continue to work at her job. Working-class men vacillate between tolerating the paid work of the women they live with because it adds to the family income and resisting the women's earning more than they do because they then lose their right to the women's domestic labor (Hochschild 1989).

Working-class women have been able to mobilize politically, but only as part of their family roles (Naples 1991a, 1991b, 1992). Their women's organizations fight for better living and working conditions and improved health care, which benefit men as well as women. Among disadvantaged racial ethnic groups, women's consciousness of their oppressed status has often been subsumed under a fight for the rights of the men of their group.[10]

Working- and middle-class women, as the nexus between the household and the economy, shop for their families and work as sales clerks; they link children and the educational system as the primary parents and as teachers; and they care for the sick and the elderly as amateur and as professional nurses. Their unwaged work, which expands domestic labor way beyond housework and child care, benefits families. Insidiously, however, it also allows employers to keep down the salaries of the women doing the work for pay (Glazer 1993). Coalitions of middle- and working-class women have organized around what are defined as women's problems—battering, child abuse, incest, rape, and prostitution. These organizations rarely present a radical critique of the gendered social order that supports men's sense of entitlement to the sexual and domestic services of women. They also do not see how the unwaged work women do as wives and mothers and the low-waged work they do as clerks, teachers, and nurses jointly oppress women (D. E. Smith 1990).

The women in the class of owners and managers are for the most part exploited as social reproducers by the men of their class because they do not own as much property or earn as much as men do. If they do, and they hire others to care for their households and children, they are the social equivalents of husbands and fathers (Rothman 1989). It is this possibility of women assuming the social status of dominant men in Western societies that those men resist the most. If women business owners, managers, and professionals were allowed to compete freely with men for the most powerful and prestigious positions, including those in government, they would attain a critical mass that would solidify their political clout. Instead, the few high-status women who do achieve positions of prestige and power are likely to be coopted by the dominant men whose support their positions depend on. They cannot afford to alienate elite men by questioning the gender order that gives those men their superior power, and so they end up "honorary men" rather than fighters for gender equality.

Providing food and supervising children's welfare are usually women's province, whether it is done privately or communally (DeVault 1991). In many countries, just producing, processing, or shopping for food takes an enormous amount of women's time; in more affluent countries, children's educational and psychological welfare are the focus of mothering work. The emotional bonds that emerge from these caretaking activities coopt women into maintaining the gendered division of labor. Their relationships with their children and with the men they love (and depend on economically) make them suppress their resentment over double days, glass ceilings, and sexual harassment. The combination of women's poor position in the economy, continued responsibility for child care and domestic labor, and delegitimation of their bids for leadership positions makes it extremely difficult for them to attain political power of any significance, and so the laws and rules that structure their life chances continue to be made by dominant men.

Men's emotional and sexual exploitation of women, their objectification of women in culture and devaluation in the world's main religions, their rendering women invisible in standard histories, and their ideological justification of legal controls over women's bodies—the patriarchal component of gender inequality—are the *means* of subordination. The psychological investment of women in their children and the stigmatization of men's and women's homosexual love and women's sexuality inscribe the gender order in men's and women's personalities and identities. Tying women to children *and* men emotionally meets men's needs for biological inheritance, emotional sustenance, and heterosexual relationships. Whether it is direct, by restricting access to contraception and abortion, or indirect, by invoking women's purported nurturant and caretaking qualities and claiming they are therefore indispensable as mothers of small children, the effect is to coopt women into a structure of gender inequality through "bonds of love" (Benjamin 1988).

More intimate parenting by men might break the cycle of the reproduction of mothering and gendered personality structures that alienate men emotionally and bond women to their children so intensely. It might also diminish the level of violence and sexual exploitation. But alone, it will not produce gender equality. Gendered parenting, personality structures, sexual exploitation, and physical violence help maintain men's control over women, but they are not the cause of institutionalized gender inequality. The basic cause is women's deprivation of rights of access to property and well-paid jobs, which makes them economically dependent and emotionally and sexually vulnerable. This deprivation has been systematic and state-supported, and it persists because it advantages men both as property owners and as workers. Married women with children whose husbands have good jobs collude in this exploitation because their material well-being and social status and that of their children are higher when they live with a man than if they try to make a life on their own. Women with children who have neither the resources of a man's economic support nor a secure position of their own in the workplace are unlikely, because of their need to rely on government assistance, to protest the system as a system. But they, of all women, experience its oppression firsthand.

Most families cannot survive economically without women's paid work. If choices have to be made between child care and paid work, women neglect, abandon, or board out their children (Boswell 1988; Fuchs 1984). As "bad mothers," they then bear the brunt of these decisions emotionally and socially (Gordon 1989). Men invest time and energy in the care and teaching of children (sometimes only sons) when it is to their advantage. The intense battles over child custody indicate that many men today want children they can claim through biological connection or through investment in time and energy (Smart and Sevenhuijsen 1989). Some men may be more willing than some women to organize their work lives around parenting, but in most countries, the structure of work denies them the opportunity, just as the lack of good child care outside the home penalizes women for their work commitments. But even where work schedules are flexible and the state provides child-care leave to either parent, as in Sweden, few men take on substantial amounts of child care and housework. As service to others, this work has emotional rewards, not the tangible monetary payoff men in industrial and postindustrial societies have been taught to seek as a mark of masculinity. The love and respect that are the rewards of family work attest to a woman's, not a man's, worth.

Women's lives serve their families and the economy. Men's lives serve not only their families and the economy but also themselves. If women work hard for their families, they get vicarious gratification as wives and mothers; if men work hard for their families, the power, prestige, and income they earn is their own.[11] Among African Americans, even women who are upwardly mobile remain linked to their families, who are often the people who helped them get an education and prepare for a career (Higginbotham and Weber 1992). In contrast, for African-American men, "self-determination and accountability . . . are at the core of the self and of manhood" (Hunter and Davis 1992, 475).

The fault lines in this gendered social order are single parenthood for women and unemployment for men; both circumstances upset the complementary role expectations that tie women to individual men in order to have a family of their own and give individual men the resources for their dominant status. Bringing up children on the poor salary of a woman's job or on assistance from a government that questions their moral status can radicalize women, just as long-term unemployment has led men to question the legitimacy of an economy that deprives them of work. Rebellious men, once they have jobs, are likely to want a secure and even traditional family life; rebellious women have the potential to challenge the whole gendered social structure that makes it so difficult for them to live both comfortably and independently.

Can You Have Gender and Equality, Too?

I have argued throughout this book that gender is a social creation, a product of human inventiveness adopted for its usefulness in allocating reciprocal rights and responsibilities, work tasks, and the physical and social reproduction of new members of any society. The gendered division of work in early societies did not separate subsistence labor and child care—women did both—and many of these societies were egalitarian or possibly even woman-dominated, given women's important contribution to the food supply and their evident role in the procreation of valued children. Accidentally or deliberately, but in any case probably quite gradually, gender got inextricably built into stratification and inequality, producing a subordinate group, "women," whose labor, sexuality, and childbearing could be exploited.

The unequal distribution of power, property, and prestige between women and men is now part of the structure of modern societies. Gender statuses today are inherently unequal, and the whole point of gendering is to produce structured gender inequality. Subordination of women is an intrinsic part of the modern social order not because men are naturally superior or dominant (if they were, there would be no subordinate men) or because women bear children (if that were true, no mother would ever be a leader in her society). The subordination of women persists because it produces a group that can be exploited as workers, sexual partners, childbearers, and emotional nurturers in the marketplace and in the household. Policies that could establish true gender equality are not seriously implemented because they would erode the exploitation of women's labor, sexuality, and emotions. Societies and communities that have tried to establish egalitarianism rarely give as much attention to gender inequality as they do to economic inequity, the main concern of men.

Given a concept of natural differences between females and males that mystifies the pervasive and continual social construction of differentiated gender categories, to make all women and men equal would need perfect and scrupulously maintained equivalence between women's and men's rights, responsibilities, and rewards to compensate for these supposed immutable sex differences. Since gender is at present a system of power and dominance mostly favoring men, redressing the imbalance would mean giving women some of men's privileges, such as freedom from housework, and men some of women's responsibilities, such as taking care of infants. Instead, men have gotten women's privileges, such as limits on the number of hours a day a paid worker can be required to work, and women have gotten men's responsibilities, such as economic support of their families (Stacey 1991, 259). Lesbians and homosexual men are able to break the microsystem of domination and subordination, since personal power differentials are not gendered in their families and their communities, but they participate in the gendered macrosystem, especially in the world of work, as women and men.[12]

A truly radical goal for feminism would be not just gender equality but "a society in which maleness and femaleness are socially irrelevant, in which men and women, as we know them, will no longer exist" (Jaggar 1983, 330), a society without gender.[13] A more pragmatic goal (but ultimately equally radical) would be a society without economic inequities, racial distinctions, or sexual exploitation, since they are all implicated in the social production of gender inequality. These goals are not really different. If gender inequality is the raison d'être for the social institution of gender today, making women and men equal in every sphere of life would undermine the need for the construction and maintenance of gender distinctions. The resultant degendered social order would not be a society of indistinguishable clones—individuality and cross-cutting groupings would produce much more variety than two genders.

Structured Equality

How can we restructure the institutionalized arrangements that subordinate and exploit women and build a society that is potentially egalitarian for women and men? Since race and class are intertwined with gender in the social arrangements that reproduce inequality, it is highly unlikely that gender inequality alone could (or should) be redressed without considering racial and economic exploitation. For example, capitalism currently exploits women as a reserve army of cheap labor, but it also exploits disadvantaged men. Socialism accumulates more surplus if some workers are paid less than others, but these lesser-paid workers are not necessarily women. These systems do not need gendered job segregation or gendered occupational stratification to survive in their current forms; they need only low-cost workers and hierarchies of management. If the low-paid and high-paid workers were a random mix of women and men, and the owners and managers were also mixed on gender, equality of women and men in each stratum could be accomplished without altering income inequalities or managerial hierarchies.

People with different social characteristics, however, are rarely randomly sorted into a stratification system because their characteristics are used to create or justify the contingencies of inequality—the structure of the education system, the rewards for different kinds of work, the allocation of responsibility for the care of dependents. Any socially constructed categories can be so used as long as structures of inequality organize a society. If we want to eliminate the exploitation of any social group by any other social group, a society has to be structured for equality. That means that all individuals within a group and all social groups within a society have to be guaranteed equal access to the valued resources of the society—education; work; sufficient income for a comfortable standard of living; satisfying emotional, sexual, and familial relationships; freedom from violence and exploitation; help in times of dependence; and the opportunity to produce knowledge, create culture, and lead in small and large ways. In order for individuals to be equal, the social groups that order their lives—their families, work organizations, schools, religions, ethnicities, sexual communities—have to be structurally equal, and within those groups, all the members have to be social equals. Equality does not mean sameness or even similarity; it means that different talents and contributions are equally valued and rewarded. *The meta-rule in a social order structured for equality is that no individual within a group and no group within the society monopolizes the economic, educational, and cultural resources or the positions of power.*

In order to make all workers equal, everyone who does any kind of socially useful work, including the caretakers of dependents, must receive a wage that sustains a comfortable standard of living. Job segregation on the basis of gender and race would then be superfluous. Shared or rotated management would flatten hierarchies, and so there would be no point for the members of any group to monopolize positions of authority. But if some people, or some groups of people, disproportionately continued to be the caretakers of dependents, and production work continued to be more highly valued than social reproduction, inequality would persist. As Cynthia Cockburn says: "Until the symbolic man-as-citizen has his mind on the cooker, his eye on a toddler and a hand on granddad's wheelchair, no constitution will guarantee social equality" (1991, 97). For true equality, care of children and the elderly would have to be made every able-bodied adult's responsibility equally, perhaps in a vertical kinship system, with each competent adult responsible for a child and an elderly parent or grandparent (Lorber 1975).

Pregnancy and childbirth are not insurmountable barriers to structures of equality. Childbearing is not most modern women's main role in life. As Connell suggests, in postindustrial societies,

> childbearing can be made a fairly short episode in any woman's life, and can be made socially equivalent to conception, pregnancy-support and infant care in men's lives. We have the knowledge and resources to share childcare and domestic work among adults to any extent desired in a balance between efficiency and privacy. Large numbers of men and women can choose to be childless without any danger of depopulation; a free choice of forms of cathexis becomes a general possibility. (1987, 280)

That is, if parenting is seen as many adults' responsibility, then social, emotional, and economic support during pregnancy and childbirth could certainly be given by the nonpregnant and the nonbirthers to the woman who gestates and delivers a child for the household. Structuring for equality would do away not with procreative differences but with social roles and patterns of behavior that assign responsibilities that have nothing to do with pregnancy and childbirth to all females, many of whom are not and never will be birth mothers. Egalitarian child care and child support are already structured into some dual-career and two-income families, joint custody arrangements, and gay and lesbian households.

If every adult in a household is to be equal, household income has to be shared equally; otherwise the one with more economic resources has greater bargaining power. Even a household of unequal earners can be structured for equality. All household income could be pooled and allocated first to food, clothing, shelter, transportation, medical care, school fees, and other household expenses (perhaps including paid child care, house cleaning, laundry), donations, gifts, entertainment, vacations, retirement, and savings for emergencies. After that, to ensure equal resources, the remainder could be split evenly among the adult members of the household for their individual use (cf. Hertz 1986, 84–113).[14] Each adult in a household should be able to claim the same amount of discretionary income, regardless of earnings, since that surplus buys the freedom to travel, donate, entertain, give gifts, save, work on private projects, and so on. Any earnings from this discretionary income should belong to the investor who is risking her or his own money. Individuals should also be able to leave what they have accumulated to whomever they want.

Any family work not done through paid services, as well as responsibility for hiring, overseeing, and transportation, would have to be evenly split or allocated by desirability, competence, convenience, and time. If all adults shared responsibility for domestic work, each would have equivalent time for educational and occupational advancement and political work. Any grouping of adults could share both the income from paid work and their domestic labor and thus provide economic support and nurturing care for the children, elderly, and sick in a household. If the economic system and the political system were also structured for equality (by equitable income distribution and rotated positions of authority), the egalitarian structure of domestic life would support and be supported by the egalitarian structure of work and government.

Freed of exploitive economic, kinship, and procreative relationships, sexuality could indeed be the result of individual desires. But all kinds of sexual behavior would not be acceptable in an egalitarian society. Relations between adults and children and those imbued with acts of violence would erase the structural conditions of equality—that no one be exploited or subordinated in any way or by any means by anyone or any social institution. Children's equality depends on the protection of adults, protection that is violated by sexual exploitation. Violence creates the ultimate condition of inequality— unequal power—and so any use or threat of physical harm of one person by another must be absolutely forbidden legally and tabooed culturally as well. But for socially competent adults, all consenting sexual relationships, including those with *fantasies* of violence, would have equal value in a society structured for equality.[15]

A structure of cultural equality would mean that all symbolic and ideological representations would have equal worth. The forms and content of culture might not even be that different from much that is produced throughout the world today, but the meanings would be different: "In a world in which the power structure was such that both men and women equally could be represented clothed or unclothed in a variety of poses and positions without any implications of dominance or submission—in a world of total and, so to speak, unconscious equality, the female nude would not be problematic" (Nochlin 1988, 30).[16] What about pornography? In a utopian social order, such as true communism, says Alan Soble, "the making of pornography . . . will surely be libidinally satisfying, but that is not why it or any other work is meaningful and satisfying. It is nonalienated labor because it would be freely chosen, the project would be collectively planned without a hierarchy of authority, its completion would involve a playful creativity, and the product would be appreciated and admired by others" (1986, 127).

Currently, the subordination, exploitation, and even extermination of some social groups by others as well as the inequality of individuals within all social groups is part of the laws, governments, and criminal justice systems of most countries, even those supposedly organized for equality. If societies are to reverse this pattern and build on their traditional or constitutional structures of equality, at a minimum every proposed law, court order, or state policy must be examined first for its effect on all the structural conditions of equality —the distribution of economic resources; production of knowledge and culture; shares of political power; help for children, the elderly, the sick, the less physically and mentally competent; valuation of ethnic traditions and religious beliefs; and acceptance of consenting adults' sexual practices.

Does a social world structured for equality mean people will be a varied, motley crew, or a version of middle-class, white, Anglo-Saxon Protestant men? It would probably take as deliberate an effort to counteract hegemonic masculine values in workplaces and other organizations as it would be to structure them for equality. That is, conscious reorganization along the lines suggested by Patricia Yancey Martin would be necessary to construct a social order based on qualities of "inclusion, participation and diversity" (1993, 290).[17] These are the necessary conditions for gender equality.

Into and Out of Noah's Ark

Human beings have constructed and used gender—human beings can deconstruct and stop using gender. The most obvious way would be to deliberately and self-consciously *not* use gender to organize social life. Gender-neutrality resonates with Western concepts of achievement, in which individual talents, ambitions, strengths, and weaknesses constitute the only basis for work roles and leadership positions. Gender-neutrality assumes that women and men who are similarly educated and trained are interchangeable and that gender equality will come when more women get the equivalent of prestigious men's jobs and positions of authority and more men participate in housework and child care.

Women and men at present are rarely interchangeable because the social order is structured to advantage men and disadvantage women. In the micropolitics of everyday life and the macropolitics of laws and state policies, dominant men are so privileged that they continue to dominate without much conscious effort. Women and subordinate men have to show that they are as good as dominant men to succeed economically, politically, or artistically— the burden of proof is on them. Social policies that ignore this structure of gender inequality and assume that remedies can take place on the individual level are doomed to failure, and the failure will be attributed to the attitudes, competencies, and motivations of the individuals concerned, both dominant and subordinate, not to the social structure.

Whether without a revolution it is possible to structure gender equality in social orders that are organized to guarantee the privileges of dominant men is questionable. To see how deeply gender inequality organizes work, parenting, leadership, politics, and culture in modern societies, consider what a world would be like where women and men equally worked in every occupation and profession, equally took care of children, governed equally, equally produced culture.

In a world of scrupulous gender equality, equal numbers of girls and boys would be educated and trained for the liberal arts and for the sciences, for clerical and manual labor, and for all the professions. Among those with equal credentials, women and men would be hired in an alternating fashion for the same type of job—or only men would be hired to do women's types of jobs and only women would be hired to do men's types of jobs until half of every workforce was made up of men and half, women.[18]

If men did women's work, would the pay increase, autonomy be encouraged, and the work gain in prestige? If women were not seen as taking over men's work, but performing it interchangeably with men, would the work be devalued, deskilled, and paid less? Would upward mobility be restricted in order to encourage rapid turnover and low wages if half of all lower-level workers were men? If a work process was degraded, all workers would suffer, and they might resist employers as a group, instead of men competing against women for the best jobs or for any jobs at all.

If men as well as women cared for children, many ways might be found to equalize responsibility for parenting: crèches at work for breast-feeding and bottle-feeding parents, men taking as much time off as women to care for sick children, "daddy tracks" if "mommy tracks" persisted (in which case, there would probably be no separate tracks for parents). Please note that in no way am I suggesting that *females* and *males* could be interchanged, only women and men. Males do not get pregnant, but they can take care of infants; females gestate and lactate, but that does not mean that only they must take parental leave. Equal child care would involve staffing community child-care centers and schools with equal numbers of men and women doing every kind of task. How would primary parents who were interchangeably women and men alter children's gendered psychological development? How would children be socialized if their caretakers and teachers were equally women and men?

What would happen if positions of responsibility were alternated between women and men? In elected positions, two women then two men could run against each other alternately to ensure that neither men nor women predominated.[19] In appointed positions, women and men of equal qualifications would be alternated. What would be the effect on concepts of authority and leadership? On training and grooming for advancement? On gendered patterns of deference? On sexual harassment?

Although some modern countries have a high percentage of doctors and lawyers who are women, professional work has been stratified by gender, with men in the more prestigious sectors and in the policy-making positions. The same is true of education; women mostly occupy the lower grades of teaching and the lower levels of administration. Scientific research in all modern countries is dominated by men. These are the arenas where knowledge is produced in response to theoretical questions and pragmatic problems. If half of all medical specialists, medical school faculties, and researchers were women; if half the police and lawyers and judges at all levels were women; if half the university professors, deans, provosts, presidents, and chancellors were women; if half the scientists in the world were women, what changes are predictable in medical practice and research priorities, in the criminal justice system and the interpretation of laws, in the knowledge produced and the knowledge taught, in the scientific problems considered important enough to command enormous resources?[20]

Suppose women had equal time with men in all cultural productions. In art museums, an equal number of acquisitions by women and men would be the rule. In concerts, an equal number of pieces composed by women and by men would be played by an equal number of women and men musicians.[21] An equal number of books by women and by men would appear on every publisher's list. An equal number of movies produced, directed, and written by women and by men would feature, in any year, an equal number of women and men heroes. The same principles would be used for every television channel's programming. How would canons of taste be affected? How would prestigious prizes be awarded? Would symbolic language change if women's experiences were as privileged as men's experiences?

In sports, every competition would have an equal number of women's and men's teams and players, the rules of competition would be the same for women and for men, and women's and men's events would receive equal time, pay, and prize money. The featured main event would alternate between women and men. The media would cover women's and men's sports and sports heroes equally. Would men begin to identify with women sports stars? Would women turn out to be physiologically similar to men in ways that are now hidden by the rules of the games?[22] Would some sports competitions become unisex?

Perhaps the most drastic upset of current ways of thinking would occur if all the armed forces were half women and half men, including combat units. In many wars and revolutions, women have fought side by side with men, both openly and disguised as men.[23] Frenchwomen played such an important part in the resistance to Nazism, running escape lines, sabotaging, spying, and printing clandestine newspapers, that they finally could no longer be denied the right to vote (M. L. Rossiter 1986, 223). According to the *New York Times* of May 2, 1993, during World War II, Russian women were machine gunners and snipers, served on artillery and tank crews, and flew in three all-woman air force fighter and bomber units. In Israel, women fought in the underground for nationhood and in the War of Independence, reaching levels as high as 20 percent of all soldiers. On April 30, 1993, the *Jerusalem Post* published the following fifty-year-old news story:

> Malka Epstein, a 22-year-old girl, is now a legendary figure in Central Poland where she leads a guerilla unit with headquarters in old quarry caves in the Kielce district. From these headquarters this girl has been conducting sabotage raids on Nazi units in the last 18 months. She is credited with having destroyed many German munition stores and with derailing trains carrying German soldiers to the Russian front.

As long as battles and wars are fought, women must be able to fight if they are to be equal with men. Otherwise, men will continue to feel that since they put their lives on the line and women do not, they are entitled to privileges and powers unavailable to women (W. Brown 1990, 25–26). Moreover, the idea of aggressive masculinity as protective of women lets men define which women are deserving of their protection. In World War II, women civilians were tortured, executed, bombed, and gassed; in all wars, they have been raped and murdered. Women should compose half of the peacemakers, but as long as there are wars, to be equal, they should be half of the fighters, too.

The other side of this exchange of expectations of men and women is that the nurturance and service to others that defines the "good woman" in Western cultures should apply to the "good man" as well. As Kay Ann Johnson points out, the Maoist utopian vision of the complete person (to-mien-shou) broke down the distinction between the intellectual and the manual laborer, the philosopher and the peasant, the artist and the artisan, but was never applied to women and men: "Never was it suggested, even in the most utopian movements, that men should learn from women . . . the value of, and how to perform, the nurturant human services" (1983, 167).

Other radical changes in concepts of femininity and masculinity would occur in a scrupulously equal world. All forms of sexuality would have to be recognized as equally valid. There would, therefore, have to be equal numbers of pornographic magazines, movies, strip shows, erotic dancers, and any other sexual productions for heterosexual, homosexual, bisexual, transvestite, and sadomasochistic women as for the same groups of men. Movies, television, books, and popular songs can be expected to show women as sexual pursuers equally with men, and homosexuality and heterosexuality as producing equally happy and tragic relationships. You might see plots revolving around heterosexual women sexually harassing and abusing heterosexual men, and gay men and lesbians sexually harassing each other and heterosexuals.[24]

Suppose all the major religions allowed women to become priests, to rise in the religious hierarchy, and to interpret the Old and New Testaments, the Qur'an, the Bhaghavad Gita. Since the practices of the world's major religions were originally based on social orders that separated women and men and assigned them different roles in life, fundamentalists could not allow women and men the same religious roles. But what would happen if religions that now profess gender equality really gave women and men an equal chance to be leaders?[25] If liturgies were completely gender-neutral? If "God" were not "the Lord," "our Father," or "King of the universe" but "the Leader," "our Parent," "Creator of the universe"?

The very radicalness of the effects of scrupulous gender equality throughout a whole social society, the cries of outrage you would predict if absolutely equal numbers of women and men had to be constantly maintained in all areas of life, the sense of unreality about a completely gender-balanced world, all make clear how very far the most progressive, most industrialized, most postmodern, most egalitarian society today would have to go to become truly gender-neutral. What government would organize a system of complete gender balance? Not only do we still want to know immediately whether an infant is a boy or girl, that information, that categorization, combined with race and other social characteristics, tells us and the infants just where in their social order they are going to be placed, and whether they are going to be encouraged to live their lives as dominant, self-confident, and central to society or as subordinate, subverted, and peripheral to the main action. When we no longer ask "boy or girl?" in order to start gendering an infant, when the information about genitalia is as irrelevant as the color of the child's eyes (but not yet the color of skin), then and only then will women and men be socially interchangeable and really equal. And when that happens, there will no longer be any need for gender at all.

Does all this equality mean that no one will criticize, satirize, parody, oppose, challenge, resist, rebel, start new groups, or live alone? I doubt it. Free of gender, race, and class inequality, what might we all be? Perhaps culturally identified women, men, heterosexuals, homosexuals, citizens of different countries, adherents of different religions, members of different occupations and professions, of different birth and social parents, and so on.[26] Perhaps people free to experience *jouissance*—the erotic passions expressed in human bodies, human identities, deeply held beliefs, work, love, spirituality.[27] Perhaps what Donna Haraway predicts—cyborgs who understand and can control the interface of humans and technology, who belong now to one group, now to another, identified with many or with none at all:

> The cyborg is a creature in a post-gender world; it has no truck with bisexuality, pre-Oedipal symbiosis, unalienated labor, or other seductions to organic wholeness through a final appropriation of all the powers of the parts into a higher unity. . . . The cyborg is resolutely committed to partiality, irony, intimacy, and perversity. It is oppositional, utopian, and completely without innocence. . . . I would rather be a cyborg than a goddess. (1985, 67, 101)

So would I.

Notes

INTRODUCTION

1. The French feminist groups of the 1970s that called themselves *Psychoanalyse et Politique* were Marxists who tried to amalgamate dialectical materialism and the Freudian and Lacanian discourse on sexuality and the unconscious.
2. In addition to Hill Collins and hooks, see Chow 1987; Christian 1988; Garcia 1989; King 1988; Spelman 1988.
3. For the new scholarship in men's studies, see Brod 1987; Hearn 1987; Hearn and Morgan 1990; Kimmel 1987b; Kimmel and Messner 1992; Staples 1982.
4. For overviews, see Marks and Courtivron 1981; Mitchell and Rose 1985; Moi 1985.
5. For debates over the politics of gender as a stable or shifting category both culturally and historically, see Alcoff 1988; de Lauretis 1989; Riley 1988; J. W. Scott 1988a, 1988b.
6. Bem 1993, 133–75; Gerson and Peiss 1985; Margolis 1985; D. E. Smith 1987a, 1990; West and Zimmerman 1987.
7. Blair 1989; Jenson 1986.
8. See Riley 1983 for the British experience with war nurseries.
9. Fuszara 1991; Moghadam 1990; Rosenberg 1991; Szalai 1991; and the special issue of *Feminist Review* entitled "Shifting Territories: Feminisms and Europe," no. 39 (1991).
10. Applebome 1991; Clymer 1991; J. Gross 1990a, 1990b; Nordheimer 1991; Schmitt 1991; M. W. Segal 1986.
11. A slightly higher percentage of women were killed, .0004 to .0003 for the men. Figures are taken from the *New York Times* story looking back one year later (Applebome 1992).
12. Francke 1991; Nordheimer 1991; Quindlen 1991a, 1992; Sciolino 1990; Stiehm 1985; and U.S. General Accounting Office 1989. For a variety of feminist

writings on women and war, see Cooper, Munich, and Squier 1989; Elshstain and Tobias 1990; Gioseffi 1988; and M. L. Rossiter 1986.

13. Ayres 1991; Gonzalez 1991; LeMoyne 1990a; McFadden 1991.
14. Not only were the servicemen unlikely to give up their privileges, but a year later there were published reports of twenty-three incidents of sex crimes against servicewomen, including rape (*New York Times,* 1992b).
15. Goode [1982]1993; Kandiyoti 1988; Klatch 1987.
16. Acker 1989b; Connell 1990; Stacey and Thorne 1985.

CHAPTER ONE   "NIGHT TO HIS DAY"

1. Gender is, in Erving Goffman's words, an aspect of *Felicity's Condition:* "any arrangement which leads us to judge an individual's . . . acts not to be a manifestation of strangeness. Behind Felicity's Condition is our sense of what it is to be sane" (1983, 27). Also see Bem 1993; Frye 1983, 17–40; Goffman 1977.
2. In cases of ambiguity in countries with modern medicine, surgery is usually performed to make the genitalia more clearly male or female.
3. See J. Butler 1990 for an analysis of how doing gender *is* gender identity.
4. Douglas 1973; MacCormack 1980; Ortner 1974; Ortner and Whitehead 1981a; Yanagisako and Collier 1987. On the social construction of childhood, see Ariès 1962; Zelizer 1985.
5. On the hijras of India, see Nanda 1990; on the xaniths of Oman, Wikan 1982, 168–86; on the American Indian berdaches, W. L. Williams 1986. Other societies that have similar institutionalized third-gender men are the Koniag of Alaska, the Tanala of Madagascar, the Mesakin of Nuba, and the Chukchee of Siberia (Wikan 1982, 170).
6. Durova 1989; Freeman and Bond 1992; Wheelwright 1989.
7. Gender segregation of work in popular music still has not changed very much, according to Groce and Cooper 1989, despite considerable androgyny in some very popular figures. See Garber 1992 on the androgyny. She discusses Tipton on pp. 67–70.
8. In the nineteenth century, not only did these women get men's wages, but they also "had male privileges and could do all manner of things other women could not: open a bank account, write checks, own property, go anywhere unaccompanied, vote in elections" (Faderman 1991, 44).
9. When unisex clothing and men wearing long hair came into vogue in the United States in the mid-1960s, beards and mustaches for men also came into style again as gender identifications.
10. For other accounts of women being treated as men in Islamic countries, as well as accounts of women and men cross-dressing in these countries, see Garber 1992, 304–52.
11. Dollimore 1986; Garber 1992, 32–40; Greenblatt 1987, 66–93; Howard 1988. For Renaissance accounts of sexual relations with women and men of ambiguous sex, see Laqueur 1990a, 134–39. For modern accounts of women passing as men that other women find sexually attractive, see Devor 1989, 136–37; Wheelwright 1989, 53–59.

12. Females who passed as men soldiers had to "do masculinity," not just dress in a uniform (Wheelwright 1989, 50–78). On the triple entendres and gender resonances of Rosalind-type characters, see Garber 1992, 71–77.

13. Also see Garber 1992, 234–66.

14. Bolin describes how many documents have to be changed by transsexuals to provide a legitimizing "paper trail" (1988, 145–47). Note that only members of the same social group know which names are women's and which men's in their culture, but many documents list "sex."

15. For an account of how a potential man-to-woman transsexual learned to be feminine, see Garfinkel 1967, 116–85, 285–88. For a gloss on this account that points out how, throughout his encounters with Agnes, Garfinkel failed to see how he himself was constructing his own masculinity, see Rogers 1992.

16. Paige and Paige (1981, 147–49) argue that circumcision ceremonies indicate a father's loyalty to his lineage elders—"visible public evidence that the head of a family unit of their lineage is willing to trust others with his and his family's most valuable political asset, his son's penis" (147). On female circumcision, see El Dareer 1982; Lightfoot-Klein 1987; van der Kwaak 1992; Walker 1992. There is a form of female circumcision that removes only the prepuce of the clitoris and is similar to male circumcision, but most forms of female circumcision are far more extensive, mutilating, and spiritually and psychologically shocking than the usual form of male circumcision. However, among the Australian aborigines, boys' penises are slit and kept open, so that they urinate and bleed the way women do (Bettelheim 1962, 165–206).

17. The concepts of moral hegemony, the effects of everyday activities (praxis) on thought and personality, and the necessity of consciousness of these processes before political change can occur are all based on Marx's analysis of class relations.

18. Other societies recognize more than two categories, but usually no more than three or four (Jacobs and Roberts 1989).

19. Carol Barkalow's book has a photograph of eleven first-year West Pointers in a math class, who are dressed in regulation pants, shirts, and sweaters, with short haircuts. The caption challenges the reader to locate the only woman in the room.

20. The taboo on males and females looking alike reflects the U.S. military's homophobia (Bérubé 1989). If you can't tell those with a penis from those with a vagina, how are you going to determine whether their sexual interest is heterosexual or homosexual unless you watch them having sexual relations?

21. Garber feels that *Tootsie* is not about feminism but about transvestism and its possibilities for disturbing the gender order (1992, 5–9).

22. See Bolin 1988, 149–50, for transsexual men-to-women's discovery of the dangers of rape and sexual harassment. Devor's "gender blenders" went in the opposite direction. Because they found that it was an advantage to be taken for men, they did not deliberately cross-dress, but they did not feminize themselves either (1989, 126–40).

23. See West and Zimmerman 1987 for a similar set of gender components.

24. On the "logic of practice," or how the experience of gender is embedded in the norms of everyday interaction and the structure of formal organizations, see Acker 1990; Bourdieu [1980] 1990; Connell 1987; Smith 1987a.

CHAPTER TWO   BELIEVING IS SEEING

1. On the "aesthetics of anatomical difference" or how anatomical drawings are complex constructions of what is seen and what is believed, see Laqueur 1990a, especially 163–69.
2. For the same reason, penile and scrotal skin is used to construct the vagina and labia for males undergoing transsexual surgery.
3. The plastic surgeons' term for these operations is "clarification of genitalia." Much of the surgery could better be done when the child is older, but parents suffer intensely from not knowing what sex their child is (Richard C. Sadove M.D., personal communication; Weiss forthcoming).
4. A fairly common condition in newborn boys is incomplete closure of the urethra and urination from the sheath rather than the tip of the penis.
5. Hermaphrodites are born with missing sex chromosomes that result in anomalous development in puberty, or have ambiguous genitalia at birth—an enlarged clitoris that resembles a penis or a very small penis that resembles a clitoris, an incompletely open vagina that resembles a scrotum or an incompletely closed scrotum that resembles a vagina, and so on. See Money and Ehrhardt 1972.
6. Also see Bourdieu [1980]1990, 66–79.
7. Birke 1986; Fausto-Sterling 1985; Hubbard 1990; Hubbard, Henifin and Fried 1979; Longino and Doell 1983, Naftolin and Butz 1981; Sayers 1982.
8. Fausto-Sterling 1985; Kemper 1990; Treadwell 1987. Recent research on male cichlid fish has found that dominance produces brain-cell and hormonal changes, not the other way around, and that testosterone produces dominance behavior in *female* hyenas (Angier 1991, 1992b).
9. In ancient Greece, women ran races in their own Olympics, as can be seen on a vase in the Vatican. Their athletic events were in honor of Hera and were performed for women spectators (Pomeroy 1975, 137).
10. Birrell 1988, 479–91; Boutilier and SanGiovanni 1983; M. A. Hall 1988; Hargreaves 1986; Messner and Sabo 1990; Moran 1992; Slatton and Birrell 1984, Willis 1982.
11. The first West Point women's basketball team was called "Sugar Smacks." It was changed to "Army Women's Basketball" by the athletic director (a man), who felt the original name was not serious enough. The women had chosen the name during their first year—"smacks" is one of the name for "plebes" (Barkalow 1990, 126).
12. For discussion, see Boutilier and SanGiovanni 1983, 183–218; Theberge and Cronk 1986.
13. Dunning 1986; Kemper 1990, 167–206; Messner 1987, 1989, 1992.
14. Fine 1987; Glassner 1992; Majors 1990.
15. Hargreaves 1986; Messner 1988; Olson 1990; Theberge 1987; Willis 1982.

16. Gallagher and Laqueur 1987; Jordanova 1989; Jacobus, Keller, and Shuttleworth 1990; Martin 1987.
17. Clinton 1982, 18−35; Fox Genovese 1988, 166, 193; J. Jones 1986, 11−29; Matthei 1982, 87−89; White 1985, 120−21.
18. A. Y. Davis 1983, 5−12; Ehrenreich and English 1973; hooks 1981, 15−49.
19. Bird and Freemont 1991; Gove 1984; Levy 1988; C. Muller 1990; Nathanson 1975; Verbrugge 1985, 1986, 1989a, 1989b.
20. Gibbs 1988a, 1988b; Jackson and Perry 1989; Nsiah-Jefferson and Hall 1989.
21. Gitlin and Pasnau 1989; Lennane and Lennane 1973; Vertinsky 1990.
22. Calhoun and Selby 1980; Greil, Leitko, and Porter 1988; Lorber 1987b, 1989; Lorber and Bandlamudi 1993; Miall 1986; Sandelowski 1990a.
23. Bertin 1989; Heitlinger 1987, 57−64; Petchesky 1979; Stellman and Henifin 1982; M. J. Wright 1979.
24. However, social groups that have segregating rituals for menstruating women often drop these rituals with modernization (Ullrich 1982).
25. Abplanalp 1983; Fausto-Sterling 1985, 90−122; Koeske 1983; Parlee 1973, 1982a; Rittenhouse 1991.
26. Goodman 1980, 1982; McCrea 1986; Perlmutter and Bart 1982.
27. For critiques, see E. Martin 1987; O'Brien 1981; Rich 1976.
28. Also see J. K. Brown 1982; Kearns 1982; A. L. Wright 1982.
29. Daly 1978; S. Laws 1983; Zita 1988.
30. Cockburn 1983; P. Edwards 1990; Fernández-Kelly and García 1988; Hartmann 1987; Hartmann, Kraut, and Tilly 1987; Kramer and Lehman 1990; Perry and Greber 1990; Rothschild 1983; Turkle and Papert 1990; Wright et al. 1987; Zimmerman 1983.
31. However, in countries that have very strict laws against drinking and driving, the man is the one who is likely to drink, the woman to stick to mineral water or nonalcoholic beer and to drive.
32. Eisenstein 1988; Goffman 1963a; Levesque-Lopman 1988, 104−13; Rothman 1989, 246−54; Vogel 1990; Zola 1982a.
33. Various devices and arrangements could cancel out these differences entirely. Wheelwright describes how at least one woman who passed as a man used a hollow tube to urinate with (1989, 25). Both women and men astronauts use catheters. Urinals could be in one room, and bathrooms with stalls and doors on them could be unisex.
34. All sperm are considered "male," even though half carry the X chromosome and will produce a female fetus. Scientific as well as popular accounts of fertilization anthropomorphize sperm and ova: "the epic of the heroic sperm struggling against the hostile uterus is the account of fertilization usually seen in contemporary introductory biology texts" (Biology and Gender Study Group 1988, 64). Now that the egg has been found to play a very active role in attracting and locking onto sperm, a revisionist metaphor has the egg acting like a Venus flytrap that engulfs a weakly wriggling sperm (E. Martin 1991). In actuality, fertilization is a series of steps in which the sperm and the egg are both active and passive biochemical interactors.

CHAPTER THREE   HOW MANY OPPOSITES?

1. Freud [1905] 1962 laid out these theories of sexuality, which focus on the mother-father-child triad. Later, object-relations theory put greater emphasis than Freud did on the mother-daughter and mother-son bond for the development of emotional, not just sexual, relationships. For feminist discussions of psychoanalytic theories of sexuality and emotions, see Benjamin 1988; J. Butler 1990; Chodorow 1989; Flax 1990; Gallop 1982; L. J. Kaplan 1991; Mitchell 1975; Mitchell and Rose 1985.

2. The question of core sexual identity as a consolidation of sexual practices is a contested area. See Bolin 1988; De Cecco and Shively 1983–84; Hansen and Evans 1985; Troiden 1988, 41–60; and the entire issues of *Journal of Homosexuality* 9(2–3), 1983–84 (Bisexual and Homosexual Identities: Critical Theoretical Issues, edited by John P. De Cecco and Michael G. Shively) and 10(3–4), 1984 (Controversies over the Bisexual and Homosexual Identities: Commentaries and Reactions). Concepts of "core identity" usually collapse gender and sexuality (see, e.g., Person 1980; Stoller 1985, 10–24).

3. For accounts of the social construction of sexuality and the discourses that support its social control, see Blackwood 1985; Caulfield 1985; Foucault 1978, 1985; Gagnon and Simon 1973; Greenberg 1988; Gutiérrez 1992; Katz 1990; Kitzinger 1987; Laws and Schwartz 1977; McIntosh 1968; Plummer 1981a; A. Rich 1980; G. Rubin 1984; Sabbah 1984a; Weeks 1985, 1989.

4. Also see Brownmiller 1975, 210–55, and A. Y. Davis 1983, 172–201. For an analysis of the social construction of evidentiary proof in rape cases, see Estrich 1987.

5. Garber 1992, 267–303, in her account of racial transvestism, especially in nineteenth-century minstrel shows, indicates that both gender and race get reversed. She also describes William and Ellen Craft's account of their escape from slavery in 1848; Ellen, lighter-skinned, became a "man," the master, while William passed as the servant "boy" (282–85). In a story by Richard Wright, entitled "Man of All Work," a Black man who is a professional cook gets a job as a housekeeper and baby sitter by dressing in his wife's clothes and passing as a woman (292–95).

6. P. H. Collins 1990, 67–90; J. Lewis 1981; Majors and Billson 1992; Staples 1982, 1992; Wallace [1978] 1990.

7. Gay men have been critical of the macho objectifying sexuality that fetishizes the penis. See Blachford 1981; Edwards 1990; Stoltenberg 1990. Diane Richardson 1988 discusses many kinds of "safe sex and safer sex" for heterosexual, male homosexual, and lesbian partners.

8. Figure 27, p. 196. The numbers of couples were gay men, 309; heterosexual cohabitators, 349; married heterosexuals, 344; and lesbians, 357.

9. On the need for new "vocabularies of desire," see Schneider and Gould 1987, 136–40.

10. For the feminist debates over sadomasochism and pornography, see Creet 1991; English, Hollibaugh, and Rubin 1981; Faderman 1991, 246–70; Ferguson et al.

1984; Hollibaugh and Moraga 1983; Phelan 1989, 81–133; B. R. Rich 1986; Vance 1984a; E. Wilson 1984. The feminist "sex wars of the 1980s" started with the 1982 Scholar and the Feminist IX conference at Barnard College in 1982. *Pleasure and Danger* (Vance 1984b) is a collection of the papers from the conference.

11. The physiology of female and male sexuality was first mapped by Masters and Johnson 1966. Also see Sherfey 1972.

12. Grimm comes up with forty-five different types of erotic and nonerotic, complementary and similar relationships (1987, tables 1–3, 74–76).

13. Identifying as a transsexual is a transitional phase; the final status is identification as a woman or a man (see Bolin 1988). On the politics of identity as a bisexual, see Rust 1992, 1993.

14. Money 1988, 179–80, lists fifty-two paraphilias, from acrotomophilia (amputee partner) to zoophilia (animal partner). L. J. Kaplan 1991, 249–50, talks of *homeovestism,* using clothes of one's own gender for arousal and orgasm. And for the future, astrophilia (spacecraft sex)? Typically, if "blushing, NASA confronts the romantic possibilities of future long missions with mixed crews," the mixture will be strictly heterosexual, married couples (see Broad 1992).

15. There is some question as to whether bisexuality is gaining recognition as a sexual orientation.

16. Also see Klein and Wolf 1985.

17. Davis and Kennedy 1986; Devor 1989; Faderman 1991, 167–74; Kennedy and Davis 1989.

18. See Blachford 1981; Edwards 1990; John Marshall 1981 for discussions of homosexual men's identity displays. See Brod 1987; Connell 1990b, 1992; Franklin 1988; Kimmel 1987b; Kimmel and Messner 1989; Staples 1982; Stoltenberg 1990 for recent research on heterosexual and homosexual masculinities.

19. See Bérubé 1989 and Bérubé and D'Emilio 1984 for lesbians in the military. For discrimination against lesbians in the work force, see Martin and Leonard 1984; Schneider 1982.

20. For the history of homosexuality from a social-construction perspective, see Duberman, Vicinus, and Chauncey 1989; Faderman 1981, 1991; Greenberg 1988; Kitzinger 1987; Plummer 1981b; Troiden 1988; Vicinus 1992. For indications of legitimation, see Bishop 1991; *New York Times* 1991a.

21. On identity politics in the gay and lesbian communities in the twentieth century, see D'Emilio 1983b; S. Epstein 1987; Escoffier 1985; Kitzinger 1987; Krieger 1982, 1983; Lockard 1985; Phelan 1989, 1993; Taylor and Whittier forthcoming. For identity politics in Hispanic gay and lesbian communities, see Arguelles and Rich 1984; Garcia 1989; Rich and Arguelles 1985. There are brief accounts of homophobia in African-American communities in almost every book on gender and race in the United States. Beck (1980) is a well-known Jewish lesbian anthology. On the overall question of gender identities and gender politics in feminism, see J. Butler 1990, 1–34.

22. Fee 1989; S. L. Gilman 1988; Luker 1975; Padgug 1989; Patton 1990; Treichler 1988. The same arguments about abstinence, use of condoms, and sexual moral-

ity that are raging around AIDS today raged around syphilis in the late nineteenth century (McLaren 1978, 199–200). In both instances, moralistic rather than pragmatic issues have been the focus of the debate.

23. Lightfoot-Klein (1989) estimated that the number of women living in Africa in the 1980s who were circumcised was 94 million (31). The procedures ranged from mild sunna (removing the prepuce of the clitoris) to modified sunna (partial or total clitoridectomy) to infibulation or pharaonic circumcision, which involves clitoridectomy and excision of the labia minora and the inner layers of the labia majora, and suturing the raw edges together to form a bridge of scar tissue over the vaginal opening, leaving so small an opening that normal bladder emptying takes fifteen minutes and menstrual blood backs up (see descriptions in Lightfoot-Klein, 32–36).

24. But those who have reinfibulation after childbirth go through the process over and over again. It is called *adlat el rujal* (men's circumcision) because it is designed to create greater sexual pleasure for men, not unlike the rationale for episiotomy and tight suturing in Western obstetrical practice (Rothman 1982, 58–59).

25. On the French *salonnières,* see Landes 1988, 23–28. For working-class women's sexuality in the twentieth century, see Nestle 1983; Peiss 1983.

26. A by-product of this change was that if a woman was raped and impregnated during the earlier period, it was taken as evidence that she had acquiesced and enjoyed the act; after the nineteenth century, that argument could no longer be used as a legal defense against the charge of rape (McLaren 1984, 27).

27. At the end of the nineteenth century, when the term *heterosexual* was invented, it first referred to abnormal, perverted, or nonprocreative "appetite" for the opposite sex. See L. J. Kaplan 1991, 201–36, for a psychoanalytic discussion of Emma Bovary.

28. Corbin 1990; Hobson, 1987; R. Rosen 1982; Walkowitz 1980.

29. Kitzinger (1987, 90–109) points out that the love-and-romance account of lesbianism, like the account that claims that women who turn lesbian have gotten in touch with their true feelings or real self, reflects the dominant liberal ideology of the salience of the private and the individual, and that these accounts depoliticize the implicit critique of men's domination lesbians represent. Weston (1991, 21–49) notes that the rhetoric on the family among homosexuals frequently reifies kinship as biological and procreative. She, too, points out the dangers of the emphasis on long-term co-residential couples with or without children as "model" gay and lesbian relationships (195–213). Also see Wittig 1980, 1981.

30. Acker, Barry, and Esseveld 1981; Cancian 1987; Hess 1981; Raymond 1986. For the classic account of women's bonding, see Smith-Rosenberg 1975.

31. Also see Farr 1988; Fine 1992; Lyman 1987; Messner 1992, 85–107.

32. Anderson 1990, 112–19; Bobroff 1983; Haug et al. 1987; Moffatt 1989, 181–270; Peña 1991.

33. Franklin 1992; Gary 1987; hooks 1990; Ladner 1971; Staples 1982; Wallace [1978] 1990.

34. Also see Cancian 1987, 69–102; L. B. Rubin 1983. Some women find an

emotional substitution in romance novels (Snitow 1983); for others, the solution to their dilemma of "loving too much" is sought in self-help books (Simonds 1992).

35. For overviews of research, debates over perspectives, and extensive biblio-graphies, see Breines and Gordon 1983; Brush 1990; Dobash et al. 1992; Frieze and Browne 1987; L. Gordon 1989, 250–88; Harlow 1991; Kurz 1989; Staples 1982, 55–71; Straus 1992; Yllö and Bograd 1988.

36. See L. J. Kaplan 1991, 212–36, for a discussion of psychologically abusive relationships and Beth Richie 1992 for a theory of gender entrapment.

37. Battering in lesbian relationships has patterns similar to battering in heterosexual relationships (Hart 1986; Schilit et al. 1991).

38. Browne 1987; Gillespie 1989; L. E. Walker 1989.

39. As Gillespie (1989) discusses, the self defense plea in Anglo-Saxon and American law is based on ideas of fairness in fights between or among men in frontierlike situations.

40. Finkelhor and Yllö 1985, Frieze 1983; D. E. H. Russell 1990.

41. In general, neither the medical system nor the law has given battered women much attention or protection. See Chaudhuri and Daly 1992; Ferraro 1989; Kurz 1987; Kurz and Stark 1988; Stark, Flitcraft, and Frazier 1979; Warshaw 1989.

42. The father's brother's son is a parallel cousin; the father's sister's son is a cross-cousin. In other societies, the defining kin are the mother's siblings.

43. A review of studies done in the United States, France, Germany, Japan, and Ireland indicates that most incest is between fathers or stepfathers and daughters and that in the cases that involved sons, fathers are as likely to be the molesters as mothers (Herman 1981, 7–21). Also see L. Gordon 1989, 204–49; D. E. H. Russell 1986; L. E. Walker 1988.

44. Also see Wattenberg 1985.

45. Ritchie (1992) found that African-American battered women, some of whom had been sexually abused as children, felt they were "special children" in their families.

46. Caputi 1987; Harlow 1991; Liz Kelly 1987, 1988; Sheffield 1987; Schneider 1991; Stanko 1990.

47. Baril 1990; Caputi 1989; Hollway 1987; P. B. Seidman 1991.

48. Also not included are homosexual rapes among men, which occur commonly in prisons but also in the same situations as heterosexual rapes, as manifestations of power (Stoltenberg 1991).

49. For successful survival strategies, see Bart and O'Brien 1985; Scully 1990, 171–82. Screaming and making a lot of noise, fighting back strongly and viciously, and running away if possible have proved successful in resisting rape without incurring serious injury.

50. Roiphe (1993) argues that the definition of date rape as any unwanted sexual relations between those who know each other is too broad and deprives women of agency.

51. Social disorganization was measured by geographical mobility, divorce, lack of religious affiliation, single-parent households, and ratio of tourists to residents.

Gender inequality was measured by economic, political, and legal indicators. The sex magazines were soft-core porn, such as *Hustler, Penthouse,* and *Playboy*. The five states with highest average annual rates of reported rape per 100,000 of population for 1980–82 were Alaska, 83.3; Nevada, 64.5; Florida, 55.5; California, 55.0; Washington, 49.6. The five with the lowest rates were Wisconsin, 14.9; Iowa, 13.4; Maine, 13.0; South Dakota, 11.8; North Dakota, 9.3.

52. These statistics reflect the prison population. In the majority of rapes in the United States, the victim and perpetrator are of the same race (Scully 1990, 145–49).

53. Chancer 1987; Martin and Hummer 1989; Sanday 1990.

54. Sexual assaults have been a common occurrence at American conventions where most of the attenders are men; see, e.g., the navy pilots' Tailhook convention, where "groups of officers in civilian dress suddenly turned violent, organizing with military precision into drunken gangs that shoved terrified women down the gauntlet, grabbing their breasts and buttocks and stripping off their clothes" (Schmitt 1992). Top admirals were eventually penalized for this event, but the officers were not (N. Lewis 1993).

55. Their sexuality was quite complex and included what they defined as lesbian relationships, although they still had male genitalia (161–73).

CHAPTER FOUR   MEN AS WOMEN AND WOMEN AS MEN

1. The passage as Colette wrote it is: "At a time when I was, when at least I believed I was insensitive to Damien, I suggested to him that he and I would make a pair of ideal traveling companions, both courteously selfish, easy to please, and fond of long silences. . . .
     'I like to travel only with women,' he answered.
     The sweet tone of his voice scarcely softened the brutality of his words. . . . He was afraid he had hurt my feelings and tried to make up, with something even worse.
     'A woman? You? I know you would like to be one . . .'" (1993, 75; ellipses in the original).

2. After reclassification, Barbin, who had been a certified and competent schoolteacher, had to look for men's work. Bolin (1988, 156–57) notes a similar problem for men-to-women transsexuals who worked in fields dominated by men.

3. Richard C. Sadove M.D., personal communication. Dr. Sadove did the reconstructive surgery.

4. Fausto-Sterling 1985, 87–88; Herdt 1990, 437–38.

5. Most of the research is on men-to-women transsexuals. For reviews, see Bolin 1987; Docter 1988. For a scathing critique of transsexual research and practice, see Stoller 1985, 152–70. For a critique of the medical construction of transsexualism as a fixed core identity, see Billings and Urban 1982.

6. See Garfinkel 1967, 116–85, for a detailed account of how Bill-Agnes managed the practical details of passing while constructing a new gendered identity.

Raymond (1979) is critical of men-to-women's gender identity because they have not had the previous experience of women's oppression.

7. Bolin's data on five transsexuals' postoperative sexual relationships indicated that three were bisexual and one was lesbian (181).

8. There have also been relationships between women-to-men and men-to-women transsexuals; these, however, are heterosexual and heterogendered (Money 1988, 93).

9. Actually, the mark of gender identity in Western culture is the penis—the person who has one of adequate size is male and a man; the person who does not, is not-male, not a man. Femaleness and womanhood seem to be more problematic and need more "work" to consturct. For an opposite point of view about masculinity, see Gilmore 1990.

10. Also see Heilbrun 1988, 32—36; L. J. Kaplan 1991, 492—500.

11. Also see Smith-Rosenberg 1985.

12. Dollimore 1986; Greenblatt 1987, 66—93; Howard 1988; Lavine 1986. On the fluidity of representations of bodily sex during the Renaissance, see Laqueur 1990, 114—34. On the "semiotics of dress" in modern life, see E. Wilson 1985.

13. Also see Wheelwright 1989, 9—15.

14. Bolin lists seventy North and South American Indian tribes that have berdaches (1987, 61n).

15. By the end of the nineteenth century, the adoption of Western sexual and gender mores led to the delegitimation of the female cross-gender status (Blackwood 1984, 39—40), but not the male, according to W. L. Williams (1986).

16. The last known castrato, Alessandro Moreschi (1858—1922), made a series of recordings in 1902 and 1903, the year Pope Pius X formally banned castrati from the papal chapel, but he sang in the Sistine Chapel choir until 1913 (Ellison 1992, 37).

CHAPTER FIVE   WAITING FOR THE GODDESS

1. Dworkin 1979; Griffin 1982; Lederer 1980b; MacKinnon 1982; 1987, 125—213; Nead 1990. For men's critiques of pornography, see Kimmel 1991. For feminist debates over pornography, see Ellis 1984; English, Hollibaugh, and Rubin 1981; Ferguson et al. 1984; Gubar and Hoff 1989; Morgan 1978; Phillipson 1984; Steinem 1978b. For a Marxist view, see Soble 1986. For a comparison of all the political views, see Berger, Searles, and Cottle 1991.

2. Alan Soble's contention that under capitalism, "the use of pornography is an attempt to recoup in the domain of sexual fantasy what is denied to men in production and politics" (1986, 81) would seem to support the radical feminist view, but Soble sees men who use pornography as powerless, whereas the radical feminists see them as powerful, domineering, and potentially if not actually dangerous to women by virtue of their participation in a culture that encourages men's violence as a means of subordinating women.

3. For a succinct, no-nonsense description of work in pornography, see Lederer 1980a.

4. Pornography for male homosexuals in a cultural context that condemns the passive partner as less than a man would not necessarily be demeaning, since a homosexual viewer could identify with the aggressive partner. See the section on gay male porn in Kimmel 1991, 247–87. Pornographic lesbian sex is mostly for men's consumption.

5. Molly Bloom is a stronger person than Penelope, her prototype in Homer's *Odyssey,* on which *Ulysses* is based. Penelope sobs or weeps copiously for over nineteen years while waiting for her husband to return from the Trojan War.

6. In languages with gendered nouns and verbs, the masculine is invariably primary or unmarked; the feminine has something added and is usually listed second in texts of grammar. As in English before feminists insisted on more linguistic precision, the masculine subsumes the feminine in plural nouns and verbs of mixed gender. The arbitrary assignment of gender to inanimate nouns is usually contrasted to the natural assignment of gender to animate nouns and pronouns; the usage in both instances is a social artifact for maintaining a symbolically gendered world.

7. Lacan's language is far more cryptic—"The phallus is the privileged signifier of that mark where the share of the logos is wedded to the advent of desire" (Mitchell and Rose 1985, 82; translated by Rose). For feminist discussions of Lacan, Freud, and psychoanalytic theories of gender, sexuality, and culture, see J. Butler 1990; Cixous and Clément [1975] 1986; Flax 1990; Irigaray [1974] 1985, [1977] 1985; L. J. Kaplan 1991; Mitchell and Rose 1985. *Differences: A Journal of Feminist Cultural Studies* did a whole issue on the phallus (4[1]: 1992).

8. De Lauretis 1984, 1987; Flax 1990; Jardine 1985; Marcus 1982; Mulvey 1989; Poovey 1988.

9. Also see G. Koch 1985.

10. Gay men's "clone culture" has, sometimes seriously and sometimes in parody, fetishized stereotypical masculine imagery; identities expressed through clothing are macho images of conventional men's occupations—cowboy, construction worker, soldier, athlete, police, biker, and elegant executive (T. Edwards 1990).

11. Most of the music we call "classical," Susan McClary (1991) claims, is tuned to the predominant male "ear" and builds up to orgasmic climaxes startlingly reminiscent of pornographic films' "money shots": "Music itself often relies heavily upon the metaphorical simulation of sexual activity for its effects. . . . Tonality itself—with its process of instilling expectations and subsequently with-holding promised fulfillment until the climax—is the principal musical means during the period from 1600 to 1900 for arousing and channeling desire. Even without texts or programs, tonal compositions ranging from Bach organ fugues to Brahms symphonies whip up torrents of libidinal energy that are variously thwarted or allowed to gush" (12–13).

12. Also see Coser 1978.

13. The theme would be truly universal if women's deaths in childbirth were included. Samuel Delaney, in a piece about homosexuals' risk of AIDS, includes a comment from "a concerned and sensitive heterosexual woman friend: . . . 'AIDS has now put gay men in the position that straight women have always been in

with sex: any unprotected sexual encounter now always carries with it the possibility of life or death'" (1991, 29).

14. A subtle evocation of brutal early death and longing for beautiful times past is John Corigliano's opera *The Ghosts of Versailles,* with a libretto by William M. Hoffman. It premiered on December 19, 1991, and was performed to sell-out audiences at the Metropolitan Opera House in New York City. None of the program notes or reviews alluded to the opera's emotional linkage to the AIDS reign of terror, even though both Corigliano and Hoffman have written explicitly on the subject, Corigliano in his Symphony No. 1 and Hoffman in his play *As Is.*

15. Chicago's great work is now locked up in crates in a warehouse because no museum will permanently display it.

16. Also see Lorde 1984; Wittig 1980, 110; 1981, 49.

17. Raymond 1986; A. Rich 1976; Rupp 1989; Taylor and Rupp 1993. For a critique, see Echols 1983.

18. For a discussion of Freud and the mirror game, see Mitchell 1975, 382–98.

19. Translated by Spivak 1988, 179–96.

20. The Brontës, George Eliot, George Sand, and other nineteenth-century women novelists were published under male pseudonyms.

21. Becker 1982, 351–71; Chadwick 1988; Frueh 1988; Lang and Lang 1990. In 1989, the ten most expensive paintings sold during the year were all by men artists (R. Reif 1989). Six of the ten were by Picasso, and two were by Van Gogh. The remaining two were an Impressionist and a Renaissance artist. For a review of laboratory studies of biases of women's and men's creative achievements, see Top 1991.

22. "Money creates taste" is one of Jenny Holzer's "Truisms" (Auping 1992, pl. 31, 88). Holzer was the first woman to represent the United States at the prestigious Venice Biennale, in 1990, and her installation won the Golden Lion Award for best pavilion (50–66).

23. For O'Keeffe, see Cowart, Hamilton, and Greenough 1987; Messinger 1988.

24. Also see Ammer 1980; J. M. Edwards 1989; Tick and Bowers 1980.

25. Zwilich was the first woman composer to win a Pulitzer Prize for music. She did so in 1983, for her Symphony No. 1 (*Three Movements for Orchestra*). There are also many operas by women going back to 1625 that almost never get produced in major opera houses (Pendle 1992). Smyth wrote several operas in the early part of this century, as did Eleanor Everest Freer, Amy Beach, and Mary Carr Moore. In the last forty years, Vivian Fine, Miriam Gideon, Peggy Glanville-Hicks, Libby Larsen, Meredith Monk, Thea Musgrave, Julia Perry, Evelyn Pittman, Louise Talma, and Judith Weir have written operas that have been praised but rarely produced. Only Musgrave and Weir have had major international productions.

26. On the failure of the avant-garde of the first half of the twentieth century to critically confront extant gender patterns and relationships, see Stimpson 1979. She notes that neither personally nor organizationally was there any challenge to men's domination.

27. For androgynous and reverse-gender choreography in modern dance, see Hann 1988, 131–36, 204–16.

28. Feminist science fiction that has transformed gender has done so by making humans alternately male and female (Le Guin 1969), creating artificial wombs and priming men with female hormones so they can breast-feed (Piercy 1976), creating multiple sexes and genders (O. E. Butler 1987, 1988, 1989), and doing away with men (Gilman 1979; Russ 1975). For an overview, see Nielsen 1984. Dystopias written by men, like Orwell's *1984,* reinforce traditional gender norms by romanticizing sexuality; women's love is the source of men's (not women's) freedom from the repressive state (Baruch 1991, 195–96, 207–29).

29. For a lengthy discussion of the oppression of women in myths in Western culture, see de Beauvoir 1953, 139–263.

30. Ironically, when the early Christian fathers attempted to differentiate their believers from Jews, they adopted more stringent sexual practices and accused Jews of sensuality and witchcraft. Jews were feminized, and Jews and women were demonized. See Farrell 1992, chap. 2. For recent feminist readings of the Judeo-Christian origin myth, see Bal 1986 and Meyers 1988, 72–121.

31. Ehrenberg 1989, 66–76; Gimbutas 1974, 1989; Marshack 1972, 281–340.

32. Knight (1991) argues that the synchronization of women's menstrual cycles around times of the moon combined with the need for men's labor in hunting led to women devising ritual taboos against sexual relations during menstruation. Women purified themselves only if the men fed them.

33. Also see Pearson 1984.

34. According to Warner (1983, 282–89), the Virgin Mary is a cultural descendant of a fertility symbol, the Queen of the May. The month of May is named after Maia, mother of Hermes and Zeus, who, with her sisters, was transformed into the Pleides, stars that appear in the sky in the month of May. Maia was assimilated to a minor fertility deity in Rome, but in medieval Europe, the Queen of the May "was crowned and sometimes married to the Green Man, in an ancient fertiliity rite" on the first of May. On the transformation of the three pre-Islamic fertility goddesses into the daughters of Allah, see Sabbah 1984, 104–06. On the goddesses of Sumer and the shift to masculine monotheism in Judaism, see Frymer-Kensky 1992. On the Teotihuacan Feathered Serpent of many Mexican cultures originally representing a goddess, see Wilford 1993. On the uprooting of the Corn Mothers, see Gutiérrez 1991. On goddesses in various religions, see Eisler 1987; Jayakar 1990; Larrington 1992; M. Stone 1976.

CHAPTER SIX   OUT OF EDEN

1. It can be found in Haraway 1989, 383.

2. Lancaster 1974, 12–41; McGrew 1981; Tanner 1981; Tanner and Zihlman 1976.

3. Slings are still in use in many parts of the world and were the prototype for a ubiquitous item of Western parental equipment today—the Snugli, patented by Ann Moore in 1984. Moore had seen slings in Africa when she was in the Peace Corps (Andrews 1990).

4. J. K. Brown 1970; Leibowitz 1986; Marwell 1975.

5. Conkey 1985; Pfeiffer 1985; Welbourn 1984.
6. Lévi-Strauss 1956, 1969; Mauss 1954; Meillassoux (1975) 1981; Redclift 1987; Siskind 1978; Yanagasako and Collier 1987.
7. Blumberg 1978; Collier 1988; Collier and Rosaldo 1981, 1984; Friedl 1975; Mukhopadhyay and Higgins 1988.
8. Also see Friedl 1975, 59–60.
9. For Leroi-Gourhan, the horse is male and bison female; for Laming, the horse is female and the bison male.
10. Collier 1988; Collier and Rosaldo 1981; Mauss 1954; Strathern 1988.
11. Blumberg 1978, 1984; Collier 1988; Engels [1884] 1972; Leacock 1981; Meillassoux [1975] 1981; Sacks 1979.
12. Collier and Rosaldo 1981; Kandiyoti 1988; Lamphere 1974.
13. Also see Mitchell 1975, 370–76.
14. Also see Chevillard and Leconte 1986, 92–93; Redclift 1987.
15. Also see Weiner 1979.
16. Ehrenberg 1989, 25–26; C. S. Wood 1979, 21–40.
17. Childe 1942, 48–68; Ehrenberg 1989, 77–99.
18. Ehrenberg 1989, 90–99; Hodder 1984; Mellaart 1967.
19. For the debate, see Barstow 1978; Ehrenberg 1988, 66–76.
20. Childe 1942, 48–68; Ehrenberg 1989, 99–107; Rohrlich-Leavitt 1977.
21. On the continuance of matrilineal social organization see Sacks 1979; Schlegel 1977; Whyte 1978. On the consequences of patrilineality for the status of women, see Chevillard and Leconte 1986; Coontz and Henderson 1986; Engels [1884] 1972; Redclift 1987.

CHAPTER SEVEN   ROCKING THE CRADLE

1. Asherah is also referred to as *Rahmay,* the word for "womb." In Hebrew, *rachmim,* the word for "pity," has the same root as *racham,* the word for "womb."
2. On the social construction of motherhood, see H. Marshall 1991; Rich 1977; Rothman 1989; Trebilcot 1983; Scheper-Hughes 1992, 340–99.
3. It is getting less and less abstract; Delaisi de Parseval and Hurstel (1987, 76) note that biological paternity can now be proved with 99.8 percent accuracy.
4. Weiss (1994) found the same phenomenon with parents of premature children who were in incubators.
5. According to an unpublished paper by Delilah Amir, the familiar admonition to women that they must bring forth children in pain should be translated from biblical Hebrew as "in sorrow shall you bring forth children" ("Soviet women talking about their experiences giving birth—labor and the state," Tel Aviv University. Paper presented at the Fifth International Interdisciplinary Congress on Women, Costa Rica, February 1993).
6. Women undergoing amniocentesis often claim they do not feel the fetus move until they know that no defects have been found that might warrant aborting (Rothman 1986). On pregnancy as a social relationship, see Rothman 1989, 97–105.
7. When infants die in the Alto do Cruzeiro, "death without weeping" is the

culturally approved response (Scheper-Hughes 1992, 416–23). On the elaborate nineteenth-century mourning practices for dead children and mothers' reconciliation to the loss, see Simonds 1988. On how women-dominated religions help mothers become reconciled to infant deaths, see Sered 1994.

8. The state often knew the name, occupation, and address of the mother, especially if she had given birth in the public maternity hospital, but the mothers frequently stated that the abandonment was temporary (Fuchs 1984, 32). There were stories of mothers presenting themselves as wet nurses so that they would be paid to care for their own children. This stratagem did not arouse official sympathy or concern for the women's welfare (41).

9. Also see Badinter 1981, 68–78; Scheper-Hughes 1992, 355–56, 364.

10. In sixth-century Italy, children were sold in the marketplace (Boswell 1988, 201). In early modern Europe, babies were sold or rented as substitutes for babies that had died (279–82). Mothers paid to dispose of an unwanted baby at the beginning of the twentieth century; a generation later, there was a black market in adoptable babies. Subsequently, payments to agencies became fees, and payments to foster parents became financial support for the child (Zelizer 1985, 169–207).

11. On deliberate infanticide, also see Dickemann 1984; Johansson 1984; Scrimshaw 1984.

12. To understand the effects of sex ratio on fertility rates, simply consider that if a group consists of one fertile woman and nine fertile men, she can have approximately one child per year. If a group consists of nine fertile women and one fertile man, the women can have nine children per year. For an overview of the issues on sex selection using sperm separation in in vitro and artificial insemination, timing of coitus around ovulation, and selective abortion after amniocentesis, see Bennett 1983. For possible effects of imbalanced gender ratios, see Guttentag and Secord 1983.

13. Also see M. K. Walker 1992.

14. On the social control of fertility, see Amir and Biniamin 1992; Anker 1985; Croll, Davin, and Kane 1985; Engelstein 1991; Ferree 1993; Gittens 1982; Goldman 1991; L. Gordon 1990a; Greer 1985; Heitlinger 1987; Laslett 1977; McLaren 1978, 1984; Mohr 1987; Reed 1978. Direct control of women's fertility under slavery is total (see Jennings 1990).

15. The overall fertility rate is the average number of children a woman would bear if she went through the reproductive ages (15–49) having children at the age-specific fertility rates observed in a given year.

16. Greil 1991; Lasker and Borg 1987; Miall 1986; Pfeffer 1987; Sandelowski 1983.

17. Callan et al. 1988; Crowe 1985; I. Koch 1990; L. S. Williams 1988.

18. An additional no-choice choice that is the result of successful fertility treatment is whether to abort some of the fetuses in a multiple pregnancy to ensure the survival of the others (see Evans et al. 1988; Fredericksen, Keith, and Sabbagha 1992).

19. These cases of "grandmother" gestators continue to be prominently reported (see *New York Times* 1991e). Strathern notes that "assisted reproduction creates the

biological parent as a separate category" (1992, 20). Where the donor of sperm, oocytes, or fertilized embryos is anonymous, the legal status of the social parents is usually not contested and does not have to be officially designated (Novaes 1989). On legal opinions in the United States, see Blankenship et al. 1993; Cohen and Taub 1989.

20. Also see Dawson [1929] 1989; N. Hall 1989; Rivière 1974.

21. On changes in custody laws and practices and their justification, see Coltrane and Hickman 1992; Grossberg 1983; J. W. Jacobs 1982; Olsen 1984; Seltzer 1991; Shanley 1989, 131—55; Smart and Sevenhuijsen 1989; Walters and Chapman 1991.

22. "Unfitness" in a mother usually means "sexual misconduct," even where it has no relevance to her fitness as a parent, whereas fathers who have beaten both the mother and the children may be given custody (Sack 1992).

23. On the changing definitions of child abuse, see L. Gordon 1989; Strauss 1991. Also see the alternative viewpoints by Demie Kurz, Donileen R. Loeske, and Joan McCord in the same issue (*Social Problems,* May 1991).

24. Also see Ruddick 1983. For her, the essence of "maternal thinking" is attention and love (223—24).

25. According to Nelson, approximately 40 percent of children under the age of one, 38 percent aged one or two and 15 percent between the ages of three and five, representing 5.1 million children, are cared for on a mostly informal basis by women in their homes in the United States (1990, 4).

26. For critiques of Rossi's 1977 paper, see Gross et al. 1979. Rossi's biosocial approach was a startling shift from her position in 1964, when she wrote a widely cited paper recommending structural social changes so that women could participate fully in the occupational world and men could equally share parenting.

27. Greif surveyed 1,136 mostly white Catholic or Protestant American fathers who had formal or informal custody after divorce, and also interviewed more than 100.

28. Also see Cohen 1987.

29. For critiques of Chodorow, see Gottlieb 1984; R. M. Jackson 1989; Lorber et al. 1981. On gay and lesbian parents, see Bozett 1987.

30. For historical changes in childbirth in the United States, see Rothman 1982; Wertz and Wertz 1989.

31. She also comments that the present prince of Wales was in the birthing room for his two sons' births; when he was born, his father was playing squash (1987, 37). For German fathers, see Nickel and Köcher 1987, 101.

32. Also see Hochschild 1989, 228—38; Jump and Haas 1987; Pleck 1987; L. Segal 1990, 26—89; Vannoy-Hiller and Philliber 1989, 104—09.

33. S. Jackson 1987; Nugent 1987; G. Russell 1987; Sagi, Koren, and Weinberg, 1987. A well-publicized slogan of one of Israel's women's organizations was "Be a man, give her a hand."

34. An unpublished study from Norway suggests that then men will define appropriate parenting behavior (Berit Brandth and Elin Kvande, "Changing masculinities: The reconstruction of fathering." University of Trondheim. Presented at the

Family Sociology–Developing the Field Conference, Voksenåsen, March 1992). Men's version of child care includes taking the child along when seeing people for work or social reasons and does not include doing the housework while child-minding.

35. These leave benefits, which vary by the country offering them, are usually a mix of the following: pregnancy and maternity leave before and after the birth, for the mother; about two weeks off after the birth, for the father; parental leave, with high, then low, compensation during the first year, which either may take, and days to care for a sick child (Kaul 1991).

36. Married men with children whose wives cut back on their labor force participation have to work longer hours to maintain the same family income. As long as women earn less than men, the pattern makes perfect sense in terms of the family economy re time and money. She spends time; he provides money (cf. Shelton 1992, 33–62).

37. For data on mothers who try to bring up their children according to feminist principles, see T. Gordon 1990. For a good exploration of meta-rules necessary to counteract the hidden assumptions of gendered parenting, see Held 1983.

38. Benston 1969; Bologh 1990, 240–65; Cancian 1985; Smith-Rosenberg 1975.

39. Also see Beer 1983, 67; Mainardi 1970, 452; Rowbotham 1973, 47–80; Zaretsky 1986.

40. Poor men have few choices, too. Boswell quotes Basil of Caesarea, an early Christian writer, on the plight of a poor father considering selling one of his children to feed the others: "If I hold on to them all, I will see all of them die of hunger, but if I sell one, how will I face the rest, having become suspect of treachery in their eyes?" (1988, 165–66).

CHAPTER EIGHT   DAILY BREAD

1. Harris 1981; Horan and Hargis 1991; White and Brinkerhoff 1987; Wilk and Netting 1984.

2. At market rates, a full-time housewife's services in the United States is estimated at $16–17,000 in 1991 dollars (Odum 1992).

3. On all these activities, see Abel and Nelson 1990; Daniels 1987; DeVault 1991; di Leonardo 1987; Finch 1983; Fishman 1978; Glazer 1990; Izraeli 1992; Komarovsky 1962; Lopata 1971, 73–136; Oakley 1974; Papanek 1979; L. B. Rubin 1976; Schooler et al. 1983; Sharma 1986; D. E. Smith 1987a, 151–226; Stivens 1981.

4. Bridenthal 1976; Calasanti and Bailey 1991; Coontz and Henderson 1986; Hill 1989; Huber 1990; Thornton and Fricke 1987; Sacks 1984; D. E. Smith 1987b; Tilly and Scott 1978.

5. Also see A. Whitehead 1981, 1984.

6. Fox-Genovese 1988, 172–87, 193; Jones 1985, 11–43.

7. Anderson and Zinsser 1988, 1:353–77; Davidoff and Hall 1987.

8. Bridget Hill notes that in poor eighteenth-century English households, urine was used for washing clothes and "persons" (1989, 111–12).

9. Acker 1988; Kessler-Harris 1990, 6–32; May 1982.
10. Also see Kessler-Harris 1990.
11. Dill 1980; Glenn 1985, 1986; Palmer 1989; Rollins 1985; Romero 1988.
12. Davidoff and Hall 1987, 357–96; Shanley 1989; Welter 1966.
13. Davidoff and Hall 1987, 387–96; Palmer 1989, 137–51.
14. R. S. Cowan 1987; B. J. Fox 1990; Glazer 1984; Nolan 1990; Rothschild 1983; Vanek 1974.
15. Baca Zinn 1990; Dill 1980; Glenn 1985, 1986, 1992; Romero 1988.
16. Also see Dugger 1988; E. Higginbotham 1983; Wilkinson 1984.
17. DeVault 1991; Glazer 1988, 1990; D. E. Smith 1987a, 181–207.
18. Daniels 1988; di Leonardo 1987; J. Nash 1990; Ostrander 1984; Stack 1975.
19. Also see Rowbotham 1973, 81–115; J. Smith 1987.
20. D. E. Smith 1984; Sokoloff 1980.
21. Gimenez 1990; Glazer 1993; J. Smith 1987.
22. Also see Arendell 1986; Glendon 1989, 148–238; Grella 1990; Smart 1984.
23. For histories of welfare policies in Western countries, see Abramovitz 1988; P. F. Clement 1992; Pascall 1986; Skocpol 1992; Ursel 1992.
24. See L. Gordon 1989, 82–115, for the policies of Massachusetts child-protection agencies toward single mothers.
25. For accounts of the rise of the modern welfare state in Europe and Canada, see Bock and Thane 1991; Haavio-Mannila and Kauppinen 1992; Holter 1984; Jenson 1986; Pascall 1986; Schirmer 1982; Ursel 1992. For policies and benefits in the United States, see Abramovitz 1988; L. Gordon 1990b; Hyde and Essex 1991; Skocpol 1992. For a comparison of Britain and the United States, see Skocpol and Ritter 1991. For Israel's policies, see Izraeli 1992.
26. Abramovitz 1988, 349–79; Amott 1990; Naples 1991c; Quadagno 1990.
27. Amott 1990; Baca Zinn 1989; Brewer 1988; Collins 1990, 115–37; Mink 1990; B. J. Nelson 1984.
28. Joan Acker, personal communication.
29. Also see Baca Zinn 1989; Brewer 1988; Fraser 1989, 144–87; McLanahan, Sørenson, and Watson 1989; Osmond and Martin 1983. For the feminization of poverty worldwide, see Goldberg and Kremen 1990.
30. For vivid ethnographic descriptions of life on welfare, see Sheehan 1975; Stack 1975. For an analysis of the importance of this hidden economy to capitalism, see J. Smith 1984.
31. Countries vary in the extent of their benefits. Sweden is purported to be the most generous, but all the European countries have maternal and child-care benefits. For comparisons of the benefits offered by European countries, see Hootsmans 1992, table 11.2, 190; Kamerman 1991, table 1.1, 18. For policies and benefits in the United States, see Hyde and Essex 1991, Appendix B, 468–89.
32. Gelb 1989, 3; Lewis and Åström 1992, 72–73; Ruggie 1984.
33. Sweden's extended parental-leave policies also encouraged an interrupted-career pattern; women who had two children in fairly rapid succession could combine two sets of leave and stay out of the labor market for several years (Lewis and

Åström 1992, 76–78). However, unlike the United States, they continued to receive a substantial portion of their wages.

34. Berk 1985; DeVault 1991, 5–13; Komter 1989. In the 1950s, when lesbians divided into "butches" and "femmes," the "femmes" were expected to do the housework (Faderman 1991, 169).

35. Hertz 1986, 185–95; Holmstrom 1972, 59–101; Hunt and Hunt 1977, 1982; Izraeli 1992; Johnson, Johnson, and Liese 1991.

36. Benería and Roldán 1987; Blumberg 1991a; Roldán 1988.

37. Malveaux 1988, 135–37; Ross 1987; Willie 1985, 274; 1988, 183.

38. Also see Blumstein and Schwartz 1983, 51–111; Hertz 1992; Jasso 1988; Pahl 1989; Treas 1993.

39. Also see Berk 1980, 1985; Blumstein and Schwartz 1983, 144–48; Calasanti and Bailey 1991; M. T. Coleman 1991; Coverman 1985, Kalleberg and Rosenfeld 1990; Kamerman 1979; Moen 1989; Pleck 1985; Ross 1987; Shelton 1992, 63–109; Vannoy-Hiller and Philliber 1989; E. O. Wright et al. 1992.

40. A more insidious consequence is that without community property laws, his payments of the mortgage on a house give him ownership in case of divorce (Smart 1984, 82–89, 101–09).

41. In relationships that seem stable on the surface, the less powerful partner may have buried resentment or feel that continued arguments are useless. See Chafetz 1980; Haavind 1984; Komter 1989.

42. Hochschild 1989a, 82–86, 220–28; Pahl 1989, 112, 169.

CHAPTER NINE   SEPARATE AND NOT EQUAL

1. A U.S. population survey of 4,018 women and 4,583 men who changed occupations between 1980 and 1981 found that 43.2 percent of the 850 women who were in occupations where at least 70 percent of the workers were men, 51.6 percent of the 1,123 women who were in relatively gender-balanced occupations, and 54.5 percent of the 2,045 women in occupations where at least 70 percent of the workers were women moved to occupations where the workers were mostly women. For the men, 62.5 percent of the 251 who worked in occupations where most of the workers were women, 69.3 percent of the 807 who worked in gender-balanced occupations, and 76.6 percent of the 3,525 who worked in occupations where most of the workers were men shifted to occupations whose workers were at least 70 percent men (J. A. Jacobs 1989b, table 7.2).

2. Also see Waite and Berryman 1985, 35–76.

3. See Collinson, Knights, and Collinson 1990, for how personnel managers produce gender segregation and rationalize doing what they know is against the law.

4. Acker 1990; Baron 1991; Feldberg and Glenn 1979; Hossfeld 1990; B. W. Jones 1984; Nash and Fernández-Kelly 1983; Thomas 1982.

5. Also see Waite and Berryman 1985, 4–34.

6. Kuhn and Bluestone 1987; Sassen 1988; Tiano 1987, 1990.

7. Acker 1990; Baron 1991; Kondo 1990a; Leidner 1991.

8. Baron, Mittman, and Newman 1991; Beechey 1987; Collinson and Knights 1986; Roos and Reskin 1984; Walby 1986.

9. For cross-national data, see Brinton 1989; Cohen, Bechar, and Raijman 1987; Lapidus 1976; Reskin and Hartmann 1986; Roos 1984, Table 3.4, 54−55.

10. For histories of women's work, see Clark [1919] 1982; Hanawalt 1986; B. Hill 1989; Kessler-Harris 1982; Lown 1990; Matthaei 1982; Pinchbeck [1930] 1981.

11. Kasson 1976, 55−106; Kessler-Harris 1982, 30-44. Young white women living in orphanages and almshouses, as well as indigent widows and their children, were literally sold as factory workers in less benign arrangements (Abramovitz 1988, 89−90).

12. I. Berger 1990; Lamphere 1985; Tilly 1981; Turbin 1984.

13. Fox-Genovese 1988; E. Higginbotham 1983; J. Jones 1986; B. J. Mason 1987; Morrissey 1989, 62−80; Mullings 1986; White 1985.

14. Acosta-Belén and Bose 1990; Benería and Sen 1981; Boserup 1970; Brydon and Chant 1989; J. Nash 1990; Tinker 1990.

15. Blumberg 1991a; Mencher 1988; Roldán 1988; Whitehead 1981.

16. See also Marglin 1978, 37−38.

17. Fernández-Kelly 1984; Lown 1990, 196−98; Nestle 1983; Peiss 1983.

18. For a discussion of the debate over protective legislation in nineteenth-century England, see Lown 1990, 182−84, 194−95, 210−19.

19. The U.S. Supreme Court recently outlawed barring pregnant women from hazardous jobs (Greenhouse 1991).

20. Crompton and Jones 1984; Davies 1982, 129−62; Glenn and Feldberg 1977; Kanter 1977a, 69−103.

21. Carter 1987; Donato and Roos 1987; Game and Pringle 1983, 80−93; Glenn and Tolbert 1987.

22. Burris 1989; Cockburn 1983, 1985; Game and Pringle 1983, 25−40; Hacker 1987, 1989, 95−139; Wajcman 1991.

23. Cockburn 1985; Tax 1980; Walsh 1977; Witz 1986.

24. Amott and Matthaei 1991; Mencher 1988; Moen and Smith 1986; Rosen 1987; Semyonov 1980; Whitehead 1981.

25. Bunster and Chaney 1989; Fernández-Kelly 1983; Rosen 1987; Westwood 1985; Westwood and Bhachu 1988.

26. Allen and Wolkowitz 1987, 59−86; Beechey and Perkins 1987; Benería and Roldán 1987; Bennett and Alexander 1987; Boris and Daniels 1989; Christensen 1988; Mies 1982.

27. Allen and Wolkowitz 1987; Benería 1987; Benería and Roldán 1987, 31−74; Carter 1987; Gottfried 1991; Elson and Pearson 1981; Fuentes and Ehrenreich 1983, Kwong 1988; Mies 1982, 103−09.

28. Also see Rosenfeld 1980.

29. Humphries 1988; Kessler-Harris 1982, 250−72; Milkman 1976. Loscocco and Robinson (1991) found the same process for women in small businesses; they tended to enter women's stereotyped fields or those unattractive to white men.

30. Acker 1991; Auster and Drazin 1988; Baron and Newman 1990; M. F. Fox 1985; Hannan, Schömann, and Blossfeld 1990; England and McCreary 1987; Lewin-

Epstein and Stier 1987; Madden 1985; Marini 1989; McLaughlin 1978; Rosenfeld 1983; Rosenfeld and Kalleberg 1990; Sorensen 1989; Swafford 1978; Tienda, Smith, and Ortiz 1987; Treiman and Roos 1983.

31. For evaluation methods, see Acker 1989a; Blum 1991; Evans and Nelson 1989; Remick 1984; Steinberg and Haignere 1987; Treiman and Hartmann 1981.

32. Acker 1989a; Blum 1991; Brenner 1987; England 1992; Evans and Nelson 1989; Steinberg 1987.

33. Acker 1989a; Malveaux 1987; Taylor and Smitherman-Donaldson 1989.

34. Acker 1989a, 199–227; Amott and Matthaei 1988; Blum 1991, 183–202; Brenner 1987; Evans and Nelson 1989, 162–73; Feldberg 1984; Steinberg 1987.

CHAPTER TEN   GUARDING THE GATES

1. On women in management cross-culturally, see Adler and Izraeli 1988b, 1993; Antal and Izraeli 1993. On the structural conditions that affect women's entry into and upward mobility in management in Israel, see Izraeli 1993.

2. Nine women won the Nobel Prize in the sciences between 1901 and 1989, 2.2 percent of the 407 awarded. Similar percentages of women were members of the prestigious national academies of science in England (3.2), France (2.3), Germany (2.1), and the United States (3.4) in the 1980s. The percentages of women who obtained doctorates in the sciences in the late 1960s and early 1970s (the feeder pool) was 9.3 percent for England, 19 percent for France, 4.8 percent for Germany, and 9.8 percent for the United States (Zuckerman 1991, 47, table 1.1).

3. Interview with Jardenia Ovadia, M.D., July 26, 1984. For the tentativeness with which women are supported for positions of authority by noncolleagues, see Chase and Bell 1990. For a review and critique of the literature on women and achievement, see Kaufman and Richardson 1982.

4. Cole and Singer 1991; M. F. Fox 1991; Reskin 1978a, 1978b.

5. The interviews took place in California, Texas, Massachusetts, and Arizona. The percentages of men in these occupations in the United States in 1990 were nursing, 5.5; elementary school teachers, 14.8; librarians, 16.7; social workers, 31.8 (table 1, 254). The proportion of Black men is greatest in social work.

6. Also see Dexter 1985; Martin, Harrison, and DiNitto 1983.

7. For a continuance of this pattern of business-family marriages well into the twentieth century in Japan, but with arranged marriages, see Hamabata 1990.

8. Lever 1976, 1978; Luria and Herzog 1991; Maccoby 1990; Thorne 1990, 1993; Thorne and Luria 1986.

9. Some teachers deliberately mix boys and girls, but in other schools, teachers routinely divide a class into boys and girls (for teams, lineup, etc.). For a history of gender practices in the public schools in the United States, see Hansot and Tyack 1988.

10. Gutek 1985, 129–52; Hochschild 1983; Tancred-Sheriff 1989, 52–55.

11. Sexist jokes and sexual remarks about and to women seem to occur among men

of all classes, in every work setting, and in many countries. See Collinson 1988; Lyman 1987; Peña 1991. These verbal acts of sexual aggression can easily turn into sexual assault if the woman is alone with a group of men and physically or psychologically vulnerable. For the concept of a continuum of sexual violence, see Liz Kelly 1987.

12. Barkalow and Raab 1990; Collinson and Collinson 1989; Fine 1987b.

13. For men nurses, see C. L. Williams 1989, 118–19; on women physicians, see Lorber 1984, 60–61.

14. Also see Cockburn 1991, 159–61.

15. See Booth-Butterfield and Booth-Butterfield 1988 for cooperation and support among women teammates.

16. See Remy (1990, 45) for a more general statement of "fratriarchy based . . . on the self-interest of the association of men itself." He equates this age-graded bonding with men's huts, blood brotherhoods, and all-male secret societies.

17. Bourdieu 1989; Coser 1986; C. F. Epstein 1988, 215–31. Because bathrooms are gender-segregated, they are used by women as well as men for networking, but women also use them for letting out anger against "them," and as places of refuge from men (Barkalow 1990, 65; Reskin 1988; Quindlen 1988, 30–33).

18. C. F. Epstein 1981; Kanter 1977a; Lorber 1984; Zuckerman 1991. In some countries, such as the former Soviet Union, most doctors are women because it is not a high-prestige profession; in some Arab countries, women doctors are needed because women patients are not allowed to be examined by men doctors.

19. For domestic arrangements among dual-career couples, see Fava and Deierlein 1989; Hertz 1986; Holmstrom 1972; Lorber 1984, 80–98; Vannoy-Hiller and Philliber 1989. For choice between career and family, see Gerson 1985.

20. Cole and Zuckerman 1991; C. F. Epstein 1981, 342–43; Kaufman 1978; Lorber 1984, 91–93; Zunz 1991.

21. Lorber 1984, 80–98, found that married women physicians tended to combine their social life with networking, and since many were married to physicians, their networks were larger than those of single women.

22. The process actually starts in childhood, with differential treatment of girls and boys in grade schools, and proliferates in the higher grades, with only bright middle-class boys being encouraged to take math and science courses (AAUW Report 1992).

23. On women in science, see Cole 1979; Keller 1983, 1985; Reskin 1978a, 1978b; M. W. Rossiter 1982; Sayre 1975; Zuckerman, Cole, and Brewer 1991; and the Sage issue on Black women in science and technology (6 [Fall] 1989). On comparisons of women's and men's careers in various professions, see Ahearn and Scott 1981; C. F. Epstein 1971, 1981, 1991; M. F. Fox 1991; Fox and Faver 1985; Judi Marshall 1989; Powell 1988, 175–206.

24. Freeland Judson says that with Linus Pauling, James Watson, and Francis Crick, "she was one of the four people closest to the discovery of the structure of DNA" (1979, 147). His account discusses the personalities and interchanges of all the players (1979, 100–98).

25. "Rosy" was a nickname used behind her back (Judson 1979, 148).
26. Freeland Judson cites a letter that he feels indicates "she had good reason to think she headed an independent team" (103).
27. According to Freeland Judson, Crick and other readers of the manuscript forced the apologia; Wilkins still had feelings of animosity toward his "dear, dead colleague" (1979, 102).
28. Mozart's own sister, Nannerl, was also a pianist, composer, and child prodigy. She and Mozart traveled around Europe together until she was fifteen and married. She may even have written some of the early works attributed to Mozart (Steinem 1992). Actually, Mozart wasn't "Mozart, the great composer," in his own day, nor was he in the nineteenth century. Mozart's high status is a modern phenomenon. The term *status shield* is Hochschild's (1983, 162–81).
29. Oswald Hall (1946, 1948, 1949) developed these concepts for medical communities. I extended them to women physicians' careers (Lorber 1984), but the concepts are valid for all kinds of colleague groups.
30. In 1977a, 206–42; also 1977b. The effects of imbalanced numbers in work situations are boundary maintenance by dominants, role encapsulation (assigning or defining the work tokens do as appropriate), performance pressures because of tokens' heightened visibility, and stereotyped informal roles, such as, for token women, mother, mascot, seductress, and "iron maiden." (I have not seen similar roles identified for token men, such as men nurses, or for Black women or men in white groups or vice versa.)
31. Barkalow and Raab 1990; S. E. Martin 1980; C. L. Williams 1989.
32. M. F. Fox 1981, 1984; Lorber 1987a, 1991.
33. For a psychological approach to women's leadership styles, see Cantor and Bernay 1992. For an anthropological perspective, see Power 1991, 166–67, who notes that among chimpanzees in the wild, "a charismatic leader . . . is any of a number of animals of either sex who are, to varying degrees, confident, self-assured, normally nonaggressive, but fearless when roused, tolerant of others, approachable and responsive, with a 'presence' through posture and bearing (rather than through size and strength) and who carry out leader-role related behaviors." For female leadership, see pp. 196–203 and De Waal 1984.
34. England 1979; Hearn and Parkin 1988; Kanter 1977a, 166–205; Powell 1988, 150–56; Wolf and Fligstein 1979a, 1979b.
35. Barkalow and Raab 1990; S. E. Martin 1980; C. L. Williams 1989.
36. Also see C. L. Williams 1990, 48–87, on the official obsession with masculinity and femininity when women entered the Marine Corps.
37. Formal theories and experiments on how status organizes interaction, particularly how beliefs about actors' social characteristics govern evaluation of performance, allocation of rewards, and the structure of power and prestige in small groups, document many of the processes described in this section. For overviews and recent developments in the field, see Fisek, Berger, and Norman 1991; Ridgeway and Berger 1988; Wagner and Berger 1991. For studies specifically on gender, see Carli 1991; Lockheed 1985; Molm 1998; Pugh and Wahrman 1983; Ridgeway 1988; Ridgeway and Diekema 1989; Stewart 1988; Wagner 1988.

38. Deaux and Major 1987; Goffman 1959; Hochschild 1983; Ridgeway 1987; Ridgeway and Johnson 1990; Scheff 1990.
39. Dovidio et al. 1988; Fishman 1978; Kollock, Blumstein, and Schwartz 1985; West 1982; Wiley and Woolley 1988; Zimmerman and West 1975.
40. Goffman 1963b, 1967, 5–95; Henley 1977. When Geraldine Ferraro was Walter Mondale's running mate, there was a whole set of rules about standing, walking, touching, and addressing each other (Dowd 1984).
41. Dabbs and Stokes 1975; F. Davis 1961; Egolf and Corder 1991; C. F. Epstein 1981, 309–14; Goffman 1963a; Hatfield and Sprecher 1986; Unger, Hilderbrand, and Madar 1982; Webster and Driskell 1983.
42. For other *New York Times* reports, columns, and stories documenting the continuing pervasiveness of sexual harassment and the micropolitics of the issue, see Apple 1991; Bray 1991; De Witt 1991; Dowd 1991a, 1991b; Goleman 1991; Kolbert 1991a, 1991b; Lewin 1991b; Quindlen 1991b, 1991c, 1991d; Schafran 1991; Warrock 1991; Wicker 1991; Lena Williams 1991; M. C. Wilson 1991. For articles and features slanted toward men's perspectives, see the special section of the *Wall Street Journal,* Sex and Power in the Office, October 18, 1991, B1–B4.
43. Professor Hill's experiences are not unusual for minority women seeking teaching positions in law schools. A recent survey of 174 of the 176 U.S. law schools found that minority women compared to minority men are more likely to begin in nontenured tracks (44 percent to 29 percent), to teach at lower-prestige law schools (-0.12 to 0.66 on a scale where 0 is average), and twice as likely to teach beginning courses (Merritt and Reskin 1992).
44. The January-February 1992 issue of *Ms. Magazine* featured an article by Anita Hill based on remarks delivered at a panel on sexual harassment and policy-making at the National Forum for Women State Legislators, which had been convened by the Center for the American Woman and Politics at Rutgers University (1992). Also see Sharpe 1992 on the reality of sexual harassment in Washington, D.C.; Williams et al. 1992 for analysis and comment by five African-American feminists. For a rebuttal of right-wing interpretations, see Mayer and Abramson 1993.
45. Dziech and Weiner 1990; Gutek 1985; MacKinnon 1979; Mathews 1991; Paludi 1990; Schneider 1982, 1985, 1991. Consensual sexual relations between equals (and even between a superior and a subordinate) is not harassment, but, in the face of refusal, persistent demands for dates or sexual relations is. Work organizations, schools, and the military usually have written and unwritten rules governing dating and sexual relations among their members, but may be less explicit about what constitutes sexual harassment. See Barkalow 1990; Cockburn 1991, 138–70; Gutek 1985, 149; Powell 1988, 135–37; Schneider 1984.
46. Also see Rowe 1977; Schneider 1982.
47. On the range of verbal and nonverbal types of sexual harassment, see Gruber 1992.
48. See L. Fraser 1991; J. Gross 1991; *Stanford-Observer* 1991 for background stories; *New York Times* 1991c for the news report.

49. Grant 1988; Lenhart et al. 1991; Lorber 1991.
50. Partly as a result of Anita Hill's experiences in front of a panel of white men, after the 1992 election, the number of U.S. senators rose from two to six; one is African-American, Carol Mosely Braun.

CHAPTER ELEVEN   THE VISIBLE HAND

1. For overviews of women's lives in Greece and Rome, see Anderson and Zinsser 1988, 1:26–66; Arthur 1977; Pomeroy 1975, 1991; Rohrlich-Leavitt 1977.
2. Communism is an ideal of shared ownership of the means of production and distribution of goods and services on the basis of need. State socialism is the term most frequently used for countries whose main economic institutions are owned by the state; workers are state employees and are paid on the basis of their jobs, but the state also subsidizes housing, health care, day care, schools at every level, retirement pensions, public transportation, and basic foods. In the modern welfare states of Western Europe, the government provides less extensive social benefits than under state socialism, but more than under capitalism. In Western European countries, the economy is a mix of public and private ownership, with the public sector employing a larger number of people than in capitalist countries such as the United States. Welfare states and capitalist countries shift back and forth on the size of the private and public sectors and the extent of public subsidies and benefits; the collapse of state socialism has opened Eastern Europe to these ideological, economic, and political debates over the advantages and disadvantages of private enterprise versus public welfare. For recent discussions of the gap between socialist theory and practice, see Buckley 1985, 1989; Haug 1991; Molyneux 1981; and the roundtable discussion in Krupps, Rapp, and Young 1989.
3. In Germany, women have experienced the vicissitudes of every twentieth-century state form. They obtained the vote and other civil rights after World War I. Some German women supported Nazism, which divested them of civil rights, and others resisted it to the point of death. After World War II, German women lived under occupation, and then those in the East lived under state socialism and those in the West under advanced capitalism. They are now in the throes of unification (Bridenthal, Grossman, and Kaplan 1984; Dölling 1991; Einhorn 1989; Ferree 1993; Koonz 1977; Oldfield 1987; Rosenberg 1991; H. G. Shaffer 1981).
4. Dölling 1991; Einhorn 1991; Moghadam 1990a; Szalai 1991; WuDunn 1992.
5. Jancar 1978, 112–18, makes this point for women in communist countries, but the same is true of political careers in any system. For women and power historically and cross-nationally, see Epstein and Coser 1981; Garlick, Dixon, and Allen 1992.
6. Also see W. Brown 1992; Boris and Bardaglio 1987; Connell 1990; Eisenstein 1984; N. Fraser 1989, 144–87; Pascall 1986; Schirmer 1982; Ursel 1992.
7. For Europe, see Anderson and Zinsser 1988 1:296–350; Coontz and Henderson 1986, 142–48; McNamara and Wemple 1974; Stone 1979, 69–89. The same

use of daughters in lieu of sons was true of precolonial Nigeria, according to Amadiume (1987). In modern Japan, in order to ensure that the family enterprise stays in the family if there are no male heirs or is managed well if the male heirs are not competent or reliable, business families have a tradition of a "male bride" who takes his wife's name and is adopted into his wife's household; the wife not only keeps the family name; she also assumes the household headship and inherits the family enterprise, becoming a social man (Hamabata 1990, 36, 45).

8. The lines of inheritance of patrilineal primogeniture are eldest son, eldest son's sons and grandsons, starting with the eldest; next eldest son and his sons, starting with the eldest, and so on until there are no sons, grandsons, or great-grandsons left. Then the line goes to the eldest daughter, her sons, grandsons, and great-grandsons, starting with the eldest; her next youngest sister and her sons, grandsons, and great-grandsons, starting with the eldest; and so on. A high death rate of infants and children and a short life span favored women's becoming queen and inheriting the Crown's property. However, in nonruling families, property was often entailed to the male line and was inherited by cousins rather than daughters, who presumably were married and belonged to different families.

9. Coontz and Henderson 1986, 148–54; L. Stone 1979, 93–146.

10. Charles de Gaulle, leader of the Free French in exile, enfranchised women on April 21, 1944, for their work in the underground fight against the Nazis and the Vichy government, and recommended that women and men of the Resistance be appointed to municipal councils in the parts of France that were liberated (M. L. Rossiter 1986, 223). Women voted in municipal elections a year later and in national elections in November, 1945. Truly universal suffrage was made part of the French constitution in 1946.

11. Wealthy women who presided over salons in seventeenth-century France influenced the intellectual debates that preceded the revolution (Landes 1988, 23–28). On the political influence of the salons of prerevolutionary Parisian aristocratic women after 1789, see Linda Kelly 1987, 20–23. On the activities of women in the French Revolution, see Graham 1977; Linda Kelly 1987; Landes 1988; Levy, Applewhite, and Johnson 1979.

12. One of the society's founding principles said: "All the members of the Society make up a family of sisters, and since an arbitrary act against one of its members must attack the whole Society, the one who suffered the violation of the laws is urged to inform the Society, which will obtain justice for her" (Levy, Applewhite, and Johnson 1979, 164).

13. In what may be the extreme of ironies, a Black woman, passing as a man, was a skilled sailor with the British Royal Navy for eleven years at the beginning of the nineteenth century. Her sex was discovered in 1815, when her estranged husband claimed part of her earnings (Wheelwright 1989, 69). See Poovey 1988 for the history and limitations of the 1857 act.

14. Glendon 1989; Holcombe 1983; Shanley 1989, 49–78, 103–30.

15. The same property rights, comparative autonomy, and ambiguous social position occurred in polygynous Mormon families in the nineteenth century. For contrasting views, see Dunfey 1984 and Iversen 1984.

16. See J. Jones 1986, 44–78, for the systematic way Black men and women were kept subordinate to whites through sharecropping after the Civil War, and Black women were systematically made unequal to Black men by the policies of the Freedmen's Bureau.

17. In an astounding concatenation of events, Campbell and Ciller won in the same week that Ruth Bader Ginsburg was chosen as President Bill Clinton's first nominee for the U.S. Supreme Court. She was confirmed easily and became the second woman justice. If Campbell and Ciller stay in power, and if Bader Ginsberg and Sandra Day O'Connor support the rights of women, the week of June 14, 1993 should go down in history. Campbell describes herself as a feminist, but she is a member of a conservative party (Farnsworth 1993).

18. According to the Inter-Parliamentary Union, a Geneva-based organization, the percentage of women in the parliaments of the countries of these women leaders as of June 1991 was Bangladesh, 10.3; Great Britain, 6.3; France, 5.7; Iceland, 23.8; India, 7.1; Ireland, 7.8; Israel, 6.7; Nicaragua, 16.3; Norway, 35.8 (the long-term woman prime minister insisted that her party have a certain percentage of women on their election lists); Pakistan, 0.9; the Philippines, 9.0; Poland 13.5; Turkey, 1.3 (Ragab 1992). Even without women prime ministers, the Scandinavian countries have had consistently high percentages of women representatives: Finland, 38.5; Denmark, 33.0; Sweden, 38.1, in 1991. As of June 1993, women had 13.5 percent of the seats in Canada's House of Commons (Farnsworth 1993). The United States' representation of women in Congress at the time was only 8.5 percent.

19. I. Berger 1990; Browning 1985; Hernes 1984; Naples 1991a, 1991b, 1992; B. J. Nelson 1984; Piven 1985; Safa 1990; Sarvasy 1992.

20. Buhle 1983; Kessler-Harris 1982; Lown 1990; Walby 1986.

21. W. Brown 1992; Connell 1990; Hernes 1984; Okin 1979, 140–66; MacKinnon 1989, 157–70; Pateman 1988. For feminist redefinitions of the concept of the citizen, see K. B. Jones 1990; Orloff 1993; Sarvasy 1992.

22. Ironically, Marx had named a woman, Harriet Law, to the General Council of the First International and had encouraged the participation of women (Landes 1989, 23).

23. Bebel's *Die Frau und der Socialismus* was enormously influential among women and men throughout the world and went through many editions and translations ([1904] 1970 is a translation of the 33rd German edition, originally published by the New York Labor News Press). Bebel's work, Engels's *The Origin of the Family, Private Property and the State,* published in 1884, whose ideas Bebel incorporated in his later editions, and Kollantai's *Social Bases of the Woman Question,* published in 1909 and based on both Bebel and Engels, were the theoretical underpinnings for socialist and communist discussions of "the woman question."

24. From the preface to Lenin [1934] 1975 written by his widow, Nadezhda Krupskaya, dated 1933, ten years after his death.

25. Clements 1979; Edmondson 1984; Holt 1977; Jancar 1978; Stites [1978] 1990; Waters 1989.

26. March 8; February 23 on the Russian calendar. See Lapidus 1978, 54–122, and

Rowbotham 1974, 134—69, for chronologies. March 8 has become International Women's Day; it was first celebrated in both the Soviet Union and China in 1924.

27. Kollantai survived Lenin's displeasure and Stalin's purges by becoming a diplomat. She was ambassador to Norway, Mexico, and Sweden. She returned to the Soviet Union with honors in 1945 and died in 1952 at the age of eighty. Rosa Luxemburg, in prison in Germany when Lenin took power in 1917, also disputed him on the necessity of dictatorship (1961). She was released in 1918, went along with an unsuccessful Communist Party putsch, did not flee the country, and was murdered on the way back to prison on January 16, 1919.

28. Clara Zetkin's report of her long conversation with Lenin in 1920 includes his chastisement of her for discussing sexual and marital problems at meetings with German working women and his criticism of a pamphlet on sex using Freudian theories that was written by a Viennese communist woman (in Lenin [1934] 1975, 101—03). After defending the relevance of the discussions as leading to an analysis of women's historical and current status and economic position, Zetkin gives in and says she herself criticized such discussions, and that "sex and marriage were no longer the focal point in lectures at discussion evenings" (103). Lenin did consider shared housework an important issue not only materially but intellectually: "his slave takes her revenge. . . . Her backwardness and her lack of understanding for her husband's revolutionary ideals act as a drag on his fighting spirit" (115).

29. On abortion rates in the Soviet Union and Central European Communist countries, 1953—73, see Jancar 1978, 70, table 28. For debates on abortion in the Soviet Union, see Engelstein 1991 and Goldman 1991.

30. Medicine was by no means a high-prestige or highly paid occupation, and many of the heads of hospitals and clinics were men. See Browning 1987, 6—8, for pre-breakup figures on women's employment.

31. Jancar's research shows similar patterns for Communist Albania, Bulgaria, Czechoslovakia, East Germany, Hungary, Poland, Romania, and Yugoslavia (1987).

32. For recent feminist activity, see Feminist Review, no. 39, 1991: "Shifting Territories: Feminisms and Europe," "Feminists and Socialism," and "Women in Action: Country by Country."

33. For firsthand accounts and analysis of life in the Soviet Union in the 1980s, see Browning 1985, 1987; Gray 1990; Hansson and Lidén 1983; Lapidus 1982; Mamonova 1984. For socialization, see Attwood 1990; for views of women in Russian culture and literature, see Gray 1990, 114—31; Mamonova 1989; for Soviet women's magazines as reinforcements of ideology, see McAndrew 1985.

34. Rowbotham (1974) entitled her chapter on the Russian Revolution "If You Like Tobogganing."

35. One account, made famous during the 1919 May Fourth Movement, is widely cited as an inspiration for Mao Zedong's concern for women's status. The bride-to-be slit her own throat with a dagger she had concealed in the bridal chair in which she was carried to the groom's home on her wedding day.

36. Leith (1973) feels that Xiang's connections to high-powered men gave her greater influence on party policy (56). The women leaders in the Guomingdang were also married to top-ranking men. Also see Witke 1973b, who says nothing about the marital politics of the women members in the CCP.

37. Skocpol 1979, 236–80, has a succinct account of Mao Zedong's guerrilla-war entrenchment tactics and how they provided his base for successful mass mobilization of the peasants.

38. Andors 1983; Croll 1980, 1983, 1984; Davin 1973, 1985a; Honig and Hershatter 1988; Jancar 1978, 129–36; Johnson 1983; Stacey 1983; Wolf 1985. For an early report, see Yang 1965. For more positive reports, see Myrdal 1965, 17–33; Sidel 1972, 1974.

39. Also see Andors 1983, 101–23.

40. Also see B. M. Barnett 1993. McAdam (1992) discusses the effect of gender on the civil rights movement in the United States and cites many works on women in other American movements. Women have been important participants in twentieth-century protest movements and revolutions in Spain (Ackelsberg 1991; Mangini 1991), South and Central America (Chinchilla 1990; Jaquette 1989; N. C. Nash 1992; L. L. Reif 1989; Safa 1990), the Middle East (A. R. Bloom 1991; Kandiyoti 1991; Moghadam 1993a, 1993b), and South Africa (Berger 1990; G. W. Seidman 1993). Also see West and Blumberg 1990.

41. The women agitators who went into the streets against the shah of Iran's Western-oriented government wore the veil as a *symbol* of protest and then had to protest against it as a reality when Ayatollah Khomeini, then in exile, called for women to wear modest Islamic dress. Once he was in power, the veil became compulsory as the symbol of the new purity of women (Mernissi 1987). Moghadam notes that there were militant pro-Islamic and anti-Islamic women in Iran (1993a, 1993b). For the variety of uses of head coverings and other modesty clothing, see Mac Leod 1991; Rugh 1986.

42. According to one observer, 70 percent of the newly unemployed in Russia are woman between the ages of forty-five and fifty-five; advertisements for new jobs are openly appealing for sexy young women to serve as secretaries (vanden Heuvel 1992). There are also proposals to close about a third of Moscow's childcare centers and to limit the hours of work for mothers with children under the age of fourteen. For the situation of women in Central Europe, see *Feminist Review,* no. 39, 1991.

43. Damian 1990; Rosenberg 1991; Szalai 1991. For the prevalence of women in rural production in socialist development, see Croll 1981.

44. Chinchilla 1990; Izraeli 1981; Moghadam 1993a; Molyneux 1985; Nazzari 1983.

45. On the tendency for revolutionary ideologies to become more radical and repressive as revolutionary authority is assailed by internal dissent and external opposition, see Goldstone 1991, 416–58.

CHAPTER TWELVE   DISMANTLING NOAH'S ARK

1. Eisenstein 1988; MacKinnon 1989; Okin 1979; Pateman 1988.

2. Also see Jaggar 1990; MacKinnon 1989, 215–34. Joan Wallach Scott (1988b)

argues that in a broader sense, the concept of equality means *indifference* to differences.

3. For analysis of the complexity of legal issues involved in gender equality and equity, see the papers in Part One of Bartlett and Kennedy 1991. The editors provide an extensive annotated bibliography on sex differences and equality theory on pp. 156–61. Also see C. F. Epstein 1990.

4. Also see F. J. Davis 1991.

5. Also see Chafetz 1990.

6. Also see Blumberg 1976. Current changes in the kibbutz movement include privatization, much more hired labor for production work, and women doing more domestic work for their own families. The effect on women's lives is likely to be similar to the effect of the shift from socialism to capitalism in Eastern Europe (Michal Palgi, personal communication).

7. Also see Redclift 1985; J. Smith 1984, Roldán 1985.

8. Benería and Sen 1982; Bennholdt-Thomsen 1981; Blumberg 1989; Fernández-Kelly 1989; Gimenez 1990; Mies 1986; Mies, Bennholdt-Thomsen, and von Werlhof 1988; Redclift 1985; J. Smith 1984.

9. See Benería and Roldán 1987; Bunster and Chaney 1989; Byerly 1986; Chaney and García Castro 1989a, 1989b; Fernández-Kelly 1983; Westwood and Bhachu 1988 for working-class women's work; and Acker 1989a; Blum 1991; Remick 1984; and Swafford 1978 for wage differentials in modern industrialized societies.

10. Chow 1987; Garcia 1989; Wallace [1978] 1990.

11. Acker 1988; Holcombe 1983; Weitzman 1985.

12. On class differences in a lesbian workplace, see Weston and Rofel 1984. On lesbian and gay families, see Bozett 1987; Weston 1991.

13. Badinter (1989, 147–190) argues that women and men in Western societies are already coming to resemble each other and that gender differences are blurring considerably.

14. For examples of egalitarian marriage contracts for different types of couples, see Weitzman 1974, 1278–88, and for a description of one couple's scrupulously equal financial arrangements, see Millman 1991, 165–70.

15. No society can be structured for equality that uses thought policing. Societies have too often suppressed categories of people on the justification of sexual or moral purity. Conversely, if people wanted to structure their lives around the principles of fundamentalist Judaism, Christianity, or Islam, they would have to be free to do so, but not to impose their views on any other groups.

16. Also see Ecker 1985.

17. Also see Cockburn 1991, 227–36; Ferguson 1984, 154–212. Without the separatism, these are similar to the values of lesbian feminism—egalitarianism, collectivism, an ethic of care, respect for experiential knowledge, pacifism, and cooperation (Taylor and Rupp 1993).

18. If a male passed as a woman or a female as a man, and no one knew, as has happened in many times and places, and still no doubt does happen, it would not matter, since the exchange is between the members of the social categories women and men.

19. In some organizations I belong to, such an arrangement is used to ensure the sometime election of *white men.*

20. Feminists have raised these epistemological questions particularly with regard to science, which is supposed to be objective but actually reflects the values of dominant men. See Haraway 1988; Harding 1986, 1991; Keller 1985; Longino 1990. For an African-American feminist perspective on law, see P. J. Williams 1991, and on social thought, see P. H. Collins 1990. Also see D. E. Smith 1987a and 1990 on the production of knowledge and power.

21. Block and Neuls-Bates (1979) found three thousand compositions by American women published from colonial times to 1920.

22. Remember that the Olympics had no marathon competition for women until fairly recently; that women's endurance is ignored in long-distance swimming and in tennis, and that in general, the rules for women's competition are based more on what the men who make the rules think women can or should do in sports than on women's actual capabilities.

23. Durova 1989; Freeman and Bond 1992; Graham 1977; Wheelwright 1989.

24. In a review of "above-the-counter sex fiction," Kendrick (1992, 36) calls Ann Rice's novels "omnisexual."

25. Jesus Christ included women as founders and leaders of congregations, but within two hundred years the established church excluded women from the priesthood, just as the Jews did, and gave husbands authority over their wives, just as the Romans did (Farrell 1992; Fiorenza 1979). Judith Plaskow (1990, 36–48) argues that Judaic history has written women leaders out as well, and that there is evidence of their leadership roles in the synagogue through the sixth century C.E.

26. See Marge Piercy's communities in *Woman on the Edge of Time* (1976).

27. On the power of the erotic, see Lorde 1984; on sexuality and spiritual passion, see Plaskow 1990, 191–97; on the definition of *jouissance* as "total access, total participation, as well as total ecstasy," see Cixous and Clément [1975] 1986, 165–66.

BIBLIOGRAPHY

The full title of *Signs* is *Signs: Journal of Women in Culture and Society.*

AAUW Report. 1992. How schools shortchange girls: A study of major findings on girls and education. Washington, D.C.: American Association of University Women Educational Foundation.

Abel, Elizabeth. 1981. (E)Merging identities: The dynamics of female friendship in contemporary fiction by women. *Signs* 6:413–35.

Abel, Emily K., and Margaret K. Nelson (eds.). 1990. *Circles of care: Work and identity in women's lives.* Albany: State University of New York Press.

Abplanalp, Judith M. 1983. Premenstrual syndrome: A selective review. *Women and Health* 8(2–3):107–23.

Abramovitz, Mimi. 1988. *Regulating the lives of women: Social welfare policy from colonial times to the present.* Boston, Mass.: South End Press.

Ackelsberg, Martha A. 1991. *Free women of Spain: Anarchism and the struggle for the emancipation of women.* Bloomington: Indiana University Press.

Acker, Joan. 1988. Class, gender, and the relations of distribution. *Signs* 13:473–97.

———. 1989a. *Doing comparable worth: Gender, class, and pay equity.* Philadelphia: Temple University Press.

———. 1989b. Making gender visible. In *Feminism and sociological theory,* edited by Ruth A. Wallace. Newbury Park, Calif.: Sage.

———. 1990. Hierarchies, jobs, and bodies: A theory of gendered organizations. *Gender & Society* 4:139–58.

———. 1991. Thinking about wages: The gendered wage gap in Swedish banks. *Gender & Society* 5:390–407.

Acker, Joan, Kate Barry, and Joke Esseveld. 1981. Feminism, female friends, and the reconstruction of intimacy. In *Research in the interweave of social roles: Friendship,* edited by Helena Z. Lopata, vol. 2. Greenwich, Conn.: JAI Press.

Acosta-Belén, Edna, and Christine E. Bose. 1990. From structural subordination to empowerment: Women and development in Third World contexts. *Gender & Society* 4:299–320.

Adams, David. 1988. Treatment models of men who batter: A profeminist analysis. In Yllö and Bograd.

Adler, Nancy J., and Dafna N. Izraeli. 1988a. Women in management world-wide. In Adler and Izraeli (eds).

———— (eds.). 1988b. *Women in management world-wide.* Armonk, N.Y.: M. E. Sharpe.

———— (eds.). 1993. *Competitive frontiers: women managers in a global economy.* Oxford and New York: Basil Blackwell.

Agassi, Judith Buber. 1989. Theories of gender equality: Lessons from the kibbutz. *Gender & Society* 3:160–86.

Ahearn, Nancy C., and Elizabeth L. Scott. 1981. *Career outcomes in a matched sample of men and women Ph.D.s: An analytical report.* Washington, D.C.: National Academy Press.

Ahmed, Leila. 1992. *Women and gender in Islam.* New Haven: Yale University Press.

Alcoff, Linda. 1988. Cultural feminism versus post-structuralism: The identity crisis in feminist theory. *Signs* 13:405–36.

Allen, Jeffner (ed.). 1990. *Lesbian philosophies and cultures.* Albany: State University of New York Press.

Allen, Sheila, and Carol Wolkowitz. 1987. *Homeworking: Myths and realities.* London: Macmillan.

Almquist, Elizabeth M. 1987. Labor market gendered inequality in minority groups. *Gender & Society* 1:400–14.

Althouse, Ann. 1989. Dare to contemplate the woman gymnast. Letter to Editor, *New York Times,* 7 August.

Amadiume, Ifi. 1987. *Male daughters, female husbands: Gender and sex in an African society.* London: Zed Books.

Amir, Delila, and Orly Biniamin. 1992. Abortion approval as a ritual of symbolic control. In *The criminalization of a woman's body,* edited by Clarice Feinman. Binghamton, N.Y.: Harrington Park Press.

Ammer, Christine. 1980. *Unsung: A history of women in American music.* Westport, Conn.: Greenwood Press.

Amott, Teresa L. 1990. Black women and AFDC: Making entitlement out of necessity. In Gordon (ed.).

Amott, Teresa, and Julie Matthaei. 1988. The promise of comparable worth: A socialist-feminist perspective. *Socialist Review* 18(2):101–17.

————. 1991. *Race, gender, and work: A multicultural economic history of women in the United States.* Boston, Mass.: South End Press.

Anderson, Bonnie S., and Judith P. Zinsser. 1988. *A history of their own: Women in Europe from prehistory to the present.* Vols. 1 and 2. New York: Harper & Row.

Anderson, Elijah. 1990. *Streetwise: Race, class and change in an urban community.* Chicago: University of Chicago Press.

Andors, Phyllis. 1983. *The unfinished liberation of Chinese women, 1949–1980.* Bloomington: Indiana University Press.

Andrews, Edmund A. 1990. Patents: An exhibition of inventions by women. *New York Times,* 20 January.

Angier, Natalie. 1991. In fish, social status goes right to the brain. *New York Times,* Science Section, 12 November.

——. 1992a. 2 experts say women who run may overtake men. *New York Times,* Science Section, 7 January.

——. 1992b. Hyenas' hormone flow puts females in charge. *New York Times,* Science Section, 1 September.

Anker, Richard. 1985. Comparative survey. In *Working women in socialist countries: The fertility connection,* edited by Valentina Bodrova and Richard Anker. Geneva: International Labor Office.

Antal, Ariane Berthoin, and Dafna N. Izraeli. 1993. Women in management: An international comparison. In Fagenson.

Apple, R. W., Jr. 1991. Spectacle of degradation. *New York Times,* 13 October.

Applebome, Peter. 1991. Ripples of pain as U.S. dips deeper into military. *New York Times,* 31 January.

——. 1992. A year after victory, joy is a ghost. *New York Times,* 16 January.

Applewhite, Harriet Branson, and Darline Gay Levy (eds.). 1990. *Women and politics in the age of the democratic revolution.* Ann Arbor: University of Michigan Press.

Ardener, Shirley. 1987. A note on gender Iconography: The vagina. In *The cultural construction of sexuality,* edited by Pat Caplan. London and New York: Tavistock.

Arendell, Terry. 1986. *Mothers and divorce: Legal, economic and social dilemmas.* Berkeley: University of California Press.

Arguëlles, Lourdes, and B. Ruby Rich. 1984. Homosexuality, homophobia, and revolution: Notes toward an understanding of the Cuban lesbian and gay male experience. Part 1. *Signs* 9:683–99.

Ariès, Philippe. 1962. *Centuries of childhood: A social history of family life,* translated by Robert Baldick. New York: Vintage.

Aronson, Lisa. 1991. African women in the visual arts. *Signs* 16:550–74.

Arthur, Marylin. 1977. "Liberated" women: The classical era. In Bridenthal and Koonz.

Ashe, Marie. 1991. Abortion of narrative: A reading of the judgment of Solomon. *Yale Journal of Law and Feminism* 4:81–92.

Ashley, Jo Ann. 1976. *Hospitals, paternalism, and the role of the nurse.* New York: Teachers College Press.

Astin, Helen S. 1991. Citation classics: Women's and men's perceptions of their contributions to science. In Zuckerman, Cole, and Bruer.

Attwood, Lynne. 1990. *The new Soviet man and woman: Sex-role socialization in the USSR.* Bloomington: Indiana University Press.

Auping, Michael. 1992. *Jenny Holzer.* New York: Universe.

Austad, Steven N. 1986. Changing sex nature's way. *International Wildlife,* May-June, 29.

Auster, Ellen R., and Robert Drazin. 1988. Sex inequality at higher levels in the hierarchy: An intraorganizational perspective. *Sociological Inquiry* 58:216–27.

Ayres, B. Drummond, Jr. 1991. Old stories with new twists told by Persian Gulf troops. *New York Times,* 11 March.

Baca Zinn, Maxine. 1989. Family, race, and poverty in the eighties. *Signs* 14:856–74.

————. 1990. Family, feminism, and race in America. *Gender & Society* 4:68–82.

Badinter, Elisabeth. 1981. *Mother love, myth and reality: Motherhood in modern history.* New York: Macmillan.

————. 1989. *The unopposite sex: The end of the gender battle,* translated by Barbara Wright. New York: Harper & Row.

Baker, Susan. 1980. Biological influences on sex and gender. *Signs* 6:80–96.

Bal, Mieke. 1986. Sexuality, sin, and sorrow: The emergence of female character (a reading of Genesis 1–3). In Suleiman.

Baril, Joan. 1990. The center of the backlash: Media's shifted focus on massacre increases misogyny. *Off Our Backs,* April, 13–15.

Barkalow, Carol, with Andrea Raab. 1990. *In the men's house.* New York: Poseidon Press.

Barnett, Bernice McNair. 1993. Invisible southern Black women leaders of the civil rights movement: The triple constraints of gender, race, and class. *Gender & Society* 7:162–82.

Barnett, Elyse Ann. 1988. *Le edad critica:* The positive experience of menopause in a small Peruvian town. In *Women and health: Cross-cultural perspectives,* edited by Patricia Whelehan and contributors. Granby, Mass.: Bergin & Garvey.

Baron, Ava. 1987. Contested terrain revisited: Technology and gender definitions of work in the printing industry, 1850–1920. In B. D. Wright.

———— (ed.). 1991. *Work engendered: Toward a new history of American labor.* Ithaca, N.Y.: Cornell University Press.

Baron, James N., and William T. Bielby. 1985. Organizational barriers to gender equality: Sex segregation of jobs and opportunities. In Rossi (ed.).

Baron, James N., Brian S. Mittman, and Andrew E. Newman. 1991. Targets of opportunity: Organizational and environmental determinants of gender integration within the California civil service, 1979–1985. *American Journal of Sociology* 96:1362–1401.

Baron, James N., and Andrew E. Newman. 1990. For what it's worth: Organizations, occupations, and the value of the work done by women and nonwhites. *American Sociological Review* 55:155–75.

Baron, Larry, and Murray A. Straus. 1987. Four theories of rape: A macrosociological analysis. *Social Problems* 34:467–89.

Barrett, Michèle. [1980] 1988. *Women's oppression today: The Marxist/feminist encounter.* Rev. ed. London: Verso.

Barry, Kathleen. 1979. *Female sexual slavery.* Englewood Cliffs, N.J.: Prentice-Hall.

Barstow, Anne. 1978. The uses of archeology for women's history: James Mellaart's work on the Neolithic goddess at Çatal Hüyük. *Feminist Studies* 4:7–18.

Bart, Pauline B., and Patricia H. O'Brien. 1985. *Stopping rape: Successful survival strategies.* New York: Pergamon.

Bartlett, Katharine T., and Rosanne Kennedy (eds.). 1991. *Feminist legal theory: Readings in law and gender.* Boulder, Colo.: Westview Press.

Baruch, Elaine Hoffman. 1991. *Women, love, and power: Literary and psychoanalytic perspectives.* New York: New York University Press.

Battersby, Christine. 1989. *Gender and genius: Towards a feminist aesthetics.* Bloomington: Indiana University Press.

Baulieu, Etienne-Emile Baulieu, with Mort Rosenblum. 1991. *The "abortion pill": RU-486, a woman's choice.* New York: Simon & Schuster.

Bebel, August. [1904] 1970. *Woman under socialism,* translated by Daniel de Leon. New York: Source Book Press.

Beck, Evelyn Torton (ed.). 1982. *Nice Jewish girls: A lesbian anthology.* Watertown, Mass.: Persephone Press.

Becker, Howard S. 1982. *Art worlds.* Berkeley: University of California Press.

Beechey, Veronica. 1987. *Unequal work.* London: Verso.

Beechey, Veronica, and Tessa Perkins. 1987. *A matter of hours: Women, part-time work and the labor market.* Minneapolis: University of Minnesota Press.

Beer, William R. 1983. *Househusbands: Men and housework in American families.* New York: Praeger.

Bellingham, Bruce. 1986. Institution and family: An alternative view of nineteenth-century child saving. *Social Problems* 6:S33-S57.

Bem, Sandra Lipsitz. 1981. Gender schema theory: A cognitive account of sex typing. *Psychological Review* 88:354–64.

———. 1983. Gender schema theory and its implications for child development: Raising gender-aschematic children in a gender-schematic society. *Signs* 8:598–616.

———. 1993. *The lenses of gender: Transforming the debate on sexual inequality.* New Haven: Yale University Press.

Bería, Lourdes and Martha Roldán. 1987. *The crossroads of class and gender: Industrial homework, subcontracting, and household dynamics in Mexico City.* Chicago: University of Chicago Press.

Bería, Lourdes, and Gita Sen. 1981. Accumulation, reproduction, and women's role in economic development: Boserup revisited. *Signs* 7:279–98.

———. 1982. Class and gender inequalities and women's role in economic development: Theoretical and practical implications. *Feminist Studies* 8:157–76.

Bería, Lourdes, and Catharine B. Stimpson (eds.). 1987. *Women, households, and the economy.* New Brunswick, N.J.: Rutgers University Press.

Benjamin, Jessica. 1988. *The bonds of love: Psychoanalysis, feminism, and the problem of domination.* New York: Pantheon.

Bennett, Neil G. (ed.). 1983. *Sex selection of children.* New York: Academic Press.

Bennett, Sheila Kishler, and Leslie B. Alexander. 1987. The mythology of part-time work: Empirical evidence from a study of working mothers. In Bería and Stimpson.

Bennholdt-Thomsen, Veronika. 1981. Subsistence production and extended reproduction. In Young, Wolkowitz, and McCullagh.

———. 1988. Why do housewives continue to be created in the Third World, too? In Mies, Bennholdt-Thomsen, and von Werlhof.

Benokraitis, Nijole V., and Joe R. Feagin. 1986. *Modern sexism: Blatant, subtle, and covert discrimination.* Englewood Cliffs, N.J.: Prentice-Hall.

Benson, Susan Porter. 1986. *Counter cultures: Saleswomen, managers, and customers in American department stores, 1890–1940.* Urbana: University of Illinois Press.

Benston, Margaret. 1969. The political economy of women's liberation. *Monthly Review* 21(Sept.):13–27.

Berger, Iris. 1990. Gender, race, and political empowerment: South African canning workers, 1940–1960. *Gender & Society* 4:398–420.

Berger, John. 1977. *Ways of seeing.* New York: Penguin.

Berger, Ronald, Patricia Searles, and Charles Cottle. 1991. *Feminism and pornography.* New York: Praeger.

Berk, Sarah Fenstermaker (ed.). 1980. *Women and household labor.* Newbury Park, Calif.: Sage.

———. 1985. *The gender factory: The apportionment of work in American households.* New York: Plenum.

Bernard, Jessie. 1981. *The female world.* New York: Free Press.

Bernstein, Richard. 1986. France jails 2 in odd case of espionage. *New York Times,* 11 May.

Berryman, Sue E., and Linda J. Waite. 1987. Young women's choice of nontraditional occupations. In Bose and Spitze.

Bertin, Joan E. 1989. Women's health and women's rights: Reproductive hazards in the workplace. In Ratcliff et al.

Bérubé, Allan. 1989. Marching to a different drummer: Gay and lesbian GIs in World War II. In Duberman, Vicinus, and Chauncey.

Bérubé, Allan, and John D'Emilio. 1984. The military and lesbians during the McCarthy years. *Signs* 9:759–75

Bettelheim, Bruno. 1962. *Symbolic wounds: Puberty rites and the envious male.* London: Thames and Hudson.

Bielby, Denise, and William T. Bielby. 1988. She works hard for the money: Household responsibilities and the allocation of work effort. *American Journal of Sociology* 93:1031–59.

Bielby, William, and James Baron. 1984. A woman's place is with other women: Sex segregation within organizations. In Reskin.

———. 1986. Men and women at work: Sex segregation and statistical discrimination. *American Journal of Sociology* 91:759–99.

———. 1987. Undoing discrimination: Job integration and comparable worth. In Bose and Spitze.

Biersack, Aletta. 1984. Paiela "women-men": The reflexive foundations of gender ideology. *American Ethnologist* 11:118–38.

Billings, Dwight B., and Thomas Urban. 1982. The socio-medical construction of transsexualism: An interpretation and critique. *Social Problems* 29:266–82.

Biology and Gender Study Group. 1988. The importance of feminist critique for contemporary cell biology. *Hypatia* 3:61–76.

Bird, Chloe E., and Allen M. Fremont. 1991. Gender, time use, and health. *Journal of Health and Social Behavior* 32:114–29.

Birdwhistell, Ray L. 1970. *Kinesics and context: Essays on body motion communication.* Philadelphia: University of Pennsylvania Press.

Birke, Linda. 1986. *Women, feminism and biology: The feminist challenge.* New York: Methuen.

Birrell, Susan J. 1988. Discourses on the gender/sport relationship: From women in sport to gender relations. In *Exercise and sport science reviews,* edited by Kent Pandolf, vol. 16. New York: Macmillan.

Birrell, Susan J., and Sheryl L. Cole. 1990. Double fault: Renée Richards and the construction and naturalization of difference. *Sociology of Sport Journal* 7:1–21.

Bishop, Katherine. 1991. Not quite a wedding, but quite a day for couples by the Bay. *New York Times,* 15 February.

Blachford, Gregg. 1981. Male dominance and the gay world. In Plummer (ed.).

Blackman, Julie. 1989. *Intimate violence: A study of injustice.* New York: Columbia University Press.

Blackwood, Evelyn. 1984. Sexuality and gender in certain Native American tribes: The case of cross-gender females. *Signs* 10:27–42.

———. 1985. Breaking the mirror: The construction of lesbianism and the anthropological discourse on homosexuality. *Journal of Homosexuality* 11(3–4):1–17.

Blair, Diane D. 1989. *The handmaid's tale* and *The birth dearth*: Prophecy, prescription and public policy. *Journal of Political Science* 17(1–2):99–113.

Blankenship, Kim M., Beth Rushing, Suzanne Onorato, and Renée White. 1993. Reproductive technologies and the U.S. courts. *Gender & Society* 7:8–31.

Bleier, Ruth. 1984. *Science and gender.* New York: Oxford University Press.

Bleier, Ruth, Stacey J. Keen, Julianne Imperato-McGinley, and Ralph E. Peterson. 1979. Why does a pseudohermaphrodite want to be a man? *New England Journal of Medicine* 301:839–40.

Block, Adrienne Fried, and Carol Neuls-Bates (eds.). 1979. *Women in American music: A bibliography of music and literature.* Westport, Conn.: Greenwood Press.

Bloom, Anne R. 1991. Women in the defense forces. In *Calling the equality bluff: Women in Israel,* edited by Barbara Swirski and Marilyn P. Safir. New York: Teacher's College Press.

Bloom, Harold. 1990. *The book of J,* translated by David Rosenberg. New York: Grove Weidenfeld.

Blum, Linda M. 1991. *Between feminism and labor: The significance of the comparable worth movement.* Berkeley: University of California Press.

Blum, Linda M., and Vicki Smith. 1988. Women's mobility in the corporation: A critique of the politics of optimism. *Signs* 13:528–45.

Blumberg, Rae Lesser. 1976. Kibbutz women: From the fields of revolution to the laundries of discontent. In *Women of the world,* edited by Lynne B. Iglitzin and Ruth Ross. Santa Barbara, Calif.: ABC-Clio.

———. 1978. *Stratification: Socioeconomic and sexual inequality.* Dubuque, Iowa: Wm. C. Brown.

———. 1984. A general theory of gender stratification. In *Sociological theory 1984,* edited by Randall Collins. San Francisco: Jossey-Bass.

———. 1989. Making the case for the gender variable: Women and the wealth and well-being of nations. Washington, D.C.: Office of Women in Development, U.S. Agency for International Development.

————. 1991a. Income under female versus male control: Hypotheses from a theory of gender stratification and data from the third world. In Blumberg (ed.).

————. (ed.). 1991b. *Gender, family, and economy: The triple overlap.* Newbury Park, Calif.: Sage.

Blumberg, Rae Lesser, and Marion Tolbert Coleman. 1989. A theoretical look at the gender balance of power in the American couple. *Journal of Family Issues* 10:225–50.

Blumstein, Philip, and Pepper Schwartz. 1983. *American couples: Money, work, sex.* New York: Pocketbooks.

————. 1991. Money and ideology: Their impact on power and the division of household labor. In Blumberg (ed.).

Bobroff, Anne. 1983. Russian working women: Sexuality and bonding patterns in the politics of daily life. In Snitow, Stansell, and Thompson.

Bock, Gisela, and Pat Thane (eds.). 1991. *Maternity and gender policies: Women and the rise of the European welfare states, 1880s-1950s.* New York and London: Routledge.

Bolin, Anne. 1987. Transsexualism and the limits of traditional analysis. *American Behavioral Scientist* 31:41–65.

————. 1988. *In search of Eve: Transsexual rites of passage.* South Hadley, Mass.: Bergin & Garvey.

Bologh, Roslyn Wallach. 1990. *Love or greatness: Max Weber and masculine thinking--a feminist inquiry.* London: Unwin Hyman.

Booth-Butterfield, Melanie, and Steve Booth-Butterfield. 1988. Jock talk: Cooperation and competition within a university women's basketball team. In *Women communicating: Studies of women's talk,* edited by Barbara Bate and Anita Taylor. Norwood, N.J.: Ablex.

Boris, Eileen, and Peter Bardaglio. 1987. Gender, race, and class: The impact of the state on the family and the economy, 1790–1945. In Gerstel and Gross.

Boris, Eileen, and Cynthia R. Daniels. 1989. *Homework: Historical and contemporary perspectives on paid labor at home.* Urbana: University of Illinois Press.

Bose, Christine E. 1987. Devaluing women's work: The undercount of women's employment in 1900 and 1980. In *Hidden aspects of women's work,* edited by Christine E. Bose, Roslyn Feldberg, Natalie Sokoloff, with the Women and Work Research Group. New York: Praeger.

Bose, Christine E., and Peter H. Rossi. 1983. Gender and jobs: Prestige standings of occupations as affected by gender. *American Sociological Review* 48:316–30.

Bose, Christine E., and Glenna Spitze (eds.). 1987. *Ingredients for women's employment policy.* Albany: State University of New York Press.

Boserup, Ester. 1970. *Women's role in economic development.* New York: St. Martin's Press.

Boswell, John. 1988. *The kindness of strangers: The abandonment of children in Western Europe from late antiquity to the Renaissance.* New York: Pantheon.

————. 1990a. Sexual and ethical categories in premodern Europe. In McWhirter, Sanders and Reinisch.

————. 1990b. Concepts, experience, and sexuality. *Differences: A Journal of Feminist Cultural Studies* 2(1):67–87.

Bourdieu, Pierre. 1989. Social space and symbolic power. *Sociological Theory* 7:14–25.

————. [1980] 1990. *The logic of practice.* Stanford, Calif.: Stanford University Press.

Bourdieu, Pierre, and Jean-Claude Passeron. [1970] 1977. *Reproduction in education, society and culture,* translated by Richard Nice. Newbury Park, Calif.: Sage.

Boutilier, Mary A., and Lucinda SanGiovanni. 1983. *The sporting woman.* Champaign, Ill.: Human Kinetics.

Boydston, Jeanne. 1986. To earn her daily bread: Housework and antebellum working-class subsistence. *Radical History Review* 35:7–25.

Bozett, Frederick W. (ed.). 1987. *Gay and lesbian parents.* New York: Praeger.

Bradley, Harriet. 1986. Technological change, management strategies, and the development of gender-based job segregation in the labor process. In Knights and Willmott.

Bray, Rosemary L. 1991. Taking sides against ourselves. *New York Times Magazine,* 17 November.

Breines, Wini, and Linda Gordon. 1983. The new scholarship on family violence. *Signs* 8:490–531.

Brenner, Johanna. 1987. Feminist political discourses: Radical versus liberal approaches to the feminization of poverty and comparable worth. *Gender & Society* 4:447–65.

Brewer, Rose M. 1988. Black women in poverty: Some comments on female-headed families. *Signs* 13:331–39.

Bridenthal, Renate. 1976. The dialectics of production and reproduction in history. *Radical America* 10(March-April):3–11.

Bridenthal, Renate, Atina Grossman, and Marion Kaplan. 1984. *When biology became destiny: Women in Weimar and Nazi Germany.* New York: Monthly Review Press.

Bridenthal, Renate, and Claudia Koonz (eds.). 1977. *Becoming visible: Women in European history.* Boston: Houghton Mifflin.

Bridges, William P., and Robert L. Nelson. 1989. Markets in hierarchies: Organizational and market influences on gender inequality in a state pay system. *American Journal of Sociology* 95:616–58.

Brinton, Mary C. 1989. Gender stratification in contemporary Japan. *American Sociological Review* 54:549–64.

Broad, William J. 1992. Recipe for love: A boy, a girl, a spacecraft. *New York Times,* Science Section, 11 February.

Brod, Harry (ed.). 1987. *The making of masculinities.* Boston: Allen & Unwin.

————. 1990. Pornography and the alienation of male sexuality. In Hearn and Morgan.

Broder, Sherri. 1988. Child care or neglect? Baby farming in late nineteenth-century Philadelphia. *Gender & Society* 2:128–48.

Brody, Jane E. 1979. Benefits of transsexual surgery disputed as leading hospital halts the procedure. *New York Times,* 2 October.

Brown, Elsa Barkley. 1989. African-American women's quilting. *Signs* 14:921–29.

Brown, Judith K. 1970. A note on the division of labor by sex. *American Anthropologist* 72:1074–78.

————. 1982. A cross-cultural exploration of the end of the childbearing years. In Voda, Dinnerstein, and O'Donnell.

Brown, Wendy. 1992. Finding the man in the state. *Feminist Studies* 18:7–34.

Browne, Angela. 1987. *When battered women kill*. New York: Free Press.

Browning, Genia. 1985. Soviet politics: Where are the women? In Holland.

———. 1987. *Women and politics in the USSR: Consciousness raising and Soviet women's groups*. New York: St. Martin's Press.

Brownmiller, Susan. 1975. *Against our will: Men, women and rape*. New York: Simon & Schuster.

Brozan, Nadine. 1978. Training linked to disruption of female reproductive cycle. *New York Times,* 17 April.

Brush, Lisa D. 1990. Violent acts and injurious outcomes in married couples: Methodological issues in the National Survey of Families and Households. *Gender & Society* 4:56–67.

Brydon, Lynn, and Sylvia Chant. 1989. *Women in the Third World: Gender issues in rural and urban areas*. New Brunswick, N.J.: Rutgers University Press.

Buckley, Mary. 1989a. The "woman question" in the contemporary Soviet Union. In Kruks, Rapp, and Young.

———. 1989b. *Women and ideology in the Soviet Union*. Ann Arbor: University of Michigan Press.

Buckley, Thomas, and Alma Gottlieb (eds.). 1988. *Blood magic: The anthropology of menstruation*. Berkeley: University of California Press.

Buhle, Mari Jo. 1983. *Women and American socialism, 1870–1920*. Urbana: University of Illinois Press.

Bullen, A. H. (ed.). 1935. *The works of Thomas Middleton,* vol. 4. London: John C. Nimmo.

Bullough, Vern, and Martha Voght. 1973. Women, menstruation and nineteenth-century medicine. *Bulletin of the History of Medicine* 47:66–82.

Bunster, Ximenia, and Elsa M. Chaney. 1989. *Sellers and servants: Working women in Lima, Peru*. Granby, Mass.: Bergin & Garvey.

Burawoy, Michael, and János Lukács. 1992. *The radiant past: Ideology and reality in Hungary's road to capitalism*. Chicago: University of Chicago Press.

Burman, Chila. 1988. There have always been great Blackwomen artists. In *Visibly female: Feminism and art today,* edited by Hilary Robinson. New York: Universe Books.

Burris, Beverly H. 1989. Technology and gender in the workplace. *Social Problems* 36:165–80.

Butler, Judith. 1990. *Gender trouble: Feminism and the subversion of identity*. New York and London: Routledge.

Butler, Octavia E. 1987. *Dawn: Xenogenesis*. New York: Popular Library.

———. 1988. *Adulthood rites*. New York: Popular Library.

———. 1989. *Imago*. New York: Popular Library.

Byerly, Victoria. 1986. *Hard times cotton mill girls: Personal histories of womanhood and poverty in the South*. Ithaca, N.Y.: ILR Press.

Calasanti, Toni M., and Carol A. Bailey. 1991. Gender inequality and the division of household labor in the United States and Sweden: A socialist-feminist approach. *Social Problems* 38:34–53.

Calhoun, Lawrence G., and James W. Selby. 1980. Voluntary childlessness, involuntary childlessness, and having children: A study of social perceptions. *Family Relations* 29:181–83.

Callan, Victor J., Belinda Kloske, Yoshihisa Kashima, and John F. Hennesscy. 1988. Toward understanding women's decisions to continue or to stop *in vitro* fertilization: The role of social, psychological, and background factors. *Journal of In Vitro Fertilization and Embryo Transfer* 5:363–69.

Callender, Charles, and Lee M. Kochems. 1985. Men and not-men: Male gender-mixing statuses and homosexuality. *Journal of Homosexuality* 11(3–4):165–78.

Cancian, Francesca M. 1985. Gender politics: Love and power in the private and public spheres. In Rossi (ed.).

———. 1987. *Love in America: Gender and self-development.* New York: Cambridge University Press.

Cancian, Francesca M., and Steven L. Gordon. 1988. Changing emotion norms in marriage: Love and anger in U.S. women's magazines since 1900. *Gender & Society* 2:308–42.

Cantor, Dorothy W., and Toni Bernay with Jean Stoess. 1992. *Women in power: The secrets of leadership.* Boston: Houghton Mifflin.

Cantor, Milton, and Bruce Laurie (eds.). 1977. *Class, sex, and the woman worker.* Westport, Conn.: Greenwood Press.

Caputi, Jane. 1987. *The age of sex crime.* Bowling Green, Ohio: Bowling Green University Popular Press.

———. 1989. The sexual politics of murder. *Gender & Society* 3:437–56.

Carli, Linda L. 1991. Gender, status, and influence. *Advances in Group Processes* 8:89–113.

Carlson, Alison. 1991. When is a woman not a woman? *Women's Sport and Fitness,* March, 24–29.

Carrigan, Tim, Bob Connell, and John Lee. 1987. Toward a new sociology of masculinity. In Brod.

Carter, Michael J., and Susan Boslego Carter. 1981. Women's recent progress in the professions or, women get a ticket to ride after the gravy train has left the station. *Feminist Studies* 7:477–504.

Carter, Valerie J. 1987. Office technology and relations of control in clerical work organization. In B. D. Wright et al.

Caulfield, Minna Davis. 1985. Sexuality in human evolution: What is "natural" in sex? *Feminist Studies* 11:343–63.

Chadwick, Whitney. 1988. Women artists and the politics of representation. In Raven, Langer, and Frueh.

Chafetz, Janet Saltzman. 1980. Conflict resolution in marriage: Toward a theory of spousal strategies and marital dissolution rates. *Journal of Family Issues* 1:397–42.

———. 1984. *Sex and advantage: A comparative macro-structural theory of sex stratification.* Totowa, N.J.: Rowman & Allenheld.

———. 1990. *Gender equity: An integrated theory of stability and change.* Newbury Park, Calif.: Sage.

Chafetz, Janet Saltzman, and Anthony Gary Dworkin. 1986. *Female revolt: Women's movements in world and historical perspective.* Totowa, N.J.: Rowman & Allenheld.

Chancer, Lynn. 1987. New Bedford, Massachusetts, March 6, 1983–March 22, 1984: The "before and after" of a group rape, *Gender & Society* 1:239–60.

Chaney, Elsa M., and Mary García Castro (eds.). 1989. *Muchachas no more: House-hold workers in Latin America and the Caribbean.* Philadelphia: Temple University Press.

Chase, Susan E. 1988. Making sense of "the woman who becomes a man." In *Gender and discourse: The power of talk,* edited by Alexandra Dundas Todd and Sue Fisher. Norwood, N.J.: Ablex.

Chase, Susan E., and Colleen S. Bell. 1990. Ideology, discourse, and gender: How gatekeepers talk about women school superintendents. *Social Problems* 37:163–77.

Chaudhuri, Molly, and Kathleen Daly. 1992. Do restraining orders help? Battered women's experiences with male violence and legal process. In *Domestic violence: The changing criminal justice response,* edited by Eve Buzawa and Carl Buzawa. Westport, Conn.: Greenwood.

Chevillard, Nicole, and Sébastian Leconte. 1986. The dawn of lineage societies: The origins of women's oppression. In Coontz and Henderson.

Childe, Gordon. 1942. *What happened in history.* Harmondsworth, England: Penguin.

Chinchilla, Norma Stoltz. 1990. Revolutionary popular feminism in Nicaragua: Ar-ticulating class, gender, and national sovereignty. *Gender & Society* 4:370–97.

Chodorow, Nancy. 1974. Family structure and feminine personality. In Rosaldo and Lamphere.

———. 1976. Oedipal asymmetries and heterosexual knots. *Social Problems* 23:454–68.

———. 1978. *The reproduction of mothering.* Berkeley: University of California Press.

———. 1989. *Feminism and psychoanalytic theory.* New Haven: Yale University Press.

Chow, Esther Ngan-Ling. 1987. The development of feminist consciousness among Asian American women. *Gender & Society* 1:284–99.

Christensen, Kathleen. 1988. *Women and home-based work: The unspoken contract.* New York: Holt.

Christian, Barbara 1988. The race for theory. *Feminist Studies* 14:67–79.

Cixous, Hélène. 1976. The laugh of the Medusa, translated by Keith Cohen and Paula Cohen. *Signs* 1:875–93.

———. 1981. Castration or decapitation? translated by Annette Kuhn. *Signs* 7:41–55.

Cixous, Hélène, and Catherine Clément. [1975] 1986. *The newly born woman,* trans-lated by Betsy Wing. Minneapolis: University of Minnesota Press.

Clark, Alice. [1919] 1982. *Working life of women in the seventeenth century.* London: Routledge.

Clark, Anna. 1987. *Women's silence, men's violence: Sexual assault in England, 1770–1845.* New York and London: Pandora.

Clément, Catherine. [1979] 1988. *Opéra, or the undoing of women,* translated by Betsy Wing. Minneapolis: University of Minnesota Press.

Clement, Priscilla Ferguson. 1992. Nineteenth-century welfare policy, programs, and poor women: Philadelphia as a case study. *Feminist Studies* 18:35–58.

Clements, Barbara Evans. 1979. *Bolshevik feminist: The life of Aleksandra Kollantai.* Bloomington: Indiana University Press.

Clements, Barbara Evans, Barbara Alpern Engel, and Christine D. Worobec (eds.). 1991. *Russia's women: Accommodation, resistance, transformation.* Berkeley: University of California Press.

Clinton, Catherine. 1982. *The plantation mistress.* New York: Pantheon.

Clymer, Adam. 1991. A home front with no parents at home. *New York Times,* 16 February.

Cockburn, Cynthia. 1983. *Brothers: Male dominance and technological change.* London: Pluto Press.

————. 1985. *Machinery of dominance: Women, men and technical know-how.* London: Pluto Press.

————. 1991. *In the way of women: Men's resistance to sex equality in organizations.* Ithaca, N.Y.: ILR Press.

Cohen, Sherrill, and Nadine Taub (eds.). 1989. *Reproductive laws for the 1990s.* Clifton, N.J.: Humana Press.

Cohen, Theodore F. 1987. Remaking men: Men's experiences becoming and being husbands and fathers and their implications for reconceptualizing men's lives. *Journal of Family Issues* 8:57–77.

Cohen, Yinon, Shlomit Bechar, and Rebecca Raijman. 1987. Occupational sex segregation in Israel, 1972–1983. *Israel Social Science Research* 5(1–2):97–106.

Cohn, Samuel. 1985. *The process of occupational sex-typing: The feminization of clerical labor in Great Britain.* Philadelphia: Temple University Press.

Cole, Jonathan R. 1979. *Fair science: Women in the scientific community.* New York: Free Press.

Cole, Jonathan R., and Burton Singer. 1991. A theory of limited differences: Explaining the productivity puzzle in science. In Zuckerman, Cole, and Bruer.

Cole, Jonathan R., and Harriet Zuckerman. 1991. Marriage, motherhood, and re-research performance in science. In Zuckerman, Cole, and Bruer.

Coleman, Emily. 1976. Infanticide in the early Middle Ages. In Stuard.

Coleman, Marion Tolbert. 1991. The division of household labor: Suggestions for future empirical consideration and theoretical development. In Blumberg (ed.).

Colette. 1933. *The pure and the impure: A case-book of love,* translated by Edith Dally. New York: Farrar & Rinehart.

Collier, Jane Fishburne. 1988. *Marriage and inequality in classless societies.* Stanford, Calif.: Stanford University Press.

Collier, Jane F., and Michelle Z. Rosaldo. 1981. Politics and gender in simple societies. In Ortner and Whitehead (eds.).

Collins, Jane L. 1990. Unwaged labor in comparative perspective: Recent theories and unanswered questions. In Collins and Gimenez.

Collins, Jane L., and Martha E. Gimenez (eds). 1990. *Work without wages: Comparative studies of domestic labor and self-employment.* Albany: State University of New York Press.

Collins, Patricia Hill. 1989. The social construction of Black feminist thought. *Signs* 14:745–73.

————. 1990. *Black feminist thought: Knowledge, consciousness, and the politics of empowerment.* Boston: Unwin Hyman.

Collinson, David L. 1988. "Engineering humor": Masculinity, joking and conflict in shop-floor relations. *Organization Studies* 9:181–99.

Collinson, David L., and Margaret Collinson. 1989. Sexuality in the workplace: The domination of men's sexuality. In Hearn et al.

Collinson, David L., and David Knights. 1986. "Men only": Theories and practices of job segregation in insurance. In Willmott and Knights.

Collinson, David L., David Knights, and Margaret Collinson. 1990. *Managing to discriminate.* New York and London: Routledge.

Coltrane, Scott. 1988. Father-child relationships and the status of women: A cross-cultural study. *American Journal of Sociology* 93:1060–95.

————. 1989. Household labor and the routine production of gender. *Social Problems* 36:473–90.

————. 1992. The micropolitics of gender in nonindustrial societies. *Gender & Society* 6:86–107.

Coltrane, Scott, and Neal Hickman. 1992. The rhetoric of rights and needs: Moral discourse in the reform of child custody and child support laws. *Social Problems* 39:400–20.

Conkey, Margaret A. 1985. Ritual communication, social elaboration, and the variable trajectories of Paleolithic material culture. In Price and Brown.

Connell, R.[Robert] W. 1987. *Gender and power: Society, the person, and sexual politics.* Stanford, Calif.: Stanford University Press.

————. 1990a. The state, gender, and sexual politics: Theory and appraisal. *Theory and Society* 19:507–44.

————. 1990b. A whole new world: Remaking masculinity in the context of the environmental movement. *Gender & Society* 4:452–78.

————. 1992. A very straight gay: Masculinity, homosexual experience, and gender. *American Sociological Review* 57:735–51.

Cook, Blanche Wiesen. 1977. Female support networks and political activism: Lillian Wald, Crystal Eastman, and Emma Goldman. *Chrysalis* 3(Autumn):43–61.

————. 1979. "Women alone stir my imagination": Lesbianism and the cultural tradition. *Signs* 4:718–39.

————.1992. *Eleanor Roosevelt: Volume One, 1884–1933.* New York: Viking.

Coontz, Stephanie, and Peta Henderson. 1986. Property forms, political power and female labor in the origins of class and state societies. In Coontz and Henderson (eds.).

————(eds.). 1986. *Women's work, men's property: The origins of gender and class.* London: Verso.

Cooper, Helen M., Adrienne Auslander Munich, and Susan Merrill Squier (eds.). 1989. *Arms and the woman: War, gender, and literary representation.* Chapel Hill: University of North Carolina Press.

Corbin, Alain. 1990. *Women for hire: Prostitution and sexuality in France after 1850,* translated by Alan Sheridan. Cambridge, Mass.: Harvard University Press.

Corley, Mary C., and Hans O. Mauksch. 1987. Registered nurses, gender, and commitment. In Statham, Miller, and Mauksch.

Coser, Rose Laub. 1978. The principle of patriarchy: The case of *The Magic Flute*. *Signs* 4:337–48.

———. 1986. Cognitive structure and the use of social space. *Sociological Forum* 1:1–26.

Cott, Nancy F. 1978. Passionlessness: An interpretation of Victorian sexual ideology, 1790–1850. *Signs* 4:219–36.

———. 1987. *The grounding of modern feminism*. New Haven: Yale University Press.

Coverman, Shelley. 1985. Explaining husbands' participation in domestic labor. *Sociological Quarterly* 26:81–97.

Covin, Teresa Joyce, and Christina Christenson Brush. 1991. An examination of male and female attitudes toward career and family issues. *Sex Roles* 25:393–415.

Cowan, Alison Leigh. 1991. Management citadel rocked by unruliness. *New York Times*, Business Section, 26 September.

Cowan, Ruth Schwartz. 1987. Women's work, housework, and history: The historical roots of inequality in work-force participation. In Gerstel and Gross.

Cowart, Jack, Juan Hamilton, and Sarah Greenough (eds.). 1987. *Georgia O'Keeffe: Art and letters*. Washington, D.C.: National Gallery of Art.

Creet, Julia. 1991. Daughter of the movement: The psychodynamics of lesbian s/m fantasy. *Differences: A Journal of Feminist Cultural Studies* 3(2):135–59.

Crenshaw, Kimberlé. 1991. Demarginalizing the intersection of race and sex: A Black feminist critique of antidiscrimination doctrine, feminist theory, and antiracist politics. In Bartlett and Kennedy.

Crimp, Douglas (ed.). 1988. *AIDS: Cultural analysis, cultural activism*. Cambridge, Mass.: MIT Press.

Croll, Elisabeth. 1978. *Feminism and socialism in China*. New York: Schocken.

———. 1981. Women in rural production and reproduction in the Soviet Union, China, Cuba, and Tanzania: Socialist development experiences and case studies. *Signs* 7:361–99.

———. 1983. *Chinese women since Mao*. London: Zed Books.

———. 1984. The exchange of women and property: Marriage in post-revolutionary China. In Hirschon.

Croll, Elisabeth, Delia Davin, and Penny Kane (ed.). 1985. *China's one-child family policy*. New York: St. Martin's Press.

Crompton, Rosemary, and Gareth Jones. 1984. *White-collar proletariat: Deskilling and gender in clerical work*. Philadelphia: Temple University Press.

Crowe, Christine. 1985. "Women want it": *In vitro* fertilization and women's motivations for participation. *Women's Studies International Forum* 8:57–62.

Crutchfield, Will. 1992. A baritone gives voice to a patchwork of emotions. *New York Times*, Arts and Leisure Section, 31 May.

Cucchiari, Salvatore. 1981. The gender revolution and the transition from bisexual horde to patrilocal band: The origins of gender hierarchy. In Ortner and Whitehead (eds.).

Dabbs, James M., Jr., and Neil A. Stokes III. 1975. Beauty is power: The use of space on the sidewalk. *Sociometry* 38:551–57.

Dahl, Tove Stang. 1984. Women's right to money, translated by Gunvor Nyquist. In Holter.

Dahlberg, Frances (ed.). 1981. *Woman the gatherer.* New Haven: Yale University Press.

Dalla Costa, Mariarosa. 1973. *The power of women and the subversion of the community.* 2d ed. Bristol, England: Falling Wall Press.

Dalsimer, Marlyn, and Laurie Nisonoff. 1987. The new economic readjustment policies: Implications for Chinese urban working women. *Review of Radical Political Economics* 16:17–43.

Daly, Mary. 1978. *Gyn/Ecology: The metaethics of radical feminism.* Boston: Beacon Press.

Daly, Mary, and Jane Caputi. 1987. *Intergalactic wickedary of the English language.* Boston: Beacon Press.

Damian, Natalia (ed.). 1990. Feminization of agriculture in Eastern Europe. *International Review of Sociology* 1:71–183.

Daniels, Arlene Kaplan. 1987. Invisible work. *Social Problems* 34:403–15.

————. 1988. *Invisible careers: Women civic leaders from the volunteer world.* Chicago: University of Chicago Press.

Davidoff, Leonore, and Catherine Hall. 1987. *Family fortunes: Men and women of the English middle class, 1780–1850.* Chicago: University of Chicago Press.

Davies, Christie. 1982. Sexual taboos and social boundaries. *American Journal of Sociology* 87:1032–63.

Davies, Margery W. 1982. *Woman's place is at the typewriter: Office work and office workers, 1870–1930.* Philadelphia: Temple University Press.

Davin, Delia. 1973. Women in the liberated areas. In Young (ed.).

Davis, F. James. 1991. *Who is Black? One nation's definition.* University Park: Pennsylvania State University Press.

Davis, Angela Y. 1983. *Women, race and class.* New York: Vintage.

Davis, Fred. 1961. Deviance disavowal: The management of strained interaction by the visibly handicapped. *Social Problems* 9:120–32.

Davis, Madeline, and Elizabeth Lapovsky Kennedy. 1986. Oral history and the study of sexuality in the lesbian community: Buffalo, New York, 1940–1960. *Feminist Studies* 12:7–26.

Davis, Nancy J., and Robert V. Robinson. 1991. Men's and women's consciousness of gender inequality: Austria, West Germany, Great Britain, and the United States. *American Sociological Review* 56:72–84.

Davis, Natalie Zemon. 1975. *Society and culture in early modern France.* Stanford, Calif.: Stanford University Press.

Dawson, Warren R. [1929] 1989. *The custom of couvade.* Dallas, Tex.: Spring.

Dean-Jones, Lesley. 1991. The cultural construct of the female body in classical Greek science. In Pomeroy (ed.).

Deaux, Kay, and Brenda Major. 1987. Putting gender into context: An interactive model of gender-related behavior. *Psychological Review* 94:369–89.

De Beauvoir, Simone. 1953. *The second sex,* translated by H. M. Parshley. New York: Knopf.

De Cecco, John P., and Michael G. Shively. 1983–84. From sexual identity to sexual relationships: A contextual shift. *Journal of Homosexuality* 9(2–3):1–26.

Dekker, Rudolf M., and Lotte C. van de Pol. 1989. *The tradition of female transvestism in early modern Europe.* New York: St. Martin's Press.

Delaisi de Parseval, Geneviève, and Françoise Hurstel. 1987. Paternity "á la française," translated by Helen Dykins. In Lamb (ed.).

Delaney, Janice, Mary Jane Lupton, and Emily Toth. 1977. *The curse: A cultural history of menstruation.* New York: New American Library.

Delany, Samuel R. 1991. Straight talk/street talk. *Differences: A Journal of Feminist Cultural Studies* 3(2):21–38.

De Lauretis, Teresa. 1984. *Alice doesn't: Feminism, semiotics, cinema.* Bloomington: Indiana University Press.

————. 1987. *Technologies of gender.* Bloomington: Indiana University Press.

————. 1989. The essence of the triangle or, taking the risk of essentialism seriously: Feminist theory in Italy, the U.S., and Britain. *Differences: A Journal of Feminist Cultural Studies* 1(2):3–37.

Delphy, Christine, and Diane Leonard. 1992. *Familiar exploitation: A new analysis of marriage in contemporary Western societies.* Cambridge, England: Polity Press.

D'Emilio, John. 1983a. Capitalism and gay identity. In Snitow, Stansell, and Thompson.

————. 1983b. *Sexual politics, sexual communities: The making of a homosexual minority in the United States, 1940–1970.* Chicago: University of Chicago Press.

Derdeyn, Andre P. 1976. Child custody contests in historical perspective. *American Journal of Psychiatry* 133:1369–76.

DeVault, Marjorie L. 1991. *Feeding the family: The social organization of caring as gender work.* Chicago: University of Chicago Press.

Devor, Holly. 1987. Gender blending females: Women and sometimes men. *American Behavioral Scientist* 31:12–40.

————. 1989. *Gender blending: Confronting the limits of duality.* Bloomington: Indiana University Press.

De Waal, Frans. 1984. *Chimpanzee politics: Power and sex among apes.* New York: Harper & Row.

De Witt, Karen. 1991. The evolving concept of sexual harassment. *New York Times,* 13 October.

Dexter, Carolyn R. 1985. Women and the exercise of power in organizations: From ascribed to achieved status. In Larwood, Stromberg, and Gutek.

Dickemann, Mildred. 1984. Concepts and classification in the study of human infanticide: Sectional introduction and some cautionary notes. In Hausfater and Hrdy.

di Leonardo, Micaela. 1987. The female world of cards and holidays: Women, families, and the work of kinship. *Signs* 12:440–53.

Dill, Bonnie Thornton. 1980. "The means to put my children through": Child-rearing goals and strategies among Black female domestic servants. In *The Black woman,* edited by La Frances Rodgers-Rose. Newbury Park, Calif.: Sage.

Dobash, R. Emerson, and Russell Dobash. 1979. *Violence against wives: A case against the patriarchy.* New York: Free Press.

Dobash, Russell P., R. Emerson Dobash, Margo Wilson, and Martin Daly. 1992. The myth of sexual symmetry in marital violence. *Social Problems* 39:71–91.

Docter, Richard F. 1988. *Transvestites and transsexuals: Toward a theory of cross-gender behavior.* New York: Plenum.

Dodd, Alexandra Dundas. 1989. *Intimate adversaries: Cultural conflict between doctors and women patients.* Philadelphia: University of Pennsylvania Press.

Dollimore, Jonathan. 1986. Subjectivity, sexuality, and transgression: The Jacobean connection. *Renaissance Drama,* n.s. 17:53–81.

Dölling, Irene. 1991. Between hope and helplessness: Women in the GDR after the "turning point." *Feminist Review,* no. 39:3–15.

Donato, Katharine M. 1990. Programming for change? The growing demand for women systems analysts. In Reskin and Roos.

Donato, Katharine M., and Patricia A. Roos. 1987. Gender and earnings inequality among computer specialists. In B. D. Wright et al.

Douglas, Mary. 1973. *Natural symbols.* New York: Vintage.

Dovidio, John F., Clifford E. Brown, Karen Heltman, Steve L. Ellyson, and Caroline F. Keating. 1988. Power displays between women and men in discussions of gender-linked tasks: A multichannel study. *Journal of Personality and Social Psychology* 55:580–87.

Dowd, Maureen. 1984. Goodbye male ticket, hello etiquette gap. *New York Times,* 18 July.

———. 1991a. The Senate and sexism. *New York Times,* 8 October.

———. 1991b. Taboo issues of sex and race explode in glare of hearing. *New York Times,* 13 October.

———. 1991c. Image more than reality became issue, losers say. *New York Times,* 16 October.

Draper, Elaine. 1993. Fetal exclusion policies and gendered constructions of suitable work. *Social Problems* 40:90–107.

Duberman, Martin Bauml, Martha Vicinus, and George Chauncey, Jr. (eds.). 1989. *Hidden from history: Reclaiming the gay and lesbian past.* New York: New American Library.

Dublin, Thomas. 1977. Women, work and protest in the early Lowell mills: "The oppressing hand of avarice would enslave us." In Cantor and Laurie.

Duff, Robert W., and Lawrence K. Hong. 1984. Self-images of women bodybuilders. *Sociology of Sport Journal* 2:374–80.

Dugger, Karen. 1988. Social location and gender-role attitudes: A comparison of Black and white women. *Gender & Society* 2:425–48.

Dunfey, Julie. 1984. "Living the principle" of plural marriage: Mormon women, utopia, and female sexuality in the nineteenth century. *Feminist Studies* 10:523–36.

Dunning, Eric. 1986. Sport as a male preserve: Notes on the social sources of masculine identity and its transformations. *Theory, Culture and Society* 3:79–90.

Durova, Nadezhda. 1989. *The cavalry maiden: Journals of a Russian officer in the Napoleonic Wars,* translated by Mary Fleming Zirin. Bloomington: Indiana University Press.

Dworkin, Andrea. 1974. *Woman hating.* New York: NAL Penguin.

———. 1981. *Pornography: Men possessing women.* New York: Perigee (Putnam).

———. 1987. *Intercourse.* New York: Free Press.

Dwyer, Daisy, and Judith Bruce (eds.). 1988. *A home divided: Women and income in the Third World.* Palo Alto, Calif.: Stanford University Press.

Dyer, Richard. 1985. Male sexuality in the media. In *The sexuality of men,* edited by Andy Metcalf and Martin Humphries. London: Pluto Press.

Dziech, Billie Wright, and Linda Weiner. 1990. *The lecherous professor: Sexual harassment on campus.* 2d ed. Boston: Beacon Press.

Echols, Alice. 1983. The new feminism of yin and yang. In Snitow, Stansell, and Thompson.

Ecker, Gisela (ed.). 1985. *Feminist aesthetics,* translated by Harriet Anderson. London: Women's Press.

Edin, Kathryn, and Christopher Jencks. 1992. Reforming welfare. In *Rethinking social policy: Race, poverty, and the underclass,* by Christopher Jencks. Cambridge, Mass.: Harvard University Press.

Edmondson, Linda Harriet. 1984. *Feminism in Russia, 1900–17.* Stanford, Calif.: Stanford University Press.

Edwards, J. Michèle. 1989. Women and music. *NWSA Journal* 1:506–18.

Edwards, Paul. 1990. The army and the microworld: Computers and the politics of gender identity. *Signs* 16:102–127.

Edwards, Richard. 1979. *Contested terrain: The transformation of the workplace in the twentieth century.* New York: Basic Books.

Edwards, Tim. 1990. Beyond sex and gender: Masculinity, homosexuality and social theory. In Hearn and Morgan.

Egolf, Donald B., and Lloyd E. Corder. 1991. Height differences of low and high job status, female and male corporate employees. *Sex Roles* 24:365–73.

Ehrenberg, Margaret. 1989. *Women in prehistory.* Norman: University of Oklahoma Press.

Ehrenreich, Barbara. 1983. *The hearts of men: American dreams and the flight from commitment.* Garden City, N.Y.: Doubleday Anchor.

Ehrenreich, Barbara, and Deirdre English. 1973. *Complaints and disorders: The sexual politics of sickness.* Westbury, N.Y.: Feminist Press.

———. 1978. *For her own good: 150 years of the experts' advice to women.* Garden City, N.Y.: Doubleday Anchor.

Ehrensaft, Diane. 1987. *Parenting together: Men and women sharing the care of their children.* Urbana: University of Illinois Press.

Ehrlichman, Howard, and Rosalind Eichenstein. 1992. Private wishes: Gender similarities and differences. *Sex Roles* 26:399–422.

Eichler, Margrit. 1989. Sex change operations: The last bulwark of the double standard. In Richardson and Taylor.

Einhorn, Barbara. 1989. Socialist emancipation: The women's movement in the German Democratic Republic. In Kruks, Rapp, and Young.

———. 1991. Where have all the women gone? Women and the women's movement in East Central Europe. *Feminist Review,* no. 39:16–36.

Eisenstein, Zillah. 1981. *The radical future of liberal feminism.* New York: Longman.

———. 1984. *Feminism and sexual equality: Crisis in liberal America.* New York: Monthly Review Press.

———. 1988. *The female body and the law.* Berkeley: University of California Press.

Eisler, Riane. 1987. *The chalice and the blade: Our history, our future.* San Francisco: Harper & Row.

Eitzen, D. Stanley, and Maxine Baca Zinn. 1989. The de-athleticization of women: The naming and gender marking of collegiate sport teams. *Sociology of Sport Journal* 6:362–70.

El Dareer, Asma. 1982. *Woman, why do you weep? Circumcision and its consequences.* London: Zed Books.

Ellis, Kate. 1984. I'm black and blue from the Rolling Stones and I'm not sure how I feel about it: Pornography and the feminist imagination. *Socialist Review* 14(3–4):103–25.

Ellison, Cori. 1992. Breaking the sound barrier: How women finally made their way to the operatic stage. *Opera News,* July, 14, 16–17, 37.

Elshtain, Jean Bethke, and Sheila Tobias (eds.). 1990. *Women, militarism, and war.* Savage, Md.: Rowman & Littlefield.

Elson, Diane, and Ruth Pearson. 1981. The subordination of women and the internationalization of factory production. In Young, Wolkowitz, and McCullagh.

Engels, Frederick. [1884] 1972. *The origin of the family, private property, and the state.* New York: International Publishers.

Engelstein, Laura. 1991. Abortion and the civic order: The legal and medical debates. In Clements, Engel, and Worobec.

England, Paula. 1979. Women and occupational prestige: A case of vacuous sex equality. *Signs* 5:252–65.

———. 1992. *Comparable worth: Theories and evidence.* New York: Aldine de Gruyter.

England, Paula, and Lori McCreary. 1987. Gender inequality in paid employment. In Hess and Marx Ferree.

English, Deirdre, Amber Hollibaugh, and Gayle Rubin. 1981. Talking sex: A conversation on sexuality and feminism. *Socialist Review* 11(4):43–62.

English, Jane. 1982. Sex equality in sports. In *Femininity, masculinity, and androgyny,* edited by Mary Vetterling-Braggin. Boston: Littlefield, Adams.

Epstein, Cynthia Fuchs. 1971. *Women's place: Options and limits in professional careers.* Berkeley: University of California Press.

———. 1981. *Women in law.* New York: Basic Books.

———. 1988. *Deceptive distinctions: Sex, gender and the social order.* New Haven: Yale University Press.

———. 1990. Faulty framework: Consequences of the difference model for women in the law. *New York Law School Law Review* 35:309–36.

———. 1991. Constraints on excellence: Structural and cultural barriers to the recognition and demonstration of achievement. In Zuckerman, Cole, and Bruer.

Epstein, Cynthia Fuchs, and Rose Laub Coser (eds.). 1981. *Access to power: Cross-national studies of women and elites.* London: George Allen & Unwin.

Epstein, Steven. 1987. Gay politics, ethnic identity: The limits of social constructionism. *Socialist Review* 17(3–4):9–54.

Escoffier, Jeffrey. 1985. Sexual revolution and the politics of gay identity. *Socialist Review* 15(4–5):119–53.

Estioko-Griffin, Agnes, and P. Bion Griffin. 1981. Woman the hunter: The Agta. In Dahlberg.

Estrich, Susan. 1987. *Real rape.* Cambridge, Mass.: Harvard University Press.

Etzioni, Amitai. 1969. *The semi-professions and their organization.* New York: Free Press.

Evans, Mark J., John C. Fletcher, Ivan E. Zador, Burritt W. Newton, Mary Helen Quigg, and Curtis D. Struyk. 1988. Selective first-trimester termination in octuplet and quadruplet pregnancies: Clinical and ethical issues. *Obstetrics and Gynecology* 71:289–96.

Evans, Sara M., and Barbara J. Nelson. 1989. *Wage justice: Comparable worth and the paradox of technocratic reform.* Chicago: University of Chicago Press.

Eyer, Diane E. 1992. *Mother-infant bonding: A scientific fiction.* New Haven: Yale University Press.

Faderman, Lillian. 1981. *Surpassing the love of men: Romantic friendship and love between women from the Renaissance to the present.* New York: William Morrow.

————. 1991. *Odd girls and twilight lovers: A history of lesbian life in twentieth-century America.* New York: Columbia University Press.

Fagenson, Ellen A. (ed.). 1993. *Women in management: Trends, issues and challenges in managerial diversity.* Newbury Park, Calif.: Sage.

Farnsworth, Clyde H. 1993. How women moved up in Canada. *New York Times,* 20 June.

Farr, Kathryn Ann. 1988. Dominance bonding through the good old boys sociability group. *Sex Roles* 18:259–77.

Farrell, Susan A. 1991. "It's our church, too!" Women's position in the Catholic church today. In *The social construction of gender,* edited by Judith Lorber and Susan A. Farrell. Newbury Park, Calif.: Sage.

————. 1992. Sexuality, gender, and ethics: The social construction of feminist ethics in the Roman Catholic church. Ph.D. diss. City University of New York Graduate School.

Farwell, Marilyn R. 1988. Toward a definition of the lesbian literary imagination. *Signs* 14:100–18.

Fausto-Sterling, Anne. 1985. *Myths of gender: Biological theories about women and men.* New York: Basic Books.

————. 1987. Society writes biology/biology constructs gender. *Daedalus,* Fall, 61–76.

————. 1993. How many sexes are there? *New York Times,* Op-ed Page, 12 March.

Fava, Sylvia F., and Kathy Deierlein. 1989. Women physicists: Nontraditional occupations and traditional family roles. In *Contemporary readings in sociology,* edited by Judith N. DeSena. Dubuque, Iowa: Kendall/Hunt.

Fee, Elizabeth. 1989. Venereal disease: The wages of sin? In Peiss and Simmons.

Feinbloom, Deborah Heller, Michael Fleming, Valerie Kijewski, and Margo P. Schulter. 1976. Lesbian/feminist orientation among male-to-female transsexuals. *Journal of Homosexuality* 2(1):59–71.

Feldberg, Roslyn L. 1984. Comparable worth: Toward theory and practice in the United States. *Signs* 10:311–28.

Feldberg, Roslyn L., and Evelyn Nakano Glenn. 1979. Job versus gender models in the sociology of work. *Social Problems* 26:524–38.

Ferber, Marianne A. 1986. Citations: Are they an objective measure of scholarly merit? *Signs* 11:381–89.

————. 1988. Citations and networking. *Gender & Society* 2:82–89.

Ferguson, Ann, Jacquelyn N. Zita, and Kathryn Pyne Addelson. 1981. On "Compulsory heterosexuality and lesbian existence": Defining the issues. *Signs* 7:158–99.

Ferguson, Ann, Ilene Philipson, Irene Diamond and Lee Quinby, and Carole S. Vance and Ann Barr Snitow. 1984. Forum: The feminist sexuality debates. *Signs* 10:106–35.

Ferguson, Kathy E. 1984. *The feminist case against bureaucracy.* Philadelphia: Temple University Press.

Fernández-Kelly, María Patricia. 1983. *For we are sold, I and my people: Women and industry in Mexico's frontier.* Albany: State University of New York Press.

————. 1984. *Maquiladoras*: The view from inside. In *My troubles are going to have trouble with me: Everyday trials and triumphs of women workers,* edited by Karen Brodkin Sacks and Dorothy Remy. New Brunswick, N.J.: Rutgers University Press.

————. 1989. Broadening the scope: Gender and international economic development. *Sociological Forum* 4:611–35.

Fernández-Kelly, María Patricia, and Anna M. García. 1988. Invisible amidst the glitter: Hispanic women in the Southern California electronics industry. In Statham, Miller, and Mauksch.

Ferraro, Kathleen J. 1989. Policing woman battering. *Social Problems* 36:61–74.

Ferree, Myra Marx. 1993. The rise and fall of "mommy politics": Feminism and unification in (East) Germany. *Feminist Studies* 19:89–115.

Fierman, Jaclyn. 1990. Why women still don't hit the top. *Fortune,* 30 July.

Finch, Janet. 1983. *Married to the job: Wives' incorporation in men's work.* London: George Allen & Unwin.

Fine, Gary Alan. 1987a. *With the boys: Little League baseball and preadolescent culture.* Chicago: University of Chicago Press.

————. 1987b. One of the boys: Women in male-dominated settings. In Kimmel (ed.).

————. 1992. The dirty play of little boys. In Kimmel and Messner.

Fine, Michelle, and Adrienne Asch. 1985. Disabled women: Sexism without the pedestal. In *Women and disability: The double handicap,* edited by Mary Jo Deegan and Nancy A. Brooks. New Brunswick, N.J.: Transaction.

Finkelhor, David, and Kersti Yllö. 1985. License to rape: Sexual abuse of wives. New York: Holt, Rinehart and Winston.

Fiorenza, Elisabeth Schüssler. 1979. Word, spirit and power: Women in early Christian communities. In *Women of spirit: Female leadership in the Jewish and Christian traditions,* edited by Rosemary Ruether and Eleanor McLaughlin. New York: Simon & Schuster.

Fisek, M. Hamit, Joseph Berger, and Robert Z. Norman. 1991. Participation in heterogeneous and homogeneous groups: A theoretical integration. *American Journal of Sociology* 97:114–42.

Fisher, Sue. 1986. *In the patient's best interest: Women and the politics of medical decisions.* New Brunswick, N.J.: Rutgers University Press.

Fishman, Pamela M. 1978. Interaction: The work women do. *Social Problems* 25:397–406.

Fister, Patricia. 1988. *Japanese women artists, 1600–1900*. Lawrence: Spencer Museum of Art, University of Kansas.

Flax, Jane. 1990. *Thinking fragments: Psychoanalysis, feminism, and postmodernism in the contemporary West*. Berkeley: University of California Press.

Folbre, Nancy. 1983. Of patriarchy born: The political economy of fertility decisions. *Feminist Studies* 9:261–84.

———. 1991. The unproductive housewife: Her evolution in nineteenth century economic thought. *Signs* 16:463–84.

Form, William, and David Byron McMillen. 1983. Women, men, and machines. *Work and Occupations* 10:147–78.

Foucault, Michel. 1972. *The archeology of knowledge and the discourse on language*, translated by A.M. Sheridan Smith. New York: Pantheon.

———. 1978. *The history of sexuality: An introduction*, translated by Robert Hurley. New York: Pantheon.

———. 1985 *The use of pleasure*, translated by Robert Hurley. New York: Pantheon.

——— (ed.). 1980. *Herculine Barbin: Being the recently discovered memoirs of a nineteenth-century French hermaphrodite*, translated by Richard McDougall. New York: Pantheon.

Fox, Bonnie J. 1990. Selling the mechanized household: 70 years of ads in *Ladies' Home Journal*. *Gender & Society* 4:25–40.

Fox, Mary Frank. 1981. Sex, salary, and achievement: Reward-dualism in academia. *Sociology of Education* 54:71–84.

———. 1984. Women and higher education: sex differentials in the status of students and scholars. In Freeman.

———. 1985. Location, sex-typing, and salary among academics. *Work and Occupations* 12:186–205.

———. 1991. Gender, environmental milieu, and productivity in science. In Zuckerman, Cole, and Bruer.

Fox, Mary Frank, and Catherine A. Faver. 1985. Men, women, and publication productivity: Patterns among social work academics. *Sociological Quarterly* 26:537–49.

Fox-Genovese, Elizabeth. 1988. *Within the plantation household: Black and white women of the old South*. Chapel Hill, N.C.: University of North Carolina Press.

Francke, Linda Bird. 1991. Hers: Requiem for a soldier. *New York Times Magazine*, 21 April.

Franklin, Clyde W., II. 1988. *Men and society*. Chicago: Nelson-Hall.

———. 1992. Black male-female conflict: Individually caused and socially structured. In Kimmel and Messner.

Franklin, Sara. 1990. Deconstructing "desperateness": The social construction of infertility in popular representations of new reproductive technologies. In *The new reproductive technologies*, edited by M. McNeil, I. Varcoe, and S. Yearley. London: Macmillan.

Fraser, Laura. 1991. The doctor's dilemma. *Vogue*, October, 306–11.

Fraser, Nancy. 1989. *Unruly practices: Power, discourse and gender in contemporary social theory*. Minneapolis: University of Minnesota Press.

Fredericksen, Marilynn C., Louis Keith, and Rudy E. Sabbagha. 1992. Fetal reduction: Is this the appropriate answer for multiple gestation? *International Journal of Fertility* 37:8–14.

Freeman, Jo (ed.). [1979] [1984] 1989. *Women: A feminist perspective*. 2d, 3d, and 4th eds. Mountain View, Calif.: Mayfield.

Freeman, Lucy, and Alma Halbert Bond. 1992. *America's first woman warrior: The courage of Deborah Sampson*. New York: Paragon.

Freud, Sigmund. [1905] 1962. *Three essays on the theory of sexuality*, translated and edited by James Strachey. New York: Basic Books.

Friedl, Ernestine. 1975. *Women and men*. New York: Holt, Rinehart and Winston.

Frieze, Irene Hanson. 1983. Investigating the causes and consequences of marital rape. *Signs* 8:532–53.

Frieze, Irene Hanson, and Angela Browne. 1989. Violence in marriage. In *Family violence,* edited by Lloyd Ohlin and Michael Tonry. Chicago: University of Chicago Press.

Frueh, Arlene. 1988. Towards a feminist theory of art criticism. In Raven, Langer, and Frueh.

Frye, Marilyn. 1983. *The politics of reality: Essays in feminist theory*. Trumansburg, N.Y.: Crossing Press.

————. 1990. Lesbian "sex." In Allen.

Frymer-Kensky, Tikva. 1992. *In the wake of the goddesses: Women, culture, and the biblical transformation*. New York: Free Press.

Fuchs, Rachel Ginnis. 1984. *Abandoned children: Foundlings and child welfare in nineteenth-century France*. Albany: State University of New York Press.

————. 1992. *Poor and pregnant in Paris: Strategies for survival in the nineteenth century*. New Brunswick, N.J.: Rutgers University Press.

Fuentes, Annette, and Barbara Ehrenreich. 1983. *Women in the global factory*. Boston, Mass.: South End Press.

Fulbright, Karen. 1987. The myth of the double-advantage: Black female managers. In Simms and Malveaux.

Fuszara, Malgorzata. 1991. Legal regulation of abortion in Poland. *Signs* 17:117–28.

Gagnon, John, and William Simon. 1973. *Sexual conduct: The social sources of human sexuality*. Chicago: Aldine.

Gailey, Christine Ward. 1987. Evolutionary perspectives on gender hierarchy. In Hess and Marx Ferree.

Gallagher, Catherine, and Thomas Laqueur (eds.). 1987. *The making of the modern body*. Berkeley: University of California Press.

Gallop, Jane. 1982. *The daughter's seduction: Feminism and psychoanalysis*. Ithaca, N.Y.: Cornell University Press.

Game, Ann, and Rosemary Pringle. 1983. *Gender at work*. Sydney: George Allen & Unwin.

Garber, Marjorie. 1989. Spare parts: The surgical construction of gender. *Differences: A Journal of Feminist Cultural Studies* 1(3):127–59.

————. 1992. *Vested interests: Cross-dressing and cultural anxiety*. New York and London: Routledge.

Garcia, Alma M. 1989. The development of Chicana feminist discourse, 1970–1980. *Gender & Society* 3:217–38.

Garfinkel, Harold. 1967. *Studies in ethnomethodology.* Englewood Cliffs, N.J.: Prentice-Hall.

Garlick, Barbara, Suzanne Dixon, and Pauline Allen (eds.). 1992. *Stereotypes of women in power: Historical perspectives and revisionist views.* Westport, Conn.: Greenwood.

Garrard, Mary D. 1989. *Artemesia Gentileschi: The image of the female hero in Italian baroque art.* Princeton: Princeton University Press.

Gary, Lawrence E. 1987. Predicting interpersonal conflict between women and men: The case of Black men. In Kimmel (ed.).

Gates, Hill. 1989. The commoditization of Chinese women. *Signs* 14:799–832.

Gelb, Joyce. 1989. *Feminism and politics: A comparative perspective.* Berkeley: University of California Press.

Gelman, Susan A., Pamela Collman, and Eleanor E. Maccoby. 1986. Inferring properties from categories versus inferring categories from properties: The case of gender. *Child Development* 57:396–404.

Gerson, Judith M., and Kathy Peiss. 1985. Boundaries, negotiation, consciousness: Reconceptualizing gender relations. *Social Problems* 32:317–31.

Gerson, Kathleen. 1985. *Hard choices: How women decide about work, career, and motherhood.* Berkeley: University of California Press.

Gerstel, Naomi, and Harriet Engel Gross (eds.). 1987. *Families and work.* Philadelphia: Temple University Press.

Gibbs, Jewelle Taylor. 1988a. Health and mental health of young Black males. In Gibbs et al.

———. 1988b. The new morbidity: Homicide, suicide, accidents, and life-threatening behaviors. In Gibbs. et al.

Gibbs, Jewelle Taylor, et al. (eds). 1988. *Young, Black and male in America: An endangered species.* Dover, Mass.: Auburn House.

Gilbert, Sandra M. 1983. Soldier's heart: Literary men, literary women, and the Great War. *Signs* 8:422–50.

Gilbert, Sandra M., and Susan Gubar. 1988. *No man's land: The place of the woman writer in the twentieth century.* 2 vols. New Haven: Yale University Press.

Gillespie, Cynthia K. 1989. *Justifiable homicide: Battered women, self-defense, and the law.* Columbus: Ohio State University Press.

Gilligan, Carol. 1982. *In a different voice.* Cambridge, Mass.: Harvard University Press.

Gilman, Charlotte Perkins. [1892] 1973. *The yellow wallpaper.* Old Westbury, N.Y.: Feminist Press.

———. 1979. *Herland.* New York: Pantheon.

Gilman, Sander L. 1988. AIDS and syphilis: The iconography of disease. In Crimp.

Gilmartin, Christina. 1989. Gender, politics, and patriarchy in China: The experiences of early women Communists, 1920–27. In Kruks, Rapp, and Young.

Gilmore, David D. 1990. *Manhood in the making: Cultural concepts of masculinity.* New Haven: Yale University Press.

Gimbutas, Marija. 1974. *The gods and goddesses of Old Europe.* Berkeley: University of California Press.

———. 1989. *The language of the goddess.* San Francisco: Harper & Row.

Gimenez, Martha E. 1990. The dialectics of waged and unwaged work: Waged work, domestic labor and household survival in the United States. In Collins and Giminez.

Gioseffi, Daniela (ed.). 1988. *Women on war: Essential voices for the nuclear age.* New York: Simon & Schuster.

Gitlin, Michael J., and Robert O. Pasnau. 1989. Psychiatric syndromes linked to reproductive function in women: A review of current knowledge. *American Journal of Psychiatry* 146:1413–21.

Gittins, Diana. 1982. *Fair sex: Family size and structure in Britain, 1900–39.* New York: St. Martin's Press.

Glass, Jennifer. 1988. Job quits and job changes: The effects of young women's work conditions and family factors. *Gender & Society* 2:228–40.

Glass, Jennifer, and Valerie Camarigg. 1992. Gender, parenthood, and job-family compatibility. *American Journal of Sociology* 98:131–51.

Glassner, Barry. 1992. Men and muscles. In Kimmel and Messner.

Glazer, Nona Y. 1984. Servants to capital: Unpaid domestic labor and paid work. *Review of Radical Political Economics* 16:61–87.

———. 1988. Overlooked, overworked: Women's unpaid and paid work in the health services "cost crisis." *International Journal of Health Services* 18:119–37.

———. 1990. The home as workshop: Women as amateur nurses and medical care providers. *Gender & Society* 4:479–99.

———. 1991. "Between a rock and hard place": Women's professional organizations in nursing and class, racial, and ethnic inequalities. *Gender & Society* 5:351–72.

———. 1993. *Women's paid and unpaid labor: The work transfer in retailing and health care.* Philadelphia: Temple University Press.

Glendon, Mary Ann. 1989. *The transformation of family law: State, law and family in the United States and Western Europe.* Chicago: University of Chicago Press.

Glenn, Evelyn Nakano. 1985. Racial ethnic women's labor: The intersection of race, gender, and class oppression. *Review of Radical Political Economics* 17:86–108.

———. 1986. *Issei, Nissei, war bride.* Philadelphia: Temple University Press.

———. 1992. From servitude to service work: Historical continuities in the racial division of paid reproductive labor. *Signs* 18:1–43.

Glenn, Evelyn Nakano, and Roslyn L. Feldberg. 1977. Degraded and deskilled: The proletarianization of clerical work. *Social Problems* 25:52–64.

Glenn, Evelyn Nakano, and Charles M. Tolbert II. 1987. Technology and emerging patterns of stratification for women of color: Race and gender segregation in computer occupations. In B. D. Wright et al.

Godelier, Maurice. 1986. *The making of great men: Male domination and power among the New Guinea Baruyea,* translated by Rupert Sawyer. Cambridge, England: Cambridge University Press.

Goffman, Erving. 1959. *The presentation of self in everyday life.* Garden City, N.Y.: Doubleday Anchor.

————. 1963a. *Stigma.* Englewood Cliffs, N.J.: Prentice-Hall.

————. 1963b. *Behavior in public places: Notes on the social organization of gatherings.* New York: Free Press.

————. 1967. *Interaction ritual: Essays in face-to-face behavior.* Hawthorne, N.Y.: Aldine.

————. 1977. The arrangement between the sexes. *Theory and Society* 4:301–33.

————. 1983. Felicity's condition. *American Journal of Sociology* 89:1–53.

Goldberg, Gertrude Schaffner, and Eleanor Kremen (eds.). 1990. *The feminization of poverty: Only in America?* Westport, Conn.: Greenwood.

Goldin, Claudia. 1990. *Understanding the gender gap: An economic history of American women.* New York: Oxford University Press.

Goldman, Wendy Zeva. 1989. Women, the family and the new revolutionary order in the Soviet Union. In Kruks, Rapp, and Young.

————. 1991. Women, abortion, and the state, 1917–36. In Clements, Engel, and Worobec.

Goldstone, Jack A. 1991. *Revolution and rebellion in the early modern world.* Berkeley: University of California Press.

Goleman, Daniel. 1991. Sexual harassment: It's about power, not lust. *New York Times,* Science Section, 22 October.

Gonzalez, David. 1991. So few died, but how it hurt those back home: 11 stories. *New York Times,* 15 March.

Goode, William J. 1959. The theoretical importance of love. *American Sociological Review* 24:38–47.

————. 1978. *The celebration of heroes.* Berkeley: University of California Press.

————. [1982] 1993. Why men resist. In *Rethinking the family: Some feminist questions,* edited by Barrie Thorne and Marilyn Yalom, 2d ed. Boston, Mass.: Northeastern University Press.

Goodman, Madeleine. 1980. Toward a biology of menopause. *Signs* 5:739–53.

————. 1982. A critique of menopause research. In Voda, Dinnerstein, and O'Donnell.

Gordon, Linda. 1989. *Heroes of their own lives: The politics and history of family violence, Boston, 1880–1960.* New York: Penguin.

————. 1990a. *Woman's body, woman's right: Birth control in America.* Rev. ed. Baltimore, Md.: Penguin.

———— (ed.). 1990b. *Women, the state, and welfare.* Madison: University of Wisconsin Press.

Gordon, Tuula. 1990. *Feminist mothers.* New York: New York University Press.

Gottfried, Heidi. 1991. Mechanisms of control in the temporary help service industry. *Sociological Forum* 6:699–713.

Gottlieb, Roger. 1984. Mothering and the reproduction of power: Chodorow, Dinnerstein, and social theory. *Socialist Review* 14(5):93–119.

Gould, Lois. 1972. X: A fabulous child's story. *Ms. Magazine,* December, 74–76, 105–06.

Gove, Walter R. 1984. Gender differences in mental and physical illness: The effects of fixed roles and nurturant roles. *Social Science and Medicine* 19:77–91.

Graham, Dee L. R., Edna Rawlings, and Nelly Rimini. 1988. Survivors of terror: Battered women, hostages and the Stockholm syndrome. In Yllö and Bograd.

Graham, Ruth. 1977. Loaves and liberty: Women in the French Revolution. In Bridenthal and Koonz.

Gramsci, Antonio. 1971. *Selections from the prison notebooks,* translated and edited by Quintin Hoare and Geoffrey Nowell Smith. New York: International Publishers.

Grant, Linda. 1988. The gender climate in medical school: Perspectives of women and men students. *Journal of the American Medical Women's Association* 43:109–10, 115–19.

Gray, Francine du Plessix. 1990. *Soviet women: Walking the tightrope.* New York: Doubleday.

Greenberg, David F. 1988. *The construction of homosexuality.* Chicago: University of Chicago Press.

Greenblatt, Stephen. 1987. *Shakespearean negotiations: The circulation of social energy in Renaissance England.* Berkeley: University of California Press.

Greenhouse, Linda. 1991. Court backs right of women to jobs with health risks. *New York Times,* 21 March.

Greer, Germaine. 1985. *Sex and destiny: The politics of human fertility.* New York: Harper & Row.

Gregersen, Edgar. 1983. *Sexual practices: The story of human sexuality.* New York: Franklin Watts.

Greif, Geoffrey L. 1985. *Single fathers.* Lexington, Mass.: Lexington Books.

Greil, Arthur L. 1991. *Not yet pregnant: Infertile couples in contemporary America.* New Brunswick, N.J.: Rutgers University Press.

Greil, Arthur L., Thomas A. Leitko, and Karen L. Porter. 1988. Infertility: His and hers. *Gender & Society* 2:172–99.

Grella, Christine E. 1990. Irreconcilable differences: Women defining class after divorce and downward mobility. *Gender & Society* 4:41–55.

Grieco, Margaret, and Richard Whipp. 1986. Women and the workplace: Gender and control in the labor process. In Knights and Willmott.

Griffin, Susan. 1982. *Pornography and silence: Culture's revenge against nature.* New York: Harper & Row.

Grigsby, Darcy Grimaldo. 1990. Dilemmas of visibility: Contemporary women artists' representations of female bodies. In *The female body, Part 1,* edited by Laurence Goldstein. Special issue of *Michigan Quarterly Review* 29:584–618.

Grimm, David E. 1987. Toward a theory of gender: Transsexualism, gender, sexuality, and relationships. *American Behavioral Scientist* 31:66–85.

Grimm, James W., and Robert N. Stern. 1974. Sex roles and internal labor market structures: The "female" semi-professions. *Social Problems* 21:690–705.

Groce, Stephen B., and Margaret Cooper. 1990. Just me and the boys? Women in local-level rock and roll. *Gender & Society* 4:220–29.

Gross, Edward. 1968. Plus ça change . . . ? The sexual structure of occupations over time. *Social Problems* 16:198–208.

Gross, Harriet Engel, Jessie Bernard, Alice J. Dan, Nona Glazer, Judith Lorber,

Martha McClintock, Niles Newton, and Alice Rossi. 1979. Considering "A biosocial perspective on parenting." *Signs* 4:695–717.

Gross, Jane. 1990a. New home front developing as women hear call to arms. *New York Times,* 18 September.

———. 1990b. Needs of family and country clash in Persian Gulf mission. *New York Times,* 12 December.

———. 1991. A woman's resignation touches a nerve at medical schools. *New York Times,* 14 July.

Grossberg, Michael. 1983. Who gets the child? Custody, guardianship, and the rise of judicial patriarchy in nineteenth-century America. *Feminist Studies* 9:235–60.

Gruber, James. 1992. A typology of personal and environmental sexual harassment: Research and policy implications for the 1990s. *Sex Roles* 26:447–63.

Gruber, James, and Lars Bjorn. 1982. Blue-collar blues: The sexual harassment of women auto workers. *Work and Occupations* 9:271–98.

Gubar, Susan, and Joan Hoff. 1989. *For adult users only: The dilemma of violent pornography.* Bloomington: Indiana University Press.

Guinan, Mary E. 1988. PMS or perifollicular phase euphoria? *Journal of the American Medical Women's Association* 43:91–92.

Gullickson, Gay L. 1991. La pétroleuse: Representing revolution. *Feminist Studies* 17:241–65.

Gutek, Barbara A. 1985. *Sex and the workplace: The impact of sexual behavior and harassment on women, men, and organizations.* San Francsico: Jossey-Bass.

Gutiérrez, Ramón A. 1992. *When Jesus came, the Corn Mothers went away: Marriage, sexuality, and power in New Mexico, 1500 -1846.* Stanford, Calif.: Stanford University Press.

Guttentag, Marcia, and Paul F. Secord. 1983. *Too many women: The sex ratio question.* Newbury Park, Calif.: Sage.

Haas, Linda. 1980. Role-sharing couples: A study of egalitarian marriages. *Family Relations* 29:289–96.

———. 1982. Determinants of role-sharing behavior: A study of egalitarian couples. *Sex Roles* 8:747–60.

———. 1991. Equal parenthood and social policy: Lessons from a study of parental leave in Sweden. In Hyde and Essex.

Haavind, Hanne. 1984. Love and power in marriage. In Holter.

Haavio-Mannila, Elina, and Kaisa Kauppinen. 1992. Women and the welfare state in Nordic countries. In *Women's work and women's lives: The continuing struggle worldwide,* edited by Hilda Kahne and Janet Z. Giele. Boulder, Colo.: Westview.

Hacker, Sally L. 1979. Sex stratification, technology and organizational change: A longitudinal study of AT&T. *Social Problems* 26:539–57.

———. 1989. *Pleasure, power and technology.* Winchester, Mass.: Unwin Hyman.

Hacker, Sally L., with Clara Elcorobairutia. 1987. Women workers in the Mondragon system of industrial cooperatives. *Gender & Society* 1:358–79.

Hadingham, Evan. 1979. *Secrets of the Ice Age: The world of the cave artists.* New York: Walker.

Hall, M. Ann. 1988. The discourse of gender and sport: From femininity to feminism. *Sociology of Sport Journal* 5:330–40.

Hall, Nor. 1989. *Broodmales: A psychological essay on men in childbirth.* Dallas, Tex.: Spring.

Hall, Oswald. 1946. The informal organization of the medical profession. *Canadian Journal of Economics and Political Science* 12:30–41.

———. 1948. The stages of a medical career. *American Journal of Sociology* 53:327–36.

———. 1949. Types of medical careers. *American Journal of Sociology* 55:243–53.

Hall, Peter Dobkin. 1978. Marital selection and business in Massachusetts merchant families, 1700–1900. In *The American family in socio-historical perspective,* edited by Michael Gordon. New York: St. Martin's Press.

Hallo, William W., and J. J. A. Van Dijk. 1968. *The exultation of Inanna.* New Haven: Yale University Press.

Hamabata, Matthews Masayki. 1990. *Crested kimono: Power and love in the Japanese business family.* Ithaca, N.Y.: Cornell University Press.

Hammel, E. A., Sheila R. Johansson, and Caren A. Ginsberg. 1983. The value of children during industrialization: Sex ratios in childhood in nineteenth-century America. *Journal of Family History* 8:346–66.

Hanawalt, Barbara A. (ed.). 1986. *Women and work in preindustrial Europe.* Bloomington: Indiana University Press.

Hanna, Judith Lynne. 1988. *Dance, sex and gender: Signs of identity, dominance, defiance, and desire.* Chicago: University of Chicago Press.

Hannan, Michael T., Klaus Schömann, and Hans-Peter Blossfeld. 1990. Sex and sector differences in the dynamics of wage growth in the Federal Republic of Germany. *American Sociological Review* 55:694–13.

Hansen, Charles E., and Anne Evans. 1985. Bisexuality reconsidered: An idea in pursuit of a definition. *Journal of Homosexuality* 11(1–2):1–6.

Hansen, Karen Tranberg. 1990. Body politics: Sexuality, gender, and domestic service in Zambia. *Journal of Women's History* 2:120–42.

Hansen, Karen V. 1989. "Helped put in a quilt": Men's work and male intimacy in nineteenth-century New England. *Gender & Society* 3:334–54.

Hansot, Elisabeth, and David Tyack. 1988. Gender in American public schools: Thinking institutionally. *Signs* 13:741–60.

Hansson, Carola, and Karin Lidén (eds.). 1983. *Moscow women: Thirteen interviews,* translated by Garry Bothmer, George Blecher, and Lone Blecher. New York: Pantheon.

Haraway, Donna. 1978a. Animal sociology and a natural economy of the body politic. Part I: A political physiology of dominance. *Signs* 4:21–36.

———. 1978b. Animal sociology and a natural economy of the body politic. Part II: The past is the contested zone: Human nature and theories of production and reproduction in primate behavior studies. *Signs* 4:37–60.

———. 1981. In the beginning was the word: The genesis of biological theory. *Signs* 6:469–81.

———. 1985. A manifesto for cyborgs. *Socialist Review* 15(2):65–107.

————. 1988. Situated knowledges: The science question in feminism and the privilege of partial perspective. *Feminist Studies* 14:575–99.

————. 1989. *Primate visions.* New York and London: Routledge.

————. 1990. Investment strategies for the evolving portfolio of primate females. In Jacobus, Keller, and Shuttleworth.

————. 1991. *Simians, cyborgs, and women: The reinvention of nature.* New York and London: Routledge.

Harding, Sandra. 1986. *The science question in feminism.* Ithaca, N.Y.: Cornell University Press.

————. 1991. *Whose science? Whose knowledge? Thinking from women's lives.* Ithaca, N.Y.: Cornell University Press.

Hare-Mustin, Rachel T., and Jeanne Marecek (eds.). 1990. *Making a difference: Psychology and the construction of gender.* New Haven: Yale University Press.

Hargreaves, Jennifer A. (ed.). 1982. *Sport, culture, and ideology.* London: Routledge and Kegan Paul.

————. 1986. Where's the virtue? Where's the grace? A discussion of the social production of gender relations in and through sport. *Theory, Culture, and Society,* 3:109–21.

Harley, Sharon. 1990. For the good of family and race: Gender, work and domestic roles in the Black community, 1880–1930. *Signs* 15:336–49.

Harlow, Caroline Wolf. 1991. *Female victims of violent crime.* Washington, D.C.: U.S. Department of Justice, Bureau of Justice Statistics.

Harris, Anne Sutherland, and Linda Nochlin. 1976. *Women artists: 1550–1950.* New York: Knopf.

Harris, Olivia. 1981. Households as natural units. In Young, Wolkowitz, and Mc-Cullagh.

Harrison, James, James Chin, and Thomas Ficarrotto. 1992. Warning: Masculinity may be dangerous to your health. In Kimmel and Messner.

Hart, Barbara. 1986. Lesbian battering: An examination. In *Naming the violence: Speaking out against lesbian battering,* edited by Kerry Lobel. Seattle: Seal Press.

Hartmann, Heidi I. 1976. Capitalism, patriarchy, and job segregation by sex. *Signs* 1(3, pt. 2):137–67.

————. 1981a. The family as the locus of gender, class, and political struggle: The example of housework. *Signs* 6:366–94.

————. 1981b. The unhappy marriage of Marxism and feminism: Towards a more progressive union. In Sargent.

———— (ed.). 1987. *Computer chips and paper clips: Technology and women's employment.* Vol. 2. Washington, D.C.: National Academy Press.

Hartmann, Heidi I., Robert E. Kraut, and Louise A. Tilly (eds.). 1986. *Computer chips and paper clips: Technology and women's employment.* Vol. 1. Washington, D.C.: National Academy Press.

Hartsock, Nancy C. M. 1983. *Money, sex, and power: Toward a feminist historical materialism.* New York: Longman.

Haskell, Molly. 1989. Hers: He drives me crazy. *New York Times Magazine,* 24 September, 26, 28.

Hatfield, Elaine, and Susan Sprecher. 1986. *Mirror, mirror: The importance of looks in everyday life.* Albany: State University of New York Press.

Haug, Frigga. 1991. The end of socialism in Europe: A new challenge for socialist feminism? *Feminist Review,* no. 39:37–48.

Haug, Frigga, et al. 1987. *Female sexualization: A collective work of memory.* London: Verso.

Hausfater, Glenn, and Sarah Blaffer Hrdy (eds.). 1984. *Infanticide: Comparative and evolutionary perspectives.* New York: Aldine.

Hayden, Dolores. 1981. *The grand domestic revolution: A history of feminist designs for American homes, neighborhoods, and cities.* Cambridge, Mass.: MIT Press.

Hearn, Jeff. 1987. *The gender of oppression: Men, masculinity and the critique of Marxism.* New York: St. Martin's Press.

Hearn, Jeff, and David Morgan (eds.). 1990. *Men, masculinities and social theory.* London: Unwin Hyman.

Hearn, Jeff, and P. Wendy Parkin. 1988. Women, men, and leadership: A critical review of assumptions, practices, and change in the industrialized nations. In Adler and Izraeli (eds.).

Hearn, Jeff, Deborah L. Sheppard, Peta Tancred-Sheriff, and Gibson Burrell (eds.). 1989. *The sexuality of organization.* Newbury Park, Calif.: Sage.

Heilbrun, Carolyn. 1988. *Writing a woman's life.* New York: Ballantine.

Heitlinger, Alena. 1979. *Women and state socialism: Sex inequality in the Soviet Union and Czechoslovakia.* Montreal: McGill-Queen's University Press.

————. 1987. *Reproduction, medicine and the socialist state.* New York: St. Martin's Press.

Held, Virginia. 1983. The obligations of mothers and fathers. In Trebilcot.

————. 1989. Birth and death. *Ethics* 99:362–88.

Hendrix, Lewellyn, and Zakir Hossain. 1988. Women's status and mode of production: A cross-cultural test. *Signs* 13:437–53.

Henley, Nancy M. 1977. *Body politics: Power, sex, and nonverbal communication.* Englewood Cliffs, N.J.: Prentice-Hall.

Hennig, Margaret, and Anne Jardim. 1976. *The managerial woman.* New York: Pocket Books.

Henriques, Diana B. 1992. Ms. Siebert, still on the barricades. *New York Times,* Business Section, 5 July.

Herdt, Gilbert. 1981. *Guardians of the flutes: Idioms of masculinity.* New York: McGraw-Hill.

————. 1990. Mistaken gender: 5α-reductase hermaphroditism and biological reductionism in sexual identity reconsidered. *American Anthropologist* 92:433–46.

Herdt, Gilbert, and Julian Davidson. 1988. The Sambia "turnim-man": Sociocultural and clinical aspects of gender formation in male pseudohermaphrodites with 5α-reductase deficiency in Papua, New Guinea. *Archives of Sexual Behavior* 17:33–56.

Herek, Gregory M. 1986. On heterosexual masculinity: Some psychical consequences of the social construction of gender and sexuality. *American Behavioral Scientist* 29:563–77.

Herlihy, David. 1976. Land, family, and women in continental Europe, 701–1200. In Stuard.

———. 1984. Households in the early Middle Ages: Symmetry and sainthood. In Netting, Wilk, and Arnould.

Herman, Judith Lewis, with Lisa Hirschman. 1981. *Father-daughter incest.* Cambridge, Mass.: Harvard University Press.

Hernes, Helga Maria. 1984. Women and the welfare state: The transition from private to public dependence. In Holter.

Herrmann, Anne. 1991. "Passing" women, performing men. In *The female body, Part 2,* edited by Laurence Goldstein. Special issue of *Michigan Quarterly Review* 30:60–71.

Hertz, Rosanna. 1986. *More equal than others: Women and men in dual-career marriages.* Berkeley: University of California Press.

———. 1992. Financial affairs: Money and authority in dual-earner marriage. In Lewis, Izraeli, and Hootsmans.

Hess, Beth B. 1981. Friendship and gender roles over the life course. In *Single life: Unmarried adults in social context,* edited by Peter J. Stein. New York: St. Martin's Press.

———. 1990. Beyond dichotomy: Drawing distinctions and embracing differences. *Sociological Forum* 5:75–93.

Hess, Beth B., and Myra Marx Ferree (eds.). *Analyzing gender* Newbury Park, Calif.: Sage.

Hewlett, Barry S. 1987. Intimate fathers: Patterns of paternal holding among Aka Pygmies. In Lamb (ed.).

———. 1992a. Husband-wife reciprocity and the father-infant relationship among Aka Pygmies. In Hewlett (ed.).

——— (ed.). 1992b. *Father-child relations: Cultural and biosocial contexts.* New York: Aldine de Gruyter.

Higginbotham, Elizabeth. 1983. Laid bare by the system: Work and survival for Black and Hispanic women. In Swerdlow and Lessinger.

———. 1987. Employment for professional Black women in the twentieth century. In Bose and Spitze.

Higginbotham, Elizabeth, and Lynn Weber. 1992. Moving up with kin and community: Upward social mobility for Black and white women. *Gender & Society* 6:416–40.

Higginbotham, Evelyn Brooks. 1992. African-American women's history and the metalanguage of race. *Signs* 17:251–74.

Hilbert, Richard A. 1987. Bureaucracy as belief, rationalization as repair: Max Weber in a post-functionalist age. *Sociology Theory* 5:70–86.

Hill, Anita. 1992. The nature of the beast. *Ms. Magazine,* January-February, 32–33.

Hill, Bridget. 1989. *Women, work, and sexual politics in eighteenth-century England.* Oxford and New York: Basil Blackwell.

Hillier, Bill, and Julienne Hanson. 1984. *The social logic of space.* Cambridge, England: Cambridge University Press.

Hillsman, Sally T., and Bernard Levenson. 1975. Job opportunities of Black and white working-class women. *Social Problems* 22:510–32.

Hirschon, Renée (ed.). *Women and property: Women as property.* London: Croom Helm.

Hobson, Barbara Meil. 1987. *Uneasy virtue: The politics of prostitution and the American reform tradition.* New York: Basic Books.

Hochschild, Arlie Russell. 1983. *The managed heart: Commercialization of human feeling.* Berkeley: University of California Press.

Hochschild, Arlie, with Anne Machung. 1989a. *The second shift: Working parents and the revolution at home.* New York: Viking.

————. 1989b. The economy of gratitude. In *The Sociology of emotions: Original essays and research papers,* edited by D. D. Franks and E. D. McCarthy. Greenwich, Conn.: JAI Press.

Hodder, Ian. 1984. Burials, houses, and women in the European Neolithic. In Miller and Tilley.

Hoerning, Erika M. 1988. The myth of female loyalty. *Journal of Psychohistory* 16:19–45.

Hoffer, Peter C., and N. E. H. Hull. 1981. *Murdering mothers: Infanticide in England and New England, 1558–1803.* New York: New York University Press.

Hoffmann, Joan C. 1982. Biorhythms in human reproduction: The not-so-steady states. *Signs* 7:829–44.

Holcombe, Lee. 1983. *Wives and property: Reform of the Married Women's Property Law in nineteenth-century England.* Toronto: University of Toronto Press.

Holder, Maryse. 1988. Another cuntree: At last, a mainstream female art movement. In Raven, Langer, and Frueh.

Holland, Barbara (ed.). 1985. *Soviet sisterhood.* Bloomington: Indiana University Press.

Holland, Dorothy C., and Margaret A. Eisenhart. 1990. *Educated in romance: Women, achievement, and college culture.* Chicago: University of Chicago Press.

Hollibaugh, Amber, and Cherríe Moraga. 1983. What we're rollin' around in bed with: Sexual silences in feminism. In Snitow, Stansell, and Thompson.

Hollway, Wendy. 1987. "I just wanted to kill a woman." Why? The Ripper and male sexuality. In *Sexuality: A reader,* edited by Feminist Review. London: Virago.

Holmstrom, Lynda Lytle. 1972. *The two-career family.* Cambridge, Mass.: Schenkman.

Holt, Alix (ed. and trans.). 1977. *Selected writings of Alexandra Kollontai.* Westport, Conn.: Lawrence Hill.

Holter, Harriet (ed.). 1984. *Patriarchy in a welfare society.* Oslo, Norway: Universitetsforlaget.

Honig, Emily, and Gail Hershatter. 1988. *Personal voices: Chinese women in the 1980s.* Stanford, Calif.: Stanford University Press.

Hood, Jane C. 1983. *Becoming a two-job family.* New York: Praeger.

hooks, bell. 1981. *Ain't I a woman: Black women and feminism.* Boston: South End Press.

————. 1984. *Feminist theory: From margin to center.* Boston: South End Press.

————. 1989. *Talking back: Thinking feminist, talking Black.* Boston: South End Press.

—. 1990. *Yearning: Race, gender, and cultural politics.* Boston: South End Press.

Hootsmans, Helen. 1992. Beyond 1992: Dutch and British corporations and the challenge of dual-career couples. In Lewis, Izraeli, and Hootsmans.

Horan, Patrick M., and Peggy G. Hargis. 1991. Children's work and schooling in the late nineteenth-century family economy. *American Sociological Review* 56:583–96.

Hossfeld, Karen J. 1990. "Their logic against them": Contradictions in sex, race, and class in Silicon Valley. In Ward.

Howard, Jean E. 1988. Crossdressing, the theater, and gender struggle in early modern England. *Shakespeare Quarterly* 39:418–41.

Hubbard, Ruth. 1990. *The politics of women's biology.* New Brunswick, N.J.: Rutgers University Press.

Hubbard, Ruth, Mary Sue Henifin, and Barbara Fried (eds.). 1979. *Women look at biology looking at women.* Boston: G. K. Hall.

Huber, Joan. 1990. Macro-micro links in gender stratification. *American Sociological Review* 55:1–10.

Huber, Joan, and Glenna Spitze. 1983. *Sex stratification: Children, housework, and jobs.* New York: Academic Press.

Hudson, Jackie. 1978. Physical parameters used for female exclusion from law enforcements and athletics. In *Women and sport: From myth to reality,* edited by Carole A. Oglesby. Philadelphia: Lea and Febiger.

Hughes, Everett C. 1971. *The sociological eye.* Chicago: Aldine-Atherton.

Humphries, Jane. 1988. Women's employment in restructuring America: The changing experience of women in three recessions. In *Women and recession,* edited by Jill Rubery. London: Routledge and Kegan Paul.

Hunt, Janet G., and Larry L. Hunt. 1977. Dilemmas and contradictions of status: The case of the dual-career family. *Social Problems* 24:407–16.

—. 1982. The dualities of careers and families: New integrations or new polarities? *Social Problems* 29:499–510.

Hunter, Andrea G., and James Earl Davis. 1992. Constructing gender: An exploration of Afro-American men's conceptualization of manhood. *Gender & Society* 6:464–79.

Hwang, Carl Philip. 1987. The changing role of Swedish fathers. In Lamb (ed.).

Hwang, David Henry. 1989. *M Butterfly.* New York: New American Library.

Hyde, Janet Shibley. 1990. Meta-analysis and the psychology of gender differences. *Signs* 16:55–73.

Hyde, Janet Shibley, and Marilyn J. Essex. 1991. *Parental leave and child care: Setting a research and policy agenda.* Philadelphia: Temple University Press.

Hymowitz, Carol, and Timothy D. Schellhardt. 1986. The glass ceiling. *Wall Street Journal,* 24 March, Section 4, 1.

Imperato-McGinley, Julianne, Luis Guerrero, Teofilo Gautier, and Ralph E. Peterson. 1974. Steroid 5α-reductase deficiency in man: An inherited form of male pseudohermaphroditism. *Science* 186:1213–15.

Imperato-McGinley, Julianne, Ralph E. Peterson, Teofilo Gautier, and Erasmo Sturla.

1979. Androgens and the evolution of male-gender identity among male pseu-pseudohermaphrodites with 5α-reductase deficiency. *New England Journal of Medicine* 300 (May 31):1233–37.

Irigaray, Luce. [1974] 1985. *Speculum of the other woman,* translated by Gillian C. Gill. Ithaca, N.Y.: Cornell University Press.

————. [1977] 1985. *This sex which is not one,* translated by Catherine Porter with Carolyn Burke. Ithaca, N.Y.: Cornell University Press.

————. 1980. When our lips speak together, translated by Carolyn Burke. *Signs* 6:69–79.

————. 1981a. And the one doesn't stir without the other, translated by Helene Vivienne Wenzel. *Signs* 7:60–67.

————. 1981b. This sex which is not one, translated by Claudia Reeder. In Marks and Courtivron.

————. 1981c. When the goods get together, translated by Claudia Reeder. In Marks and Courtivron.

Irvine, Janice M. 1990. *Disorders of desire: Sex and gender in modern American sexology.* Philadelphia: Temple University Press.

Iversen, Joan. 1984. Feminist implications of Mormon polygyny. *Feminist Studies* 10:505–22.

Izraeli, Dafna N. 1981. The Zionist women's movement in Palestine, 1911–1927: A sociological analysis. *Signs* 7:87–114.

————. 1984. The attitudinal effects of gender mix in union committees. *Industrial and Labor Relations Review* 37:212–21.

————. 1992. Culture, policy, and women in dual-earner families in Israel. In Lewis, Izraeli, and Hootsmans.

————. 1993. Outsiders in the promised land: Women managers in Israel. In Adler and Izraeli.

Jackson, Irene V. 1981. Black women and music: A survey from Africa to the New World. In *The Black woman cross-culturally,* edited by Filomena Chioma Steady. Cambridge, Mass.: Schenkman.

Jackson, Jacquelyn Johnson, and Charlotte Perry. 1989. Physical health conditions of middle-aged and aged Blacks. In Markides.

Jackson, Robert Max. 1989. The reproduction of parenting. *American Sociological Review* 54:215–32.

Jackson, Sonia. 1987. Great Britain. In Lamb (ed.).

Jacobs, Jerry A. 1989a. Long-term trends in occupational segregation by sex. *American Journal of Sociology* 95:160–73.

————. 1989b. *Revolving doors: Sex segregation and women's careers.* Stanford, Calif.: Stanford University Press.

Jacobs, John W. 1982. The effect of divorce on fathers: An overview of the literature. *American Journal of Psychiatry* 139:1235–41.

Jacobs, Sue-Ellen, and Christine Roberts. 1989. Sex, sexuality, gender, and gender variance. In *Gender and anthropology,* edited by Sandra Morgen. Washington, D.C.: American Anthropological Association.

Jacobus, Mary, Evelyn Fox Keller, and Sally Shuttleworth (eds.). 1990. *Body/politics: Women and the discourses of science.* New York and London: Routledge.

Jaggar, Alison M. 1983. *Feminist politics and human nature.* Totowa, N.J.: Rowman & Allanheld.

——— ———. 1990. Sexual difference and sexual equality. In Rhode.

James, George. 1991. In trash, a brief life and a note of love. *New York Times,* 1 May.

Jancar, Barbara Wolfe. 1978. *Women under Communism.* Baltimore, Md.: Johns Hopkins University Press.

Janofsky, Michael. 1992. Yamaguchi has the delicate and golden touch. *New York Times,* 22 February.

Jaquette, Jane (ed.). 1989. *The women's movement in Latin America: Feminism and the transition to democracy.* Winchester, Mass.: Unwin Hyman.

Jardine, Alice A. 1985. *Gynesis: Configurations of woman and modernity.* Ithaca, N.Y.: Cornell University Press.

Jasso, Guillermina. 1988. Employment, earnings, and marital cohesiveness: An empirical test of theoretical predictions. In Webster and Foschi.

Jay, Nancy. 1981. Gender and dichotomy. *Feminist Studies* 7:38–56.

Jayakar, Pupul. 1990. *The earth mother: Legends, ritual arts, and goddesses of India.* San Francisco: Harper & Row.

Jencks, Christopher, Lauri Perman, and Lee Rainwater. 1988. What is a good job? A new measure of labor-market success. *American Journal of Sociology* 93:1322–57.

Jenness, Valerie. 1990. From sex as sin to sex as work: COYOTE and the reorganization of prostitution as a social problem. *Social Problems* 37:403–20.

Jennings, Thelma. 1990. "Us colored women had to go through aplenty": Sexual exploitation of African-American slave women. *Journal of Women's History* 1:45–74.

Jenson, Jane. 1986. Gender and reproduction: Or, babies and the state. *Studies in Political Economy* 20:9–46.

Johansson, Sheila Ryan. 1984. Deferred infanticide: Excess female mortality during childhood. In Hausfater and Hrdy.

Johnson, Cynda Ann, Bruce E. Johnson, and Bruce S. Liese. 1991. Dual-doctor marriages: The British experience. *Journal of the American Medical Women's Association* 46:155–59, 163.

Johnson, Kay Ann. 1983. *Women, the family and peasant revolution in China.* Chicago: University of Chicago Press.

Johnson, Richard A., and Gary I. Schulman. 1989. Gender-role composition and role entrapment in decision-making groups. *Gender & Society* 3:355–72.

Jones, Beverly W. 1984. Race, sex, and class: Black female tobacco workers in Durham, North Carolina, 1920–1940, and the development of female consciousness. *Feminist Studies* 10:441–51.

Jones, Jacqueline. 1986. *Labor of love, labor of sorrow: Black women, work, and the family from slavery to the present.* New York: Vintage.

Jones, Kathleen B. 1990. Citizenship in a woman-friendly polity. *Signs* 15:781–812.

Jordanova, Ludmilla. 1989. *Sexual visions: Images of gender in science and medicine between the eighteenth and twentieth centuries.* Madison: University of Wisconsin Press.

Joseph, Gloria I., and Jill Lewis. 1981. *Common differences: Conflicts in Black and white feminist perspectives.* Garden City, N.Y.: Doubleday Anchor.

Joyce, James. [1922] 1986. *Ulysses.* New York: Random House.

Judson, Horace Freeland. 1979. *The eighth day of creation: The makers of the revolution in biology.* New York: Simon & Schuster.

Jump, Teresa L., and Linda Haas. 1987. Fathers in transition: Dual-career fathers participating in child care. In Kimmel (ed.).

Kalleberg, Arne L., and Rachel A. Rosenfeld. 1990. Work in the family and in the labor market: A cross-national, reciprocal analysis. *Journal of Marriage and the Family* 52:331–46.

Kamerman, Sheila B. 1979. Work and family in industrialized societies. *Signs* 4:634–50.

————. 1991. Parental leave and infant care: U.S. and international trends and issues, 1978–1988. In Hyde and Essex.

Kandiyoti, Deniz. 1988. Bargaining with patriarchy. *Gender & Society* 2:274–90.

———— (ed.). 1991. *Women, Islam and the state.* Philadelphia: Temple University Press.

Kando, Thomas. 1973. *Sex change: The achievement of gender identity among feminized transsexuals.* Springfield, Ill.: Charles C Thomas.

Kanter, Rosabeth Moss. 1977a. *Men and women of the corporation.* New York: Basic Books.

————. 1977b. Some effect of proportions on group life: Skewed sex ratios and responses to token women. *American Journal of Sociology* 82:965–90.

Kaplan, E. Anne. 1983. Is the gaze male? In Snitow, Stansell, and Thompson.

Kaplan, Louise J. 1991. *Female perversions: The temptations of Emma Bovary.* New York: Doubleday.

Kasson, John F. 1976. *Civilizing the machine: Technology and republican values in America, 1776–1900.* New York: Penguin.

Katz, Jonathan Ned. 1990. The invention of heterosexuality. *Socialist Review* 20(1):7–34.

Kaufman, Debra R. 1978. Associational ties in academe: Some male and female differences. *Sex Roles* 4:9–21.

Kaufman, Debra R., and Barbara L. Richardson. 1982. *Achievement and women: Challenging the assumptions.* New York: Free Press.

Kaul, Hjørdis. 1991. Who cares? Gender inequality and care leave in Nordic countries. *Acta Sociologica* 34:115–25.

Kay, Herma Hill. 1985. Models of equality. *University of Illinois Law Review* 1985 (1):39–88.

Kearns, Bessie Jean Ruley. 1982. Perceptions of menopause by Papago women. In Voda, Dinnerstein, and O'Donnell.

Keddie, Nikki R., and Beth Baron (eds.). 1991. *Women in Middle Eastern history: Shifting boundaries in sex and gender.* New Haven: Yale University Press.

Keller, Evelyn Fox. 1983. *A feeling for the organism: The life and work of Barbara McClintock.* New York: W. H. Freeman.

————. 1985. *Reflections on gender and science.* New Haven: Yale University Press.

Kelly, Joan. 1984. *Women, history, and theory.* Chicago: University of Chicago Press.

Kelly, Linda. 1987. *Women of the French Revolution.* London: Hamish Hamilton.

Kelly, Liz. 1987. The continuum of sexual violence. In *Women, violence and social control,* edited by Jalna Hanmer and Mary Maynard. Atlantic Highlands, N.J.: Humanities Press.

————. 1988. *Surviving sexual violence.* Minneapolis: University of Minnesota Press.

Kemper, Theodore D. 1990. *Social structure and testosterone: Explorations of the socio-bio-social chain.* New Brunswick, N.J.: Rutgers University Press.

Kemper, Theodore D., and Randall Collins. 1990. Dimensions of microinteraction. *American Journal of Sociology* 96:32–68.

Kendrick, Walter. 1992. Increasing our dirty-word power: Why yesterday's smut is today's erotica. *New York Times Book Review,* 31 May, 3, 36.

Kennedy, Elizabeth Lapovsky, and Madeline Davis. 1989. The reproduction of butch-fem roles: A social constructionist approach. In Peiss and Simmons.

Kessler, Suzanne J. 1990. The medical construction of gender: Case management of intersexed infants. *Signs* 16:3–26.

Kessler, Suzanne J., and Wendy McKenna. [1978] 1985. *Gender: An ethnomethodological approach.* Chicago: University of Chicago Press.

Kessler-Harris, Alice. 1982. *Out to work: A history of wage-earning women in the United States.* New York: Oxford University Press.

————. 1990. *A woman's wage: Historical meanings and social consequences.* Lexington: University Press of Kentucky.

Kibria, Nazli. 1990. Power, patriarchy, and gender conflict in the Vietnamese immigrant community. *Gender & Society* 4:9–24.

Kilborn, Peter T. 1991. Employers left with many decisions. *New York Times,* 21 March.

Kim, Seung-Kyung. 1990. *Capitalism, patriarchy and autonomy: Women factory workers in the Korean economic miracle.* Ph.D. diss., City University of New York Graduate School.

Kimmel, Michael S. 1987a. Men's responses to feminism at the turn of the century. *Gender & Society* 1:261–83.

———— (ed.). 1987b. *Changing men: New directions in research on men and masculinity.* Newbury Park, Calif.: Sage.

———— (ed.). 1991. *Men confront pornography.* New York: Meridian.

Kimmel, Michael S., and Michael A. Messner (eds.). 1992. *Men's lives.* 2d ed. New York: Macmillan.

Kincaid, Jamaica. 1978. Girl. *The New Yorker,* 26 June.

King, Deborah K. 1988. Multiple jeopardy, multiple consciousness: The context of a Black feminist ideology. *Signs* 14:42–72.

Kingson, Jennifer A. 1988. Women in the law say path is limited by "mommy track." *New York Times,* 8 August.

Kingston, Maxine Hong. 1976. *The woman warrior.* New York: Vintage.

Kiss, Yudit. 1991. The second "no": Women in Hungary. *Feminist Review,* no. 39:49–57.

Kitzinger, Celia. 1987. *The social construction of lesbianism*. Newbury Park, Calif.: Sage.

Klatch, Rebecca. 1987. *Women of the new right*. Philadelphia: Temple University Press.

Klein, Fritz, Barry Sepekoff, and Timothy J. Wolf. 1985. Sexual orientation: A multi-variable process. *Journal of Homosexuality* 11(1—2):35—49.

Klein, Fritz, and Timothy J. Wolf (eds.). 1985. *Two lives to lead: Bisexuality in men and women*. New York: Harrington Park Press.

Klein, Renate, Janice Raymond, and Lynette Dumble. 1991. *RU 486: Misconceptions, myths, and morals*. East Haven, Conn.: Inland.

Knight, Chris. 1988. Menstrual synchrony and the Australian rainbow snake. In Buckley and Gottlieb.

———. 1991. *Blood relations: Menstruation and the origins of culture*. New Haven: Yale University Press.

Knights, David, and Hugh Willmott (eds.). 1986. *Gender and the labor process*. Hampshire, England: Gower.

Koch, Gertrud. 1985. Why women go to men's films. In Ecker.

Koch, Lene. 1990. IVF: An irrational choice? *Issues in Reproductive and Genetic Engineering* 3:235—42.

Koeske, Randi Daimon. 1982. Toward a biosocial paradigm for menopausal research: Lessons and contributions from the behavioral sciences. In Voda, Dinnerstein, and O'Donnell.

———. 1983. Lifting the curse of menstruation: Toward a feminist perspective on the menstrual cycle. *Women and Health* 8(2—3):1—15.

Kohn, Melvin L. 1963. Social class and parent-child relationships. *American Journal of Sociology* 68:471—80.

Kohn, Melvin L., and Kazimierz M. Slomczynski. 1991. *Social structure and self-direction: A comparative analysis of the United States and Poland*. Cambridge, Mass.: Basil Blackwell.

Kolata, Gina. 1992a. Track federation urges end to gene test for femaleness. *New York Times*, 12 February.

———. 1992b. Dr. Barbara McClintock, 90, gene research pioneer, dies. *New York Times*, 4 September.

Kolbert, Elizabeth. 1991a. Sexual harassment at work is pervasive, survey says. *New York Times*, 11 October.

———. 1991b. Most in national survey say judge is the more believable. *New York Times*, 15 October.

Kollock, Peter, Philip Blumstein, and Pepper Schwartz. 1985. Sex and power in interaction: Conversational privileges and duties. *American Sociological Review* 50:34—46.

Komarovsky, Mirra. 1962. *Blue-collar marriage*. New York: Random House.

———. 1976. *Dilemmas of masculinity: A study of college youth*. New York: Norton.

———. 1985. *Women in college: Shaping new feminine identities*. New York: Basic Books.

———. 1992. The concept of social role revisited. *Gender & Society* 6:301—13.

Komter, Aafke. 1989. Hidden power in marriage. *Gender & Society* 3:187—216.

Kondo, Dorinne K. 1990a. *Crafting selves: Power, gender, and discourses of identity in a Japanese workplace.* Chicago: University of Chicago Press.

———. 1990b. *M. Butterfly*: Orientalism, gender, and a critique of essentialist identity. *Cultural Critique,* no. 16 (Fall):5–29.

Koonz, Claudia. 1977. Mothers in the Fatherland: Women in Nazi Germany. In Bridenthal and Koonz.

Kraditor, Aileen S. [1965] 1981. *The ideas of the woman suffrage movement, 1890–1920.* New York: Norton.

Kramer, Pamela E., and Sheila Lehman. 1990. Mismeasuring women: A critique of research on computer ability and avoidance. *Signs* 16:158–72.

Krieger, Susan. 1982. Lesbian identity and community: Recent social science literature. *Signs* 8:91–108.

———. 1983. *The mirror dance: Identity in a woman's community.* Philadelphia: Temple University Press.

Kristeva, Julia. 1981. Women's time, translated by Alice Jardine and Harry Blake. *Signs* 7:13–35.

———. [1974] 1977. *About Chinese women,* translated by Anita Burrows. New York: Urizen Books.

Kristof, Nicholas D. 1991. Stark data on women: 100 million are missing. *New York Times,* Science Section, 5 November.

———. 1993. Chinese turn to ultrasound; scorning baby girls for boys. *New York Times,* 21 July.

Kruks, Sonia, Rayna Rapp, and Marilyn B. Young (eds.). 1989. *Promissory notes: Women in the transition to socialism.* New York: Monthly Review Press.

Kuhn, Sarah, and Barry Bluestone. 1987. Economic restructuring and the female labor market: The impact of industrial change on women. In Benería and Stimpson.

Kuhn, Thomas S. 1970. *The structure of scientific revolutions.* 2d ed. Chicago: University of Chicago Press.

Kurz, Demie. 1987. Emergency department response to battered women: A case of resistance. *Social Problems* 34:501–13.

———. 1989. Social science perspectives on wife abuse: Current debates and future directions. *Gender & Society* 3:489–505.

Kurz, Demie, and Evan Stark. 1988. Not-so-benign neglect: The medical response to battering. In Yllö and Bograd.

Kwong, Peter. 1988. American sweatshops 1980s style: Chinese women garment workers. In *Genes & Gender V. Women at work: Socialization toward inequality,* edited by Georgine M. Vromen, Dorothy Burnham, and Susan G. Gordon. New York: Gordian Press.

Ladner, Joyce A. 1971. *Tomorrow's tomorrow: The Black woman.* Garden City, N.Y.: Doubleday.

Lamb, Michael E. 1987a. Introduction: The emergent American father. In Lamb (ed.).

——— (ed.). 1987b. *The father's role: Cross-cultural perspectives.* Hillsdale, N.J.: Lawrence Erlbaum.

Laming, Annette. 1959. *Lascaux and engravings.* Harmondsworth England: Penguin.

Laming-Empéraire, Annette. 1971. *Un hypothèse de travail pour un nouvelle approche des sociétés préhistoriques* [A working hypothesis for a new approach to prehistoric societies]. In *Mélanges offerts à A. Varagnac.* Paris: Ecole Pratique des Historique Etudes.

Lamp, Frederick. 1988. Heavenly bodies: Menses, moon, and the rituals of license among the Temne of Sierra Leone. In Buckley and Gottlieb.

Lamphere, Louise. 1974. Strategies, cooperation, and conflict among women in domestic groups. In Rosaldo and Lamphere.

————. 1985. Bringing the family to the work: Women's culture on the shop floor. *Feminist Studies* 11:519–40.

————. 1987. *From working daughters to working mothers: Immigrant women in a New England industrial community.* Ithaca, N.Y.: Cornell University Press.

Lancaster, Jane Beckman. 1974. *Primate behavior and the emergence of human culture.* New York: Holt, Rinehart and Winston.

Landes, Joan B. 1988. *Women and the public sphere in the age of the French Revolution.* Ithaca, N.Y.: Cornell University Press.

————. 1989. Marxism and the "woman question." In Kruks, Rapp, and Young.

Lang, Gladys Engel, and Kurt Lang. 1990. *Etched in memory: The building and survival of artistic reputation.* Chapel Hill: University of North Carolina Press.

Lapidus, Gail Warshofsky. 1976. Occupational segregation and public policy: A comparative analysis of American and Soviet patterns. *Signs* 1:119–36.

————. 1978. *Women in Soviet society: Equality, development, and social change.* Berkeley: University of California Press.

———— (ed.). 1982. *Women, work, and family in the Soviet Union.* Armonk, N.Y.: M. E. Sharpe.

Laqueur, Thomas. 1990a. *Making sex: Body and gender from the Greeks to Freud.* Cambridge, Mass.: Harvard University Press.

————. 1990b. The facts of fatherhood. In *Conflicts in feminism,* edited by Marianne Hirsch and Evelyn Fox Keller. New York and London: Routledge.

Larrington, Carolyne (ed.). 1992 *The feminist companion to mythology.* London: Pandora Press.

Larwood, Laurie, Ann H. Stromberg, and Barbara A. Gutek (eds.). 1985. *Women and work: An annual review.* Vol. 1. Newbury Park, Calif.: Sage.

Lasker, Judith N., and Shirley Borg. 1987. *In search of parenthood.* Boston: Beacon Press.

Laslett, Barbara, and Johanna Brenner. 1989. Gender and social reproduction: Historical perspectives. *Annual Review of Sociology* 15:381–404.

Laslett, Peter. 1977. *Family life and illicit love in earlier generations.* Cambridge, England: Cambridge University Press.

Lavine, Laura. 1986. Men in women's clothing: Anti-theatricality and effeminization from 1579 to 1642. *Criticism* 28:121–43.

Laws, Judith Long. 1975. The psychology of tokenism: An analysis. *Sex Roles* 1:51–67.

Laws, Judith Long, and Pepper Schwartz. 1977. *Sexual scripts: The social construction of female sexuality.* New York: Holt, Rinehart and Winston.

Laws, Sophie. 1983. The sexual politics of premenstrual tension. *Women's Studies International Forum* 6:19–31.

Leacock, Eleanor. 1981. Women's status in egalitarian society: Implications for social evolution. In *Myths of male dominance*. New York: Monthly Review Press.

Lederer, Laura. 1980a. Then and now: An interview with a former pornography model. In Lederer (ed.).

———. (ed.). 1980b. *Take back the night: Women on pornography.* New York: Morrow.

Leeton, John, L. K. Chan, and Jayne Harmon. 1986. Pregnancy established in an infertile patient after transfer of an embryo fertilized in vitro where the oocyte was donated by the sister of the recipient. *Journal of In Vitro Fertilization and Embryo Transfer* 3:379–82.

Leeton, John, Catriona King, and Jayne Harmon. 1988. Sister-sister in vitro fertilization surrogate pregnancy with donor sperm: The case for surrogate gestational pregnancy. *Journal of In Vitro Fertilization and Embryo Transfer* 5:245–48.

Le Guin, Ursula K. 1969. *The left hand of darkness.* New York: Ace.

———. 1975. *The dispossessed.* New York: Avon.

Leibowitz, Lila. 1986. In the beginning . . .: The origins of the sexual division of labor and the development of the first human societies. In Coontz and Henderson (eds.).

Leidner, Robin. 1991. Serving hamburgers and selling insurance: Gender, work, and identity in interactive service jobs. *Gender & Society* 5:154–77.

Leith, Suzette. 1973. Chinese women in the early Communist Movement. In Young (ed.).

LeMoyne, James. 1990a. Army women and the Saudis: The encounter shocks both. *New York Times*, 25 September

———. 1990b. Ban on driving by women reaffirmed by Saudis. *New York Times,* 15 November.

Lenhart, Sharyn A., Freada Klein, Patricia Falcao, Elizabeth Phelan, and Kevin Smith. 1991. Gender bias against and sexual harassment of AMWA members in Massachusetts. *Journal of the American Medical Women's Association* 46:121–25.

Lenin, V. I. [1934] 1975. *The emancipation of women.* New York: International Publishers.

Lennane, K. Jean, and R. John Lennane. 1973. Alleged psychogenic disorders in women—a possible manifestation of sexual prejudice. *New England Journal of Medicine* 288:288–92.

Lerner, Gerda. 1979. The lady and the mill girl: Changes in the status of women in the Age of Jackson, 1800–1840. In *A heritage of her own,* edited by Nancy F. Cott and Elizabeth Pleck. New York: Simon & Schuster.

———. 1986. *The creation of patriarchy.* New York: Oxford University Press.

Leroi-Gourhan, André. 1968. *The art of prehistoric man in Europe.* London: Thames and Hudson.

———. 1981. *The dawn of European art.* Cambridge, England: Cambridge University Press.

Lever, Janet. 1976. Sex differences in the games children play. *Social Problems* 23:478–87.

————. 1978. Sex differences in the complexity of children's play and games. *American Sociological Review* 43:471–83.

Levesque-Lopman, Louise. 1988. *Claiming reality: Phenomenology and women's experience.* Totowa, N.J.: Rowman & Littlefield.

Levine, Martin P., and Robin Leonard. 1984. Discrimination against lesbians in the work force. *Signs* 9:700–10.

Levinson, Richard M. 1975. Sex discrimination and employment practices: An experiment with unconventional job inquiries. *Social Problems* 22:533–42.

Lévi-Strauss, Claude. 1956. The family. In *Man, culture, and society,* edited by Harry L. Shapiro. New York: Oxford.

————. [1949] 1969. *The elementary structures of kinship,* translated by J. H. Bell and J. R. von Sturmer. Boston: Beacon Press.

Levy, Darline Gay, Harriet Branson Applewhite, and Mary Durham Johnson (eds.). 1979. *Women in revolutionary Paris, 1789–1795.* Urbana: University of Illinois Press.

Levy, Judith A. 1988. Intersections of gender and aging. *Sociological Quarterly* 29:479–86.

Lewin, Tamar. 1991a. Nude pictures are ruled sexual harassment. *New York Times,* 23 January.

————. 1991b. A case study of sexual harassment. *New York Times,* 11 October.

Lewin-Epstein, Noah, and Haya Stier. 1987. Labor market structure, gender and socio-economic inequality in Israel. *Israel Social Science Research* 5(1–2):107–20.

Lewis, Neil A. 1993. Tailhook affair brings censure of 3 admirals. *New York Times,* 16 October.

Lewis, Jane, and Gertrude Åström. 1992. Equality, difference, and state welfare: Labor market and family policies in Sweden. *Feminist Studies* 18:59–87.

Lewis, Jill. 1981. The subject of struggle: Feminism and sexuality. In Joseph and Lewis.

Lewis, Susan, Dafna N. Izraeli, and Helen Hootsmans (eds.). 1992. *Dual-earner families: International perspectives.* London: Sage.

Lightfoot-Klein, Hanny. 1989. *Prisoners of ritual: An odyssey into female circumcision in Africa.* New York: Harrington Park Press.

Lim, Linda Y. C. 1990. Women's work in export factories: The politics of a cause. In Tinker.

Lin, Nan, and Yanjie Bian. 1991. Getting ahead in urban China. *American Journal of Sociology* 97:657–88.

Lipman-Blumen, Jean. 1976. Toward a homosocial theory of sex roles: An explanation of sex segregation in social institutions. *Signs* 1(Spring, pt. 2):15–31.

Lisak, David. 1991. Sexual aggression, masculinity, and fathers. *Signs* 16:238–62.

Lockard, Denyse. 1985. The lesbian community: An anthropological approach. *Journal of Homosexuality* 11(3–4):83–95.

Lockheed, Marlaine E. 1985. Sex and social influence: A meta-analysis guided by theory. In *Status, rewards, and influence: How expectations organize behavior,* edited by Joseph Berger and Morris Zelditch, Jr. San Francsico: Jossey-Bass.

Longino, Helen E. 1990. *Science as social knowledge*. Princeton: Princeton University Press.

Longino, Helen E., and Ruth Doell. 1983. Body, bias, and behavior: A comparative analysis of reasoning in two areas of biological science. *Signs* 9:206–27.

Lopata, Helena Znaniecki. 1971. *Occupation: Housewife*. New York: Oxford University Press.

Lopata, Helena Znaniecki, and Joseph H. Pleck (eds.). 1983. *Research in the interweave of social roles: Jobs and families*. Vol. 3. Greenwich, Conn.: JAI Press.

Lorber, Judith. 1967. Deviance as performance: The case of illness. *Social Problems* 14:302–10.

———. 1975. Beyond equality of the sexes: The question of the children. *Family Coordinator* 24:465–72.

———. 1981. The limits of sponsorship for women physicians. *Journal of the American Medical Women's Association* 36:329–38.

———. 1984. *Women physicians: Careers, status, and power*. London and New York: Tavistock.

———. 1985. More women physicians: Will it mean more humane health care? *Social Policy* 16(Summer):50–54.

———. 1986. Dismantling Noah's ark. *Sex Roles* 14:567–80.

———. 1987a. A welcome to a crowded field: Where will the new women physicians fit in? *Journal of the American Medical Women's Association* 42:149-52.

———. 1987b. *In vitro* fertilization and gender politics. *Women & Health* 13:117–33.

———. [1979] 1989a. Trust, loyalty, and the place of women in the informal organization of work. In Freeman.

———. 1989b. Choice, gift, or patriarchal bargain? Women's consent to *in vitro* fertilization in male infertility. *Hypatia* 4:23–36.

———. 1991. Can women physicians ever be true equals in the American medical profession? In *Current research in occupations and professions*, edited by Judith A. Levy. Vol. 6. Greenwich, Conn.: JAI Press.

Lorber, Judith, and Lakshmi Bandlamudi. 1993. Dynamics of marital bargaining in male infertility. *Gender & Society* 7:32–49.

Lorber, Judith, Rose Laub Coser, Alice S. Rossi, and Nancy Chodorow. 1981. On *The reproduction of mothering*: A methodological debate. *Signs* 6:482–514.

Lorber, Judith, and Martha Ecker. 1983. Career development of female and male physicians. *Journal of Medical Education* 58:447–56.

Lorber, Judith, and Dorothy Greenfeld. 1990. Couples' experiences with *in vitro* fertilization: A phenomenological approach. In *Advances in assisted reproductive technologies*, edited by S. Mashiach et al. New York: Plenum.

Lorde, Audre. 1984. *Sister outsider*. Trumansberg, N.Y.: Crossing Press.

Loscocco, Karyn A., and Joyce Robinson. 1991. Barriers to women's small-business success in the United States. *Gender & Society* 5:511–32.

Lown, Judy. 1990. *Women and industrialization: Gender at work in nineteenth-century England*. Minneapolis: University of Minnesota Press.

Luker, Kristin. 1975. *Taking chances: Abortion and the decision not to contracept*. Berkeley: University of California Press.

————. 1984. *Abortion and the politics of motherhood.* Berkeley: University of California Press.

Luria, Zella, and Eleanor W. Herzog. 1991. Sorting gender out in a children's museum. *Gender & Society* 5:224–32.

Luxemburg, Rosa. 1961. *The Russian Revolution.* Ann Arbor: University of Michigan Press.

Lydon, Mary. 1991. Calling yourself a woman: Marguerite Yourcenar and Colette. *Differences: A Journal of Feminist Cultural Studies* 3(3):26–44.

Lyman, Peter. 1987. The fraternal bond as a joking relationship: A case study of the role of sexist jokes in male group bonding. In Kimmel (ed.).

Maccoby, Eleanor. 1990. Gender and relationships: A developmental account. *American Psychologist* 45:513–20.

MacCormack, Carol P. 1980. Nature, culture and gender: A critique. In *Nature, culture and gender,* edited by Carol P. MacCormack and Marilyn Strathern. Cambridge, England: Cambridge University Press.

MacKinnon, Catharine A. 1979. *Sexual harassment of working women.* New Haven: Yale University Press.

————. 1982. Feminism, Marxism, method, and the state: An agenda for theory. *Signs* 7:515–44.

————. 1983. Feminism, Marxism, method and the state, Part II. *Signs* 8:635–58.

————. 1987. *Feminism unmodified.* Cambridge, Mass.: Harvard University Press.

————. 1989. *Toward a feminist theory of the state.* Cambridge, Mass.: Harvard University Press.

————. 1990. Legal perspectives on sexual difference. In Rhode.

MacLeod, Arlene Elowe. 1991. *Accommodating protest: Working women, the new veiling and change in Cairo.* New York: Columbia University Press.

Madden, Janice Fanning. 1985. The persistence of pay differentials: The economics of sex discrimination. In Larwood, Stromberg, and Gutek.

Mainardi, Patricia. 1970. The politics of housework. In *Sisterhood is powerful,* edited by Robin Morgan. New York: Vintage.

Majors, Richard. 1990. Cool pose: Black masculinity in sports. In Messner and Sabo.

Majors, Richard, and Janet Mancini Billson. 1992. *Cool pose: The dilemmas of Black manhood in America.* New York: Lexington Books.

Malveaux, Julianne. 1987. Comparable worth and its impact on Black women. In Simms and Malveaux.

————. 1988. The economic statuses of Black families. In *Black families,* edited by Harriette Pipes McAdoo. 2d. ed. Newbury Park, Calif.: Sage.

Mamonova, Tatyana (ed.). 1984. *Women and Russia: Feminist writings from the Soviet Union.* Boston: Beacon Press.

————. 1989. *Russian women's studies: Essays on sexism in Soviet culture.* New York: Pergamon.

Mangan, J. A., and Roberta J. Park. 1987. *From fair sex to feminism: Sport and the socialization of women in the industrial and post-industrial eras.* London: Frank Cass.

Mangini, Shirley. 1991. Memories of resistance: Female activists from the Spanish Civil War. *Signs* 17:171–86.

Marcus, Jane. 1982. Storming the toolshed. *Signs* 7:622–40.

————. 1987. *Virginia Woolf and the languages of patriarchy.* Bloomington: Indiana University Press.

Marglin, Stephen A. 1978. What do bosses do? The origins and functions of hierarchy in capitalist production. In *The division of labor: The labor process and class-struggle in modern capitalism,* edited by Andre Gorz. Hassocks, England: Harvester Press.

Margolis, Diane Rothbard. 1985. Redefining the situation: Negotiations on the meaning of woman. *Social Problems* 32:332–47.

Marini, Margaret Mooney. 1989. Sex differences in earnings in the United States. *Annual Review of Sociology* 15:343–80.

Marini, Margaret Mooney, and Mary C. Brinton. 1987. Sex typing in occupational socialization. In Bose and Spitze.

Markides, Kyriakos S. (ed.). 1989. *Aging and health: Perspectives on gender, race, ethnicity and class.* Newbury Park, Calif.: Sage.

Marks, Elaine, and Isabelle de Courtivron (eds.). 1981. *New French feminisms.* New York: Schocken.

Marsh, Barbara. 1991. Women in the work force (Tables). *Wall Street Journal,* 18 October, B3.

Marshack, Alexander. 1972. *The roots of civilization.* New York: McGraw-Hill.

Marshall, Harriette. 1991. The social construction of motherhood: An analysis of childcare and parenting manuals. In *Motherhood: Meanings, practices and ideologies,* edited by Ann Phoenix, Anne Woollett, and Eva Lloyd. Newbury Park, Calif.: Sage.

Marshall, John. 1981. Pansies, perverts and macho men: Changing conceptions of male homosexuality. In Plummer (ed.).

Marshall, Judi. 1989. Re-visioning career concepts: A feminist invitation. In *Handbook of career theory,* edited by Michael B. Arthur, Douglas T. Hall, and Barbara S. Lawrence. Cambridge, England: Cambridge University Press.

Martin, Emily. 1987. *The woman in the body: A cultural analysis of reproduction.* Boston: Beacon Press.

————. 1991. The egg and the sperm: How science has constructed a romance based on stereotypical male-female roles. *Signs* 16:485–501.

Martin, Lynn. 1991. *A report on the glass ceiling initiative.* Washington, D.C.: U.S. Department of Labor.

Martin, Patricia Yancey. 1991. Gender, interaction, and inequality in organizations. In Ridgeway.

————. 1993. Feminist practice in organizations: Implications for management. In Fagenson.

Martin, Patricia Yancey, Dianne Harrison, and Diana DiNitto. 1983. Advancement for women in hierarchical organizations: A multilevel analysis of problems and prospects. *Journal of Applied and Behavioral Science* 19:19–33.

Martin, Patricia Yancey, and Robert A. Hummer. 1989. Fraternities and rape on campus. *Gender & Society* 3:457–73.

Martin, Susan Ehrlich. 1980. *Breaking and entering: Police women on patrol.* Berkeley: University of California Press.

Marwell, Gerald. 1975. Why ascription? Parts of a more or less formal theory of the functions and dysfunctions of sex roles. *American Sociological Review* 40:445–55.

Mason, Beverly J. 1987. Jamaican working-class women: Producers and reproducers. In Simms and Malveaux.

Mason, Karen Oppenheim. 1985. *The status of women: A review of its relationships to fertility and mortality.* New York: Rockefeller Foundation.

Masters, William H., and Virginia E. Johnson. 1966. *Human sexual response.* Boston: Little, Brown.

Mathews, Susan M. 1991. Title VII and sexual harassment: Beyond damages control. *Yale Journal of Law and Feminism* 3:299–320.

Matthaei, Julie A. 1982. *An economic history of women's work in America.* New York: Schocken.

Maurois, André. 1955. *Lelia: The life of George Sand,* translated by Gerard Hopkins. New York: Harper.

Mauss, Marcel. 1954. *The gift.* Glencoe, Ill.: Free Press.

May, Martha. 1982. The historical problem of the family wage: The Ford Motor Company and the five-dollar day. *Feminist Studies* 8:399–424.

Mayer, Jane, and Jill Abramson. 1993. The surreal Anita Hill. *New Yorker,* 24 May.

McAdam, Doug. 1992. Gender as a mediator of the activist experience: The case of Freedom Summer. *American Journal of Sociology* 97:1211–40.

McAndrew, Maggie. 1985. Soviet women's magazines. In Holland.

McClary, Susan. 1991. *Feminine endings: Music, gender, and sexuality.* Minneapolis: University of Minnesota Press.

McClintock, Martha. 1979. Considering "A biosocial perspective on parenting." *Signs* 4:703–10.

McConnell, Joyce E. 1992. Beyond metaphor: Battered women, involuntary servitude and the Thirteenth Amendment. *Yale Journal of Law and Feminism* 4:207–53.

McCorriston, Joy, and Frank Hole. 1991. The ecology of seasonal stress and the origins of agriculture in the Near East. *American Anthropologist* 93:46–69.

McCrea, Frances B. 1986. The politics of menopause: The "discovery" of a deficiency disease. In *The sociology of health and illness,* edited by Peter Conrad and Rochelle Kern. New York: St. Martin's Press.

McCullough, Joan. 1973. The 13 who were left behind. *Ms. Magazine,* September.

McFadden, Robert D. 1991. New Jersey pilot, a woman, dies in crash in Gulf. *New York Times,* 4 March.

McGaw, Judith A. 1982. Women and the history of American technology. *Signs* 7:798–828.

McGrew, W. C. 1981. The female chimpanzee as a human evolutionary prototype. In Dahlberg.

McIntosh, Mary. 1968. The homosexual role. *Social Problems* 16:182–92.

———. 1978. The state and the oppression of women. In *Feminism and materialism: Women and modes of production,* edited by Annette Kuhn and AnnMarie Wolpe. London: Routledge and Kegan Paul.

McLanahan, Sara S., Annemette Sørenson, and Dorothy Watson. 1989. Sex differences in poverty, 1950–1980. *Signs* 15:102–22.

McLaren, Angus. 1978. *Birth control in nineteenth century England.* New York: Holmes & Meier.

———. 1984. *Reproductive rituals: The perception of fertility in England from the sixteenth century to the nineteenth century.* London and New York: Methuen.

McLaughlin, Steven D. 1978. Occupational sex identification and the assessment of male and female earnings inequality. *American Sociological Review* 43:909–21.

McNamara, Jo Ann, and Suzanne Wemple. 1974. The power of women through the family in medieval Europe, 500–1100. In *Clio's consciousness raised: New perspectives on the history of women,* edited by Mary S. Hartman and Lois Banner. New York: Harper Colophon.

McWhirter, David P., Stephanie A. Sanders, and June Machover Reinisch (eds.). 1990. *Homosexuality/heterosexuality: Concepts of sexual orientation.* New York: Oxford University Press.

Meillassoux, Claude. [1975] 1981. *Maidens, meal and money: Capitalism and the domestic community.* Cambridge, England: Cambridge University Press.

Mellaart, James. 1967. *Çatal Hüyük: A Neolithic town in Anatolia,* New York: McGraw-Hill.

Mellars, Paul A. 1985. The ecological basis of social complexity in the Upper Paleolithic of southwestern France. In Price and Brown.

Mencher, Joan. 1988. Women's work and poverty: Women's contribution to household maintenance in South India. In Dwyer and Bruce.

Mernissi, Fatima. 1987. *Beyond the veil: Male-female dynamics in Muslim society.* Bloomington: Indiana University Press.

Merritt, Deborah J., and Barbara F. Reskin. 1992. The double minority: Empirical evidence of a double standard in law school hiring of minority women. *Southern California Law Review* 65:2299–2359.

Merton, Robert K. 1968. The Matthew effect in science. *Science* 159:56–63.

Messinger, Lisa Mintz. 1988. *Georgia O'Keeffe.* New York: Metropolitan Museum of Art.

Messner, Michael A. 1987. The meaning of success: The athletic experience and the development of male identity. In Brod.

———. 1988. Sports and male domination: The female athlete as contested ideological terrain. *Sociology of Sport Journal* 5:197–211.

———. 1989. Masculinities and athletic careers. *Gender & Society* 1:71–88.

———. 1992. *Power at play: Sports and the problem of masculinity.* Boston: Beacon Press.

Messner, Michael A., Margaret Carlisle Duncan, and Kerry Jensen. 1993. Separating the men from the girls: The gendered language of televised sports. *Gender & Society* 7:121–37.

Messner, Michael A., and Donald F. Sabo (eds.). 1990. *Sport, men, and the gender order: Critical feminist perspectives.* Champaign, Ill.: Human Kinetics.

Meyers, Carol. 1988. *Discovering Eve: Ancient Israelite women in context.* New York: Oxford University Press.

Miall, Charlene E. 1986. The stigma of involuntary childlessness. *Social Problems* 33:268–82.

Michelow, M. C., J. Bernstein, M. J. Jacobson, J. L. McLoughlin, D. Rubenstein, A. I. Hacking, S. Preddy, and I. J. van der Wat. 1988. Mother-daughter in vitro fertilization triplet surrogate pregnancy. *Journal of In Vitro Fertilization and Embryo Transfer* 5:31–34.

Mies, Maria. 1982. *The lace makers of Narsapur: Indian housewives produce for the world market.* London: Zed Books.

———. 1986. *Patriarchy and accumulation on a world scale.* London: Zed Books.

Mies, Maria, Veronika Bennholdt-Thomsen, and Claudia von Werlhof. 1988. *Women: The last colony.* London: Zed Books.

Milkman, Ruth. 1976. Women's work and the economic crisis: Some lessons of the Great Depression. *Review of Radical Political Economics* 8:73–97.

———. 1987. *Gender at work.* Urbana: University of Illinois Press.

Miller, Daniel, and Christopher Tilley (eds.). 1984. *Ideology, power, and prehistory.* Cambridge, England: Cambridge University Press.

Miller, Eleanor M. 1986. *Street women.* Philadelphia: Temple University Press.

Millett, Kate. 1970. *Sexual politics.* Garden City, N.Y.: Doubleday.

Millman, Marcia. 1991. *Warm hearts and cold cash: The intimate dynamics of families and money.* New York: Free Press.

Mine, Anne. 1988. The changing economy of attention. *Socialist Review* 18(2):87–99.

Mink, Gwendolyn. 1990. The lady and the tramp: Gender, race, and the origins of the American welfare state. In Gordon (ed.).

Mitchell, Juliet. 1975. *Psychoanalysis and feminism.* New York: Vintage.

Mitchell, Juliet, and Jacqueline Rose (eds.). 1985. *Feminine sexuality: Jacques Lacan and the école freudienne.* New York: Norton.

Moen, Phyllis. 1989. *Working parents: Transformations in gender roles and public policies in Sweden.* Madison: University of Wisconsin Press.

Moen, Phyllis, and Ken R. Smith. 1986. Women at work: Commitment and behavior over the life course. *Sociological Forum* 1:450–75.

Moers, Ellen. 1977. *Literary women: The great writers.* Garden City, N.Y.: Doubleday Anchor.

Moffatt, Michael. 1989. *Coming of age in New Jersey: College and American culture.* New Brunswick, N.J.: Rutgers University Press.

Moghadam, Valentine M. 1989. Revolution, the state, Islam, and women: Sexual politics in Iran and Afghanistan. *Social Text* 22:40–61.

———. 1990a. Gender and restructuring: Perestroika, the 1989 revolutions, and women. WIDER Working Paper 87. Helsinki, Finland: World Institute for Development Economics Research, United Nations University.

———. 1990b. Gender, development and policy: Toward equity and empowerment. Helsinki, Finland: World Institute for Development Economics Research, United Nations University.

———. 1992. Development and patriarchy: The Middle East and North Africa in economic and demographic transition. WIDER Working Paper 99. Helsinki, Finland: World Institute for Development Economics Research, United Nations University.

———. 1993a. *Modernizing women: Gender and social change in the Middle East.* Boulder, Colo.: Lynne Rienner.

————— (ed.). 1993b. *Gender and national identity: The woman question in Algeria, Iran, Afghanistan, and Palestine.* London: Zed Books.

Mohr, James C. 1978. *Abortion in America: The origins and evolution of national policy, 1800–1900.* New York: Oxford University Press.

Moi, Toril. 1985. *Sexual/textual politics: Feminist literary theory.* New York: Methuen.

Molm, Linda D. 1988. Status generalization in power-imbalanced dyads: The effects of gender on power use. In Webster and Foschi.

Molotch, Harvey. 1988. The restroom and equal opportunity. *Sociological Forum* 3:128–32.

Molyneux, Maxine. 1981. Women in socialist societies: Problems of theory and practice. In Young, Wolkowitz, and McCullagh.

—————. 1985. Mobilization without emancipation? Women's interests, the state and revolution in Nicaragua. *Feminist Studies* 11:227–54.

Money, John. 1988. *Gay, straight and in-between: The sexology of erotic orientation.* New York: Oxford University Press.

Money, John, and Anke A. Ehrhardt. 1972. *Man & woman, boy & girl.* Baltimore, Md.: Johns Hopkins University Press.

Moore, Gwen. 1990. Structural determinants of men's and women's personal networks. *American Sociological Review* 55:726–35.

Moore, Henrietta L. 1989. *Feminism and anthropology.* Minneapolis: University of Minnesota Press.

Moran, Malcolm. 1992. Title IX: A 20-year search for equity. *New York Times,* Sports Section, 21, 22, 23 June.

Morgan, Robin. 1978. How to run the pornographers out of town (and preserve the First Amendment). *Ms. Magazine,* November.

Morrill, Calvin. 1991. Conflict management, honor, and organizational change. *American Journal of Sociology* 97:585–621.

Morris, Jan. 1975. *Conundrum.* New York: Signet.

Morrison, Ann M., Randall P. White, Ellen Van Velsor and the Center for Creative Leadership. 1987. *Breaking the glass ceiling.* Reading, Mass.: Addison-Wesley.

Morrison, Toni. 1987. *Beloved.* New York: Knopf.

Morrissey, Marietta. 1989. *Slave women in the New World: Gender stratification in the Caribbean.* Lawrence: University Press of Kansas.

Mossé, Claude. 1991. Women in the Spartan revolutions of the third century B.C., translated by Sarah Pomeroy. In Pomeroy (ed.).

Ms. Magazine. 1991. Reinventing the wheel. March.

Mueller, Eva. 1982. The allocation of women's time and its relation to fertility. In *Women's roles and population trends in the third world,* edited by Richard Anker, Mayra Buvinic, and Nadia H. Youssef. London: Croom Helm.

Mukhopadhyay, Carol C., and Patricia J. Higgins. 1988. Anthropological studies of women's status revisited: 1977–1987. *Annual Review of Anthropology* 17:461–95.

Muller, Charlotte. 1990. *Health care and gender.* New York: Russell Sage Foundation.

Muller, Viana. 1985. Origins of class and gender hierarchy in Northwest Europe. *Dialectical Anthropology* 10:93–105.

Mullings, Leith. 1986. Uneven development: Class, race, and gender in the United States before 1900. In *Women's work: Development and the division of labor by gender,* edited by Eleanor Leacock and Helen I. Safa. South Hadley, Mass.: Bergin & Garvey.

Mulvey, Laura. 1989. *Visual and other pleasures.* Bloomington: Indiana University Press.

Myrdal, Jan. 1965. *Report from a Chinese village.* New York: Pantheon.

Nadler, Ronald D. 1990. Homosexual behavior in nonhuman primates. In McWhirter, Sanders, and Reinisch.

Naftolin, F., and E. Butz (eds.). 1981. Sexual dimorphism. *Science* 211:1263–1324.

Nanda, Serena. 1984. The hijiras of India: A preliminary report. *Medicine and Law* 3:59–75.

———. 1986. The hijiras of India: Cultural and individual dimensions of an institutionalized third gender role. *Journal of Homosexuality* 11(3–4):35–54.

———. 1990. *Neither man nor woman: The hijiras of India.* Belmont, Calif.: Wadsworth.

Naples, Nancy. 1991a. Contradictions in the gender subtext of the war on poverty: The community work and resistance of women from low-income communities. *Social Problems* 38:301–17.

———. 1991b. "Just what needed to be done": The political practice of women community workers in low-income neighborhoods. *Gender & Society* 5:478–94.

———. 1991c. A socialist feminist analysis of the Family Support Act of 1988. *Affilia* 6:23–38.

———. 1992. Activist mothering: Cross-generational continuity in the community work of women from low-income urban neighborhoods. *Gender & Society* 6:441–63.

Nash, June. 1990. Latin American women in the world capitalist crisis. *Gender & Society* 4:338–53.

Nash, June, and María Patricia Fernández-Kelly (eds.). 1983. *Women, men, and the international division of labor.* Albany: State University of New York Press.

Nash, Nathaniel C. 1992. Shining Path women: So many and so ferocious. *New York Times,* 22 September.

Nathanson, Constance A. 1975. Illness and the feminine role: A theoretical review. *Social Science and Medicine* 9:57–62.

Nazzari, Muriel. 1983. The woman question in Cuba: An analysis of material constraints on its solution. *Signs* 10:246–63.

Nead, Lynda. 1990. The female nude: Pornography, art, and sexuality. *Signs* 15:323–35.

Nelson, Barbara J. 1984. Women's poverty and women's citizenship: Some political consequences of economic marginality. *Signs* 10:209–31.

———. 1990. The origins of the two-channel welfare state: Workmen's compensation and mothers' aid. In Gordon (ed.).

Nelson, Margaret K. 1990. *Negotiated care: The experience of family day care providers.* Philadelphia: Temple University Press.

Nestle, Joan. 1983. My mother liked to fuck. In Snitow, Stansell, and Thompson.

Netting, Robert McC., Richard R. Wilk, and Eric J. Arnould (eds.). 1984. *Households: Comparative and historical studies of the domestic group.* Berkeley: University of California Press.

New, Rebecca S., and Laura Benigni. 1987. Italian fathers and infants: Cultural constraints on paternal behavior. In Lamb (ed.).

Newton, Esther. 1984. The mythic mannish lesbian: Radclyffe Hall and the new woman. *Signs* 9:557–75.

New York Times. 1989a. Musician's death at 74 reveals he was a woman. 2 February.

———. 1989b. Gymnastic girls, not women. 1 August.

———. 1990. Woman is acquitted in trial for using the men's room. 3 November.

———. 1991a. Paper includes gay couples on what was wedding page. 22 March.

———. 1991b. Woman to lead Annapolis midshipmen. 28 April.

———. 1991c. Citing sexism, Stanford doctor quits. 4 June.

———. 1991d. Should women be sent into combat? Week in Review, 21 July.

———. 1991e. Woman gives birth for daughter. 13 October.

———. 1992a. Few women found in top public jobs. 3 January.

———. 1992b. Sex crimes in Gulf cited. 18 July.

Nickel, Horst, and Ellen M. T. Köcher. 1987. West Germany and the German-speaking countries. In Lamb (ed.).

Nielsen, Joyce McCarl. 1984. Women in dystopia/utopia: *1984* and beyond. *International Journal of Women's Studies* 7:144–54.

Nochlin, Linda. 1988. *Women, art, and power and other essays.* New York: Harper & Row.

Nolan, Mary. 1990. Housework made easy: The Taylorized housewife in Weimar Germany's rationalized economy. *Feminist Studies* 16:549–77.

Nordheimer, Jon. 1991. Women's role in combat: The war resumes. *New York Times,* 26 May.

Novaes, Simone B. 1989. Giving, receiving, paying: Gamete donors and donor policies in reproductive medicine. *International Journal of Technology Assessment in Health Care* 5:639–57.

Nsiah-Jefferson, Laurie, and Elaine J. Hall. 1989. Reproductive technology: Perspectives and implications for low-income women and women of color. In Ratcliff et al.

Nugent, Kevin. 1987. The father's role in early Irish socialization: Historical and empirical perspectives. In Lamb (ed.).

Nuss, Shirley, with Ettore Denti and David Viry. 1989. *Women in the world of work: Statistical analysis and projections to the year 2000.* Geneva: International Labor Office.

Oakley, Ann. 1974. *The sociology of housework.* New York: Pantheon.

———. 1976. *Women's work: The housewife, past and present.* New York: Vintage.

———. 1980. *Becoming a mother.* New York: Schocken.

O'Brien, Mary. 1981. *The politics of reproduction.* New York: Routledge.

———. 1989. *Reproducing the world: Essays in feminist theory.* Boulder, Colo.: Westview Press.

Odum, Maria. 1992. If the G.N.P. counted housework, would women count for more? *New York Times,* News of the Week, 5 April.

Oehninger, Sergio, John F. Stecker, and Anibal A. Acosta. 1992. Male infertility: The impact of assisted reproductive technologies. *Current Opinion in Obstetrics and Gynecology* 4(April):185–96.

Offen, Karen. 1988. Defining feminism: A comparative historical approach. *Signs* 14:119–57.

Off Our Backs. 1990. Romania: Pregnancy police. February.

Okin, Susan Moller. 1979. *Women in Western political thought.* Princeton: Princeton University Press.

Oldfield, Sybil. 1987. German women in the resistance to Hitler. In Reynolds (ed.).

Olsen, Fran. 1984. The politics of family law. *Law and Inequality* 2:1–19.

Olson, Jon, and Jon Miller. 1983. Gender and interaction in the workplace. In Lopata and Pleck.

Olson, Wendy. 1990. Beyond Title IX: Toward an agenda for women and sports in the 1990s. *Yale Journal of Law and Feminism* 3:105–51.

O'Meara, J. Donald. 1989. Cross-sex friendship: Four basic challenges of an ignored relationship. *Sex Roles* 21:525–43.

Omolade, Barbara. 1983. Hearts of darkness. In Snitow, Stansell, and Thompson.

Orloff, Ann Shola. 1993. Gender and the social rights of citizenship: The comparative analysis of gender relations and welfare states. *American Sociological Review* 58:303–28.

Ortner, Sherry B. 1974. Is female to male as nature is to culture? In Rosaldo and Lamphere.

Ortner, Sherry B., and Harriet Whitehead. 1981a. Introduction: Accounting for sexual meanings. In Ortner and Whitehead (eds.).

———— (eds.). 1981b. *Sexual meanings: The cultural construction of gender and sexuality.* Cambridge, England: Cambridge University Press.

Ory, Marcia G., and H. R. Warner. 1990. *Gender, health and longevity.* New York: Springer.

Osmond, Marie Withers, and Patricia Yancey Martin. 1983. Women, work, and welfare: A comparison of Black and white female heads of households. *International Journal of Sociology of the Family* 13:37–56.

Ostrander, Susan A. 1984. *Women of the upper class.* Philadelphia: Temple University Press.

Otis, Leah L. 1986. Municipal wet nurses in fifteenth-century Montpellier. In Hanawalt.

Overall, Christine. 1992. What's wrong with prostitution? Evaluating sex work. *Signs* 17:705–24.

Padgug, Robert A. 1989. Gay villain, gay hero: Homosexuality and the social construction of AIDS. In Peiss and Simmons.

Pahl, Jan. 1989. *Money and marriage.* New York: St. Martin's Press.

Paige, Karen Ericksen, and Jeffrey M. Paige. 1981. *The politics of reproductive ritual.* Berkeley: University of California Press.

Palmer, Phyllis. 1989. *Domesticity and dirt: Housewives and domestic servants in the United States, 1920–1945.* Philadelphia: Temple University Press.

Paludi, Michele A. (ed.). 1990. *Ivory power: Sexual harassment on campus.* Albany: State University of New York Press.

Papanek, Hanna. 1979. Family status production: The "work" and "non-work" of women. *Signs* 4:775–81.

———. 1990. To each less than she needs, from each more than she can do: Allocations, entitlements, and value. In Tinker.

Pareles, Jon. 1990. On the edge of the permissible: Madonna's evolving persona. *New York Times*, Arts and Leisure Section, 11 June.

Parker, Stephen. 1990. *Informal marriage, cohabitation and the law, 1750–1989*. New York: St. Martin's Press.

Parlee, Mary Brown. 1973. The premenstrual syndrome. *Psychological Bulletin* 80:454–65.

———. 1982a. The psychology of the menstrual cycle: Biological and psychological perspectives. In *Behavior and the menstrual cycle,* edited by Richard C. Friedman. New York: Marcel Dekker.

———. 1982b. Changes in moods and activation levels during the menstrual cycle in experimentally naive subjects. *Psychology of Women Quarterly* 7:119–31.

Parsons, Talcott. 1951. *The social system*. Glencoe, Ill.: Free Press.

Pascall, Gillian. 1986. *Social policy: A feminist analysis*. London and New York: Tavistock.

Pateman, Carole. 1988. *The sexual contract*. Stanford, Calif.: Stanford University Press.

Pearce, Diana. 1990. Welfare is not *for* women: Why the war on poverty cannot conquer the feminization of poverty. In Gordon (ed.).

Pearson, Carol S. 1984. Of time and revolution: Theories of social change in contemporary feminist science fiction. In *Women in search of utopia: Mavericks and mythmakers,* edited by Ruby Rohrlich and Elaine Hoffman Baruch. New York: Schocken.

Peiss, Kathy. 1983. "Charity girls" and city pleasures: Historical notes on working-class sexuality, 1880–1920. In Snitow, Stansell, and Thompson.

Peiss, Kathy, and Christina Simmons (eds.). 1989. *Passion and power: Sexuality in history*. Philadelphia: Temple University Press.

Peña, Manuel. 1991. Class, gender, and machismo: The "treacherous-woman" folklore of Mexican male workers. *Gender & Society* 5:30–46.

Pendle, Karin. 1992. Lost voices. *Opera News,* July.

Penelope, Julia. 1990. The lesbian perspective. In Allen.

Perlmutter, Ellen, and Pauline B. Bart. 1982. Changing views of "the change": A critical review and suggestions for an attributional approach. In Voda, Dinnerstein, and O'Donnell.

Perman, Lauri, and Beth Stevens. 1989. Industrial segregation and the gender distribution of fringe benefits. *Gender & Society* 3:388–404.

Perry, Mary Elizabeth. 1987. The manly woman: A historical case study. *American Behavioral Scientist* 31:86–100.

Perry, Ruth, and Lisa Greber. 1990. Women and computers: An introduction. *Signs* 16:74–101.

Person, Ethel Spector. 1980. Sexuality as the mainstay of identity: Psychoanalytic perspectives. *Signs* 5:605–30.

Petchesky, Rosalind Pollack. 1979. Workers, reproductive hazards, and the politics of protection: An introduction. *Feminist Studies* 5:233–45.

————. 1984. *Abortion and woman's choice: The state, sexuality, and reproductive freedom.* Boston: Northeastern University Press.

Petry, Carl F. 1991. Class solidarity versus gender gain: Women as custodians of property in later medieval Egypt. In Keddie and Baron.

Pfeffer, Naomi. 1987. Artificial insemination, in vitro fertilization and the stigma of infertility. In *Reproductive technologies: Gender, motherhood and medicine,* edited by Michelle Stanworth. Minneapolis: University of Minnesota Press.

Pfeiffer, John E. 1985. *The creative explosion: An inquiry into the origins of art and religion.* Ithaca, N.Y.: Cornell University Press.

Phelan, Shane. 1989. *Identity politics: Lesbian feminism and the limits of community.* Philadelphia: Temple University Press.

————. 1993. (Be)coming out: Lesbian identity and politics. *Signs* 18:765–90.

Philipson, Ilene. 1984. Beyond the virgin and the whore. *Socialist Review* 14(3–4):127–36.

Phillips, Anne, and Barbara Taylor. 1980. Sex and skill: Notes towards a feminist economics. *Feminist Review* 6:79–88.

Phipps, William E. 1989. *Genesis and gender: Biblical myths of sexuality and their cultural impact.* New York: Praeger.

Piercy, Marge. 1976. *Woman on the edge of time.* New York: Fawcett Crest.

Pinchbeck, Ivy. [1930] 1981. *Women workers and the Industrial Revolution, 1750–1850.* London: Virago.

Piven, Frances Fox. 1985. Women and the state: Ideology, power, and the welfare state. In Rossi (ed.).

Plaskow, Judith. 1990. *Standing again at Sinai: Judaism from a feminist perspective.* New York: Harper & Row.

Pleck, Joseph H. 1977. The work-family role system. *Social Problems* 24:417–27.

————. 1983. Husbands' paid work and family roles: Current research issues. In Lopata and Pleck.

————. 1985. *Working wives/working husbands.* Newbury Park, Calif.: Sage.

————. 1987. American fathering in historical perspective. In Kimmel (ed.).

Plummer, Kenneth. 1981a. Building a sociology of homosexuality. In Plummer (ed.).

———— (ed.). 1981b. *The making of the modern homosexual.* Totowa, N.J.: Barnes & Noble.

Pogrebin, Letty Cottin. 1987. *Among friends: Who we like, why we like them and what we do with them.* New York: McGraw-Hill.

Polatnick, M. Rivka. 1983. Why men don't rear children: A power analysis. In Trebilcot.

Poll, Carol. 1978. No room at the top: A study of the social processes that contribute to the underrepresentation of women on the administrative levels of the New York City school system. Ph.D. diss. City University of New York Graduate School.

Pomeroy, Sarah B. 1975. *Goddesses, whores, wives, and slaves: Women in classical antiquity.* New York: Schocken.

———— (ed.). 1991. *Women's history and ancient history.* Chapel Hill: University of North Carolina Press.

Poovey, Mary. 1988a. Feminism and deconstruction. *Feminist Studies* 14:51–65.

———. 1988b. Covered but not bound: Caroline Norton and the 1857 Matrimonial Causes Act. *Feminist Studies* 14:467–85.

Powell, Gary N. 1988. *Women and men in management.* Newbury Park, Calif.: Sage.

Power, Margaret. 1991. *The egalitarians—human and chimpanzee: An anthropological view of social organization.* Cambridge, England: Cambridge University Press.

Powers, Marla N. 1980. Menstruation and reproduction: An Oglala case. *Signs* 6(1, pt. 2):54–65.

Price, T. Douglas, and James A. Brown (eds.). 1985. *Prehistoric hunter-gatherers: The emergence of cultural complexity.* Orlando, Fla.: Academic Press.

Prior, Jerilynn C., Yvette M. Vigna, Martin T. Schechter, and Arthur E. Burgess. 1990. Spinal bone loss and ovulatory disturbances. *New England Journal of Medicine* 323:1221–27.

Proctor, Candice E. 1990. *Women, equality, and the French Revolution.* Westport, Conn.: Greenwood.

Ptacek, James. 1988. Why do men batter their wives? In Yllö and Bograd.

Pugh, M. D., and Ralph Wahrman. 1983. Neutralizing sexism in mixed-sex groups: Do women have to be better than men? *American Journal of Sociology* 88:746–62.

Quadagno, Jill. 1990. Race, class, and gender in the U.S. welfare state: Nixon's failed family assistance plan. *American Sociological Review* 55:11–28.

Quindlen, Anna. 1988. *Living out loud.* New York: Ivy Books.

———. 1991a. Women warriors. *New York Times,* Op-Ed Page, 3 February.

———. 1991b. Listen to us. *New York Times,* Op-Ed Page, 9 October.

———. 1991c. An American tragedy. *New York Times,* Op-Ed Page, 12 October.

———. 1991d. The perfect victim. *New York Times,* Op-Ed Page, 16 October.

———. 1992. Women in combat. *New York Times,* Op-Ed Page, 8 January.

Ragab, Marie-Jose. 1992. Women in parliaments. *National NOW Times,* June.

Ranke-Heinemann, Uta. 1990. *Eunuchs for the kingdom of heaven: Women, sexuality and the Catholic church,* translated by Peter Heinegg. New York: Penguin.

Ratcliff, Kathryn Strother, Myra Marx Ferree, Gail O. Mellow, Barbara Drygulski Wright, Glenda D. Price, Kim Yanoshik, and Margie S. Freston (eds.). 1989. *Healing technology: Feminist perspectives.* Ann Arbor: University of Michigan Press.

Raven, Arlene, Cassandra L. Langer, and Joanna Fruch (eds.). 1988. *Feminist art criticism.* Ann Arbor, Mich.: UMI Research Press.

Raymond, Janice G. 1979. *The transsexual empire: The making of the she-male.* Boston: Beacon Press.

———. 1986. *A passion for friends: Toward a philosophy of female affection.* Boston: Beacon Press.

Redclift, Nanneke. 1985. The contested domain: Gender, accumulation and the labor process. In Redclift and Mingione.

———. 1987. Rights in women: Kinship, culture, and materialism. In *Engels revisited: New feminist essays,* edited by Janet Sayers, Mary Evans, and Nanneke Redclift. London and New York: Tavistock.

Redclift, Nanneke, and Enzo Mingione (eds.). 1985. *Beyond employment: Household, gender and subsistence.* Oxford and New York: Basil Blackwell.

Reed, Evelyn. 1978. *Sexism and science.* New York: Pathfinder Press.

Reed, James. 1978. *From private vice to public virtue: The birth control movement in American society since 1830.* New York: Basic Books.

Reif, Linda Lobao. 1989. Women in revolution: The mobilization of Latin American women in revolutionary guerrilla movements. In Richardson and Taylor.

Reif, Rita. 1989. Art prices are still astonishing, but fever seems to be cooling. *New York Times,* Arts and Leisure Section, 6 December.

Remick, Helen (ed.). 1984. *Comparable worth and wage discrimination: Technical possibilities and political realities.* Philadelphia: Temple University Press.

Remy, John. 1990. Patriarchy and fratriarchy as forms of androcracy. In Hearn and Morgan.

Reskin, Barbara F. 1978a. Sex differentiation and the social organization of science. *Sociological Inquiry* 48:6–37.

———. 1978b. Scientific productivity, sex, and location in the institution of science. *American Journal of Sociology* 83:1235–43.

——— (ed.). 1984. *Sex segregation in the workplace: Trends, explanations, remedies.* Washington, D.C.: National Academy Press.

———. 1988. Bringing the men back in: Sex differentiation and the devaluation of women's work. *Gender & Society* 2:58–81.

Reskin, Barbara F., and Heidi I. Hartmann (eds.). 1986. *Women's work, men's work: Sex segregation on the job.* Washington, D.C.: National Academy Press.

Reskin, Barbara F., and Patricia A. Roos. 1990. *Job queues, gender queues: Explaining women's inroads into male occupations.* Philadelphia: Temple University Press.

Reverby, Susan M. 1987. *Ordered to care: The dilemma of American nursing, 1850–1945.* Cambridge, England: Cambridge University Press.

Reynolds, Siân. 1987a. Marianne's citizens? Women, the Republic and universal suffrage in France. In Reynolds (ed.).

——— (ed.). 1987b. *Women, state and revolution: Essays on power and gender in Europe since 1789.* Amherst: University of Massachusetts Press.

Rhode, Deborah L. (ed.). 1990. *Theoretical perspectives on sexual difference.* New Haven: Yale University Press.

Rich, Adrienne. 1977. *Of woman born: Motherhood as experience and as institution.* New York: Norton.

———. 1980. Compulsory heterosexuality and lesbian existence. *Signs* 5:631–60.

Rich, B. Ruby. 1986. Review essay: Feminism and sexuality in the 1980s. *Feminist Studies* 12:525–61.

Rich, B. Ruby, and Lourdes Arguelles. 1985. Homosexuality, homophobia, and revolution: Notes toward an understanding of the Cuban lesbian and gay male experience, Part II. *Signs* 11:120–36.

Richards, Renée, with Jack Ames. 1983. *Second serve.* New York: Stein and Day.

Richardson, Dianne. 1988. *Women and AIDS.* New York: Methuen.

Richardson, Laurel, and Verta Taylor (eds.). 1989. *Feminist frontiers II.* New York: Random House.

Richie, Beth E. 1992. Gender entrapment: An exploratory study of the links between gender identity, violence against women, and crime among battered African-American women. Ph.D. diss., City University of New York Graduate School.

Ridgeway, Cecilia L. 1987. Nonverbal behavior, dominance, and the basis of status in task groups. *American Sociological Review* 52:683–94.

———. 1988. Gender differences in task groups: A status and legitimacy account. In Webster and Foschi.

——— (ed.). 1991. *Gender, interaction, and inequality.* New York: Springer-Verlag.

Ridgeway, Cecilia L., and Joseph Berger. 1988. The legitimation of power and prestige orders in task groups. In Webster and Foschi.

Ridgeway, Cecilia L., and David Diekema. 1989. Dominance and collective hierarchy formation in male and female task groups. *American Sociological Review* 54:79–93.

Ridgeway, Cecilia L., and Cathryn Johnson. 1990. What is the relationship between socioemotional behavior and status in task groups? *American Journal of Sociology* 95:1189–1212.

Riley, Denise. 1983. *War in the nursery: Theories of the child and mother.* London: Virago.

———. 1988. *Am I that name? Feminism and the category of women in history.* Minneapolis: University of Minnesota Press.

Ríos, Palmira N. 1990. Export-oriented industrialization and the demand for female labor: Puerto Rican women in the manufacturing sector, 1952–1980. *Gender & Society* 4:321–37.

Risman, Barbara J. 1987. Intimate relationships from a microstructural perspective: Men who mother. *Gender & Society* 1:6–32.

Rittenhouse, C. Amanda. 1991. The emergence of premenstrual syndrome as a social problem. *Social Problems* 38:412–25.

Rivière, P. G. 1974. The couvade: A problem reborn. *Man,* n.s. 9:423–35.

Rodgers, Fran Susser, and Charles Rodgers. 1989. Business and the facts of family life. *Harvard Business Review,* November-December, 121–29.

Rogers, Mary F. 1992. They were all passing: Agnes, Garfinkel, and company. *Gender & Society* 6:169–91.

Rohrlich-Leavitt, Ruby. 1977. Women in transition: Crete and Sumer. In Bridenthal and Koonz.

Roiphe, Katie. 1993. *The morning after: Sex, fear and feminism on campus.* Boston: Little, Brown.

Roldán, Martha. 1985. Industrial outworking, struggles for the reproduction of working-class families and gender subordination. In Redclift and Mingione.

———. 1988. Renegotiating the marital contract: Intrahousehold patterns of money allocation and women's subordination among domestic outworkers in Mexico City. In Dwyer and Bruce.

Rollins, Judith. 1985. *Between women: Domestics and their employers.* Philadelphia: Temple University Press.

Romero, Mary. 1988. Day work in the suburbs: The work experience of Chicana private housekeepers. In Statham, Miller, and Mauksch.

Ronnen, Meir. 1992. Canaanite fertility figure found in the Negev. *Jerusalem Post,* 10 November.

Roos, Patricia A. 1985. *Gender and work: A comparative analysis of industrial societies.* Albany: State University of New York Press.

———. 1990. Hot-metal to electronic composition: Gender, technology, and social change. In Reskin and Roos.

Roos, Patricia A., and Barbara F. Reskin. 1984. Institutional factors contributing to sex segregation in the workplace. In Reskin (ed.).

Rosaldo, Michelle Zimbalist, and Louise Lamphere (eds.). 1974. *Woman, culture and society.* Stanford, Calif.: Stanford University Press.

Rose, Sonya O. 1987. Gender segregation in the transition to the factory: The English hosiery industry, 1850–1910. *Feminist Studies* 13:163–84.

Rose, Suzanna M. 1985. Same- and cross-sex friendships and the psychology of homosociality. *Sex Roles* 12:63–74.

Rosen, Ellen Israel. 1987. *Bitter choices: Blue-collar women in and out of work.* Chicago: University of Chicago Press.

Rosen, Ruth. 1982. *The lost sisterhood: Prostitution in America, 1900–1918.* Baltimore, Md.: Johns Hopkins University Press.

Rosenberg, Dorothy J. 1991. Shock therapy: GDR women in transition from a socialist welfare state to a social market economy. *Signs* 17:129–51.

Rosenfeld, Rachel A. 1980. Race and sex differences in career dynamics. *American Sociological Review* 45:583–609.

———. 1983. Sex segregation and sectors: An analysis of gender differences in returns from employer changes. *American Sociological Review* 48:637–55.

Rosenfeld, Rachel A., and Arne L. Kalleberg. 1990. A cross-national comparison of the gender gap in income. *American Journal of Sociology* 96:69–106.

Ross, Catherine E. 1987. The division of labor at home. *Social Forces* 65:816–33.

Rossi, Alice S. 1964. Equality between the sexes: An immodest proposal. *Daedalus* 93:607–52.

———. 1977. A biosocial perspective on parenting. *Daedalus* 106:1–31.

———. 1980. Life span theories and women's lives. *Signs* 6(1, pt. 2):4–32.

———. 1984. Gender and parenthood. *American Sociological Review* 49:1–19.

——— (ed.). 1985. *Gender and the life course.* Hawthorne, N.Y.: Aldine.

Rossi, Alice S., and Peter Eric Rossi. 1977. Body time and social time: Mood patterns by menstrual cycle phase and day of the week. *Social Science Research* 6:273–308.

Rossi, Alice S., and Peter H. Rossi. 1990. *Of human bonding: Parent-child relations across the life course.* New York: Aldine de Gruyter.

Rossiter, Margaret L. 1986. *Women in the resistance.* New York: Praeger.

Rossiter, Margaret W. 1982. *Women scientists in America: Struggles and strategies to 1940.* Baltimore, Md.: Johns Hopkins University Press.

Rothman, Barbara Katz. 1982. *In labor: Women and power in the birthplace.* New York: Norton.

———. 1986. *The tentative pregnancy.* New York: Viking.

———. 1989. *Recreating motherhood: Ideology and technology in a patriarchal society.* New York: Norton.

Rothschild, Joan. 1983. Technology, housework, and women's liberation: A theoretical analysis. In *Machina ex dea: Feminist perspectives on technology,* edited by Joan Rothschild. New York: Pergamon.

Rowbotham, Sheila. 1973. *Women's consciousness, man's world.* New York: Penguin.

——. 1974. *Women, resistance and revolution: A history of women and revolution in the modern world.* New York: Vintage.

——. 1976. *Hidden from history: Rediscovering women in history from the seventeenth century to the present.* New York: Vintage.

——. 1989. *The past is before us: Feminism in action since the 1960s.* Boston: Beacon Press.

Rowe, Mary P. 1977. The Saturn's rings phenomenon: Microinequities and unequal opportunities in the American economy. Proceedings of the Conference on Women's Leadership and Authority in the Health Professions, Santa Cruz, Calif.

Rubin, Gayle. 1975. The traffic in women: Notes on the political economy of sex. In *Toward an anthropology of women,* edited by Rayna R[app] Reiter. New York: Monthly Review Press.

——. 1984. Thinking sex: Notes for a radical theory of the politics of sexuality. In Vance (ed.).

Rubin, Lillian Breslow. 1976. *Worlds of pain: Life in the working-class family.* New York: Basic Books.

——. 1983. *Intimate strangers: Men and women together.* New York: Harper & Row.

——. 1991. *Erotic wars: What happened to the sexual revolution?* New York: Harper-Collins.

Ruddick, Sara. 1983. Maternal thinking. In Trebilcot.

Ruggie, Mary. 1984. *The state and working women: A comparative study of Britain and Sweden.* Princeton: Princeton University Press.

Rugh, Andrea B. 1986. *Reveal and conceal: Dress in contemporary Egypt.* Syracuse, N.Y.: Syracuse University Press.

Rupp, Leila J. 1989. "Imagine my surprise": Women's relationships in mid-twentieth century America. In Duberman, Vicinus, and Chauncey.

Russ, Joanna. 1975. *The female man.* New York: Bantam.

Russell, Diana E. H. 1986. *The secret trauma: Incest in the lives of girls and women.* New York: Basic Books.

——. 1990. *Rape in marriage.* Rev. ed. Bloomington: Indiana University Press.

Rust, Paula C. 1992. The politics of sexual identity: Attraction and behavior among lesbian and bisexual women. *Social Problems* 39:366–86.

——. 1993. "Coming out" in the age of social constructionism: Sexual identity formation among lesbian and bisexual women. *Gender & Society* 7:50–77.

Sabbah, Fatna A. 1984. *Woman in the Muslim unconscious,* translated by Mary Jo Lakeland. New York: Pergamon.

Sack, Laura. 1992. Women and children first: A feminist analysis of the primary caretaker standard in child custody cases. *Yale Journal of Law and Feminism* 4:291–328.

Sacks, Karen [Brodkin]. 1979. *Sisters and wives.* Urbana: University of Illinois Press.

——. 1984. Generations of working-class families. In *My troubles are going to have trouble with me,* edited by Karen Brodkin Sacks and Dorothy Remy. New Brunswick, N.J.: Rutgers University Press.

—————. 1989. Toward a unified theory of class, race, and gender. *American Ethnologist* 16:534–50.

Safa, Helen Icken. 1981. Runaway shops and female employment: The search for cheap labor. *Signs* 7:418–33.

—————. 1990. Women's social movements in Latin America. *Gender & Society* 4:354–69.

Safa-Isfahani, Kaveh. 1980. Female-centered world views in Iranian culture: Symbolic representations of sexuality in dramatic games. *Signs* 6:33–53.

Sagi, Abraham, Nina Koren, and Mayah Weinberg. 1987. Fathers in Israel. In Lamb (ed.).

Salmon, Marylynn. 1979. "Life, liberty, and dower": The legal status of women after the American Revolution. In *Women, war, and revolution,* edited by Carol R. Berkin and Clara M. Lovett. New York: Holmes and Meier.

Sanday, Peggy Reeves. 1981a. *Female power and male dominance: On the origins of sexual inequality.* Cambridge, England: Cambridge University Press.

—————. 1981b. The socio-cultural context of rape: A cross-cultural study. *Journal of Social Issues* 37:5–27.

—————. 1990. *Fraternity gang rape: Sex, brotherhood, and privilege on campus.* New York: New York University Press.

Sandelowski, Margarete. 1990a. Fault lines: Infertility and imperiled sisterhood. *Feminist Studies* 16:33–51.

—————. 1990b. Failures of volition: Female agency and infertility in historical perspective. *Signs* 15:475–99.

—————. 1993. *With child in mind: Studies of the personal encounter with infertility.* Philadelphia: University of Pennsylvania Press.

Sanders, Paula. 1991. Gendering the ungendered body: Hermaphrodites in medieval Islamic law. In Keddie and Baron.

Sandqvist, Karin. 1992. Sweden's sex-role scheme and commitment to gender equality. In Lewis, Izraeli, and Hootsmans.

Sapiro, Virginia. 1990. The gender basis of American social policy. In Gordon (ed.).

Sargent, Lydia (ed.). 1981. *Women and revolution: A discussion of the unhappy marriage of Marxism and feminism.* Boston: South End Press.

Sarvasy, Wendy. 1992. Beyond the difference versus equality policy debate: Post-suffrage feminism, citizenship, and the quest for a feminist welfare state. *Signs* 17:329–62.

Sassen, Saskia. 1988. *The mobility of labor and capital: A study in international investment and labor flow.* Cambridge, England: Cambridge University Press.

Sattel, Jack W. 1976. The inexpressive male: Tragedy or sexual politics? *Social Problems* 23:469–77.

Sayers, Janet. 1982. *Biological politics: Feminist and anti-feminist perspectives.* London and New York: Tavistock.

Sayre, Anne. 1975. *Rosalind Franklin and DNA.* New York: Norton.

Schafran, Lynn Hecht. 1991. The harsh lessons of Professor Hill. *New York Times* Business Section, 13 October.

Scharff, Virginia. 1991. *Taking the wheel: Women and the coming of the motor age*. New York: Free Press.

Scheff, Thomas J. 1988. Shame and conformity: The deference-emotion system. *American Sociological Review* 53:395–406.

———. 1990. *Microsociology: Discourse, emotion, and social structure*. Chicago: University of Chicago Press.

Scheper-Hughes, Nancy. 1992. *Death without weeping: The violence of everyday life in Brazil*. Berkeley: University of California Press.

Schilit, Rebecca, Gwat-Yong Lie, Judy Bush, Marilyn Montagne, and Lynne Reyes. 1991. Intergenerational transmission of violence in lesbian relationships. *Affilia* 6:72–87.

Schirmer, Jennifer G. 1982. *The limits of reform: Women, capital, and welfare*. Cambridge, Mass.: Schenkman.

Schlegel, Alice (ed). 1977. *Sexual stratification: A cross-cultural view*. New York: Columbia University Press.

Schmitt, Eric. 1991. War puts U.S. servicewomen closer than ever to combat. *New York Times*, 22 January.

———. 1992. Wall of silence impedes inquiry into a rowdy Navy convention. *New York Times*, 14 June.

Schneider, Beth E. 1982. Consciousness about sexual harassment among heterosexual and lesbian women workers. *Journal of Social Issues* 38:75–98.

———. 1984. The office affair: Myth and reality for heterosexual and lesbian women workers. *Sociological Perspectives* 27:443–64.

———. 1985. Approaches, assaults, attractions, affairs: Policy implications of the sexualization of the workplace. *Population Research and Policy Review* 4:93–113.

———. 1991. Put up and shut up: Workplace sexual assaults. *Gender & Society* 5:533–48.

Schneider, Beth E., and Meredith Gould. 1987. Female sexuality: Looking back into the future. In Hess and Marx Ferree.

Schooler, Carmi, Melvin Kohn, Karen A. Miller, and Joanne Miller. 1983. Housework as work. In *Work and personality: An inquiry into the impact of social stratification*. Norwood, N.J.: Ablex.

Schulte, Regina. 1984. Infanticide in rural Bavaria in the nineteenth century. In *Interest and emotion: Essays on the study of family and kinship*, edited by Hans Medick and David Warren Sabean. Cambridge, England: Cambridge University Press.

Schultz, Martin. 1992. Occupational pursuits of free American women: Analysis of newspaper ads, 1800–1849. *Sociological Forum* 7:587–607.

Schultz, Martin, and Herman R. Lantz. 1988. Occupational pursuits of free women in early America: An examination of eighteenth-century newspapers. *Sociological Forum* 3:89–109.

Schwendinger, Julia R., and Herman Schwendinger. 1983. *Rape and inequality*. Newbury Park, Calif.: Sage.

Schweninger, Loren. 1990. Property-owning free African-American women in the South. *Journal of Women's History* 1:13–44.

Sciolino, Elaine. 1990. Battle lines are shifting on women in war. *New York Times*, 23 January.

Scott, Bonnie Kime. 1990. *The gender of modernism.* Bloomington: Indiana University Press.

Scott, Joan Wallach. 1988a. *Gender and the politics of history.* New York: Columbia University Press.

————. 1988b. Deconstructing equality-versus-difference: Or, the uses of post-structuralist theory for feminism. *Feminist Studies* 14:33–50.

Scrimshaw, Susan C. M. 1984. Infanticide in human populations: Societal and individual concerns. In Hausfater and Hrdy.

Scully, Diana. 1990. *Understanding sexual violence: A study of convicted rapists.* Boston: Unwin Hyman.

Segal, Lynne. 1990. *Slow motion: Changing masculinities, changing men.* New Brunswick, N.J.: Rutgers University Press.

Segal, Mady Wechsler. 1986. The military and the family as greedy institutions. *Armed Forces and Society* 13:9–38.

Segura, Denise A. 1989. Chicana and Mexican immigrant women at work: The impact of class, race, and gender on occupational mobility. *Gender & Society* 3:37–52.

Seidman, Gay W. 1993. "No freedom without the women": Mobilization and gender in South Africa, 1970–1992. *Signs* 18:291–320.

Seidman, Paul B. 1991. The Montreal massacre and the war against women: The means to an end get meaner. *Changing Men,* no. 22 (Winter-Spring):11.

Seltzer, Judith A. 1991. Legal custody arrangements and children's economic welfare. *American Journal of Sociology* 96:895–929.

Semyonov, Moshe. 1980. The social context of women's labor force participation: A comparative analysis. *American Sociological Review* 86:534–50.

Sen, Amartya K. 1990. Gender and cooperative conflicts. In Tinker.

Sered, Susan Starr. 1994. *Priestess, mother, sacred sister: Religions dominated by women.* New York: Oxford University Press.

Shaffer, Harry G. 1981. *Women in the two Germanies: A comparative study of a socialist and a non-socialist society.* New York: Pergamon.

Shaffer, Peter. 1980. *Amadeus.* New York: Harper & Row.

Shanley, Mary Lyndon. 1989. *Feminism, marriage, and the law in Victorian England, 1850–1895.* Princeton: Princeton University Press.

Shapiro, Ann-Louise. 1991. Love stories: Female crimes of passion in fin-de-siècle Paris. *Differences: A Journal of Feminist Cultural Studies* 3(3):45–68.

Sharma, Ursula. 1986. *Women's work, class, and the urban household: A study of Shimla, North India.* London and New York: Tavistock.

Sharpe, Rochelle. 1992. Capitol Hill's worst kept secret: Sexual harassment. *Ms. Magazine* January-February.

Sheehan, Susan. 1975. *A welfare mother.* New York: New American Library.

Sheehy, Jeanne. 1987. The training and professional life of Irish women artists before the twentieth century. In *Irish women artists.* Dublin: National Gallery of Ireland and Douglas Hyde Gallery.

Sheffield, Carole J. 1987. Sexual terrorism: The social control of women. In Hess and Marx Ferree.

Shelton, Beth Anne. 1992. *Women, men and time: Gender differences in paid work, housework and leisure.* Westport, Conn.: Greenwood Press.

Sherfey, Mary Jane. 1973. *The nature and evolution of female sexuality.* New York: Vintage.

Sherrod, Drury. 1987. The bonds of men: Problems and possibilities in close male relationships. In Brod.

Showalter, Elaine. 1987. Critical cross-dressing: Male feminists and the woman of the year. In *Men in feminism,* edited by Alice Jardine and Paul Smith. New York: Methuen.

Sidel, Ruth. 1972. *Women and child care in China: A firsthand report.* New York: Hill and Wang.

————. 1974. *Families of Fengsheng: Urban life in China.* Baltimore: Penguin.

Silver, Allan. 1990. Friendship in commercial society: Eighteenth-century social theory and modern sociology. *American Journal of Sociology* 95:1474–1504.

Simmons, Martin. 1992. The truth about male friendships. In Kimmel and Messner.

Simms, Margaret C., and Julianne Malveaux (eds.). 1987. *Slipping through the cracks: The status of Black women.* New Brunswick, N.J.: Transaction Books.

Simonds, Wendy. 1988. Confessions of loss: Maternal grief in *True Story,* 1920–1985. *Gender & Society* 2:149–71.

————. 1992. *Women and self-help culture: Reading between the lines.* New Brunswick, N.J.: Rutgers University Press.

Simson, Rennie. 1983. The Afro-American female: The historical context of the construction of sexual identity. In Snitow, Stansell, and Thompson.

Siskind, Janet. 1978. Kinship and mode of production. *American Anthropologist* 80:860–71.

Siu, Bobby. 1982. *Women of China: Imperialism and women's resistance, 1900–1949.* London: Zed Books.

Skocpol, Theda. 1979. *States and social revolutions: A comparative analysis of France, Russia, and China.* New York: Cambridge University Press.

————. 1992. *Protecting soldiers and mothers: The political origins of social policy in the United States.* Cambridge, Mass.: Harvard University Press.

Skocpol, Theda, and Gretchen Ritter. 1991. Gender and the origins of modern social policies in Britain and the United States. *Studies in American Political Development* 5 (Spring):36–93.

Slatton, Bonnie, and Susan Birrell (eds.). 1984. The politics of women's sport. *Arena Review* 8 (July):entire issue.

Smart, Carol. 1984. *The ties that bind: Law, marriage and the reproduction of patriarchal relations.* London: Routledge and Kegan Paul.

Smart, Carol, and Selma Sevenhuijsen (eds.). 1989. *Child custody and the politics of gender.* New York and London: Routledge.

Smith, Dorothy E. 1987a. *The everyday world as problematic: A feminist sociology.* Toronto: University of Toronto Press.

————. 1987b. Women's inequality and the family. In Gerstel and Gross.

————. 1990. *The conceptual practices of power: A feminist sociology of knowledge.* Toronto: University of Toronto Press.

Smith, Joan. 1984. Nonwage labor and subsistence. In Smith, Wallerstein, and Evers.

————. 1987. Transforming households: Working-class women and economic crisis. *Social Problems* 34:416–36.

Smith, Joan, Immanuel Wallerstein, and Hans-Dieter Evers (eds.). 1984. *Households and the world economy.* Newbury Park, Calif.: Sage.

Smith-Rosenberg, Carroll. 1975. The female world of love and ritual: Relations between women in nineteenth-century America. *Signs* 1:1–29.

————. 1985. *Disorderly conduct: Visions of gender in Victorian America.* New York: Knopf.

Smuts, Barbara B., and David J. Gubernick. 1992. Male-infant relationships in nonhuman primates: Paternal investment or mating effort? In Hewlett (ed.).

Snitow, Ann [Barr]. 1983. Mass market romance: Pornography for women is different. In Snitow, Stansell, and Thompson.

Snitow, Ann, Christine Stansell, and Sharon Thompson (eds.). 1983. *Powers of desire: The politics of sexuality.* New York: Monthly Review Press.

Soble, Alan. 1986. *Pornography: Marxism, feminism and the future of sexuality.* New Haven: Yale University Press

Sokoloff, Natalie J. 1980. *Between money and love.* New York: Praeger.

————. 1988. Evaluating gains and losses by Black and white women and men in the professions, 1960–1980. *Social Problems* 35:36–53.

Sorensen, Elaine. 1989. Measuring the effect of occupational sex and race composition on earnings. In *Pay equity: Empirical inquiries,* edited by Robert T. Michael, Heidi I. Hartmann, and Brigid O'Farrell. Washington, D.C.: National Academy Press.

South, Scott J., Charles M. Bonjean, Judy Corder, and William T. Markham. 1982a. Sex and power in the federal bureaucracy: A comparative analysis of male and female supervisors. *Work and Occupations* 9:233–54.

South, Scott J., Charles M. Bonjean, William T. Markham, and Judy Corder. 1982b. Social structure and intergroup interaction: Men and women of the federal bureaucracy. *American Sociological Review* 47:587–99.

Spelman, Elizabeth. 1988. *Inessential woman: Problems of exclusion in feminist thought.* Boston: Beacon Press.

Spencer, Dee Ann. 1988. Public schoolteaching: A suitable job for a woman? In Statham, Miller, and Mauksch.

Spivak, Gayatri Chakravorty. 1988. *In other worlds: Essays in cultural politics.* New York and London: Routledge.

Srole, Carole. 1987. "A blessing to mankind, and especially to womankind": The typewriter and the feminization of clerical work, Boston, 1860–1920. In B. D. Wright et al.

Stacey, Judith. 1983. *Patriarchy and socialist revolution in China.* Berkeley: California University Press.

————. 1991. *Brave new families: Stories of domestic upheaval in late twentieth century America.* New York: Basic Books.

Stacey, Judith, and Barrie Thorne. 1985. The missing feminist revolution in sociology. *Social Problems* 32:301–16.

Stack, Carol B. 1975. *All our kin: Strategies for survival in a Black community.* New York: Harper & Row.

Stanford-Observer. 1991. Neurosurgeon resigns, cites sexism. May-June.

Stanko, Elizabeth. 1990. *Everyday violence: How women and men experience sexual and physical danger.* London: Pandora.

Staples, Robert. 1982. *Black masculinity: The Black male's roles in American society.* San Francsico: Black Scholar Press.

———. 1992. Stereotypes of Black sexuality: The facts behind the myths. In Kimmel and Messner.

Stark, Evan, Anne Flitcraft, and William Frazier. 1979. Medicine and patriarchal violence: The social construction of a "private" event. *International Journal of Health Services* 9:461–93.

Statham, Anne, Eleanor M. Miller, and Hans O. Mauksch (eds.). 1988. *The worth of women's work.* Albany: State University of New York Press.

Staves, Susan. 1990. *Married women's separate property in England, 1660–1833.* Cambridge, Mass.: Harvard University Press.

Steil, Janice M., and Karen Weltman. 1991. Marital inequality: The importance of resources, personal attributes, and social norms on career valuing and the allocation of domestic responsibilities. *Sex Roles* 24:161–79.

Stein, Arlene. 1989. Three models of sexuality: Drives, identities and practices. *Sociological Theory* 7:1–13.

Steinberg, Ronnie. 1987. Radical challenges in a liberal world: The mixed success of comparable worth. *Gender & Society* 4:466–75.

Steinberg, Ronnie, and Lois Haignere. 1987. Equitable compensation: Methodological criteria for comparable worth. In Bose and Spitze.

Steinem, Gloria. 1978a. If men could menstruate. *Ms. Magazine,* October.

———. 1978b. Erotica and pornography: A clear and present difference. *Ms. Magazine,* November.

———. 1992. Seeking out the invisible woman. *New York Times,* Arts and Leisure Section, 13 March.

Stellman, Jeanne M., and Mary Sue Henifin. 1982. No fertile women need apply: Employment discrimination and reproductive hazards in the workplace. In *Biological woman—the convenient myth,* edited by Ruth Hubbard, Mary Sue Henifin, and Barbara Fried. Cambridge, Mass.: Schenckman.

Stewart, Penni. 1988. Women and men in groups: A status characteristics approach to interaction. In Webster and Foschi.

Stiehm, Judith Hicks. 1985. The generations of U.S. enlisted women. *Signs* 11:155–75.

Stimpson, Catharine R. 1979. The power to name: Some reflections on the avant-garde. In *The prism of sex: Essays in the sociology of knowledge,* edited by Julia A. Sherman and Evelyn Torton Beck. Madison: University of Wisconsin Press.

Stites, Richard. [1978] 1990. *The women's liberation movement in Russia: Feminism, nihilism, and Bolshevism, 1860–1930.* Princeton: Princeton University Press.

Stivens, Maila. 1981. Women, kinship and capitalist development. In Young, Wolkowitz, and McCullagh.

Stoller, Robert J. 1985. *Presentations of gender.* New Haven: Yale University Press.

Stoltenberg, John. 1990. *Refusing to be a man: Essays on sex and justice.* New York: Meridian.

———. 1991. A coupla things I've been meaning to say about really confronting male power. *Changing Men,* no. 22 (Winter-Spring):8–10.

Stone, Lawrence. 1979. *The family, sex and marriage in England, 1500–1800.* New York: Harper Colophon.

———. 1990. *Road to divorce: England, 1530–1987.* New York: Oxford University Press.

Stone, Merlin. 1976. *When god was a woman.* San Diego: Harcourt Brace Jovanovich.

Strang, David, and James N. Baron. 1990. Categorical imperatives: The structure of job titles. *American Sociological Review* 55:479–95.

Strathern, Marilyn. 1988. *The gender of the gift.* Berkeley: University of California Press.

———. 1992. *Reproducing the future: Anthropology, kinship and the new reproductive technologies.* New York and London: Routledge.

Straus, Murray A. 1991. Discipline and deviance: Physical punishment of children and violence and other crime in adulthood. *Social Problems* 38:133–54.

———. 1992. Sociological research and social policy: The case of family violence. *Sociological Forum* 7:211–37.

Strober, Myra H. 1984. Toward a general theory of occupational sex segregation. In Reskin (ed.).

Strom, Stephanie. 1992. Fashion Avenue's $100 million woman. *New York Times,* Business Section, 17 May.

Stuard, Susan Mosher (ed.). 1976. *Women in medieval society.* Philadelphia: University of Pennsylvania Press.

Suleiman, Susan Rubin (ed.). 1986. *The female body in Western culture: Contemporary perspectives.* Cambridge, Mass.: Harvard University Press.

Sunstein, Cass R. (ed.). 1990. *Feminism and political theory.* Chicago: University of Chicago Press.

Sussman, George. 1982. *Selling mother's milk: The wet-nursing business in France, 1715–1914.* Urbana: University of Illinois Press.

Swafford, Michael. 1978. Sex differences in Soviet earnings. *American Journal of Sociology* 43:657–73.

Swerdlow, Amy, and Hanna Lessinger (eds.). 1983. *Class, race, and sex: The dynamics of control.* Boston: G. K. Hall.

Swerdlow, Marian. 1989. Men's accommodations to women entering a nontraditional occupation: A case of rapid transit operatives. *Gender & Society* 3:373–87.

Szalai, Julia. 1991. Some aspects of the changing situation of women in Hungary. *Signs* 17:152–70.

Tancred-Sheriff, Peta. 1989. Gender, sexuality and the labor process. In Hearn et al.

Tangri, Sandra Schwartz. 1976. A feminist perspective on some ethical issues in population programs. *Signs* 1:895–904.

Tanner, Nancy Makepeace. 1981. *On becoming human.* Cambridge, England: Cambridge University Press.

Tanner, Nancy, and Adrienne Zihlman. 1976. Women in evolution. Part I: Innovation and selection in human origins. *Signs* 1:585–608.

Tax, Meredith. 1980. *The rising of the women: Feminist solidarity and class conflict, 1880–1917.* New York: Monthly Review Press.

Taylor, Dalmas A., and Geneva Smitherman-Donaldson (eds.). 1989. Special Issue: African-American women and affirmative action. *Sex Roles* 21:1–160.

Taylor, Verta, and Leila J. Rupp. 1993. Women's culture and lesbian feminist activism: A reconsideration of cultural feminism. *Signs* 19(1), in press.

Taylor, Verta, and Nancy E. Whittier. Forthcoming. Collective identity in social movement communities: Lesbian feminist mobilization. In *Frontiers of social movement theory,* edited by Aldon Morris and Carol Mueller. New Haven: Yale University Press.

Terry, Don. 1989. A week of rapes: The jogger and 28 not in the news. *New York Times,* 29 May.

Theberge, Nancy. 1987. Sport and women's empowerment. *Women's Studies International Forum* 10:387–93.

Theberge, Nancy, and Alan Cronk. 1986. Work routines in newspaper sports departments and the coverage of women's sports. *Sociology of Sport Journal* 3:195–203.

Thomas, Barbara J., and Barbara F. Reskin. 1990. A woman's place is selling homes: Occupational change and the feminization of real estate sales. In Reskin and Roos.

Thomas, Robert J. 1982. Citizenship and gender in work organization: Some considerations for theories of the labor process. In *Marxist inquiries: Studies of labor, class, and states,* edited by Michael Burawoy and Theda Skocpol. Supplement to *American Journal of Sociology* 88.

Thorne, Barrie. 1990. Children and gender: Constructions of differences. In Rhode.

———. 1993. *Gender play: Girls and boys at school.* New Brunswick, N.J.: Rutgers University Press.

Thorne, Barrie, and Zella Luria. 1986. Sexuality and gender in children's daily worlds. *Social Problems* 33:176–90.

Thornton, Arland, and Thomas E. Fricke. 1987. Social change and the family: Comparative perspectives from the West, China, and South Asia. *Sociological Forum* 2:746–79.

Tiano, Susan. 1987. Gender, work, and world capitalism: Third World women's role in development. In Hess and Marx Ferree.

———. 1990. *Maquiladora* women: A new category of workers? in Ward.

Tick, Judith, and Jane Bowers (eds.). 1980. *Women making music: Studies in the social history of women musicians and composers.* Berkeley: University of California Press.

Tienda, Marta, Shelley A. Smith, and Vilma Ortiz. 1987. Industrial restructuring, gender segregation, and sex differences in earnings. *American Sociological Review* 52:195–210.

Tilly, Louise A. 1981. Paths of proletarianization: Organization of production, sexual division of labor, and women's collective action. *Signs* 7:400–17.

Tilly, Louise A., and Joan W. Scott. 1978. *Women, work and family.* New York: Holt, Rinehart, and Winston.

Tinker, Irene (ed.). 1990. *Persistent inequalities: Women and world development.* New York: Oxford University Press.

Top, Titia J. 1991. Sex bias in the evaluation of performance in the scientific, artistic, and literary professions: A review. *Sex Roles* 24:73–106.

Toren, Nina, and Vered Kraus. 1987. The effects of minority size on women's position in academia. *Social Forces* 65:1090–1100.

Tournaye, Herman, Paul Devroey, Michel Camus, Catherine Staessen, Nico Bollen, Johan Smitz, and Andre C. Van Steirteghem. 1992. Comparison of in vitro fertilization in male and tubal infertility. *Human Reproduction* 7(February):218–22.

Treadwell, Perry. 1987. Biologic influences on masculinity. In Brod.

Treas, Judith. 1993. Money in the bank: Transaction costs and the economics of marriage. *American Sociological Review* 58:723–34.

Trebilcot, Joyce (ed.). 1983. *Mothering: Essays in feminist theory.* Totowa, N.J.: Rowman and Allenheld.

Treichler, Paula A. 1988. AIDS, homophobia, and biomedical discourse: An epidemic of signification. In Crimp.

Treiman, Donald J., and Heidi I. Hartmann (eds.). 1981. *Women, work and wages: Equal pay for jobs of equal value.* Washington, D.C.: National Academy Press.

Treiman, Donald J., and Patricia A. Roos. 1983. Sex and earnings in industrial society: A nine-nation comparison. *American Journal of Sociology* 89:612–50.

Trimberger, Ellen Kay. 1983. Feminism, men, and modern love: Greenwich Village, 1900–1925. In Snitow, Stansell, and Thompson.

Trinh, T. Minh-ha. 1989. *Woman, native, other: Writing postcoloniality and feminism.* Bloomington: Indiana University Press.

Troiden, Richard R. 1988. *Gay and lesbian identity: A sociological analysis.* Dix Hills, N.Y.: General Hall.

Trombley, Stephen. 1982. *All that summer she was mad: Virginia Woolf, female victim of male medicine.* New York: Continuum.

Trotsky, Leon. 1970. *Women and the family,* translated by John Fairlie et al. New York: Pathfinder Press.

Tsurumi, E. Patricia. 1990. *Factory girls: Women in the thread mills of Meiji Japan.* Princeton: Princeton University Press.

Tuchman, Gaye. 1975. Woman and the creation of culture. In *Another voice,* edited by Marcia Millman and Rosabeth Moss Kanter. Garden City, N.Y.: Doubleday Anchor.

Tuchman, Gaye, with Nina Fortin. 1989. *Edging women out: Victorian novelists, publishers, and social change.* New Haven: Yale University Press.

Turbin, Carole. 1984. Reconceptualizing family, work and labor organizing: Working women in Troy, 1860–90. *Review of Radical Political Economics* 16:1–16.

Turkle, Sherry, and Seymour Papert. 1990. Epistemological pluralism: Styles and voices within the computer culture. *Signs* 16:128–57.

Ucko, Peter J., and Andrée Rosenfeld. 1967. *Paleolithic cave art.* New York: McGraw-Hill.

Ulrich, H. E. 1992. Menstrual taboos among Havik Brahmin women: A study of ritual change. *Sex Roles* 26:19–20.

Unger, Rhoda K., Marcia Hiderbrand, and Theresa Madar. 1982. Physical attractiveness and assumptions about social deviance: Some sex-by-sex comparisons. *Personality and Social Psychology Bulletin* 8:293–301.

United Nations. 1980. *Program of action for the second half of the United Nations decade for women: Equality, development and peace.* New York: United Nations.

U. S. General Accounting Office. 1989. Women in the military: Career progression not a current problem but concerns remain. Briefing Report GAO/NSLAD-89–210BR.

Ursel, Jane. 1992. *Private lives, public policy: 100 years of state intervention in the family.* Toronto: Women's Press.

Valverde, Mariana. 1985. *Sex, power and pleasure.* Toronto: Women's Press.

Vance, Carole S. 1984a. Epilogue and addenda: The scholar and the Feminist IX Conference. In Vance (ed.).

——— (ed.). 1984b. *Pleasure and danger: Exploring female sexuality.* Boston: Routledge and Kegan Paul.

Vanden Heuvel, Katrina. 1992. Women of Russia, unite! *New York Times,* Op-Ed Page, 12 September.

van der Kwaak, Anke. 1992. Female circumcision and gender identity: A questionable alliance? *Social Science and Medicine* 35:777–87.

Vanek, Joann. 1974. Time spent in housework. *Scientific American* 231:116–20.

Van Gennep, Arnold. 1960. *The rites of passage,* translated by Monika B. Vizedom and Gabrielle L. Caffee. Chicago: University of Chicago Press.

Vannoy-Hiller, Dana, and William W. Philliber. 1989. *Equal partners: Successful women in marriage.* Newbury Park, Calif.: Sage.

Verbrugge, Lois M. 1985. Gender and health: An update on hypotheses and evidence. *Journal of Health and Social Behavior* 26:156–82.

———. 1986. Role burdens and physical health of women and men. *Women & Health* 11:47–77.

———. 1989a. The twain meet: Empirical explanations of sex differences in health and mortality. *Journal of Health and Social Behavior* 30:282–304.

———. 1989b. Gender, aging, and health. In Markides.

Vertinsky, Patricia. 1990. *The eternally wounded woman: Women, doctors and exercise in the late nineteenth century.* Manchester, England: Manchester University Press.

Vecsey, George. 1990. Cathy Rigby, unlike Peter, did grow up. *New York Times,* 19 December.

Veyne, Paul. 1985. Homosexuality in ancient Rome. In *Western sexuality: Practice and precept in past and present times,* edited by Philippe Ariès and André Béjin, translated by Anthony Forster. Oxford and New York: Basil Blackwell.

Vicinus, Martha. 1992. "They wonder to which sex I belong": The historical roots of the modern lesbian identity. *Feminist Studies* 18:467–97.

Voda, Anne M., Myra Dinnerstein, and Sheryl R. O'Donnell (eds.). 1982. *Changing perspectives on menopause.* Austin: University of Texas Press.

Vogel, Lise. 1977. Hearts to feel and tongues to speak: New England mill women in the early nineteenth century. In Cantor and Laurie.

———. 1990. Debating difference: Feminism, pregnancy, and the workplace. *Feminist Studies* 16:9–32.

Von Werlhof, Claudia. 1988. The proletarian is dead: Long live the housewife! In Mies, Bennholdt-Thomsen, and von Werlhof.

Wagner, David G. 1988. Gender inequalities in groups: A situational approach. In Webster and Foschi.

Wagner, David G., and Joseph Berger. 1991. Status characteristics theory: The growth of a program. In *Theoretical research programs: Studies in the growth of theory,* edited by Joseph Berger and Morris Zelditch, Jr. Stanford, Calif.: Stanford University Press.

Waite, Linda J., and Sue E. Berryman. 1985. *Women in nontraditional occupations: Choice and turnover.* Santa Monica, Calif.: Rand.

Wajcman, Judy. 1991. *Feminism confronts technology.* University Park: Pennsylvania State University Press.

Walby, Sylvia. 1986. *Patriarchy at work: Patriarchal and capitalist relations in employment.* Minneapolis: University of Minnesota Press.

———. 1990. *Theorizing patriarchy.* Oxford and New York: Basil Blackwell.

Waldron, Ingrid. 1976. Why do women live longer than men? *Social Science and Medicine* 10:349–62.

Walker, Alice. 1983. *In search of our mothers' gardens: Womanist prose.* New York: Harcourt Brace Jovanovich.

———. 1992. *Possessing the secret of joy.* New York: Harcourt Brace Jovanovich.

Walker, Lenore E. 1984. *The battered woman syndrome.* New York: Springer.

———. 1988. *Handbook on sexual abuse of children: Assessment and treatment issues.* New York: Springer.

———. 1989. *Terrifying love: Why battered women kill and how society responds.* New York: Harper & Row.

Walker, Molly K. 1992. Maternal reactions to fetal sex. *Health Care for Women International* 13:293–302.

Walkowitz, Judith R. 1980. *Prostitution and Victorian society: Women, class, and the state.* Cambridge, England: Cambridge University Press.

Wallace, Michele. [1978] 1990. *Black macho and the myth of the superwoman.* London: Verso.

Walsh, Mary Roth. 1977. *"Doctors wanted: No women need apply": Sexual barriers in the medical profession, 1835–1975.* New Haven: Yale University Press.

———. 1992. Before and after Frances Conley. *Journal of the American Medical Women's Association* 48:119–21.

Walters, Lynda Henley, and Steven F. Chapman. 1991. Changes in legal views of parenthood: Implications for fathers in minority cultures. In *Fatherhood and families in cultural context,* edited by Frederick W. Bozett and Shirley M. H. Hanson. New York: Springer.

Ward, Kathryn (ed.). 1990. *Women workers and global restructuring.* Ithaca, N.Y.: ILR Press.

Warner, Marina. 1982. *Joan of Arc: The image of female heroism.* New York: Vintage.

———. 1983. *Alone of all her sex: The myth and the cult of the Virgin Mary.* New York: Vintage.

Warrock, Anna M. 1991. Objects of the game. *New York Times,* Op-Ed Page, 11 October.

Warshaw, Carole. 1989. Limitations of the medical model in the case of battered women. *Gender & Society* 3:506–17.

Waters, Elizabeth. 1989. In the shadow of the Comintern: The Communist women's movement, 1920–43. In Kruks, Rapp, and Young.

Watson, James D. 1968. *The double helix: A personal account of the discovery of the structure of DNA.* New York: Atheneum.

Watson, Tracey. 1987. Women athletes and athletic women: The dilemmas and contradictions of managing incongruent identities. *Sociological Inquiry* 57:431–46.

Wattenberg, Esther. 1985. In a different light: A feminist perspective on the role of mothers in father-daughter incest. *Child Welfare* 64:203–11.

Weber, Max. 1964. *The theory of social and economic organization,* edited by Talcott Parsons, translated by A. M. Henderson and Talcott Parsons. New York: Free Press.

Webster, Murray, Jr., and James E. Driskell, Jr. 1983. Beauty as status. *American Journal of Sociology* 89:140–65.

Webster, Murray, Jr., and Martha Foschi (eds.). 1988. *Status generalization: New theory and research.* Stanford, Calif.: Stanford University Press.

Weeks, Jeffrey. 1985. *Sexuality and its discontents: Meanings, myths and modern sexualities.* New York and London: Routledge.

———. 1989. *Sex, politics and society: The regulation of sexuality since 1800.* 2d ed. London and New York: Longman.

Weiner, Annette B. 1979. Trobriand kinship from another view: The reproductive power of women and men. *Man,* N.S. 14:328–48.

Weir, Lorna, and Leo Casey. 1984. Subverting power in sexuality. *Socialist Review* 14(3–4):139–57.

Weisman, Steven R. 1989. Tokyo journal. Sex harassment: Glare of light on man's world. *New York Times,* 13 November.

Weiss, Meira. 1994. *Conditional love: Parental relations toward handicapped children.* Westport, Conn.: Greenwood Press.

———. Forthcoming. Fence sitters: Parents' reactions to sexual ambiguities in their newborn children. *Semiotica.*

Weitzman, Lenore J. 1974. Legal regulation of marriage: Tradition and change. *California Law Review* 62:1172–1278.

———. 1985. *The divorce revolution: The unexpected social and economic consequences for women and children in America.* New York: Free Press.

Welbourn, Alice. 1984. Endo ceramics and power strategies. In Miller and Tilley.

Welter, Barbara. 1966. The cult of true womanhood, 1820–1860. *American Quarterly,* Summer, 151–74.

Wertz, Richard W., and Dorothy C. Wertz. 1989. *Lying-in: A history of childbirth in America.* Expanded ed. New Haven: Yale University Press.

Wessel, Lois. 1991. Reproductive rights in Nicaragua: From the Sandinistas to the government of Violeta Chamorro. *Feminist Studies* 17:537–49.

West, Candace. 1982. Why can't a woman be more like a man? An interactional note on organizational game-playing for managerial women. *Work and Occupations* 9:5–29.

————. 1984. *Routine complications: Troubles with talk between doctors and patients.* Bloomington: Indiana University Press.

West, Candace, and Don Zimmerman. 1987. Doing gender. *Gender & Society* 1:125–51.

West, Guida, and Rhoda Lois Blumberg. (eds.). 1990. *Women and social protest.* New York: Oxford University Press.

Weston, Kathleen M. 1991. *Families we choose: Lesbians, gays, kinship.* New York: Columbia University Press.

Weston, Kathleen M., and Lisa B. Rofel. 1984. Sexuality, class, and conflict in a lesbian workplace. *Signs* 9:623–46.

Westwood, Sallie. 1985. *All day, every day: Factory and family in the making of women's lives.* Urbana: University of Illinois Press.

Westwood, Sallie, and Parminder Bhachu (eds.). 1988. *Enterprising women: Ethnicity, economy, and gender relations.* New York and London: Routledge.

Wharton, Amy S., and James N. Baron. 1987. So happy together? The impact of gender segregation on men at work. *American Sociological Review* 52:574–87.

Wheelock, Jane. 1990. *Husbands at home: The domestic economy in a post-industrial society.* New York and London: Routledge.

Wheelwright, Julie. 1989. *Amazons and military maids: Women who cross-dressed in pursuit of life, liberty and happiness.* London: Pandora Press.

White, Deborah Gray. 1985. *Ar'n't I a woman? Female slaves in the plantation South.* New York: Norton.

White, Lynne K., and David B. Brinkerhoff. 1987. Children's work in the family: Its significance and meaning. In Gerstel and Gross.

Whitehead, Ann. 1981. "I'm hungry, Mum": The politics of domestic budgeting. In Young, Wolkowitz, and McCullagh.

————. 1984. Men and women, kinship and property: Some general issues. In Hirschon.

Whitehead, Harriet. 1981. The bow and the burden strap: A new look at institutionalized homosexuality in native North America. In Ortner and Whitehead (eds.).

Whyte, Martin K. 1978. *The status of women in preindustrial societies.* Princeton: Princeton University Press.

Wicker, Tom. 1991. Blaming Anita Hill. *New York Times,* Op-Ed Page, 10 October.

Wikan, Unni. 1982. *Behind the veil in Arabia: Women in Oman.* Baltimore, Md.: Johns Hopkins University Press.

Wiley, Mary Glenn, and Dale E. Woolley. 1988. Interruptions among equals: Power plays that fail. *Gender & Society* 2:90–102.

Wilford, John Noble. 1993. Mysterious Mexican culture yields its secrets. *New York Times,* Science Section, 29 June.

Wilk, Richard R., and Robert McC. Netting. 1984. Households: Changing forms and functions. In Netting, Wilk, and Arnould.

Wilkinson, Doris. 1984. Afro-American women and their families. In *Women and the family: Two decades of change,* edited by Beth B. Hess and Marvin Sussman. New York: Haworth.

Williams, Christine L. 1989. *Gender differences at work: Women and men in nontraditional occupations.* Berkeley: University of California Press.

———. 1992. The glass escalator: Hidden advantages for men in the "female" professions. *Social Problems* 39:253–67.

Williams, Lena. 1991. Blacks say the blood spilled in the Thomas case stains all. *New York Times,* 14 October.

Williams, Linda. 1989. *Hard core: Power, pleasure, and the "frenzy of the visible."* Berkeley: University of California Press.

Williams, Linda S. 1988. "It's going to work for me": Responses to failures of IVF. *Birth* 15:153–56.

Williams, Patricia J. 1991. *The alchemy of race and rights.* Cambridge, Mass.: Harvard University Press.

Williams, Patricia J., Barbara Smith, Rebecca Walker, Marcia Ann Gillespie, and Eleanor Holmes Norton. 1992. Refusing to be silenced. *Ms. Magazine,* January-February.

Williams, Walter L. 1986. *The spirit and the flesh: Sexual diversity in American Indian culture.* Boston: Beacon Press.

Willie, Charles Vert. 1985. *Black and white families: A study in complementarity.* Dix Hills, N.Y.: General Hall.

———. 1988. *A new look at Black families.* 3d ed. Dix Hills, N.Y.: General Hall.

Willis, Paul. 1982. Women in sport in ideology. In Hargreaves.

Wilson, Edward O. 1975. *Sociobiology: The new synthesis.* Cambridge, Mass.: Harvard University Press.

———. 1978. *On human nature.* Cambridge, Mass.: Harvard University Press.

Wilson, Elizabeth. 1984. Forbidden love. *Feminist Studies* 10:213–26.

———. 1985. *Adorned in dreams: Fashion and modernity.* London: Virago Press.

Wilson, Marie C. 1991. Just a day at the office. *New York Times,* Op-Ed Page, 11 October.

Witke, Roxane. 1973a. Mao Tse-tung, women and suicide. In Young (ed.).

———. 1973b. Woman as politician in China of the 1920s. In Young (ed.).

Wittig, Monique. 1971. *Les guérillères.* New York: Viking.

———. 1980. The straight mind. *Feminist Issues* 1:103–11.

———. 1981. One is not born a woman. *Feminist Issues* 2:47–54.

Witz, Anne. 1986. Patriarchy and the labor market: Occupational control strategies and the medical division of labor. In Knights and Willmott.

Wolf, Margery. 1985. *Revolution postponed: Women in contemporary China.* Stanford, Calif.: Stanford University Press.

Wolf, Wendy C., and Neil D. Fligstein. 1979a. Sex and authority in the workplace: The causes of sexual inequality. *American Sociological Review* 44:235–52.

———. 1979b. Sexual stratification: Differences in power in the work setting. *Social Forces* 58:94–107.

Wood, Corinne Shear. 1979. *Human sickness and health.* Palo Alto, Calif.: Mayfield.

Wood, Elizabeth. 1980. Women in music. *Signs* 6:283–97.

Woodhouse, Annie. 1989. *Fantastic women: Sex, gender, and transvestism.* New Brunswick, N.J.: Rutgers University Press.

Wright, Ann L. 1982. Variation in Navajo menopause: Toward an explanation. In Voda, Dinnerstein, and O'Donnell.

Wright, Barbara Drygulski, et al. (eds.). 1987. *Women, work, and technology: Transformations.* Ann Arbor: University of Michigan Press.

Wright, Erik Olin, Karen Shire, Shu-ling Hwang, Maureen Dolan, and Janeen Baxter. 1992. The non-effects of class on the gender division of labor in the home: A comparative study of Sweden and the United States. *Gender & Society* 6:252–82.

Wright, Michael J. 1979. Reproductive hazards and "protective" discrimination. *Feminist Studies* 5:302–09.

WuDunn, Sheryl. 1991. China's castaway babies: Cruel practice lives on. *New York Times,* 26 February.

———. 1992. Women face increasing bias as China focuses on profits. *New York Times,* 28 July.

Yanagisako, Sylvia Junko, and Jane Fishburne Collier. 1987. Toward a unified analysis of gender and kinship. In *Gender and kinship: Essays toward a unified analysis,* edited by Jane Fishburne Collier and Sylvia Junko Yanagisako. Berkeley: University of California Press.

Yang, C. K. 1965. *Chinese Communist society: The family and the village.* Cambridge, Mass.: M.I.T. Press.

Yankauskas, Ellen. 1990. Primary female syndromes: An update. *New York State Journal of Medicine* 90:295–302.

Yllö, Kersti. 1984. The status of women, marital equality, and violence against wives. *Journal of Family Issues* 5:307–20.

Yllö, Kersti, and Michele Bograd (eds.). 1988. *Feminist perspectives on wife abuse.* Newbury Park, Calif.: Sage.

Yoder, Janice D. 1989. Women at West Point: Lessons for token women in male-dominated occupations. In Freeman.

———. 1991. Rethinking tokenism: Looking beyond numbers. *Gender & Society* 5:178–92.

Yoder, Janice D., Penny L. Crumpton, and John F. Zipp. 1989. The power of numbers in influencing hiring decisions. *Gender & Society* 3:269–76.

Young, Iris Marion. 1990. *Throwing like a girl and other essays in feminist philosophy and social theory.* Bloomington: Indiana University Press.

Young, Kate, Carol Wolkowitz, and Roslyn McCullagh (eds.). 1981. *Of marriage and the market: Women's subordination in international perspective.* London: CSE Books.

Young, Kathleen Z. 1989. The imperishable virginity of Saint Maria Goretti. *Gender & Society* 3:474–82.

Young, Marilyn B. (ed.). 1973. *Women in China: Studies in social change and feminism.* Ann Arbor: University of Michigan Center for Chinese Studies.

————. 1989. Chicken Little in China: Women after the Cultural Revolution. In Kruks, Rapp, and Young.

Zaretsky, Eli. 1986. *Capitalism, the family, and personal life.* Rev. ed. New York: Harper & Row.

Zelizer, Viviana A. 1985. *Pricing the priceless child: The changing social value of children.* New York: Basic Books.

Zick, Cathleen D., and Jane L. McCullough. 1991. Trends in married couples' time use: Evidence from 1977–1978 and 1987–1988. *Sex Roles* 24:459–87.

Zihlman, Adrienne L. 1978. Women and evolution, Part II: Subsistence and social organization among early hominids. *Signs* 4:4–20.

————. 1981. Women as shapers of the human adaptation. In Dahlberg.

Zimmer, Lynn. 1988. Tokenism and women in the workplace: The limits of gender-neutral theory. *Social Problems* 35:64–77.

Zimmerman, Don H., and Candace West. 1975. Sex roles, interruptions and silences. In *Language and sex: Difference and domination,* edited by Barrie Thorne and Nancy Henley. Rowley, Mass.: Newbury House.

Zimmerman, Jan (ed.). 1983. *The technological woman: Interfacing with tomorrow.* New York: Praeger.

Zita, Jacquelyn. 1988. The premenstrual syndrome: "Dis-easing" the female cycle. *Hypatia* 3:77–99.

Zola, Irving Kenneth. 1982a. *Missing pieces: A chronicle of living with a disability,* edited by Irving Kenneth Zola. Philadelphia: Temple University Press.

————. 1982b. Tell me, tell me. In *Ordinary lives: Voice of disability and disease.* Cambridge, Mass.: Apple-wood Books.

Zuckerman, Harriet. 1977. *Scientific elite: Nobel laureates in the United States.* New York: Free Press.

————. 1991. The careers of men and women scientists: A review of current research. In Zuckerman, Cole, and Bruer.

Zuckerman, Harriet, Jonathan R. Cole, and John T. Bruer (eds.). 1991. *The outer circle: Women in the scientific community.* New York: Norton.

Zunz, Sharyn. 1991. Gender-related issues in the career development of social work managers. *Affilia* 6:39–52.

INDEX